KU-737-045

**LIAONING, JILIN, & HEILONGJIANG**
*Pages 436–455*

**BEIJING**
*Pages 78–119*

**HEBEI, TIANJIN, & SHANXI**
*Pages 120–139*

**SHANDONG & HENAN**
*Pages 140–159*

**SHAANXI**
*Pages 160–171*

**GUANGDONG & HAINAN**
*Pages 294–305*

**FUJIAN**
*Pages 284–293*

Harbin

THE NORTHEAST

Jilin

Shenyang

Hohhot

Beijing · Tianjin

Taiyuan · Shijiazhuang · Ji'nan

Yinchuan

BEIJING & THE NORTH

YELLOW SEA

Xining

Lanzhou

Zhengzhou

Xi'an

Nanjing · Shanghai

Hefei

Hangzhou

Chengdu

Wuhan

CENTRAL CHINA

Nanchang

Chongqing

Changsha

Fuzhou

THE SOUTHWEST

Guiyang

THE SOUTH

Kunming

Guangzhou

Nanning

Hong Kong & Macau

Haikou

SOUTH CHINA SEA

0 kilometers     400

0 miles     400

# EYEWITNESS TRAVEL

# CHINA

LONDON, NEW YORK,
MELBOURNE, MUNICH AND DELHI
www.dk.com

PROJECT EDITORS  Hugh Thompson, Kathryn Lane
PROJECT ART EDITOR  Gadi Farfour
EDITOR  Vandana Mohindra
DESIGNERS  Mathew Kurien, Maite Lantaron,
Pallavi Narain, Rebecca Milner
PICTURE RESEARCHER  Ellen Root
RESEARCH ASSISTANT  Monica Yue Hua Ma
MAP CO-ORDINATORS  Uma Bhattacharya, Casper Morris
DTP DESIGNER Jason Little

MAIN CONTRIBUTORS
Donald Bedford, Deh-Ta Hsiung, Christopher Knowles,
David Leffman, Simon Lewis,
Peter Neville-Hadley, Andrew Stone

CONSULTANTS
Christopher Knowles, Peter Neville-Hadley

PHOTOGRAPHERS
Demetrio Carrasco, Ian Cumming, Eddie Gerald, Nigel Hicks,
Colin Sinclair, Chris Stowers, Linda Whitwham

ILLUSTRATORS
Richard Bonson, Stephen Conlin, Gary Cross, Richard Draper, Kevin
Goold, Paul Guest, Claire Littlejohn, John Mullany, Chris Orr,
Arun Pottirayil

Reproduced by Colourscan, Singapore
Printed in Malaysia by Vivar Printing Sdn. Bhd.

First published in Great Britain in 2005
by Dorling Kindersley Limited
80 Strand, London WC2R 0RL
A Penguin Company

12 13 14 15 10 9 8 7 6 5 4 3 2 1

**Reprinted with revisions 2008, 2010, 2012**

Copyright 2005, 2012 © Dorling Kindersley Limited, London

A CIP catalogue record is available from the British Library.

ISBN 978-1-4053-6890-2

FLOORS ARE REFERRED TO IN ACCORDANCE WITH AMERICAN USAGE, IE THE
"FIRST FLOOR" IS AT GROUND FLOOR LEVEL

*Front cover main image: Decorations at Donyue Temple, Beijing*

MIX
Paper from
responsible sources
FSC
www.fsc.org   FSC™ C018179

Confucius (551–479 BC)

# CONTENTS

## INTRODUCING
## CHINA

## BEIJING & THE
## NORTH

## CENTRAL CHINA

◁ The Great Wall meandering along the ridges of northern China's mountainous terrain

*Pailou*, a decorative gate, leading to Gao Miao in Zhongwei, Ningxia

Dramatic karst hills in the town of Guilin, Guangxi

Fengxian Si, the largest of the Buddhist Longmen Caves, Henan

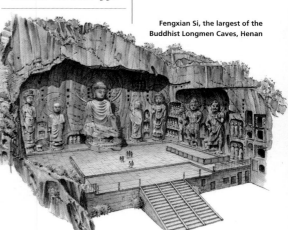

# HOW TO USE THIS GUIDE

This Eyewitness Travel Guide helps you to get the most from your visit to China, providing expert recommendations as well as detailed practical information. The opening chapter *Introducing China* maps the country and and sets it in its historical and cultural context. Each of the seven regional sections is divided into area chapters that cover from one to three provinces each. Here you will find descriptions of the most important sights with maps, pictures, and illustrations. Hotel and restaurant recommendations can be found in *Travelers' Needs*. The *Survival Guide* contains practical information on everything from transport to personal safety.

**1 At a Glance**

*A map-based feature introduces each of the seven regional sections, giving an illustrated overview of the area. The map indicates major cities and sights.*

**Getting Around** gives a brief description of long-distance transport in the region.

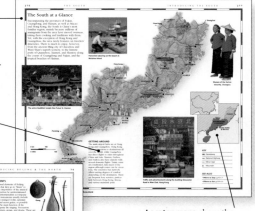

**Locator maps** show the color-coded chapter divisions within the section.

**2 Regional Feat**
*Each regional introduction highlights aspects of the area's culture, history, geography, and cuisine. Fascinating features are sprinkled throughout the area chapters as well.*

**3 Chapter Introduction**
*Each chapter is coded a different color. For easy reference, all sights in the area are numbered and plotted on a map. The black bullet numbers also indicate the order in which the sights are covered in the chapter.*

**A map** shows cities, passenger rail routes, and all major roads.

## 4 Town Map

*Within each chapter, important towns and cities are described in detail, and numerous sights recommended. A Visitors' Checklist gives practical information and a handy map locates the main sights and transport hubs.*

**Visitors' Checklist** provides the address, opening times, transport information, and more.

**A sight list** corresponds to the bullets on the map.

## 5 Major Sights

*Historic buildings are intricately illustrated; museums have color-coded floor plans to help locate the best exhibits; and natural parks have maps with walking routes.*

**Stars indicate** the features that no visitor should miss.

## 6 Major City Map

*Beijing, Hong Kong, and Shanghai each have their own chapters with introductory maps – sights are plotted with numbered bullets. Hong Kong and Beijing have detailed Street Finder maps as well.*

**Bulleted sights** are listed in alphabetical order.

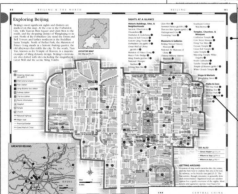

**Each chapter** has color-coded thumb tabs. See the inside front cover for a map plotting all chapters.

## 7 Detailed Information

*Along with practical information, each sight is described and written in Chinese characters. The entries appear in the same order as the numbering on the map at the beginning of the chapter.*

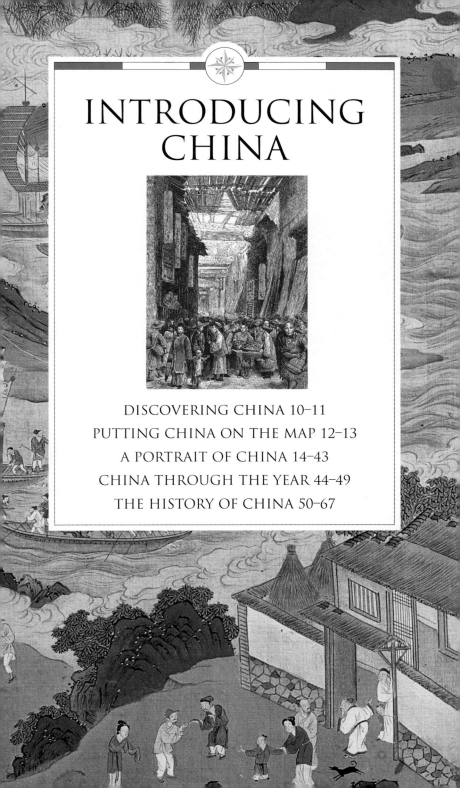

# INTRODUCING CHINA

# DISCOVERING CHINA

Guangxu-era porcelain plate

China is famed for the marathon meanderings of its Great Wall, the towering high-altitude palaces of Tibet, and the great cave-temple complexes that dot the ancient silk-trade routes. Within this vast country are lush sub-tropical landscapes, high snowy wildernesses, and neat rice terraces, farmed for thousands of years. The people are as different as the lands they inhabit, and their temples and domestic architecture just as varied. Few other countries can offer as much in a single visit, and China is rapidly becoming one of the world's most popular destinations.

Beijing's spectacular Forbidden City

## BEIJING & THE NORTH

- **Beijing's Forbidden City**
- **The Great Wall of China**
- **Xi'an's Terracotta Army**
- **Ancient Pingyao**

Northern China contains many of the country's most iconic sights. Visitors can lose themselves for hours among the labyrinthine passageways and lavish pavilions of Beijing's former Ming and Qing Imperial Palace, the **Forbidden City** (see pp86–9). Also to the north is the mighty **Great Wall of China** (see pp106–8), built to protect imperial rule. Various sections can easily be reached as day trips from the capital. The former capital of Xi'an offers the eerie ranks of the first emperor's **Terracotta Army** (see pp168–9) and the surrounding countryside is littered with Tang dynasty tombs. Shanxi also has most of China's oldest wooden buildings such as those in **Datong** (see p131) and **Wutai Shan** (see pp134–6), and the best-preserved walled city of all at **Pingyao** (see pp138–9).

## CENTRAL CHINA

- **Booming Shanghai**
- **Suzhou's gardens**
- **Ming-era Tunxi and Shexian**
- **Hangzhou's West Lake**

Zhejiang is now China's richest province, and it is along the coastline that much of the country's wealth can be found, in former treaty ports such as Ningbo and Wenzhou. **Shanghai** (see pp183–201), the "Paris of the East" in the 1920s, is once

The neon lights of Shanghai's bustling Nanjing Road

again mainland China's brightest and most booming city. Its old concession-era buildings, renewed as restaurants and bars, now face a forest of cranes and sci-fi towers in the Pudong district. Nearby are the gentler charms of **Suzhou's gardens** (see pp204–15). Inland are the humble Ming-era houses and the striking whitewashed mansions of the wealthy merchants of **Tunxi**, **Shexian**, **Hongcun**, and **Xidi** (see p234). **West Lake** (see p242), is particularly scenic and is China's most famous lake.

Traditional sail boat, a good way to see the city of Hong Kong

## THE SOUTH

- **Hong Kong**
- **Xiamen's colonial mansions**
- **Multi-cultural Quanzhou**
- **Yongding's earthern *tulou***

Much of the interest of the southeast lies in the impact of foreigners. Orderly, cosmopolitan, and formerly British **Hong Kong** (see pp307–25) is everything the mainland cities aspire to be, and its seaside Manhattan-with-mountains skyline is one of the world's most spectacular. The pre-revolution foreign community of **Xiamen** (see pp286–7) left behind elaborate European mansions, while hundreds of years earlier communities of Catholics and Muslims left a surprising assortment of religious monuments at **Quanzhou** *(see p291)*. In the region's mountainous interior, the giant earthen fortresses *(tulou)* of the Hakka people at **Yongding** *(see p290)* were villages in their own right: home to hundreds of people and livestock.

Typical cobbled street in Lijiang's Old Town

## THE SOUTHWEST

- **Guangxi's limestone peaks**
- **Towns of Dali and Lijiang**
- **Natural bridges of Sanjiang**

China's scenic southwest enjoys mild weather and is home to a wide variety of ethnic minority peoples, known for their lively festivals and extraordinary architecture. The toothy limestone peaks of **Guangxi** *(see pp397–413)* are one of China's most famous attractions, and the cruise between them along the Li River from Guilin *(see pp414–7)* is a popular day

trip. The well-preserved Yunnan mountain towns of **Dali** *(see pp386–8)* and **Lijiang** *(see pp390–3)* have winding lanes lined by streams. Around Guangxi's **Sanjiang** *(see pp420–1)* are timber drum towers and covered bridges like elongated temples.

## THE NORTHEAST

- **Concession-era architecture of Dalian and Harbin**
- **Qing palaces of Shenyang**
- **Waterfalls of Changbai Shan**

The northeast offers respite from China's scorching summer heat. The architecture of **Dalian** *(see pp444–5)* and **Harbin** *(see pp450–1)*, dating back to periods of Russian and Japanese occupation, is some of the country's best-preserved. **Shenyang** *(see pp438–9)* still houses a Qing palace complex, and the last emperor Pu Yi, ruled a Japanese-controlled Manchuria from a palace in **Changchun** *(see p446)*. Volcanic **Changbai Shan** *(see pp448–9)* offers views of the waters of Tian Chi (Heaven's Lake), which straddles the border with North Korea.

## INNER MONGOLIA & THE SILK ROADS

- **Mogao Caves**
- **Taklamakan Desert oases**
- **Tibetan monasteries**

Many of the great trade routes with Central Asia and beyond once passed through the region, leaving elaborate

Buddhist monuments. The greatest of these is the **Mogao Caves** at Dunhuang *(see p497)* where fresco-lined caves record the passage of Buddhism into China and the ebb and flow of power in the region. The oases around the **Taklamakan Desert** include **Turpan** *(see pp504–5)*, with its substantial vineyards; **Kuqa** *(see p509)* with its warren of adobe housing, and rapidly changing **Kashgar** *(see pp510-13)* with its mosque and Sunday livestock market. The Tibetan monasteries of **Xining** *(see p498)* and **Xiahe** *(see p482)* offer a more accessible alternative to Tibet, and the rebuilt fort at **Jiayuguan** *(see pp492–3)* marks the end of the brick-clad Ming-era Great Wall.

The majestic splendor of Lhasa's Potala Palace

## TIBET

- **Rail journey to Lhasa**
- **Lhasa's Potala Palace**
- **Everest Base Camp**

The rail route to **Lhasa** *(see pp528–37)* is China's most spectacular rail journey, and the world's highest. The highlands of the Tibetan plateau still have areas off-limits to foreigners, and the special permits needed hint at the territory's history as a hermit, forbidden kingdom. The slab-sided **Potala Palace** *(see pp534–5)* towers over Lhasa and is an awe-inspiring sight. The side trip to **Everest Base Camp** *(see pp546–7)* from the Friendship Highway to Nepal offers unbeatable views of Everest and other peaks over 26,000 ft (8,000 m).

Dramatic limestone peaks dot the mountainous landscape of Guangxi

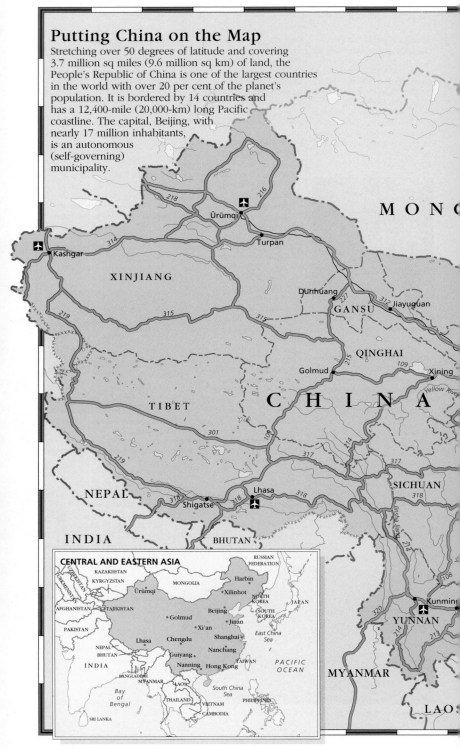

# Putting China on the Map

Stretching over 50 degrees of latitude and covering 3.7 million sq miles (9.6 million sq km) of land, the People's Republic of China is one of the largest countries in the world with over 20 per cent of the planet's population. It is bordered by 14 countries and has a 12,400-mile (20,000-km) long Pacific coastline. The capital, Beijing, with nearly 17 million inhabitants, is an autonomous (self-governing) municipality.

MONGO

Ürümqi

Turpan

Kashgar

XINJIANG

Dunhuang

GANSU

Jiayuguan

QINGHAI

Golmud

Xining

Yellow River

C H I N A

TIBET

SICHUAN

NEPAL

Shigatse

Lhasa

INDIA

BHUTAN

Kunming

YUNNAN

LAOS

218

216

314

219

315

315

227

312

215

109

301

109

317

214

317

318

318

318

320

214

213

108

**CENTRAL AND EASTERN ASIA**

RUSSIAN FEDERATION

KAZAKHSTAN

KYRGYZSTAN

MONGOLIA

Harbin

Xilinhot

NORTH KOREA

JAPAN

Ürümqi

UZBEKISTAN

TURKMENISTAN

AFGHANISTAN

TAJIKISTAN

PAKISTAN

Golmud

Beijing

SOUTH KOREA

Jinan

East China Sea

Xi'an

Shanghai

Chengdu

Lhasa

NEPAL

BHUTAN

INDIA

BANGLADESH

Guiyang

Nanchang

TAIWAN

PACIFIC OCEAN

MYANMAR

LAOS

Nanning

Hong Kong

South China Sea

Bay of Bengal

THAILAND

VIETNAM

CAMBODIA

PHILIPPINES

SRI LANKA

◁ Detail of a *History of the Emperors of China*, a series of silk paintings created in c.17th century

KEY
- ✈ International airport
- ═══ Expressway
- ═══ National Highway
- ─── Railroad
- ▬ ▬ International border
- ▬ ▬ Provincial border
- ××× Disputed border

RUSSIAN FEDERATION

*Argun*

*Amur (Heilong Jiang)*

HEILONGJIANG

Qiqiha'er

Harbin

*Xingkai Hu*

301

202

221

301

111

301

JILIN

Changchun

Jilin

Xilinhot

INNER MONGOLIA

208

Shenyang

LIAONING

NORTH KOREA

Anshan

101

111

Hohhot

Baotou

Datong

BEIJING

Tianjin

TIANJIN

BO HAI

Dalian

SOUTH KOREA

Yinchuan

210

208

*Yellow River*

HEBEI

Shijiazhuang

110

Taiyuan

SHANXI

*Yellow River*

Ji'nan

Qingdao

YELLOW SEA

307

NINGXIA

109

309

211

309

SHANDONG

Lanzhou

210

Luoyang

Zhengzhou

Xuzhou

JIANGSU

HENAN

*Huai He*

310

Xi'an

Huainan

206

Nanjing

Shanghai

SHAANXI

108

Hefei

SHANGHAI

213

269

ANHUI

Hangzhou

Ningbo

*Yangzi*

HUBEI

Wuhan

ZHEJIANG

Chengdu

CHONGQING

EAST CHINA SEA

Chongqing

*Yuan Jiang*

*Zi Shui*

Nanchang

104

213

HUNAN

Changsha

JIANGXI

FUJIAN

Guiyang

209

207

323

316

Fuzhou

GUIZHOU

379

323

Xiamen

TAIWAN

GUANGXI

GUANGDONG

105

Nanning

Guangzhou

Shenzhen

207

Hong Kong

Macau

VIETNAM

SOUTH CHINA SEA

Haikou

HAINAN

225

Sanya

0 km        200

0 miles        200

# A PORTRAIT OF CHINA

*Thirty years after the late Deng Xiaoping's "reform and opening" policy allowed foreign travelers back into China, the country remains largely as mysterious and undiscovered as it was in the 19th century, when gunboat diplomacy by foreign superpowers forced the last tottering dynasty to open up the country to foreign trade and exploration.*

Drawn by this air of mystery, the number of visitors coming to China has been rising rapidly. Not one visitor will fail to be impressed by the splendor of China's greatest sights.

The Great Wall has been completely rebuilt in parts in modern times, but its dizzying loops across the horizon still leave most visitors lost for words. The Forbidden City, at the heart of Beijing, draws crowds that make its original majesty hard to imagine, but the labyrinth of side passages still leaves the more inquisitive visitor spellbound. Although images of Xi'an's Terracotta Warriors are familiar, nothing prepares visitors for coming face to face with

**A rural worker**

an army of thousands. China may not be quite the rapidly modernizing economic success of investment fable, but nor is it the medieval backwater of travelers' tales – the truth lies somewhere in between. Not far from the excitement and wealth of the shiny, high-rise cities, water buffalo pull the plow, and donkey carts are still a popular form of transport.

The success of the 2008 Olympics was a defining moment for China in terms of economic development and ability to host a global event on such a huge scale. However, the legacy of the games was overshadowed by the global economy crashing just weeks after.

Shanghai's high-rise skyline, a symbol of China's booming prosperity

◁ Timeless scenery in southern China's karst hills as a fisherman takes his cormorants night fishing

The dizzying, hill-hugging loops of the Great Wall of China

## MODERN CHINA

China's vast population, despite famines and civil wars, has grown from 400 million to approximately 1.3 billion in less than a century. This increase has driven a boom in consumerism, most evident in the cities where advertising hoardings for coffee, computers, and the latest fashions line streets of shops selling fast food, phones, and face-lifts.

Shanghai is said to represent the new entrepreneurial China, and visitors will immediately notice the billboards, the towers, and the giant HDTV screens on the sides of shiny malls. Urban Shangai received a massive facelift in preparation for the 2010 World Expo,

and scores of office blocks, roads, and metro lines were built. However, Shanghai is only one city, 70% of the Chinese people work in agriculture, and the majority of commercial enterprises are still in state ownership or have state majority shareholdings.

There has been obvious, rapid economic development – luxury hotels, convenient public transport, and excellent restaurants. However, these welcome refinements have been tempered for the visitor by the destruction of traditional housing for the construction of highways soon choked with traffic. And yet for some people this commercialism has provided the disposable income to fund a return to traditional hobbies and pastimes.

Today, former occupants of crumbling courtyard houses may find themselves exiled to unfinished towers in the suburbs, but in the spaces between the blocks, they've revived the tradition of walking their snuffling Pekinese. Songbirds flutter and call from delicate bamboo cages

Traditional courtyard housing in Lijiang, southwest China

while their owners sit and chat. On bridges over ring roads, old men gather to fly colorful kites – now made from supermarket shopping bags.

### GROWING TOO FAST?

As population growth drives a consumer boom, China's energy needs are fast outstripping its capacity and a major expansion of its network of coal-fired generating stations is planned. But China is already the planet's biggest polluter – in many cities the atmosphere is furry enough to stroke.

With few opportunities for work in the countryside, tens of millions are moving to the cities in search of a better life. Living in poor conditions and often left unpaid after building the new towers, they send whatever they can to families back home. Others staff the restaurants and run a million small businesses from shoe-shining to knife-sharpening. If your taxi driver doesn't know where he's going, it's often because he hasn't been in town long.

Those better off in the city blame the migrants for the rise in urban crime (although most countries would envy China's crime figures), but complain when the services they provide vanish at Chinese New Year due to the workers returning home for the holiday.

European architecture on the Bund, Shanghai

### POLITICS

The end of the 20th century has seen communist regimes toppled across Europe, but the present government has made it all too clear that there will be no political change in China in the foreseeable future. Politics, although almost invisible to visitors, still enters every aspect of life, including the training of tour guides to provide cultural and historical information that supports the view of China the Party wishes to promote.

The Chinese people are removed from politics, because as individuals they can make little difference.

The Hong Kong rush hour – much the same as in any international metropolis

Dissatisfaction is widespread and increasing, particularly with regards to corruption, pollution, environmental degradation, and the expensive, rising cost of living. The global recession has hit certain sectors, such as manufacturing very hard, and unemployment is rising.

Traditional modes of transport in Beijing

### FAMILY LIFE

Eight out of ten of the parents of the current generation of twenty-year-olds had their spouses chosen and approved by their work unit, but today's urban youth experiment early, live together outside marriage (until recently still illegal), and try a few partners before settling down.

Divorce, unheard of until the end of the last century, is now common, and is attributed to an increase in work demands and extra-marital affairs. Attitudes to children, too, are changing. There are hints that the one-child policy, long breached by anyone with connections or cash, may be relaxed a little. And there are signs that many members of the urban middle class, although still a tiny percentage of the total population, wish to enjoy the treats they can now afford rather than have children. While 20 years ago it was considered fortunate

Minority mother and child

to own a bicycle, now aspiring, young urbanites can work towards owning a car and an apartment.

### UNIFIED BY LANGUAGE

The whole nation may have felt proud when Yang Liwei became the country's first astronaut in 2003, heralding China's entry to the exclusive club of space nations. The government likes to use such occasions to promote Han unity – "Han" is the name the Chinese majority use for themselves, as opposed to the 50 or so officially recognized minorities within China's borders (*see pp24–25*). There's been a tendency to treat these minorities as unpredictable pets, and their mostly colorful costumes and traditional festivals have been put at the forefront of tourism promotion in recent years. It may not be ideal but it is a great improvement on the forced assimilation of past times.

Almost everyone is educated in Mandarin (*Putonghua*), the official language of China, but there are five completely different regional versions of Chinese, and a strong sense of local culture and tradition goes with them.

Popstars performing an outdoor concert in Beijing

The Chinese people's common love of food also helps differentiate them, with preferences for spicy, vinegary, sweet, and other flavors being distributed geographically. Visitors to Sichuan and Yunnan will find the locals rightly proud of their uniquely fiery cuisine, while those visiting Guangdong and Guangxi will be astonished at the subtlety and delicacy of Cantonese food.

### CULTURE AND RELIGION

While traditional opera is now largely confined to shows for foreign tourists, modern art, films, and popular music have all flourished. Not all of it is good by any means but art galleries now feature on tourist itineraries, resident students crowd bars to hear Chinese punk bands, and millions around the world flock to see big-budget martial arts epics.

Religion and superstition are making a small come-back which the government regards warily – it fears organizations of any kind not directly under its control. Many people are still struggling to cope with the end of government-organized everything, and for some the structure of organized religion provides a

**A space nation – China's first astronaut Yang Liwei**

substitute. There may be many more opportunities to start businesses and make money, and all kinds of employment that simply didn't exist before Deng Xiaoping's reform policy kick-started the economy, but jobs no longer come with housing, healthcare, or any guarantees they'll last.

But the Chinese are used to turbulence, and are incredibly stoic about it. Their attitude to visitors varies from the studied indifference of the smart metropolitans, to the close interest in foreign wallets of the tourist touts, via frank curiosity, and the casual warmth and generosity of everyday folk.

**China's modern consumer society – a smart shopping mall in Xi Dan, Beijing**

# Landscape and Wildlife – West

**Forest butterfly**

The west of China is made up of a high, arid mountain plateau and, further north, a harsh, dry desert. These areas are not suited to agriculture and therefore sparsely populated by humans – only specialist animals that have adapted to the conditions survive here. At the eastern edge of the Tibetan plateau lie the mountains and wooded hills of central and west China, home to pockets of bamboo forest – the habitat of one of China's most famous and unique animals, the giant panda. Watered by rivers of melted snow from Tibet, the forests are also home to a great number of other animals, trees, and especially beautiful flowers *(see pp344–5)*.

**KEY**

① Tibetan High Plateau

② Mountains of Central & West

③ Deserts of North & Northwest

④ Bamboo Forest

## TIBETAN HIGH PLATEAU

The vast, rocky Qinghai-Tibet Plateau lies between the Kunlun Mountains in the north, the Karakoram in the west and the Himalayas to the south. The average altitude is about 15,994 ft (4,875 m), making it the highest plateau in the world.

**The Blue poppy** *is one of the most famous Himalayan flowers. About 15 species of this genus* (Meconopsis) *grow in Yunnan and Tibet, and are used in traditional medicine.*

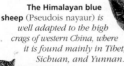

**The Himalayan blue sheep** (Pseudois nayaur) *is well adapted to the high crags of western China, where it is found mainly in Tibet, Sichuan, and Yunnan.*

**Snow leopards** (Panthera (Uncia) uncia) *have thick fur to protect them. Though protected, they are still poached for their valuable pelts.*

## MOUNTAINS OF CENTRAL & WEST CHINA

The central ranges have large areas of natural forest habitats, and are major wildlife refuges. Covering over 20,000 sq miles (52,000 sq km), they are home to many species, including the endangered golden monkey *(Rhinopithecus).*

**Rhesus macaques** (Macaca mulatta) *are common in Chinese forests. Though able to fend for themselves, they are used to people, and can be a nuisance begging for food.*

**Chinese fir** (Cunninghamia lanceolata) *is a common conifer, found typically in mixed needle-leaved-broadleaved forests in high sub-tropical sites.*

**The silver pheasant** (Lophura nycthemera) *is one of China's most beautiful birds. It is common in evergreen forests and bamboo thickets in southern and eastern areas.*

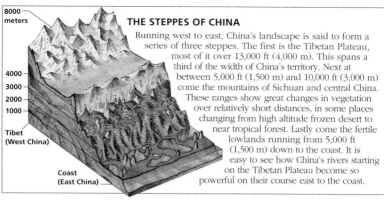

## THE STEPPES OF CHINA

Running west to east, China's landscape is said to form a series of three steppes. The first is the Tibetan Plateau, most of it over 13,000 ft (4,000 m). This spans a third of the width of China's territory. Next at between 5,000 ft (1,500 m) and 10,000 ft (3,000 m) come the mountains of Sichuan and central China. These ranges show great changes in vegetation over relatively short distances, in some places changing from high altitude frozen desert to near tropical forest. Lastly come the fertile lowlands running from 5,000 ft (1,500 m) down to the coast. It is easy to see how China's rivers starting on the Tibetan Plateau become so powerful on their course east to the coast.

## DESERTS OF NORTH & NORTHWEST

Deserts cover about 20% of China's landmass – mainly in the northwest. This is a challenging environment and plants and animals adapted to the deserts are few: reptiles and small rodents such as jerboas predominate.

**Only about 600** *of the two-humped Bactrian camel* (Camelus bactrianus) *survive in the deserts of China.*

**Wormwoods** (Artemisia spp.) *are typical low shrubs of dry steppe communities and can tolerate periodic droughts and even salty soils.*

**The deserts** *of northern China, close to Mongolia, are the habitat of the rare goitered gazelle* (Gazella subgutturosa); *despite its rarity it is still targeted by trophy hunters.*

## BAMBOO FOREST

China has some 500 species of bamboo covering about 3% of the total forest area. They are found in 18 provinces and are not only a vital habitat for wildlife, but with their almost indestructible culms (stems), are also a valuable resource.

**Tall forests of muso bamboo** (Phyllostachys pubescens) *are managed to provide a sustainable crop of culms, which local people use in many ways (see p411).*

**Golden pheasant** (Chrysolophus pictus) *is native to scrubby hillsides and forests in central southern China, from 2,625–8,200 ft (800–2,500 m).*

**The giant panda** (Ailuropoda melanoleuca), *symbol of conservation, is slowly increasing in forest reserves in central and western China.*

# Landscape & Wildlife – East

China has the most diverse flora and fauna of any country in the temperate zone, with around 30,000 plant species, 500 mammal species, and 1,200 bird species. Although much of lowland China has been intensively cultivated for centuries, there still remains vast areas of important wild habitat including 29 million acres (12 million hectares) of lakes, and 31 million acres (13 million hectares) of marsh, bog, and coastal saltmarsh. The rugged nature of northeast China's borderlands has prevented the loss of its forest to agriculture, and, despite heavy logging, it is the largest area of forest in China. The accessibility of the steppe, however, has seen much of it lost to agriculture.

**Sacred Lotus**

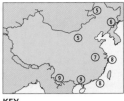

## KEY

- ⑤ Steppe Grasslands
- ⑥ Forests of Northeast China
- ⑦ Fertile Lowlands
- ⑧ Wetlands & Coasts
- ⑨ Jungle

## STEPPE GRASSLAND
The specialized grasses and drought resistant herbs of the steppe are an important source of food to the nomadic herders. In addition, their roots hold together the topsoil helping prevent erosion and desertification. Heavy cultivation in recent years has led to sandstorms in Beijing.

## FORESTS OF NORTHEAST CHINA
Forests here consist mainly of coniferous trees. Along with the evergreen fir, spruce, and pine, the deciduous larch is also common. To the south of these forest regions are mixed temperate broadleaf forests with oaks and birch prominent.

**The steppe cat** (Felis libyca) *is common in the shrubby steppe habitats of the Heavenly Mountains (Tian Shan) of the northwest. It feeds on small mammals, birds, and reptiles.*

**Asiatic black bears** (Ursus thibetanus) *are found in many regions – even as far south as Hainan. In colder areas they hibernate in winter.*

**The great bustard** (Otis tarda) *is, at up to 33 lb (15 kg), the heaviest flying bird. It nests in the open, on hummocks of dry grass.*

**The false acacia** (Robinia pseudoacacia), *though native to eastern North America, has been extensively planted in China.*

**The saiga antelope** (Saiga tatarica) *is one of the strangest steppe creatures. Its large nose filters dust and heats the air it breathes.*

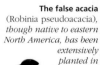

**The beautiful azure-winged magpie** (Cyanopica cyana) *is a sociable species, moving in noisy flocks through the trees of forests and parks.*

## UNDER THREAT

Pollution of the air, soil, and waterways, is threatening many of China's delicate environments, special animals, and plants, especially when faced with large building projects like the Three Gorges Dam. In addition, the use of rare animals in medicinal "remedies" means that many species face extinction from poaching. However, the Chinese government is now paying some attention to conservation and reports that the giant panda, great crested ibis, and Chinese alligator are all increasing in numbers thanks to the protection of their habitat and improved ecosystems. Nevertheless there is still a long way to go.

## JUNGLE

Tropical forests occur in the deep south of China – mainly on the island of Hainan, and also the basins of Yunnan. Many forests are secondary, or have been replaced through felling and grazing by a kind of savanna or by plantations, especially of rubber.

## FERTILE LOWLANDS

Intensively cultivated and denuded of natural vegetation, the huge lowland flood-plains of major rivers, notably the Yellow and Yangzi, are a seemingly endless patchwork of fields. Grain crops, dominated by rice, are broken up by ponds with fish, ducks, and frogs.

## WETLANDS AND COASTS

Wetlands are some of the country's most diverse ecosystems, being prime habitats for rare or endemic plants and animals. The lakes and flooded river valleys are also vital staging posts for migrating birds, such as waterfowl and species of endangered crane.

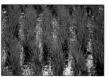

**Rice fields** *or paddies occupy much of the fertile lowlands and hillsides in central and southern China.*

**The water arum** (Calla palustris) *grows around marshes and bogs in the northeast at altitudes of up to 3,600 ft (1,100m).*

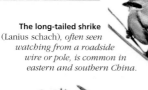

**The long-tailed shrike** (Lanius schach), *often seen watching from a roadside wire or pole, is common in eastern and southern China.*

**The mandarin duck** (Aix galericulata) *looks exotic and is a tree-hole nester, found mainly along wooded streams in the northeast.*

**Water Buffalo** (Bubalus arnee) *are beasts of burden and used for plowing. They are at home in the muddy wet paddy fields of the south.*

**Hawksbill turtles** (Eretmochelys imbricata) *still breed on a few beaches along the southern tropical coast but are at risk from humans.*

# China's Peoples

There are about 55 different ethnic minorities in China, each with their own distinctive customs, costumes and, in many cases, languages. Though rich in culture, and varied, together they make up only about seven percent of the population, with the main group, known as Han Chinese, accounting for the rest. Modernization of society and intermarriage are inevitably leading to a dilution of these differences, but many groups remain proud of their heritage and retain their traditional beliefs and customs. Many have beautiful styles of dress (especially the women), and these costumes and cultures have become a major attraction to visitors, who bring trade to communities.

**Over 1 million Kazakh**
*Muslims live in the north of Xinjiang Province. Renowned for their horsemanship, the Kazakhs center their lives around their precious horses and farming.*

**There are around**
*8 million Uighur, a Muslim people with a language close to Turkish. They inhabit Xinjiang Province in China's far northwest.*

KAZAKHSTAN

KAZAKHSTAN

Kazakh

MON

KYRGYZSTAN

Kyrgyz

Uighur

## NORTHWEST
A variety of mostly Islamic people inhabit this area dominated by desert, semi-desert, and mountains. The Uighur are the dominant minority and have their own Autonomous Region. Other groups include the Hui, Kazakhs, Kyrgyz, Uzbeks, Tajiks, and Tatars.

Tibetan

C    H    I

**Naxi of Lijiang** have strong traditions and are guardians of an ancient script.

NEPAL

**Bai** *people live mainly in Sichuan, Yunnan, Guizhou, and Hunan, and number some 1.6 million. Their capital is Dali (Yunnan). Although traditionally farmers and fishermen, their colorful costumes attract a lot of tourism.*

BHUTAN

Naxi
Lisu
Bai

MYANMAR

Ha
Dai

LAO

## SOUTHWEST
The Tibetan plateau is home to more than 4.5 million Tibetans. With around 20 different minorities the southwest of China has the most ethnic diversity. The Yi, the largest group in this region (6.6 million), live in Sichuan, Yunnan, and Guizhou.

**The Dai and Hani** *of Xishuangbanna in southern Yunnan in the tropical south are mainly Buddhist farmers, and have a deep respect for the natural world.*

## NORTHEAST

As well as the Mongolians, there are a few small groups of minorities in the northeast. These include about a few thousand Daur as well as the Oroqen, Hezhen and Ewenki. There are also around 2 million Koreans (Chaoxian) while the largest group are the Manchu, with about 9.8 million.

**The Muslim Hui** *have their own so-called Autonomous Region of Ningxia but have established communities in cities across China.*

**The Oroqen** *is one of China's smallest minority, with a population of about 7,000. They live mainly in Inner Mongolia and in Heilongjiang Province. They live in conical houses with birch bark or skin roofs, supported by poles (see p455).*

## CENTRAL & EAST

The 630,000 She live mainly in Fujian and Zhejiang Provinces. They are farmers, with a strong artistic tradition using bamboo. Another small group, the Gaoshan (about 400,000) are from Taiwan, but many have settled on the eastern mainland, notably in Fujian Province.

**The Tujia** *of Hunan, Hubei and Sichuan have a history stretching back over 2,000 years. There are about 5.7 million Tujia.*

## SOUTH

The largest minority in China is the Zhuang (15.5 million), who live mainly in their Autonomous Region of Guangxi, famous for the dramatic dragon-back rice terraces of Longsheng. They have linguistic and cultural links with the Dai who are ethnically related to Thai peoples. Renowned for their crafts and colorful festivals *(see pp406–9)*, the Miao (7.4 million) inhabit many areas in the southern provinces.

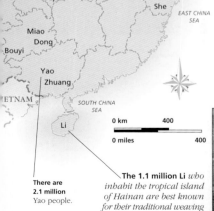

RUSSIAN FEDERATION

Oroqen

Hezhe

Manchu

Korean

NORTH KOREA

Mongolian

Hui

YELLOW SEA

N      A

ang      Tujia

She

EAST CHINA SEA

Miao
Dong

Bouyi

Yao

Zhuang

ETNAM

SOUTH CHINA SEA

Li

0 km          400

0 miles          400

There are 2.1 million Yao people.

**The 1.1 million Li** *who inhabit the tropical island of Hainan are best known for their traditional weaving skills, producing colorful woven articles.*

# Language and Script

The Chinese script can be traced back to the oracle bones of the Shang dynasty (16th–11th centuries BC) that were inscribed with symbols representing words and used for divination. Despite changes brought about by different writing materials, Chinese characters have remained remarkably consistent. It is said that to read a newspaper takes knowledge of at least 3,000 characters but an educated person would be expected to know over 5,000. Since 1913 the official spoken language has been *Putonghua* (Mandarin) but there are many regional dialects. Although people from different parts of China may not be able to understand each other, they can use a shared written script.

**Cang Jie**, *minister of the legendary Yellow Emperor, was supposedly inspired to invent the Chinese script one morning after seeing bird and animal tracks in the snow.*

## A BEAUTIFUL SCRIPT

Writing was elevated to an art form considered on a par with painting as a visual aesthetic *(see pp38–9)*. As the process changed from inscribing bone, brass or stone to using a brush on silk and paper, a more fluid writing style became possible.

**Seal, in red cinnabar** – this may be a name seal, or inscribed with other characters.

**Oracle bones** *display China's first examples of seal script. Questions were inscribed on the bones which were then burnt – the way cracks divided the inscriptions was deemed significant.*

**Bamboo slats** *were used from around the 5th century BC. These were tied together to make the earliest type of books. Used for administrative and philosophical texts, the script runs from top to bottom.*

**Writing materials** were silk, stone, or paper, which was first invented around the 2nd century BC.

**Cursive script** *(cao shu)* has strokes that run into each other. Fluid and dynamic, it allows for great expressiveness.

**The Diamond Sutra (AD 868)** *is the world's first block-printed book to bear a date. Printing was probably invented about a century earlier. Movable block printing was developed in the 11th century but had less social impact than in Europe because of the thousands of symbols required.*

## CHINESE CHARACTERS

May be composed of pictographic, ideographic and phonetic elements. The radical (or root), an element that appears on the left or at the top of a character, usually gives a clue as to sense. Here, in the character for "good," pronounced *"hao,"* the radical combines with another meaning element "child." The concept, therefore, is that "woman" plus "child" equals "good."

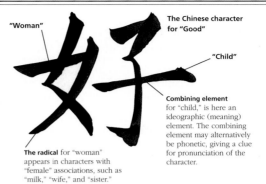

"Woman"

The Chinese character for "Good"

"Child"

Combining element for "child," is here an ideographic (meaning) element. The combining element may alternatively be phonetic, giving a clue for pronunciation of the character.

The radical for "woman" appears in characters with "female" associations, such as "milk," "wife," and "sister."

Pinyin is a Romanization *system that was introduced in 1956. While Pinyin will never replace the character forms, it is an easier method for children to start learning the language and useful for input to computers.*

## STYLES OF CALLIGRAPHY

**Zhuanshu**, or seal script, was developed during the Zhou era and used for engraved inscriptions.

**Lishu**, or clerical script, probably evolved during the Han era and was used for stone inscriptions.

**Kaishu**, or regular script, developed from Lishu after the Han era, is the basis of modern type.

**Cao shu**, or cursive script, literally grass script, has strokes that are reduced to abstract curves or dots.

**Xingshu**, or running script, has strokes that run together, and is a semicursive script.

**Simplified** script was introduced in 1956 to make it easier for peasants to learn to read.

**Chinese typewriters** *were very difficult to use. The typist had to find each character in a tray of thousands. Computers have made typing Simplified script much easier – the user types in the Pinyin and gets a sub-menu of several possible characters.*

# Chinese Literature

Dating back to the sixth century BC, the earliest Chinese
texts were primarily philosophic, such as the Confucian
*Analects* and Daoist *Daode Jing*. History as a literary
genre was not established until the Han period
(206 BC–AD 220) with Sima Qian's *Historical Records*:
thereafter each dynasty wrote a history of the preceding
one. As for the novel, a fully fledged Chinese example
did not appear until the Ming period (1368–1644) and
was developed during the Qing dynasty until it was
eventually stifled by Communism. Since the 1980s
Chinese authors have been allowed greater freedom of
expression, although, in 2000, news of exiled writer Gao
Xingjian's Nobel Prize for Literature was suppressed.

**Confucius, author of the *Analects*,
and his disciples**

## CLASSICS

Post-Qin dynasty, once Confucianism
had become the state orthodoxy, five
early works were canonized as the Five
Classics: *the Book of Changes, Book of
Documents, Book of Songs, Spring and
Autumn Annals* and *Book of Ritual*.
These books were established as the
basis for Chinese education.

**The scholar class or literati** *achieved the
status of government official through
success in the civil service examinations,
based on detailed knowledge of the Classics
and accomplishment in writing.*

## TANG POETS

With early beginnings in the *Book of Songs* and *Elegies of
Chu*, Chinese poetry reached its height more than twelve
hundred years later in the Tang period (618–907). The
two greatest Tang poets are considered to be Du Fu and
Li Bai. Others include the Buddhist Wang Wei, also 8th-
century, and slightly later Bai Juyi (772–846).

**Jia Baoyu** prefers to flirt with
the women rather than obey
his father and study hard to
advance his career.

**Du Fu** *(AD c. 712–770) wrote of
suffering in war, as well as of family
life. His keynote is compassion,
considered a Confucian virtue. His
poems display enormous erudition.*

**Li Bai** *(AD c. 701–761) was a
more ebullient figure. A prolific
poet, his favorite subjects were
moon gazing and carousing.
The theme of freedom from
constraint is a Daoist one.*

## EPIC NOVELS

In the Ming era, the novel developed from folk tales and myths into classics such as *Journey to the West*, *Romance of the Three Kingdoms* and *The Water Margin* – a tale of the heroic fight against corruption. Later, the Qing novels used a more elevated language and subtle characterization, culminating in the romantic novel, *Dream of the Red Chamber*. These novels contain many characters that reoccur in other cultural contexts from Beijing Opera to popular television serials and films.

**Guandi, God of War**, *derives from Guan Yu, a general of the state of Shu, portrayed in* Romance of the Three Kingdoms. *This novel was based on historical figures from the Three Kingdoms Era (AD 220–80). A symbol for justice, honesty, and integrity, his figurines are found in temples throughout China.*

**Journey to the West** *is a comic fantasy based on the pilgrimage to India of the Buddhist monk Xuanzang. The late Ming novel centers on Monkey, one of the monk's companions who represents carefree genius, bravery, and loyalty.*

### DREAM OF THE RED CHAMBER

Perhaps the greatest Chinese novel, this portrays the decline of an aristocratic Qing household. Infused with a Daoist sense of transcendence, it focuses on the life and loves of the idle Jia Baoyu and twelve perceptively drawn female characters.

## 20TH CENTURY

In the early 20th century, fiction writers and playwrights addressed social issues in a new realist style. However Communism demanded revolutionary themes. After the persecution of writers during the Cultural Revolution *(see pp64–5)*, experimental forms and styles gradually emerged. However, the books of Chinese authors may still be banned if they are openly critical of the government or are "spiritual pollutants"; nevertheless pirated versions are often widely available.

**Mo Yan** *is a post-Cultural Revolution fiction writer. Best known for his novel* Red Sorghum *(1986), made into a major film, he writes in a rich style, often graphic, fantastic, and violent.*

**Lu Xun**, *early 20th-century writer of short stories and novellas, is known as the father of modern Chinese literature. His realist, satirical style is indebted to such writers as Dickens. He is renowned for his humorous depiction of Ah Q, an illiterate but enthusiastic peasant, done down by the forces of convention.*

# Religion and Philosophy

Traditionally, the three strands in Chinese religion and philosophy are Confucianism, Daoism, and Buddhism. An eclectic approach to religion allows the three to coexist, often within a single temple. Confucianism, the first to gain real influence, can be seen as a manifestation of the public, socially responsible self. Daoism represents a personal and wilder side; its emphasis on the relativity of things contrasts with Confucian concern for approved roles. Buddhism, a foreign import, is spiritual and otherworldly, offering an alternative to Chinese pragmatism. During the Cultural Revolution, religion was outlawed as contrary to Communist ideas. Today, people are largely able to express their beliefs.

**Laozi, Buddha, and Confucius**

## CONFUCIANISM

Originated by Confucius (551–479 BC) and developed by later thinkers, Confucianism advocates a structured society in which people are bound to each other by the moral ties of the five familial relationships: parent-child, ruler-subject, brother-brother, husband-wife, and friend-friend. In Imperial China, Confucianism was the philosophy of the elite scholar-gentleman class. For much of the Communist era, it was reviled as a reactionary philosophy linked to the former ruling aristocracy.

**Filial piety**, *or* xiao, *another Confucian precept, consists of obedience to and reverence for one's parents, and by extension respect for other family members and one's ruler.*

**Confucius** *was a thinker and teacher whose philosophy of family obligations and good government is based on the principles of* ren *(benevolence) and* yi *(righteousness). He died unknown, his disciples spreading his teachings.*

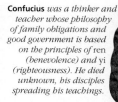

**The paying of respects** *to one's ancestors is based on filial piety and runs throughout Chinese culture. During the Qing Ming festival in April, Chinese traditionally clean and upkeep their ancestors' tombs.*

**The birth of Confucius** *is celebrated in the philosopher's home town of Qufu (see pp142–3) in late September. Many thousands of his descendants, all surnamed Kong, still live in the city.*

**Scholars** *collated the Confucian Classics including the* Lunyu *(Analects), a series of Confucius's sayings, well after his death. The Classics were the basis of education until 1912.*

## DAOISM

Strongly linked with early folk beliefs, Daoism incorporates the traditional concepts of an ordered universe, *yin* and *yang*, and directed energy, *qi* (see pp32–3). Over time, Daoism developed into a complex religion with an extensive pantheon. Daoist philosophy encourages following one's intuition and following the grain of the universe by living in accordance with the Dao.

**Laozi**, *the founder of Daoism, is a shadowy figure, who may have lived in the 6th century BC. The* Daode Jing, *which introduces the idea of Dao or the Way that permeates reality, is attributed to him.*

**Han Xiangzi**, *one of the Eight Immortals, a popular group of Daoist adepts, is believed to have fallen from a sacred peach tree, which bestowed eternal life. He is usually shown playing a flute.*

**Daoist alchemists** *aimed to find an elixir for eternal life, winning influence with emperors. Daoism influenced scientific development, and contributed to the discovery of gunpowder in the 9th century.*

**In "Peach Blossom Spring"** *by Daoist poet Tao Qian, a fisherman chances upon a lost idyllic world and encounters Immortals. Daoist reverence for nature led to the creation of numerous paradises.*

## BUDDHISM

In China the Mahayana school of Buddhism, which promises salvation to anyone who seeks it, is followed. Enlightened ones, *bodhisattvas*, remain in this world to help enlighten others. Through deeds and devotion believers gain merit and maintain their connections with the *bodhisattvas*, bringing them closer to nirvana.

**The Laughing Buddha**, *or Milefo, is an adaptation of the Maitreya, the Future Buddha. His large belly and laughing face are signs of abundance and he is worshiped in the hopes of a happy, affluent life.*

**The Guardian King** *of the South (left) is coiled by a snake; the King of the North holds a parasol. Kings of the four directions guard the entrance to many temples protecting the main deity from evil influences.*

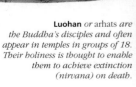

**Luohan** *or arhats are the Buddha's disciples and often appear in temples in groups of 18. Their holiness is thought to enable them to achieve extinction (nirvana) on death.*

**A Buddhist supplicant** *burns sticks of incense in aid of prayer. Buddhist temples throb with spiritual energy, as worshipers pray and make offerings to gain merit.*

# The Power of *Qi*

The Chinese philosophical notion of a cosmic *qi* or breath that permeates the universe dates from the Shang and Zhou periods. *Qi* is regarded as having created the cosmos and the Earth, and given rise to the complementary opposing negative and positive forces of *yin* and *yang*. Every physical change that occurs in the world is seen as a product of the working of *qi*. In the Daoist *Daode Jing*, *qi* is synonymous with Dao ("the Way"). The *qi* character *(right)* represents a bowl of rice with steam, where the rice's power or *qi* is manifested, rising above. The concept of *qi* runs through all areas of Chinese thought: it is a guiding principle in both traditional science and the arts.

Chinese character for *qi*, resembling a steaming bowl of rice

## HARNESSING *QI*
*Qi* informs multiple practical and applied fields. When Chinese medicine became formalized during the 2nd century BC, for example, *qi* was established as its central concept. It was seen as the vital substance of living things, circulating in the body through a network of channels or meridians *(see p232).*

**Acupressure** *and acupuncture rely on the idea of* qi *circulating in the body. A person may suffer from inadequate or excessive* qi, *and the aim is to release or dampen the* qi *as appropriate.*

**The *cun* trigram** is very *yin*. Its attributes are devotion and reception and it is connected to the element of earth.

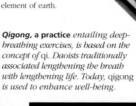

**Qigong, a practice** *entailing deep-breathing exercises, is based on the concept of* qi. *Daoists traditionally associated lengthening the breath with lengthening life. Today,* qigong *is used to enhance well-being.*

**Martial arts** *emphasize the cultivation of* qi. *Through concentration, practitioners, such as monks of the Shaolin Monastery, perform extraordinary feats of fitness and endurance.*

A **feng shui** *practitioner sets up a* bagua *chart and other instruments to trace the flow of* qi *within an office building.* Feng shui *is popular in Hong Kong, where it is less frowned on as a superstitious practice.*

## FENG SHUI

Chinese geomancy, or *feng shui* ("wind and water"), is based on ideas of *qi*. *Feng shui* posits that the appropriate layout of a building or room, for example the position of doorways, affects the flow of *qi* and hence the inhabitants' general well-being.

**The Ming Tombs** *(see pp104–5), constructed for the Ming emperors, were sited and built in accordance with* feng shui. *Evil influences from the north were supposedly warded off by the Jundu Shan mountain range.*

**The HSBC building** *on Hong Kong's Statue Square (see p310) is thought to enjoy outstanding* feng shui, *with harbor views and a large atrium allowing the free flow of* qi.

**The *qian* trigram,** *the trigram in which* yang qi *is strongest, consists of three unbroken lines.*

**The *yin-yang*** symbol, repre- sents the interdependency of *yin* (negative) and *yang* (positive).

## YIJING

The Chinese classic, the *Yijing (I Ching)*, or *Book of Changes,* has been consulted as a divination guide book for thousands of years. In it the *bagua* are combined into 64 hexagrams of six *yin* or *yang* lines each. The hexagrams represent even more complex states of *qi* than the *bagua*.

**Confucius,** *in his later years, became very inter- ested in the* Yijing, *and wrote numerous annota- tions to the text. Here he randomly divides yarrow sticks to create hexagrams and consults the* Yijing *to determine their meaning.*

## BAGUA CHART

Eight *bagua,* or trigrams, ranged around a *yin-yang* symbol make up the basic *bagua* chart, an attempt to codify the working of *qi.* Each trigram consists of three lines – *yin* (broken) or *yang* (unbroken). Together they make up all possible permu- tations of such sets of lines and describe potential movement between different *qi* states.

**Divination sticks** *are often consulted nowadays to divine the future. Outside temples in Hong Kong, worshipers can be seen scattering the sticks on the ground. A practiced diviner reads the pattern by picking out* bagua *shapes.*

# Architecture

For over two thousand years, the Chinese have used the same architectural model for both imperial and religious buildings. This has three elements: a platform, post-and-beam timber frames, and non-loadbearing walls. Standard

**Tiled imperial dragon**

features of building complexes include a front gate, four-sided enclosures or courtyards, and a series of halls in a linear formation running north. Most Chinese buildings were built of wood, but because wooden buildings tend to catch fire, only a few structures remain; the earliest date from the Tang period.

**Aerial view of the Forbidden City, showing the traditional linear layout**

## HALL

In every context, the Chinese hall or *tang* follows the same pattern: a platform of rammed earth or stone, and timber columns arranged in a grid. The front of the hall always has an odd number of bays. Between the columns and beams are brackets *(dougong)*, cantilevers that support the structure, allowing the eaves to overhang. The timber is brightly painted, the roof aesthetically curved, and tiled or thatched.

**Gate of Heavenly Purity** (see pp88)
*An archetypal Chinese hall, the central doorway and uneven number of bays emphasize the processional element.*

**Base gives monumentality**

**Bay, or space between columns**

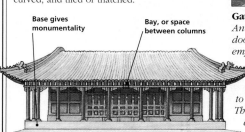

**Standard Hall**
*Buildings in China conformed to a set of rules about proportions. This uniform architecture created a sense of identity – useful in a large and disparate country.*

## STORIED BUILDING *(LOU)* AND STORIED PAVILION *(GE)*

Multi-story buildings in China predate pagodas and varied from two-storied private homes to huge seven- or more story towers built to enjoy the scenery. Storied pavilions were used for storage and had doors and windows only at the front. Both types of building kept the standard elements of base, columns, and hanging walls.

**Storied Pavilion**
*These were used for storing important items, such as libraries of Buddhist sutras or colossal statues.*

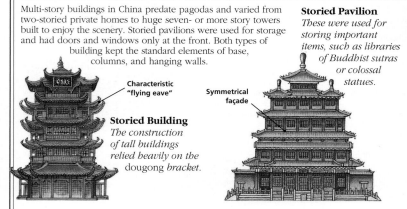

**Characteristic "flying eave"**

**Symmetrical façade**

**Storied Building**
*The construction of tall buildings relied heavily on the dougong bracket.*

## PAGODA

Based on the Indian stupa, the Chinese pagoda, or *ta*, was developed in the first century AD along with the arrival of Buddhism. Multi-storied pagodas appeared in Buddhist temple complexes (although later they often stood on their own) and were often intended to house a religious statue. They were built of brick, stone, or wood *(see p165)*.

Top resembles Indian stupa

Base, usually with an underground chamber

## ORNAMENTAL ARCHWAY

The *pailou*, or *paifang*, is a memorial or decorative archway. Made of wood, brick, or stone, and sometimes with glazed tiles, it often bears an edifying inscription. *Pailou* were erected at crossroads, temples, bridges, government offices, parks, and tombs.

Ornamental, multi-sectioned roof

Inscription typically four characters

## CITY WALLS

Early defensive walls, like other early architectural forms, were made of earth – either pounded hard by pestles or moistened to make a clay and pressed around reed frames. Later walls were often built using brick. City walls were traditionally square, with the main gate to the south. The Chinese for "city" *(cheng)* also means "wall."

Easy to defend with a bow

Gate tower, often a two-story *lou*

**Pingyao City Walls**
*Made of rammed earth and brick, rising 33 ft (10 m) high, the ramparts and watchtowers were an effective defense. The current structure, collapsed in parts, is from the Ming dynasty.*

**City wall and gate**
*The towers on top of walls can vary from small buildings to palatial multi-story structures.*

## ARCHITECTURAL DETAILS

It is interesting to interpret the architectural detail on Chinese buildings. The use of yellow tiles, for example, was reserved for the emperor. The Nine-Dragon Screen, which occurs in the Forbidden City and elsewhere, is also imperial since the dragon symbolizes the *yang*, or male principle, and by extension the emperor.

**Chiwen**
*Able to douse flames with water, the Chiwen often appears at the end of a roof ridge (see p87) as a protection against fire.*

**Dougong**
*A bracket (dougong), transmits the load from roof to column. It's a traditionally complex, nail-free, and ornamental construction method.*

# Chinese Inventions

**Pocket compass**

Printed books, porcelain, silk, umbrellas and kites are just a few of the everyday objects that originated in China and are used today throughout the world. Remarkably, the Chinese developed the technology to produce fine porcelain over 1,000 years before Europe. Philosophy played a part in two of the most famous Chinese discoveries. Seeking the elixir of life, Daoist alchemists stumbled upon gunpowder, while the magnetic compass was developed from an instrument used for geomancy and *feng shui*.

**Wheelbarrow:** *used in agriculture, industry, and by the military. Like the plow, it vastly increased the efficiency of manual workers.*

**Cast iron:** *made by lowering the ore's melting point with phosphorus before heating it in very hot blast furnaces that had been developed over hundreds of years of firing pottery.*

**The decimal system** developed alongside the writing system and led to mathematical advances.

**The first paper** was made from mulberry bark, bamboo, hemp, linen, and silk.

**The crossbow** had better range, penetration, and accuracy than the standard bow.

| 2000 | 1800 | 1600 | 1400 | 1200 | 1000 | 800 | 600 | 400 | 200 |
|------|------|------|------|------|------|-----|-----|-----|-----|

**BC**

| 2000 | 1800 | 1600 | 1400 | 1200 | 1000 | 800 | 600 | 400 | 200 |
|------|------|------|------|------|------|-----|-----|-----|-----|

**High-fired stoneware:** *first produced in the Shang dynasty, at the same time as the early glazes that added strength color, and waterproofing.*

**Kuan or moldboard plow:** *increased the efficiency of farmers. A cast-iron blade could cut through and plow previously unplowable land.*

## GREAT LEAPS FORWARD

Early advances in technology spawned an agricultural revolution in China. Iron-bladed plows increased the amount of land that could be farmed and multiplied its productivity, enabling a larger population to be sustained. Paper, paper money, and printing were key to the efficient administration of a vast populous, centrally controlled state. Increased manpower, organization, and technology advanced industrial production in mining and porcelain factories, for example, as well as boosting China's military might.

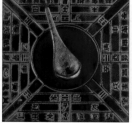

**Magnetic compass:** *used for geomancy, the first compasses consisted of a loadstone spoon and bronze plate. Later examples would help Chinese sailors make huge voyages on trading trips.*

**Porcelain:** *ceramic technology reached a new peak in the 6th century with the discovery of "true" porcelain; hard, white and translucent, it rings to the touch. Production methods would stay a closely guarded secret, keeping its value for export (see p254).*

**Stirrup:** *this increased the efficiency of horses as tools for communication, transportation, and warfare.*

**Printing:** *woodblock printing was used to spread Buddhist teachings, and was well-developed by the time of the Diamond Sutra (see p26). In 1041–8, Bi Sheng carved individual characters on pieces of clay, inventing movable block type.*

## PRINTING

The discovery of movable type did not really impact upon Chinese society, and most printers continued to carve the individual characters into a block. In Europe 400 years later, however, the discovery of movable type revolutionized society. This is because it is much easier to handle the 26 or so different blocks in a Roman alphabet than the around 3,000 or more characters needed for a Chinese newspaper – not even allowing for duplicates. Woodblock carving therefore required far fewer resources.

| 200 | 400 | 600 | 800 | 1000 | 1200 | 1400 | 1600 | 1800 | 2000 |
|-----|-----|-----|-----|------|------|------|------|------|------|

AD ..................................................................................... AD

| 200 | 400 | 600 | 800 | 1000 | 1200 | 1400 | 1600 | 1800 | 2000 |
|-----|-----|-----|-----|------|------|------|------|------|------|

**Paper money:** *developed by merchants as certificates of exchange. Lighter than coins, bills were soon adopted by the government.*

**Gun powder:** *first discovered by necromancers. It was originally used for fireworks and mining and not for warfare until the 8th century.*

**Cargo ship:** *designed with compartments, and equipped with fore-and-aft lugsails and stern-post rudders, these multi-masted ships were larger and technically superior to their European counterparts.*

**Seismometer:** *invented by Chang Heng. It identified the direction of an earthquake when a ball fell from one of the dragons into a frog's mouth.*

**The abacus:** *invented during the Yuan dynasty. Because it is able to perform complex calculations, it is often referred to as the first computer and is still used in China today.*

# Traditional Arts

**Funerary bronze bell**

The earliest Chinese artifacts were found in royal tombs. These include bronzes, ceramics, and jades from the Shang and Zhou period, as well as terracotta warriors from the Qin period. Of the many rich art forms that subsequently developed in China, painting and pottery are perhaps the most important, and have reached the highest aesthetic level. Other significant art forms include sculpture, notably the Buddhist sculpture of Western China. There are also many distinctive and popular forms of Chinese decorative art.

**Buddhist sculpture in the Gandharan style**

**Ritual bronze tripod** *from an early royal tomb, decorated with a mythical animal design known as a* taotie.

**Wet and dry ink** used to give the detail of the trees.

## POTTERY

Since inventing porcelain, China developed a huge range of potting, decorating, and glazing techniques that were imitated from Europe to Japan. Chinese ceramics led the world in aesthetic taste and technique up until the demise of the Qing dynasty.

**Textured strokes** give the rocks depth.

**Tang earthenware tomb figure** *representing a fierce warrior, with typical rough* sancai *(three-color) drip glaze. This was a lead-based glaze, fired at a low temperature.*

**Song celadon bowl**, *with incised floral design. Celadon was the European name given to the refined gray-green glaze of this type of stoneware and porcelain.*

**Ming vase** *in the blue-and-white style known and imitated internationally. The technique involves underglaze painting in cobalt blue before the pot is fired.*

**Qing famille-rose vase,** *a delicate porcelain in a distinctive palette. The name comes from the use of bright pink enamel.*

**Bird-and-flower painting** *(including the depiction of fruit and insects) reveals the Chinese Daoist interest in observing the natural world. Despite the lightness of subject, the paintings have an intense, quasi-scientific depth.*

## CHINESE PAINTING

Considered the highest traditional art form, Chinese painting is executed on silk or paper using a brush and inks or watercolors. **Landscape painting**, associated with the scholar class, reached a highpoint in the Northern Song and Yuan periods. Huang Gongwang *(see below)*, a master of the Yuan, was admired for his simple calligraphic style.

**Religious painting** *first appeared along the Silk Road with the arrival of Buddhism from India. The Chinese soon developed an individual style.*

**Ink wash** is used for the hills in the distance.

**Bamboo painting** *was a genre of the scholar class. Bamboo symbolized the scholar-gentleman who would bend but not break in the face of adversity.*

## TRADITIONAL CRAFTS

As well as the traditional high art forms of painting and pottery, China has a wealth of beautiful decorative arts. Delicate carvings in lacquer, ivory and jade are popular, as are colorful cloisonné items, decorated inksticks (or cakes), snuff bottles, and fans.

**Snuff bottles** *were produced in large numbers during the Qing period. Made of glass, jade, mother-of-pearl, or semi-precious stones, they were delicately carved or painted on the inside in exquisite detail.*

**Lacquer carving** *is distinctive for its deep red color and floral designs, and is often used on boxes.*

**Cloisonné** *is a style of enameling. Individual metal cloisons, usually made of copper, are soldered together and inlaid with different colored enamels. The object is then fired and polished.*

# Modern Arts

The birth of modern art in China at the start of the 20th century coincided with greater contact with the West. Experiments with new materials and styles in the visual arts, Western-style music, "spoken drama" *(huaju)*, cinema, and modern literary forms such as free verse all took root at this time. However, after 1949, this creativity was stifled by Soviet-influenced Socialist Realism. During the Cultural Revolution many artists were even persecuted on the grounds that their works were "reactionary." Since the 1980s and 1990s, however, there has been some liberalization in the arts and new, exciting forms have developed.

**The Oriental Pearl TV Tower**, *Pudong, Shanghai is one example of China's high-rise architecture boom since the early 1990s.*

**This example of performance art** *is by Cang Xin, a Beijing-based conceptual artist, active since the mid-1990s. The title of this piece,* Unification of Heaven and Man, *alludes to classical Chinese philosophical concepts.*

Shaven-headed man

### MODERN ART

This painting, *Series 2 No. 2*, is by Fang Lijun, leader of the Cynical Realism school, which came about as a reaction to the demise of the pro-democracy movement in 1989. Rejecting idealism, these artists comment on problems in China.

**Sculpture** *entitled* Torso, *by Zhan Wang, a Shanghai-based conceptual artist. Zhan uses reflective steel sheets to give the illusion of solidity.*

**Orchestral and chamber music** *has been popular in China since the early 20th century. Today, there are many schools specializing in Western-style music, and several high-quality ensembles and artists on the world scene.*

## CHINESE CINEMA

From early classics such as *Street Angel* (1937), made in the (then) foreign enclave of Shanghai, Chinese cinema has scaled new heights of international success, with the work of such acclaimed directors as Zhang Yimou.

**Farewell My Concubine (1993)**, *directed by Chen Kaige, a post-Cultural Revolution filmmaker, who gave expression to new moral uncertainties, is set in the world of traditional Chinese Opera.*

**The Hong Kong film industry** *followed its own path and became primarily famous for its action movies. Renowned martial arts star Jackie Chan, seen above in an early acting and directorial debut,* Fearless Hyena, *made many films and successfully crossed over from Hong Kong to Hollywood.*

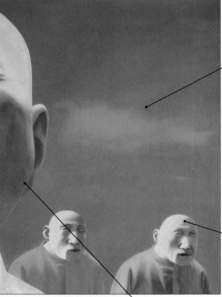

**Background is a hazy blue, making it appear dream-like**

**Wei Wei** *is one of the bestselling pop stars in China today. Rock music only took off in the 1980s: Cui Jian, the "grandad" of Chinese rock still performs but is seen as a rebel by the authorities. Hong Kong's less controversial Canto-pop singers, in contrast, have had more freedom.*

**Anonymous figures seem threatening**

**Main figure is yelling or yawning – is he angry or just bored?**

**Ballet** *in contemporary China mixes traditional Chinese and Western influences. Here, the ballet version of Zhang Yimou's film* Raise the Red Lantern *is performed by members of the National Ballet.*

**Modern theater** *provides an expression of Chinese life in the 21st century. Here, a scene from* Toilet *(2004), a black comedy, is performed by the National Theater company in Beijing. The play broke taboos with its frank portrayal of urban life and treatment of homosexuality.*

# Festivals

An important part of Chinese culture and tradition, festivals are generally happy and colorful affairs that reaffirm ancient beliefs and customs. The biggest and most important festival is Spring Festival, or Chinese New Year. This brings families together for several days: the home is cleaned and everyone dresses up in new clothes; decorations are put up and gifts exchanged; and finally there is always time for a lively and noisy carnival climaxing in a brilliant display of pyrotechnics. Nearly all the festival elements and rituals are geared towards bringing good luck and prosperity. In business, all debts should be settled by Chinese New Year. Overall, the festivities last about 15 days but the whole country closes down for only four.

**Hongbao**
*These decorative red envelopes symbolize luck and wealth and bring about both as they contain money – they are typically given to children on New Year's Eve.*

**Lion Dance**
*Performed at New Year and other festivals. Usually two people are required to play the lion. The dance demands more martial arts skills than the Dragon Dance, also performed on these occasions.*

**Fireworks exploding over Hong Kong's Victoria Harbour**

**Firecrackers**
*Strings of firecrackers are set off at New Year making the streets noisy and, potentially, dangerous places. Beijing tried to ban these in the center of the city supposedly driving people out to the suburbs for noisy fun.*

**Drummers**
*At the Spring Festival, processions of dancers and drummers march over the New Year period up until the Lantern Festival. Like the firecrackers, the noise of the drumming is supposed to keep the evil spirits away.*

### FESTIVAL FOOD

**A type of mooncake**

Each festival has its special food: *jiaozi* (boiled dumplings) are usually eaten for New Year especially in the North of China; *yuanxiao* (glutinous rice balls) feature during the Lantern Festival and can be made with a sweet or savory filling; and *zongzi* (sticky rice pyramids wrapped in bamboo leaves) are served at the Dragon Boat Festival. The Mid-Autumn Festival, which falls on a full moon, brings mooncakes. Made to a thousand recipes with savory or sweet fillings, the cake symbolizes the moon.

**Rice pyramids or *zongzi***

### SPECTACULAR FIREWORKS

New Year would not be complete without fireworks. Some major cities put on impressive all-night displays. Fireworks were originally intended to ward off evil spirits, or perhaps wake up the dragon who would create rain in the coming year and guarantee a good harvest.

**Colorful lanterns**
*Coinciding with the full moon, the Lantern Festival marks the end of the two-week New Year period. Lanterns may bear auspicious characters or be in animal shapes.*

**Tangerines**
*A New Year symbol of luck, tangerines are put on display at home – along with fresh flowers. The word for "tangerine" sounds like "luck" in Chinese while flowers signify a new beginning.*

**Duilian**
*These red scrolls at either side of the doorway bear Spring Couplets in classical Chinese expressing good wishes for the family in the coming year.*

**Traditional papercut of an astrological chart**

### CHINESE ASTROLOGY

Each year is associated with one of twelve animal signs, which repeat in a cycle. At New Year people talk of welcoming, for example, the "Year of the Dog." In Chinese astrology, people born under a specific animal sign are supposed to have some of the characteristics attributed to the animal.

**Dragon** 2012, symbol of China, the emperor, and the positive Yang element (*see pp32–3*).

**Snake** 2013, an ancient ancestor, Fuxi, was thought to be half-human and half-snake.

**Horse** 2014, symbol of freedom.

**Sheep** 2015, signifying peace and creativity.

**Monkey** 2016, associated with fun and genius, as in the story of the Monkey King.

**Rooster** 2017 has 5 virtues: refinement, courage, assertiveness, benevolence, and reliability.

**Dog** 2018, considered lucky in Chinese mythology.

**Pig** 2019, associated with fertility and virility.

**Rat** 2020, welcomed as a clever protector and bringer of wealth.

**Ox** 2021, Laozi, the Daoist philosopher, is often shown sitting on an ox.

**Tiger** 2022, in China he is deemed the king of the animals.

**Rabbit** 2023, associated with longevity and believed to live in the moon.

# CHINA THROUGH THE YEAR

The traditional Chinese festivals are tied to the lunar calendar, which has 29.5 days a month, and this means the solar dates change every year. Festivals associated with Communism – National Day and Labor Day, for example – are usually fixed to the Western calendar. Religious festivals, kept alive in Hong Kong, Tibet, and other areas of the Chinese-speaking world, are gradually making a comeback in the

A red lantern – lucky symbol

People's Republic of China (PRC), and outlying areas such as Inner Mongolia have their own distinctive festivals. Some celebrations of foreign origin such as Christmas are also observed. Before the important New Year Festival, there are weeks of preparation. Most offices and shops are closed for three days, but many tend to take a week-long break at this time. As most Chinese return to their family home, travel is very difficult.

Colorful parade celebrating Chinese New Year

## SPRING (FEB–APR)

This is the time of year when Chinese people try to settle old debts and make time to meet with friends and family members. The arrival of peach blossom is a signal of rejuvenation and the Spring Festival celebrates the start of the ancient cycle of plowing and sowing.

### 1ST LUNAR MONTH

**Spring Festival (Chun Jie)**
The main festival – Chinese New Year (see pp42–3). Gifts and red envelopes filled with money are exchanged and new shoes and clothes worn.
**Lantern Festival** (Feb–Mar) Coinciding with a full moon, this festival marks the end of the fifteen-day New Year period. A great many lanterns bearing auspicious characters or in animal

shapes can be seen. *Yuanxiao* (sticky rice balls) are eaten.

### 2ND LUNAR MONTH

**Tibetan New Year** Tibetan New Year is marked by the eating of "barley crumb"

A highly elaborate Tibetan butter sculpture

food and an exchange of Tashi Delek blessings. It is followed by Monlam, the great prayer festival later in the month, and the butter lamp festival.
**Hong Kong Arts Festival** *(Feb/Mar)* A major international arts festival as well as the premier arts event in Hong Kong. A mix of overseas and local artists provide music, theater, dance, popular entertainment, film and exhibition programs over three or four weeks.
**International Women's Day** *(Mar 8)* Women have a half or even a whole day's holiday, while men continue to work.

### 3RD LUNAR MONTH

**Tree-planting Day** *(Apr 1)* Promoted since the late 1970s by the reformist government, but not an official holiday, this is part of a greening campaign.
**Weifang International Kite Festival** *(Apr)* Flying kites is part of Qingming celebrations. Over 1,000 contestants compete at this festival in Shandong.
**Water Sprinkling Festival** *(mid-Apr)* Exclusive to the Dai people (Xishuangbanna, Yunnan, see p383). Marks the Dai lunar New Year, and involves blessing others by sprinkling or splashing them with water, which represents the quelling of the flames of a mythical tyrant demon.

Qing Ming Festival, sweeping or tending the ancestors' graves

**Qing Ming Festival** *(Apr)*
Festival for sweeping the graves and honoring the dead. Food is left on the grave and families often take a picnic with them.

**Hainan Coconut Festival** *(Apr)* Set up in 1992, and a showcase for the local coconut harvest.

**Third Moon Fair** *(Apr)* Dali area. This festival is exclusive to the Buddhist Bai minority in Yunnan. Events include fairs, horse-racing, singing, and dancing.

**Tin Hau Festival** *(Apr–May)* Celebrated in Hong Kong and coastal areas such as Fujian, the birthday of the Heavenly Queen or Mazu *(see p149)*, who looks after those at sea, is important for fishermen and sailors.

## SUMMER (MAY–JUL)

Once the summer arrives, festivals are often held outdoors. May sees the start of the traveling season as many people go on trips around the country to see family and friends.

## 4TH LUNAR MONTH

**International Labor Day** *(May 1)* A week-long holiday around May Day during which travel can be difficult.

**Youth Day** *(May 4)* Commemorates the student movements of 1919, which sparked the evolution of modern China.

**Buddha's Birthday** An important religious festival in Tibet but not officially observed in the PRC, though Buddhists may now do so privately. The festival has a higher profile in Hong Kong, where it is also known as the Festival of the Ten Thousand Buddhas. Buddhists pray for the washing away of sin and the attainment of wisdom and peace.

**"Meet in Beijing" Festival** *(May)* International music and arts festival, including opera, dance, instrumental and vocal concerts.

## 5TH LUNAR MONTH

**Children's Day** *(Jun 1)* Cinemas and other places of entertainment are free to children, who are also showered with presents.

**Dragon Boat Festival (or Fifth Moon Festival)** *(Jun)* commemorates the patriotic poet Qu Yuan who drowned himself. Originally religious but now just fun. Teams of rowers compete in long, decorated boats. Rice cakes *(zongzi)* are eaten. Hong Kong has several very colorful events, one with international teams.

**Shanghai International Film Festival** *(Jun)* First held in October 1993, this is the only accredited A Category international film festival in mainland China.

Dragon Boat Festival – colorful, lively, and exciting to watch

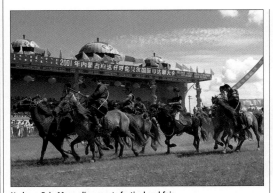

Nadaam Fair, Mongolian sports festival and fair

## 6TH LUNAR MONTH

**Founding of Chinese Communist Party** *(Jul 1)* A day to mark the event that took place in 1921 in Shanghai.

## AUTUMN (AUG–OCT)

The weather may still be warm in the sub-tropical south, but in the high uplands and central areas it is cooling down. As the leaves turn golden, this is a popular time of the year to travel to festivals.

## 7TH LUNAR MONTH

**Army day** *(Aug 1)* Marks the first Communist uprising against the Nationalists in 1927. The theme is unity between the army and the people.
**Lovers' festival** *(Aug)* A romantic day, this celebrates the story of the earthly cowherd and celestial weaving girl who were separated by the gods but who are annually reunited in the heavens by a bridge of magpies on the seventh day of the seventh moon. It is also known as Seven Sisters Festival.
**Shoton (Yoghurt festival)** *(Aug/Sep)* Tibetan festival of opera. Takes its name from the yoghurt served by pilgrims to the monks.
**Nadaam Fair** *(Aug)* (Inner Mongolia) Held in Hohhot,
Bayanbulak and elsewhere, Inner Mongolia. Horse-racing, wrestling and archery. Women wear their traditional dress. It's also a trading fair.
**Nakchu Horse Race Festival** (Tibet) *(Aug)* The most important folk festival in Tibet. This takes place in Nakchu. Over a thousand herdsmen then compete in the traditional Tibetan sports of archery horse-racing, and general horsemanship.
**Zhongyuan (Hungry Ghost Festival)** Similar to Halloween, a traditional festival combining elements of ancestor worship and Buddhism, suppressed under Communism. Considered an inauspicious time to move house or marry.

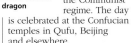

Mid-Autumn festival dragon

**Qingdao International Beer Festival** *(Aug)* Held in the eastern port city of Qingdao, Shandong, home of Tsingtao Beer, brewed from the spring waters of nearby Lao Shan *(see p146)*.

## 8TH LUNAR MONTH

**Teachers' Day** *(Sep 1)* Not an established holiday, but it began in the 1980s in response to the anti-intellectualism of the Cultural Revolution.
**Mid Autumn Festival or Zhong Qiu** *(Sep)* Harvest or moon festival when moon cakes are eaten throughout the country and family reunions take place *(see p43)*.
**Shaolin International Martial Arts Festival** *(Sep)* Annual event since 1991 in the city of Zhengzhou.
**Confucius' Birthday** *(Sep 28)* Gradually regaining popularity in the PRC, after vilification of the sage (born in 551BC) under the Communist regime. The day is celebrated at the Confucian temples in Qufu, Beijing and elsewhere.
**International Fashion Festival** (mid-Sep) Dalian. Two weeks of fashion shows by Asian designers, with a spectacular opening parade.

Qingdao International Beer Festival dancers

National day, well-drilled troops on the march

## 9TH LUNAR MONTH

**National Day** *(Oct 1)* A great rush of holiday-making takes place during this week-long break. Parades celebrate the founding of the PRC in 1949. **Double-ninth (Chongyang) Festival** *(Oct)* Double nine signifies double *yang* (in the *yin-yang* duality), connected with male assertiveness and strength. Traditionally, people do symbolic things like climb to high places, carry a sprig of dogwood, and drink chrysanthemum wine to drive away evil spirits at this festival, though it's not observed everywhere.

## WINTER (NOV–JAN)

This season brings a drop in temperatures and relief from the humidity in the south, while central and northern regions usually experience bitter winters. The main traveling season is over but everyone enjoys the lengthy preparations for the Chinese New Year at home.

## 10TH LUNAR MONTH

**Zhuang Song Festival** *(Nov)* The Zhuang minority in Guangxi have their own distinctive folk-song and dance tradition. Since 1999

an International Folk Song and Arts Festival has been held in Nanning.

## 11TH LUNAR MONTH

**Winter Solstice** Chinese astronomers identified this day as early as the Han period. Historically, it has been an important festival, though less so now. In the north, people often eat dumpling soup or dumplings on this day to keep them warm. In the south, people may eat red-bean and sticky rice to drive away evil spirits. **Christmas Day** *(Dec 25)* Although only a tiny number of the population is Christian, the commercial side of this celebration has taken off with Christmas trees and Shengdan Laoren, a Chinese version of Father Christmas, seen as a popular image. It's a public holiday in Hong Kong.

## 12TH LUNAR MONTH

**Corban Festival** *(Dec/Jan)* Celebrated in Xinjiang, Ningxia, and among Hui people across China, this is a Muslim festival remembering Abraham's last-minute reprieve to sacrifice a goat instead of his son. Animals are slaughtered for a feast, with singing and dancing.

**New Year's Day** *(Jan 1)* Overshadowed by the massive Chinese New Year celebrations that take place later in January or February, but it is still a recognized public holiday.

### PUBLIC HOLIDAYS

**New Year's Day** (Jan 1)

**Chinese New Year or Spring Festival** (Jan/Feb)

**Qing Ming Festival** (Apr)

**International Labor Day** (May 1–3)

**Dragon Boat Festival** (May)

**National Day** (Oct)

**Weekend Shifting**
The weekends before and after the Spring Festival and October holidays are often shifted from year to year *toward* the 3-day block to allow for a continuous run of 7 days' holiday. To add to the confusion, the exact days of the holiday are usually not finalized until shortly beforehand. You may wish to avoid traveling during this period because many facilities are closed. Try to confirm the exact dates with a travel agent beforehand.

# The Climate of China

With many different climate zones across its vast landmass, China experiences all extremes of weather ranging from the hot, wet summers and warm winters of the sub-tropical southwestern coast and high temperatures of the Turpan Depression to the cool summers and long, dry winters of its mountainous regions. Rainfall is sparse in the arid northern uplands and the near-Siberian northeast but plentiful in the humid south and east.

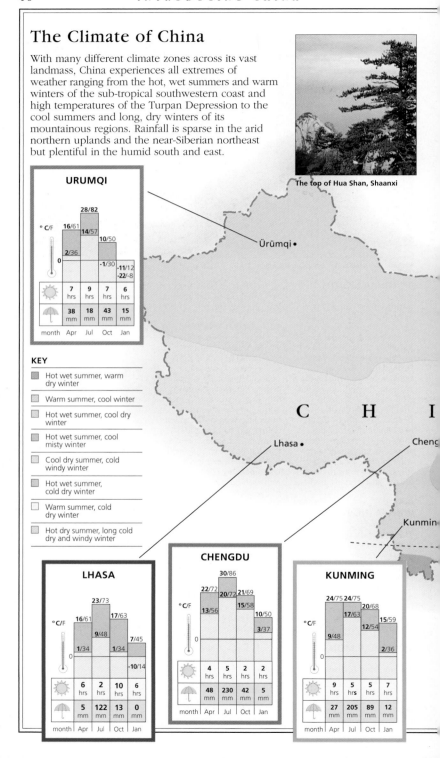

The top of Hua Shan, Shaanxi

**URUMQI**

| °C/F | 16/61 | 28/82 | 10/50 | |
| | | 14/57 | | |
| | 2/36 | | -1/30 | -11/12 |
| 0 | | | | -22/-8 |
| ☀ | 7 hrs | 9 hrs | 7 hrs | 6 hrs |
| ☂ | 38 mm | 18 mm | 43 mm | 15 mm |
| month | Apr | Jul | Oct | Jan |

Ürümqi •

**KEY**

| | |
|---|---|
| ▮ | Hot wet summer, warm dry winter |
| ▢ | Warm summer, cool winter |
| ▮ | Hot wet summer, cool dry winter |
| ▮ | Hot wet summer, cool misty winter |
| ▢ | Cool dry summer, cold windy winter |
| ▮ | Hot wet summer, cold dry winter |
| ▢ | Warm summer, cold dry winter |
| ▮ | Hot dry summer, long cold dry and windy winter |

C    H    I

Lhasa •

Cheng

Kunmin

**LHASA**

| °C/F | 16/61 | 23/73 | 17/63 | |
| | | 9/48 | | 7/45 |
| | 1/34 | | 1/34 | |
| 0 | | | | -10/14 |
| ☀ | 6 hrs | 2 hrs | 10 hrs | 6 hrs |
| ☂ | 5 mm | 122 mm | 13 mm | 0 mm |
| month | Apr | Jul | Oct | Jan |

**CHENGDU**

| °C/F | 22/72 | 30/86 | 21/69 | |
| | 13/56 | 20/72 | 15/58 | 10/50 |
| | | | | 3/37 |
| 0 | | | | |
| ☀ | 4 hrs | 5 hrs | 2 hrs | 2 hrs |
| ☂ | 48 mm | 230 mm | 42 mm | 5 mm |
| month | Apr | Jul | Oct | Jan |

**KUNMING**

| °C/F | 24/75 | 24/75 | 20/68 | |
| | | 17/63 | | 15/59 |
| | 9/48 | | 12/54 | |
| 0 | | | | 2/36 |
| ☀ | 9 hrs | 5 hrs | 5 hrs | 7 hrs |
| ☂ | 27 mm | 205 mm | 89 mm | 12 mm |
| month | Apr | Jul | Oct | Jan |

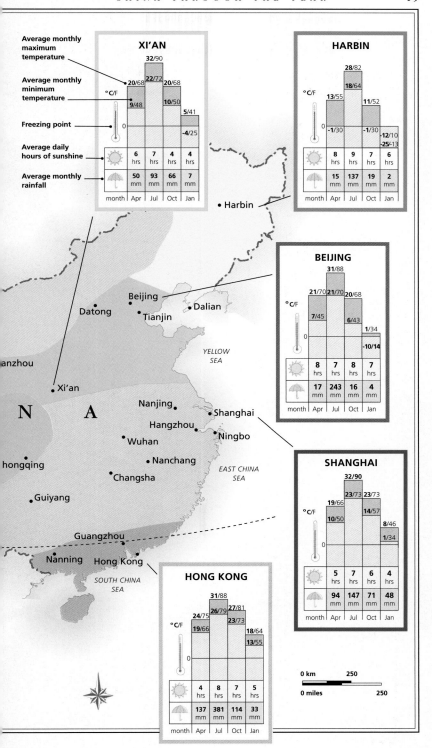

**XI'AN**

Average monthly maximum temperature
Average monthly minimum temperature
Freezing point
Average daily hours of sunshine
Average monthly rainfall

°C/F

| | 20/68 | 32/90 | 20/68 | 5/41 |
| | 9/48 | 22/72 | 10/50 | -4/25 |

0

| | 6 hrs | 7 hrs | 4 hrs | 4 hrs |
| | 50 mm | 93 mm | 66 mm | 7 mm |
| month | Apr | Jul | Oct | Jan |

**HARBIN**

°C/F

| | 13/55 | 28/82 | 11/52 | -12/10 |
| | -1/30 | 18/64 | -1/30 | -25/-13 |

0

| | 8 hrs | 9 hrs | 7 hrs | 6 hrs |
| | 15 mm | 137 mm | 19 mm | 2 mm |
| month | Apr | Jul | Oct | Jan |

**BEIJING**

°C/F

| | 21/70 | 31/88 | 20/68 | 1/34 |
| | 7/45 | 21/70 | 6/43 | -10/14 |

0

| | 8 hrs | 7 hrs | 8 hrs | 7 hrs |
| | 17 mm | 243 mm | 16 mm | 4 mm |
| month | Apr | Jul | Oct | Jan |

**SHANGHAI**

°C/F

| | 19/66 | 32/90 | 23/73 | 8/46 |
| | 10/50 | 23/73 | 14/57 | 1/34 |

0

| | 5 hrs | 7 hrs | 6 hrs | 4 hrs |
| | 94 mm | 147 mm | 71 mm | 48 mm |
| month | Apr | Jul | Oct | Jan |

**HONG KONG**

°C/F

| | 24/75 | 31/88 | 27/81 | 18/64 |
| | 19/66 | 26/79 | 23/73 | 13/55 |

0

| | 4 hrs | 8 hrs | 7 hrs | 5 hrs |
| | 137 mm | 381 mm | 114 mm | 33 mm |
| month | Apr | Jul | Oct | Jan |

• Harbin

Datong •
Beijing •  • Dalian
Tianjin •

anzhou

• Xi'an

N    A

Nanjing •
Hangzhou •  • Shanghai
Wuhan •  • Ningbo
hongqing  • Nanchang
Changsha •

• Guiyang

Guangzhou •

Nanning •  Hong Kong •

YELLOW SEA

EAST CHINA SEA

SOUTH CHINA SEA

0 km    250
0 miles    250

# THE HISTORY OF CHINA

C*hina boasts one of the longest single unified civilizations in the world. Its history is characterized by dramatic shifts in power between rival factions, periods of peace and prosperity when foreign ideas were assimilated and absorbed, the disintegration of empire through corruption and political subterfuge, and the cyclical rise of ambitious leaders to found each new empire.*

### FIRST SETTLERS

From around 8000 BC, settlements of populations based on a primitive agricultural economy began to emerge in the eastern coastal regions and along the rich river deltas of the Huang He (Yellow River), the Yangzi, and the Wei. These civilizations focused on hunting, gathering, and fishing, and the cultivation of millet in the north and rice in the south. Each civilization is notable

Yangshao pottery amphora

for its own distinct style of pottery, such as the bold earthenware of the Yangshao (5000–3000 BC) and the black ceramics of the Longshan (3000–1700 BC).

### BRONZE AGE CHINA AND THE FIRST KINGDOMS

The first dynasty in China was founded by the Shang around 1600 BC. The Shang lived in large, complex societies and were the first to mass-produce cast bronze. Power centered on the ruling elite who acted as shamans of a sort, communicating with their ancestors and gods through diviners.

Elaborate bronze food and wine vessels were used both for banqueting and for making ancestral offerings. Inscriptions on oracle bones provide the first evidence of writing, dating from around 1300 BC.

In 1066 BC, the Zhou seized power, establishing their western capital at present-day Xi'an. The Western Zhou initially sustained many of the traditions of the Shang, but later reorganized the political system, and replaced the use of oracle bones with inscriptions on bronze and, later, writing on silk and strips of bamboo.

The Eastern Zhou (770–221 BC) is divided into the Spring and Autumn period (770–475 BC) and the Warring States period (475–221 BC). The Eastern Zhou period was dominated by political conflict and social unrest, as rival factions jockeyed for power. It also saw economic expansion and development as the use of iron revolutionized agriculture. It was in this climate of unrest that the philosophical ideologies of Confucianism, Daoism, and Legalism emerged.

## TIMELINE

| 8000 BC | 6000 BC | 4000 BC | 2000 BC | 1000 BC | 500 BC |
|---|---|---|---|---|---|

**8000– 6500 BC**
Neolithic period

**5000–3000 BC**
Yangshao culture based around the Wei river

**2200–1600 BC**
Existence of semimythical first dynasty, the Xia

**1300 BC** First writing on oracle bones

**c. 551–479 BC**
Life of Confucius

**475–221 BC**
Eastern Zhou: Warring States

**6500–5000 BC**
Earliest settlements in northern China

**1600–1050 BC**
Shang dynasty

**1066 –771 BC** Power seized by Zhou

**770–476 BC**
Eastern Zhou: Spring and Autumn period

**513 BC** First mention of iron casting

*Bronze food vessel, Shang*

◁ **Detail from "The first Emperor of the Han Dynasty Entering Kuan Tung" by Song painter Chao Po Chu**

# Dynasty Timeline

China was ruled by a succession of dynasties, broken by periods of fragmentation and civil war. The emperor's authority was divinely granted through a mandate of heaven and was thus unlimited. Leaders of succeeding dynasties claimed that the previous leadership had displeased the gods and had therefore had its heavenly mandate withdrawn.

## SHANG DYNASTY

### 1600–1050 BC

The Shang dynasty marked the emergence of Bronze Age China and palace culture. A semi-divine king acted as a shaman and communicated with the gods.

*Bronze tripod food vessel, Shang*

## WESTERN HAN

### 206 BC–AD 9

| | |
|---|---|
| Gaozu | 206–195 BC |
| Huidi | 195–188 BC |
| Shaodi | 188–180 BC |
| Wendi | 180–157 BC |
| Jingdi | 157–141 BC |
| Wudi | 141–87 BC |
| Zhaodi | 87–74 BC |
| Xuandi | 74–49 BC |
| Yuandi | 49–33 BC |
| Chengdi | 33–7 BC |
| Aidi | 7–1 BC |
| Pingdi | 1 BC–AD 6 |
| Ruzi | AD 7–9 |

*Broken terracotta heads found at Jingdi's tomb*

## EASTERN HAN

### AD 25–220

| | | | |
|---|---|---|---|
| Guang Wudi | 25–57 | Chongdi | 144–145 |
| Mingdi | 57–75 | Zhidi | 145–146 |
| Zhangdi | 75–88 | Huandi | 146–168 |
| Hedi | 88–105 | Lingdi | 168–189 |
| Shangdi | 106 | Xiandi | 189–220 |
| Andi | 106–125 | | |
| Shundi | 125–144 | | |

## TANG

### 618–907

| | | | |
|---|---|---|---|
| Gaozu | 618–626 | Jingzong | 824–827 |
| Taizong | 626–649 | Wenzong | 827–840 |
| Gaozong | 649–683 | Wuzong | 840–846 |
| Zhongzong | 684 & 705–710 | Xuanzong | 846–859 |
| Ruizong | 684–690 | Yizong | 859–873 |
| | & 710–712 | Xizong | 873–888 |
| Wu Zetian | 690–705 | Zhaozong | 888–904 |
| Xuanzong | 712–756 | Aidi | 904–907 |
| Suzong | 756–762 | | |
| Daizong | 762–779 | | |
| Dezong | 779–805 | | |
| Shunzong | 805 | | |
| Xianzong | 805–820 | | |
| Muzong | 820–824 | | |

*Sancai-glazed dancing tomb figures*

## FIVE DYNASTIES & TEN KINGDOMS

### 907–960

Based north of the Yangzi, five successive dynasties swiftly usurped one another, with no dynasty lasting for more than three reigns. The Ten Kingdoms to the south went through a similarly turbulent period.

Throughout this period and most of the Song dynasty, the northern frontiers were dominated by the semi-nomadic Liao dynasty (907–1125) in the east, and by the Western Xia (990–1227) in the west. In 1115, the Liao were overthrown by the Jin (1115–1234), who forced the Song southwards in 1127.

## YUAN

### 1279–1368

Genghis Khan (1162–1227) united numerous Mongol speaking tribes and captured Beijing in 1215. His grandson, Kublai, completed the conquest of China by finally defeating the Southern Song in 1279.

| | |
|---|---|
| Kublai Khan | 1279–1294 |
| Temur Oljeitu | 1294–1307 |
| Khaishan | 1308–1311 |

| | |
|---|---|
| Ayurbarwada | 1311–1320 |
| Shidebala | 1321–1323 |
| Yesun Temur | 1323–1328 |
| Tugh Temur | 1328–1329, |
| | 1329–1333 |
| Khoshila | 1329 |
| Toghon Temur | 1333–1368 |

## MING

### 1368–1644

| | | | |
|---|---|---|---|
| Hongwu | 1368–1398 | Longqing | 1567–1572 |
| Jianwen | 1399–1402 | Wanli | 1573–1620 |
| Yongle | 1403–1424 | Taichang | 1620 |
| Hongxi | 1425 | Tianqi | 1621–1627 |
| Xuande | 1426–1435 | Chongzhen | 1628–1644 |
| Zhengtong | 1436–1449 | | |
| Jingtai | 1450–1457 | | |
| Tianshun | 1457–1464 | | |
| (Zhengtong restored) | | | |
| Chenghua | 1465–1487 | | |
| Hongzhi | 1488–1505 | | |
| Zhengde | 1506–1521 | | |
| Jiajing | 1522–1567 | | |

## WESTERN ZHOU DYNASTY

**1066–771 BC**

The Zhou founded their capital at Chang'an (Xi'an). They continued some Shang traditions, but reorganized the political system, dividing the nobility into grades. The feudal system of the Western Zhou broke down after the capital was sacked and the king slain.

## EASTERN ZHOU DYNASTY

**770–221 BC**

**Spring and Autumn**
770–475 BC

**Warring States**
475–221 BC

The Zhou dynasty ruled at its eastern capital of Luoyang alongside numerous rival states. This long period of almost constant warfare was brought to an end when the Qin emerged victorious.

## QIN DYNASTY

**221–206 BC**

| | |
|---|---|
| Qin Shi Huang | 221–210 BC |
| Er Shi | 210–207 BC |

*Statue of attendant from the tomb of Qin Shi Huangdi*

## PERIOD OF DISUNITY

**220–589**

China was divided into the warring Wei, Wu, and Shu kingdoms. The Wei briefly re-united China under the Western Jin (280–316), the first of the six Southern Dynasties (280–589), with their capital at Jiankang (Nanjing). The north was ruled by a succession of ruling houses – the 16 Kingdoms (304–439). The nomadic Toba Wei set up the Northern Wei dynasty, the first of five Northern Dynasties (386–581) with a capital first at Datong, then at Luoyang.

## SUI

**581–618**

China was once more united by the short and decisive rule of the Sui.

| | |
|---|---|
| Wendi | 581–604 |
| Yangdi | 604–617 |
| Gongdi | 617–618 |

*Emperor Wendi's flotilla on the Grand Canal*

## NORTHERN SONG

**960–1126**

| | | | |
|---|---|---|---|
| Taizu | 960–976 | Shenzong | 1068–1085 |
| Taizong | 976–997 | Zhezong | 1086–1101 |
| Zhenzong | 998–1022 | Huizong | 1101–1125 |
| Renzong | 1022–1063 | Qinzong | 1126–1127 |
| Yingzong | 1064–1067 | | |

*Painting by Emperor Huizong*

## SOUTHERN SONG

**1127–1279**

| | |
|---|---|
| Gaozong | 1127–1162 |
| Xiaozong | 1163–1190 |
| Guangzong | 1190–1194 |
| Ningzong | 1195–1224 |
| Lizong | 1225–1264 |
| Duzong | 1265–1274 |
| Gongdi | 1275 |
| Duanzong | 1276–1278 |
| Di Bing | 1279 |

## QING

**1644–1911**

| | |
|---|---|
| Shunzhi | 1644–1661 |
| Kangxi | 1661–1722 |
| Yongzheng | 1723–1735 |
| Qianlong | 1736–1795 |
| Jiaqing | 1796–1820 |
| Daoguang | 1821–1850 |
| Xianfeng | 1851–1861 |
| Tongzhi | 1862–1874 |
| Guangxu | 1875–1908 |
| Xuantong (Pu Yi) | 1909–1912 |

*The Zhengde Emperor's love of leisure led to a relaxation of imperial control*

*Imperial dragon detail on the back of a eunuch's official court robe*

## FOUNDATION OF IMPERIAL CHINA

The Warring States Period was finally brought to an end as the Qin emerged victorious. In 221 BC, Qin Shi pronounced himself the first emperor (huangdi) of China and ruled over a short yet decisive period of history. The Qin state was based on the political theories of Legalism, which established the role of the ruler as paramount and espoused a system of collective responsibility. Following unification, Qin Shi conscripted thousands of workers to join together the defensive walls to the north, creating the Great Wall. He standardized the system of money, and weights and measures, and laid the foundations for a legal system. A ruthless ruler, Qin Shi died in the belief that his famous terracotta army would protect him in the afterlife from his numerous enemies.

**Archer from Qin terracotta army**

The founding of the Han dynasty (206 BC–AD 220) heralded a "golden age" in Chinese history. Emperor Gaodi (r. 206–195 BC) established the capital of the Western Han (206 BC–AD 9) at Chang'an (Xi'an), and retained much of the centralized administration established by the Qin. Subsequent emperors developed the civil service examination to select able men for state office. Han society was founded on the principles propounded by Confucius, and the Confucian classics formed the basis of the civil service examination. Daoism and *yin-yang* theory coexisted with ancestor worship and would form the basis of indigenous Chinese belief *(see pp30–33)*.

The Han empire expanded with regions of Central Asia, Vietnam, and Korea being brought under Chinese control. In 138 BC, General Zhang Qian was sent to establish diplomatic links with Central Asia and returned with tales of rich pastures and "heavenly horses." The fine thoroughbreds of Ferghana (in modern Uzbekistan) were traded in exchange for Chinese silk, starting the flow of goods along the fabled Silk Road *(see pp464–5)*.

Han rule was briefly interrupted as Wang Mang seized power in AD 9, only to be restored by Guang Wudi (r. AD 25–57), who established the Eastern Han capital in Luoyang. Once more, the Han expanded Chinese territory. Paper was by now in use for much official documentation and the first Chinese dictionary was produced. Buddhism began its spread to China with the first Buddhist communities being established in Jiangsu province.

Chariot and footmen, impressed into a tomb's brick, Han

## TIMELINE

Tomb figure, Qin

**213 BC** Burning of the books as part of process of "unification"

**221–206 BC** Qin dynasty under first emperor, Qin Shi

**206 BC–AD 9** Western Han capital established at Chang'an (Xi'an)

**165 BC** First official examinations for the selection of civil servants

**c. 139–126 BC** Official envoy Zhang Qian establishes first diplomatic and trading links of Silk Road

**AD 2** First known census: 57,671,400 individuals

*Bronze horse and rider, Han*

**25–220** Eastern Han dynasty capital at Luoyang

**c. 100** First dictionary *Shuo Wen* produced with more than 9,000 characters

**65** First mention of Buddhist community established at court of Prince Ying of Chu

| 200 BC | 100 BC | 1 | AD 100 |
|---|---|---|---|

Sui emperors Yangdi and Wendi in a detail from "Portraits of the 13 Emperors" by Tang painter Yen Li Pen

## PERIOD OF DIVISION

From the rule of Hedi (r. AD 88–105), the Eastern Han declined. Civil war finally split the country in 220. The next 350 years were characterized by almost constant warfare as China was ruled by over 14 short-lived dynasties and 16 "kingdoms."

China was divided into the Northern and Southern dynasties (265–581), each region taking on its own distinct character. Foreign peoples took control of the North, such as the Toba branch of the Xianbei, who founded the Northern Wei in 386. These rulers were receptive to foreign ideas and religions, creating some of the finest Buddhist cave complexes first at Yungang, near their capital in Datong, and from 494, at Longmen, when they moved their capital to Luoyang.

Apsara from Buddhist cave, Northern Wei

As foreign invaders took control of the North, the Han Chinese retreated south to establish their new capital at Jiankang (Nanjing). In a climate of relative stability, the south became the economic and cultural center as the population shifted to the Yangzi delta. Philosophy and the arts flourished alongside a renewed interest in Daoism and a growing interest in Buddhism.

## UNIFICATION AND STABILITY

Following military successes against the Liang and the Chen, the Northern Zhou general Yang Jian (541–604) pronounced himself emperor, taking the name Wendi, and founded the Sui dynasty in 581. This brief but significant dynastic rule established political and social stability. He undertook an extensive program of works including extending the Great Wall and the beginnings of the Grand Canal. The second emperor, Yangdi (569–617), restored diplomatic relations with Japan and Taiwan and extended trade to Central Asia.

**190** Communications with central Asia are cut

**late 3rd c.** Renewed interest in Daoism

**220** Civil war breaks out between the kingdoms of Wei, Shu, and Wu

**265–581** China divided into Northern and Southern dynasties

**310** Massive exodus of Chinese upper classes to South

*Colossal Buddha at Yungang Caves, Northern Wei*

**386–535** Northern Wei, first of the ruling houses to adopt Buddhism

**581–618** Sui dynasty, initiated by Wendi's reunification of China

**c. 6th C** First true porcelain produced

**c. 7th C** Woodblock printing first used in China

| 200 | 300 | 400 | 500 | 600 |

# Tang Dynasty

The Tang Dynasty is widely regarded as one of China's golden ages, characterized by economic prosperity, territorial expansion, and political stability. During this period China reached its largest size to date: from Korea to Vietnam and across Central Asia to southern Siberia. Trade flourished by land and sea, stimulating the flow of luxury goods between East and West. Foreign religions were tolerated and Buddhism gained popular and imperial patronage. The arts and literature of the Tang are still considered to be among China's finest, notably the famous poets Li Bai and Du Fu.

 Tang rule AD 750

**This pottery figure,** *decorated in three-color or sancai glaze, depicts life along the Silk Route. Merchants and pilgrims traveled the legendary route bringing with them objects crafted in gold and silver, textiles, exotic foods, and fine horses.*

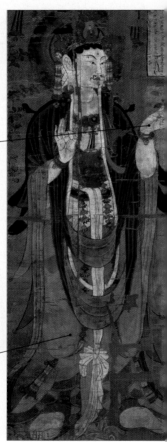

**The similar figures** carry typical attributes of Avalokitesvara: this one holds a flower; the other a vase and a sprig of willow.

**Foreign envoys,** *including Koreans (the figure on the right) and westerners (standing next to the Korean), traveled to the Tang court for delegations and giving tribute, as seen in this tomb mural.*

**Ample, draped robes,** **typical of Tang style**

**This silver cup,** *part of a board of buried treasure dug up in 1970, shows distinct western influence, although the relief decoration is lavishly Tang.*

**Chang'an's (Xi'an's)** *elaborate city walls enclosed a population of one million by the seventh century, making Chang'an the largest city in the world. The cosmopolitan capital was populated by Sogdians, Turks, Uighurs, Arabs, and Persians.*

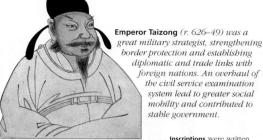

**Emperor Taizong** (r. 626–49) was a great military strategist, strengthening border protection and establishing diplomatic and trade links with foreign nations. An overhaul of the civil service examination system lead to greater social mobility and contributed to stable government.

**Inscriptions** were written for wealthy donors who commissioned paintings on behalf of themselves or loved ones in order to accrue religious merit.

**Avalokitesvara,** one of the most popular bodhisattvas, is identified by the Amitabha Buddha in his crown.

**Wu Zetian** (r. 690–705), the only empress in Chinese history, manipulated her weak husband, Emperor Gaozong, and ruthlessly eradicated her opposition. Despite her scandalous nature, she became a strong ruler and brought peace and prosperity.

**Emperor Xuanzong** (r. 712–56) or Minghuang, the Brilliant Emperor, ruled over a glorious period. A great scholar and patron of the arts, he poured his wealth into temple construction and founded the Academy of Letters (Hanlin-yuan) in 754.

## DUNHUANG SILKS

During the Tang Dynasty, Buddhism gained popular and imperial support, particularly under the rule of the devout Wu Zetian. Buddhist communities became important centers for the transla-tion of *sutras* and the production of Buddhist arts, such as the fine silk paintings of Dunhuang.

## AN EMPEROR'S LOVE AND DEMISE

In his later years, the Xuanzong emperor increasingly neglected his official duties as he became infatuated with his concubine, Yang Guifei. Intrigue and factions at court bred instability and in AD 750, General An Lushan, half Sogdian half Turkish by descent, seized control of the northeastern frontier. In 755 An Lushan stormed the capital forcing the court to flee for Sichuan. As they reached Mawai, Xuanzong's troops mutinied and demanded the emperor hand over Yang Guifei. She was strangled before his eyes, and the tragic story of their love affair has been immortalised by poets. Although An Lushan was eventually defeated, the Tang dynasty fell into decline.

**Yang Guifei's plump figure became a classic *sancai* form**

## GLORY OF THE TANG

The Tang dynasty (AD 618–907) marks a high point in Chinese history (*see pp56–7*). During this golden age, China enjoyed an extended period of peace and prosperity. The arts flourished and were enriched by foreign styles, motifs, and techniques such as silverworking. Foreign religions, such as Nestorian Christianity, were tolerated and coexisted alongside native Daoism and Confucianism. Woodblock printing was invented by the Chinese some time during the 7th century and hastened the spread of Buddhism.

*Sancai* **glazed horse, Tang**

Following the An Lushan rebellion of 755, the Tang became increasingly inward looking. The great Buddhist persecution of 841–46 was symptomatic of a dynasty in decline, which finally fell in 907.

### THE LIAO DYNASTY (907–1125)

The Liao dynasty, which at its largest covered much of Mongolia, Manchuria, and northern China, was ruled by semi-nomadic and pastoral people, the Qidan. The Liao maintained a dual administration, Qidan and Chinese, and even a prime-ministership, to ensure the survival of their own customs and traditions whilst utilizing the efficiency of Tang structures of government. In 1115, the Qidan were overthrown by another semi-nomadic people, the Ruzhen (Jurchen).

With the support of the Northern Song, the Ruzhen took control of the north and founded the Jin dynasty. The Liao were forced westwards to the region of the Tian mountain range in present-day Xinjiang, where they established the Western Liao (1125–1211). The rest of northwest China was dominated by the Western Xia, a Tibetan related people who recognized the Liao as their overlords.

### FIVE DYNASTIES AND TEN KINGDOMS (907–960)

While the north of China was dominated by the insurgence of semi-nomadic peoples from the steppe regions, the south was ruled by a series of short military dictatorships. The Song dynasty was founded in 960 by Zhao Kuangyin, a military commander of the later Zhou (951–960), whose imperial name became Shizong. In the Yangzi delta and regions to the south, the Ten Kingdoms existed in relative peace and stability and were reunited by the Song in 979.

**Painting of an official celebrating, Five Dynasties (923–938)**

## TIMELINE

| | | | | | | |
|---|---|---|---|---|---|---|
| **618–907** Tang Dynasty heralds new golden age | **690–705** Empress Wu Zetian rules as first empress of China | **755–763** An Lushan rebellion drives emperor and court from Chang'an to Sichuan | **806** Earliest dated printed manuscript, the Diamond Sutra | **907–60** Period of division known as Five Dynasties and Ten Kingdoms | **10th c.** Gunpowde and fire ar first used |
| | **700** | **750** | **800** | **850** | **900** |
| **661** Chinese administration in Kashmir, Bokhara, and the borders of eastern Iran | **705** Famous poet Li Bai born | *Tang silver* | **806–820** First bankers' bill | **907–1125** Qidan people rule northeastern China as the Liao dynasty, making Beijing their southern capital | |
| | | | **770** Death of great poet Du Fu | | |

## THE SONG DYNASTY (960–1279)

The Song presided over a period of cultural brilliance and unprecedented growth in urban life during which the social makeup of China fundamentally changed. Less territorially ambitious than the Tang, the Song stimulated economic development through improved communications and transport. New industries based on mass production began to emerge, notably the porcelain industry based in Jiangxi province. During the Southern Song, China underwent an industrial revolution producing quantities of raw materials such as salt and iron on a scale that would not be seen in Europe until the 18th century.

In this buoyant economic climate a new middle-class emerged, stimulating demand for the new range of consumer goods. Power shifted from the aristocratic elite to government bureaucrats, who spent their spare time practising the arts of poetry, calligraphy, and painting. Collecting and connoisseurship led to an artistic renaissance and the founding of the first Imperial collections. Emperor Huizong was a great patron of the arts who used ancient precedents and values to buttress his own position.

Neo-Confucianism and a renewed interest in Daoism marked a return to indigenous beliefs and traditional structures of power.

The Northern Song repeatedly came under attack from the Western Xia in the northwest and the Jin in the northeast. Only 12 years after joining forces with the Song against the Liao, the Jin invaded the

Illustration of Song Emperor Huizong, r. 1101–1125

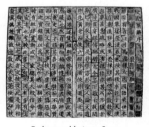

Early movable type, Song

Northern Song capital at Bianliang (Kaifeng), capturing emperor Qinzong and forcing the court to flee southwards. The capital of the Southern Song (1127–1279) was established at Lin'an (Hangzhou) south of the Yangzi.

## JIN DYNASTY (1115–1234)

The Jin were a semi-nomadic Tungusic people originating from Manchuria. War with the Song and persistent attacks from the Mongols resulted in a weakening of the Jin state which by the early 13th century formed a buffer state between the Song in the south and the Mongols in the north. In 1227, Mongol and Chinese allied forces defeated the Jin and in 1234 the Jin emperor committed suicide. The Jin state was integrated into the rapidly expanding Mongol empire.

---

**960–1126** Northern Song reunites China and bases capital at Bianliang (Kaifeng)

*Detail of painting by Emperor Huizong*

**1127–1279** Southern Song dynasty with capital at Hangzhou, after being forced south by the Jin

**1154** First issue of paper money (Jin)

**1206–1208** Song and Jin at war

| 950 | 1000 | 1050 | 1100 | 1150 | 1200 |
|---|---|---|---|---|---|

**990–1227** Western Xia people establish kingdom dominating northwest China

**1041–8** First attempts at printing with movable type

**1090** First attested use of compass on Chinese ships

**1115–1234** Jin dynasty founded in northeast China forcing Liao westwards

**1214** Jin move capital from Beijing to Kaifeng in Henan province

## MONGOL RULE (1279–1368)

The Mongol leader Genghis Khan (*see p471*) united the various Mongol-speaking tribes of the steppes and in 1215 conquered northern China. He divided his empire into four kingdoms, each ruled by one of his sons. His grandson Kublai Khan (r. 1260–94), ruler of the eastern Great Khanate, finally defeated the Southern Song in 1279 and proclaimed himself emperor of the Yuan dynasty. China now became part of a vast empire which stretched from the East China Sea across Asia as far as Poland, Hungary and Bohemia. Two capitals were maintained at Dadu or Khanbalik (present-day Beijing) and Yuanshangdu (Xanadu). The Silk Routes opened once more, connecting China to the Middle East and Medieval Europe. Direct contact was now made for the first time between the Mongol court and European diplomats, Franciscan missionaries, and merchants. According to the writings of Marco Polo, the

**Buddhist deity, Yuan**

Italian merchant spent 21 years in the service of Kublai and his court.

The Mongols ruled through a form of military government, in contrast to the bureaucratic civil service established by the Chinese. Although Chinese and Mongol languages were both used for official business, the Chinese were not encouraged to take up official posts. Muslims from Central and Western Asia took their place, and the Chinese increasingly retreated from official life.

As there were no clear rules for succession, civil war broke out in 1328 between Mongol nobles. The secret societies of the Red Turbans and the White Lotus led peasant rebellions and in 1368 General Zhu Yuanzhang forced the Mongols out of China, becoming the first emperor of the Ming dynasty.

## MING DYNASTY (1368–1644)

The Ming (literally "brilliant") dynasty was one of the longest and most stable periods in China's history. The founder of the Ming, Zhu Yuanzhang, rose from humble beginnings to become a general, ruling as the Hongwu emperor ("vast military accomplishment"). During his reign, Hongwu introduced radical changes to both central and local government, which he made binding on his successors. The emperor's role became more autocratic as Hongwu dispensed with the position of Prime Minister, taking direct responsibility for overseeing all six ministries himself.

Hongwu appointed his grandson to be his successor. Upon his death, his son the Prince of Yan, who controlled the region around Beijing, led an army

**Genghis Khan (c.1162–1227), Persian miniature**

## TIMELINE

**1215** Mongols capture Beijing

**1234** Jin emperor commits suicide and Jin integrated into Mongol empire

*Mongol on horseback*

**1368–1644** Ming dynasty, founded by rebel leader General Zhu Yuanzhang

**1403** Construction of Great Walls in North China

| 1250 | 1300 | 1350 | 1400 |

**1227** Genghis Khan dies, having united various Mongol-speaking tribes of the steppe

**1279–1368** Kublai Khan defeats Southern Song and rules China as emperor of the Yuan dynasty

**1328** Civil war breaks out between Mongol nobles

*Jade elephant, Ming*

**The existing battlements of the Great Wall, reinforced and joined together during the Ming dynasty**

against his nephew, taking Nanjing and proclaiming himself emperor Yongle ("Eternal Joy"). Yongle (r. 1403–24) moved the capital to his power base in Beijing, where he created a new city based on traditional principles of Chinese city planning. At its core lay the Forbidden City *(see pp86–9)*, the imperial palace and offices of government, surrounded by a grid system of streets, with four imperial altars at the cardinal points. The entire city was walled to provide both protection and enclosure. In 1421, Beijing became the official capital and would remain so until the present day. The Great Wall was reinforced, extended and faced with brick during the Ming dynasty.

By the 15th century, China had become a significant maritime power, its ships dwarfing those of contemporary Europe. Blue and white porcelain, silk, and other luxury items were in high demand in the foreign markets of Japan, Southeast Asia, and the Middle East. Yongle sent six maritime expeditions under the Muslim eunuch admiral Zheng He, which

**Wedding jewelry, Ming**

reached as far as the east coast of Africa. In 1514 Portuguese traders first landed in China, purchasing tea which then became a fashionable drink in European society. Porcelain provided ballast for the ships, and other luxury items were brought back along with the cargo. Trade was dominated by the Dutch in the 17th century, only to be surpassed by the British a hundred years later. Jesuit missionaries, who arrived in the 16th century, claimed few converts but gained access to the emperor and the inner court.

The arts thrived under the Xuande emperor (r. 1425–35), an artist and poet, who patronized the arts, notably the porcelain industry at Jingdezhen. In literature, the late Ming is noted for its great dramas and classical novels, such as *Journey to the West (see p29)*. Philosophy of the time reinforced the Neo-Confucianism of the Song.

The late Ming was dominated by peasant uprisings, incursions by Japanese pirates and Mongolian tribes, and excessive eunuch power. Rebellions within China eventually joined with external forces to end Ming rule.

| | | | | | |
|---|---|---|---|---|---|
| **1425–35** Xuande emperor becomes first Ming emperor to patronize the arts extensively | **1514** Portuguese land in China, becoming the first Europeans to trade in tea and porcelain | *Gilt bronze bowl, Ming* | **1573–1620** Wanli reign begins well but dynasty declines as emperor takes little interest in duties | **1620** The Taichang emperor poisoned by eunuchs | |
| **1450** | | **1500** | | **1550** | **1600** |
| **1420** Construction of the Forbidden City in Beijing completed | **Early 16th century** Later Ming monarchs neglect duties of government and eunuch power increases | **1538** Jesuit Father Matteo Ricci enters southern China and begins missionary duties | **1570** Popular novel *Xi Yu Ji* (Journey to the West) published | **1600s** Dutch dominate European trade with China | **1601** Jesuit missionary Matteo Ricci allowed to enter Beijing |

## QING RULE (1644–1911)

The Manchu leader Nurhachi established the Later Jin in 1616, organizing the scattered tribes of the north into eight banner units *(see p432–3)*. In 1636, the Manchu ruler Abahai changed the name to Qing, literally "pure," and prepared the way for the capture of Beijing in 1644. Under Manchu control, China was once more ruled by a foreign people. The Manchus were keen to adopt the Chinese method of rule, encouraging Chinese scholars into the service of the new empire. Dual administration at national and provincial levels meant Manchu and Chinese bureaucrats worked side by side using first Manchu and later Chinese as the official languages of government. However, despite the close interaction of Manchu and Chinese, the ruling Manchus were careful to maintain a distinct separation in order to protect their own privileges and cultural traditions.

**Emperor Kangxi, r. 1661–1722**

The first emperors of the Qing were enlightened rulers who presided over one of the largest and most populous countries in the world. The territorial aspirations of the Kangxi emperor brought the regions of Central Asia and southern Siberia once more under Chinese control. Kangxi *(see p122)* was succeeded by the Yongzheng emperor. It was his fourth son, the Qianlong emperor, "Lasting Eminence," (r. 1735–96) who heralded another golden age. An ambitious ruler, Qianlong was determined to extend China's borders beyond those of the Tang, personally leading campaigns to Burma, Vietnam, and Central Asia.

During the 18th century, contact with the west increased through Jesuit missionaries and trade. By the mid-18th century, the Chinese sought to control trade by refusing all official contact with Westerners and opening only Canton to foreign merchants. Pressure from European embassies increased as the British sent Lord Macartney in 1792–94 to establish diplomatic relations and open China to trade. China refused to grant a single concession to the British.

### THE DECLINE OF THE EMPIRE

The 19th century is one of the most turbulent periods of Chinese history, as internal uprisings, natural disasters, and the relentless encroachment of the West culminated in the end of the empire. A succession of weak rulers were manipulated and controlled by

**Lord Macartney's massive entourage arriving at Qianlong's tent**

## TIMELINE

| | | |
|---|---|---|
| **1644–1800** Military expansion into Central Asia and Siberia; colonization of new territories Yunnan and Xinjiang | **1723–1735** Kangxi's son Yin Zhen seizes power ruling under name of emperor Yongzheng | *The Shunzhi emperor, r. 1644–61* **1747** Qianlong builds Yuanming Yuan *(see p103)* in western style |

| 1650 | 1675 | 1700 | 1725 | 1750 |
|---|---|---|---|---|

| | | | | |
|---|---|---|---|---|
| **1644–1911** Manchus establish ng dynasty | **1650** First Catholic church in Beijing | **1661–1722** Rule of Kangxi emperor. Appoints Jesuits to run Board of Astronomy | **1735–1796** Qianlong, a great patron of the arts, rules over another golden age | **1757** Chinese restrict all foreign trade to Canton |

A merchant testing tea quality in a Cantonese warehouse

In 1900 the Boxers allied with imperial troops and attacked the foreign legations in Beijing (see p433). An eight-nation army defeated the onslaught, and Cixi fled to Xi'an, blaming everything on the emperor. The Chinese government paid once more for the loss of life and Cixi returned to Beijing until her death in 1908. The child emperor Pu Yi lived in the Forbidden City as the last emperor until his abdication. On 1 January 1912 the Republican leader Sun Yat-sen inaugurated the Chinese Republic.

the Dowager Empress Cixi, who ruled for much of the late Qing from "behind the curtain." The Taiping Rebellion of 1850–64 devastated south and central China (see p422).

Western powers, frustrated by the reluctance of the Chinese to open to foreign trade, brought the Chinese under increasing pressure. Keen to protect the trade of opium from their colonies in India, the British engaged in the First Opium War (1840–42), which culminated in the Treaty of Nanjing, resulting in the opening of four new ports to trade, known as "Treaty Ports", the payment of huge indemnities, and the ceding of Hong Kong to Britain. Following the Arrow War (Second Opium War) with Britain and France (1856), the European forces divided China into "spheres of influence" – the British strongest along the Yangzi and in Shanghai, the Germans controlling Shandong province, and the French controlling the borders with Vietnam.

Sun Yat-sen, 1866–1925

## FROM EMPIRE TO REPUBLIC
In the final years of the empire, many Chinese intellectuals recognized the need to modernize. Supporters of the Reform Movement of 1898 propounded the adoption of western technology and education, and, following the Boxer Rebellion, a number of reforms were adopted. Elected regional assemblies were set up, further undermining the power of the Qing. In 1911 the empire collapsed completely. Sun Yat-sen (see p297) was elected provisional President of China, but was soon forced to resign in favor of general Yuan Shikai, who sought to become emperor. Yuan was forced to back down when governors revolted and he died soon after in 1916. China then came under the control of a series of regional warlords until it was united once more with the founding of the People's Republic of China in 1949.

| 1796–1805 White Lotus Rebellion damages prestige and wealth of dynasty | | 1816 Lord Amherst leads British envoy seeking to open China to trade | 1850–64 Taiping Rebellion | 1856–58 Arrow War (Second Opium War) with Britain and France | 1898 The Guangxu emperor imprisoned by Empress Cixi | 1900 Boxer uprising |
|---|---|---|---|---|---|---|
| 1775 | 1800 | 1825 | 1850 | 1875 | 1900 | |

| | 1792–94 Lord Macartney leads embassy to Beijing and unsuccessfully attempts to establish trade relations with England | | 1861 Empress Dowager Cixi begins "rule from behind the screen" | | | 1908 Death of Empress Dowager Cixi |
|---|---|---|---|---|---|---|
| Jade pendant, Qing | | | 1840–42 First Opium War with Britain | | Cixi's nail covers | 1894 Sino-Japanese war |

# The Cultural Revolution

Actor in opera

In 1965, Mao Zedong set in motion a chain of events that were to unleash the turmoil now known as the Cultural Revolution. Having socialized industry and agriculture, Mao called on the masses to transform society itself – all distinctions between manual and intellectual work were to be abolished and class distinction disappear. The revolution reached its violent peak in 1967, with the Red Guards spreading social unrest. The People's Liberation Army (PLA) finally restored order, but the subsequent years were characterized by fear, violence, and mistrust.

**Children were encouraged** *to take part in the Revolution. Their enthusiasm led to the destruction of family photographs and possessions. In some cases, children denounced their own parents.*

## THE RED GUARD

Mao appealed to students to form the Red Guard, in whom he entrusted the fate of the revolution. The movement rapidly gathered momentum and the Red Guard, who raised Mao to godly status, traveled China spreading Mao Zedong "Thoughts," smashing remnants of the past, vandalizing temples, and wreaking havoc.

**Mass public meetings** *were held as part of the Socialist Education Movement, a precursor of the Cultural Revolution intended to reverse "capitalist" and "revisionist" tendencies perceived in social and economic life. Everyone was required to attend.*

**An injured cadre** *is carried away after being denounced. Shamings became the bench mark of public meetings. Many politicians and teachers were paraded and accused, leading to job loss and, in some cases, suicide.*

**The** *Little Red Book* was essential to the Red Guard and issued to every soldier under Lin Biao's command.

**Demonstrating their opposition** *to Soviet-style communism and their support for Maoism, Red Guards change a Beijing street sign in front of the Soviet Embassy from East Yangwei to Fanxiu Lu (Anti-revisionism Road).*

**Lin Biao spread the study** *of the "Thoughts of Mao" and compiled the Little Red Book which became obligatory reading for his army recruits. As head of the PLA, Lin Biao provided essential military backing and was Mao's named successor. He died in a plane crash over Siberia in 1971 amid rumors of an imminent usurpation.*

**Model operas** *were the pet project of Mao's third wife, Jiang Qing. She set about creating a politically correct revolutionary culture. Many artists and intellectuals were sent to the countryside for re-education.*

**May 7 Cadre Schools** *were set up by the central government in 1968. 100,000 officials plus 30,000 family members were sent to perform manual labor and undergo ideological re-education. An unknown number of lower-ranking cadres were sent to thousands of other cadre schools.*

**Liu Shaoqi** *(right), president from 1959–66, was one of a number of high officials to be denounced, imprisoned, and paraded in "struggle rallies." He died from his experiences.*

## GANG OF FOUR

The Gang of Four, as they became known, orchestrated attacks on intellectuals and writers, high officials, the party, and the state and were responsible for some of the worst excesses of the Cultural Revolution. Zhang Chunqiao, critic and propagandist, Yao Wenyuan, editor-in-chief of *Shanghai Liberation Army Daily,* Wang Hongwen, a young worker, and Mao's third wife Jiang Qing, an ex-film star, dominated the political center unchallenged until Mao's death in 1976. Millions of Chinese citizens watched their televized trial in 1980–81. Jiang Qing, who was singled out by propagandists and became one of the most hated figures in China, was defiant until the end, railing against her prosecutors throughout the trial. She took her own life in 1991, while serving her life sentence.

**Lynched effigies of members of the Gang of Four hanging from a tree**

**Chiang Kai-shek (1887–1975), leader of the KMT**

## COMMUNISTS AND NATIONALISTS

After the fall of the empire, the political landscape changed dramatically and became dominated by two forces, the Nationalist Party or Kuomintang (KMT) and the Communist Party, founded in 1921. The Nationalists were led first by Sun Yat-sen from his power base in Guangzhou, then by General Chiang Kai-shek who seized power in 1926. In 1923 the two Parties formed a "united front" against the warlords, but in 1926 the Communists were expelled from the KMT. Chiang Kai-shek led his army to Nanjing where he tried to establish a Nationalist capital, and betrayed the Communist-led workers of Shanghai who were massacred by underworld gangsters. The Communists were driven underground and Mao Zedong retreated to the countryside.

High in the mountains of Jiangxi province, Mao and Zhu De founded the Jiangxi Soviet in 1930. From this inaccessible base, the communists began to redistribute land to the peasants and institute new marriage laws. In 1934, Chiang Kai-shek drove the communists from the area, forcing Mao to embark on the legendary Long March (*see pp256–7*). Yan'an, where the march ended, became the new Communist Party headquarters and would remain so until 1945.

## JAPANESE ATTACK

Domestic turmoil laid China open to attack, and in 1931 the Japanese occupied Manchuria, founding the puppet state of Manchukuo and placing the last Qing emperor, Pu Yi, at its head (*see p446*). By 1937 the Japanese had occupied much of northern China, Shanghai, and the Yangzi valley ruthlessly taking cities, wreaking death and devastation. The Japanese were finally driven from Chinese soil in 1945, and China was plunged into civil war.

## THE EAST IS RED

By 1947, the Communist policy of land reform was reaping rewards and gaining the support of people in the countryside. In 1948–9, the Communists gained decisive victories over the KMT. On 1 October 1949 Chairman Mao pronounced the founding of the People's Republic of China in Beijing. Chiang Kai-shek fled to Taiwan, establishing a Nationalist government and taking with him many Imperial treasures.

毛主席革命路线胜利万岁
**Communist poster depicting Mao surrounded by the masses**

## TIMELINE

| | | | | |
|---|---|---|---|---|
| **1912** Abdication of emperor Pu Yi marks the end of Imperial China | **1921** Founding of the Chinese Communist Party | **1945** End of World War II; Japan defeated | **1958** Radical reform of the Great Leap Forward | **1965** Mao launches Cultural Revolution |
| | | **1937** Japanese take much of northern China | **1947** Civil War breaks out in China | |
| **1910** | **1920** | **1930** | **1940** | **1950** | **1960** |
| | **1926** Chiang Kai-shek seizes leadership of National Party | **1934** Mao leads the Red Army on Long March | **1951–2** Rural co-ops established | |
| *Last Emperor Pu Yi* | **1931** Japanese invasion of Manchuria | **1949** Mao proclaims founding of People's Republic of China | |

In the early years of the People's Republic, the Chinese worked hard to re-build a country devastated by 100 years of turmoil. New laws sought to redress inequities of the past, redistributing land and outlawing arranged marriages.

Zhou Enlai with President Nixon

In 1957 the Party launched the Hundred Flowers movement, which initially encouraged freedom of expression. Unprepared for the storm of criticism which resulted, the Party promptly branded intellectuals as "rightists" and sent them to the countryside for re-education. Frustrated with the slow rate of change, Mao launched the Great Leap Forward in 1958. Large communes providing food and childcare replaced the family, releasing manual labor and improving productivity. But unrealistic productivity targets and the falsification of statistics concealed the disastrous effect of Mao's experiment. Agricultural failure coupled with natural disasters resulted in the starvation of millions.

Having reformed agriculture and industry, Mao sought to transform society and launched the Cultural Revolution in 1965 *(see pp64–5)*. The greatest excesses of the period were over by 1971, but the country was tightly controlled and directed until Mao's death in 1976. Deng Xiaoping emerged as leader, implementing economic reforms which returned land to the peasants and encouraged greater economic freedom.

The economic liberalization of the 1980s stimulated the economy but was unmatched by political freedom. On 4 June 1989 the democracy movement called for political reform and an end to corruption, but was brutally suppressed in Beijing's Tian'an Men Square and in other large cities. Whilst many students and intellectuals fled abroad, others remain incarcerated in China's jails. Deng Xiaoping pressed on with economic reform, and the 1990s saw the opening of Special Economic Zones and stock exchanges in Shenzhen and Shanghai. By 1992, the economy had become one of the largest in the world.

The unprecedented rate of economic growth in the 1990s was matched by the transformation of the landscape as traditional buildings made way for modern highrises. The former colonies of Hong Kong and Macau were returned to China and foreign investment flooded in, with entrepreneurs prospering. Disbanding the state economy has also spawned inequity, and the gap between rich and poor grows

Chinese traders on the Stock Exchange

increasingly wider. How the most populous nation on earth resolves the many issues it faces is of compelling interest to the rest of a world on whose future a re-awakened China is going to have a massive impact.

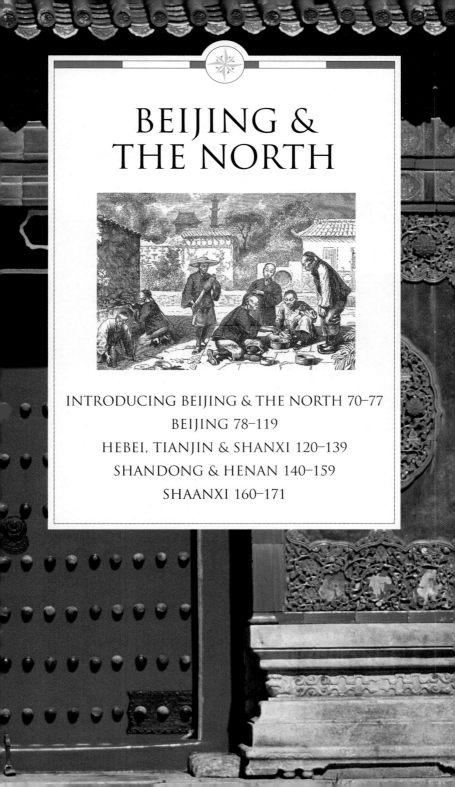

# BEIJING &
# THE NORTH

# Beijing & the North at a Glance

Threaded by the yellow river and the Great Wall, China's north encompasses the six provinces of Hebei, Tianjin, Shanxi, Shandong, Henan, and Shaanxi, as well as Beijing, the nation's capital. From this vast domain, six ancient capitals governed China, leaving behind a wealth of dynastic sites, such as Beijing's magnificent Forbidden City, the Terracotta Warriors near Xi'an, and the Buddhist carvings at Longmen and Yungang. The region's religious sites include the Daoist peaks of Hua Shan and Tai Shan, the Buddhist Wutai Shan, and the Shaolin Temple. Along the coast are the ports of Tianjin and Qingdao, preserves of European architecture, and Shanhaiguan, where the Great Wall meets the sea.

**Practicing *tai ji quan*, Temple of Heaven, Beijing**

**Vividly painted cave interior at the Yungang Caves, Datong, Shanxi**

DATON

TAIYUAN

PINGYAO

YAN'AN

LINFEN      CHANGZHI

108

↑ *Yinchuan*

*Lanzhou*

*Baoji*

LUOYANG

ZHENGZH

LINGBAO

XI'AN

SHANGZHOU

312

207

NANYANG

210

*Hanzhong*

SHIQUAN

316

108

✈ *Xiangfan*

Yellow River (Huang He)

208

207

## GETTING AROUND

Beijing has good air, rail, and bus links to the surrounding region. There are daily flights to Xi'an, Luoyang, Qingdao, Kaifeng, Hong Kong, Guangzhou, Chengde, Kunming, and Zhengzhou. Express trains link Beijing directly with all the region's large cities, while many smaller towns are served by slower trains. Tianjin is a major north-south rail junction. There is also a comprehensive long-distance bus service, while faster private buses ply the popular tourist routes.

**KEY**

▬▬▬ Expressway

▬▬ National Highway

═══ Minor road

▲ Mountain area

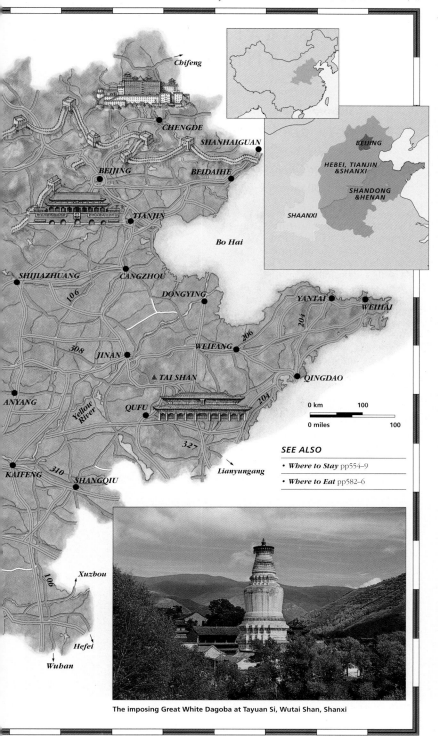

Chifeng

CHENGDE

SHANHAIGUAN

BEIJING

BEIDAIHE

TIANJIN

Bo Hai

BEIJING

HEBEI, TIANJIN
&SHANXI

SHANDONG
&HENAN

SHAANXI

SHIJIAZHUANG

CANGZHOU

DONGYING

YANTAI

WEIHAI

106

308

JINAN

WEIFANG

206

204

QINGDAO

▲ TAI SHAN

ANYANG

Yellow
River

QUFU

204

0 km          100

0 miles          100

327

Lianyungang

KAIFENG

310

SHANGQIU

### SEE ALSO

- **Where to Stay** pp554–9

- **Where to Eat** pp582–6

106

Xuzhou

Hefei

Wuhan

**The imposing Great White Dagoba at Tayuan Si, Wutai Shan, Shanxi**

# A PORTRAIT OF BEIJING & THE NORTH

*T*he yellow river, the wellspring of Chinese culture and civilization, carves a course through the country's parched northern terrain, the historic homeland of the Han Chinese and location of the most significant monuments. Thus most visitors to the Middle Kingdom usually concentrate on these historic sites, beginning with the nation's capital, Beijing.

For millennia, the Yellow River (Huang He) has nurtured the communities strung along its banks while sporadically washing away their settlements. The great river flows through the provinces of Shaanxi, Shanxi, Henan, and Shandong, often forming a natural boundary between provinces. It also features in the names of Henan (South of the River) and Hebei (North of the River). In its long and looping journey it traverses a land rich in historic sights and cities, before spilling into Bo Hai (Bo Sea), north of the sacred mountain, Tai Shan. Occasionally, it comes across the vestiges of that other barrier, the Great Wall. Now a largely disintegrating bastion, the wall crawls across the face of North China, a reminder of the

**Defender of the Buddha, Longmen**

region's vulnerable position so close to the border with Inner Mongolia and erstwhile Manchuria. Although the Great Wall was built as a defensive fortification, it could not prevent the hordes of nomadic tribes, the so-called "barbarians," from entering China.

Neolithic finds and archeological sites wrote the province of Henan into the earliest pages of Chinese history. Here, South of the Yellow River, Luoyang and Kaifeng are two of the country's most important dynastic capitals; another ancient city, Anyang, was capital of the Shang dynasty. However, it is Xi'an in Shaanxi province that is more eclipsed by its past than any other ancient capital.

The Tower of the Fragrance of the Buddha overlooking Kunming Lake at the Summer Palace, Beijing

The modern skyline of Qingdao, Shandong Province on China's east coast

Xi'an's most magnificent treasures are the Terracotta Warriors *(see pp168–9)*, created to guard the tomb of Qin Shi Huangdi, the Qin emperor who unified China. However Xi'an reached its zenith during the Tang dynasty *(see pp56–7)*, prospering because of its position at the eastern end of the Silk Road. The Grand Mosque and sizable Muslim population testify to Xi'an's cosmopolitan grandeur during that time.

**Lighting incense sticks Beijing's Lama Temple**

Toward the end of the 13th century, the Mongol Kublai Khan established Beijing as his capital. But it was only in 1407, when the Ming emperor Yongle moved his seat of power here, that Beijing achieved imperial status. Still organized along its grand Ming and Qing dynasty lines, it is a city of straight, wide boulevards and narrow, winding alleys around an ancient palatial core, the Forbidden City. The temples and palaces are today complemented by slick shopping streets and the commercial buzz of a people coming into their own in the 21st century.

The two adjoining provinces of Hebei and Shanxi are griddles in summer and iceboxes in winter, although Hebei's eastern seaboard towns benefit from cooling sea breezes. Shanxi, on the other hand, is sometimes affected by seasonal sand storms blowing in from the Gobi Desert. Hebei's fertile soil and productive agrarian economy contrast with landlocked Shanxi's mineral-rich terrain. Both provinces are heavily industrialized but there are still many sights that demand attention, such as the Buddhist monastery of Chongshan Si *(see p137)*, the holy mountain Tai Shan, and the port of Tianjin, Hebei's former capital. Despite modernization, Tianjin has preserved its European architecture, a legacy of its past as a foreign trading post. The Buddhist sculptures at the UNESCO World Heritage Site of the Longmen Caves in Luoyang *(see pp154–5)* are remarkable while Shandong is best known for Qufu, the birthplace of Confucius, the eminent philosopher-sage, whose teachings, which greatly influenced Chinese culture, are acceptable once more.

The kind of scenery that has inspired Chinese poets and artists for thousands of years, Hua Shan, Shaanxi

# Beijing Opera

**Souvenir mask**

One among many hundreds of local operas across China, Beijing Opera began in the Qing dynasty. It is said that Emperor Qianlong (r.1736–96), on a tour of the south, was rather taken by the operas of Anhui and Hebei and brought these troupes back to Beijing, where a new form of opera was established. The Guangxu emperor and Dowager Empress Cixi were also keen devotees and helped develop the art form. Beijing Opera has proved remarkably resilient, surviving the persecution of actors and the banning of most of the plays during the Cultural Revolution.

**Emperor Qianlong, credited with starting Beijing Opera**

## BEIJING OPERA

Visually stunning and with a distinct musical style, the plays are based on Chinese history and literature. Beijing Opera is a form of "total theater" with singing, speech, mime, acrobatics, and symbolic visual effects.

**Monkey** *is one of the favorite characters – clever, resourceful, and brave. He appears in Chinese classic literature (see p28–9).*

**The colors of the painted faces** *symbolize the individual character's qualities. Red, for example, represents loyalty and courage; purple, solemnity and a sense of justice; green, bravery and irascibility.*

**Riding a horse** *is represented by raising a tasseled horsewhip. Other actions and movement on the stage are similarly stylized rather than realistic.*

**The acrobatics** *of Beijing Opera combine graceful gymnastics and movements from the martial arts. Training is notoriously hard. The costumes are designed to make the jumps seem more spectacular by billowing out as they spin.*

## MUSICAL INSTRUMENTS

Despite the dramatic visual elements of Beijing Opera, the Chinese say that they go to "listen" to opera, not to see it. The importance of the musical elements should not therefore be underestimated. Typically six or seven instrumentalists accompany the opera. The stringed instruments usually include the *erhu* or Chinese two-stringed violin, *sanxian* or three-stringed lute, and moon guitar, or possibly *pipa* (traditional lute). The main function of the instruments is to accompany the singing. Percussion instruments include clappers, gongs, and drums. These are used largely to punctuate the action; movement and sound are intimately linked. Wind instruments also sometimes feature, such as the Chinese horn, flute, and *suona*.

Gong

Suona    Pipa    Erhu

**Mei Lanfang** *was the foremost interpreter of the female role type or* dan *during the opera's heyday in the 1920s and 1930s. Traditionally all female roles were played by male actors, although that has now changed.*

## THE FOUR MAIN ROLES

There are four main role types in Beijing Opera: the *sheng* (male) and *dan* (female) roles have naturalistic make-up. The *jing* or "painted faces," in contrast, have stylized patterned, colored faces, while the *chou* are comic characters.

**Sheng:** these may be young or old, with beard or without.

**Dan:** there are six parts within this role from virtuous girl to old woman.

**Chou:** with a white patch on his face, the *chou* is usually dim but amusing.

**Jing:** the most striking looking, they also have the most forceful personality.

# Regional Food: Beijing & the North

Communities developed beside the Yellow River before 6000 BC, but it is not until about 1500 BC, when written records started, that a picture of the dietary habits of the ancient Chinese becomes clear. They kept pigs and grew millet, wheat, barley, and rice and even fermented their grain to make alcoholic beverages. Later (around 1100 BC), soybeans were added to the Chinese diet, soon followed by by-products such as soy sauce and beancurd (tofu). Beijing never had a distinctive cuisine of its own, but as the center of the empire it imported elements and influences from a variety of sources.

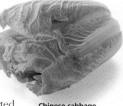

Chinese cabbage

Candied apples on the street, a feature of northern cuisine

### THE PALACE KITCHEN

Kublai Khan made Beijing the capital in 1271 and brought simple Mongolian influences to the northern Chinese cuisine – lamb, roasting, and the hot pot. Prior to that, the national capitals had been centered around the Yellow River valley in Xi'an, Luoyang, or Kaifeng. Elaborate preparation and expensive ingredients – shark's fin, bird's nest soup, and abalone, all imported from the south – feature as well as artistic presentation and poetic names. Imperial cuisine can be summed up as the distillation of the creations of generations of Imperial Palace chefs over almost a millennium.

### SHANDONG

As the birthplace and home of Confucius, the cuisine of Shandong is generally regarded as the oldest and best in China. Shandong has produced the largest number of famous master chefs, and it is even said that the iron wok originated here as well.

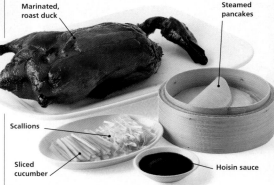

Marinated, roast duck

Steamed pancakes

Scallions

Sliced cucumber

Hoisin sauce

A whole Peking duck with traditional accompaniments

### REGIONAL DISHES AND SPECIALTIES

Peking duck – an Imperial meal – must be the best known dish in north Chinese cuisine. The duck, a local Beijing variety, is carefully dried, and then brushed with a sweet marinade before being roasted over fragrant woodchips. Finally it is carved by the chef and eaten wrapped in pancakes with a special duck sauce, slivered scallions, and cucumbers. To accompany the duck, diners might also be served duck liver pâté, and duck soup to finish. Another specialty of the region is Mongolian Hotpot; a simple one-pot dish which suited the nomadic way of life. Other regional specialties are made with local resources – carp from the Yellow River, king prawns and yellow croakers from the coast of Shandong, and not forgetting the aromatics – garlic, leeks, and scallions.

Duck pears – like a duck's head

**Mu Shu Pork:** *stir-fried tiger lily buds, scrambled egg, black fungus, and shredded pork – eaten with pancakes.*

Shandong cuisine is popular in Beijing. As one of the most important agricultural areas of China, Shandong supplies Beijing with most of its food; its main crops are wheat, barley, sorghum, millet, and corn as well as soybeans and peanuts. Additionally, fisheries are widely developed along the Yellow River and the north China coast, particularly around the rocky Shandong peninsula where the specialties are fish, prawns, shellfish, abalones, sea slugs, and sea urchins. Fruits are also a Shandong specialty, and wines and beers – especially the famous Tsingtao beer (see p146) – are exported worldwide.

Some of the wide variety of foods on display at a night food market

The art of pouring tea, shown in a Beijing restaurant

## TIANJIN

One of the largest cities in China, Tianjin occupies a rather unique position in Chinese cuisine. As a treaty port, Tianjin has acquired a cosmopolitan nature in many aspects of its daily life, particularly showing Russian and Japanese influences. Hence you will find a large number of beef and lamb dishes here, and the city is famous for its dumplings.

## MONGOLIAN & MUSLIM CUISINE

The Chinese Muslim school of cooking derives mainly from the Hui, the Uighur, and the Mongolian minorities. The Hui are distributed throughout China, but their traditional area of settlement is in the north. The Uighur are mainly in the northwest, while the Mongols are traditionally nomadic and spread throughout the north. As Muslims they do not eat pork, so beef, lamb, and mutton cooked on skewers are important foods in their daily diet. Hand-made noodles and flat breads also feature.

### ON THE MENU

**Drunken Empress Chicken**
Supposedly named after Yang Guifei, an imperial concubine overly fond of her alcohol.

**Stir-fried Kidney-flowers**
These are actually pork kidneys criss-cross cut into "flowers" and stir-fried with bamboo shoots, water chestnuts, and black fungus.

**Fish Slices with Wine Sauce**
Deep-fried fish fillet braised in a wine sauce.

**Phoenix-tail Prawns**
King prawn tails coated in batter and bread crumbs, then deep-fried.

**Lamb in Sweet Bean Sauce**
Tender fillet of lamb sliced and cooked in sweet bean paste with vinegar to give it that classic sweet and sour taste.

**Hot Candied Apples**
A popular Chinese dessert.

**Lamb & Scallions:** *sliced lamb rapidly stir-fried with garlic, leeks or scallions, and sweet bean paste.*

**Mongolian Hotpot:** *thinly sliced lamb, vegetables, and noodles dipped in boiling water and an array of sauces.*

**Sweet & Sour Carp:** *the quintessential Shandong dish traditionally made with Yellow River carp.*

# BEIJING

The capital of the People's Republic of China is one of the world's largest cities with a population of over 19 million. Beijing first became an imperial capital during the Mongol Yuan dynasty (1279–1368), and both the Ming and Qing emperors ruled from the Forbidden City at its heart. Today, an all-pervading spirit of change has added an exciting new dimension to the city.

Expanding in concentric rings from the Forbidden City at its core, the grid-like layout of modern-day Beijing still echoes its Ming dynasty blueprint. Old Beijing survives in its temples, palaces, and old alleyways (*hutong*) that crisscross the city outside the second ring road, which itself charts the loop of the demolished City Wall. Within this ancient outline are huge avenues, vaulting flyovers, towering skyscrapers, shopping malls, and the vast expanse of Tian'an Men Square. The city that the 13th-century Mongol warlord Genghis Khan once put to the torch is undergoing a new, dramatic facelift, as a result of a culmination of a quarter-century of reform, the pressures of a growing population, and the 2008 Olympics. Beijing is a microcosm of modern China and all its contradictions, a bustling mix of affluent shoppers, trendy youths, beggars, and plain-clothes police. Bars and cafés proliferate, and entertainment options range from traditional Beijing opera and spectacular acrobatics to modern jazz and even raucous punk clubs. And in the capital's many restaurants, China's diverse cuisine can be sampled across its range – from the fierce spices of Sichuan to the dainty morsels of Cantonese *dim sum*. On the roads, the city's army of bicycles may be under pressure from the huge influx of new cars, but for the time being pedal power is still one of the best ways to get around Beijing.

Pleasure cruise on Kunming Lake, Summer Palace

◁ Red flags flying next to Zhengyang Men, Tian'an Men Square

# Exploring Beijing

Beijing's most significant sights and districts are
marked on this map. At the core is the Forbidden
City, with Tian'an Men Square and Qian Men to the
south, and the shopping district of Wangfujing to its
east. North of the Forbidden City stand the Drum and
Bell Towers and farther northeast is the Buddhist
Lama Temple. North of Beihai Park, the Mansion of
Prince Gong stands in a historic *hutong* quarter, the
old alleyways that riddle the city. To the south, Tian
Tan, known as the Temple of Heaven, is a majestic
example of Ming dynasty design. Beijing's environs
are also dotted with sites including the magnificent
Great Wall and the scenic Ming Tombs.

**LOCATOR MAP**
*See Map pp70–71*

**KEY**

<table>
<tr><td>▨</td><td>Street-by-Street area:<br>see pp82–3</td></tr>
<tr><td>✈</td><td>International airport</td></tr>
<tr><td>🚉</td><td>Train station</td></tr>
<tr><td>🚌</td><td>Long distance bus station</td></tr>
<tr><td>Ⓜ</td><td>Subway station</td></tr>
<tr><td>🚍</td><td>City bus station</td></tr>
<tr><td>ℹ</td><td>Tourist information</td></tr>
<tr><td>✚</td><td>Hospital</td></tr>
<tr><td>卍</td><td>Temple</td></tr>
<tr><td>✝</td><td>Church</td></tr>
<tr><td>━</td><td>National highway</td></tr>
<tr><td>━</td><td>Major road</td></tr>
<tr><td>┅</td><td>Provincial border</td></tr>
<tr><td>▨</td><td>Great Wall of China</td></tr>
</table>

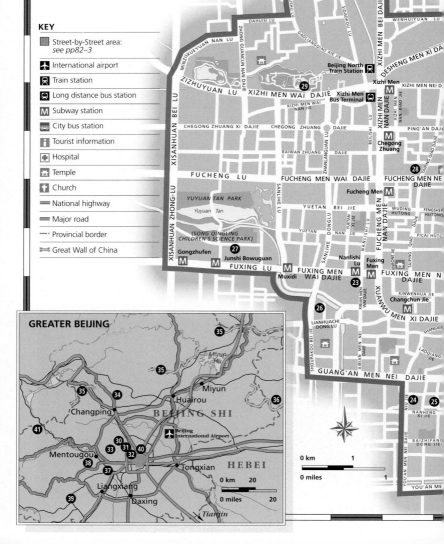

## SIGHTS AT A GLANCE

### Historic Buildings, Sites & Neighborhoods
Ancient Observatory ⑲
Chuandixia ㊶
Dazhalan & Liulichang ⑥
Drum & Bell Towers ⑫
Eastern Qing Tombs ㊱
*Forbidden City pp86–9* ⑧
*Great Wall of China pp106–9* ㉟
Marco Polo Bridge ㊲
*Ming Tombs pp104–5* ㉞
National Olympic Stadium ㊵
Peking Man Site ㊴
Prince Gong's Mansion ⑪

Qian Men ③
*Summer Palace pp100–2* ㉚
*Tian'an Men Square pp82–3* ①
Underground City ④
Yuanming Yuan ㉛

### Museums & Galleries
Beijing Capital Museum ㉓
Beijing Planning Exhibition Hall ⑤
Beijing Natural History Museum ㉑

Chinese Military History Museum ㉗
National Museum of China ②
National Art Museum of China ⑰
Southeast Corner Watchtower ⑳

### Temples, Churches & Mosques
Confucius Temple ⑭
Cow Street Mosque ㉔
Dong Yue Miao ⑯
Fayuan Temple ㉕
Great Bell Temple ㉜
Lama Temple ⑬
Miaoying Temple White Dagoba ㉘
South Cathedral ⑦
Tanzhe Temple ㊳
*Temple of Heaven pp96–7* ㉒
White Clouds Temple ㉖

### Shops & Markets
Wangfujing Street ⑱

### Parks & Zoos
Bei Hai Park ⑩
Beijing Zoo ㉙
Di Tan Park ⑮
Jing Shan Park ⑨
Xiang Shan Park ㉝

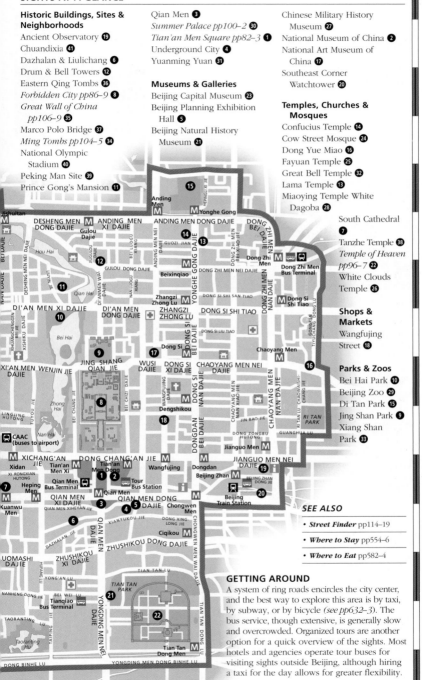

### SEE ALSO

- *Street Finder* pp114–19
- *Where to Stay* pp554–6
- *Where to Eat* pp582–4

### GETTING AROUND

A system of ring roads encircles the city center, and the best way to explore this area is by taxi, by subway, or by bicycle (*see pp632–3*). The bus service, though extensive, is generally slow and overcrowded. Organized tours are another option for a quick overview of the sights. Most hotels and agencies operate tour buses for visiting sights outside Beijing, although hiring a taxi for the day allows for greater flexibility.

# Street-by-Street: Tian'an Men Square ❶
天安门广场

**Chairman Mao**

Tian'an Men Guangchang – the Square of the Gate of Heavenly Peace – is a vast open concrete expanse at the heart of modern Beijing. With Mao's Mausoleum at its focal point, and bordered by 1950s Communist-style buildings and ancient gates from Beijing's now leveled city walls, the square is usually filled with visitors strolling about as kites flit overhead. The square has also traditionally served as a stage for popular demonstrations and is most indelibly associated with the student protests of 1989 and their gory climax.

**Cyclists along Chang'an Jie**

**Great Hall of the People**
*Seat of the Chinese legislature, the vast auditorium and banqueting halls are open for part of the day except when the National People's Congress is in session.*

**★ Zhengyang Men**
*Along with the Arrow Tower this tower formed a double gate known as the Qian Men. It now houses a museum on the history of Beijing.*

**The Arrow Tower or Jian Lou**,
like Zhengyang Men, was first
built in the Ming dynasty.

**★ Mao's Mausoleum**
*Flanked by revolutionary statues, the building contains the embalmed body of Chairman Mao. His casket, raised from its refrigerated chamber, is on view mornings and afternoons.*

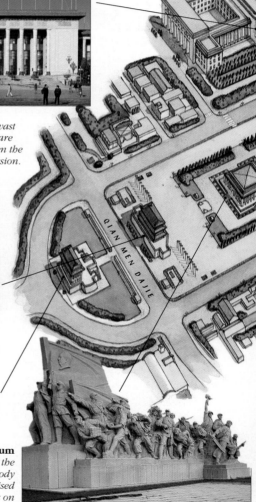

QIAN MEN DAJIE

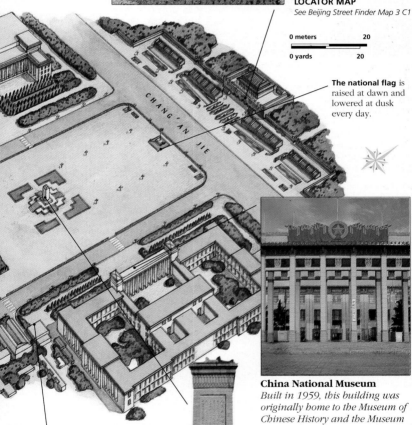

### ★ Tian'an Men
*Mao proclaimed the founding of the People's Republic of China on October 1, 1949 from this Ming dynasty gate, where his huge portrait still remains.*

**LOCATOR MAP**
*See Beijing Street Finder Map 3 C1*

| 0 meters | 20 |
| 0 yards | 20 |

**The national flag is** raised at dawn and lowered at dusk every day.

**China National Museum**
*Built in 1959, this building was originally home to the Museum of Chinese History and the Museum of the Revolution, now merged. It reopened to great fanfare in 2011 after three years of renovation. The halls also host exhibitions from other world class museums.*

**Bags, coats, and cameras** must be left here before visiting Mao's Mausoleum.

### Monument to the People's Heroes
*Erected in 1958, the granite monument is decorated with bas-reliefs of episodes from China's revolutionary history and calligraphy from Communist veterans Mao Zedong and Zhou Enlai.*

**STAR SIGHTS**

★ Mao's Mausoleum

★ Zhengyang Men

★ Tian'an Men

Zhengyang Men, Qian Men – part of Beijing's central fortifications

# National Museum of China ❷
中国国家博物馆

Tian'an Men Square. **Map** 3 C2. Ⓜ
*Tian'an Men Dong.* **Tel** *(010) 6511
9207.* ◯ *9am–5pm Tue–Sun.* Ⓟ
🖥 **www.chnmuseum.cn**

The National Museum of China
reopened in March 2011 after a
three-year program of renovation. Reported to be the
largest museum in the world,
it now stands at more than
2 million sq ft (185,806 sq m),
with 49 rooms holding around
a million cultural relics,
including the cowboy hat
worn by Deng Xiaoping on a
trip to the United States and
other noteworthy artifacts.
Two permanent exhibitions
cover China's ancient history
and from 1840 to the present
day, although the chaos of
the Cultural Revolution is
glossed over with just a single
photograph.

# Qian Men ❸
前门

Qian Men Dajie. **Map** 3 C2. Ⓜ *Qian
Men.* ◯ *8:30am–3:30pm daily.* 🖼

Qian Men or the Front Gate
consists of two towers, the
**Zhengyang Men**,
on the southern
edge of Tian'an
Men Square, and
the **Jian Lou**
(Arrow Tower) just
to the south.
Zhengyang Men (Facing the
Sun Gate) was the most
imposing of the nine gates of
the inner city wall that divided
Beijing's imperial quarters in
the Forbidden City from the
"Chinese City," where, during
the Manchu Qing dynasty, the
Chinese inhabitants lived.
    Rising 131 ft (40 m), the
gate stands on the north-
south axis that runs through
the Tian'an Men and the
Forbidden City. Its museum

has dioramas of the old city
walls, and photographs of
Beijing's old streets.

🚇 **Zhengyang Men**
**Tel** *(010) 6522 9386.* ◯ *daily.* 🖼

# Underground City ❹
北京地下城

62 Xi Damo Hutong. **Map** 4 D2.
Ⓜ *Qian Men.* **Tel** *(010) 6702 2657.*
● *until 2012/13 for repairs, call to
check before visiting.* 🖼 📷

At the height of the Sino-
Soviet rift in the 1960s, Mao
Zedong gave orders to carve
out a vast network of bomb-
proof tunnels beneath
Beijing. The resulting maze
of tunnels was equipped
with weapons, hospitals, and
large stocks of water and
    food. The Underground City
    has been open to
    visitors in the past,
    but is currently
    closed due to
    damaged and
    blocked tunnels.

战备医院
War  Hospital

**War Hospital sign,
Underground City**

# Planning and Exhibition Hall ❺
展览馆

20 Qian Men Dong Dajie. **Map** 3 C2.
Ⓜ *Qian Men.* **Tel** *(010) 6701 7074.*
◯ *9am–5pm Tue–Sun.* 🖼 📷

This impressive museum, just
east of the historic Qian Men
area, offers a glimpse into what
Beijing's future has in store.

---

## BEIJING'S CITY WALLS

The earliest defensive walls around Beijing (then called
Yanjing, later Zhongdu) were erected in the Jin dynasty
(1115–1234) and modeled on the wall around Kaifeng (see
p150). The Mongol Kublai Khan rebuilt Zhongdu, naming it
Dadu, and encompassed it with a 19-mile (30-km) wall. It
was only during the Ming era (1368–1644) that the walls
took on their final shape of an Outer Wall with seven gates,
and an Inner Wall with nine gates. The magnificent Inner
Wall was 38 ft (11.5 m) high and 64 ft (19.5 m) wide. The
walls and most of their gates were unfortunately demolished
in the 1950s and 60s to make way for roads. Of the inner
wall, only Qian Men and Desheng Men survive, while the
outer wall retains only Dongbian Men (see p95). The old
gates live on as place names on the second ring road, and as
the names of stations on the Beijing Underground Loop line.

**Arrow Tower of Qian Men**

Shop selling Communist memorabilia, Dazhalan Jie

The highlight is a huge scale model of what the city should look like in 2020, complete with a sound and light show. In contrast, the museum also has models and historical photographs of old Beijing.

## Dazhalan & Liulichang ❻
### 大栅栏和琉璃厂

**Map** 3 C2. **M** *Qian Men.*

South of Qian Men are the narrow and lively *hutongs (see p91)* of the old Chinese quarter. The inner city wall and its gates separated the "Inner City" containing the imperial quarters of the Manchu emperors from the "Chinese City," where the Chinese lived apart from their

Cyclists on restored Liulichang Jie

Qing overlords. The district has been renovated to create a Qing dynasty appearance, complete with a tourist tram. Running west off the northern end of Qian Men Dajie is Dazhalan Jie, whose name "Big Barrier Street" refers to the now-demolished gates that were closed every night to fence off the residents from Qian Men and the Inner City. There are *hutong* tours by rickshaw – drivers just wait in the street in Dazhalan.

The area is a great place for browsing, and has several quaint Qing-era specialty shops. Located down the first alley on the left from Dazhalan Jie is the century-old pickle shop **Liubiju**, while **Ruifuxiang**, on the right-hand side of Dazhalan, is renowned for its silks and traditional Chinese garments. On the south side of Dazhalan Jie is the Chinese medicine shop **Tongrentang Pharmacy**, which has been in business since 1669 and enjoyed imperial patronage. On the same side of the road, the **Zhangyiyuan Chazhuang** or Zhangyiyuan Teashop has been supplying fine teas since the early 20th century. West of Dazhalan Jie is Liulichang Jie, a fascinating place to wander – it has everything from ceramics to antique Chinese books. Beware of so-called "antiques" which should be judiciously examined before buying.

## South Cathedral ❼
### 南堂

141 Qian Men Xi Dajie. **Map** 3 A2. **M** *Xuanwu Men.*

The first Catholic church to be built in Beijing, South Cathedral (Nan Tang) stands close to the Xuanwu Men

underground station, on the site of Jesuit Matteo Ricci's former residence. Ricci was the first Jesuit missionary to reach Beijing. Arriving in 1601, he sent gifts of European curiosities such as clocks, mathematical instruments, and a world map to the Wanli emperor, thus gaining his goodwill, and was eventually given permission to establish a church.

Like many of China's churches, this restored building has suffered much devastation. Construction first began in 1605, and it subsequently burned down in 1775. It was rebuilt a century later, only to be destroyed once again during the Boxer Rebellion of 1900. The cathedral was rebuilt in 1904. Also known as St. Mary's Church, it is the city's largest functioning Catholic cathedral, and has regular services in a variety of languages including Chinese, English, and Latin. Service timings are posted on the noticeboard. A small gift shop is located near the south gate.

Stained glass at the South Cathedral (Nan Tang)

# Forbidden City ❽
## 故宫

**Decorative wall relief**

Forming the very heart of Beijing, the Forbidden City, officially known as the Palace Museum (Gugong), is China's most magnificent architectural complex and was completed in 1420. The huge palace is a compendium of imperial architecture and a lasting monument of dynastic China from which 24 emperors ruled for nearly 500 years. The symbolic center of the Chinese universe, the palace was the exclusive domain of the imperial court and dignitaries until the abdication in 1912. It was opened to the public in 1949.

**Chinese Lions**
*Pairs of lions guard the entrances of halls. The male is portrayed with a ball under his paw, while the female has a lion cub.*

**★ Golden Water**
*Five marble bridges, symbolizing the five cardinal virtues of Confucianism, cross the Golden Water, which flows from west to east in a course designed to resemble the jade belt worn by officials.*

**Storehouses**

**Offices of the imperial secretariat**

**OUTER COURT**
At the center of the Forbidden City, the Outer Court is easily its most impressive part. Most of the other buildings in the complex were there to service this city within a city.

**Meridian Gate (Wu Men)**
*From the balcony the emperor would review his armies and perform ceremonies marking the start of a new calendar.*

**Gate of Supreme Harmony**
*Originally used for receiving visitors, the 78-ft (24-m) high, double-eaved hall was later used for banquets during the Qing dynasty (1644–1912).*

★ **Marble Carriageway**
*The central ramp carved with dragons chasing pearls among clouds was reserved for the emperor.*

**VISITORS' CHECKLIST**

North of Tian'an Men Square.
**Map** 1 C5. **Tel** *(010) 6513 2255.*
⬛ *Apr–Oct:* 8:30am–5pm daily;
*Nov–Mar:* 8:30am–4:30pm daily.
📷 🔶 🔶 ⬛ 🔶 ⬛
**www**.dpm.org.cn

**Hall of Preserving Harmony**

**Bronze cauldrons** were filled with water in case of fire.

**Gate of Heavenly Purity**

**The Hall of Middle Harmony** received the emperor before official ceremonies.

**Imperial sundial**

★ **Hall of Supreme Harmony**
*The largest hall in the palace, this was used for major occasions such as the enthronement of an emperor. Inside the hall, the ornate throne sits beneath a fabulously colored ceiling.*

**Roof Guardians**
*An odd number of these figures, all associated with water, are supposed to protect the building from fire.*

**STAR FEATURES**

★ Golden Water

★ Marble Carriageway

★ Hall of Supreme Harmony

**DESIGN BY NUMBERS**

The harmonious principle of *yin* and *yang* is the key to Chinese design. As odd numbers represent *yang* (the preferred masculine element associated with the emperor), the numbers three, five, seven, and the ultimate odd number – nine, recur in architectural details. It is said that the Forbidden City has 9,999 rooms and, as nine times nine is especially fortunate, the doors for imperial use usually contain 81 brass studs.

**Palace door with a lucky number of studs**

# Exploring the Forbidden City

A short distance north through the Gate of Heavenly Purity lies the Inner Court with three impressive inner palaces. Further on through the Imperial Flower Garden stands the Shenwu Gate, the north gate of the Forbidden City, an exit from the palace that leads to a walk across to Jing Shan Park *(see p90)*. On the western and eastern flanks of the Inner Court, it is also possible to explore numerous halls, some of which house museum collections (entry fee payable).

**The Pavilion of a Thousand Autumns in the Imperial Gardens**

### 🏯 The Inner Court

Beyond the Hall of Preserving Harmony (Outer Court) lies a large but narrow courtyard with gates leading to the open areas east and west of the Outer Court and a main gate, the **Gate of Heavenly Purity**, leading to the Inner Court. Here lie three splendid palaces, mirroring those of the Outer Court but on a smaller scale. The double-eaved **Palace of Heavenly Purity** was used as the imperial sleeping quarters and for the reception of officials. It was here that the last Ming emperor, Chongzhen, wrote his final missive in red ink, before getting drunk, killing his 15-year-old daughter and his concubines, and then hanging himself on Jing Shan *(see p90)*, just north of the palace, as peasant rebels swarmed through the capital. Beyond lie the **Hall of Union**, used as a throne room by the empress, and the **Palace of Earthly Tranquillity**, the living quarters of the Ming empresses. During the Qing dynasty, the hall was used for Manchurian shaman rites, including animal sacrifice.

### 🏯 The Imperial Gardens

The **Imperial Flower Garden**, north of the three inner palaces and the Gate of Earthly Tranquillity, dates from the reign of the Ming Yongle emperor. It is symmetrically laid out with pavilions, temples, and halls as well as a rock garden and ancient trees. On the west and east sides of the garden are the charming Thousand Autumns Pavilion and Ten Thousand Springs Pavilion, each topped with a circular roof. Positioned centrally in the north of the garden, the **Hall of Imperial Peace** formerly served as a temple, and, on top of the lofty rockery in the northeast of the garden, the Imperial View Pavilion rises with long views over the gardens and beyond. During the Qing dynasty, sacrifices were performed in the gardens on the seventh day of the seventh lunar month (China's equivalent of Valentine's Day) by the emperor, empress, and imperial concubines to a pair of stars that represent lovers.

### 🏯 Eastern Palaces

On the east side of the Inner Court lies a much closer knit series of smaller palaces and courtyards formerly used as the residences of imperial concubines. Nowadays, some of these areas serve as museums of jade, paintings, enamels, and antique collectibles, including the impressive Clock Exhibition Hall (housed in the **Palace of Eternal Harmony**) with its

**Imperial five-clawed dragons on a glazed Nine Dragon Screen**

### CHINESE DRAGONS

The Chinese dragon is a curious hybrid of sometimes many animal parts – snake's body, deer horns, bull's ears, hawk's claws and fish scales. Endowed with magical characteristics, it can fly, swim, change into other animals, bring rainfall and ward off evil spirits. The five-clawed dragon represented the power of the emperor, and therefore could only adorn his imperial buildings. The Chinese dragon is a beneficent beast offering protection and good luck, hence its depiction on screens and marble carriageways, and its significance, even today, in festivals such as Chinese New Year.

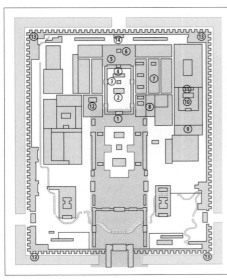

## THE FORBIDDEN CITY

① Gate of Heavenly Purity
② Palace of Heavenly Purity
③ Hall of Union
④ Palace of Earthly Tranquillity
⑤ Imperial Flower Garden
⑥ Hall of Imperial Peace
⑦ Palace of Eternal Harmony
⑧ Palace of Abstinence
⑨ Nine Dragon Screen
⑩ Imperial Zenith Hall
⑪ Palace of Peaceful Longevity
⑫ Hall of Mental Cultivation
⑬ Arrow Tower
⑭ Gate of Divine Prowess

| 0 meters | 300 |
| 0 yards | 300 |

### KEY

☐ Imperial buildings

☐ Area illustrated (see pp86–7)

sizeable and fascinating display. Note that these are occasionally moved to other halls and at some an entry fee is payable. Among the collection are elaborate Chinese, British, and French timepieces, donated or collected by Qing emperors. In the southeast of the inner court is the **Palace of Abstinence**, where the emperor fasted before sacrificial ceremonies. Further southeast stands a beautiful **Nine Dragon Screen**, a 100-ft (31-m) long spirit wall made from richly glazed tiles and similar to the screen in Beihai Park (see p90). Screens were used to shield areas from sight and allow visitors to make themselves presentable. The screen leads on to the jewelry displays housed in a series of halls in the northeast of the complex, including the **Imperial Zenith Hall** and the **Palace of Peaceful Longevity**. These halls contain an array of decorative objects and tools used by the emperor. Northwest of the Palace of Peaceful Longevity is its flower garden, a tranquil strip of rockeries and pavilions.

**Tile relief by the Hall of Mental Cultivation**

### ♛ Western Palaces

Much of the western flank of the Forbidden City is closed to visitors, but the halls west of the three inner palaces are accessible. **The Hall of Mental Cultivation** was used by Yongzheng (see p109) for his residence, rather than the Hall of Heavenly Purity, where his father, Kangxi, had lived for 60 years. The East Warm Chamber of the Hall of Mental Cultivation was the site of the formal abdication by Henry Pu Yi, the last emperor, on February 12, 1912 (see p446).

### ♛ The Palace Walls

The wall around the Forbidden City is marked at each corner by an elaborate **Arrow Tower**, notable for its many eaves. The northern gate of the palace is called the **Gate of Divine Prowess** or Shenwu Men, and served as a combined bell and drum tower. The palace wall was enclosed within a moat and another wall ran around the grounds of the Imperial City. Beyond this lay the inner and outer city walls of Beijing. Damaged in the 1950s and 1960s, only a few parts of the Imperial City wall survive, while the city walls have all but vanished. However, the wall of the Forbidden City and its four gates have survived intact and can still be admired.

**One of four arrow towers at each corner of the palace wall**

**Bei Hai with Jing Shan's summit in the background**

## Jing Shan Park **9**
景山公园

44 Jingshan Xi Jie, Xicheng. **Map** 1 C4. Ⓜ *Dong Si.* **Tel** *(010) 6404 4071.* ⏰ *6:30am–7:30pm daily.* 🎫

Situated on Beijing's north-south axis, Jing Shan Park has its origins in the Yuan dynasty (1279–1368). Its hill was created from earth that was excavated while building the palace moat during the reign of the Ming Yongle emperor. In the early years of the Ming dynasty it was known as Wansui Shan (Long Life Hill), but was renamed Jing Shan (View or Prospect Hill) in the Qing era. Foreign residents also referred to it as Coal Hill (Mei Shan), supposedly because coal was stored at the foot of the hill although other theories exist.
Until the fall of the Qing, Jing Shan was linked to the Forbidden City and was restricted to imperial use. The hill's purpose was to protect the imperial palaces within the Forbidden City from malign northern influences, which brought death and destruction according to classical *feng shui*. However, it failed to save the last Ming emperor Chongzhen, who hanged himself from a locust tree (*huaishu*) in the park in 1644, when rebel troops forced their way into Beijing. Another tree, planted after the original tree was cut down, marks the spot in the park's southeast. The park is dotted

with several pavilions and halls, but the highlight of any visit is the superb view of the Forbidden City from the hill's Wanchun Ting (Wanchun Pavilion).

## Bei Hai Park **10**
北海公园

1 Wenjin Jie, Xicheng. **Map** 1 C4. Ⓜ *Tian'an Men Xi.* **Tel** *(010) 6403 3225.* ⏰ *6am–8pm daily.* 🎫 📷

An imperial garden for more than 1,000 years, Bei Hai Park was opened to the public in 1925. Filled with artificial hills, pavilions, and temples, it is associated with Kublai Khan, who redesigned it during the Mongol Yuan dynasty. The Tuancheng (Round City), near the south entrance, has a huge, decorated jade urn belonging to him.
The park is named after its extensive lake, **Bei Hai**, whose southern end is bordered by the inaccessible Zhong Nan Hai, the Commu-nist Party Headquarters. In the middle of Bei Hai, Jade Island was supposedly made from the earth excavated while creating the lake. It is topped by the 118-ft (36-m) high **White Dagoba**, a Tibetan-style stupa built to honor the visit of the fifth Dalai Lama in 1651. Beneath the huge dagoba, **Yongan Si** comprises a series of ascending halls. The lake's northern shore has several sights, including the massive **Nine Dragon Screen**, an 89-ft

**White Dagoba, Bei Hai Park**

(27-m) long spirit wall made of colorful glazed tiles. Depicting nine intertwining dragons, it was designed to obstruct evil spirits. The Xiao-xitian Temple lies to the west.

## Prince Gong's Mansion **11**
恭王府

17 Qianhai Xi Jie, Xicheng. **Map** 1 B3. Ⓜ *Gulou.* **Tel** *(010) 8328 8149.* ⏰ *8:30am–4:30pm daily.* 🎫

Beijing's most complete example of a historic mansion is situated in a charming *hutong* district west of Qian Hai. It was supposedly the inspiration behind the residence portrayed by Cao Xueqin in his classic 18th-century novel *Dream of the Red Chamber (see pp28–29)*. Built during the reign of the Qianlong emperor, the house is extensive and its charming garden is a pattern of open corridors and pavilions, dotted with pools and gateways. Originally built for Heshun, a Manchu official and the emperor's favorite, the residence was appropriated by the imperial household after he was found guilty of using regal motifs in his mansion design. It was later bequeathed to Prince Gong in the Xianfeng emperor's reign (r.1851–61). The house is popular with tour groups, so early morning is the best time to visit and afterwards, the local *hutongs* can be explored. Beijing Opera is performed in its Grand Opera House.

**Elaborate arched gateway, Prince Gong's Mansion**

# Beijing's Courtyard Houses

At first glance, Beijing seems a thoroughly modern city, but a stroll through the city's alleyways *(hutong)* reveals the charm of old Beijing. These *hutong* – weaving across much of central Beijing – are where many Beijing residents *(Beijingren)* still live. Typically running east to west, *hutong* are created by the walls of courtyard houses *(siheyuan)*. Formerly the homes of officials and the well-to-do,

**Washing the laundry in public**

many were taken over by the state but they are now increasingly privately owned. The *hutong* are very easy to find, try the alleyways between the main streets south of Qian Men, or around Hou Hai and Qian Hai. The modernization of Beijing has destroyed many traditional *siheyuan*, but a few have been converted into hotels *(see pp554–6)*, allowing the visitor a closer look at this disappearing world.

**The main hall** was the most northerly and usually reserved for the eldest of the family, such as the grandparents.

**Crowded courtyards**
*As space became an issue in Beijing, additional buildings filled in the large courtyards. Several families may be living together in one siheyuan.*

**Wall** adds privacy and keeps out spirits as they are unable to turn corners.

**The open courtyard** lets in both the sunlight and the wind and cold.

**The number of halls** and courtyards determines the grandeur of the residence.

**Entrance** is at the southeastern corner as prescribed by *feng shui.*

**Walls** were important to the Chinese psyche – even in the secure capital, they felt the need to retreat behind them.

**Social housing**
*With several families living together, a strong community spirit is fostered, while the* hutong *outside becomes an extension of the home.*

**Typical Beijing hutong**
*You can take organized rickshaw tours of the* hutong, *sometimes with a visit to Prince Gong's Mansion (see p90), but it can be more fun to explore them by yourself.*

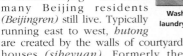

A view of the Bell Tower from Beijing's Drum Tower

# Drum & Bell Towers ⑫

鼓楼

Northern end of Di'an Men Wai Dajie, Dongcheng. **Map** 1 C2. Ⓜ *Gulou.* **Tel** *(010) 8402 7869.* ◯ *9am–5pm daily.* 

Located on the north-south meridian that bisects the Forbidden City and Tian'an Men Square, the Drum Tower (Gu Lou) rises up from a historic Beijing *hutong* district *(see p91)*. The squat structure seen today was originally built in 1420 during the reign of the Ming Yongle emperor. Visitors can climb the steep stairs to look out over the city and inspect the 25 drums there. The one large and 24 smaller drums were beaten to mark the hours of the day. According to the official Chinese accounts, the original drums were destroyed by the foreign soldiers of the international army that relieved Beijing during the Boxer Rebellion *(see p433)*.

A short walk north of the Drum Tower, the Bell Tower (Zhong Lou) is an edifice from 1745, which replaced an earlier tower that had burnt down. Suspended within the tower is a 15-ft (4.5-m) high and 42-ton (42,674-kg) bell, that was cast in 1420. Visitors can pay to ring the bell for good luck.

# Lama Temple ⑬

雍和宫

12 Yonghe Gong Dajie, Dongcheng. **Map** 2 E2. Ⓜ *Yonghe Gong.* **Tel** *(010) 6404 3769.* ◯ *9am–4pm daily.* 

Beijing's most spectacular temple complex, the Lama Temple (Yonghegong) was constructed during the 17th century and converted into a Tibetan lamasery in 1744. Its five main halls are a stylistic blend of Han, Mongol, and Tibetan motifs. The first hall has a traditional display – the plump laughing Buddha, Milefo, is back-to-back with Wei Tuo, the Protector of Buddhist Doctrine, and flanked by the Four Heavenly Kings. **Yonghe Hall** beyond has three manifestations of Buddha, flanked by 18 *luohan* – those freed from the cycle of rebirth. Even farther back, the Tibetan-styled **Falun Hall** or Hall of the Wheel of Law has a statue of Tsongkhapa, the founder of the Yellow Hat sect of Tibetan Buddhism *(see pp522–3)*.

The highlight, however, is encapsulated within the towering **Wanfu Pavilion** (Wanfu Ge) – a vast 55-ft (17-m) high statue of Maitreya (the Future Buddha), carved from a single block of

The striking main gateway of the colorful Lama Temple

*For hotels and restaurants in Beijing see pp554–6 and pp582–4*

**Statue of Confucius at the main entrance, Confucius Temple**

sandalwood. The splendid exhibition of Tibetan Buddhist objects at the temple's rear includes statues of the deities Padmasambhava (Guru Rinpoche), and the Tibetan equivalent of Guanyin, Chenresig, alongside ritual objects such as the scepter-like *dorje* (thunderbolt) and *dril bu* (bell), symbols of the male and female energies. Few captions are in English.

# Confucius Temple 孔庙

13 Guozijian Jie, Dongcheng. **Map** 2 E2. M *Yonghe Gong.* **Tel** *(010) 8401 1977.* 9am–5pm daily.

Adjacent to the Lama Temple, the Confucius Temple is the largest in China outside Qufu, the philosopher's birthplace in Shandong province (see *p142*). The alley leading to the temple has a fine *pailou* (decorative archway), few of which survive in Beijing. First built in 1302 during the Mongol Yuan dynasty, the temple was expanded in 1906 in the reign of Emperor Guangxu. It is a tranquil place that offers respite from the city's bustle. Around 200 ancient stelae stand in the silent courtyard in front of the main hall (Dacheng Dian), inscribed with the names of those who successfully passed

the imperial civil service exams. Additional stelae are propped up on the backs of *bixi* (mythical cross between a tortoise and a dragon), within pavilions surrounded by cypress trees. On a marble terrace in the main hall are statues of Confucius and some of his disciples.

# Di Tan Park 地坛公园

N of the Lama Temple, Dongcheng. **Map** 2 E1. M *Yonghe Gong.* **Tel** *(010) 6421 4657.* 6am–9pm daily.

An ideal place to stroll amidst trees, Di Tan Park was named after the Temple of Earth (Di Tan), which was the venue for imperial sacrifices. The park's altar (Fangze Tan) dates to the Ming dynasty and its square shape represents the earth. Under the Ming, five main altars were established at the city's cardinal points – Tian Tan (Temple of Heaven) in the south, Di Tan in the north, Ri Tan (Temple of the Sun) in the east, Yue Tan (Temple of the Moon) in the west, and Sheji Tan (Temple of Land and Grain) in the center. Mirroring ancient ceremonies, a lively temple fair *(miaohui)* is held during the Chinese New Year (see *pp42–3*), to welcome the spring planting season and appease the gods.

# Dong Yue Miao 东岳庙

141 Chaoyang Men Wai Dajie, Chaoyang. **Map** 2 F4. M *Chaoyang Men.* **Tel** *(010) 6551 0151.* 8:30am–4:30pm Tue–Sun.

On Beijing's eastern side near Chaoyang's Workers' Stadium, the mesmerizing Dong Yue Miao takes its name from the Daoist Eastern Peak, Dong Yue, also known as Tai Shan (see *pp144–5*). It is fronted by a fabulous glazed Ming dynasty *paifang* inscribed with the characters "Zhisi Daizong," meaning "offer sacrifices to Mount Tai (Tai Shan) in good order."

This colorful and active temple, dating to the early 14th century, was restored at considerable cost in 1999, and is tended by Daoist monks. The main courtyard leads into the Hall of Tai Shan, where there are statues of the God of Tai Shan and his attendants. The greatest attractions here are over 70 "Departments," filled with vivid Daoist gods and demons, whose functions are explained in English captions. In Daoist lore, the spirits of the dead go to Tai Shan, and many Departments dwell on the afterlife. The Department for Increasing Wealth and Longevity, for example, offers cheerful advice.

**Guardian at entrance, Dong Yue Miao**

**Corn laid out to form Chinese characters, temple festival, Di Tan Park**

# National Art Museum of China ⑰
## 中国美术馆

1 Wusi Dajie, Dongcheng. **Map** 2 D4.
Ⓜ *Dong Si.* **Tel** *(010) 6401 7076.*
◯ *9am–5pm daily, last entry 4pm.*
**www**.namoc.org

Hosting exhibitions of Chinese and international art, as well as occasional photographic displays, the National Art Museum of China (Zhongguo Meishuguan) has 14 halls over three levels. This quite ordinary building holds an exciting range of Chinese modern art, which suffers less censorship than other media, such as film or literature. Magazines such as *Time Out Beijing* and *The Beijinger* carry details of current and forthcoming exhibitions.

# Wangfujing Street ⑱
## 王府井

**Map** 4 D1. Ⓜ *Wangfujing.* **Night Market** ◯ *5:30pm–10pm daily.* **St. Joseph's Church** 74 Wangfujing Dajie. **Tel** *(010) 6524 0634.* ◯ *early morning during services.*

Bustling Wangfujing Street (Wangfujing Dajie), Beijing's original shopping street, is filled with department stores and giant malls such as the Sun Dong'an Plaza *(see p112)*. Everything from curios, *objets d'art*, antiques, clothes, and books are available here. The huge **Foreign Language**

The imposing façade of St. Joseph's Church, Wangfujing Street

**Bookstore** is a good place to buy a more detailed map of Beijing. The street has a lively mixture of pharmacies, laundry and dyeing shops, as well as stores selling silk, tea, and shoes.

However, the street's highlight is the **Night Market**, with its endless variety of traditional Chinese snacks, including skewers of beef, and more exotic morsels such as scorpions. Other offerings include pancakes, fruit, shrimps, squid, flat bread, and more. The Wangfujing Snack Street, south of the Night Market, also has a range of colorful restaurants.

The impressive triple-domed **St. Joseph's Church**,

known as the East Cathedral, is at 74 Wangfujing Dajie. One of the city's most important churches, it has been restored at a cost of US$2 million. It was built on the site of the former residence of Jesuit Adam Schall von Bell (1591–1669) in 1655, and has been rebuilt a number of times after being successively destroyed by earthquake, fire, and then during the Boxer Rebellion. It is fronted by an open courtyard and an arched gateway.

# Ancient Observatory ⑲
## 古观象台

**Map** 4 F1. Ⓜ *Jianguo Men.* **Tel** *(010) 6512 8923.* ◯ *summer: 9am–6pm daily; winter: 9am–4:30pm daily.*

Ecliptic armillary sphere, Ancient Observatory

Beijing's ancient observatory (Gu Guanxiangtai) stands on a platform alongside a flyover off Jianguo Men Nei Dajie. Dating to 1442, it is one of the oldest in the world. A Yuan dynasty (1279–1368) observatory was also located here, but the structure that survives today was built after the Ming emperors relocated their capital from Nanjing to Beijing. In the early 17th century, the Jesuits, led by Matteo Ricci (1552–1610) and followed by Adam Schall von Bell, impressed the emperor and the imperial astronomers with their scientific knowledge, particularly the accuracy of their predictions of eclipses.

The Belgian Jesuit Father Verbiest (1623–88) was appointed to the Imperial Astronomical Bureau, where he designed a set of astronomical instruments in 1674. Several of these were appropriated by German soldiers during the Boxer Rebellion of 1900, and were only returned after World War I. A collection of reproduction astronomical devices lies in

Delicious street food at the Night Market, just off Wangfujing Street

*For hotels and restaurants in Beijing see pp554–6 and pp582–4*

The atmospheric Red Gate Gallery, Southeast Corner Watchtower

the courtyard on the ground floor, some decorated with fantastic Chinese designs including dragons. Steps lead to the roof, where there are impressive bronze instruments, including an azimuth theodolite, used to measure the altitude of celestial bodies, and an armillary sphere, for measuring the coordinates of planets and stars.

Southeast Corner Watchtower (Dongbian Men Jian Lou)

## Southeast Corner Watchtower ⑳
东边门箭楼

Off Jianguo Men Nan Dajie, Chongwen. **Map** 4 F2. Ⓜ *Beijing Zhan.* **Red Gate Gallery** *Tel (010) 6525 1005.* ⬜ *9am–5pm daily.* 🖳 *For exhibition details visit* **www**.redgategallery.com

About 2 km (1 mile) south of the Ancient Observatory, an imposing chunk of the Beijing City Walls *(see p85)* survives in the form of the 15th-century Southeast Corner Watchtower (Dongbian Jiao

Lou). After climbing onto the Ming dynasty battlements, visitors can walk along the short but impressive stretch of attached wall to admire the towering bastion, pitted with archers' windows, and look down on the city below. The walls of the tower are engraved with graffiti left by soldiers of the international army that marched into the city to liberate the Foreign Legations during the Boxer Rebellion in 1900.

Within its splendid, cavernous interior, accessed from the battlements, the rooms reveal enormous red wooden columns and pillars, crossed with beams. The **Red Gate Gallery**, one of Beijing's most appealing art galleries, is situated within this superb setting. Originally founded in 1991 by Brian Wallace, an Australian who came to Beijing to learn Chinese, the gallery exhibits works in a wide variety of media by up-and-coming contemporary Chinese and foreign artists. Forthcoming exhibitions are listed on the gallery's website *(see above).*

## Beijing Natural History Museum ㉑
自然历史博物馆

126 Tianqiao Nan Dajie, Chongwen. **Map** 3 C3. Ⓜ *Qian Men, then taxi.* **Tel** *(010) 6702 3096.* ⬜ *9am–5pm Tue–Sat.* **www**.bmnh.org.cn

This museum is the largest of its type in China, with about 5,000 specimens arranged into three collections. The Paleontology Hall displays a selection of the prehistoric animals that populated China millions of years ago. The zoology section explains and illustrates the course of evolution, and a basement houses a macabre display of human cadavers, pickled corpses, limbs, and organs. The botany collection is less impressive.

## Temple of Heaven ㉒

*See pp96–7.*

## Beijing Capital Museum ㉓
北京首都博物馆

16 Fuxingmenwai Dajie. Ⓜ *Muxidi.* **Tel** *(010) 6337 0491.* ⬜ *9am–5pm Tue–Sun.* 🖳 🍴 ♿

Beijing's premier museum has a collection of 200,000 of the best Chinese art and antiquities over five floors. An interesting film telling the story of Beijing is screened every 30 minutes. English captions on the exhibits are limited, so it is worth hiring an audio guide.

Dinosaur skeletons in the Paleontology Hall, Natural History Museum

# Temple of Heaven ㉒

天坛

**Gate to the Round Altar**

Completed during the Ming dynasty, the Temple of Heaven, more correctly known as Tian Tan, is one of the largest temple complexes in China and a paradigm of Chinese architectural balance and symbolism. Now a UNESCO World Heritage Site, it was here that the emperor would make sacrifices and pray to heaven and his ancestors at the winter solstice. As the Son of Heaven, the emperor could intercede with the gods, represented by their spirit tablets, on behalf of his people and pray for a good harvest. Off-limits to the common people during the Ming and Qing dynasties, the Temple of Heaven is situated in a large and pleasant park that now attracts early morning practitioners of *tai ji quan (see p273).*

**Qinian Dian, where the emperor prayed for a good harvest**

**Name plaques** are often written in the calligraphy of an emperor.

**Circular roof symbolizes the sky.**

## THE TIAN TAN COMPLEX

The main parts of the temple complex are all connected on the favored north-south axis by the Red Step Bridge (an elevated pathway) to form the focal point of the park. The Round Altar is made up of concentric rings of stone slabs in multiples of nine, the most auspicious number. The circular Echo Wall is famed for its supposed ability to carry a whisper from one side of the wall to the other.

① Hall of Prayer for Good Harvests
② Red Step Bridge
③ Echo Wall
④ Imperial Vault of Heaven
⑤ Round Altar

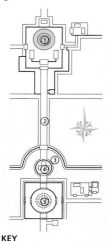

**KEY**

☐ Area illustrated

**Triple gates for emperor (east), officials (west) and gods (center)**

**Imperial Vault of Heaven, store for the spirit tablets of the gods**

**The Round Altar, site of the emperor's sacrifice**

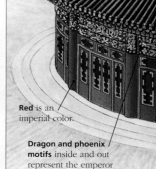

**Red** is an imperial color.

**Dragon and phoenix motifs** inside and out represent the emperor and empress.

## STAR FEATURES

★ Caisson Ceiling

★ Dragon Well Pillars

**The golden finial**
is 125 ft (38 m) high
and prone to lightning
strikes.

## VISITORS' CHECKLIST

Tian Tan Dong Lu (East Gate),
Chongwen. **Map** 4 E4. **Tel** (010)
6702 8866. Ⓜ Tiantan Dong
Men. 🚌 34, 6, 35. Park. ◯ 6am
–8pm daily. **Temple Buildings** ◯
8:30am–6pm. 🈲 📷 🎫 🚻 🛗

### ★ Caisson Ceiling
*The splendid circular caisson
ceiling has a gilded dragon
and phoenix at its center. The
hall is entirely built of wood
without using a single nail.*

**Blue** represents
the color of
heaven.

### ★ Dragon Well Pillars
*The roofs of the hall are supported
on 28 highly-decorated pillars. At
the center, the four huge columns,
known as Dragon Well pillars,
represent the seasons, while the
other 24 smaller pillars symbolize
the months in a year plus the two-
hour time periods in a day.*

**Tablets** in memory
of his ancestors
were worshipped
by the emperor.

**Symbolic
offerings**

### QINIAN DIAN
Originally built in 1420,
the Qinian Dian, or Hall of
Prayer for Good Harvests,
is often incorrectly called
the Temple of Heaven.
There is in fact no single
temple building as such
at Tian Tan, a more literal
translation of which is
Altar of Heaven – referring
to the whole complex.

### Marble Platform
*Three tiers of marble form a
circle 300 ft (90 m) in
diameter and 20 ft (6 m) high.
The balusters on the upper tier
are decorated with dragon
carvings to signify the imperial
nature of the structure.*

# Cow Street Mosque ㉔
## 牛街清真寺

18 Niu Jie, Xuanwu. **Map** 3 A3.
Ⓜ Caishikou, then taxi. **Tel** (010)
6353 2564. ⬜ 8am–6pm daily.
Avoid Fri (holy day). 🈳

Beijing's oldest and largest
mosque dates back to the
10th century. It is located in
the city's Hui district, near
numerous Muslim restaurants
and shops. The Hui, a Chinese
Muslim minority group mainly
from Ningxia province, are
now scattered throughout
China and number around
200,000 in Beijing. The men are
easily identified by their beards
and characteristic white hats.
   The Cow Street Mosque
is an attractive edifice, with
Islamic motifs and Arabic
verses decorating its halls
and stelae. Its most prized
possession is a 300-year-old,
hand-written copy of the
Koran (Gulanjing).
   Astronomical observations
and lunar calculations were
made from the tower-like
**Wangyue Lou**. The graves of
two Yuan dynasty Arab missionaries engraved with Arabic
inscriptions can be seen here.
The courtyard is lush with
greenery, making it an idyllic
escape from Beijing's busy
streets. Visitors are advised to
dress conservatively (you can
hire clothes if necessary).
Non-Muslims are not allowed
to enter the prayer hall.

Buddhist statuary in the main hall, Fayuan Temple

# Fayuan Temple ㉕
## 法源寺

7 Fayuan Si Qian Jie, Xuanwu. **Map** 3
A3. Ⓜ Caishikou. **Tel** (010) 6353
4171. ⬜ 8:30am–3:30pm daily. 🈳

A short walk east from Cow
Street Mosque, the Fayuan
Temple dates to AD 696 and
is probably the oldest temple
in Beijing. It was consecrated
by the Tang Taizong emperor
(r.626–49), to commemorate
the soldiers who perished in
an expedition against the
northern tribes. The original
Tang era buildings were
destroyed by a succession of
natural disasters, and the
current structures date from
the Qing era.
   The temple's layout is
typical of Buddhist temples.
Near the gate, the incense
burner (lu) is flanked by the
Drum and Bell Towers to the
east and west. Beyond, the

Hall of the Heavenly Kings
(Tianwang Dian) is guarded
by a pair of bronze lions, and
has statues of Milefo (the
Laughing Buddha) and his
attendant Heavenly Kings.
Ancient stelae stand in front
of the main hall, where a
gilded statue of Sakyamuni
(the Historical Buddha) is
flanked by bodhisattvas and
luohan – those freed from
the cycle of rebirth.
   At the temple's rear, the
Scripture Hall stores sutras,
while another hall contains
a 16-ft (5-m) Buddha statue.
The grounds are busy with
monks who attend the
temple's Buddhist College.

# White Clouds Temple ㉖
## 白云寺

6 Baiyuanguan Jie, Xuanwu. Ⓜ
Nanlishi Lu, then taxi. **Tel** (010) 6344
3666. ⬜ 8:30am–4pm daily. 🈳

Home to the China Daoist
Association, the White Clouds
Temple (Baiyun Guan) was
founded in AD 739 and is
Beijing's largest Daoist shrine.
Known as the Temple of
Heavenly Eternity, it was one
of the three ancestral halls of
the Quanzhen School of
Daoism, which focused on
right action and the benefits
of good karma. Built largely
of wood, the temple burnt to
the ground in 1166, and since
then has been repeatedly
destroyed and rebuilt. The
structures that survive date
largely from the Ming and
Qing dynasties. A triple-gated
Ming pailou (decorative

Resplendent interior of the Cow Street Mosque

archway) stands at the entrance. It is believed that rubbing the carved monkey on the main gate brings good luck. The major halls are arranged along the central axis, with more halls on either side. The Hall of the Tutelary God has images of four marshals who act as temple guardians, while the Hall of Ancient Disciplines is dedicated to the Seven Perfect Ones, disciples of Wang Chongyang, the founder of the Quanzhen School. The Hall of Wealth is popular with pilgrims who seek blessings from the three spirits of wealth, while the infirm patronize the Hall of the King of Medicine.

The temple grounds are full of Daoist monks with their distinctive topknots. It is most lively during the Chinese New Year *(see pp42–3)*, when a temple fair *(miaohui)* is held.

## Chinese Military History Museum **㉗**
军事博物馆

9 Fuxing Lu, Haidian. **M** *Junshi Bowuguan*. **Tel** *(010) 6686 6244.* ☐ *8am–5pm daily.*

Topped by a gilded emblem of the People's Liberation Army, the Chinese Military History Museum is devoted to weaponry and revolutionary heroism. It is close to Muxidi, where the People's Liberation Army killed scores of civilians in 1989. Visitors are greeted by paintings of Mao, Marx, Lenin, and Stalin. The ground floor exhibits defunct F-5 and F-7 jet fighter planes, tanks,

Buddhist monks, Miaoying Temple White Dagoba

and surface-to-air missiles. The top gallery chronicles with pride many of China's military campaigns.

## Miaoying Temple White Dagoba **㉘**
妙应寺

Fucheng Men Nei Dajie, Xicheng. **Map** 1 A4. **M** *Fucheng Men.* **Tel** *(010) 6616 0211.* ☐ *9:30am–4pm daily.* 🖼

Celebrated for its distinctive Tibetan-styled, 167-ft (51-m) white *dagoba* (stupa or funerary mound) designed by a Nepalese architect, the

Miaoying Temple (Miaoying Si) dates to 1271, when Beijing was under Mongol rule. In addition to its conventional Drum and Bell Towers, Hall of Heavenly Kings, and Main Halls, this Buddhist temple has a remarkable collection of small Tibetan Buddhist statues in one of its halls. Another hall has a collection of 18 bronze *luohan* (disciples).

## Beijing Zoo **㉙**
北京动物园

137 Xizhi Men Wai Dajie, Haidian. **M** *Xizhi Men, then taxi.* **Tel** *(010) 6831 4411.* ☐ *7:30am–5pm (to 6pm spring & summer).* 🖼 *extra to see pandas.*

West of the Beijing Exhibition Hall, Beijing Zoo has improved somewhat but still has some outdated concrete and glass cages. The Panda Hall is one of its better enclosures, and the bears are at their liveliest in the mornings. The real reason for visiting is the huge **Aquarium**, with coral reefs, an Amazon rainforest, and an impressive shark pool. There is also an array of aquatic mammals, including whales and dolphins.

F-5 fighter planes, Chinese Military History Museum

# Summer Palace ⑩

颐和园

**Bronze dragon**

The sprawling grounds of the Summer Palace (Yihe Yuan) served the Qing Dynasty as an imperial retreat from the stifling summer confines of the Forbidden City. Despite existing as an imperial park in earlier dynasties, it was not until the time of Emperor Qianlong, who reigned from 1736 to 1795, that the Summer Palace assumed its current layout. The palace is most associated, however, with Cixi who had it rebuilt twice: once following its destruction by French and English troops in 1860, and again in 1902 after it was plundered during the Boxer Rebellion.

**★ Longevity Hill**
*The Tower of the Fragrance of the Buddha dominates this slope covered with impressive religious buildings.*

Temple of the Sea of Wisdom

**Marble Boat**
*Cixi paid for this extravagant folly with funds meant for the modernization of the Imperial Navy. The superstructure of the boat is made of wood painted white to look like marble.*

Boat pier

## PLAN OF GROUNDS

The grounds of the Summer Palace cover 716 acres (290 hectares), with Kunming Lake lying to the south of Longevity Hill. South Lake Island is just off the east shore and a stroll around the entire shoreline takes about two hours.

① Jade Belt Bridge
② West Causeway
③ South Lake Island
④ Bronze ox

Kunming Lake

West Lake

South Lake

**The Bronze Pavilion**, weighing 207 tons (188 tonnes), is a highly-detailed replica of a timber-framed building.

### STAR SIGHTS

★ Longevity Hill

★ Garden of Virtue and Harmony

★ Long Corridor

**KEY**

☐ Area illustrated

0 meters 800
0 yards 800

## EMPRESS DOWAGER CIXI

Together with Tang-dynasty Empress Wu Zetian *(see p57)*, Cixi is remembered as one of China's most powerful women. Having borne the Xianfeng emperor's son as an imperial concubine, Cixi later seized power as regent to both the Tongzhi and and Guangxu emperors (her son and nephew respectively). Cixi prevented Guangxu from implementing state reforms and, in her alliance with the Boxer Rebellion, paved the way for the fall of the Qing Dynasty in 1911.

**Empress Cixi, 1835–1908**

### VISITORS' CHECKLIST

6 miles (10 km) NW of Beijing. ***Tel*** (010) 6281 2244. Ⓜ *Suzhou Jie then 5 min taxi.* 🚌 *from Yuyuan Tan Park, and Exhibition Center near zoo (not in winter).* ◻ *Apr–Oct: 6:30am–6pm, Nov–Mar: 7am–5pm.* 📷 🖥 🛗

**Suzhou Street**

**Back Lake**

★ **Garden of Virtue and Harmony**
*This three-story building served as a theater, where the court's 348-member opera troupe entertained Cixi, who watched from the surrounding gallery.*

**The Garden of Harmonious Pleasures** was Cixi's favorite fishing spot.

**Hall of Happiness and Longevity**

**Hall of Jade Ripples**

**East Palace Gate (main entrance)**

★ **Long Corridor**
*The beams along the length of this 2,388-ft (728-m) walkway are decorated with over 14,000 scenic paintings.*

**Hall of Benevolence and Longevity**
*The principal ceremonial hall, this single-eaved building houses the throne upon which Cixi sat.*

# Exploring the Summer Palace

Like the imperial resort at Chengde *(see pp122–5)*, the palace grounds are arranged as a microcosm of nature, its hills *(shan)* and water *(shui)* creating a natural composition further complemented by bridges, temples, walkways, and ceremonial halls. Even after repeated restoration, the Summer Palace tastefully harmonizes the functional and fanciful, with administrative and residential quarters leading to the pastoral vistas of the grounds, as well as numerous peaceful temples and shrines.

Seventeen-arch Bridge linking South Lake Island to the mainland

The grounds of the Summer Palace are extensive, but the main buildings can all be visited by those with a bit of energy and time. The main entrance at the **East Palace Gate** (Gong Dong Men) leads to the official and residential halls of the palace complex. Just inside the main gate stands the **Hall of Benevolence and Longevity** (Renshou Dian). Note the bronze statues in front of this ceremonial hall, including the symbol of Confucian virtue, the mythical *qilin*, a hybrid, cloven-hoofed animal with horns and scales. You will see signs here for **Suzhou Street**, which houses over-priced snack and souvenir stalls, and is not worth the extra entry fee.

By the lakeside to the west, the **Hall of Jade Ripples** (Yulan Tang) is where Cixi incarcerated the Guangxu emperor after the abortive 1898 Reform Movement. Cixi's residence, the **Hall of Happiness and Longevity** (Leshou Tang) is to the west

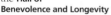

Bronze ox, believed to pacify the waters and prevent floods

of the **Garden of Virtue and Harmony** (Dehe Yuan) and north of the jetty from where Cixi would set sail across the lake. From here, the **Long Corridor** (Chang Lang) follows the lakeside, interrupted along its length by four pavilions. At the corridor's halfway point, a series of religious buildings ascends the slopes of **Longevity Hill** (Wanshou Shan), a sequence marked at the lakeside by a fabulous decorative gate *(pailou)*, beyond which stands **Cloud Dispelling Gate,** with two bronze lions sitting alongside it. The first main hall, the **Cloud Dispelling Hall** (Paiyun Dian) is a double-eaved structure, above which rises the prominent, octagonal **Tower of the Fragrance of the Buddha** (Foxiang Ge). Behind the tower sits the rectangular brick and tile 18th-century **Temple of the Sea of Wisdom** (Huihai Si), its exterior decorated with green and yellow

tiles and glazed Buddhist effigies, many of which have been vandalized. From here you can look down to the **Back Lake** (Hou Hu). West of the Tower of the Fragrance of the Buddha is the **Precious Clouds Pavilion** (Baoyun Ge), also called the **Bronze Pavilion**. Dating from the 18th century, the building is one of a handful that survived the destruction wrought by foreign troops.

The buildings at the north end of the lake are more than enough to fill a single day, however the southern end of the grounds can be blissfully free of crowds. Boat trips to **South Lake Island** depart from the jetty near the Marble Boat (north of which are the imperial boathouses). Alternatively, if time will allow, hire a boat for a leisurely row around Kunming Lake. **Dragon King Temple** (Longwang Miao) on South Lake Island is dedicated to the god of rivers, seas, and rain. The island is connected to the eastern shore by the elegant **Seventeen-arch Bridge** (Shiqi Kong Qiao). A marble lion crowns each of the 544 balusters along the bridge's length, and a large bronze ox, dating back to 1755, reposes on the eastern shore. On the opposite shore, steep-sloped **Jade Belt Bridge** links the mainland to the West Causeway which slices through the lake to its southern point.

The unusual Bronze Pavilion, fashioned entirely from metal

Remnants of the Yuanming Yuan, once said to resemble Versailles

# Yuanming Yuan ③¹
## 圆明园

28 Qinghua Xi Lu, Haidian. Ⓜ
Yuanming Yuan. **Tel** (010) 6262
8501. ◯ 7am–7pm daily. 🖼️

The yuanming yuan (Garden
of Perfect Brightness, sometimes called the Old Summer
Palace), now sits isolated from
the main Summer Palace, but
was a collection of princely
gardens fused into the main
mass by the Qing Qianlong
emperor in the mid-18th century. He commissioned Jesuits
at his court to design and construct a set of European-style
buildings in one corner, which
they likened to Versailles.
Unfortunately, all the traditional
Chinese halls were burned
down by British and French
troops during the Second
Opium War in 1860. Later the
European-style buildings were
pulled down, and much of the
remains carted away by the
locals for building purposes.
Chinese narrations of the
devastation criticize both the
marauding European troops
and the ineffectual Qing rulers.
  Today, Yuanming Yuan is
a jumble of sad, yet graceful
fragments of stone and marble strewn in the **Eternal
Spring Garden** in the park's
northeastern corner. A small
museum displays images and
models of the palace, depicting
its scale and magnificence. The
**Palace Maze** has been recreated in concrete to the west of
the ruins. The rest of the park
is a pleasant expanse of lakes,
pavilions, gardens, and walks.

# Great Bell Temple ³²
## 大钟寺

31a Beisanhuan Xi Lu, Haidian. Ⓜ
Dazhong Si. 🚌 300, 367. **Tel** (010)
6255 0819. ◯ 8:30am–4pm daily. 🖼️

Home to a fascinating collection of bells, the 18th-century
Dazhong Si follows a typical
Buddhist plan, with the
Heavenly Kings Hall, Main
Hall, and the
Guanyin Bodhisattva
Hall. Its highlight is
the 46.5 ton (47,
246 kg) bell – one of
the world's largest –
that is housed in the
rear tower. The bell
was cast between
1403 and 1424, and
brought here from
Wanshou Temple in the
reign of the Qianlong
emperor. Buddhist *sutras* in
Chinese and Sanskrit embellish its surface. During the Ming
and Qing dynasties, the bell
was struck 108 times to bring
in the New Year, and could be
heard for 25 miles (40 km). The
gallery above has a display on
bell casting, and visitors can
toss a coin into the bell for
luck. Hundreds of bells from
the Song, Yuan, Ming, and
Qing eras can be seen in a
separate hall on the west side.

# Xiang Shan Park ³³
## 香山公园

Wofosi Lu, Xiang Shan, Haidian district.
Ⓜ *Bagou, then taxi.* 🚌 *333 from
Summer Palace, 360 from Zoo.*
◯ *6am–6pm.* 🖼️ **Botanical
Gardens** ◯ *9am–4pm daily.* 🖼️

This wooded parkland
area, also known as
Fragrant Hills Park, is at its
scenic best in the fall, when
the maples turn a flaming red.
Its main attractions are the
fine views from **Incense
Burner Peak**, accessible by
a chairlift, and the splendid
**Biyun Temple**, or Azure
Cloud Temple, close to the
main gate. The temple is
guarded by the menacing
deities Heng and Ha in the
Mountain Gate Hall. A
series of halls leads
to the Sun Yat-sen
Memorial Hall,
where his coffin was
stored in 1925, before
being taken to Nanjing.
At the temple's rear is
the distinctive 112-ft
(34-m) high Diamond
Throne Pagoda. About
a mile (2 km) east of
Xiang Shan Park are
the **Beijing Botanical
Gardens**, with some 3,000
plant species. The gardens'
**Sleeping Buddha Temple** is
renowned for its magnificent
bronze statue of a reclining
Buddha. China's last emperor,
Pu Yi (*see p446*), ended his
days here as a gardener.

Heng, Biyun
Temple deity

The Great Bell Temple or Dazhong Si

# Ming Tombs: Chang Ling 🌐
## 明十三陵

**Mythical *qilin*
on Sacred Way**

The resting place for 13 of the 16 Ming
emperors, the Ming Tombs (Shisan Ling)
are China's finest example of imperial tomb
architecture. The site was originally selected
because of its auspicious *feng shui*
alignment; a ridge of mountains to the
north cradles the tombs on three sides,
opening to the south and protecting the dead from the
evil spirits carried on the north wind. The resting place
of the Yongle emperor (1360–1424), the Chang Ling is
the most impressive tomb and the first to be built. It has
been beautifully restored, although the burial chamber,
where Yongle, his wife, and 16 concubines are thought
to be buried, has never been excavated.

★ **Sacred Way**
*Part of the 4-mile (7-km)
approach to the tombs, the Sacred
Way is lined with 36 stone statues
of officials, soldiers, animals,
and mythical beasts.*

★ **Hall of Eminent Favor**
*One of China's most
impressive surviving Ming
buildings, this double-
eaved sacrificial hall is
erected on a three-
tiered terrace.*

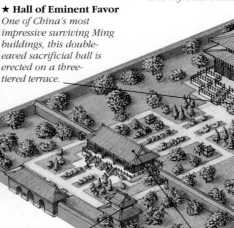

**RECONSTRUCTION
OF CHANG LING**
This shows the Chang
Ling tomb at the time of
the burial of the Yongle
emperor in the 15th century.

**The Stele Pavilion**
bears inscriptions
dating from the Qing
dynasty which revered
the Ming emperors.

**Gate of
Eminent Favor**

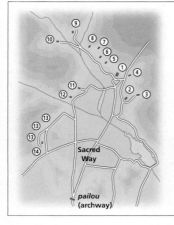

### THE MING TOMBS

The 13 tombs are spread over 15 square miles
(40 sq km), so are best visited by taxi. Chang Ling,
Ding Ling, and Zhao Ling have been restored and are
very busy. Unrestored, the rest are open yet quiet.

① Chang Ling (1424)
② Yong Ling (1566)
③ De Ling (1627)
④ Jing Ling (1435)
⑤ Xian Ling (1425)
⑥ Qing Ling (1620)
⑦ Yu Ling (1449)

⑧ Mao Ling (1487)
⑨ Tai Ling (1505)
⑩ Kang Ling (1521)
⑪ Ding Ling (1620)
⑫ Zhao Ling (1572)
⑬ Concubine cemeteries
⑭ Si Ling (1644)

Sacred
Way

*pailou*
(archway)

0 kilometers   4
0 miles   4

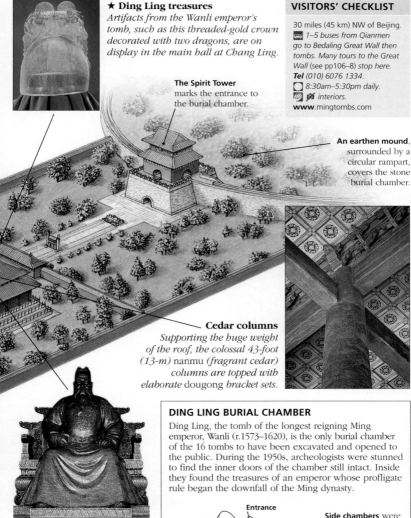

★ **Ding Ling treasures**
*Artifacts from the Wanli emperor's tomb, such as this threaded-gold crown decorated with two dragons, are on display in the main hall at Chang Ling.*

**VISITORS' CHECKLIST**

30 miles (45 km) NW of Beijing.
1–5 buses from Qianmen go to Bedaling Great Wall then tombs. Many tours to the Great Wall (see pp106–8) stop here.
*Tel* (010) 6076 1334.
8:30am–5:30pm daily.
interiors.
**www**.mingtombs.com

**The Spirit Tower** marks the entrance to the burial chamber.

**An earthen mound,** surrounded by a circular rampart, covers the stone burial chamber.

**Cedar columns**
*Supporting the huge weight of the roof, the colossal 43-foot (13-m) nanmu (fragrant cedar) columns are topped with elaborate* dougong *bracket sets.*

**Statue of the Yongle emperor**
*Yongle, the third Ming emperor, moved the capital from Nanjing to Beijing, where he then oversaw the construction of the Forbidden City.*

## STAR FEATURES

★ Hall of Eminent Favor

★ Sacred Way

★ Ding Ling treasures

## DING LING BURIAL CHAMBER

Ding Ling, the tomb of the longest reigning Ming emperor, Wanli (r.1573–1620), is the only burial chamber of the 16 tombs to have been excavated and opened to the public. During the 1950s, archeologists were stunned to find the inner doors of the chamber still intact. Inside they found the treasures of an emperor whose profligate rule began the downfall of the Ming dynasty.

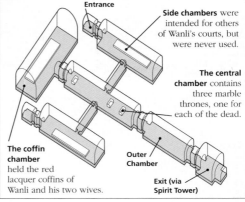

**Entrance**

**Side chambers** were intended for others of Wanli's courts, but were never used.

**The central chamber** contains three marble thrones, one for each of the dead.

**The coffin chamber** held the red lacquer coffins of Wanli and his two wives.

**Outer Chamber**

**Exit (via Spirit Tower)**

# Great Wall of China ㉟
长城

A symbol of China's historic detachment and sense of vulnerability, the Great Wall snakes over deserts, hills, and plains for several thousand miles. Originally a series of disparate earthen ramparts built by individual states, the Great Wall was created only after the unification of China under Qin Shi Huangdi (221–210 BC). Despite impressive battlements, the wall ultimately proved ineffective; it was breached in the 13th century by the Mongols and then, in the 17th century, by the Manchu. Today a UNESCO World Heritage Site, only select sections of its crumbling remains have been fully restored.

**Crumbling ruin**
*Most of the wall is still unrestored and has crumbled away leaving only the core remaining.*

**★ Panoramic views**
*Because the wall took advantage of the natural terrain for defensive purposes following the highest points and clinging to ridges, it now offers superb panoramic views.*

**Ramparts** enabled the defending soldiers to fire down on their attackers with impunity.

**Surface of stone slabs and bricks**

**Tamped layer of earth and rubble**

**Bigger rocks and stones**

**Kiln-fired bricks, cemented with a mortar of lime and glutinous rice**

**Large, locally quarried rocks**

## RECONSTRUCTION OF THE GREAT WALL

This shows a section of the wall as built by the most prolific wall builders, the Ming dynasty (1368–1644). The section at Badaling, built around 1505, is similar to this and was restored in the 1950s and 1980s.

## STAR FEATURES

★ Panoramic views

★ Watchtowers

**★ Watchtowers**
*A Ming addition, these served as signal towers, forts, living quarters, and storerooms for provisions.*

*For hotels and restaurants in Beijing see pp554–6 and pp582–4*

**Towers** were spaced two arrow shots apart to leave no part unprotected.

**Cannons**
*Another Ming addition, cannons were used to defend the wall and summon help.*

**Signal beacons** were used to warn of attack by burning dried wolf dung.

## TIPS FOR VISITORS

• The wall is exposed to the elements so be prepared for all outcomes: wear layers of clothing and a waterproof top, but also bring some suncream.
• Bring plenty of water.
• The wall can be very steep in places, so make sure you have strong footwear with a good grip such as hiking boots or tough waterproof runners.

**The carriageway** is on average 8 m (26 ft) high and 7 m (21 ft) wide.

**Multi-function wall**
*The wall enabled speedy communications via smoke, flares, drums, and bells, as well as allowing for the rapid transport of troops across the country.*

## THE GREAT WALL OF CHINA (MING DYNASTY)

0 kilometers 400

0 miles 400

Inner Mongolia

Yellow River

Datong

Beijing

Taiyuan

Tianjin

Bo Hai

Qinghai Lake

Lanzhou

Yellow Sea

Most visitors travel to the wall from Beijing (*see p108*), but it is worth seeing the wall anywhere along its length. Also impressive are the restored forts at Juyong Guan, Jiayu Guan, and Shanhaiguan.

**Places to visit**
① Jiayu Guan (*see pp498–9*)
② Badaling & Juyong Guan
③ Mutianyu & Huanghua Cheng
④ Simatai
⑤ Shanhaiguan (*see p128*)

# Exploring the Great Wall of China

A trip to the wall is a must for any visitor to Beijing. Most hotels will be able to organize this for you, usually combined with a visit to the Ming Tombs (see pp104–5). However, be sure to find out whether there are any unwanted diversions planned to cloisonné workshops, jade factories, or Chinese medicine clinics. Small groups can have a more personalized visit, and see the more remote parts of the wall, by hiring a taxi for the day from Beijing and sharing the cost.

Ruins at Huanghua Cheng clinging to the steep hillside

Stall selling tourist paraphernalia at the Great Wall, Badaling

### 🏯 Badaling

44 miles (70 km) northwest of Beijing. *Tel (010) 6912 1268.* 🚃 *1 from Qian Men.* ⏱ *6:30am–6:30pm daily.* 🎫 🚠 🚻 🍴

Equipped with guardrails, cable car, pristine watchtowers, and tourist facilities, the restored Ming fortification at Badaling is the most popular section of the Great Wall. The reward for coming to Badaling is the breathtaking view of the wall winding its way over the hills. To fully appreciate this, get away from the crowds by walking as far as you can along the wall either east or west of the entrance. The ticket includes admission to the Great Wall Museum. The pass at **Juyong Guan** is on the way to Badaling and although restored, it is often quieter than Badaling. With unscalable mountains on either side it is easy to see why this spot was chosen for defense. There are also some authentic Buddhist carvings on a stone platform, or "cloud terrace," in the middle of the pass that date back to the Yuan dynasty (1279–1368).

### 🏯 Mutianyu

56 miles (90 km) north of Beijing, Mutianyu Town, Huairou County. 🚃 *6 from Xuanwu Men.* 🚌 *916 from Dongzhimen then taxi.* ⏱ *7:30am–6pm daily.* 🎫 🚠 *& chair lifts.*

The appeal of Mutianyu lies in its dramatic hilly setting and slightly less intrusive tourist industry. With a series of watchtowers along its restored length, the wall you can see here dates from 1368 and was built upon the foundations of the wall built during the Northern Qi dynasty (AD 550–77).

### 🏯 Huanghua Cheng

37 miles (60 km) north of Beijing, Huairou County. 🚌 *916 from Dongzhimen then taxi.* ⏱ *daily.* 🎫 🚠

Situated on the same stretch of wall as Mutianyu, Huanghua is an exhilarating section of Ming wall that is far less developed than other parts of the wall, although it has still been renovated. The great barrier is split into two here by a large reservoir; most travelers take the right hand route on the other side of the reservoir, as the left-hand section is more difficult to reach. Devoid of guardrails,

the crumbling masonry at Huanghua Cheng can be uneven and fairly treacherous in parts, so be careful. This is the best option for accommodation if you want to stay near the Great Wall.

### 🏯 Simatai

68 miles (110 km) northeast of Beijing, Miyun County. 🚃 *6 from Xuanwu Men.* ▣ *for renovations.* 🎫 🚠 *(Apr–Nov).*

The wall at Simatai has only been partially repaired, affording a more genuine impression of the original wall. The steep and hazardous parts of the wall are also a lot riskier to navigate. Most visitors clamber along the eastern section of wall at Simatai, which leads to much steeper sections of wall, and later, impassable ruins, however this whole section is currently closed for renovations. There is a four-hour trek from Simatai to Jingshanling that provides spectacular vistas, too.

The restored section of the wall at Badaling, northwest of Beijing

## Eastern Qing Tombs 36
清东陵

77 miles (125 km) east of Beijing, Zunhua County, Hebei Province. ☐ *May–Oct: 8am–5pm daily; Nov–Apr: 9am–4:30pm daily.*

The remoteness of the Eastern Qing Tombs east of Beijing and over the border in Hebei province makes them far less popular than the Ming ones *(see pp104–5)*, despite the fact that the setting is even more splendid. In fact, the Eastern Qing tombs make up the largest and most complete imperial cemetery in China, built on as grand a scale as the Forbidden City itself *(see pp86–9)*. Of the many tombs scattered throughout the area,

**Spirit Way to Emperor Shunzhi's tomb at the Eastern Qing Tombs**

**Incense burners in front of a spirit tower at the Eastern Qing Tombs**

only five are the burial places of Qing emperors: the tombs of the Shunzhi emperor (r. 1644–61), Kangxi (r. 1661–1722), Qianlong (r. 1736–95), and Xianfeng (r. 1851–61) are open, while that of the Tongzhi emperor (r. 1862–74), at a distance from the main tomb grouping, is not. A 3-mile (5-km) Spirit Way, an approach lined with guardian figures, leads to Shunzhi's tomb, Xiao Ling, at the heart of the main tomb cluster, while several of the other tombs have their own smaller Spirit Ways. Southwest of here lies Yuling, Qianlong's tomb, with its incredible chamber adorned with Buddhist carvings and Tibetan and Sanskrit scriptures (rare features at imperial and principally Confucian tombs). The devious Empress Cixi

*(see p101)* is buried at Ding Dong Ling to the west, in the right-hand tomb of a complex of twin tombs, the other being the resting place of Ci'an, eldest wife of the Xianfeng emperor. Although both tombs were built in 1879, Cixi had her magnificent tomb lavishly restored in 1895. The marble carriageway up to the Hall of Eminent Favor notably locates the carving of the phoenix *(feng)*, symbol of the empress, above the carving of the dragon *(long)*, symbol of the emperor. West of Ding Dong Ling, Ding Ling is partially open and approached via a set of stone animal statues. Look for the smaller tombs of imperial concubines, their roofs tiled in green (not the yellow of emperors and empresses).

### EMPEROR YONGZHENG

The son of the Kangxi emperor and a maidservant, Yongzheng (r.1723–35) chose not to be buried at the Eastern Qing Tombs, but perversely started a necropolis as far away as possible in the Western Qing Tombs (Yixian County, Hebei Province). Perhaps, racked with guilt, he could not face burial alongside his father, whose will he had thwarted. For after Kangxi's death, Yongzheng seized the throne from his brother (his father's chosen successor), and declared himself the legitimate heir, ruthlessly eliminating any other brothers who may have been a threat to his rule. Despite this shaky start, Yongzheng was an able ruler and a devout Buddhist, punishing dishonesty among his officials and seeking to improve the morals and education of his people. Another possible reason for the switch was that he just wasn't satisfied with the Eastern Tombs and chose an area with a better natural setting. Whatever the reason, those keen on Chinese tomb architecture will enjoy the peace of the Western Qing Tombs. Nearby, moved in 1995 to a commercial cemetery, are the remains of Pu Yi, the last emperor of China.

**Yongzheng in robes embroidered with symbols of his power**

Brick stupas at Talin Si or Stupa Forest Temple

occupation of Beijing and a full-scale war. For those with a keen interest in this period of history, the incident is marked by some rather gruesome displays in Wanping's **Memorial Hall**.

## Tanzhe Temple ㊳
潭柘寺

Mentougou district. 28 miles (45 km) W of Beijing. Ⓜ *to Pingguo Yuan (1 hr), then bus 931, tourist bus 7, or taxi.* **Tel** *(010) 6086 2505.* ◯ *8am–5pm daily.* 🅿

This enormous temple dates back to the 3rd century AD, when it was known as Jiafu Si. It was later renamed Tanzhe Temple, after the adjacent mountain Tanzhe Shan, which in turn got its name from the nearby Dragon Pool (Long Tan) and the surrounding cudrania (*zhe*) trees. It has a splendid mountainside setting, and its halls rise up the steep incline. The temple is especially famous for its ancient trees, among which is a huge ginkgo known as the Emperor's Tree. A slightly smaller tree close by is called The Emperor's Wife.

The most fascinating sight, however, is the **Stupa Forest Temple** (Talin Si) near the parking lot, with its marvellous collection of brick stupas hidden among the foliage. Each stupa was constructed in memory of a renowned monk. The towering edifices were built in a variety of designs, including the graceful *miyan ta* or dense-eave stupa, characterized by ascending layers of eaves. The earliest among them dates from the Jin dynasty (1115–1234).

## Marco Polo Bridge ㊲
芦沟桥

Wanping town, Fengtai District. 10 miles (16 km) SW of city center. Ⓜ *Wukesong, then bus 624.* 🚌 *339 from Beijing's Lianhuachi bus station.* ◯ *7am–7pm daily.* 🅿 **Memorial Hall** *101 Wanpingcheng Nei Jie.* ◯ *8am–5pm Tue–Sun.* 🅿

Straddling the Yongding River in Wanping town, the 876-ft (267-m) long marble bridge was first built during the Jin dynasty in 1189 but destroyed by a flood. The current structure dates to 1698. Known as Lugou Qiao in Chinese, the bridge acquired its English name after Marco Polo described it in his famous treatise *The Travels (see p243)*. At the bridge's eastern and western ends are stelae inscribed by the Qing emperors, Kangxi and Qianlong. The poetic observation by Qianlong on a stele at the eastern end reads "*lugou xiaoyue*," meaning "Moon at daybreak at Lugou."

The balustrades along the length of the bridge are decorated by more than 400 carved stone lions, each one slightly different in appearance. Local legend has it that these fierce-looking statues come alive during the night. Despite the widening and extensive restoration work done over the centuries, a surprising amount of the bridge is original. In addition to its antiquity, it is significant as the site of the disastrous Marco Polo Bridge Incident. This is where, on July 7, 1937, the Japanese Imperial Army and Nationalist Chinese soldiers exchanged fire – an event that led to the Japanese

**Stone lion, Marco Polo Bridge**

The 11-arched Marco Polo Bridge known locally as Lugou Qiao

# Peking Man Site ㊴
## 周口店北京猿人遗址

Zhoukoudian Village. 30 miles (48 km) SW of Beijing. ⛟ 917 from Beijing's Tianqiao bus station to Fangshan, then bus 2 or taxi to site.
🔲 8:30am–4:30pm daily. 🌐

Unearthed from a cave at Zhoukoudian in the 1920s, the 40-odd fossilized human bones and primitive implements were identified as the prehistoric remains of Peking Man (*Homo erectus Pekinensis*), who lived here over 500,000 years ago. It was thought that this exciting discovery provided the much sought-after missing link between Neanderthals and modern humans. Designated a UNESCO World Heritage Site, the area is geared toward specialists, although the small museum has an interesting display of tools, ornaments, and bone fragments. Sadly, Peking Man himself is not actually here and the site has suffered neglect.

The futuristic structure of the National Olympic Stadium

The prehistoric Peking Man Site at Zhoukoudian

# National Olympic Stadium ㊵
## 奥林匹克体育中心

Olympic Green. Ⓜ Olympic Green.
⛟ 🔲 10am–5pm daily. 🌐
**www**.beijing2008.com

Beijing's National Olympic Stadium was designed to be the stunning centerpiece of China's massive building program for the 2008 Olympics. It is part of the city's "Olympic Green" development, which includes a large landscaped park, an Olympic Village, and many other stadia including the National Indoor Stadium and Swimming Center.

Swiss architects Herzog and de Meuron won the competition for the stadium with a bird's nest-like structure of apparently random, intertwined ribbons of steel and concrete that simultaneously form both façade and structure. The gaps in the concrete lattice of the roof are filled with translucent inflated bags, making the building waterproof while allowing light to filter down to the spectators.

The National Stadium is one of the most striking buildings to be found anywhere in the world, and visitors are able to take tours around it. During the winter it is turned into a ski center. Plans are in place to turn the area around the stadium into a shopping and entertainment complex.

# Chuandixia ㊶
## 川底下

Near Zhaitang town. 56 miles (90 km) NW of Beijing. Ⓜ to Pingguo Yuan (1 hr), then bus 929 to Zhaitang (3 hrs) or taxi. 🔲 daily. 🌐

Despite the rather laborious expedition required to get here, a trip to the tiny village of Chuandixia (Under the River) is well worth the effort as the crumbling hamlet survives as a living museum of Ming and Qing dynasty village architecture. Situated on a steep mountainside, it is a picturesque outpost of courtyard houses (*siheyuan*) and rural Chinese buildings. Because of the close-knit nature of the original village all the courtyards were inter-connected by small lanes. The entry ticket allows access to the entire village, all of which can be explored within a few hours. Look out for the Maoist graffiti and slogans that survive on the boundary walls; similar graffiti from the Cultural Revolution has been white-washed in most other towns.

Chuandixia's population consists of about 70 people spread over a handful of families. Accommodations can be arranged for those wanting to explore the surrounding hills or simply experience the rural hospitality. Alive to the opportunities brought by tourism, quite a few of the old homesteads provide basic facilities at a reasonable price.

Traditional Ming and Qing dynasty houses, Chuandixia village

# Shopping & Entertainment in Beijing

**Mao Memorabilia,
Liulichang**

Beijing's shopping scene has undergone a dramatic change and slick department stores co-exist with older retail outlets. Its vast array of retail options range from shopping malls and department stores to specialist stores, boutiques, antique and silk markets, and street vendors. The main shopping street Wangfujing Dajie *(see p94)* is very popular with Beijingers and visitors from out of town, but a raft of malls offer up stiff competiton. Regrettably, many of the traditional shops no longer exist with the exception of those on Dazhalan Jie *(see p85)*. Beijing also has a lively entertainment scene, with a growing number of pubs, bars, and clubs, and numerous venues for traditional Beijing Opera, theater, and music.

## SHOPPING

Visitors can buy anything from traditional handicrafts, collectibles, carpets, and silks to electronic goods, furniture, antiques, and designer clothing in Beijing. Many of the stores listed here arrange packaging and shipping as part of their service.

### ANTIQUES, CRAFTS & CURIOS

Genuine antiques *(gudong)* are hard to find. Objects dating between 1939 and 1795 cannot be taken out of the country without a certificate, anything older may not be exported at all *(see pp598–9)*. The most interesting market for antiques and curios is **Panjiayuan Market** in the southeast of town. Open all week, for the best deals and pickings, visitors should aim to get there at sunrise during weekends to rummage through the Bodhisattva statues, ceramics, screens, calligraphy, and variety of ornaments. The **Beijing Curio City** nearby also has a vast collection of ceramics, furniture, jewelry, and Tibetan art on several floors. The large **Hong Qiao Market** near the Temple of Heaven *(see pp96–7)* is good for collectibles, souvenirs, and pearls, especially the section on the third and fourth floors. Be aware, however, that many of the goods on sale here are not original items. Visitors

could spend a few hours browsing through **Liulichang** *(see p85)* for its lacquerware, ceramics, paintings, and crafts. **Huayi Classical Furniture** sells classical antique, restored, and reproduction furniture.

### BOOKS

It is advisable to take your own reading material when traveling to China, as the choice of imported and English-language fiction in Beijing is quite limited. But a fine selection of photographic, cultural, and travel books on China can be found. The **Foreign Languages Bookshop** is conveniently located, but its selection of English-language titles is small. Beijing's largest bookshop *(shudian)*, the **Tushu Dasha**, has English-language books on its third and fourth floors, but can get busy and noisy.

    **The Bookworm** should be your first choice for books; it has a great selection to either buy or borrow.

### DEPARTMENT STORES & SHOPPING MALLS

Despite fierce competition from new specialized outlets, huge department stores are still popular with the Chinese. Xidan Dajie is known for its concentration of stores. In a frenzy of consumerism, giant new malls have sprung up everywhere

(there are a lot around Xi Dan subway station), stocked with a wide range of branded items and clothing. Try **The Village** in Sanlitun Lu, which is great for named brands, or **Shin Kong Place**, near Dawang Lu subway, for designer stores.

### CARPETS & TEXTILES

Beijing's markets sell a variety of carpets *(ditan)* from Tibet, Gansu, and Xinjiang, but visitors should bargain hard on all purchases. The **Qian Men Carpet Company** on Xingfu Dajie has fine handmade carpets from Xinjiang, Mongolia, and Tibet. Other shops worth visiting are **Antique Carpets**, the carpet stores on **Liulichang**, the **Liangma Antique Market**, and the stalls at **Panjiayuan Market**.

    The cramped confines of Silk Street Alley Market have been transformed into the multi-story **New Silk Street Alley Market**; experienced shoppers say it lacks the character of the old place and visitors should still haggle for good prices. The popular **Yuanlong Silk Corporation** sells silk fabric and a large selection of ready-made silk garments, and the **Beijing Silk Store** south of Qian Men has good value silk. For upscale clothes try **Na-Li**, where it is still fine to haggle. The **Yaxiu Clothing Market** has four floors of clothes, fabric, and curios.

### ENTERTAINMENT

The arts scene in Beijing received a huge boost with the opening of the futuristic **National Center for Performing Arts**, better known as The Egg. Entertainment is largely based on the performance arts, such as Beijing Opera and traditional theater. English-language theater is increasingly popular, as are art exhibitions and music concerts. The rock, punk, and jazz live music scene is rapidly expanding.

    Cinemas show a limited range of English-language films, as there are only a small number of foreign films admitted each year. Many embassies and bars show movies (either in English or with subtitles). There is a good cinema at The Village in Sanlitun. All European and Hollywood films are pirated on release, and appear in the markets as DVDs and VCDs of variable quality. Check out the listings in the English-language entertainment magazines found in the expat pubs on Sanlitun Lu, as well as in hotels. *The Beijinger* has good listings.

## BEIJING OPERA

Traditional performances of Beijing Opera *(jingju)* are staged in the splendid **Zhengyici Theater**, the sole surviving wooden theater in China that was formerly a temple. Shows begin on most nights at 7:30pm. The **Huguang Guildhall** has a similarly distinguished setting, with daily performances at 7:15pm. During the warmer

months, there are evening shows in the marvellous **Prince Gong's Mansion** *(see p90)* at 7:30pm. Visitors who are part of tour groups are usually taken to the Liyuan Theater in the Jianguo Hotel.

## TRADITIONAL THEATER

The city's numerous teahouses are excellent venues for the enjoyment of a variety of performances such as traditional Chinese music, storytelling, Chinese opera, acrobatics, and martial arts.

The extraordinary body-bending feats of Chinese acrobats *(zaji)* can be seen at several places in the capital. Popular performances are held nightly at the **Chaoyang Theater** at 5:15 and 7:15pm, and the Beijing Acrobat Troupe stages performances at 7pm at the **Wan Sheng Theater**. Performances are also held at the **Universal Theater** every night at 7pm.

Shows featuring opera and acrobatics take place at the **Lao She Teahouse** throughout the afternoon and evenings. The **Tianqiao Happy Teahouse** also stages similar performances every evening at 6:30pm.

## PUBS, BARS & CLUBS

The capital city's expat bar scene has for years concentrated along Sanlitun Lu in Beijing's Chaoyang district – east of Dong Si Shi Tiao subway station. For a more laid-back experience, try bars around the shore where Hou Hai and Qian Hai lakes meet, such as the stylish **World of Suzie Wong**, with its Ming Dynasty beds. One of the first, and still considered to be one of the best, the **No Name Bar** near Hou Hai is well worth a visit. For a more upscale mood, try one of the bars at any of the city's four- and five-star hotels.

# DIRECTORY

## ANTIQUES, CRAFTS & CURIOS

**Beijing Curio City**
21 Dongsanhuan Nan Lu, W of Huawei Bridge, Chaoyang District.

**Hong Qiao Market**
Hong Qiao Lu, Chaoyang District. **Map** 4 E3.

**Huayi Classical Furniture**
89 Xiaodian Dongwei Lu, Chaoyang District.

**Panjiayuan Market**
Panjiayuan Lu, Chaoyang District.
◻ *6am–3pm daily.*

## BOOKS

**Foreign Languages Bookshop**
235 Wangfujing Dajie.
**Map** 2 D5.

**The Bookworm**
Building 4, Nan Sanlitun Lu.

**Tushu Dasha**
17 Xi Chang'an Jie, Xi Cheng District. **Map** 3 B1.

## DEPARTMENT STORES & MALLS

**The Village**
Sanlitun Lu, Shin Kong Place, 87 Jianguo Lu.

## CARPETS & TEXTILES

**Antique Carpets**
4A6 Gongti Donglu, Chaoyang District.

**Beijing Silk Store**
5 Zhubaoshi, Qian Men Dajie. **Map** 3 C2.

**Liangma Antique Market**
27 Liangmaqiao Lu, Chaoyang District.

**Na-Li**
Sanlitun Beilu, Chaoyang District.

**Qian Men Carpet Company**
F1, Building 3, 59 Xingfu Dajie. **Map** 4 F3.

**Yaxiu Clothing Market**
58 Gongti Bei Lu, Chaoyang District.

## Yuanlong Silk Corporation
15 Yongding Men Dong Jie. **Map** 4 D4.

## BEIJING OPERA

**Huguang Guildhall**
3 Hufangqiao Lu.
**Map** 3 B3.
*Tel (010) 6351 8284.*

**Prince Gong's Mansion**
17 Qianhai Xi Jie.
**Map** 1 B3.
*Tel (010) 8328 8149.*

**Zhengyici Theater**
220 Qian Men Xiheyan Dajie. **Map** 3 C2.
*Tel (010) 8315 1650.*

## TRADITIONAL THEATER

**Chaoyang Theater**
36 Dongsanhuan Bei Lu.
*Tel (010) 6507 2421.*

**Lao She Teahouse**
3 Qian Men Xi Dajie, Xuanwu. **Map** 3 C2.
*Tel (010) 6303 6830.*

## National Center for Performing Arts
Xi Chang'an Jie.
*Tel (010) 6655 0000.*

**Tianqiao Happy Teahouse**
1 Bei Wei Lu, Xuanwu District. **Map** 3 C3.
*Tel (010) 6304 0617.*

**Universal Theater**
10 Dong Zhi Men Nan Dajie. **Map** 2 F3.
*Tel (010) 6416 9893.*

**Wan Sheng Theater**
95 Tianqiao Shichang Street. **Map** 3 C3.
*Tel (010) 6303 7449.*

## BARS & CLUBS

**No Name Bar**
Qianhai Dong Yan, E. of the Yinding Bridge.
**Map** 1 C3.
*Tel (010) 6401 8541.*

**World of Suzie Wong**
1A Nongzhanguan Lu, Chaoyang District.

# BEIJING STREET FINDER

The map references given for all sights, hotels, restaurants, shopping, and entertainment venues described in this chapter refer to the following two maps. The page grid superimposed on the schematic map below shows which parts of Beijing's city center are covered in this *Street Finder*. An index of the street names marked on the maps follows on the opposite page. The key, set out below, indicates the scales of the maps and shows what other features are marked on them, including subway, train, and bus terminals, hospitals, and tourist information centers. Beijing has extended a long way beyond the main city center and the Greater Beijing map on page 80 gives an idea of the area to the north, west, and south of central Beijing. Getting used to the directional system of road naming *(see opposite)* is vital to getting around easily in cities.

Cycling, a good way to get around

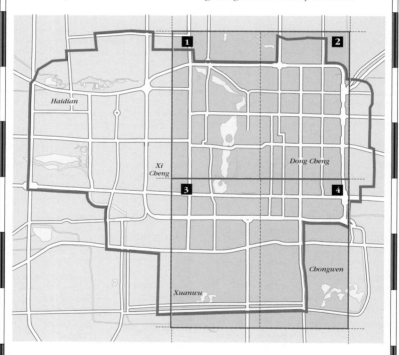

**KEY TO STREET FINDER**

| | |
|---|---|
| ■ Major sight | ℹ Tourist information |
| ■ Place of interest | ✚ Hospital |
| ▫ Other important building | ⊠ Post office |
| 🚆 Train station | ⌂ Temple |
| 🚌 Long distance bus station | ✝ Church |
| Ⓜ Subway station | C Mosque |
| 🚍 City bus station | |

**SCALE OF MAP ABOVE**

0 km             2
0 miles          2

**SCALE OF MAPS 1–4**

0 meters       500
0 yards        500

# Street Finder Index

In street names, the suffix "*jie*" meaning street, or "*lu*" meaning road are often interchangeable. Therefore, when asking for directions or an address, note that Tian Tan Jie may also be known as Tian Tan Lu. Many streets are also called "*dajie*" or avenue. Directionals such as "*zhong*" (middle), and the four cardinal points – "*dong*" (east), "*xi*" (west), "*bei*" (north), and "*nan*" (south) – are often added to street names. The other key word mentioned here is "*hutong*" (alleyway).

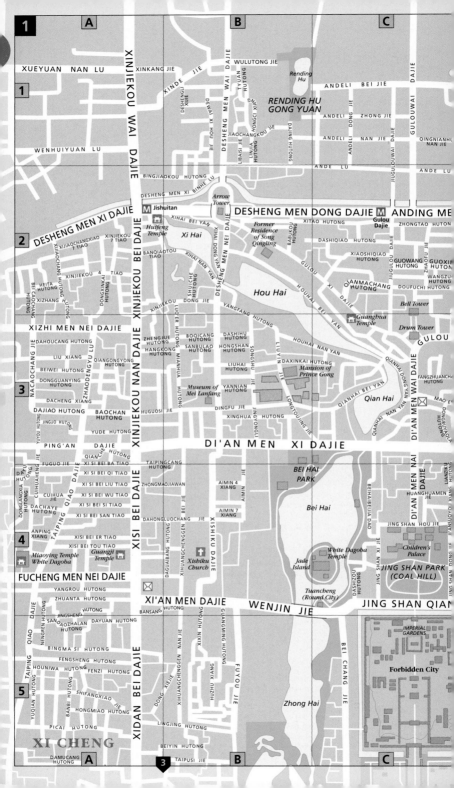

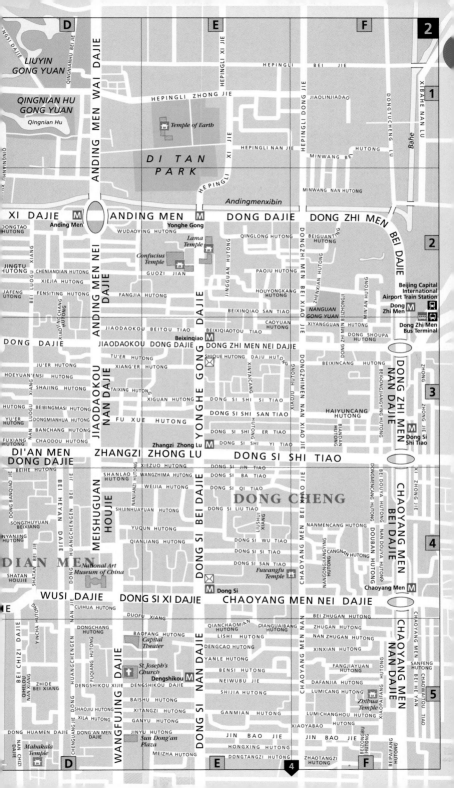

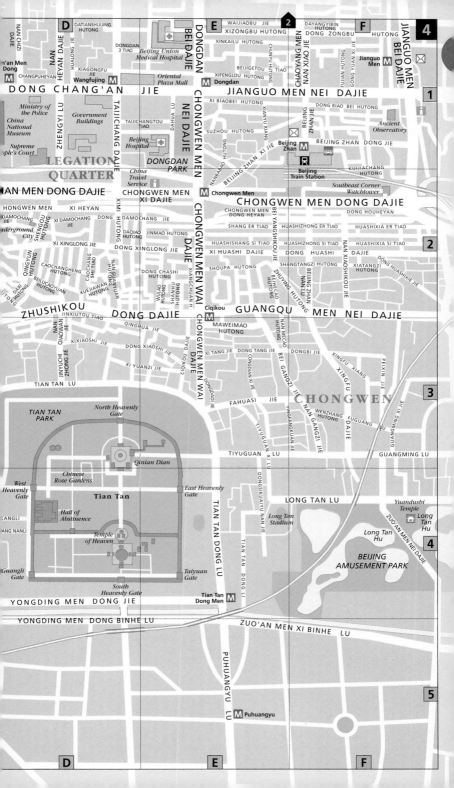

# HEBEI, TIANJIN & SHANXI

With its northern borders adjoining Inner Mongolia and the western tip of erstwhile Manchuria, Hebei divides into a long southern plateau and a mountainous north, dotted with fragments of the Great Wall. Despite these barriers, the Manchu army flowed through the Shanhaiguan Pass in 1644 to impose 250 years of foreign rule on the Chinese. Hebei borders Shanxi to the west and envelops the wealthy conurbations of Beijing and Tianjin – Hebei's former capital and a repository of foreign concession-era architecture.

Shanxi (West of the Mountains), its northern edge protected by the Great Wall, was once a buffer zone against the hostile Mongol and Turkic tribes. It is largely a mountainous plateau, heavily industrialized, with the Yellow River (Huang He) flowing the length of its western border. Leaving Beijing, most visitors first explore Chengde, with its imperial park and temple architecture, or the celebrated Buddhist carvings at Yungang, outside Datong. Other key sights include the magnificent Hanging Temple clinging to the cliff face, the peaceful hills around Wutai Shan, one of China's four sacred Buddhist mountains and the charming Ming and Qing architecture in the ancient walled town of Pingyao.

## SIGHTS AT A GLANCE

**Towns & Cities**
Beidaihe ②
Datong ⑥
Pingyao pp138–9 ⑪
Shanhaiguan ③
Shijiazhuang ⑤
Taiyuan ⑩
Tianjin ④

**Temples & Monasteries**
Chengde pp122–5 ①
Hanging Temple ⑧
Shuanglin Si ⑫

**Areas of Natural Beauty**
Wutai Shan pp134–6 ⑨
Yungang Caves pp132–3 ⑦

**Historic Sites**
Qiao Jia Dayuan ⑬

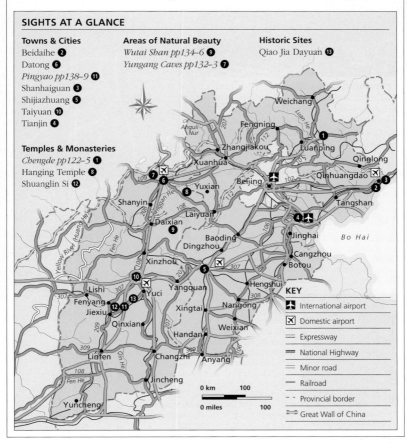

◁ **Detail of the Imperial Dragon from the Jiulong Bi (Nine Dragon Screen), Datong**

# Chengde ●

## 承德

The mountain resort at Chengde (Bishu Shanzhuang) was chosen by the Kangxi emperor in 1703 as a means of eluding the hot summers in the Forbidden City. Set in a river valley surrounded by mountains, the park was strategically secure and allowed the hardy Manchu to engage in hunting and martial sports. The rural setting beyond the Great Wall reminded the Manchu rulers of their homelands to the northeast. The eclectic temple design of the surrounding Eight Outer Temples put visiting Mongol and tribal chieftains at ease, so the emperor could exploit their allegiances.

**Incense burner**

Tibetan Buddhist designs to make the Mongol allies feel at home

Shuxiang Si

Putuozongcl Miao

Northwest Gate

**★ Putuozongcheng Miao**

*Built to resemble the Potala Palace in Lhasa, the temple is the largest of the Eight Outer Temples and has displays of* thangkas *(Tibetan religious scrolls), Tibetan religious ornaments, and two scaled-down sandalwood pagodas.*

BISHU SHANZHUANG

### KEY

| | Town area |
| --- | --- |
| = | Road |

**The wall** is over 6 miles (10 km) long

West Gate

### THE KANGXI EMPEROR

Kangxi (1654–1722) was the second Qing emperor to reign from Beijing, and held on to power for 61 years, the longest reign in China's history. His rule was, in comparison with other emperors, frugal, practical, and conscientious. During his reign the empire increased in size and wealth, and generally enjoyed peace and prosperity. He taxed the farmers moderately and protected the peasantry, building up a healthy rural economy. An outstanding militarist, he was also a patron of the arts and sciences inviting Jesuit scholars to the Chinese court. He was followed by his fourth son, Yongzheng (r.1723–35), and then his grandson Qianlong (r.1736–95), who idolized him so much that he resigned as emperor after sixty years so as not to outdo him.

**The Kangxi emperor pictured in his library**

CHENGDE CITY

### STAR SIGHTS

★ Putuozongcheng Miao

★ Puning Si

★ Bishu Shanzhuang

## Xumifushou Zhi Miao

*This temple was built to impress the visiting Panchen Lama who came to Chengde on the occasion of the Qianlong emperor's birthday in 1780.*

### VISITORS' CHECKLIST

Chengde. 150 miles (250 km) NE of Beijing. 🚗 🚌 🚐 5, 7, 11, 15 from Chengde station. 🚐 **Bishu Shanzhuang** ◯ 5:30am–6:30pm daily. 🎫 🏠 🚻 📷 **Outer Temples** ◯ daily (temples not all open at the same time). 🎫

### ★ Puning Si

*This temple combines Han Chinese designs at the front with typical Tibetan structures at the back. The highlight is the majestic wooden statue of Guanyin in the main hall (see pp124–5).*

### Pule Si

*The most impressive hall in Pule Si, the Temple of Universal Joy, is the yellow-tiled twin conical-roofed hall which has strong echoes of the Temple of Heaven in Beijing.*

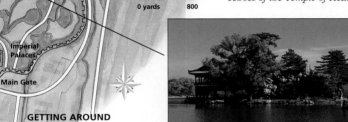

### ★ Bishu Shanzhuang

*The southern section of the resort contains an array of simple but elegant palaces, cool shaded lakes and waterside pavilions, best viewed from a rowing boat.*

### GETTING AROUND

It is possible to see the temples and resort in a one-day minibus tour. However, it is quite a tough day. If time allows, try a more leisurely walk around the resort one day and hire a taxi for the temples the next.

Map labels:
Puning Si
PUYOU SI
Xumiushou Zhi Miao
East Gate
Anyuan Miao
Yongyousi Pagoda
Puren Si
0 meters 800
0 yards 800
Imperial Palaces
Main Gate

# Puning Si, Chengde

普宁寺

**Incense burner**

One of the most impressive outer temples at the Imperial Summer Retreat at Chengde, Puning Si (Puning Temple) was built in 1755 by the Qianlong emperor to commemorate the defeat of Mongol rebels. The whole temple complex is a harmonious synthesis of Chinese and Tibetan styles of architecture. As part of a series of halls ascending the slope of a mountain, the temple's pinnacle is the Mahayana Hall, in which towers one of the world's largest wooden statues, a vast 72-ft (22-m) high representation of the Buddhist goddess of compassion, Guanyin.

**Amitabha Buddha,** Guanyin's teacher, is shown perched on the top of her head.

**Viewing gallery**

**Buddhist Symbols**
*Guanyin's hands hold an array of Buddhist symbolic instruments – the pure sound of the bell is said to drive away evil spirits.*

**One of two attendant statues**

**The terrace buildings** form a three-dimensional mandala *(see p536)*, a physical representation of Buddhist cosmology.

**Diyu** houses a macabre display of Buddhist punishments.

★ **Guanyin**
*The huge effigy of Guanyin, also known to Buddhists as Avalokitesvara, is fashioned from five different types of wood. Viewing galleries can be climbed for views above ground level.*

**Monks**
*Puning Si is the only working temple at Chengde and the monks can be seen praying in the morning.*

**STAR FEATURES**

★ Guanyin

★ Mayahana Hall

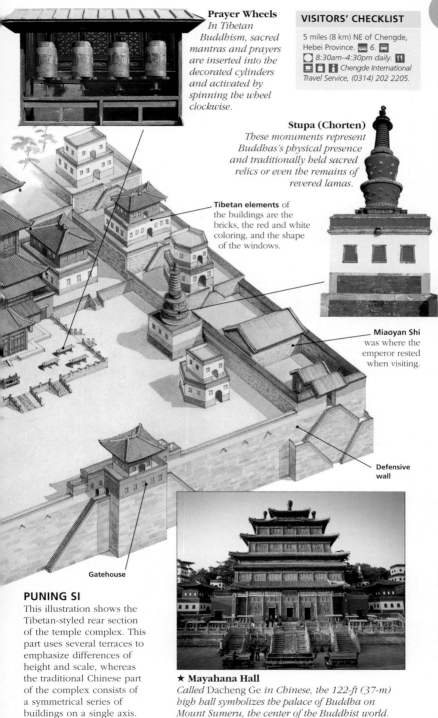

**Prayer Wheels**
*In Tibetan Buddhism, sacred mantras and prayers are inserted into the decorated cylinders and activated by spinning the wheel clockwise.*

**VISITORS' CHECKLIST**

5 miles (8 km) NE of Chengde, Hebei Province. 🚌 6. 🚗
⏰ 8:30am–4:30pm daily. 🍴
🔲 📷 ℹ️ Chengde International Travel Service, (0314) 202 2205.

**Stupa (Chorten)**
*These monuments represent Buddhas's physical presence and traditionally held sacred relics or even the remains of revered lamas.*

**Tibetan elements** of the buildings are the bricks, the red and white coloring, and the shape of the windows.

**Miaoyan Shi** was where the emperor rested when visiting.

**Defensive wall**

**Gatehouse**

**PUNING SI**
This illustration shows the Tibetan-styled rear section of the temple complex. This part uses several terraces to emphasize differences of height and scale, whereas the traditional Chinese part of the complex consists of a symmetrical series of buildings on a single axis.

**★ Mayahana Hall**
*Called* Dacheng Ge *in Chinese, the 122-ft (37-m) high hall symbolizes the palace of Buddha on Mount Sumeru, the center of the Buddhist world.*

Beidaihe, one of northern China's premier resorts

# Beidaihe ❷
## 北戴河

186 miles (300 km) E of Beijing. ✈ to Qinhuangdao, 9 miles (15 km) NE of Beidaihe, then express bus. 🚃 🚌

Despite its immense coastline, China has very few good quality beaches, except perhaps in Hainan Island in the south. Nevertheless, the coastal town of Beidaihe, North China's breezy seaside retreat, is a pleasant enough escape from Beijing's intolerable summer heat. Discovered in the 19th century by British railway engineers, it soon became popular with foreign nationals from Tianjin, and villas, summer holiday homes, and golf courses soon sprang up. These were later taken over by Chinese Communist Party cadres, and party leaders still gather in Beidaihe for their annual conference in August.

Sadly, many of the elegant European-style villas are now obscured by garish modern seafront properties. During summer (April–October), Beidaihe's beaches are packed with hawkers and domestic holiday-makers. The best way to spend one's time is to sample the array of seafood, or hire a bike or tandem from one of the outlets on Zhonghaitan Lu for panoramic rides along the coast. The hilly **Lianfeng-shan Park** in the west of town is covered in cypresses and pines, and its hilltop Sea-Viewing Pavilion provides a good vantage point for views of the coast. The restored

**Guanyin Temple**, dedicated to the Goddess of Compassion, is also located here. Beidaihe's three beaches are dotted with statues of revolutionary workers. **Middle Beach** is the most popular, while West Beach is quieter. Nearby, **Tiger Rocks** is a popular spot to watch the sunrise. **East Beach**, 4 miles (6 km) northeast of Beidaihe, gets covered in seaweed and shells at low tide.

# Shanhaiguan ❸
## 山海关

218 miles (350 km) E of Beijing. ✈ to Qinhuangdao, 8 miles (13 km) SW of Shanhaiguan, then express bus. 🚃 🚌

A short hop up along the coast from Beidaihe, Shanhaiguan (The Pass Between the Mountain and the Sea) is where the Great Wall meets the sea. Although less affluent than Beidaihe,

the town is steeped in history and is fortified by a Ming-era wall. The charming area within the walls is segmented by *hutong* (historic alleys), and serviced by a few hotels.

Shanhaiguan promotes its Great Wall links. **The First Pass Under Heaven** in the east of town is a formidable section of wall attached to a huge gatehouse. The Manchus overcame half-hearted resistance here and headed for Beijing to establish the Qing dynasty. Visitors can climb up on the ramparts, or access its tower, which displays Qing weapons and costumes. To the south is the **Great Wall Museum**, worth visiting for its photographs and models of the wall. Also on display are tools that were used to build it, as well as the various weapons that were used in its defense. There are some English captions, and the exhibits are well displayed.

A more stirring section of the wall lies 2 miles (3 km) north of town at **Jiao Shan**, where bracing climbs can be made up its steep incline – or take a cable car. **Lao Long Tou** (Old Dragon Head) marks the end of the Great Wall at the sea, 3 miles (4 km) south of town. This part of the wall has been completely reconstructed and, despite the tour buses, is worth visiting. Visitors can head west along the beach to explore Haishen Miao (Temple of the Sea God).

🏛 **Great Wall Museum**
🕐 8am–5pm daily. 🎟

The aptly named Lao Long Tou, where the Great Wall reaches the sea

◁ The Temple of Universal Joy at Pule Si, Chengde

# Tianjin ④
天津

50 miles (80 km) SE of Beijing.
🏙 10,000,000. ✈ 🚇 *Main Train Station, North Train Station, West Train Station. High speed train from Beijing's South Station takes 30 mins.* 🚌 *West Bus Station, Northeast Bus Station, Bus Station No. 1, CAAC (buses to airport), South Bus Station.* ⛴ *Tanggu Harbor.* 🛈 *22 Youyi Lu, (022) 2835 4860.*

Hebei's former capital, the municipality of Tianjin is China's fourth largest city and a major seaport. The city's appeal lies in its Western Concession architecture, a legacy of its past as a foreign trading post since 1858. The former powers, led by Britain and France, and followed by Japan, Germany, Austro-Hungary, Italy, and Russia, built schools, banks, and churches.

In the north of town, the **Ancient Culture Street** is a recreation of an ancient Chinese street. The **Tianhou Temple**, dedicated to the Goddess of the Sea, is on the street's west side. To the southwest, close to the Old Chinese Town, the **Confucius Temple** was damaged during the Cultural Revolution, and restored in 1993. About a mile (0.6 km) northeast across the River Hai is the gaunt **Wang Hai Lou Cathedral** (Wang Hail Lou Jiao Tang). Outside, a plaque in Chinese relates the church's turbulent history. It was destroyed by a mob in 1870, and again during the 1900 Boxer Rebellion. The 1976 Tang Shan earthquake damaged it for the third time, and it was repaired in 1983. North of the cathedral, the Qing-era **Dabei Monastery** is reached via a colorful market selling incense sticks and Buddhist talismans.

**Deity, Street Market**

People pay their respects to Milefo (the Laughing Buddha) at the entrance and to Guanyin in her own hall. A popular attraction is the **Tianjin Eye**, one of the tallest ferris wheels in the world, standing at 394 ft (120 m). On **Jiefang Bei Lu** are many of Tianjin's colonial buildings, including the Astor Hotel, whose guests included

**Beautiful tiled wall at the Tianhou Temple, Tianjin**

China's last emperor, Pu Yi. The excellent **Antique Market** on Shenyang Dao is a riveting sprawl of collectibles. Among the most interesting items on sale are Communist regalia including pin badges, portraits, and frayed photographs adorned with Chairman Mao's image. To the south, at the end of Binjiang Dao, Tianjin's biggest thoroughfare and shopping area, are the three green domes of the French-built **Xi Kai Cathedral** (Xi Kai Jiao Tang), open on Sundays.

🏛 **Dabei Monastery**
40 Tianwei Lu. ◯ *daily.* 🎫

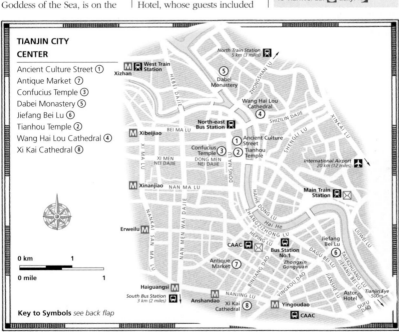

**TIANJIN CITY CENTER**

Ancient Culture Street ①
Antique Market ⑦
Confucius Temple ③
Dabei Monastery ⑤
Jiefang Bei Lu ⑥
Tianhou Temple ②
Wang Hai Lou Cathedral ④
Xi Kai Cathedral ⑧

0 km                1
0 mile              1

**Key to Symbols** *see back flap*

*For hotels and restaurants in this region see pp556–7 and pp584–5*

# Shijiazhuang ❺
石家庄

155 miles (250 km) SW of Beijing.
🏙 9,300,000. ✈ 🚉 🚍
ℹ️ 26 Donggang Lu, (0311) 858
98765.

The capital of Hebei often suffers from unfair comparisons to both Beijing and the former provincial capital, Tianjin. An industrial town dating from the modern railway age, Shijiazhuang has just a few sights including the **Hebei Provincial Museum** in the east of town, which displays musical instruments that are over 2,300 years old, historical relics such as a jade burial suit, and an entire miniature terracotta army. To the west along Zhongshan Lu is the **Martyrs' Memorial**, a park which honors two doctors as Heroes of the Revolution. Both men, a Canadian named Norman Bethune and an Indian named Dwarkanath Kotnis, served the Communist Party in the early 20th century.

🏛 **Hebei Provincial Museum**
◯ 9am–5pm Tue–Sun.

**Environs:** Most of the area's main sights lie outside Shijiazhuang, and are easily accessed by train, bus, or minibus. Lying a short train or bus journey 9 miles (15 km) north of town, the ancient walled town of **Zhengding** is

known for its temples and pagodas. The most renowned is **Dafo Si** (Great Buddha Temple), also known as Longxing Si. Its highlight is the gargantuan 69-ft (21-m) high bronze statue of Guanyin (the Goddess of Compassion) that stands in the Dabei Ge (Pavilion of Great Mercy). Fashioned over 1,000 years ago during the Song dynasty, the multi-armed statue is a riveting sight. Visitors can climb the gallery surrounding the statue for a closer look.

West of Dafo Si, the 135 ft (41 m) **Lingxiao Ta** (Lingxing Pagoda) in Tianning Si is a restored Tang dynasty structure built from wood and brick, while **Kaiyuan Si's** Tang-dynasty pagoda rises up just off Yanzhao Dajie, Zhengding's main street. Also situated here is China's sole surviving Tang dynasty Bell Tower (Zhong Lou). Dotted around Zhengding are several temples and pagodas, including the Confucian Temple, Chengling Ta (Chengling Pagoda) at Linji Si, and the Hua Ta (Hua Pagoda) at Guanghui Si, with its many intriguing motifs that represent the Buddhas, elephants, and whales.

About 25 miles (40 km) southeast of Shijiazhuang, near Zhaoxian town, the 1,400-year old **Zhaozhou Bridge** (Zhaozhou Qiao) is a graceful feat of engineering. Built over ten years by the mason Li Chun and completed in

**Kaiyuan Si's Tang pagoda, Zhengding**

**Qiao Lou at Cangyan Shan Si (Hanging Palace), Cangyang Shan**

AD 605, the 167-ft (51-m) long bridge satisfied several requirements. The gentle bow had to be level enough to convey imperial soldiers, yet high enough to evade flood waters, while relying on the soft riverbanks for support. The main arch (forming an arc rather than a semicircle) is an effortless span of 28 stone blocks. Supported on each end of the arch are two smaller ones that are designed to lighten the structure of the bridge and allow the passage of flood waters.

About 50 miles (80 km) southwest of Shijiazhuang is a surprising group of monasteries and pagodas tucked away among the cypresses and sheer drops of **Cangyan Shan** (Cangyan Mountains). The Cangyan Shan Si also known as the Hanging Palace, situated hundreds of steps up the mountainside, dates from the Sui dynasty. One hall, the Qiao Lou, is spectacularly slung between two cliffs, suspended on a bridge over the void. In the valleys and on the slopes beyond, the trail continues to explore the dramatic landscape, passing several shrines.

🏛 **Dafo Si**
◯ 8am–5pm daily. 🎫
🏛 **Zhaozhou Bridge**
◯ daily. 🎫
🏛 **Cangyan Shan**
🚍 from Shijiazhuang. ◯ daily. 🎫

**The graceful, stone Zhaozhou Bridge (Zhaozhou Qiao)**

For hotels and restaurants in this region see pp556–7 and pp584–5

# Datong 6
## 大同

165 miles (265 km) SW of Beijing.
3,000,000. CITS
Datong, (0352) 510 1326.

Situated near the southern flank of Inner Mongolia, Datong has some splendid sights worth exploring despite the coal mines and power stations that blight the surrounding landscape.

The city was twice a dynastic capital, under the Northern Wei (AD 386–534), and the Liao (AD 907–1125), both non-Chinese. The Northern Wei were fervent Buddhists who carved and decorated the **Yungang Caves** nearby, while a significant relic of the Liao era survives in the **Huayan Si** (Huayan Temple), located in an alley off Da Xi Jie, west of the crossroads in the old town. Completed by the Jin, the temple was much restored by later dynasties. Raised up on a 13-ft (4-m) terrace, Huayan Si's Great Treasure Hall (Daxiong Bao Dian) is one of China's largest Buddhist halls. Within the hall sit five gilded and enthroned Ming-era statues with attendants. The ceiling panels are decorated with Sanskrit letters, flowers, and dragons. A short walk east of the crossroads on Da Dong Jie is **Jiulong Bi** (Nine

**Gilded Buddhist statuary, Mahavira Hall, Huayan Si, Datong**

Dragon Screen), a 148-ft (45-m) tiled spirit wall built to front the palace of the 13th son of Hongwu, the first Ming emperor. Less than a mile south of the crossroads on Da Nan Jie is the **Shanhua Si**. Erected during the Tang era, it was subsequently destroyed by fire and rebuilt in the 12th century. The main hall has five Buddhist statues, flanked by 24 divine generals.

**Huayan Si**
8:30am–5:30pm daily.

**Shanhua Si**
8:30am–5pm daily. 17.

# Yungang Caves 7

*See pp132–3.*

# Hanging Temple 8
## 悬空寺

40 miles (65 km) SE of Datong.
from Datong to Hunyuan, then taxi. **Tel** (0352) 832 7417.
8am–6:30pm daily.

One of China's five sacred Daoist mountains, Heng Shan is also known as Beiyue (Northern Peak). The mountain range is a huge draw, its highest peak daring climbers to scale its 6,600 ft (2,000 m) slopes – a tradition started by the first emperor, Qin Shi Huangdi, and kept alive by later rulers. Its main attraction, however, is the spectacular Xuankong Si. Supported by slender wooden pillars, the temple seemingly clings precariously to the canyon's walls. The Northern Wei were the first to build here, but flood waters from the Heng River below regularly washed the buildings away. The current edifice dates from the Qing dynasty. The temple's 40-odd halls are hewn from natural caves and hollows in the rock, and are covered with wooden façades. They are connected by walkways and bridges, and contain statues of Confucian, Buddhist, and Daoist gods in stone, iron, and bronze. The Sanjiao Dian (Three Religions Hall) has statues of Confucius, Buddha, and Laozi all seated together.

**The spectacular Hanging Temple (Xuankong Si), Heng Shan**

# Yungang Caves ⑦

## 云岗石窟

**Lively *arhat*, Cave 18**

Carved into sandstone cliffs, the caves at Yungang are one of China's most celebrated accomplishments of Buddhist art. The assembly of over 51,000 statues was started by the Northern Wei dynasty in AD 453 to atone for their persecution of Buddhism. Hellenistic, Persian, Central Asian, and Indian influences are evident in the carvings, testifying to the many influences entering China via the Silk Road. When the capital moved from Datong to Luoyang, in AD 494, work at Yungang all but stopped. The statues are accompanied by English explanations. One third of the caves are currently closed for renovations.

**★ Exterior of Cave 6**
*The wooden temple façade has protected the beautifully carved 50-ft (16-m) stone pagoda and the rest of the sculptures within.*

**Cave 16**
Has finely featured carving especially Buddha's head.

**Cave 13**
Look for the small figure supporting the Buddha's arm.

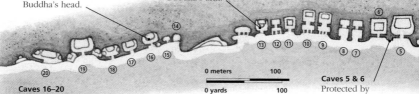

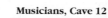

| 0 meters | 100 |
| 0 yards | 100 |

**Caves 5 & 6**
Protected by wooden frontage.

**Caves 16–20**
These are the oldest caves, built between AD 453 and 462 by the monk Tan Hao.

**★ Main Buddha, Cave 20**
*The simplicity and balance of the tableau shows great artistic merit. This cave would have been shielded by a wooden screen.*

**Detail of Cave 10**
*Built as a pair along with Cave 9, this cave is also divided into two chambers. The interior is densely decorated with colorful bas reliefs and statues in niches.*

**Musicians, Cave 12**
*This cave is decorated with devotees of music and dance. The colorful walls provide excellent evidence for the development and use of musical instruments in China at the time.*

**★ Seated Buddha, Cave 5**
*Marking a move from the more stylized earlier Buddhas, this one has a more corpulent and naturalistic air. Protected by the wooden façade, the cave is in good condition.*

## STAR SIGHTS

★ Cave 20

★ Cave 6

★ Cave 5

For hotels and restaurants in this region see pp556–7 and pp584–5

## VISITORS' CHECKLIST

10 miles (16 km) W of Datong.
*Tel* (0352) 510 2265, CITS
Datong. 🚌 3-1 from bus station.
🚉 3-2 from train station or CITS
tour booked at train station. ⬜
8:30am–5:30pm daily. 🖼 📷 🛒

View of the central section of the Yungang Caves, Datong

### Interior, Cave 3
*The Buddhas here have rounded fleshy faces and full lips, indicating that they are later creations, perhaps Sui dynasty (AD 581–618).*

### Pagoda in Cave 2
*Nearly square in construction, this cave has a carved square pagoda linking ceiling and floor. The statues in the cave have suffered a little due to exposure to the weather.*

④    ③                                        ② ①

## ARTISTIC INFLUENCES, CAVE 18

The colossal Buddha recalls the style of Gandhara (*see p465*). This Buddhist stronghold and meeting point for many of the Silk Roads sought to recreate the solemnity, dignity, and awe-inspiring nature of Buddha. A more realistic style can be seen in the five smaller *arhats* on each side and the crown worn by the Bodhisattva.

**The bared shoulder was replaced by the more Chinese robe and girdle** (*see Cave 5*)

**The realistic faces of these *arhats* show the personal input by the artists**

**Statue has webbed fingers one of the marks of Buddha**

The exterior of Cave 18 with the colossal Buddha

# Wutai Shan ⑨

五台山

The monastic village of Taihuai, nestling in the valley ringed by Wutai Shan's five mountain peaks (or terraces), has the largest concentration of temples as well as most of Wutai Shan's hotels and restaurants. Wutai Shan was the site of over 300 temples during the Qing dynasty, but many were destroyed. Tsongkhapa, the founder of the Buddhist Yellow Hat Sect (which has the Dalai Lama as its head), lived here and the mountains and its shrines are revered by Lamaist Buddhists. In winter, the roads are often closed due to snow. Late spring and summer is the best time to visit, but also the most crowded.

**Incense burner**

**Luohou Si**
*Inside this temple is a wooden lotus flower decorated with eight wooden petals that, when rotated, open to reveal carved Buddhist figures.*

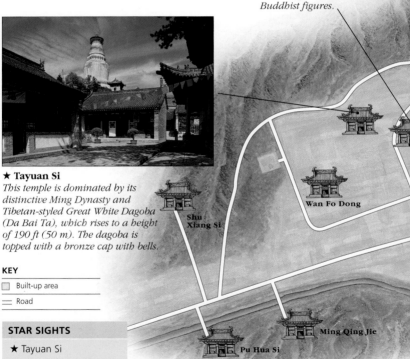

**★ Tayuan Si**
*This temple is dominated by its distinctive Ming Dynasty and Tibetan-styled Great White Dagoba (Da Bai Ta), which rises to a height of 190 ft (50 m). The dagoba is topped with a bronze cap with bells.*

Wan Fo Dong

Shu Xiang Si

Ming Qing Jie

Pu Hua Si

**KEY**

▢ Built-up area

═ Road

**STAR SIGHTS**

★ Tayuan Si

★ Xian Tong Si

★ Pusa Ding

**Taihuai**
*West of the Qingshui River, the village is thronging with pilgrims, monks, and lamas. Visitors come for its Buddhist temples and to shop for religious talismans.*

### ★ Xian Tong Si

*The highlight of this, the largest temple on Wutai Shan, is the Bronze Hall. Made entirely from metal, it is decorated with thousands of small Buddhist figures.*

**Shou Ning Si** is a little bit off the beaten track in the hills.

**an Ta Si**

### ★ Pusa Ding

*To reach Pusa Ding (Bodhisattva Summit), a temple complex dating from the Ming and Qing dynasties, there is a climb of 108 steps. A significant number – it is the number of beads on a Buddhist rosary.*

**Guang Hua Si**

**Jin Jie Si**

### Qi Fo Si

*This temple is not visited as much as the other more famous temples and as such will be a quieter spot to take in the scenery. It also has a white stone pagoda.*

**Shang Cai Dong** sits at the foot of the hills in view of the cable car to the north.

0 meters 100
0 yards 100

### THE CULT OF MANJUSRI

Known as Wenshu in China, Manjusri is the Buddhist bodhisattva of Wisdom and the patron deity of Wutai Shan. A disciple of Sakyamuni (Buddha), Manjusri is often portrayed riding a lion or holding a sword – for cleaving both ignorance and suffering. Many of Wutai Shan's temples and halls are dedicated to Wenshu and the deity's association with the mountain dates as far back as the first century AD, when a visiting Indian monk had a vision of the bodhisattva. Many more sightings have been recorded since.

**Manjusri or Wenshu, patron deity of Wutai Shan**

# Exploring Wutai Shan

Wutai shan was originally worshiped by followers of the Dao (Daoists) pursuing the secrets of immortality, before attracting devotees of Buddha who built many temples in his name. If visitors explore around Taihuai they will find many temples scattered among the peaks and in more distant parts of the region. Most can be reached without much difficulty, with a chairlift to some parts, and the effort rewards the adventurous with the chance to admire some of China's oldest buildings.

The thickly wooded slopes of Wutai Shan

### 🏯 Wutai Shan's Temples

The first temples appeared on Wutai Shan during the Eastern Han Dynasty. The five peaks of Wutai Shan are each topped with a temple, but they are hard to reach and tend to attract only devout pilgrims. Several temples can be visited either by hiking, by bus, or by minibus tour from Taihuai (including those through CITS), although other trips, such as to Nanchan Si, involve longer expeditions.

With lovely views over the valley, **Nanshan Si** (South Mountain Temple), around 2 miles (3 km) south of Taihuai, is one of the largest temples on Wutai Shan, most notable for its 18 superbly crafted *arhat* effigies. Three miles (5 km) southwest of Taihuai, immediately above Nanshan Si and part of the same temple complex, is **Youguo Si**. **Longquan Si** (Dragon Spring Temple), at the top of 108 steps through a marvelous marble archway, features the Hall of Heavenly Kings (with an effigy of Milefo – the future Buddha, also known in this chubby incarnation as the Laughing Buddha), the attractively decorated Puji Pagoda, and the Guanyin Hall, among other structures.

Two more temples within easy reach of Taihuai include the Ming dynasty **Bishan Si**, which contains some intriguing Buddhist sculptures, and **Zhenhai Si**.

Considerably farther away is the remote **Nanchan Si**, about 44 miles (70 km) south of Taihuai on the road to Taiyuan, which contains one of China's oldest surviving wooden halls (782 AD). The main hall has somehow avoided destruction – a miracle considering the many anti-Buddhist purges during China's history. Despite much restoration work, the hall's original Tang-dynasty design, a rarity in Chinese temple hall architecture, is preserved. **Foguang Si** (Buddha's Light Temple), about 25 miles (40 km) south of Taihuai, also features a Tang dynasty hall dating to the 9th century. The hall is especially notable for its fine *dougong (see p35)* bracket work, Tang and Song dynasty wall paintings, and collection of Ming dynasty *arhats*.

The elaborately carved archway at Longquan Si

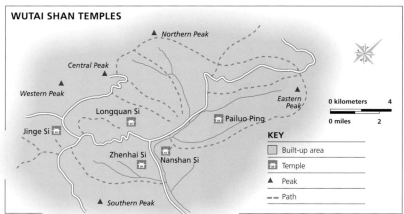

## WUTAI SHAN TEMPLES

▲ Northern Peak

Central Peak ▲

Western Peak ▲

Eastern Peak ▲

Longquan Si 🏯

Pailuo Ping 🏯

Jinge Si 🏯

Zhenhai Si 🏯    Nanshan Si 🏯

▲ Southern Peak

0 kilometers    4

0 miles    2

### KEY

⬜ Built-up area

🏯 Temple

▲ Peak

== Path

The Buddhist Chongshan Si, Taiyuan

# Taiyuan ⑩
太原

254 miles (408 km) SW of Beijing.
🏠 1,900,000. ✈ 🚌 🚃 ℹ CITS 38
Pingyang Lu, (0351) 821 1109.

A heavily industrialized city,
Taiyuan lies on the banks
of the Fen River at the heart
of Shanxi and makes a
convenient base for trips to
Pingyao (see p138) and Wutai
Shan (see pp134–6).
Between the years
471–221 BC Taiyuan
was the capital of
the Zhao Kingdom,
and became a
flourishing center
of Buddhism by the
6th century AD.
Because of its
strategic position,
bordering the
hostile nomadic
tribes to the north,
the city underwent
heavy fortification during the
Tang dynasty. However,
fearing its ambitions, the Song
ruler had it torched to the
ground. The city was rebuilt a
few years later.

The Buddhist monastery
**Chongshan Si** is hidden
down an alleyway northeast
of Wuyi (May 1) Square. A
temple has existed here since
the 7th century, although the
current building dates from
the 14th century. A fire
reduced much of the temple
to ashes in 1864, but considerable rebuilding has taken
place. The Hall of Great
Compassion (Dabei Dian)
houses the striking Qianshou
Guanyin (Thousand-Armed
Goddess of Compassion), the
central figure in the trinity of

**Guardian deity, Jinci
Temple**

statues. The multi-armed and
multi-eyed goddess stands
over 26 ft (8 m), her arms
fanned out behind her. Also
displayed in the temple are
*sutras* (Buddhist scriptures)
and scrolls from the Song,
Yuan, and Ming eras. In the
east of town, the **Twin Pagoda
Temple** (Shuangta Si) was
built on imperial instruction
during the late Ming era. Also
known as Yongzuo Temple,
its 13-story, 164-ft (50-m)
high pagodas have come
to symbolize Taiyuan.
Formerly housed in
Chunyang Temple, the
**Shanxi Provincial
Museum** is now
located in a modern,
purpose-built facility
on the banks of the
River Fen. Its
collections are
arranged over
four floors and
are beautifully
presented, although there are
few explanations of the items
in English. Displays include
relics, bronzes, Chinese
currency, statuary, and a
collection of Buddhist *sutras*.

---

📷 **Chongshan Si**
🕐 8am–4:30pm daily. 📷

🏛 **Shanxi Provincial
Museum**
🕐 9am–5pm Tue–Sun.

**Environs:** The bustling **Jinci
Si**, 15 miles (25 km) southwest of town at the base of
Xuanwang Shan (Xuanwang
Mountain), dates to the
Northern Wei, although much
of its architecture is from the
Song period. The main
entrance leads straight to the
Ming-era Mirror Terrace,
originally used as a theatrical
stage. To the west, a canal
runs through the temple complex, crossed by a bridge that
leads to a terrace supporting
four fierce iron statues. Lying
beyond is the impressively
carved Hall of the Sacred
Mother (Shengmu Dian), one
of China's oldest surviving
wooden buildings. Inside the
hall, a group of ceramic Song-
era figures waits on a central
figure of the Sacred Mother.
About 25 miles (40 km)
southwest of Taiyuan, the
**Tianlong Shan Grottoes**
in the Tianlong Mountains
constitute a small, but
significant, collection of
Buddhist cave art. A total of
21 caves dot the eastern
and western sides of the
mountain, with worn and
damaged statues dating from
the Eastern Wei to the Tang
dynasties. The best-preserved
specimen is the large seated
Buddha in Cave No. 9.

📷 **Jinci Si**
🕐 8am–5pm daily. 📷

⛰ **Tianlong Shan Grottoes**
🕐 9am–6pm daily. 📷

The temple spring at Jinci Si, Taiyuan

# Pingyao ⓫
平遥

**Traditional red lantern**

Surrounded by one of China's few intact Ming city walls, Pingyao's streets are lined with a wealth of traditional Chinese buildings, including courtyard houses, temples, and more than 3,000 historic shops. Pingyao's treasure trove of Ming and Qing architecture is a legacy of the town's affluent days as a banking center, which ceased when the Qing dynasty defaulted on loans and abdicated, leaving the banks empty. The transferral of the country's finances to Shanghai and Hong Kong turned the city into a backwater, saving it from development and, ultimately, preserving its character.

★ **Rishenchang**
*This extensive museum of early banking is the site of China's first draft bank, founded in 1824.*

West Gate, train station

**County Magistrate's Residence**
*Pingyao's justice department during the Ming and Qing dynasties, these offices represented the secular world while the Daoist temples, mirroring the County Yamen on the other side of Nan Dajie, represented the spiritual realm.*

## STAR SIGHTS

- ★ City Walls
- ★ Rishenchang
- ★ Bell Tower

**SOUTHEAST PINGYAO**
The most notable part of the car-free town, the southeast corner and center of Pingyao has the largest concentration of sights, museums, and heritage architecture.

South Gate (Ying Xun Men)

★ **City Walls**
*The 39-ft (12-m) high, crenellated enclosure dating from 1370 is said to resemble the outline of a tortoise. Its head lies at the south gate, its four feet at the east and west gates, and its tail at the north gate.*

**Furniture Museum**
*As well as this rickshaw, there are rooms in this typical Qing dynasty compound that are furnished as bedrooms, kitchens, and opium dens.*

| 0 meters | 30 |
|---|---|
| 0 yards | 30 |

**North Gate**
(Gonji Men)

**The Tianjixiang Museum** has a small collection of local artifacts.

**These three adjoining** Daoist temples were last rebuilt in 1859, after burning down during a temple fair.

DONG DAJIE

HENG CHANG MIAO JIE

**Upper East Gate**

★ **Bell Tower**
*Rising above Nan Dajie, the Bell Tower is a charming structure decorated with ornamented eaves.*

### VISITORS' CHECKLIST

62 miles (100 km) S of Taiyuan.
🚶 40,000. 🚉 🚌
**City Walls** *access at West Gate.*
⭘ *daily.* 🎫 *(joint ticket for admission to all the town's attractions).*

**Watchtowers** punctuate the length of the wall every 164 ft (50 m).

**Kuixing Tower**
*This extravagant and unusually designed eight-sided pavilion rises above the battlements. It is named after a star in the 28 constellations of the Chinese zodiac.*

# Shuanglin Si ⑫
双林寺

4 miles (6 km) SW of Pingyao. 🚌
⭘ 8:30am–6:30pm daily (until 5pm in winter). 🎫

This temple has a long history, dating back 1,500 years to the Northern Wei, which had its capital at Datong. The current temple was built during the Ming and Qing dynasties and contains over 2,000 Buddhist statues, some from the Song dynasty. The effigies are arranged in ten halls around three courtyards. The expertly fashioned figures' expressions vary from the sublime through the comic to the sinister. The lifelike *luohan* in the second hall each reveal an individual persona and the bodhisattvas in the third hall are well worth seeking out.

Classic courtyard at the extensive Qiao Jia Dayuan

# Qiao Jia Dayuan ⑬
乔家大院

12 miles (20 km) N of Pingyao. 🚌
between Taiyuan and Pingyao can drop you off. 🚌 from Pingyao.
⭘ 8am–5:30pm daily. 🎫

This magnificent courtyard house was the setting for director Zhang Yimou's classic 1991 film *Raise the Red Lantern*, starring Gong Li. Dating from the 18th century, the vast complex, comprising 313 rooms, is an exquisite exercise in architectural balance, its linked courtyards pervaded by a sense of equilibrium. Enclosed by a 33-ft (10-m) high, fortified wall, the house was built by Qiao Guifa, a merchant who made his fortune in tofu and tea.

# SHANDONG & HENAN

The swathe of territory comprising Shandong and Henan, irrigated by the final sweep of the Yellow River (Huang He), sustained some of China's earliest settled societies. The Shandong Chinese are proud of their many treasures, which include sages Confucius and Mencius, the Yellow River, and Tai Shan, China's holiest Daoist peak, and the former German colony of Qingdao, with its Bavarian cobbled streets and Teutonic architecture. (Qingdao may be testament to humiliating 19th-century foreign ambitions, but it was German expertise that helped brew China's famous Tsingtao beer.) The Yellow River enters Shandong (East of the Mountains) from the west, after slicing Henan (South of the River) into two uneven chunks. Henan's historic sights cluster around the river in the province's north, in an area that was the cradle of Chinese civilization as early as 6000 BC. The ancient capitals of Anyang, Kaifeng, and Luoyang are located here. The impressive Longmen Caves, with their Buddhist carvings, lie outside Luoyang. Other sights include the sacred Daoist mountain of Song Shan, home to the Shaolin Temple and its band of warrior monks, and the Northern Song capital of Kaifeng, with its fine Buddhist architecture and historic Judaic links.

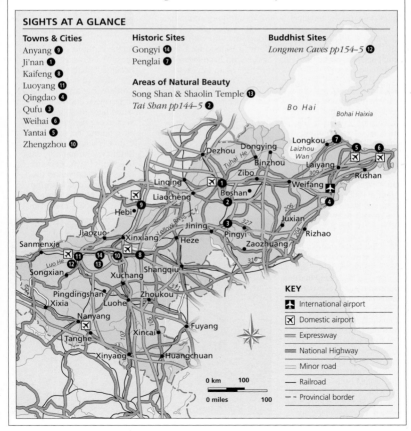

## SIGHTS AT A GLANCE

**Towns & Cities**
Anyang ⑨
Ji'nan ①
Kaifeng ⑧
Luoyang ⑪
Qingdao ④
Qufu ③
Weihai ⑥
Yantai ⑤
Zhengzhou ⑩

**Historic Sites**
Gongyi ⑭
Penglai ⑦

**Areas of Natural Beauty**
Song Shan & Shaolin Temple ⑬
*Tai Shan pp144–5* ②

**Buddhist Sites**
*Longmen Caves pp154–5* ⑫

### KEY

| ✈ | International airport |
| ✕ | Domestic airport |
| ▬ | Expressway |
| ▬ | National Highway |
| — | Minor road |
| — | Railroad |
| - - | Provincial border |

◁ **Buddha, Celestial King, and Defender of the Buddha at Fengxian Si, Longmen Caves**

Ji'nan's modern skyline, with the Yellow River in the distance

# Ji'nan ❶
济南

216 miles (350 km) S of Beijing.
👥 5,900,000. ✈ 🚉 🚌 ℹ (0531)
8267 6211.

South of the Yellow River as
it makes its final thrust for
the sea, Shandong's capital is
visited primarily by travelers
en route to the popular sights
of Tai Shan, Qingdao, and
Qufu. It was known for its
natural springs, many of
which have since dried up.
The most famous of these, the
**Black Tiger Spring**, still flows
somewhat erratically out of
tiger-headed spouts.

In the north of town, the
park surrounding **Daming
Hu** (Big Brilliant Lake) is
filled with ponds, gardens,
and temples, and is a good
place for a stroll. To the
southwest is the **Li Qingzhao
Memorial Hall**, which
commemorates one of China's
most famous female poets
who lived in the 12th century.
There is a statue of her as
well as portraits and extracts
from her writings.

In the southeast of the city,
the slopes of **Thousand Buddha
Mountain** (Qianfo Shan) are
dotted with Buddhist statues.
Several temples are situated on
the summit, which is over an
hour's climb up the steps. A
cable car service is available.
The earliest statuary dates from
the 6th century, with many
additions compensating for
those broken by Red Guards. A
short walk north of the mountain is the **Shandong Provincial
Museum**. Its exhibits include
Buddhist carvings, Neolithic

pottery fragments (some from
Long Shan nearby), and dinosaur fossils. Also on display is
China's oldest existing book
made from strips of bamboo.

**Environs:** Near Liubu village,
21 miles (33 km) southeast of
Ji'nan, the **Si Men Pagoda**
(Four Gate Pagoda) is known
for its antiquity and unusual
design. This squat, one-story
stone structure with four
doors is topped by a steeple,
and would have housed the
remains of an important
monk. The pagoda, erected in
AD 611, is the oldest of its
kind in China.

🏯 **Thousand Buddha
Mountain**
18 Jing Shiyi Lu, off Qianfoshan Lu.
◻ 5am–9pm daily. 🎫
🏛 **Shandong Provincial
Museum**
14 Jingshiyi Lu. ◻ 9am–5pm
Tue–Sun.

# Tai Shan ❷

See pp144–5.

# Qufu ❸
曲阜

112 miles (180 km) S of Ji'nan.
👥 160,000. 🚉 🚌 from Ji'nan.
ℹ CITS 36 Hongdao Lu, (0537)
449 149.

As the birthplace of China's
most revered sage, Qufu
occupies a hallowed place in
the minds of not only the
Chinese, but also the legions
of Japanese and Koreans who
come here on pilgrimage. In
September the town comes
alive during the annual festival
that celebrates Confucius's
birthday. Although the sage
lived in relative obscurity, his
descendents dwelt in the
grand **Confucius Mansion**
(Kong Fu) in the heart of
town. Wielding immense

Covered corridor to the Confucius Temple at Qufu

political authority and wealth, the Kong family – referred to by the Chinese as the First Family Under Heaven – built a palatial mansion occupying over 40 acres (16 ha). Arranged on a traditional north-south axis, the mansion is divided into residential and administrative quarters, with a temple in the east and a garden at the rear. Most of the halls date from the Ming era. The Gate of Double Glory in the north was used for the emperor's visits, while to the east stands the Tower of Refuge, where the family assembled in times of strife.

Mencius Temple at Zoucheng, south of Qufu

Next to the mansion, the **Confucius Temple** (Kong Miao) is a lengthy complex of memorial gateways, courtyards, halls, stele pavilions, auxiliary temples, gnarled cypresses, and ancestral shrines. Originally a simple shrine in 478 BC, the year after Confucius's death, the temple grew gradually over the centuries before suddenly expanding during the Ming and Qing eras. Beyond the entrance stand 198 stone stelae, listing the names of as many as 50,000 successful candidates in the imperial examinations, during the Yuan, Ming, and Qing dynasties. Some are supported on the backs of mighty

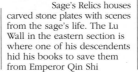

Carved column, Confucius Temple

*bixi*, primitive, turtle-like dragons. A long succession of gateways leads to the 11th-century Kuiwen Pavilion, a triple-roofed building. Confucius instructed his disciples from the Apricot Pavilion, accessed through the Great Achievements Gate. On top of a marble terrace with columns that are elaborately carved with dragons, the Great Achievements Hall (Dacheng Dian) forms the temple's splendid nucleus. Beyond, the Hall of the Sage's Relics houses carved stone plates with scenes from the sage's life. The Lu Wall in the eastern section is where one of his descendents hid his books to save them from Emperor Qin Shi

Huang (259–210 BC), who wished to burn them. The books were rediscovered during the Han era.

In the north of town, the walled **Confucius Forest** (Kong Lin) contains the grave of Confucius and other members of the Kong clan. The forest is mostly pines and cypresses interspersed with shrines and tombstones.

Not far south of Qufu, **Zoucheng** (now a city), is the hometown of Mencius (372–289 BC), the Confucian philosopher, second in importance only to Confucius himself. The tranquil Mencius Temple consists of 64 halls set around five large courtyards. As in Qufu, the philosopher has a Mansion and Graveyard.

**Confucius Mansion**
8 am–5 pm daily.

**Confucius Temple**
8am–5pm daily.

## CONFUCIUS

The teachings of Confucius (551–479 BC), China's most renowned philosopher, profoundly influenced the culture of China as well as other nations, including Japan, Korea, and Vietnam. Born in the state of Lu during an age of uninterrupted war, Confucius (whose name was derived from his Chinese name, Kong Fuzi or Master Kong) was prompted by the suffering around him to develop a practical philosophy built upon the principle of virtue *(ren)*, in the hope that rulers would govern in a just manner. Finding no audience among his native rulers, he communicated his beliefs to a body of disciples and embarked on a journey in search of a ruler who would apply his rules of governance. He died unrecognized and never recorded his philosophy in writing, but his thoughts were compiled by his followers into a volume called the *Analects (Lunyu)*, and promulgated. Championed by successive thinkers including Mencius, Confucius's philosophy later achieved predominance and formed the basis for the civil service examination system, a major hurdle to a career in officialdom right until the 20th century.

The philosopher-sage, Confucius

# Tai Shan ❷

泰山

Porter carrying
supplies to peak

Having played a part in China's earliest creation myths, Tai Shan (Peaceful Mountain) has held sway over the Chinese imagination for millennia. It is ascended year-round by legions of pilgrims and travelers, making it China's most sacred and most climbed mountain. Despite the crowds, a super-natural presence permeates Tai Shan, best experienced via a slow ascent with plenty of pit stops at wayside shrines and monuments. Many tourists stay overnight at hotels on the mountain and watch the sunrise from the cloud-wreathed peak, which is where Tai Shan's most significant temples can be found, attracting droves of devout worshipers.

**Bixia Ci,** dedicated to the Princess of the Azure Clouds, attracts would-be mothers to the summit.

HOU
WU

TAOHUA
YUAN

★ **Yuhuang Miao**
*Dedicated to the supreme deity of Daoism, the Jade Emperor Temple marks the conclusion of the ascent at 5,070 ft (1,545 m) and houses a statue of the Jade Emperor and wall paintings.*

Huima Ling

★ **Shiba Pan**
*The last and most punishing part of the climb, the steep Path of Eighteen Bends is visible from Zhong Tian Men (the halfway point), and brings weary travelers to Nan Tian Men, the last gate on Tai Shan, but not the summit.*

Longtan
Shuiku

**Heilong Tan
(Black Dragon
Pool)**

Dazhong
Qiao

**Puzhao Si**
*Tai Shan's shrines are not exclusively Daoist and this temple – with a typically Buddhist name (the Temple of Universal Light) – is easily visited if taking the Western Route up the mountain.*

## STAR SIGHTS

★ Shiba Pan

★ Yuhuang Miao

★ Dai Miao

## MOUNTAIN OF EMPERORS

The most exalted of China's five Daoist mountains, Tai Shan has been an essential imperial climb since the time of Qin Shi Huangdi. Emperors ascended Tai Shan to gain assurance that their heavenly mandate would be maintained; an abortive ascent could signal Heaven's favor was in question. Several sights have imperial associations: Huima Ling (Horse Turns Back Ridge) marks the spot where emperor Zhenzong's horse refused to go any farther and the ruler had to continue by sedan chair. Tai Shan's importance is further evinced by two other notables who clambered up its slopes: Confucius and Mao Zedong.

**Qin Shi Huangdi, first emperor of China**

### VISITORS' CHECKLIST

Tai'an, 45 miles (70 km) S of Jinan. ✈ at Ji'nan. 🚌 🚍 ℹ️ near Train Station, (0538) 827 2114. 🎫 Tai Shan Race (Sep). 🕑 7:40am–5pm; cable car: 8am–6pm. 🎫 🏛️

### KEY

🚠 Cable car

🏛️ Temple

═ Minor road

╌ Path

▢ Built–up area

## CLIMBING TAI SHAN

Two routes lead to the summit. The Central Route is more popular, following the traditional imperial way and taking travelers past the most notable monuments. Despite having fewer historical sights and not being particularly well-marked, the Western Route boasts lovely natural scenery, including Heilong Tan. Many travelers ascend by the Central Route and descend by the Western Route.

**Stone Sutra Valley**
*North of Doumu Gong is a further Buddhist contribution to this Daoist peak, a large flat rock carved with the text of the Diamond Sutra, one of Buddhist literature's most important passages.*

JINSHI YU
(STONE SUTRA VALLEY)

🏛️ **Doumu Gong**

**Hong Men Gong**
*This Ming dynasty temple, Red Gate Palace, is the first of numerous shrines dedicated to the Princess of the Azure Clouds (Bixia).*

**Yi Tian Men
(First Gate
under Heaven)**

| 0 metres | 800 |
| 0 yards | 800 |

TAI'AN

**★ Dai Miao**
*This temple is the town's main attraction and a natural departure point for climbing the mountain. The main building, the Tiankuang Dian, is an immense yellow-eaved hall that contains a massive dimly-lit Song dynasty fresco depicting the Zhenzong emperor as the God of Tai Shan.*

# Qingdao ❹
## 青岛

A world away from China's drab industrial towns, the breezy seaside city of Qingdao is a colorful port on the Shandong Peninsula. Known to foreign nationals as Tsingtao, where its namesake beer is brewed, pretty Qingdao's charms derive from its German textures, namely its cobbled streets, red roof tiles, distinctive stonework, and tree-lined avenues. Its German legacy dates from 1897, when the city came under German jurisdiction, but was returned to China in 1922. Selected as the host city for the sailing competitions of the 2008 Olympics, modern-day Qingdao is a clean, entrepreneurial, and forward-thinking city, a kind of miniature Shanghai with high ambitions.

The former Governor's Residence

face. Built in 1910, its exterior has sandy yellow walls and red clay tiles, while the frugal interior is open to visitors. The 128-ft (39-m) clocktower is also open, and visitors can climb up its steep stairway to enjoy the view of the coast. Farther east in Xinhao Shan Park is the former **Governor's Residence**. This grand mansion once played host to Yuan Shikai and Mao Zedong. A short walk to the south, the **Qingdao Museum** is worth exploring for its collection of relics, including several huge stone Buddha statues dating

## QINGDAO CITY CENTER

*Jiaozhou Bay*

Local Ferry Terminal

Long Distance Bus Station

*Tuandao Bay*

*Qingdao*

**Key to Symbols** *see back flap*

### Exploring Qingdao
In 1897, Kaiser Wilhelm took over Qingdao after two German missionaries were killed by the Boxers *(see p433)*. The Qing court was forced to cede the city to Germany for 99 years, but it was returned to China in 1922, after eight years under Japanese occupation. The Japanese took over the port again between 1938 and 1945.

Wandering about at leisure is the best way to see Qingdao's main sights, most of which lie in the **German Concession** in the southwest of town, that roughly stretches between Tai'an Lu and Xiaoyu Shan Park. The Germans built the imposing train station, equipped with a belfry, to mark the end of the line they laid to the provincial capital of Ji'nan. Reproduced on the label of Tsingtao beer, the octagonal Huilai Pavilion, which hosts craft exhibitions, lies at the tip of **Zhanqiao Pier**. The 1,444 ft (440 m) pier juts into Qingdao Bay off the frenetic

No. 6 beach. The busy Zhongshan Lu running north is Qingdao's premier shopping street. To the east is **St. Michael's Church**, whose twin spires preside over an atmospheric part of town filled with steep cobbled streets and iron balconies. Southeast of the Catholic church is the charming **Protestant Church**, with its distinctive clocktower and white clock

### CHINESE BEER

**Tsingtao beer can**

Tsingtao, which swears by its magic ingredient of mineral water from Lao Shan, is China's most famous beer *(pijiu)*. Built by homesick Germans in 1903, the Tsingtao brewery is China's largest, with exports to over 40 countries. Once the best (and most expensive) in China, Tsingtao faces stiff local competition as international breweries invest heavily in joint ventures in what is the fastest growing beer market in the world. Vast amounts of beer are drunk during the town's Beer Festival in August. You can visit the brewery and receive free samples.

An expanse of sand on one of Qingdao's many beaches

to AD 500, and paintings from the Yuan and Ming eras. Visitors can stroll down Qingdao's waterfront past its many beaches. No. 1 beach is the longest and busiest, while farther east, No. 2 beach is more attractive. Its clean stretch of sand leads to **Huashi Lou**, a stone mansion with a turret, that was once the residence of a Russian aristocrat. The genteel **Badaguan** area to the north is known for its villas and sanatoriums set amidst charming tree-lined streets.

🛉 **St Michael's Church**
15 Zhejiang Lu. ◯ *8am–5pm daily; services 7am, 6pm Sun.*

🛉 **Protestant Church**
15 Jiangsu Lu. ◯ *8:30am–5pm daily; services on Sun.*

🏛 **Qingdao Museum**
27 Meiling Lu. ◯ *daily.* 🖼

### VISITORS' CHECKLIST

200 miles (330 km) E of Ji'nan. 🚉 2,300,000. ✈ 🚆 Train Station. 🚌 Long Distance Bus Station, CAAC (buses to airport). ⛴ Passenger Ferry Terminal, Local Ferry Terminal. 🛈 9 Nanhai Lu, (0532) 389 3062. 🎉 Beer Festival (Aug).

**Environs:** An easy 25-mile (40-km) bus ride from Qingdao, the vast mountainous region of **Lao Shan** is a famous retreat with temples, waterfalls, and hiking trails. The area is steeped in Daoist lore and throughout the ages envoys were dispatched here in search of the elixir of life. The Song-era **Great Purity Palace** is located a third of the way up Mount Lao Shan. The palace was built by the first Song emperor as a place to perform Daoist rituals for the dead. From the palace, paths lead to the summit. Visitors can either climb the stairs located halfway up, or take the cable car for dramatic views. The area was once dotted with Daoist temples, but only a few survive today. The most famous is the Song-dynasty **Taiqing Temple** near the coast, not far from where the Shandong writer Pu Songling (1640–1715) lived. Many more temples survive on Lao Shan's slopes along with caves, the highest and deepest of which is the Mingxia cave in front of Xuanwu Peak. Lao Shan is also known for its mineral water, an essential ingredient of Tsingtao beer.

[Map of Qingdao showing: Passenger Ferry Terminal, XINJIANG LU, HUAYANG LU, Zhushuishan Gongyuan, LIAONING LU, REHE LU, YAN'AN YI LU, DAXUE LU, Qingdaoshan Gongyuan, St Michael's Church (2), CAAC, JIANGSU LU, Protestant Church (4), Governor's Residence (3), DAXUE LU, Zhongshan Gongyuan, Zhanshan Si, Lao Shan, Xiaoyu Shan Gongyuan, WENDENG LU, XIANGGANG XI LU, CONCESSION (5), Qingdao Museum, LAIYANG LU, NAN HAI LU, BADAGUAN (7), ZHENGYANGGUAN LU, QINGHAI XI LU, Zhanqiao Pier, Huilai Pavilion, Luxun Gongyuan, Number 1 Beach, SHANGHAIGUAN LU, Number 2 Beach, Huashi Lou (6), Number 3 Beach, Huiquan Bay, Taiping Bay, Huiquanjiao Horn, Taipingjiao Horn]

0 meters 800
0 yards 800

Qingdao's skyline, similar to the modern architecture of Pudong, Shanghai

Gateway to the Yantai Museum, housed in a fine Qing-era guild hall

# Yantai ❺
烟台

149 miles (240 km) NE of Qingdao.
🏯 6,500,000. ✈ 🚌 🚉 ⛴ to
Shanghai, Dalian & Tianjin. ❗ 180
Jiefang Lu, (0535) 623 4144.

Formerly known as Chefoo and overshadowed by the dynamic port of Qingdao to the south, Yantai is a deepwater harbor town situated on the north coast of the Shandong Peninsula, famous for its clocks, fruit, and locally produced wine. The name Yantai, meaning "Smoke Terrace," refers to the wolf-dung-burning beacons erected along the coast in the Ming dynasty to warn of sudden raids by pirates or the Japanese. In 1863, the city became a British treaty port and a substantial number of foreign merchants moved here, although its rise was eclipsed by the development of Qingdao at the end of the 1900s. The British were followed by the Germans, the Americans, and finally the Japanese. Despite its history as a treaty port, very little foreign architecture survives here, as the town never had a foreign concession.

Most travelers pass through en route to Penglai to the west, but the **Yantai Museum** is definitely worth a visit. Housed in a splendid Qing dynasty guild hall built for

Ornate Qing dynasty doors, Yantai Museum

sailors and merchants, the museum's exhibits pale by comparison to the building's elaborate architectural detail and wood and stone carvings.

The impressive main hall, known as the Palace of the Empress of Heaven, was dedicated to Tianhou, the Empress of Heaven and Protector of Seafarers, by sailors from Fujian, who had taken shelter in Yantai during a fierce storm. All the component parts of the hall were designed by craftsmen from the southern provinces of Fujian and Guangdong, and shipped to Yantai where it was assembled in 1864. It is a fine example of the southern style, with a double roof decorated in mythical ceramic, stone, and wood figures. The entrance hall to the guild hall is elaborately carved with parables and episodes from Chinese literature and mythology,

including the Eight Immortals who Crossed the Sea, battle scenes, figures, fabulous creatures, and several scenes from the *Romance of the Three Kingdoms* (see p29). Arab figures playing musical instruments lie beneath the eaves, while the beams take the shape of a woman with her infant child. The temple has a garden and is equipped with a stage, employed for performances and events celebrating the Goddess Tianhou.

Yantai also has several parks, including the small and central **Yuhuangding Park**, and **Yantai Shan Park**, a hillside haven above the sea. East of here are Yantai's two rather forlorn beaches. Both are a bit of a disappointment, and are surrounded by buildings and construction. The town's waterfront, however, is a pleasant place for a leisurely stroll. Toward the eastern headland, fishermen can be seen repairing their nets or simply relaxing.

🏛 **Yantai Museum**
257 Nan Dajie. ◯ 8am–5pm Tue–Sun. 🎫

# Weihai ❻
威海

37 miles (60 km) E of Yantai.
🏯 2,500,000. ✈ 🚌 🚉 to Yantai,
Qingdao, Beijing & Shanghai. ❗ CITS
96 Guzhai Dong Lu, (0631) 581 8616.
🛳 daily to Dalian, three times a week
to Inch'on (South Korea).

The port city of Weihai was the site of the mauling of China's European-built North Sea (Beiyang) Fleet by a Japanese flotilla during the 1894–5 Sino-Japanese War.

Museum of the 1895 Sino-Japanese War, Weihai

The Penglai Pavilion, mythical abode of the Eight Immortals

Afterwards, between 1898 and 1930, the city was a rather unproductive British Concession and was known as Port Edward, but little remains of the town's British heritage. Today, Weihai's chief diversion is **Liugong Island** (Liugong Dao), 3 miles (5 km) off the coast, reached by ferry. Providing shelter for Weihai harbor, the island forms a natural stronghold and served as the base for the doomed Chinese North Sea Fleet.

The island's main sight is the **Museum of the 1895 Sino-Japanese War**. The conflict between the two nations resulted in the ceding of Taiwan and the Liaodong Peninsula (including Dalian) to Japan. Not far from the jetty, the museum functions for the "patriotic education" of Chinese visitors, with displays of photographs and artifacts salvaged from ships, as well as reminders of the island's days as a station for the British Royal Navy.

The rest of the island is a pleasant place to explore, with several hiking trails heading off into the forested hills. Its International Beach is popular for its long stretches of sand and calm waters. Ferries connect Weihai with Dalian and Inchon in South Korea. No accommodation is available on the island.

🏛 **Museum of the 1895 Sino-Japanese War**
Liugong Island. 🚢 from Weihai (20 minutes). Ferry back to Weihai: summer 7am–6pm, every 8 mins; winter 8:30am–4:30pm, every 30 mins. ◯ daily. 🗲

# Penglai ❼
蓬莱

43 miles (70 km) NW of Yantai.
🚌 from Yantai.

Associated with the Eight Immortals of Daoism, who drank wine here before making their mythical crossing of the sea without the aid of boats, the castle-like pavilion complex of **Penglai Ge** affords dramatic views out to sea from its breezy clifftop perch. Accessible by boat or bus, the pavilion dates back to 1061, though Penglai entered folklore when China's first emperor, Qin Shi Huangdi, foraged in the area for herbs that bestow immortality.

The imposing complex has a large network of buildings, pavilions, halls, temples,

gardens, and crenellated walls. Many of the buildings are thickly covered in ivy and vines. Among its six main halls, which have been extensively renovated, the Tianhou Palace is dedicated to Tianhou, the Empress of Heaven, and enshrines a golden statue of the goddess. The statue is backed by a fine mural of dragons frolicking in the sea and amongst the clouds. The castle is at its liveliest on the occasion of the goddess's birthday, on the 23rd day of the third month of the Chinese lunar calendar (see p45), when a lively temple fair is held. The goddess is invoked with incense sticks and prayer. The complex now has a cable car and a theater.

Penglai Ge is also known for the mirage that is supposed to occur here every few decades. Witnesses have described seeing an island, complete with buildings, inhabitants, and trees arising from the mist. Visitors can watch a video recording of the mirage in the Tianhou Palace for a small fee. Penglai is usually busy on weekends when large tour groups visit the pavilion. It is quieter on weekdays, and can be easily visited as a daytrip from Yantai.

🎫 **Penglai Ge**
🚢 from Penglai (90 mins) every 20 mins. ◯ daily. Last entry at 5pm. 🗲

---

## THE EMPRESS OF HEAVEN

The Empress of Heaven, Tianhou, is also known by the Chinese as Mazu, Niangniang, and Tianshang Shengmu. She is the Daoist equivalent of Guanyin, the Buddhist Goddess of Compassion. In the coastal provinces of

Guangdong and Fujian, she is worshiped as the Goddess of the Sea, and is the guardian deity of seafarers. She was supposedly originally a woman named Lin Mo, born in AD 960 on Meizhou Island in Fujian (see p290). From a tender age, Lin Mo was famous for helping sailors in distress, and after her death at age 27, her red-clothed apparition was seen by fishermen and sailors in danger. Confusingly, in Cantonese, her name is pronounced as Tinhau, and she is also known as A-Ma in Macau.

**Goddess Tianhou depicted on a Chinese pirate flag**

# Kaifeng ⑧
开封

South of the Yellow River as it snakes into Shandong Province is the ancient walled city of Kaifeng, the capital of seven dynasties, which reached its zenith as the capital of the Northern Song (AD 960–1126). Its glory days as a burgeoning Song city are pictorially recorded in the 16-ft (5-m) long scroll "Going Upriver during the Qingming Festival," now kept in Beijing's Forbidden City. However, its prosperity could not prevent the Yellow River from repeatedly flooding the city, with a heavy loss of life. Significant buildings were also washed away, including the synagogue. Today, Kaifeng is an attractive city with fine examples of temple and pagoda architecture and some lively markets.

The ornately decorated Shanshaan Gan Guild Hall

### Exploring Kaifeng

Much of modern Kaifeng lies within the old city walls. In the west of the city is the large and peaceful Baogong Hu (Baogong Lake). Within walking distance to the south of the lake, the Kaifeng Museum on Yingbin Lu houses three stelae that originally stood outside the old Jewish synagogue. They record the history of the city's Jewish community. The No. 4 People's Hospital on Beitu Jie sits on the remains of the synagogue in the Jewish quarter. All that can be seen today is the iron cover over an old well. Outside the city walls, 6 miles (10 km) to the north, is the Yellow River Viewing Point. From the pavilion, there are expansive views across the vast silt plain of the winding river. Adjacent to the pavilion stands an iron statue of an ox, that was originally a charm to protect the city from floods.

### 🏯 Shanshan Gan Guild Hall

Xufu Jie, off Shudian Jie. ◯ 8am–5:30pm daily. 🎫

The exuberant Qing-dynasty hall was built by merchants of Gansu, Shanxi, and Shaanxi provinces, as housing. It sports a drum and bell tower, as well as a spirit wall. The building's eaves have vivid scenes from merchant life, while the eaves in the main hall are carved with animals, birds, and gold bats (symbols of luck).

### 🏯 Da Xiangguo Si

Ziyou Lu. 🚌 5, 9. ◯ 8am–6pm daily. 🎫 **Yanqing Guan** Baogong Hu Dongbei Shengli Jie. ◯ daily. 🎫 📷

Kaifeng's most celebrated temple is Da Xiangguo Si (Prime Minister's Temple). Originally built in AD 555, it was China's principal temple during the Song era when it accommodated 64 halls and a huge legion of monks. Swept away by flood waters in AD 1642 at the end of the Ming

dynasty, it was rebuilt around 1766. The octagonal pavilion at the back of the temple houses a remarkable statue of Guanyin, known as Qianshou Guanyin or the Thousand-Armed Goddess of Compassion. Carved from a single tree and covered in gold leaf, it is the temple's finest statue, and its four-sided arrangement is a rare feature. The main hall has a frieze of *luohan* (see p31). A sprawling open-air market lies near the temple.

To the west is the **Yanqing Guan** (Yanqing Temple), a small Daoist shrine known for the unusual design of its Pavilion of the Jade Emperor. This ornate, octagonal building, covered in turquoise tiles and carved brickwork, has a bronze image of the Jade Emperor inside.

### 🏯 Iron Pagoda

Iron Pagoda Park, Beimen Dajie. ◯ 8am–6pm daily. 🎫

The 13-story Iron Pagoda (Tie Ta) rises up just within the Song dynasty ramparts in the northeast of the city. This brick pagoda was built in AD 1049 and is covered with brown glazed tiles, which give the tower its metallic luster as well as its name. Visitors can climb the narrow interior staircase for views over the city and its walls. The pagoda is Kaifeng's best known landmark.

The magnificent Qianshou Guanyin, Da Xiangguo Si

**Prayer flags in front of Da Xiangguo Si**

### ♣ Longting Park

North of Zhongshan Lu. ◻ daily. 🎫
**Millennium City** ◻ daily. 🎫

Songdu Yu Jie, built on the
Imperial Way – Kaifeng's
main thoroughfare during the
Song dynasty – leads north
up to Longting Park. It
features reproduction Song-
dynasty restaurants and shops
selling antiques, calligraphy,
and knick-knacks. The street
gets progressively more
touristy as it heads northward
to Yangjia Hu (Yangjia Lake),
originally part of the imperial
park, and now surrounded
by tourist attractions and
amusement parks such as the
popular **Millennium City**.
Longting Park itself stands on
the site of the Song-dynasty
Imperial Palace and its
surrounding park. The Xibei
Hu and Yangjia Hu lakes lie to

its northwest and
south respectively. The
park is marked by
several amusement
rides for children, as
well as the Qing-
dynasty Dragon
Pavilion, and is an
excellent place to watch
the locals relaxing in
their leisure time.

### 🏯 Fan Pagoda

1 mile (1.5 km) southeast of Kaifeng.
🚌 15. ◻ 8am–5pm daily. 🎫

Hidden away (albeit
reachable by bus) south of
the city walls and just west of
the pleasant Yuwangtai Park
(Yuwangtai Gongyuan), the

### VISITORS' CHECKLIST

44 miles (70 km) E of Zhengzhou.
🏯 4,800,000. ✈ Zhengzhou.
🚉 Train Station. 🚌 Southern
Bus Station, West Bus Station. 🛈
98 Yingbin Lu, (0378) 398 4593.

Northern Song-dynasty Fan
Pagoda (Po Ta) is Kaifeng's
oldest Buddhist structure, and
was built in AD 997. Known
for its carved brickwork, the
three-story pagoda once
stood nine stories and 263 ft
(80 m) high. Visitors can
climb right to the top for
views of the surrounding
factories and houses.

### CHINA'S JEWS

It is not known when Jews *(youtairen)* first came to Kaifeng,
but evidence suggests that Jewish merchants arrived in China
in the 8th century, along the Silk Routes. It is recorded that
Chinese Jews were given seven surnames (Ai, Jin, Lao, Li, Shi,
Zhang, and Zhao) by imperial decree in the Ming era.
According to one story, in 1605 Jesuit Matteo Ricci traveled to
Kaifeng because he was told there was a community here
who believed in one god. Expecting to meet Catholics he was
surprised to find they were in fact Jewish. The community
struggled in isolation over the years, and all but disappeared
after the synagogue, damaged by flooding, was torn down in
the 19th century. Many Kaifeng Jews do not reveal themselves
due to official state disapproval.

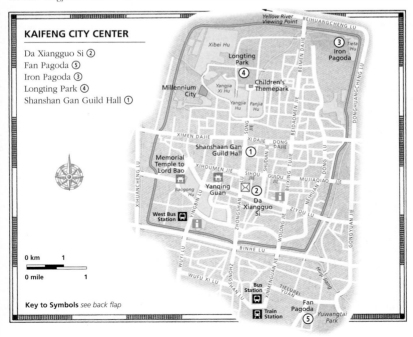

### KAIFENG CITY CENTER

Da Xiangguo Si ②
Fan Pagoda ⑤
Iron Pagoda ③
Longting Park ④
Shanshan Gan Guild Hall ①

0 km        1

0 mile      1

**Key to Symbols** see back flap

# Anyang
安阳

124 miles (200 km) N of Zhengzhou.
🏯 5,250,000. ✕ 🚃 🚉

Archeological excavations have identified that Anyang in northern Henan was the site of Yin, the capital of the Shang dynasty. In the late 19th century, peasants unearthed bones etched with ancient Chinese symbols, identified as "oracle bones" or bones used for divination (see p26). Further discoveries of bronzes, jade, and royal tombs, helped form a picture of the long forgotten city of Yin. The **Museum of Yin Ruins** (Yinxu Bowuguan), in the north of town, exhibits fragments of oracle bones, pottery, and bronze vessels, as well as six chariots, drawn by skeletal horses. To the east is the ostentatious **Tomb of Yuan Shikai**, a general who helped force the Qing abdication in return for the presidency, but later tried to have himself enthroned as emperor. The bustling **Old City**, centered around the Bell Tower south of Jiefang Lu, is also worth exploring. To the southwest, stands the octagonal, multi-eaved **Wenfeng Pagoda**, originally built in the 10th century and restored during the Ming era.

**Wenfeng Pagoda, Anyang**

🏛 **Museum of Yin Ruins**
🚃 🔘 8am–5:30pm daily. 📷
⚰ **Tomb of Yuan Shikai**
🚌 8, 23. 🚃 🔘 8am–5pm daily. 📷

---

Traditional three door gateway, Baima Si (White Horse Temple), Luoyang

# Zhengzhou ⑩
郑州

440 miles (700 km) SW of Beijing.
🏯 7,000,000. ✕ 🚃 🚉 ℹ Nongye Lu (Crn Huayuan Lu), (0371) 585 2339.

Henan's capital is used primarily as a stopover en route to Kaifeng, Luoyang, and the Shaolin Temple. The **Shang City Walls** to the east of town are all that remain of the city that existed here 3,000 years ago. To the west is **Chenghuang Miao** (Temple of the City God), with its roof sculptures of dragons and phoenixes. The pyramidal **Henan Provincial Museum**, in the north of town, has a superb collection of more than 130,000 relics with English captions, while the fourth floor houses a dinosaur gallery. For fine views of the Yellow River, visit the **Yellow River Park**, 17 miles (28 km) northwest of town.

🏛 **Henan Provincial Museum**
8 Nongye Lu. 🔘 9am–4pm daily.

---

# Luoyang ⑪
洛阳

75 miles (121 km) W of Zhengzhou.
🏯 6,400,000. ✕ 🚃 🚉
ℹ Jiudu Xi Lu, (0379) 432 3212.

Luoyang's industrial face conveys little of its impressive history. The city was the site of the ancient Zhao court, where the sage Laozi was keeper of the archives. It was also the site of China's first university in 29 BC, and was capital to 13 dynasties from Neolithic times till AD 937.

East of Wangcheng Park is the **Luoyang City Museum**, which exhibits Shang bronzes, jade carvings, and Tang era *sancai* (three-color) porcelain. Visitors flock here each spring to attend the Peony Festival, when hundreds of peonies – brought here on the orders of the Tang Empress Wu Zetian – bloom in Wangcheng Park.

Most of Luoyang's sights lie outside the city. **Guanlin**, 4 miles (7 km) south, is dedicated to Guan Yu (see p29), a heroic general of the Three Kingdoms period. The buildings are ornately decorated, and stone lionesses line the path to the main hall housing an impressive statue of Guan Yu. About 8 miles (12 km) east of town is **Baima Si** (White Horse Temple). Claiming to be China's oldest Buddhist monastery (AD 68), Baima Si remains active, with a constant stream of worshipers. The monks' tombs lie in the first courtyard, while the main hall has a statue of the Buddha.

🏛 **Luoyang City Museum**
🔘 8am–5pm daily.
🏛 **Guanlin Si**
🔘 8am–6pm daily. 📷

---

A Shang-era war chariot and charioteer from an imperial tomb, Anyang

# The Yellow River

China's second-longest river, at 3,400 miles (5,464 km), the Huang He or Yellow River gets its name from its vast silt load, picked up as it carves its way through the soft clay of the loess plateau. As the river slows, it deposits much of this silt elevating the river bed above the surrounding plains – outside Kaifeng it is up to 35 ft (10 m) higher than the city – making flooding likely. It has also changed its path completely many times, sometimes running south of the Shandong peninsula, each time with widespread devastation. In 1642 an estimated 300,000 people died when the river broke through the dykes and took the southern route. These disasters have earned the river the nickname "China's Sorrow." Rapid economic growth has lead to vastly increased water usage in north China and the Yellow River now regularly runs dry in its lower reaches.

*Banpo pottery
Yellow River*

⑤ **Pumping into the sea,**
*the yellow river's silt is
clearly visible. Over the
years the millions of tonnes
of sediment have increased
the land mass of China.*

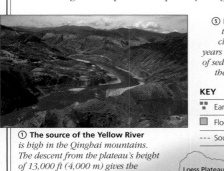

① **The source of the Yellow River**
*is high in the Qinghai mountains.
The descent from the plateau's height
of 13,000 ft (4,000 m) gives the
river its incredible power.*

**KEY**

░ Early settlement

▮ Flood plain

--- Southern route of river

Loess Plateau

Beijing ●

② ● Xining ●Lanzhou ② ⑤ Bo Hai

①

Yellow River

**MOTHER OF CHINA**
Evidence of some of the earliest Chinese settlements, dating back as far as 6000 BC, have been discovered beside the Yellow River, earning it another title "Mother of China."

Xi'an  Luoyang ④

Yellow Sea

Huai He

Yangzi

Nanjing ●

Shanghai ●

0 kilometers   400

0 miles   400

② **The river fills with
sediment** *as it cuts through
the soft loess plateau in the
north. Seemingly boiling
with energy, each cubic yard
(meter) of water carries over
82 lb (37 kg) of sediment.*

③ **As the river slows**
*it deposits its silt and
enriches the soil making
the local farmland one
of the most productive
areas of China.*

④ **As the silt raises the
riverbed** *those living close to the
river have to work together to
rebuild the dykes and keep the
river banks in good condition.*

# Longmen Caves ⑫
龙门石窟

**Flower, roof of the Lotus Cave**

This outstanding collection of religious statuary was started by the Buddhist Northern Wei rulers (386–534 AD) – creators of the Yungang Caves *(see pp132–3)* – after they moved their capital from Datong to Luoyang. The ensuing Sui and Tang dynasties further added to the grottoes especially during the rule of Tang dynasty Empress Wu Zetian, before anti-Buddhist purges abruptly halted its development. The tragic number of headless statues as a result of vandalism and theft creates a solemn mood, although today the caves are obviously well cared for.

**View across the river Yi looking onto Fengxian Si and the west bank caves**

## FENGXIAN SI ①
This cave, on the western bank, is largest of all the caves and dates back to AD 675.

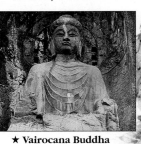

**★ Vairocana Buddha**
*Over 56 ft (17 m) tall, this colossal statue's face was reputedly modeled after the empress Wu Zetian. The statue's enigmatic smile has earned it the nickname the "Eastern Mona Lisa."*

**Ananda**
*This statue is of Ananda, a disciple of Sakyamuni, the founder of Buddhism. A master of memory, he compiled the Buddhist sutras.*

**Smashed Ananda**
*Some statues were damaged in the late-Tang dynasty, as Buddhism fell out of favor. Other figures were stolen by souvenir hunters or attacked by Red Guards during the Cultural Revolution.*

## STAR FEATURES

★ Vairocana Buddha

★ Heavenly King

**★ Heavenly King**
*Holding a votive pagoda in one hand and crushing a demon under his feet, this sculpture of a Heavenly King is remarkable for its sense of movement and realistic posture.*

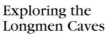

# Exploring the Longmen Caves

There are around 2,000 caves or niches and over 100,000 statues (with English captions) in total clustered inside a few caves, largely within a half-mile (1-km) section on the western bank of the Yi River.

The well-preserved **Lotus Flower Cave** ② was built c.527 and is important as it was built as a complete entity, and not added to over the years. It derives its name from the large lotus flower in the center of its domed roof, surrounded by musical water spirits – *apsarases*. The **Ten Thousand Buddha Cave** ③ is a typical Tang dynasty cave built in 680. The many figures of Buddha create an overwhelming sense of the presence of the great teacher. The **Prescription Cave** ④ is so called because it has 140

inscriptions recording many treatments for a wide variety of diseases and conditions carved on the walls on either side of the entrance. The list has been added to over a period of 150 years and so provides a unique record of typological changes over time. The three **Binyang San Dong** ⑤ caves took 24 years to build and were completed in AD 523. On the main wall there are five very large Buddhist images: the central one, of Sakyamuni, is flanked by four bodhisattvas all in the ascetic and rather formal Northern Wei style. Together with the statues on the side walls, the three groups of figures symbolize the Buddhas of the past, present, and future. There were two large reliefs of the Emperor and Empress worshiping Buddha, but these were stolen in the 1930s and they now reside in museums in the USA. The southern Binyang cave has some beautiful sculptures that were completed in 641. These figures have serene features and can clearly be seen as a transition between the artistic styles of the solemn, austere Northern Wei and the lively naturalism of the Tang artists as displayed at Fengxian Si.

Seated Buddha, Sakyamuni, in the central cave Binyang Si

# LONGMEN CAVES

The east bank of the river provides a great vantage point to appreciate the grandeur of the carvings of Fengxian Si. There is also a temple and a few minor caves.

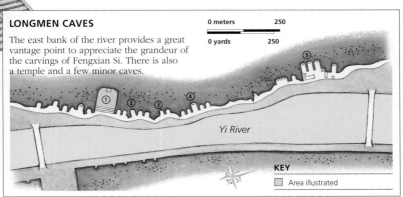

*Yi River*

**KEY**
Area illustrated

The monumental Forest of Stupas, Shaolin Temple

# Song Shan & Shaolin Temple ⑬

嵩山和少林寺

50 miles (80 km) W of Zhengzhou.
🚉 from Luoyang & Zhengzhou to Dengfeng & Shaolin Temple. 🚌 🈶
**Dengfeng** 🚉 203 Beihuan Lu, (0371) 6288 3442.

The Central Peak of China's five sacred Daoist peaks, Song Shan soars 4,895 ft (1,492 m) high. Its sights can be best explored by staying at **Dengfeng**, at the foot of Taishi Shan, where numerous trails lead past temples and pagodas, and offer splendid views. Just 3 miles (5 km) east is the vast **Zhongyue Miao** (Central Peak Temple). Possibly China's oldest Daoist shrine, it was consecrated over 2,200 years ago, although what exists today is more recent.

About 2 miles (3 km) north of Dengfeng is the **Songyang Academy**. A Confucian college that was one of China's four great centers of learning, its courtyard has two tall cypresses, said to have been planted 2,000 years ago by the Han emperor Wudi. Farther uphill, the 12-sided **Songyue Si Pagoda**, dating from the 6th century AD, is China's oldest brick pagoda. Just 6 miles (10 km) southeast of Dengfeng, the Gaocheng Observatory dates from the Yuan era. Its pyramidal tower is China's oldest intact observatory. Shaolin, literally

"Young Forest," is the name of the fighting order of monks who reside in the Buddhist **Shaolin Temple**, 8 miles (13 km) northwest of Dengfeng. Founded in the 5th century AD, it acquired its martial spirit under Bodhidarma, an Indian monk who arrived here in AD 527. He devised a system of exercises that evolved into *shaolin quan*, or Shaolin Boxing, the origin of all the great Chinese martial arts. The temple has burned down repeatedly and today its mystique has been dulled by commercialization. It remains a place of pilgrimage for martial arts devotees, who flock here to develop *gong fu* (skill), popularly known as kung fu, although many schools have moved to Dengfeng. The large temple has several halls. Toward the back, the Standing in the Snow Pavilion marks the spot where the monk Huihe chopped off his arm to

Bodhidarma statue, Shaolin Temple

commune more closely with Zen Buddhism. Behind, the Pilu Pavilion's floor is marked with pits where monks practiced their footwork. Within the Chuipu Hall, terracotta figures depict various styles of Shaolin Boxing.

The Forest of Stupas, a short walk from the temple, is a large assembly of brick pagodas, commemorating renowned Shaolin monks. Each September, the famous *wushu* (martial arts) festival is held here. The cave where Bodhidarma reputedly sat in meditation for nine years is up the mountainside.

🏛 **Shaolin Temple**
🈺 🚌 🚻 ⬤ 8am–5pm daily. 🈶
🏛 **Zhongyue Miao**
⬤ 8am–5pm daily. 🈶

# Gongyi ⑭

工艺

50 miles (80 km) W of Zhengzhou.
🚉 from Luoyang or Zhengzhou.

Just outside the sleepy town of Gongyi a historic collection of Song-era imperial tombs and a group of Buddhist grotto art can be found. The seven surviving tombs of Song emperors are marked by burial mounds and statuary. Scattered over a vast area southeast of town, the tombs can be seen from buses shuttling between Luoyang and Zhengzhou. About 5 miles (8 km) north of Gongyi, the **Buddhist Grottoes** (*shiku*) have some carvings from the Northern Wei period.

🏛 **Buddhist Grottoes**
🈺 🚌 🚻 ⬤ 8am–6pm daily. 🈶

Buddhist carvings in the grottoes outside Gongyi

◁ **Striking sculptures of the Heavenly King and Defender of the Buddha, Longmen Caves**

# Kung Fu

Chinese Martial Arts are loosely referred to as kung fu or *gong fu* in the West. *Gong fu* means "skill" and can describe the accomplishments of a calligrapher or pianist, as much as a martial artist. No one is certain when the fighting arts came to the country, but it is clear that China has the largest number and most colorful of fighting styles, including Drunken Boxing and Praying Mantis Fist. Although there is considerable blurring between

**Kung fu sword**

them, kung fu divides into internal *(neijia)* and external *(waijia)* schools. The internal schools tend to stress internal power or *qi (see pp32–3)*, using evasion and softness to lead an attacker off balance, while *waijia* forms seek to overwhelm an opponent with physical strength and power. Kung fu employs many weapons, including the spear broadsword, pole, and whip and even encompasses training in the use of everyday objects, such as the fan, umbrella, or stool, as weapons.

**Bodhidarma,** *the founder of Chan (Zen) Buddhism, was an Indian monk who visited the Shaolin Temple. He invented a system of exercises for the monks who were often seated in meditation. It was from these exercises that Shaolin Boxing developed.*

**Shaolin monks** *endure a rigorous training regimen. Here, they perform an acrobatic version of the horse stance (mabu), a painful exercise that is essential for developing a powerful stance and a deep "root" for stability while fighting.*

**Xingyi Quan** *(Shape Mind Fist) is, of the* neijia *practices, probably the closest to a hard school. Although its strikes and blocks are linear and powerful, relaxation is paramount. The basics of this explosive fighting style are simple to learn, but tricky to master.*

**Bagua Zhang** *(Eight Trigram Palm), an internal art, incorporates circular movements into all footwork and strikes. Bagua practitioners were traditionally seen by other stylists as unpredictable, elusive, and ferocious adversaries.*

**Bruce Lee *(right)* in The Chinese Connection**

## KUNG FU FILM INDUSTRY

The Chinese and Hong Kong film industry entertains its audience with stylized versions of kung fu in movie plots that typically hinge on themes of vengeance and retribution. Famous actors have included Bruce Lee, Jackie Chan, and Jet Li and a host of lesser known B-movie actors and actresses. Hallmark films include *Drunken Master 2* (Jackie Chan), *Enter the Dragon* (Bruce Lee), *Crouching Tiger, Hidden Dragon* (Zhang Ziyi and Yun-Fat Chow), and the *Once Upon a Time in China* series (Jet Li). The martial arts employed in cinema are very different from the real thing. Movements are choreographed and stunts are practiced repeatedly to give the impression of a real fight, without the dangers inherent in real combat.

# SHAANXI

At the heart of China, bordered by the Yellow River to the east, the dusty province of Shaanxi has had its lion's share of splendor. In 1066 BC, the Western Zhou dynasty established its capital at Hao, near modern-day Xi'an (see pp162–7). It was from here, about 850 years later, that China was unified by its first emperor, Qin Shi Huangdi (see p54). This set the stage for Xi'an to serve as the seat of political power to successive dynasties including the Western Han, the Sui, and the Tang, for over a millennium. By the 9th century, Xi'an, known then as Chang'an, was the largest and wealthiest city in the world, immersed in the riches that spilled along the Silk Road. At the peak of the Tang era, Xi'an's population of over a million

people worshiped at as many as 1,000 temples within the confines of a vast city wall.

The city's treasures are abundant, from the silent army of Terracotta Warriors just northeast of Xi'an, fashioned to guard the tomb of China's first emperor, to the impressive Shaanxi History Museum, with over 3,000 exhibits ranging from Shang and Zhou bronze vessels to Tang-era ornaments and funerary items.

Xi'an's other key sights include the extensive Eight Immortals Temple associated with Daoist legends, and the two Goose Pagodas with their strong connections to Tang-era Buddhism. Many visitors also make a trip to the holy mountain of Hua Shan, to the east of Xi'an, for its stimulating combination of energetic hiking opportunities and quiet sanctity.

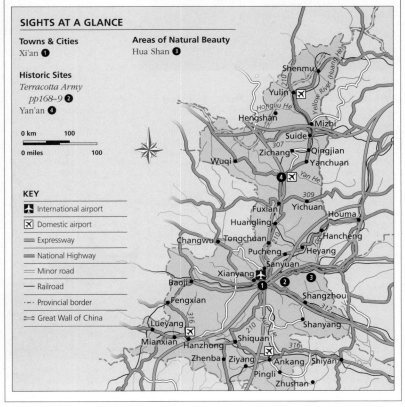

**SIGHTS AT A GLANCE**

**Towns & Cities**
Xi'an ❶

**Historic Sites**
*Terracotta Army*
   *pp168–9* ❷
Yan'an ❹

**Areas of Natural Beauty**
Hua Shan ❸

0 km          100

0 miles        100

**KEY**

✈ International airport

✕ Domestic airport

═ Expressway

═ National Highway

═ Minor road

─ Railroad

-·- Provincial border

⚊ Great Wall of China

◁ **Adventurous tourists at the top of South Peak, the highest of Hua Shan's summits**

# Xi'an ❶
西安

**Drum at Xi'an Drum Tower**

Capital of modern Shaanxi, Xi'an has served as capital to 11 dynasties over a period of 4,000 years, including the Western Zhou, Western Han, Qin, Western Wei, Northern Zhou, Sui, and Tang. The Chinese trace its lineage back even further to the mythical Yellow Emperor, who made Xianyang his capital (2200–1700 BC). Xi'an peaked during the Tang dynasty, when its position at the eastern end of the Silk Road *(see pp464–5)* transformed it into a bustling metropolis, luring foreign merchants and faiths, including Nestorian Christians, Muslims, Zoroastrians, Manicheans, and Buddhists. The city declined later but has some splendid sights and a thriving tourist economy.

**Detail from the Nestorian tablet at the Forest of Stelae Museum**

Imperial Academy in Xi'an. The Daqin Nestorian Tablet in the second hall may be of more interest to visitors. The stele is topped with a cross and was carved in 781 to commemorate the arrival of Nestorian Christianity in Xi'an. The characters at the top of the stele refer to Rome (or Daqin), and Nestorian Christianity, the "Revered Religion." Branded heretical for believing in the separation of Christ's human and divine attributes, the first Nestorians arrived in Xi'an in AD 635. They thrived in the city for two centuries before suddenly vanishing altogether.

Inside the third hall, an engraved map of Chang'an reveals the scale of the city at the height of its glory. The fourth hall houses calligraphic renditions of poems by Su Dongpo (1037–1101) and other Chinese poets, and illustrations including etchings of Bodhidarma, the Indian founder of Chan (Zen) Buddhism *(see pp158–9)*. Useful reference material for the study of local history and society during the Song, Yuan, Ming, and Qing eras can be found preserved in the fifth hall. The museum's side halls display further historical and religious artifacts.

**A view of the South Gate, Xi'an City Walls**

## 🏯 Xi'an City Walls
🕐 *Spring and summer: 8am–7pm; autumn and winter: 8:30am–5pm.*
📷 🖥️

Unlike many city walls in China, including Beijing's mighty ramparts – now mostly flattened – Xi'an's walls are still intact, forming a 9-mile (14-km) long rectangle around the city center. In 1370, during the reign of Hongwu, the first Ming emperor, these walls were built on the foundations of the Tang imperial palace, using rammed earth, quicklime, and glutinous rice extract. The 39-ft (12-m) high bastions have bases up to 59 ft (18 m) thick. Visitors can climb the walls at several locations, particularly at the steps east of the South Gate or at the West Gate, for walks along the busy ramparts. Though striking in themselves, the walls are modest compared to the mighty bastion that once encompassed 30 sq miles (78 sq km) of Chang'an, Xi'an's name during the Tang era.

## 🏛 Forest of Stelae Museum
🕐 *8am–6pm daily.* 🖼️
A short distance east of the South Gate, this museum's seven halls house over 1,000 stelae – stone pillars carved for commemorative purposes – the earliest dating from the Han dynasty. The tablets bearing dense reams of classical Chinese may only interest scholars, but others are engraved with maps and illustrations. The stelae in the first hall comprise a record of the 12 Confucian classics, including the *Book of Songs (Shijing)*, the *Book of Changes (Yijing or I Ching)*, and the *Analects (Lunyu)*. These were carved on 114 stone tablets in 837, upon the orders of the Tang Wenzong emperor, as the standard texts to eliminate copyist's errors, and were kept at the

**The façade of the Forest of Stelae Museum, once the Temple of Confucius**

### 🥁 Drum & Bell Towers
◷ 8:30am–5:30pm daily. 🎫

The enormous Bell Tower, with its distinctive green three-tiered roof, is situated in the center of Xi'an, where the city's four main streets converge. Standing on a brick platform, this wooden structure was first built in 1384, two blocks west of here, before being relocated to its current site in 1582. It was later restored in 1739. The tower,

**Iron bell in the Bell Tower**

which formerly housed a large bronze bell that was struck each morning, now stores a collection of bells, chimes, and musical instruments. A balcony running all along the outside offers splendid views of the town's main roads and heavy traffic. The Drum Tower, built in 1380, is situated to the west of the Bell Tower on the edge of the old Muslim Quarter, for centuries the home of Xi'an's Hui minority currently numbering around 30,000. Within its restored interior, there is a display of drums, and drumming performances take place daily.

### 🕌 The Great Mosque
◷ 8am–6:30pm daily. 🎫

First built during the Tang dynasty, and located in the heart of the Muslim Quarter west of the Bell Tower, Xi'an's Chinese-styled Great Mosque (Da Qingzhen Si) is one of the largest in China. Originally built in 742, when Islam was still a young religion, the mosque's surviving buildings date to the Qing dynasty and have been restored. A serene oasis of tranquility, the mosque has four courtyards, the first of which

**Arabic script on a stone arch in the Great Mosque's courtyard**

### VISITORS' CHECKLIST

744 miles (1,200 km) SW of Beijing. 🏙 8,000,000. ✈ Xiguan Airport, Xianyang 25 miles (40 km). 🚌 Xi'an Train Station. 🚌 Xi'an Bus Station, CAAC (buses to airport), West Bus Station. ℹ Xi'an CITS (029) 852 23170.

contains a 30-ft (9-m) high decorated wooden arch, built in the 17th century, while the third houses the Introspection Minaret, an octagonal pagoda with a triple-eaved roof. Housed within the hall to the south of the minaret is a Ming-dynasty handwritten copy of the holy Koran. Located beyond two fountains is the main prayer hall, capped in turquoise tiles, its ceiling carved with inscriptions from the Koran. The prayer hall is usually closed to non-Muslims. Avoid visiting the mosque on Fridays, the Muslim holy day.

Also worth exploring is the charming Muslim Quarter, with its winding streets, low houses, narrow lanes, excellent ethnic cuisine, and resident Hui community.

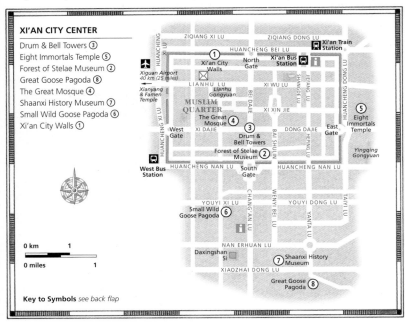

### XI'AN CITY CENTER

Drum & Bell Towers ③
Eight Immortals Temple ⑤
Forest of Stelae Museum ②
Great Goose Pagoda ⑧
The Great Mosque ④
Shaanxi History Museum ⑦
Small Wild Goose Pagoda ⑥
Xi'an City Walls ①

0 km                    1
0 miles                 1

Key to Symbols *see back flap*

### Eight Immortals Temple

9am–5:30pm daily.

East of Xi'an's walls, this is its largest Daoist shrine, built on the site of a temple originally consecrated to the Thunder God, whose presence had been indicated by subterranean rumblings. It was later named Baxian Gong, after the Eight Immortals of Daoist mythology, who were glimpsed here during the Song dynasty. The halls and courtyards of this active temple teem with monks and nuns. Of particular interest are a series of slabs attached to the wall in the main courtyard, inscribed with Daoist literature and illustrations, including extracts from the *Neijing*, the bible of Daoist yogis and alchemists. Other plaques are etched with curious Daoist designs, including a tablet illustrated with the five mystic symbols denoting the Five Daoist sacred mountains. On the left and right of the **Lingguan Hall** are statues of the guardian beings, the White Tiger and Green Dragon, and an effigy of Wang Lingguan, the protector of Daoism. Statues of the Eight Immortals line either side of their hall.

Stele Pavilion Eight Immortals Temple

At the rear of the complex, the **Doumu Hall** is dedicated to the important Daoist Goddess Doumu, also called Doulao, the Queen of the Big Dipper. Also at the rear is the Hall of Master Qiu, where the dowager-Empress Cixi and the Guangxu emperor sought refuge when they fled Beijing's Forbidden City at the end of the Boxer Rebellion in 1900 *(see p433)*. Above the door of the hall is a tablet inscribed with the characters *yuqing zhidao*, meaning the Dao of Jade Purity, Cixi's dedication to the abbot. The temple hosts a popular religious festival on the first and fifteenth day of every lunar month. An excellent street market of curios, fakes, and memorabilia is held on Wednesdays and Sundays in the road outside the temple.

**The Small Goose Pagoda, originally 15 storys high**

### Small Goose Pagoda

Youyi Xi Lu. 7, 8, 40, 46. 8am–5pm daily.

Southwest of the South Gate, the 43-m (141-ft) high Small Goose pagoda, Xiaoyan Ta, is attached to the remains of a temple, Jianfu Si. One of the city's Tang relics, it was built to store *sutras* (scriptures) brought back from India. Its brick tower, completed in AD 709, was meant to protect the *sutras* from fire, which often destroyed wooden temples. The pagoda's top was jolted off by an earthquake. At the back of the complex is the **Xi'an Museum**, storing 130,000 cultural relics.

### Shaanxi History Museum

*See pp166–7.*

### Great Goose Pagoda

Yanta Lu. 5, 21,501. 8am–6pm daily. (separate fee to climb the pagoda).

This Tang-dynasty pagoda, built in AD 652, is attached to the extant Ci'en Si (Ci'en Temple). Known as Dayan Ta, the pagoda was built in memory of the Gaozong emperor's mother, Empress Wende. The monk Xuanzang, who traveled to India via Central Asia and returned with bundles of *sutras (see p487)*, officiated at the temple, translating the hundreds of scriptures from Sanskrit into Chinese. The 210-ft (64-m) high pagoda, built on his orders for their storage, is a square, sturdy structure with a brick exterior and wood interior. At the height of the Tang dynasty, Xi'an's extent was almost seven times larger than it is today, enclosing within its walls both the temple and pagoda.

The Dayan Ta can be climbed, and visitors throw money from the windows for good luck. The large temple complex, smaller now than during its Tang heyday, can also be explored. Its main hall contains three statues of the Buddha flanked by 18 *luohan* or *arhats (see pp30–1)*.

At the back of the pagoda is a huge relief depicting scenes from Xi'an's history. North of the pagoda is a giant fountain which has nightly shows timed to music.

**A visitor lighting a candle in the courtyard, Great Goose Pagoda**

# History of the Pagoda

Considered an archetypal element of Chinese architecture, the pagoda originates from India in concept and form as a development from the Buddhist stupa. However, Chinese architectural forms and styles were soon used in the design of pagodas, as can be seen by the pillar pagodas in the Yungang caves that clearly show multi-storied buildings. Over 1,500 years pagodas developed a variety of forms from pillars to squat tombs to soaring multi-story towers. Made of stone, brick, or wood, they could also be square or multi-sided. As they became uniquely Chinese they were also used slightly differently. Originally the focal point of the temple, they were superseded in this by the more functional hall. *Feng shui* led to pagodas being built without a temple on hills outside towns or overlooking rivers, to bring good luck or prevent floods.

**Yungang pillar pagoda**

**The Indian stupa** *was a symbolic tomb and receptacle for Buddhist relics that inspired the pagoda. However the stupa form was largely dropped until the 13th century when the Yuan imported Tibetan Buddhist stupas (also known as dagobas), popularizing the form for later dynasties.*

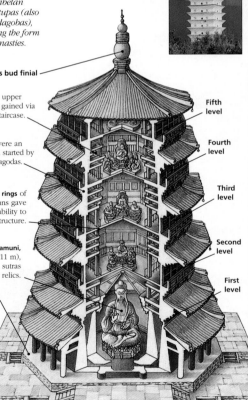

**This Dali pagoda** *is a beautiful example of a stone close-eaved pagoda. From a square base it is 260-ft (69-m) high, tapering to a lotus bud spike that recalls the Indian stupas.*

**Lotus bud finial**

**Access** to upper Buddhas gained via narrow staircase.

**Galleries** were an innovation started by wooden pagodas.

**Two rings** of columns gave extra stability to the structure.

**Sakyamuni,** (33 ft/11 m), stored sutras and relics.

**Base**

**Fifth level**
**Fourth level**
**Third level**
**Second level**
**First level**

**Octagonal pagodas** *may have come about as a result of Tantric Buddhism which used a cosmology with eight cardinal points.*

## YINGXIAN PAGODA
The wooden pagoda at the Fogong Si, Yingxian is one of the finest surviving pagodas. Built in 1056, the octagonal building is called the Sakyamuni Pagoda.

# Shaanxi History Museum
陕西历史博物馆

Ancient crossbow

One of Xi'an's premier attractions, this roomy, modern museum contains over 370,000 relics chronicling Shaanxi civilization and culture from as far back as prehistoric times. The collection is strong in ceramics, bronzes, jade pieces, gold and silver items, ancient coins, and calligraphy mainly from the pre-Ming periods, reflecting Xi'an's later decline. Look out also for some interesting Tang-dynasty frescoes and the chance to examine some of the renowned terracotta soldiers (*see pp168–9*) up close. Exhibits are well displayed and accompanied by both Chinese and English captions.

**Tang-dynasty style architecture of the modern Shaanxi History Museum**

**★ Shang Cooking Pot**
*The ogre-mask motif of this vessel is indicative of the Shang society's absorption in the world of nature spirits and supernatural beings. The bronzes of the Shang era are regarded as the dynasty's most significant creative achievement.*

**Zhou Wine Decanter**
*Capped with a lid in the shape of a tiger and incorporating a tail-shaped handle, this ox-shaped zun (a type of wine vessel) was excavated in 1967. The elaborate surface pattern is typical of Zhou-dynasty animistic design.*

**Entrance**

## KEY TO FLOORPLAN

- ☐ Pre-history
- ☐ Shang and Zhou Dynasties
- ☐ Qin Dynasty
- ☐ Han Dynasty
- ☐ Northern and Southern Dynasties
- ☐ Tang Dynasty
- ☐ Song to Qing Dynasties
- ☐ Special exhibitions
- ☐ Non-exhibition space

**Tiger-shaped Tally**
*Inscribed with the archaic script used for Qin official texts, this remarkable bronze artifact was issued to generals to authorize the mobilization of troops.*

## STAR SIGHTS

★ Shang Cooking Pot

★ Tang *Sancai* Horse

*For hotels and restaurants in this region see pp558–9 and pp585–6*

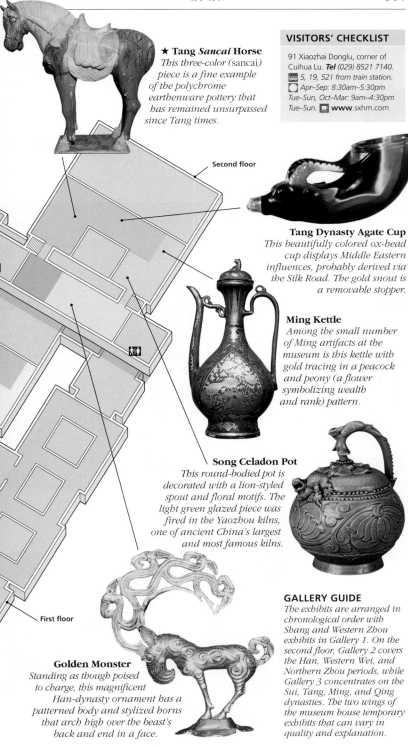

★ **Tang *Sancai* Horse**
This three-color (sancai)
piece is a fine example
of the polychrome
earthenware pottery that
has remained unsurpassed
since Tang times.

Second floor

**Tang Dynasty Agate Cup**
This beautifully colored ox-head
cup displays Middle Eastern
influences, probably derived via
the Silk Road. The gold snout is
a removable stopper.

**Ming Kettle**
Among the small number
of Ming artifacts at the
museum is this kettle with
gold tracing in a peacock
and peony (a flower
symbolizing wealth
and rank) pattern.

**Song Celadon Pot**
This round-bodied pot is
decorated with a lion-styled
spout and floral motifs. The
light green glazed piece was
fired in the Yaozhou kilns,
one of ancient China's largest
and most famous kilns.

First floor

**Golden Monster**
Standing as though poised
to charge, this magnificent
Han-dynasty ornament has a
patterned body and stylized horns
that arch high over the beast's
back and end in a face.

**GALLERY GUIDE**
The exhibits are arranged in
chronological order with
Shang and Western Zhou
exhibits in Gallery 1. On the
second floor, Gallery 2 covers
the Han, Western Wei, and
Northern Zhou periods, while
Gallery 3 concentrates on the
Sui, Tang, Ming, and Qing
dynasties. The two wings of
the museum house temporary
exhibits that can vary in
quality and explanation.

# Terracotta Army ❷

兵马俑

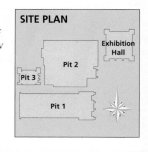

The Terracotta Army was discovered in 1974 by peasants digging a well. The awesome ranks of life-size pottery figures, modeled from yellow clay, were made to guard the tomb of Qin Shi Huangdi, despotic ruler who unified China over 2,200 years ago *(see p54)*. Excavations yielded three pits and over 7,000 soldiers, archers, and horses. Pit 1 contains the infantry; Pit 2 (still being excavated) is filled with cavalry and soldiers; and Pit 3 (partially unexcavated) seems to be the command center, with 70 high-ranking officers. Each warrior, originally colored with pigment and holding a weapon, has an individually crafted expression.

**Bell, tomb of Shi Huangdi**

## SITE PLAN

Exhibition Hall

Pit 2

Pit 3

Pit 1

### ★ Army in Pit 1

*The most impressive pit contains over 6,000 warriors, arrayed in battle formation. The rear of the vault is strewn with smashed heads and fragments yet to be assembled.*

### High-ranking Officer

*Dressed commandingly in a long, two-layered knee-length tunic, this imposing figure is distinguished both by his regalia and by being taller than the pottery infantry figures he appears to oversee.*

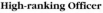

**The pottery horses** have been assembled from broken fragments, like the warriors around them.

### Original Decoration

*All of the figures were originally painted in vivid colors similar to this replica. Some retain traces of paint, but most of them faded after exposure to air.*

## STAR SIGHTS

★ Army in Pit 1

★ Kneeling Archer

### Infantry

*The pottery warriors were originally equipped with weapons, including swords, spears, and bows and arrows, many of which have rotted.*

★ **Kneeling Archer**
*Cloaked in upper-body armor and kneeling in a state of preparation, this archer is alert although his wooden bow has disintegrated. His square-toed shoes are studded for extra grip.*

**The earth-walled corridors** that house the warriors were originally roofed with wooden rafters.

**Individual details**
*The intricacy is astonishing, especially in the careful execution of individual hairstyles on the hand-sculpted heads. Further artistry is evident in the detailed belts, clothing, and footwear.*

**Restoring the army**
*The work to excavate and restore the terracotta figures continues to this day. Each warrior is unique and must be painstakingly reassembled by a team.*

## QIN SHI HUANGDI'S TOMB

The Terracotta Army is just one part, the defending army, of a complex necropolis. A mile west of the pits, a large hill, yet to be fully excavated, is believed to be the burial mound of emperor Qin Shi, a tyrant preoccupied with death and the legacy he would leave behind. He spared no expense, enlisting 700,000 people over 36 years in the tomb's construction. Historical sources portray a miniature plan of his empire: a floor cut by rivers of mercury beneath a ceiling studded with pearls to represent the night sky. The complex is also said to contain 48 tombs for concubines who were buried alive with the emperor, a fate also reserved for workers, to prevent the location and design of the tomb from becoming known. Two marvelous bronze chariots, originally housed in wooden coffins, were unearthed near the burial mound, and laboriously reassembled. Half actual size, one is made up of over 3,600 metal pieces.

**One of the bronze chariots, on display in the Exhibition Hall**

Colorful fresco in the tomb of Yi De, Qian Ling

## Xi'an: Farther Afield

The several worthwhile sights around Xi'an are best visited by the Western Tour buses that depart from Xi'an train station in the morning. Located 15 miles (25 km) northeast, the modern city of Xianyang, China's first dynastic capital, is mainly visited for its museum and the surrounding imperial tombs. Housed in a former Confucian Temple, the **Xianyang City Museum** displays relics from Qin and Han times, and its highlight is an army of 3,000 miniature terracotta soldiers excavated from a nearby tomb. **Mao Ling** (Mao Tomb), 25 miles (40 km) west of Xi'an, is the tomb of the Han emperor Wudi (141–87 BC). The largest of the Han tombs in the surrounding region, it has a museum that houses stone sculptures and further relics from the tomb complex. The impressive **Qian Ling** (Qian Tomb), 50 miles (80 km) northwest of Xi'an, is the burial site of the Tang

**Stele in Yi De's Tomb, Qian Ling**

Gaozong emperor and his wife, the indomitable Wu Zetian (see pp58–9). The Imperial Way is lined with stone figures, while the southeast section of the area contains 17 lesser tombs, including the vividly frescoed tombs of Prince Zhang Huai, the emperor's second son, and crown prince Yi De, the emperor's grandson. The mountainside mausoleum of the Tang Taizong emperor lies at **Zhao Ling** (Zhao Tomb), 43 miles (70 km) northwest of Xi'an.

Situated 74 miles (120 km) northwest of Xi'an, the remote **Famen Temple** is well worth the long journey. This shrine is one of China's first Buddhist temples, and a venerated place for Buddhist pilgrims the world over. It was built in the 2nd century AD to house a finger bone of Sakyamuni (the Historical Buddha) donated by the Indian king Ashoka, who was dispensing Buddhist relics (sarira) among Buddhist lands.

The sacred bone enjoyed extensive veneration, and was periodically removed from the temple crypt and paraded through the streets of Xi'an during the height of the Tang era. After the dynasty's fall, the crypt was lost in obscurity, possibly as a result of anti-Buddhist purges. It is surprising that the crypt remained hidden for so long, as pagodas often have vaults for storing relics and Buddhist ornaments. In the 1980s, an exploration following a partial collapse of the pagoda exposed the crypt, along with its relics and Tang-dynasty riches. Today, the finger bone is once again preserved in a crypt, while the temple museum displays many Tang-era artifacts. The sacred bone is occasionally taken abroad, as it was in 2003, when it went to Taipei in Taiwan.

🏛 **Xianyang City Museum**
Zhongshan Lu. ☐ 8am–5pm Tue–Sun.

🚍 **Mao, Qian & Zhao Ling**
🚌 number 3 from Xi'an station.
🚗 ☐ daily. 🎫

🚍 **Famen Temple**
🚌 from Xi'an station, 4 shuttles daily from 7:30am. 🚗 ☐ 8am–5:30pm daily. 🎫

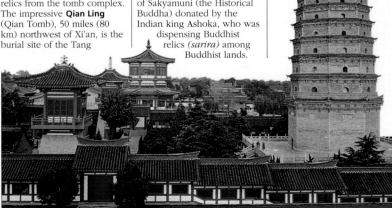

The 12-storied pagoda at the Famen Temple, now restored to its former glory

Pilgrims and hikers winding their way up North Peak, Hua Shan

# Hua Shan ❸
## 华山

*75 miles (120 km) E of Xi'an.* 🚉 *from X'ian to Menyuan, then bus.* 🚉 *from X'ian train station to Huayin, then shuttle to entrance.* 🚡 *Cable car available.*

The westernmost and loftiest of China's five Daoist peaks, the 8,563-ft (2,610-m) high Hua Shan is characterized by steep ascents, precipitous gullies, and peerless views. Crowned by five peaks (North, South, East, West, and Central), and towering southwest of the Yellow River as it loops east along the Henan-Shanxi border, Hua Shan (Flower Mountain) was traditionally likened to a lotus bloom. Also known by its other name, Xiyue (Western Peak), the mountain is believed to be presided over by the Daoist God of Hua Shan. For centuries, it was a magnet for hermits and ascetics in pursuit of immortality, and its crags and crannies still teem with Daoist myths. Its numerous temples have dwindled over the years, although several survive perched on the mountain.

Hikers can either drift to North Peak by cable car from the station at the eastern base, or make the strenuous 3–5 hour trek along with hordes of pilgrims from Huayin. From North Peak, you can either descend or follow the trail along the ridge to the other four peaks lying to the south. Spring and autumn are the best seasons to climb Hua Shan, since summers and winters are extreme. Nighttime ascents can also be made. It is best to carry food with you, though refreshments are available from vendors and at hotels along the trail. Wear shoes or boots with a rugged grip as certain sections are treacherous. Near the summits, bunches of padlocks hang on chains. According to the custom, couples have their names engraved on them and then lock them here forever. Accommodation is available in Huayin and on the mountain itself for overnight stays and watching the sunrise from East Peak.

# Yan'an ❹
## 延安

*155 miles (250 km) N of Xi'an.* 🏛 *200,000.* ✈ 🚉 *from Xi'an and Beijing.* 🚌

The quiet town of Yan'an, set within the ribbed loess hills of northern Shaanxi, is best explored by train from Xi'an. Yan'an lures Mao fans, since the town was the Communist Party's headquarters for a decade after the culmination of the Long March (*see p256*) in October 1935. In the north of town, the **Yan'an Revolutionary Museum** houses a display of Communist relics, including Mao's stuffed horse, weapons, photographs, and uniforms (few captions are in English). Not far from the museum lies the **Wangjiaping Revolution Headquarters Site**, where Mao and other front-rank party leaders worked and lived. The **Fenghuang Shan Lu Revolution Headquarters Site**, the early residence of the Communists, houses memorabilia of prominent officers. Perched on a hill southeast of town, and with impressive views, is the Ming-dynasty **Yan'an Bao Pagoda**, which sometimes features Communist memorabilia.

🏛 **Yan'an Revolutionary Museum**
Zaoyuan Lu. ⏰ *8am–5pm daily.* 🎫
🏯 **Wangjiaping Revolution Headquarters Site**
Zaoyuan Lu. ⏰ *7:30–11:30am, 2:30–5:30pm daily.* 🎫

Padlocks engraved with couples' names, Hua Shan

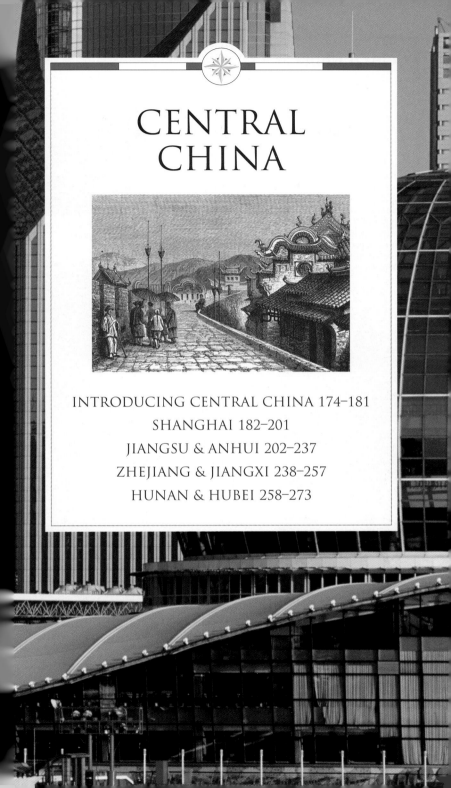

# CENTRAL CHINA

# Central China at a Glance

Dominated by the mighty Yangzi River, China's central region encompasses the east coast port city of Shanghai and the six provinces of Jiangsu, Anhui, Zhejiang, Jiangxi, Hunan, and Hubei, that fan out from it to the north, south, and west. The region is rich in historic sights as well as natural beauty, including the attractive city of Nanjing, with its largely intact city wall, and the splendid scenery around Zhejiang's West Lake and Anhui's Huang Shan mountain. The cultured cities of Hangzhou and Suzhou lie on the banks of the Grand Canal, one of the greatest engineering feats in China's early history. A more up-to-date colossal feat of construction, the Three Gorges Dam, on the Yangzi River in Hubei, is the world's largest.

View from Jiuhua Shan, a sacred Buddhist mountains

Tranquil scene in Shizi Lin (Lion Grove Garden), Suzhou

Hanzhong

WUDANG SHAN
XIANGFAN
207
318
YICHANG
ENSHI
WUHAN
Yangzi Jiang
WULINGYUAN
YUEYANG
107
319
CHANGSHA
320
HENGSHAN
322
TONGDAO
YONGZHOU
JINGGANG SI
Liuzhou
106
DAOXIAN
323
Xiao Shui
Wuzhou

## GETTING AROUND

The region's main airport hub is Shanghai, although other international airports include Nanjing, Hangzhou, Wuhan, Ningbo, and Changsha. Many towns and cities in the region have domestic airports, but unless time is really an issue, it can be more pleasurable to travel by train. The rail network has been upgraded and high speed CRH "bullet" trains operate on selected inter-city routes. Both the Grand Canal and the Yangzi River operate tourist ferry or canal-boat services, but in the remote mountainous regions such as Wudang Shan in northern Hubei, and Jinggang Shan in southern Jiangxi, bus travel is the most expedient means of transport.

### KEY

≡ Expressway

═ National Highway

── Minor road

▲ Mountain area

◁ Futuristic architecture along the banks of the Huangpu River, Pudong, Shanghai

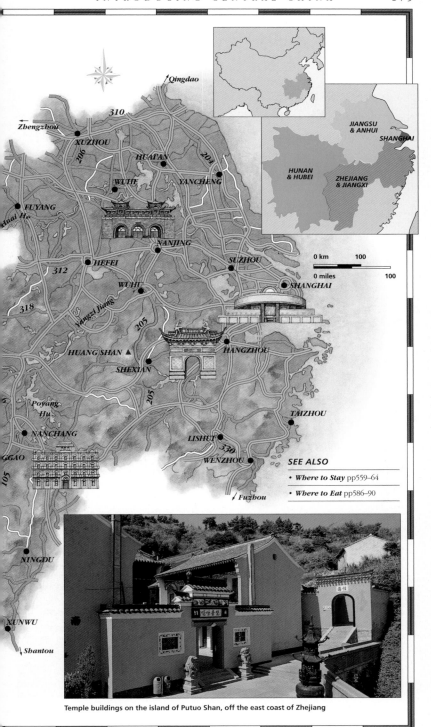

Qingdao

Zhengzhou

310

JIANGSU & ANHUI

SHANGHAI

HUNAN & HUBEI

ZHEJIANG & JIANGXI

XUZHOU

206

HUAI'AN

204

WUHE

YANCHENG

FUYANG

Huai He

312

NANJING

HEFEI

SUZHOU

0 km 100

318

WUHU

SHANGHAI

0 miles 100

Yangzi Jiang

205

HUANG SHAN ▲

HANGZHOU

SHEXIAN

205

Poyang Hu

TAIZHOU

NANCHANG

LISHUI

GGAO

330

WENZHOU

105

**SEE ALSO**

• *Where to Stay* pp559–64

• *Where to Eat* pp586–90

NINGDU

XUNWU

Shantou

Fuzhou

Temple buildings on the island of Putuo Shan, off the east coast of Zhejiang

# A PORTRAIT OF CENTRAL CHINA

*From the modern city of* Shanghai *to the historic and picturesque canal towns, Central China encapsulates the essence of the country and its culture. The region can also be considered the crucible of modern China, as many of the stirring historical events that shaped the nation took place here in the early 20th century.*

The Yangzi (Chang Jiang), which flows into the East China Sea just below Shanghai, is the thread that binds all of Central China together. The combination of water and silt has fertilized vast areas, especially around Wuhan, referred to as "China's Grain Basket", or the "Land of Fish and Rice." Despite its tendency to flood, the river has for centuries been a vital conduit for China's trade, crowded with sampans and junks, as observed by Marco Polo in the 13th century, as well as tea clippers in the 19th century and ferries and cruise ships today. The river has also accelerated the country's development: without the Yangzi there would have been no Grand Canal and no Shanghai. Now, with the controversial construction of the Three Gorges Dam, the river has been used again to supply the requirements of China's vast, clamorous population.

Ornately-styled garden gate in Yangzhou

Shanghai, which actually sits on the Huangpu River, a small tributary of the Yangzi, is something of an upstart, despite its reputation. A small provincial town until the mid-19th century, it evolved to become China's greatest city. Even after the Cultural Revolution it remained the country's fashion and shopping capital as well as a great industrial powerhouse. It is, today, one of the most visible symbols of "new" China's vitality and dynamism. A comprehensive urban makeover took place ahead of Shanghai hosting the 2010 World Expo, and the city has positioned itself as a world financial center.

View of the futuristic Pudong skyline from the Bund promenade, Shanghai

Tour boats on one of Tongli's many canals

Politically too, Shanghai's impact has been enormous; it was the site of the first meeting of the Chinese Communist Party and the spawning ground for the Cultural Revolution and the Gang of Four, all of whom had strong connections with the city.

In fact, nearly all of the major political events of 20th-century China took place in its central provinces. Nanjing, the first Ming capital, was also Chiang Kai-shek's Republican center. Chairman Mao was born and educated, and began his revolutionary activities in Hunan. In Jiangxi, the 1927 Nanchang Uprising was the rallying point for the creation of the Red Army, while the same province was the starting point of the Long March. That revolution should ignite so easily was not surprising, since Anhui, Hunan, and Jiangxi, large parts of which are mountainous and remote from the Yangzi and seats of power, have always been associated with appalling poverty.

However, long before the fall of the last emperor, this was where many of the greatest features of

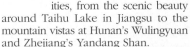

Detail from the Ming Palace Ruins, Nanjing

pre-Revolutionary Chinese culture flowered during the brilliance of the Song and Ming dynasties. Before establishing their capital in Peking, the Ming left their mark on Nanjing, as evidenced by the huge Ming tomb and formidable city wall, while Hangzhou, a former Song capital, is the location of the West Lake, one of China's most scenic places. Just as remarkable are the region's gardens and workshops producing silk embroidery and porcelain. Suzhou, in Jiangsu, has to some extent retained some of its ancient charm and is renowned for its private gardens, which have survived the upheavals of recent history largely intact. Porcelain production continues alongside the historic imperial kilns of Jingdezhen, while silk, produced throughout parts of the region, is still a major export, as it was a thousand years ago.

Considering that Central China is a heavily populated region largely shaped by man's manipulation of nature, it is surprising that there are still large areas of wilderness to enjoy. This is best illustrated in the legend of the Wild Man, China's equivalent of the Yeti, who is said to haunt Shennongjia in Hubei. For those wishing to escape urban or pastoral China, there are many opportunities, from the scenic beauty around Taihu Lake in Jiangsu to the mountain vistas at Hunan's Wulingyuan and Zhejiang's Yandang Shan.

Suspension bridge at the Divine Cliffs, Yandang Shan

# Traditional Chinese Gardens

**Lotus, a favorite symbolic flower**

The Chinese garden developed as a synthesis of two concepts linked in Daoist philosophy *(see p31)* – scenery and serenity: the contemplation of nature in isolated meditation led to enlightenment. Therefore, the educated and wealthy built natural-looking retreats for themselves within an urban environment. The garden creates poetic and painterly concepts, and aims to improve on nature by creating a picture that looks natural but is in fact entirely artificial. For this the Chinese garden designer used four main elements: rocks, water, plants, and architecture.

**Classical Chinese garden design** *was considered a type of three-dimensional landscape painting or solid poetry.*

**Rocks:** *There were two main kinds of rock – the eroded limestones from lakes, often used as sculptures, or the yellow rock piled up to recall mountains and caves to the mind of the viewer. The beauty and realism of the rockery usually determined the success or failure of the garden.*

**Water:** *An essential element of life, water also could be used in the garden as a mirror and so appear to increase the size of the garden. Water also serves as a contrasting partner and therefore a balance to the hard stone. Finally it is a home for goldfish, symbols of good fortune.*

**Corridors, paths, and bridges** *link the different areas and give the artist control over how the views are presented to the visitor.*

**Interiors** *of pavilions were important as the venues for creativity. A lot of care was taken to select an appropriate and poetic name for each building.*

**Patterns and mosaics** *brighten up the garden and are also symbolic. Cranes represent longevity, while the yin and yang symbol often appears where a path forks in two.*

## GARDEN VIEWS

Using these four elements the garden is like a series of tableaux painted onto a roll of silk. One by one they come before your eyes just as the artist intended them to. As you follow the paths, you see just what he wanted you to see. These may be borrowed views, where the scenery from somewhere else is made to look part of the picture; hidden views, where you round a corner to come upon an unexpected scene; or contrasting views where leafy bamboo softens the view of rock, or opposite views as the *yin* element water balances the *yang* element rock.

**A moon gate** *is a round door that neatly frames a view as though it were a picture. Gates can be square-, jar-, or even book-shaped.*

**Patterned screens** *allow in a certain amount of light and may be used to cast patterned shadows on white walls. They are also sometimes used to give tempting partial views through to other areas of the garden.*

**Plants:** *Plants were used sparingly and usually for their symbolic qualities. Thus the lotus is purity, as it flowers from the mud; bamboo is resolve, it is difficult to break; plum is vigor, as it blooms in winter; the pine is longevity, for it is an evergreen; the imperial peony, is wealth.*

**Buildings:** *An intrinsic part of the garden, these pavilions and waterside halls provide a place for contemplation and more importantly a specific viewpoint, as well as shelter from the sun and rain. They could range from open kiosks to multi-story halls and meeting rooms.*

## PENJING

Dating as far back as the Tang dynasty (618–907), *penjing* is the art of creating a miniature landscape in a container. Not limited to small trees, the artist may use rocks and specially cultivated plants to portray a scene of natural beauty, as though it were a landscape painting. As well as being beautiful, the harmony in these creations is seen as the spiritual expression of man's relationship with nature, the meeting of the temporal with the omnipresent. Often part of a Chinese garden will be devoted to the display or cultivation of this delicate art.

**The Chinese art of** *penjing,* **the forerunner to Japanese bonsai**

# Regional Food: Central China

Traditionally referred to as the "Lands of Fish and Rice," Central China is one of the country's leading agricultural regions with some of the most fertile land. Both wheat and rice are grown here as well as barley, corn, sweet potatoes, peanuts, and soybeans. Freshwater fisheries abound in the network of lakes and rivers, while deep-sea fishing has long been established in the coastal provinces. In the holy mountains of Huang Shan and Jiuhua Shan, Buddhist vegetarianism has also influenced the region's cuisine. Hunan's cuisine is like Sichuanese food but even spicier *(see pp346–7)*.

**Garlic chives and bok choi**

**Market stall displaying the wide variety of dried goods available**

## SHANGHAI

The characteristics of Shanghai cuisine are summarized as "exquisite in appearance, rich in flavor, and sweet in taste." A favorite winter delicacy is the hairy crab from the Yangzi estuary (although over-fishing means they come from elsewhere). A relatively new city, Shanghai has not really developed its own cuisine,

although it has its own famous filled dumplings called *xiao long bao*. Instead the city's main influences are older schools of cuisine – Huaiyang and Suzhe. Another culinary influence is the Buddhist school of cuisine. Strangely, the best Buddhist vegetarian restaurants are to

be found in Shanghai – a city with a racy reputation. Maybe the sinners want to redeem themselves by abstaining from meat occasionally. Often these dishes have similar names to meat dishes and, thanks to the skilful use of soy sauce, tofu, gluten, and agar, they can look and even taste like meat.

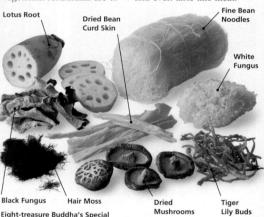

**Lotus Root**

**Dried Bean Curd Skin**

**Fine Bean Noodles**

**White Fungus**

**Black Fungus**   **Hair Moss**

**Eight-treasure Buddha's Special**

**Dried Mushrooms**

**Tiger Lily Buds**

## REGIONAL DISHES AND SPECIALTIES

Two of the area's great cities, Nanjing and Hangzhou, were at different times capitals in central China. Whenever there was a change of capital, the vast Imperial kitchens changed location bringing the staff with them, which resulted in a cross-fertilization of recipes and methods from one region to another. One favorite imperial dish despite its lowly name is Beggar's Chicken – a whole chicken is stuffed with vegetables and herbs, wrapped in lotus leaves, and encased in clay before being baked. The clay container is then broken at the table releasing the beautiful aromas. A central China specialty (but actually enjoyed all over) is red fermented bean curd. This has a pungent, cheese-like flavor that is also very savory and appears in vegetarian and meat dishes alike. Fresh water crabs are best during October and November, simply steamed with spring onions, ginger, soy, sugar and vinegar.

**Fermzented Bean Curd**

**Lions' Heads** *pork meatballs braised with Chinese leaf – meant to look like lions' heads and manes.*

## HUAIYANG & SUZHE

Based specifically around the deltas of the Huai and Yangzi Rivers, Huaiyang cuisine is most famous for its excellent fish and shellfish – the freshwater crabs from Tai Hu are superb. Suzhe cuisine, however, covers a wider area – the provinces of Jiangsu and Zhejiang – and includes culinary centers such as Nanjing and Hangzhou that both served as capital cities. Along with stews flavored with a light stock, the region is famous for its "red cooking" – food braised in soy sauce, sugar, ginger, and rice wine. "Chinkiang Vinegar" is black rice vinegar from Zhenjiang, Jiangsu, and is acknowledged to be the best

**Eels, a popular ingredient from the rivers of central China**

rice vinegar in China.

The province of Zhejiang, of course, produces China's best rice wines from Shaoxing and top quality hams from Jinhua. It is also worth trying the Long Jing (Dragon Well) green tea grown around West Lake in Hangzhou.

**Park cafés – popular places to snack on some filled dumplings**

## ANHUI

Further inland is the little known Anhui cuisine, which has a long history, but is often overlooked by visitors. Despite being landlocked, Anhui still enjoys a lot of fish thanks to its network of lakes and rivers. The province is also one of the leading agricultural regions in China, producing a great number and variety of crops and vegetables. One of Anhui's famed ingredients are its tender white bamboo shoots. These crisp shoots feature prominently in the vegetarian cuisine prepared in the lofty Buddhist mountain retreats and are often combined with a variety of exotic woodland mushrooms. Finally the world-famous Keemun red tea – it is actually black – comes from the humid hills of Qimen in south Anhui.

### ON THE MENU

**Beggars Chicken** A whole chicken stuffed with flavorings and cooked in a clay pot.

**Fried Prawns in Shells** Prawns still in their shells are rapidly fried and then braised in a soy and tomato sauce.

**Three-layer Shreds** Steamed shredded ham, chicken, and pork with bamboo shoots and black mushroom – should be called five-layer shreds.

**Fresh Water Crabs** Simply steamed with scallions, ginger, soy, sugar, and vinegar.

**Steamed Belly Pork with Ground Rice** Also known as Double-braised Pork, this long-cooked dish literally melts in your mouth.

**Eight-treasure Buddha's Special** A generic name for a delicious vegetarian dish which can actually contain any number of different ingredients.

**Tofu Casserole** *tofu with sea cucumbers, ham, prawns, mushrooms, bamboo shoots, and bok choi in a stew pot.*

**Squirrel Fish** *a bream is filleted, coated with batter, deep-fried, and served with a sweet-and-sour sauce.*

**Sweet & Sour Spare Ribs** *Deep-fried bite-size pork spare ribs braised in soy, sugar, and vinegar.*

# SHANGHAI

*Straddling both banks of the Huangpu River, close to the mouth of the mighty Yangzi on China's eastern seaboard, Shanghai is the nation's largest and most dynamic city, with a population of more than 19 million people. It is an autonomous municipality, and an explosion of economic and industrial development has made it one of the fastest growing cities in the world.*

By Chinese standards, the development of Shanghai, which means "above the sea," is a recent phenomenon. In the 13th century it became a minor county seat and so it remained until the mid-19th century when British commercial ambitions led to war with China. The ensuing Treaty of Nanking allowed the British to trade freely from certain ports, including Shanghai. The city soon became an outpost of glamor, high living, and ultimately decadence. It was divided into "concessions," where foreign nationals lived in miniature versions of first Britain, then France, the US, and Japan. The Bund or quay along the Huangpu is still lined with concession-era buildings, evidence of a time when Shanghai was the third largest financial center in the world. In 1949, the Communists took over and the city was stripped of its grandeur.

However, in 1990, the Pudong area across the river from the Bund was declared a Special Economic Zone, and a revival started. Investments poured in; flyovers, malls, and hotels sprang up, and shining metal and glass skyscrapers towered above the Huangpu. This infrastructure boom has skyrocketed into the new millennium. Both airports have been upgraded, an international cruise port has opened, and new roads, subway lines, hotels, and offices were built for the 2010 World Expo.

Exterior of the renowned Shanghai Museum

◁ Visitors throng the zig-zag bridge to the Huxingting Teahouse in Shanghai's Old City

# Exploring Shanghai

Of Shanghai's three main areas, the Old City to the south is typically Chinese, with alleys, markets, and temples. It is also the site of the Yu Gardens (Yu Yuan), Shanghai's finest traditional garden. The former concession areas comprise the French Concession to the Old City's west and the British and American Concessions – collectively known as the International Settlement – to its north. Here are the Bund, the riverside promenade lined with grand colonial buildings, including the Fairmont Peace Hotel and the Waldorf Astoria Hotel, and the city's two main shopping streets, Nanjing Road and Huaihai Road. Pudong, Shanghai's newest district, on the Huangpu's east bank, has some of the world's highest commercial buildings.

**LOCATOR MAP**
See Map pp174–75

**SEE ALSO**

## SIGHTS AT A GLANCE

**Historic Buildings, Sites & Neighborhoods**
*The Bund pp186–7* ❶
French Concession ❾
Longhua Cemetery of Martyrs ⓰
Pudong ❺
Shanghai Exhibition Center ❿
Site of the First National Congress of the Chinese Communist Party ❼
Soong Qingling's Former Residence ⓮

**Temples & Churches**
Jade Buddha Temple ⓬
Jing'an Temple ⓫
Xujiahui Catholic Cathedral ⓯

**Parks & Gardens**
Fuxing Park ❽
Hongkou Park ⓭
People's Park & Square ❸
*Yu Gardens & Bazaar pp192–3* ❻

**Museums**
*Shanghai Museum pp190–91* ❹

**Towns**
Song Jiang ⓲

**Shops & Markets**
Nanjing Road ❷

**Areas of Natural Beauty**
She Shan ⓱

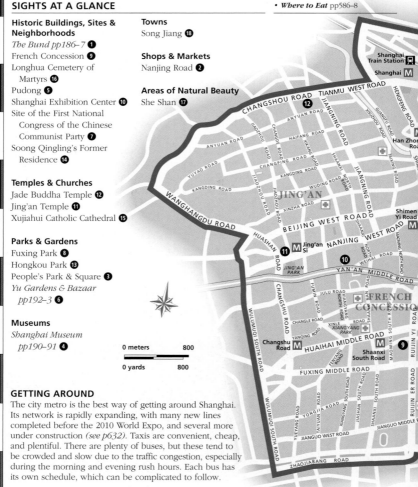

0 meters 800
0 yards 800

## GETTING AROUND

The city metro is the best way of getting around Shanghai. Its network is rapidly expanding, with many new lines completed before the 2010 World Expo, and several more under construction (*see p632*). Taxis are convenient, cheap, and plentiful. There are plenty of buses, but these tend to be crowded and slow due to the traffic congestion, especially during the morning and evening rush hours. Each bus has its own schedule, which can be complicated to follow.

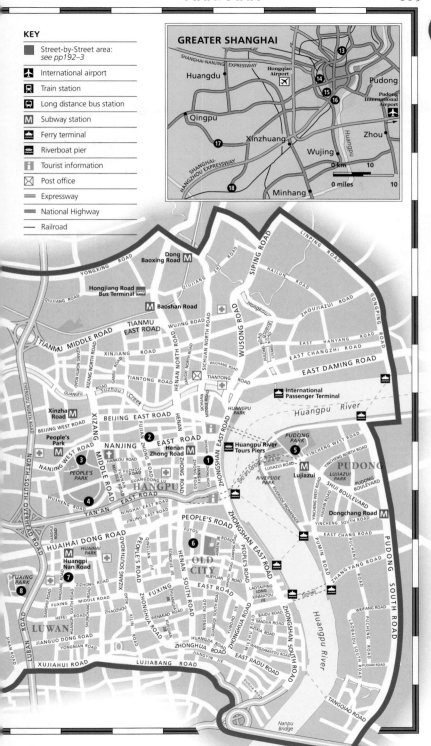

## KEY

- Street-by-Street area: *see pp192–3*
- ✈ International airport
- 🚆 Train station
- 🚌 Long distance bus station
- Ⓜ Subway station
- ⛴ Ferry terminal
- 🚢 Riverboat pier
- 🛈 Tourist information
- ⊠ Post office
- ═ Expressway
- ═ National Highway
- — Railroad

### GREATER SHANGHAI

SHANGHAI–NANJING EXPRESSWAY

Huangdu

Hongqiao Airport ✈

**13**

**14**

Pudong

**15**

**16**

Pudong International Airport ✈

Qingpu

Zhou

**17**

Xinzhuang

Huangpu

Wujing

0 km        10

0 miles     10

SHANGHAI–HANGZHOU EXPRESSWAY

**18**

Minhang

### Map labels

YONGXING ROAD

Dong Baoxing Road Ⓜ

SIPING ROAD

LINPING ROAD

Hongjiang Road Bus Terminal

QIUJIANG ROAD

HAILUN ROAD

Ⓜ Baoshan Road

ZHOUJIAZUI ROAD

GONGPING ROAD

TIANMU MIDDLE ROAD

TIANMU EAST ROAD

WUJING ROAD

WUSONG ROAD

Hongkou

EAST HANYANG ROAD

XINJIANG ROAD

SICHUAN NORTH ROAD

EAST CHANGZHI ROAD

XIZANG NORTH ROAD

HENAN NORTH ROAD

JIANGXI NORTHROAD

WUCHANG ROAD

EAST DAMING ROAD

TIANTONG ROAD

GANSU ROAD

⊠

TIANTONG ROAD

GUANGFU

Suzhou Creek

SICHUAN MIDDLE ROAD

HUANGPU PARK

International Passenger Terminal

Huangpu River

Xinzha Road Ⓜ

BEIJING WEST ROAD

BEIJING EAST ROAD

FUJIAN ROAD

HENAN ROAD

ZHONG ROAD

People's Park

XIZANG

NANJING EAST ROAD

**2**

Henan Zhong Road

🛈

ZHONGSHAN EAST ROAD

**1**

PUDONG PARK

**5**

Huangpu River Tours Piers

YINCHENG WEST ROAD

**3**

MIDDLE ROAD

Hankou Road

FUZHOU ROAD

GUANGDONG LU

Yan'an Dong Tunnel

Ⓜ Lujiazui

LUJIAZUI ROAD

YINCHENG NORTH ROAD

PUDONG

NANJING WEST ROAD

PEOPLE'S PARK

HUANGPU

RIVERSIDE PARK

LUJIAZUI PARK

PUDONG BOULEVARD

**4**

WUSHENG ROAD

YAN'AN EAST ROAD

NINGHAI EAST ROAD

JINLING EAST ROAD

SHIJI BOULEVARD

Dongchang Road Ⓜ

NORTH-SOUTH OVERHEAD ROAD

PEOPLE'S ROAD

YINCHENG SOUTH ROAD

HUAIHAI DONG ROAD

HUAIHAI PARK

FUYOU

PEOPLE'S ROAD

EAST CHANG ROAD

Huangpi Nan Road Ⓜ

DASHIJIE ROAD

PEOPLE'S ROAD

QINGLIAN

SONGXUE JIE

ANREN

DAJING ROAD

DAMING

PUMIN ROAD

PUDONG SOUTH ROAD

**6**

OLD CITY

XUEYUAN

PUCHENG ROAD

ZHANG YANG ROAD

FUXING PARK

**7**

ZIZHONG ROAD

XIZANG SOUTH ROAD

ZHANGJIA

HENAN SOUTH ROAD

FUXING EAST ROAD

GUANGQI

ZHONGHUA ROAD

LAOTAIPING LONG

XINMATOU XIN

ZHONGSHAN EAST ROAD

Tunnel

WEIFANG ROAD

**8**

MADANG ROAD

FUXING MIDDLE ROAD

HEFEI ROAD

BROADWAY

ZHAOZHOU

XILIN

NINGHE

GUANGJ

JIE

BAIDU ROAD

MAOJIA ROAD

SUJIA ROAD

BAIDU ROAD

WANGJIAMATOU ROAD

Tunnel

LAOBAIDU SOUTH ROAD

PUCHENG SOUTH ROAD

LUWAN

DANSHUI ROAD

JIANGUO DONG ROAD

YONGNIAN ROAD

ZHONGHUA ROAD

NINGHE ROAD

HUANGJIA

ZHONGHUA

JIANGYIN JIE

METAU JIE

EAST JIADU ROAD

ZHONGSHAN SOUTH ROAD

PUDIAN ROAD

SHAN ROAD

LUBAN ROAD

XUJIAHUI ROAD

LUJIABANG ROAD

DUOTA ROAD

TANGQIAO ROAD

Huangpu River

Nanpu Bridge

# The Bund ❶
## 外滩

**Lion, symbol of colonial power**

Some places are forever associated with a single landmark and in the case of Shanghai it is surely the Bund. Also known as Zhongshan East 1 Road, the Bund was at the heart of the post-1842 concession era, flanked on one side by the Huangpu River and on the other by the hotels, banks, offices, and clubs that were the grandiose symbols of western commercial power. Most of the old buildings are still in place and a walk along here can easily absorb a couple of pleasant hours. The area was redeveloped for the 2010 World Expo.

**The Bund, at its peak the third biggest financial center in world**

★ **Shanghai Pudong Development Bank**
*Built in 1921, it was said to be the most beautiful building in Asia. Inside there are delightful murals.*

★ **Customs House**
*The entrance hall is decorated with some handsome marine mosaics.*

**The bronze lions'** paws and head are rubbed for good luck.

**Russo-Asiatic Bank Building**

**Former Bank of Communications**

★ **River promenade**
*The riverside of the Bund is a wonderful place for taking a stroll, watching the river traffic, and viewing the varied Pudong skyline.*

## STAR SIGHTS

★ River promenade

★ Shanghai Pudong Development Bank

★ Customs House

★ Views of Pudong

★ **Views of Pudong**
*In the evening the Bund throngs with people enjoying the river breeze and the spectacular lights of Pudong's modern skyline (see p189).*

**Bank of China**
*Blending 1920s American and traditional Chinese styles, this impressive block was built by a rival of Sassoon, H.H. Kung.*

**Former Palace Hotel**
*The Palace Hotel was built in 1906 and was one of the best hotels in Shanghai. It is now called the Swatch Art Palace Hotel.*

**Chartered Bank Building** of India, Australia, and China.

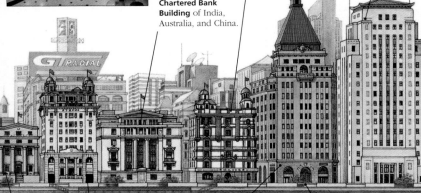

**Former Bank of Taiwan**

**North China Daily News Building**

**Chen Yi's statue**
*The bronze statue looking down the Bund is not Chairman Mao but Chen Yi, revolutionary commander and first mayor of Shanghai after 1949.*

**Fairmont Peace Hotel**
*The most distinctive building on the Bund was built in 1930 by the millionaire, Sir Victor Sassoon. Famous visitors include actor Charlie Chaplin and playright Noel Coward.*

# Nanjing Road ❷
## 南京路

Ⓜ *Nanjing Road West (for Nanjing Road).*

Running west from the Bund, Nanjing Road has historically been considered Shanghai's foremost shopping street, despite competition from areas such as chic Huaihai Road. The street is divided in two – Nanjing Road East runs from the Bund to People's Square, after which it becomes Nanjing Road West, a total length of 6 miles (10 km). The traditional "shopper's paradise" is along pedestrianized Nanjing Road East, which is filled with upscale brand malls, stores, and boutiques. Theaters, cinemas, restaurants, beauty salons, and crowds of shoppers complete the picture. Before 1949, all the major stores were located here. One of them, the Sun Department Store, is now the **Shanghai No.1 Department Store**, which attracts 100,000 customers every day with its exotic window displays. As window shopping is such a popular pastime, the pedestrianized section of Nanjing Road East between People's Park and the Bund, with its numerous 1930s European-style buildings, is perpetually busy. The road culminates on People's Square in front of the **Pacific Hotel**,

The impressive Shanghai Grand Theater

with its impressive exterior and fine plasterwork interior, and the dark and brooding **Park Hotel**, once one of the city's most fashionable hotels, as well as China's tallest building when it was built in 1934. Farther west, the area between Nanjing Road West and Jing'An Temple metro station was formerly known as Bubbling Well Road after the well near Jing'an Temple. It is more upscale and less crowded, with exclusive shopping and residential developments such as Plaza 66, Westgate Mall, and the **Shanghai Center** (*see p200*). There is a clutch of designer shops, restaurants, and apartments around the Portman Ritz-Carlton Hotel, opposite the Shanghai Exhibition Center.

# People's Park & Square ❸
## 人民广场

Nanjing Road West. Ⓜ *People's Square.* ◯ *7am–6pm daily.*

Opposite The Park Hotel is the oval-shaped former Racecourse, now occupied by People's Square and incorporating the pleasantly landscaped People's Park (Renmin Gong Yuan), the Shanghai Museum and Shanghai Grand Theater. Most people visit the park to walk, gossip, exercise, or simply watch the world go by. The park is ringed by gleaming

glass and metal skyscrapers. Facing it on its eastern side is **Mu'en Tang**, the Merciful Baptism Church that was built in 1929 as the American Baptist Church. An inter-denominational survivor of China's many revolutions, it is open to all and foreign nationals are welcome, but the services are only in Chinese.

Within the park itself is the elegant glass box of **MOCA Shanghai**, the Museum of Contemporary Art. Its two floors house regularly changing exhibitions of cutting-edge art and design. At the northwest corner of the park, the **Shanghai Art Museum** occupies the lower floors of an elegant old racecourse clubhouse. The collection is composed of a great many traditional Chinese paintings, along with some experimental works.

Opposite the Shanghai Museum is the **Shanghai Urban Planning Exhibition Hall**, which traces the huge urban development projects which have taken place in recent years. The highlight is a whole floor dedicated to a scale model of Shanghai, showing all existing and approved buildings.

At the northwest corner of People's Square is the **Shanghai Grand Theater** (*see p200*), made almost entirely of glass and topped by a spectacular convex roof. It is definitely worth a visit, for a meal with a view

The Park Hotel, formerly one of the most fashionable addresses in town

*For hotels and restaurants in this region see pp559–61 and pp586–8*

or just to look around, and tours are also available.

**Mu'en Tang**
*328 Xizang Middle Rd.* daily. *daily services, see entrance for times.*

**MOCA Shanghai**
*10am–6pm daily.*

**Shanghai Art Museum**
*9am–5pm daily.*

**Shanghai Urban Planning Exhibition Hall** *daily.*

**Shanghai Grand Theater**
*9–11am & 1–4pm daily.*

# Shanghai Museum ❹

*See pp190–91.*

# Pudong ❺
浦东

East bank of Huangpu. *from People's Square to Lujiazui.* *People's Square.* *Cross-River Ferry Terminal.*

In the mid-20th century, Pudong, facing the Bund on the other side of Huangpu, was the city's poorest quarter, a squalid huddle of slums and brothels and also the home of the notorious gangster Du Yuesheng or Big-Eared Du. In 1990, it acquired the status of Special Economic Zone, and

became one of the largest building sites in the world, supposedly festooned with a third of the world's large cranes. The transformation has been remarkable – a forest of skyscrapers has grown as investment poured in. The 1,500-ft (457-m) **Oriental Pearl TV Tower** offers views across the city from halfway up, and houses the interesting **Shanghai History Museum**. Pudong is also the site of the 1,379-ft (421-m) **Jinmao Tower**, one of the tallest buildings in

China, whose 88th-floor observation deck has views down on the Pearl. Both are surpassed by the 1,614-ft (492-m) **Shanghai World Financial Center**, which will itself be bettered in 2014 by the 124-floor, 2,073-ft (632-m) **Shanghai Tower Pudong**.

**Oriental Pearl TV Tower**
*1 Century Blvd.* **Tel** *(021) 5879 1888.* *8am–9pm daily.*

**Shanghai History Museum**
**Tel** *(021) 5879 1888.* *8am–9pm.*

The futuristic and ever-evolving skyline of Pudong

# Shanghai Museum ⊙
## 上海博物馆

**Bronze coin (AD 927–51)**

With a collection of over 120,000 pieces, the Shanghai Museum displays some of the best cultural relics from China's neolithic period to the Qing dynasty, a span of over 5,000 years. While the highlights are the bronze ware, ceramics, calligraphy, and painting, it also has excellent displays of jade, furniture, coins, and Chinese seals or "chops." The museum was established in 1952, and the current building opened in 1995 with a design that recalls some of the exhibits and symbolizes "a round heaven and a square earth."

Shanghai Museum, reminiscent of a Shang-dynasty bronze *ding* pot

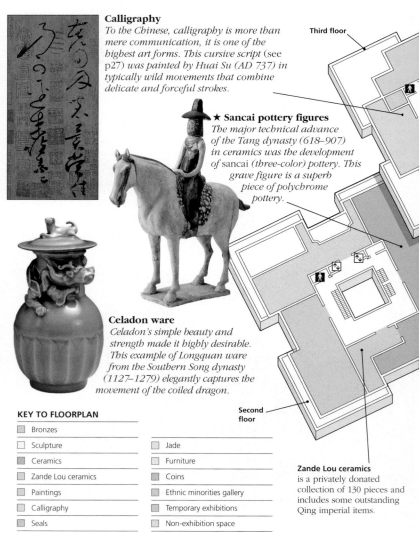

### Calligraphy
*To the Chinese, calligraphy is more than mere communication, it is one of the highest art forms. This cursive script (see p27) was painted by Huai Su (AD 737) in typically wild movements that combine delicate and forceful strokes.*

Third floor

### ★ Sancai pottery figures
*The major technical advance of the Tang dynasty (618–907) in ceramics was the development of sancai (three-color) pottery. This grave figure is a superb piece of polychrome pottery.*

### Celadon ware
*Celadon's simple beauty and strength made it highly desirable. This example of Longquan ware from the Southern Song dynasty (1127–1279) elegantly captures the movement of the coiled dragon.*

Second floor

### Zande Lou ceramics
is a privately donated collection of 130 pieces and includes some outstanding Qing imperial items.

**KEY TO FLOORPLAN**

| | |
|---|---|
| ▢ Bronzes | |
| ▢ Sculpture | ▢ Jade |
| ▢ Ceramics | ▢ Furniture |
| ▢ Zande Lou ceramics | ▢ Coins |
| ▢ Paintings | ▢ Ethnic minorities gallery |
| ▢ Calligraphy | ▢ Temporary exhibitions |
| ▢ Seals | ▢ Non-exhibition space |

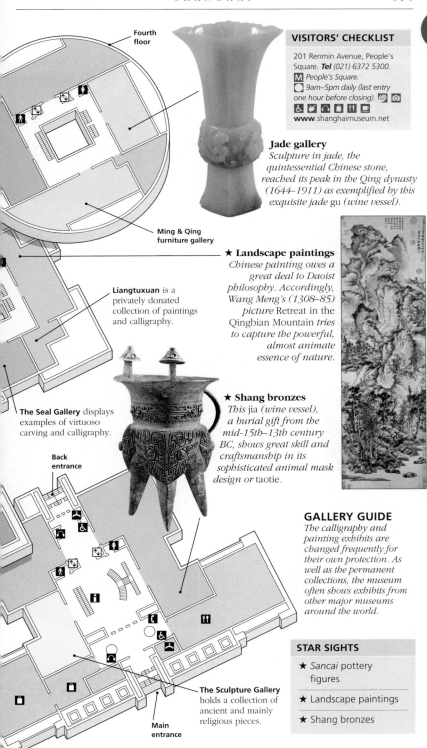

**Fourth floor**

**Ming & Qing furniture gallery**

**Liangtuxuan** is a privately donated collection of paintings and calligraphy.

**The Seal Gallery** displays examples of virtuoso carving and calligraphy.

**Back entrance**

**The Sculpture Gallery** holds a collection of ancient and mainly religious pieces.

**Main entrance**

**VISITORS' CHECKLIST**

201 Renmin Avenue, People's Square. *Tel* (021) 6372 5300.
M *People's Square.*
◯ 9am–5pm daily (last entry one hour before closing).
www.shanghaimuseum.net

**Jade gallery**
Sculpture in jade, the quintessential Chinese stone, reached its peak in the Qing dynasty (1644–1911) as exemplified by this exquisite jade gu (wine vessel).

**★ Landscape paintings**
Chinese painting owes a great deal to Daoist philosophy. Accordingly, Wang Meng's (1308–85) picture Retreat in the Qingbian Mountain tries to capture the powerful, almost animate essence of nature.

**★ Shang bronzes**
This jia (wine vessel), a burial gift from the mid-15th–13th century BC, shows great skill and craftsmanship in its sophisticated animal mask design or taotie.

**GALLERY GUIDE**
The calligraphy and painting exhibits are changed frequently for their own protection. As well as the permanent collections, the museum often shows exhibits from other major museums around the world.

**STAR SIGHTS**

- ★ Sancai pottery figures
- ★ Landscape paintings
- ★ Shang bronzes

# Yu Gardens and Bazaar ❻
豫园

**Chinese lion statue**

The old-style buildings of the Yu Gardens bazaar are not really old, but the fanciful roofs are nevertheless very appealing. The shops here peddle everything from tourist souvenirs to traditional medicines and, despite inflated prices, the area is incredibly popular. It is best to arrive early and go straight to the beautiful and relatively peaceful Ming-dynasty Yu Gardens (Yu Yuan). A dumpling lunch, before the restaurants get too busy, will set you up for a hectic afternoon of shopping and haggling, followed by a cup of tea in the quaint Huxinting teahouse.

Yu Gardens Bazaar, modern shops in old-fashioned buildings

**Restaurants** surround the lake – you can see the dumplings being made in the morning.

**Yu Gardens Bazaar**
*Despite being a bit of a tourist trap, there is plenty of fun to be had wandering among the stalls and haggling over prices.*

**Street performers**
*Every now and then a colorful troupe of performers appears bearing young children on top of poles to entertain the thronging crowds.*

Shanghai Old Street (Fangbang Road) and an entrance to the Bazaar

**★ City God Temple**
*Dating back to the Ming era, the temple once housed the patron god of Shanghai and encompassed an area as large as the bazaar. Now this small restored temple is very popular with tourists.*

### STAR SIGHTS

★ City God Temple

★ Huxinting Teahouse

★ Huge rockery, Yu Gardens

## ★ Huxinting Teahouse
*This charming building, built in 1784 by cotton merchants, only became a teahouse in the late 19th century. The zigzag bridge protects the structure, as evil spirits can't turn corners.*

## VISITORS' CHECKLIST

269 Fangbang Middle Road (Shanghai Old Street), Old City. 🚌 6. 🚇 **Tel** *(021) 6386 8649.* **City God Temple** ⬤ *8:30am–4:30pm daily.* 🌙 📷 **Yu Gardens** ⬤ *8:30am–4:30pm daily.* 🌙 🖼 🛡 📷 **Huxinting Teahouse** ⬤ *8:30am–9pm daily.* 🛡 🍴

### ★Huge rockery
*Reputed to be one of the best Ming rockeries, it is surely one of the largest. The rockery recalls the peaks, caves, and gorges of southern China.*

**Garden entrance**

### Dragon wall
*The white walls in the garden are topped by an undulating dragon. Note how it only has four claws and not five like an imperial dragon, so as not to incur the emperor's wrath.*

### Yu Gardens scenic areas
*The walls divide the garden into six scenic areas, which makes it feel like a maze and seem larger than it really is. As a result, the garden gets very busy in the afternoon and on weekends.*

**Entrance, First National Congress of the Chinese Community Party**

# Site of the First National Congress of the Chinese Communist Party ❼
中共一大会址纪念馆

374 Huangpi South Rd. [M] *Huangpi South Rd.* ◐ *9am–4pm.* 🎫

This house in the French Concession was the venue for a historic meeting, where representatives of China's communist cells met to form a national party on July 23, 1921. Officially, there were 12 participants including Mao Zedong, but it is believed that many others also attended. The police discovered the meeting and the delegates were forced to escape to a boat on Lake Nan, in Zhejiang. The house has a reconstruction of the meeting, with the original chairs and teacups used by the delegates. The exhibition hall tells the history of the Chinese Communist Party.

# Fuxing Park ❽
复兴公园

Fuxing Middle Rd. [M] *Huangpi South Road.* **Sun Yat Sen Memorial Residence** 7 Xingshan Rd. **Tel** *(021) 6437 2954.* ◐ *9am–4pm daily.* 🎫 **Zhou Enlai's Former Residence** 73 Sinan Rd. ◐ *9am–4pm daily.* 🎫

The French bought this private garden, located in the French Concession, in 1908. It was known then as the "French Park," and has

elements of a formal Parisian *jardin,* with meandering paths flanked by cherry trees. It was renamed Fuxing, meaning "revival," in 1949.

Close by on Xiangshan Road is the **Sun Yat-Sen Memorial Residence**, a typical Shanghai villa where the leader and his wife, Soong Qingling, lived between 1918 and 1924. The interior is just as it was in Sun's time, with many of his personal items such as his gramophone and books. South of the park, 73 Rue Massenet (now Sinan Road) was the **Former Residence of Zhou Enlai**, who lived here when he was head of the city's Communist Party in the 1940s. It is furnished in a spartan style and is another excellent example of a European-style Shanghai villa.

**Statue of Sun Yat Sen, Sun Yat Sen Memorial**

# French Concession ❾
法国花园

[M] *Shaanxi South Road.*

The former French Concession, stretching from the western edge of the Old City to Avenue Haig (Huashan Road), comprises European-style villas and

tree-lined boulevards, shops, and cafés, and its residents were mainly White Russians and Chinese. It had its own electrical system, judiciary, and police force, whose highest ranking officer "Pockmarked Huang," was the leader of the infamous Green Gang which controlled the opium trade.

Today, the Concession is centered around **Huaihai Road** and Yan'an Road – vibrant streets lined with megamalls, boutiques, restaurants, and bars – and the area around the stylish Art Deco façades of the **Jinjiang Hotel** complex. The hotel's compound includes the Grosvenor Residence, pre-war Shanghai's most exclusive property. The VIP Club, in the hotel's old wing, retains its 1920s architecture. The surrounding streets come alive at night with lively bars and clubs *(see p201).* Another interesting building is the **Ruijin Guesthouse** at the corner of Fuxing Middle Road and Shaanxi South Road. This Tudor-style manor is now a hotel. **The Children's Palace** at the western end of Yan'an Road was part of an early-1920s estate, and is now a children's arts center.

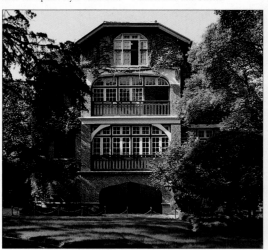

**The European-style villa that was Zhou Enlai's former residence**

# The Huangpu River

The Huangpu River is a mere 68 miles (110 km) in length from its source, Dianshan Lake, to its junction with the Yangzi River, 17 miles (28 km) downstream from Shanghai. As a spectacle, however, it is fascinating and there is much for the eye to take in, from the redeveloped waterfront at the Bund, and burgeoning modern metropolis on Pudong, to the

**Cargo ships, Huangpu River**

bustling docks that line the Huangpu all the way to the wide, windblown mouth of the Yangzi. The boat departs from the wharves on the Bund south of Yan'an Road *(see pp184–5)*. The one-hour trip takes visitors as far as the Yangpu Bridge, but there is also the longer three-and-a-half hour trip, all the way to the Yangzi River.

**The Yangzi River ⑦**
The color of the water changes markedly here, as the oily Huangpu meets the muddy and turbulent Yangzi. A lighthouse marks the confluence of the two.

**Shanghai Docks ④**
The Shanghainese proudly claim that nearly a third of all China's international trade enters via the perennially busy Huangpu river.

**Wusong Fort ⑥**
The site of a decisive battle against the British in 1842, it consisted of a crescent-shaped fort with ten imported cannons.

**Yangpu Bridge ③**
Built in 1993, this is one of the world's longest cable-stay bridges – cables are anchored to each tower.

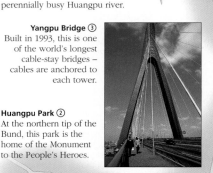

**Gongqing Forest Park ⑤**
This large and pleasantly landscaped park was reclaimed from marshland and is popular with the Shanghainese on weekends.

**Huangpu Park ②**
At the northern tip of the Bund, this park is the home of the Monument to the People's Heroes.

*Huangpu River*

② 
① *Pudong*          ③

④

| 0 km | 6 |
|---|---|
| 0 miles | 3 |

**The Bund ①**
The central road area of the Bund was redeveloped for the 2010 World Expo. Most traffic has been diverted underground and the roads turned into parks and walkways.

## TIPS BOX

*Length:* 37 miles (60 km).
One-hour trip: 10 miles (16 km).
*Boat trips:* The boats vary in size and facilities, so make sure you know what you are getting. The more expensive ones do food and even entertainment of sorts.
*Times:* 9am, 2pm, 7pm Mon–Fri; 11am, 3:30pm, 8pm Sat–Sun. The one-hour trips leave more frequently (times can vary).

Façade of the Soviet-style Shanghai Exhibition Center

## Shanghai Exhibition Center ⑩
### 上海展览中心

1000 Yan'an Middle Rd. **Tel** (021) 2216 2216. Ⓜ Jing'an Temple. ☐ 9am–4pm daily.

The enormous Shanghai Exhibition Center is one of the few reminders of the influence the Soviet Union once had in Shanghai. Built in 1954, it was known as the Palace of Sino-Soviet Friendship, and was designed as a place for exhibiting China's techno-logical and agricultural advances since the founding of the People's Republic in 1949. Ironically, the building stands on the site of the estate of millionaire Silas Hardoon – Shanghai's biggest capitalist in the 1920s. The Center is worth seeing for its grimly florid Soviet-style architecture. It has an impressively ornate entrance, with columns decorated with red stars, and a gilded spire. Today, it is an exhibition and convention center.

Nearby on Xinle Road, in the former French Conces-sion, is the old **Russian Ortho-dox Church** with its distinctive onion-shaped domes. It served thousands of refugees from the Russian Revolution in 1917. The area around Julu Road and Changle Road, nearby, has a number of interesting Art Deco and early 20th-century villas and mansions constructed by Shanghai's wealthy residents.

## Jing'an Temple ⑪
### 静安寺

1686 Nanjing West Rd (near Huashan Rd). Ⓜ Jing'an Temple. ☐ 7:30am–5pm daily.

Located opposite the attractive Jing'an Park, which contains the old Bubbling Well Cemetery, Jing'an Temple (Temple of Tranquility) is one of the city's most revered places for ancestor worship. Originally founded in the Three Kingdoms Period, it re-opened in 2006 after being completely rebuilt. In the 1930s, it was Shanghai's wealthiest Buddhist temple, headed by the influencial abbot Khi Vehdu, who was also a gangster with a harem of concubines and White Russian bodyguards. It is said that his bodyguards went with him everywhere, carrying bulletproof briefcases as shields in the event of an attack. The temple was closed during the Cultural Revolution, but has reopened to become one of the best examples of an active Buddhist shrine in the city. It is a popular place to offer coins and pray for financial success.

## Jade Buddha Temple ⑫
### 玉佛寺

170 Anyuan Rd. **Tel** (021) 6266 3668. Ⓜ Hanzhong Rd then taxi. ☐ 8:30am–4:30pm daily.

The most famous of Shanghai's temples, Jufo Si lies in the northwest part of the city. It was built in 1882 to enshrine two beautiful jade Buddha statues that were brought from Burma by the abbot Wei Ken. The temple was originally located elsewhere, but shifted here in 1918, after a fire damaged the earlier structure. After being closed for almost 30 years, it reopened in 1980, and today has some 100 monks. Built in the southern Song-dynasty style, it has sharply curved eaves and figurines on the roof. Its three main halls are connected by two courts. The first hall is the **Heavenly King Hall**, where the four Heavenly Kings line the walls. The **Grand Hall of Magnificence** houses three incarnations of the Buddha, while

Wall detail, Jade Buddha Temple

the **Jade Buddha Chamber** contains the first jade statue – that of a large reclining Buddha. The finer of the two statues, however, lies upstairs. Carved from a single piece of jade, this jewel-encrusted seated Buddha is exquisite. Visitors should note that photography is forbidden here.

Golden Buddhas in the Jade Buddha Temple

*For hotels and restaurants in Shanghai see pp559–61 and pp586–8*

# Old Shanghai

Until 1842 Shanghai was a minor Chinese river port, worthy of a protective rampart but otherwise undistinguished. In that year the Chinese government capitulated to western demands for trade concessions resulting in a number of ports along China's eastern seaboard, including Shanghai, becoming essentially European outposts. Their key feature was that of extra-territoriality – foreign residents were answerable only to the laws of their own country. Thus the Americans, British, and French had their own "concessions" – exclusive areas within the city with their own police forces and judiciary – a situation that attracted not only entrepreneurs, but refugees, criminals, and revolutionaries. This mix was a potent one and Shanghai's reputation for glamor and excess derives from the politically combustible period between the two world wars. It all came to an end in the 1940s with the Japanese invasion and wartime occupation of Shanghai.

Calendar girls, 1930s

**The Bund**, *also known as Zhongshan East No. 1 Road or, more colloquially, "Waitan," was the wide thoroughfare running along Huangpu River. This was where all the major financial players in Shanghai commerce built their offices and created the distinctively grandiose skyline.*

**The Great World** *was a quintessential Shanghai creation, a mixture of freakishness, fashion, sex, and theater under one roof, owned by the gangster Pockmarked Huang.*

**The Race Course**, *located in the area of today's People's Square, was a part of expatriate life, where, just as in the numerous clubs and institutions for non-Chinese, wealthy expats could socialize as if they were home.*

**Opium, trafficked commercially** *with claims for free-trade by British companies like Jardine Matheson, was the foundation of Shanghai's prosperity and dens dotted the city. When the mercantile veneer was jettisoned, opium became the currency of Shanghai's gangster underworld.*

**Nanking Road** *was, and still is, Shanghai's retail hub. Divided in two parts (the western end is Bubbling Well Road), it was home to China's first department stores, where Chinese and expatriates mixed on an equal footing.*

Brightly colored boats alongside the lake pier at Hongkou Park (Lu Xun Park)

# Hongkou Park ⑬
# 虹口公园

146 Dong Jiangwan East Rd.
Ⓜ *Hongkou.* ⬜ *daily.* 🎫

To the north of Suzhou Creek and Waibaidu Bridge lies the Japanese section of the former International Settlement, which once had a Zen temple, a Japanese school, and specialist Japanese shops. The area's most interesting spot is Hongkou Park, which is a pleasant place to pass the time and watch the Chinese taking boat rides on the lake, playing chess, practising *tai ji quan* or simply relaxing. It is also known as Lu Xun Park due to its strong associations with the great Chinese novelist Lu Xun (1881–1936), who lived nearby. His most famous work is *The True Story of Ah Q*, which lampooned the Chinese national character. Lu Xun was also an early proponent of the *baihua* or plain speech movement, which championed the simplification of the Chinese script and the use of spoken Chinese in literature. **Lu Xun's Tomb**, where his ashes were interred in 1956 to mark the 20th anniversary of his death, is also in the park. To the right of the park's main entrance lies a **Memorial Hall** dedicated to the novelist, where visitors can view early editions of his work and his correspondence with various intellectuals including George Bernard Shaw. Just south of

Statue, Lu Xun's Tomb

Hongkou Park is **Lu Xun's Former Residence**, where the novelist spent the last three years of his life at a house on Shanyin Road. It is an interesting example of a typical 1930s Japanese-style residence, but is perhaps even more sparsely furnished than other houses of the time. Lu Xun's rattan chairs and writing desk are also on display.

**🏛 Lu Xun's Former Residence**
9 Dalu Xincun, Shanyin Rd. ⬜ 9am–4pm. 🎫

# Soong Qingling's Former Residence ⑭
# 宋庆龄故居

1843 Huaihai Middle Rd.
Ⓜ *Hengshan Rd.* ⬜ 9–11am & 1–4:30pm daily. 🎫

At the southwestern edge of the city is the fine villa that was the residence of Soong Qingling, wife of the revolutionary leader Dr. Sun Yat Sen. All the Soong siblings – three sisters and a brother – came to wield a lot of influence in China. Of the three sisters, Soong Meiling married Chiang Kai-shek, the head of the Nationalist Republic of China from 1928 to 1949; Ailing married H.H. Kung, the director of the Bank of China, and Soong Qingling married Sun Yat-sen. Her brother, known as T.V. Soong, became Chiang Kai-shek's finance minister. Soong Qingling stayed in China once the Communists took over and became an honorary Communist heroine. She lived in Shanghai after her husband's death, initially in the house they had shared in the former French Concession (*see p194*), before moving to this villa. She died in Beijing in 1981.

The house is a charming example of a mid-20th-century Shanghai villa. It has some wonderful wood paneling and lacquerwork. Her limousines are still parked in the garage, and some of her personal items are also displayed.

**Soong Qingling's Former Residence – a charming early 20th-century villa**

*For hotels and restaurants in Shanghai see pp559–61 and pp586–8*

# Xujiahui Catholic Cathedral ⑮
## 徐家汇堂

158 Puxi Rd. *Tel (021) 6438 2595.*
Ⓜ *Xujiahui.* ◯ *1–4pm Sat, Sun.*

The redbrick Gothic Cathedral of St. Ignatius that stands at a southwestern corner of Shanghai has long been associated with foreign nationals. The land originally belonged to a member of the Xu clan, Xu Guangqi (1562–1633), who was converted to Catholicism by Matteo Ricci. Upon his death, Xu left land to the Jesuits for the building of a church, seminary, and observatory. The cathedral, with its 164-ft (50-m) twin towers, was built in 1906. It was partly destroyed during the Cultural Revolution, but was rebuilt, and now holds Sunday services attended by over 2,000 worshipers. The interior is an interesting mix of traditional Catholic decoration and Chinese embellishment. Xu Guangqi is buried nearby in Nandan Park.

# Longhua Cemetery of Martyrs ⑯
## 龙华烈士陵园

180 Longhua West Rd. Ⓜ *Shanghai Stadium then taxi. Tel (021) 6468 5995.* 🚌 *No. 41.* ◯ *8:30am–4pm Tue–Sun.* 📷 **Longhua Si** 2853 Longhua West Rd. ◯ *7am–4:30pm daily.* 📷

This site honors those who died for the communist cause before the People's Republic was established in 1949. At the center is a Memorial Hall, while many commemorative sculptures dot the park. The cemetery is situated on the site of the Nationalist Party's execution ground, where several hundred Communists were put to death in 1927 by gangs working for Chiang Kai-shek.
Nearby is **Longhua Temple** and an octagonal pagoda. A temple has existed on this site since AD 687, and a pagoda since AD 238–251. The foundations of the current pagoda, with its upturned

**Commemorative statue at the Longhua Cemetery of Martyrs**

eaves, date to AD 977, while the temple buildings were built during the late Qing era. The temple has several halls and is very active. The surrounding area is pretty in spring.

# She Shan ⑰
## 佘山

22 miles (35 km) SW of Shanghai. Ⓜ *Sheshan.* 🚌 *from Wenhua Guangchang bus stop or Xi Qu bus station in Shanghai.*

She Hill or She Shan is a mere 328-ft (100-m) high, and is surmounted by a grand, redbrick Catholic church, **Our Lady of China**. In the 1850s, European missionaries built a small chapel here. Later, a bishop took refuge in the area and vowed to build a church. The basilica was built between

**Exterior of the grand She Shan church, Our Lady of China**

1925–35. Services, often in Latin, take place on Christian holidays and particularly in May, when pilgrims stream here. The impressive cathedral is worth a closer look. The route to the top represents the Via Dolorosa (The Way of Suffering), the road that Christ took to his crucifixion. It is a pleasant walk past bamboo groves, but there is a cable car that goes to the summit. The hill also has an ancient observatory that houses an ingenious earthquake-monitoring device of a jar with dragon heads around the outside and a pendulum inside. Each dragon has a steel ball in its mouth. When an earthquake occurred, the pendulum would swing, knock a dragon, causing its mouth to open and a ball to drop out and thereby point out the quake's direction.

# Song Jiang ⑱
## 松江

25 miles (40 km) SW of Shanghai. Ⓜ *Song Jiang Xincheng.* 🚌 *from Xi Qu bus station in Shanghai.*

Situated on the Shanghai-Hangzhou railway line, Song Jiang is a small county town with a handful of sights. These include a Song-dynasty square pagoda, and close by, a 13-ft (4-m) high and 20-ft (6-m) long Ming screen wall, decorated with carvings of legendary beasts. West of Song Jiang is an old mosque, part of which dates to the Yuan dynasty and is said to be one of the oldest Islamic buildings in China. It is still a place of worship.

# Shopping & Entertainment in Shanghai

**Mao Memorabilia, Dongtai Road Market**

Shanghai has always been China's premier shopping destination. Before World War II, the city's glamorous foreign community demanded the finest goods, and Shanghai's reputation for novelty and quality continues today, with stores that cater to all tastes and budgets. This is also a culturally vibrant city, with regular performances of opera, theater, acrobatics, Western classical music, and jazz. The city's nightlife is buzzing with plenty of fashionable bars and restaurants, as well as cinemas and nightclubs.

## SHOPS & MARKETS

Shanghai's best-known shopping street is Nanjing Road, which is lined with stores *(see p188)*. **Plaza 353**, in the historic Dong Hai Plaza, is a hip mall with stores and dining options. The most interesting local market is just off Nanjing Road, on Jiangyin Road. Huaihai Road in the former French Concession is also well known, and packed with upscale fashion boutiques and stores.

## CLOTHES & TEXTILES

All the major brand names from around the world are represented here, along with some Hong Kong chain stores, though the latter often don't have sizes that fit foreign visitors. The main streets are Nanjing Road, Shaanxi South Road, Huaihai Road, and Maoming Road, as well as the malls of Pudong. For reasonably priced silk, try the **No. 1 Department Store** *(see p188)*, but the best quality is sold at stores such as **Isetan**. For fashion boutiques, there are a number of independent stores clustered at Taikang Road and at Xinle Road for youth fashion. The city has also revived its tradition of fine tailoring, and **W.W. Chan & Sons Tailor Ltd** is quality at good prices.

## ANTIQUES

Although Shanghai offers a range of antiques, there are two potential hazards in buying them. First, the market is flooded with fakes which visitors might mistake for the real thing, and second, it is illegal to export antiques that do not bear a government-approved seal. Bargains are hard to come by and the best quality items are not likely to be much cheaper than at home. The main markets are near the Old City on **Dongtai Road**, **Fuyou Road** (open Sunday only), and **Fangbang Road**. Fangbang Road's *(see p192)* **Hubao Building Basement Market** is the largest indoor antique market in Shanghai, while Hongkou district's **Duolun Road** has a row of restored shops selling antiques, books, and art.

## ARTS & CRAFTS

All traditional Chinese arts and crafts are widely available in Shanghai. The **Yu Gardens Bazaar** is great for items such as tea, teapots, teaware, and other souvenirs, but remember to always bargain hard. For porcelain, the best buys are the fine reproductions of classical porcelain, available at the **Shanghai Museum**, which although expensive, are far better than anything else in the market. Handicrafts made by China's ethnic minorities such as Tibetans, as well as by people of neighboring countries such as Nepal, are available at specialist shops on Nanjing Road. Jewelry shops abound all over the city, and jade, although available, is difficult to classify. Cultured pearls however, are a safer bet, and are available in stores such as **Shanghai Pearl City**. For Chinese art, there are galleries around Moganshan Road near Suzhou Creek.

## ENTERTAINMENT GUIDES & TICKETS

There are a number of English language publications, such as the bi-weekly *City Weekend* and monthly *that's Shanghai* and *Time Out Shanghai*, which carry details of current events, as well as restaurant reviews. Mainstream events are listed in local Chinese newspapers. Mypiano.com is the city's primary ticket agency for theater, concerts, and sports events. Tickets can also be arranged through the tourist office, directly at the venue or even through your hotel.

## PERFORMING ARTS & MUSIC

Shanghai can boast a wide variety of performing arts. There are several international-standard venues such as the **Shanghai Grand Theater** *(see p188)* and **Shanghai Oriental Art Center** that stage national and international opera performances, music, dance, and theater. Another very popular cultural venue is the **Shanghai Center** *(see p188)*, which also puts on classical Western music and opera, as well as nightly performances of the city's most famous acrobatic troupe. A hot venue is the **Mercedes-Benz Arena**, which was built for the World Expo and now hosts international concerts, theater, music and dance shows, and sports events. Traditional Chinese opera can be seen at the **Tianchan Yifu Theater** and occasionally at the old **Lyceum Theater** (Lan Xin). The **Majestic Theater** also has a programme of ballet and local opera, while modern Chinese theater is performed at the **Shanghai Dramatic Arts Center**. There are also concerts on Sunday evenings at the **Shanghai Music Conservatory Auditorium**. Jazz, which is most famously available at the **House of Blues & Jazz**, can also be heard at the **JZ Club** on Fuxing Road.

## CINEMA

Apart from Chinese and Hong Kong films, films from Europe and the US are also screened in cinemas and bars. Halls such as **UME International Cineplex**, **Shanghai Film Art Center**, and **Studio City** show foreign films (often censored), either in their original language with Chinese subtitles or dubbed into Chinese with English subtitles.

## BARS & NIGHTCLUBS

Shanghai's nightlife is China's most brash, diverse, and pulsing. Bars come and go, and what's "in" one month may close down the next. Bars tend towards the avant-garde, and are heavily influenced by what is fashionable in Tokyo, New York, and London. Prices for drinks can be high, and many bars have dancing, live music, film nights, and comedy spots. The best areas are the Bund, Xintiandi, Fuxing West Road, Yongfu Road, and Sinan Road. **Boxing Cat Brewery** on Fuxing Road is popular for happy hour beers and southern US bar food. **Malone's**, an American style bar, and close by is the **Big Bamboo**, a Canadian bar and one of the city's most popular late night hangouts. Popular cocktail lounges include **Mesa/ Manifesto** and **The Alchemist**, located at the trendy Sinan Mansions (a redevelopment of a clutch of heritage villas), plus **El Coctel**, a classy upscale lounge. **Lola** is a hip club and lounge with DJs and dancing. **Yucca** is a hot Latin-themed club, lounge, and tapas bar. The **Glamour Bar** at the corner of Guangdong Lu is decorated like a 1930s Hollywood film set. Current reviews, including details of which clubs have DJs from London and New York, are to be found in *that's Shanghai* and *Time Out Shanghai*, as well as online at www.smartshanghai.com.

# DIRECTORY

### SHOPS & MARKETS

**Plaza 353**
Nanjing East Rd.
*Tel (021) 6353 5353.*

### CLOTHES & TEXTILES

**Isetan**
527 Huaihai Middle Rd.
*Tel (021) 5306 1111.*

**Number 1 Department Store**
830 Nanjing East Rd.
*Tel (021) 6322 3344.*

**W.W. Chan & Sons Tailor Ltd.**
129-A02 Maoming South Rd. *Tel (021) 5404 1469.*

### ARTS & CRAFTS

**Duoyun Xuan**
422 Nanjing East Rd.
*Tel (021) 6351 0060.*

**Room With a View**
M50 Moganshan Rd.
*Tel (021) 6266 3369.*

**Shanghai Museum**
201 Renmin Dadao.
*Tel (021) 6372 5300.*

**Shanghai Pearl City**
3721 Hongmei Rd,
Hongqiao.
*Tel (021) 6465 0000.*

**Yu Gardens Bazaar**
260 Fangbang Middle Rd
(Shanghai Old Street).
*Tel (021) 6386 8649.*

### PERFORMING ARTS & MUSIC

**House of Blues & Jazz**
60 Fuzhou Rd.
*Tel (021) 6323 2779.*

**JZ Club**
46 West Fuxing Rd (near Yongfu Rd).
*Tel (021) 6431 0269.*

**Lyceum Theater**
57 Maoming South Rd.
*Tel (021) 6217 8530.*

**Majestic Theater**
66 Jiangning Rd.
*Tel (021) 6217 4409.*

**Mercedes-Benz Arena**
1200 Expo Avenue.
*Tel 400 181 6688.*

**Shanghai Center**
1376 Nanjing West Rd.
*Tel (021) 6279 8600.*

**Shanghai Dramatic Arts Center**
288 Anfu Rd.
*Tel (021) 6473 4567.*

**Shanghai Grand Theater**
300 People's Square.
*Tel (021) 6327 6740.*

**Shanghai Music Conservatory Auditorium**
20 Fenyang Rd.
*Tel (021) 6437 0137.*

**Shanghai Oriental Art Center**
425 Dingxiang Rd, Pudong.
*Tel (021) 6854 7793.*

**Tianchan Yifu Theater**
701 Fuzhou Rd.
*Tel (021) 6351 4668.*

### CINEMAS

**Shanghai Film Art Center**
172 Xinhua Rd.
*Tel (021) 6280 8995.*

**Studio City**
10/F, 1038 Nanjing West Rd.
*Tel (021) 6218 7109.*

**UME International Cineplex**
4/F No. 6,
Lane 123, Xingye Rd.
*Tel (021) 6373 3333.*

### BARS & NIGHTCLUBS

**Big Bamboo**
132 Nanyang Rd.
*Tel (021) 6256 2265.*

**Boxing Cat Brewery**
82 Fuxing Rd.
*Tel (021) 6431 2091.*

**El Coctel**
2/F, 47 Yongfu Rd.
*Tel (021) 6433 6511.*

**Glamour Bar**
at M on the Bund, 6/F, 20 Guangdong Rd. *Tel (021) 6329 3751.*

**Lola**
Building 4,
570 Yongjia Rd.
*Tel (021) 6073 7628.*

**Long Bar**
Waldorf Astoria Hotel,
2 The Bund.
*Tel (021) 6322 9988.*

**Malone's**
255 Tongren Rd. *Tel (021) 6247 2400.*

**Mesa/Manifesto**
748 Julu Rd.
*Tel (021) 6289 9108.*

**The Alchemist**
Block 32, Sinan Mansions,
45 Sinan Rd.
*Tel (021) 6426 0660.*

**Yucca**
Block 26F, Sinan Mansions,
45 Sinan Rd.
*Tel (021) 3368 9525.*

# JIANGSU & ANHUI

The provinces of Jiangsu and Anhui lie to the north and west of Shanghai respectively. Jiangsu, one of China's most fertile and populated areas, is largely rural. Its southern region is dominated by the Yangzi River, along which lie the major cities including Nanjing, the provincial capital, with a profusion of historic sights, and the cities of Suzhou and Yangzhou, known for their gardens, canals, and silk production. The province is developing fast but still retains its charm, especially in the small towns where traditional architecture can be seen. Anhui's main sights lie in the south, where vast spreads of paddy fields are watered by the Huai River. The area south of the Yangzi River is dominated by mountain ranges offering spectacular scenery. Huang Shan, the Yellow Mountain, is Anhui's most popular scenic area, while the Buddhist mountain, Jiuhua Shan, is more serene. The towns of Shexian and Yixian in the southeast are renowned for their traditional old houses with fine wooden carvings.

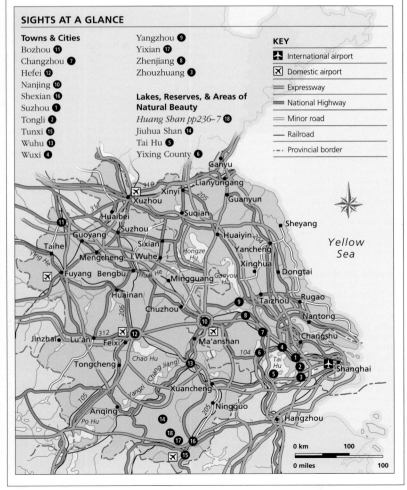

## SIGHTS AT A GLANCE

**Towns & Cities**
Bozhou ⑪
Changzhou ⑦
Hefei ⑫
Nanjing ⑩
Shexian ⑯
Suzhou ①
Tongli ②
Tunxi ⑮
Wuhu ⑬
Wuxi ④

Yangzhou ⑨
Yixian ⑰
Zhenjiang ⑧
Zhouzhuang ③

**Lakes, Reserves, & Areas of Natural Beauty**
Huang Shan pp236–7 ⑱
Jiuhua Shan ⑭
Tai Hu ⑤
Yixing County ⑥

**KEY**

✈ International airport

☒ Domestic airport

═ Expressway

▬ National Highway

─ Minor road

── Railroad

-·-· Provincial border

A farmer wades through rice fields irrigated by the Yangzi River

# Suzhou ❶

苏州

**Milefo Buddha at the base of Beisi Ta**

A network of canals, bridges, and canal-side housing characterizes the city of Suzhou. Its history dates back to the 6th century BC, when the first canals were built to control the area's low water table. The construction of the Grand Canal (see p217), 1,000 years later, brought prosperity as silk, the city's prized commodity, could be exported northwards. During the Ming dynasty, Suzhou flourished as a place of refinement, drawing an influx of scholars and merchants, who built themselves numerous elegant gardens. The city has plenty of sights, and is dissected by broad, busy roads laid out in a grid.

## 🏯 Beisi Ta

1918 Renmin Rd. ⬜ daily. 📷
The northern end of Renmin Rd is dominated by the Beisi Ta (North Pagoda), a remnant of an earlier temple complex, which has been rebuilt. The pagoda's main structure dates from the Song dynasty, but its foundations supposedly date to the Three Kingdoms era (AD 220–265). Towering 249 ft (76 m) high, it is octagonal in shape, and has sharply upturned eaves. Visitors can climb right to the top, from where there are good views of the city, including Xuanmiao Guan and the Ruiguang Pagoda (see pp212–13).

## 🏛 Suzhou Silk Museum

2001 Renmin Rd. **Tel** (0512) 8211 2636. ⬜ 9am–4:30pm daily. 📷
The Suzhou Silk Museum is a pleasure to visit, mainly because its exhibits are well-documented with English captions. It traces the history of silk production (see pp208–9) and its use from its beginnings in about 4000 BC to the present day. Exhibits include old looms with demonstrations of their workings, samples of ancient silk patterns, and a section explaining the art of sericulture. The museum's most interesting exhibit is its room full of live silk worms, eating mulberry leaves and spinning cocoons.

## 🏛 Suzhou Museum

204 Dongbei Jie. **Tel** (0512) 6754 1534. ⬜ 9am–4pm daily. 📷

**The octagonal Beisi Ta**

The municipal museum was formerly housed in the villa which was part of the adjoining Humble Administrator's Garden. The villa was occupied by Li Xiucheng, one of the leaders of the Taiping Heavenly Kingdom Rebellion (see p422) in 1860. The museum was rebuilt in a contemporary-meets-traditional style by the architect IM Pei in 2006. It houses more than 30,000 cultural relics, including excavated artifacts, Ming and Qing dynasty paintings and calligraphy, and ancient arts and crafts.

## 🌿 Humble Administrator's Garden

See pp206–7.

## 🌿 Shizi Lin

23 Yuanlin Rd. ⬜ daily. 📷
The Lion Grove Garden is considered by many the finest in Suzhou. However, visitors unfamiliar with the subtleties of Chinese garden design may find it rather bleak, as rocks are its main feature. Ornamental rocks were a crucial element of classical gardens, and symbolized either the earth or China's sacred mountains. Dating to 1342, the garden was originally built as part of a temple. The large pool is spanned by a zigzag bridge and buildings with unusually fine latticework, while part of the rockery forms a labyrinth.

## 🌿 Ou Yuan

Cang Jie. ⬜ 7:30am–5pm daily. 📷
The Ou Yuan (Double Garden) is not as busy as many of the city's other classical gardens, and is a pleasure to visit. It takes its name from its two garden areas, separated by buildings and corridors. A relaxing place, Ou Yuan has rockeries, a pool, and a fine, open pavilion at its center that is surrounded by several teahouses. It is situated in a charming locality filled with some of the most attractive houses, canals, and bridges in the city.

**The charming Ou Yuan Garden**

**Mural in the Hall of Literary Gods, Xuanmiao Guan**

### VISITORS' CHECKLIST

32 miles (50 km) NW of Shanghai. *6,000,000.* 🚃 *Suzhou Train Station.* 🚌 *Beimen Station, Nanmen Station, Wu Xianshi Station.* ⛴ *ferries to Hangzhou.* 🚢 *tours of Grand Canal.* ℹ️ *345 Shiquan St, (0512) 6530 5887.* www.classicsuzhou.com

### 🏛 Museum of Opera & Theater

14 Zhongzhangjia Xiang. *Tel (0512) 6727 3334.* ☐ *8:30am–4:30pm daily.* 📷

Housed in a beautiful Ming dynasty theater of latticed wood, the Museum of Opera and Theater (Xiqu Bowuguan) is a fascinating and highly visual museum. Its display halls are filled with examples of old musical instruments, delicate hand-copied books of scores and lyrics, masks, and costumes. Other exhibits include a life-size orchestra and vivid photographs of dramatists and actors. Traditional Suzhou Opera, known as *kun ju*, is renowned as the oldest form of Chinese opera, with a history of about 5,000 years.

The museum is the venue for occasional performances, while the adjacent teahouse stages daily shows of *kun*-style opera and music.

### 🏛 Xuanmiao Guan

94 Miaoqian Jie. *Tel (0512) 6777 5479.* ☐ *7:30am–4:15pm daily.* 📷
The Daoist Temple of Mystery was founded during the Jin dynasty but like many Chinese temples, has been rebuilt many times. The Hall of the Three Pure Worshipers dates to the Song dynasty, and is the largest ancient Daoist hall in China. The intricate structure of the roof in particular is worth scrutiny. Located in Suzhou's commercial center, the temple was associated with popular street entertainment, and although the musicians and jugglers have gone, it retains a casual atmosphere.

0 meters     800
0 yards      800

**Key to Symbols** *see back flap*

# Humble Administrator's Garden
拙政园

Tai Hu rock display

Suzhou's largest garden, Zhuozheng Yuan, the Humble Administrator's Garden is also considered the city's finest. It was established in the 16th century by a retired magistrate, Wang Xianchen, and developed over the years as subsequent owners made changes according to the fashion of the day. A 16th-century painting shows that originally the garden was less decorative than it is now. The garden is separated into three principal parts, east, central, and west. The eastern section has colorful flowers but is of less interest than the other two. There is also a museum that explains the history and philosophy of Chinese gardens.

Covered walkway – a way to enjoy the garden even in the hot sun

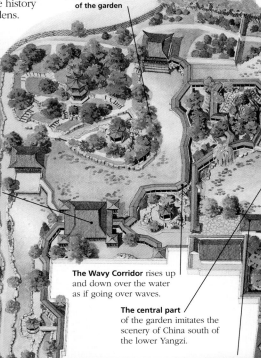

Western section of the garden

**★ Mandarin Duck Hall**
*Split into two equal rooms, this arrangement allowed visitors to enjoy the cooler north-facing chamber in summer, and the warmer south-facing one in winter.*

**The Wavy Corridor** rises up and down over the water as if going over waves.

**The central part** of the garden imitates the scenery of China south of the lower Yangzi.

## STAR SIGHTS

★ Fragrant Isle

★ Mandarin Duck Hall

★ Hall of Distant Fragrance

**★ Fragrant Isle**
*This pavilion and terrace is supposed to resemble the deck and cabin of a boat. As it projects out over the water, it gives excellent views of the garden from all sides.*

## THE HUMBLE ADMINISTRATOR'S GARDEN

Area illustrated below

1. Entrance
2. Eastern Garden
3. Garden Museum
4. Penjing Nursery (see p179)

0 meters 100
0 feet 300

### VISITORS' CHECKLIST

178 Dongbei Jie, Suzhou.
**Tel** (0512) 6751 0286.
7:30am–5pm daily (last admission 5pm). includes the Garden Museum.
**www**.szzzy.cn

**Orange Pavilion**
*Artificial mountains were an important element in Chinese gardens and were ideal for contemplation.*

**Little Flying Rainbow Bridge**

**Entrance to the central section**

**Secluded Pavilion of Firmiana Simplex and Bamboo**
*The most famous view of the garden, the "borrowed view" (see p179) of Beisi Ta, the Northern Pagoda reflected in the water, is visible from here.*

★ **Hall of Distant Fragrance**
*The main hall of the garden, is named after the perfume of the large lotus pond nearby that delicately wafts in.*

# The History of Chinese Silk

According to legend it was the Empress Xi Ling who, in 2640 BC, encouraged silkworm breeding on a large scale. Trading vast quantities of the material around the world, China profited massively from the industry. It remained a Chinese monopoly for the next 3,000 years or so until refugees smuggled the secret to Korea and Japan. Another story tells that a Chinese princess who married the Prince of Khotan secretly brought silkworms with her as a gift for her husband. The western world, which knew China as Seres, or Land of Silk, learnt the secret of silk production via two monks, who hid silkworms in their bamboo staffs.

**Statue of a silkworker, Silk Museum**

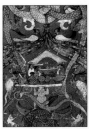

**Silk burial offering dating from c.200 BC**

**IMPERIAL GIFT**
Silk was originally reserved for use by the imperial household, an example of which is this gorgeous robe embroidered with the imperial symbol of the five-clawed dragon. The imperial yellow symbolizes the earth.

**Silk was traded** *(see pp464–5) extensively as an important source of income and indeed was often used as a form of payment of taxes or for payment of salaries.*

**This traditional pattern** suggests waves and mountains and therefore the boundless nature of the Chinese empire.

**Justinian** *was the Byzantine emperor who stole the secret of silk in AD 600. Silk had for long been fashionable in the Roman Empire but they had no idea how it was made, even thinking that it grew on trees.*

**Women produced silk** *in their own home – and it took up a large part of the day for six months of the year. The state also had many workshops producing and weaving silk. By the Tang dynasty, all classes of society in China were allowed to wear silk.*

**Silk embroidery** *became an important art and the women of distinguished families could make a considerable fortune by skilful embroidery.*

## THE PRODUCTION OF SILK

Thousands of years of intensive breeding have rendered the silk moth, *Bombyx mori*, a blind, flightless, egg-laying machine whose larvae hold the secret of silk. The genius of the Chinese lay in the discovery of the potential of its ancestor, a wild, mulberry-eating moth unique to China.

**Farming silkworms:** *the eggs are first kept at 65° F (18° C) rising to 77° F (25° C), at which point they hatch. The silkworms (actually caterpillars) are now kept at a constant temperature and fed mulberry leaves at 30-minute intervals day and night, until fattened they are ready to enter the cocoon stage.*

## MEANING OF SYMBOLS

 **Axe** *is one of the twelve symbols of sovereignty that were reserved for the emperor. The axe stands for the power to punish.*

 **Bat** *is not only for emperors but is a lucky symbol for everyone. The Chinese word for bat (fu) also sounds like good luck.*

 **Double chi** *is another of the twelve imperial symbols that represents the emperor's power to judge his subjects.*

**Silken saliva:** *the silkworms' saliva glands secrete a clear liquid, that solidifies into silk threads as it dries, and a gum that sticks these together.*

**Cocoons:** *when they are ready to pupate, with a figure-of-eight motion, they spin their sticky secretion into cocoons.*

**Making silk:** *the cocoons are steamed to kill the pupae and soaked to soften the sticky gum and allow the silk strands to be separated. Several strands are woven to make one silk thread.*

**Chinoiserie** *was popular in Europe and America at various times from the 17th century onwards. Chinese factories created a range of Chinese-style designs solely for export.*

**Silk** *has special qualities in that it retains warmth, and yet is lightweight and cool and can therefore be worn in comfort both in winter and summer.*

**China's silk industry** *is still strong today although a lot of the "silk" that is on display in cheap markets is actually rayon.*

**The octagonal Song dynasty twin pagodas, Shuang Ta**

### 🔲 Shuang Ta
Dinghui Si Xiang. ☐ daily. 🖾

Once part of a temple, these 98-ft (30-m) high twin pagodas date to the early Song era. According to an inscription, they were first built in AD 982 by the students Wang Wenhan and his brother in honor of their teacher, who helped them pass the imperial civil service exams. Twin pagodas are commonly found in India but are a rarer feature of Chinese temples, since pagodas were largely built as single edifices.

### 🍁 Yi Yuan
343 Renmin Rd. ☐ 7:30am–midnight daily. 🖾

The Garden of Happiness is one of Suzhou's newer gardens, dating from the late Qing dynasty. It was built by a government official who utilized rocks and landscape designs from other abandoned gardens. The garden appears to have originally covered a larger area; today its central feature is a pool encircled by rockeries and spanned by a zigzag bridge. The best viewpoint is from the Fragrant Lotus Pavilion, while another pavilion that juts into the pool is known for catching cooling breezes. Look out for the calligraphy by famous scholars and poets.

### 🏛 Silk Embroidery Research Institute
280 Jingde Rd. ☐ daily. 🖾

Housed in the Huan Xiu Shan Zhuang Garden (Surrounded by Majestic Mountains), this institute creates exquisitely fine silk embroidery, work that is mainly done by women. In order to produce the painting-like effect of their designs, the women sometimes work with silk strands that are so fine, they are almost invisible. They specialize in double-sided embroidery – for example, a cat with green eyes on one side and blue on the other.

### 🍁 Wangshi Yuan
Kuojia Xiang. **Tel** (0512) 6571 0286. ☐ 7:30am–5pm daily. 🖾

It is said that the Master of the Nets Garden was named after one of its owners – a retired official who wished to become an accomplished fisherman. Dating to 1140, it was completely remodeled in 1770 and for many people, is the finest of all Suzhou's gardens. Although small, it succeeds, with great subtlety, in introducing every element considered crucial to the classical garden (see pp178–9). It includes a central lake, discreet connecting corridors, pavilions with miniature courtyards, screens, delicate latticework, and above all, points which "frame a view", as if looking at a perfectly balanced photograph. The best known building is the Pavilion for Watching the Moon, from where the moon can be viewed in a mirror, in the water, and in the sky. Regular evening performances of Chinese opera, including local *kun ju*, take place here.

### 🍁 Canglang Ting
3 Canglang Ting Jie, Renmin Rd. ☐ 7:30am–5pm daily (to 4pm mid-Apr–Oct). 🖾

The Dark Blue Wave Pavilion Garden – whose name is suggestive of a relaxed and pragmatic approach to life – is perhaps Suzhou's oldest garden, first laid out in 1044 by a scholar, Su Zimei, on the site of an earlier villa. His successor, a general in the imperial army, enlarged it in the 12th century, and it was rebuilt in the 17th century. It is known for its technique of "borrowing a view", allowing the scenery beyond the garden's confines to play a role in its design. Here, it is achieved by lowering walls

**The Pavilion for Watching the Moon, Wangshi Yuan**

**Gateway to the Confucian Temple**

on the north side of some of the pavilions, allowing views across water; elsewhere the southwest hills can be seen. The central feature is a mound that is meant to resemble a wooded hill. Gardens were ideal places for contemplation and writing poetry, clearly visible in the engravings of verses and poems dotting Canglang Ting.

### 🍀 Liu Yuan & Xi Yuan

**Liu Yuan** 338 Liuyuan Rd. **Tel** *(0512) 6533 7903.* ◯ *7:30am–4:30pm daily.* 🖼 **Xi Yuan** Xiyuan Rd. **Tel** *(0512) 6533 4126.* ◯ *5:30am–7pm daily.* 🖼
Originally a pair, these two gardens lie near each other to the west of the old moated area. The Liu Yuan (Garden for Lingering in), was restored in 1953, and its four scenic areas are connected by a long corridor. The Xi Yuan (West Garden) once belonged to a devout Buddhist, and is more temple than garden. The Jiechang Temple, with its tiled roof and red beams, is a fine example of southern-style architecture. Adjoining it is the Hall of Five Hundred Louhan.

### 🏯 Pan Men Scenic Area

*See pp212–13.*

### 🏯 Confucian Temple

Renmin Rd. **Tel** *(0512) 6519 4343.* ◯ *daily.* 🖼
The original Song dynasty temple was rebuilt in 1864 after it was destroyed in the Taiping Rebellion *(see p422).* Its main hall, dating from the Ming dynasty, has several stone carvings including China's oldest surviving city map, depicting Suzhou, or

Pingjiang as it was known in 1229. A star chart dating from 1247 maps the positions of stars and celestial bodies in the heavens. It is one of the earliest surviving maps of its kind.

### 🍃 Tiger Hill

8 Sanmen Nei Rd. **Tel** *(0512) 6723 2305.* ◯ *7:30am–5pm daily.* 🖼
In the city's north-west is the popular Tiger Hill (Huqiu Shan), the burial place of He Lu, the King of Wu and founder of Suzhou. His spirit is said to be guarded by a white tiger who appeared three days after his death and refused to leave.

The main attraction is the Song-dynasty leaning pagoda (Yunyan Ta or Cloud Rock Pagoda), built in brick, which leans more than 7-ft (2-m) from the perpendicular at its highest point. Some 10th-century Buddhist *sutras* and a record of the year that it was

**Ceremonial urn, Tiger Hill**

constructed (959–961) were discovered during one of the attempts to prevent it from falling. The park is quite large, with pools and flower-beds filled with blooms in spring and early summer. One of the many boulders is split in two, allegedly the result of He Lu's swordsmanship. He is supposedly buried nearby along with 3,000 swords.

### 🏯 Hanshan Si

24 Hanshansi Long. **Tel** *(0512) 6533 6634.* ◯ *8:30am–4pm daily.* 🖼
First constructed in the Liang dynasty, the Cold Mountain Temple was named after a Tang-dynasty poet-monk. A stone rendition of him and his fellow monk, Shi De, is to be seen here. The temple was rebuilt in the 19th century, after it was destroyed during the Taiping Rebellion. Located close to the Grand Canal, it was immortalized by the Tang-dynasty poet Zhang Ji, who arrived here by boat and anchored nearby. His poem "Anchored at Night by the Maple Bridge" is inscribed on a stone stele, and contains the lines that made Hanshan Si famous: "Beyond Suzhou lies Hanshan Temple; at midnight the clang of the bell reaches the traveler's boat." The bell alluded to here was subsequently lost, and the temple's current bell was presented by Japan in 1905. Nearby, a quaint arched bridge offers views along the Grand Canal.

**Incense burners in the grounds of Hanshan Si**

# Pan Men Scenic Area
盘门

**Stone Buddha, Ruigang Pagoda**

Set in the southwest corner of the old city of Suzhou, this once overlooked area has been extensively restored – gone are the pretty canalside shacks – but it still contains some of the city's most interesting historical sights. Pan Men is a unique fortified gate that once controlled access to the city by both land and water. It is said to date back to 1351, although most of the present construction is more recent. Other highlights include the charming Wu Men Bridge and the views of the city and canals from the Ruigang Pagoda.

**Hall of Attractive Scenery**
*This three-story pavilion houses a tranquil tea room with views to the platform of the Western Stage in front.*

**★ Pan Men**
*This gate and attached section of wall (dating back to 1351) are all that remains of the city's ancient fortifications. It is the only land and water gate in China.*

**Wu Zixu's Memorial Temple**

**Double-doored water gate**

### STAR SIGHTS

★ Wu Men Bridge

★ Pan Men

★ Ruigang Pagoda

**★ Wu Men Bridge**
*This graceful bridge spanning the Grand Canal is the tallest in Suzhou and its design dates back to the Song dynasty, although it has since been rebuilt a few times. It has steps built into it and a lovely view from the top.*

**View from Ruigang Pagoda**
*After a climb up narrow stairs, looking down into the heart of Suzhou itself reveals a city dotted with large pockets of green – the beautiful gardens that have made the city so famous.*

**Entrance Gate**
This is the main entrance to the park. Pay here for access to the park and also a separate fee to climb the pagoda.

**Ornamental**
*pailou* or gate

**300-ft (90-m)
section of
city wall**

**★ Ruigang Pagoda**
*This seven-story, 140-ft (43-m) high pagoda dates back to the Song dynasty. It is constructed of brick with wooden platforms, and has simple Buddhist carvings at its base.*

**Hall of Four Auspicious Merits**
*The name of this hall is inspired by Buddhist teachings. At each side of the hall at the end of covered walkways are smaller pavilions, one containing a drum and the other a bell.*

Houses fronting canals in Zhouzhuang's old town

# Tongli ❷
同里

16 miles (25 km) SE of Suzhou.
👥 45,000. 🚌

A pretty little water town typical of the region, Tongli gives visitors a good idea of what Suzhou must have been like in its heyday. All its houses open out on to a network of canals that are spanned by dozens of stone bridges and are busy with transportation and trading boats. Some of its buildings are open to the public, such as **Jiayin Hall**, the former home of Liu Yazi, an early 20th-century actor renowned for his rather bizarre collection of gauze caps. The other interesting sight is **Tuisi Yuan**, a classical garden dating from the late Qing period.

🌸 **Tuisi Yuan**
⏰ 7:45am–5:30pm daily. 🔲

Sightseeing boats on one of Tongli's numerous canals

# Zhouzhuang ❸
周庄

12 miles (20 km) W of Shanghai.
👥 32,000. 🚌 Shanghai, Suzhou. 🚌 to Tongli. **Old Town** tickets from Quangong Rd.

A small town on the Jinghang Canal, which links Suzhou and Shanghai, Zhouzhuang was once a flourishing port, specializing in silk, pottery, and grain. It attracted scholars and officials who built fine bridges and houses between the Yuan and Qing eras. The charming **Old Town** can be explored on foot or via a boat tour on the canals. Among the sights are the Ming-era Hall of Zhang Residence with 70 rooms, and the Hall of Shen's Residence, with 100 rooms connected to the main hall. The Chengxu Temple, located near the museum, is a Song-dynasty Daoist shrine.

# Wuxi ❹
无锡

25 miles (40 km) NW of Suzhou.
👥 4,500,000. 🚉 🚌 🚌 services to Hangzhou & Suzhou. 🛈 88 Chezhan Lu. **Tel** (0510) 401 6081.

The highlights of a trip to Wuxi are the scenic Tai Hu (Lake Tai) and the Grand Canal, and the lakeside cherry blossoms in spring. According to legend, the town was established 3,500 years ago as the capital of the Wu Kingdom and was a center for the production of tin. When the mines ran dry (Wuxi means "without tin"), the capital moved west, but Wuxi

remained significant due to its location on the Grand Canal. **Xihui Park** in the west of town was established in 1958, and houses the Jichang Yuan garden. At the park's entrance, a path leads to the Dragon Light Pagoda on top of Xi Shan. A cable car connects Xi Shan to nearby Hui Shan. The **Wuxi Museum** has exhibits dating back 6,000 years.

🌸 **Xihui Park**
Huihe Rd. ⏰ 6am–6pm daily. 🔲
🏛 **Wuxi Museum**
71 Huihe Rd. ⏰ 9am–4pm daily. 🔲

The scenic cable car ride, Xihui Park, Wuxi

# Tai Hu ❺
太湖

3 miles (5 km) SW of Wuxi.

One of China's largest lakes, Tai Hu is famous for its rocks, an indispensable feature of a traditional garden (see pp178–9). The lake's northern shores are fringed with scenic spots including **Mei Yuan** (Plum Garden), spectacular in spring when its 4,000 fruit trees blossom. **Yuantou Zhu** (Turtle Head Promontory) is a favorite with the Chinese, with tea houses and pretty lake views. Nearby, **Sanshan Island** is a former bandit's haunt with temples and tall Buddha statues. However, none is as tall as the 289-ft (88-m) Lingshan Buddha on Ma Shan peninsula, a short bus ride from the other sights. The area also has a handful of lakeside theme parks.

🌸 **Mei Yuan & Yuantou Zhu**
⏰ 7am–5pm daily. 🔲

# The Grand Canal

The Grand Canal, started in 486 BC, was built in sections over the next one thousand years, with the aim of linking the Yangzi with the Yellow River, and one capital with another. It remains the world's largest man-made waterway. The earliest northern section was built for military reasons but large-scale construction began in the 7th century under the Sui Wendi emperor,

**Boat for canal cruises**

involving over 5 million conscripted males aged between 15 and 55, supervised by a vast and brutal police force. Linking the comparatively populous north with the southern rice-producing region, it reached Beijing only in the 13th century. In the early 20th century, a combination of the altered course of the fickle Yellow River and the rise of the railways saw its gradual demise.

**This map** *shows the route of the 1,112-mile (1,900-km) canal from Beijing to Hangzhou. Crossing the traditional battlefields between north and south, the canal supplied food throughout the empire. The hilly terrain led to the first recorded use of double locks in AD 984.*

**KEY**

▬ Grand Canal

**The Sui Yang Di emperor** *is said to have celebrated the completion of his work by touring the canal with a flotilla of dragon boats hauled by the empire's most beautiful women.*

**Tourist boats** *are now the only way to enjoy a journey on the canal as road and rail transport is favored by the locals. Regular tourist boats operate overnight services between Hangzhou and Suzhou or Wuxi, whilst boats can also be chartered for day-trips between the major tourist stops.*

**Barges splutter** *their way along the canal laden with agricultural produce and factory supplies. The busiest sections are in the south and north of the Yangzi to the border with Shandong.*

**The canal banks** *are lively with people performing domestic tasks. Families, even if they have houses, may live on board the boats when they are working.*

Pottery shop selling typical ceramic items, Ding Shan

# Yixing County ⑥
## 宜兴

25 miles (40 km) SW of Suzhou. 🚌 bus service between Wuxi & Yixing.

The county's main town, Yixing, is a busy transport hub that provides connections to the entire region. This fertile area of canals and farmland is known for its pottery, produced at **Ding Shan** for 3,000 years. Its name *yixing* or "purple sand" is derived from its distinctive deep maroon color. The town's streets are lined with factories and pottery shops, the latter full of items such as traditional little pots in all shapes and sizes. Ding Shan's tourist office also organizes factory visits.

A short journey from town, the **Pottery Exhibition Hall** displays a range of objects, from fine, early Yixingware to the prized miniature teapots. Nearby are the **Karst Caves**, comprising three groups – Zhanggong, Linggu, and Shanjuan. The highlight of Zhanggong's 72 caves is the

Hall of the Sea Dragon King, that can hold several thousand people, while Linggu has an underground waterfall.

🏛 **Pottery Exhibition Hall**
150 Ding Shan Beilu. ☐ *daily.* 🖾

🕳 **Karst Caves**
☐ *daily.* 🖾

# Changzhou ⑦
## 常州

25 miles (40 km) NW of Wuxi.
🚶 3,500,000. 🚉 🚌

Often overlooked, this city on the Grand Canal is worth visiting for its old center, crisscrossed by streets of traditional houses and canals. The two main streets, Bei and Nan Dajie, are lined with shops selling silks and the locally-made painted combs. The 7th-century **Tianning Si** has 83 Buddha statues decorating its roof, while the Song-era **Yizhou Pavilion** is associated with the poet Su Dongpo, who stayed here when he visited the city.

# Zhenjiang ⑧
## 镇江

31 miles (50 km) E of Suzhou. 🚶 3,000,000. 🚉 🚌
ℹ 92 Zhongshan Xi Rd.

Attractively set on the banks of the Yangzi River, Zhenjiang's prosperity was linked to the construction of the Grand Canal *(see p217)*. In the 19th century, the city was ceded to foreign powers. The former **Royal Hotel** is a fine example of European pastiche, while the old British Consulate now houses the **Zhenjiang Museum**. Its exhibits include a photograph of the *Amethyst*, the British ship that sailed upriver in 1949 to bring aid to the British in Nanjing. After coming under heavy fire, it ran aground, and was stranded for months. The ship finally made a dash for freedom, and miraculously, managed to rejoin its fleet.

To the museum's west, **Jin Shan Park** is the site of the Jin Shan Temple, founded in the Eastern Jin dynasty, and the Cishou Pagoda, one of a pair built in the Tang era. The climb to the top reveals splendid views of the Yangzi. To the city's northeast lies **Beigu Shan** hill with its beautiful **Lingyun Ting** pagoda. Farther east is **Jiao Shan**, an island famed for its scenery, accessible by cable car or boat. Above the island's fortifications, Xijiang Lou tower offers fine views of the river.

🏛 **Zhenjiang Museum**
85 Boxian Rd. ☐ *daily.* 🖾

🌲 **Jin Shan Park**
62 Jinshan Xilu. ☐ *daily.* 🖾

The southern-style Tianning Si (Temple of Heavenly Peace), Changzhou

# Calligraphy

Calligraphy raises ordinary Chinese script into a high art form and is traditionally regarded as highly as painting or poetry as a method of self-expression. The beauty of calligraphy may seem hard to appreciate for most visitors who do not read Chinese. Freestyle calligraphy, however, which transforms ordinary characters almost into figurative and abstract paintings, can easily be appreciated for its artistry. The Chinese viewer, taught from a young age the basic sequence of strokes, can mentally trace the characters as they were created by the artists and so experience their spiritual world. As they are limited to the same eight strokes, the artists' individual styles – the variations in stroke weight, angle, and vigor – are easily appreciated. Experts consider the balance and proportional weight of the strokes, the structure of the character and its unity and harmony.

**Decorative ink stone**

## THE FOUR TREASURES
The main tools of the calligrapher are known as "The Four Treasures of the Study" – ink sticks, ink stone, brushes, and paper. Anhui is especially famed for the quality of its ink and brushes.

**Ink sticks** *are made from soot – pine wood or tung oil – mixed with glue and even spices. Inks are usually black although colors are available.*

**Each character** is made up of eight types of stroke performed in a set order.

**Thinner dashes look less crowded**

**The seal** *is carefully positioned on the page. The cinnabar ink stamp may be the name of the artist or some poetry.*

**The ink stone** *is used to grind the ink stick with the right amount of water. A thick ink is glossy and strong, while thin ink can be lively or subtle.*

**Graceful downstroke to the left**

**Finely tapered hook stroke**

**Paper**, *invented around AD 100, was made from mulberry or bamboo fibers. Much cheaper than the silk it replaced, paper is classed by its weight, as this affects how fast it absorbs the ink.*

**Brush rests** *were used to hold other brushes or so the artist could put down his brush and contemplate.*

**Brushes** *permitted greater freedom for expression than engraving bone or stone (see p26) and led to more fluid scripts. Supposedly made from many varieties of fur, the tip should be round yet pointed, even and strong.*

**Practice** *is crucial. The hand must always know what it is about to do; there is no room for indecision. There are three levels of practice – tracing, copying and working from memory. Each step up allows the artist to add more individuality.*

# Yangzhou ❾

扬州

**Pagoda,
Daming Si**

One of the Yangzi River delta's great cities, Yangzhou has always been known for its prosperity, culture, and cuisine. Its location on the Grand Canal dictated the rise and fall of its fortunes. The city declined with the fall of the Song dynasty and the diminished use of the canal, but revived again in the Ming era, when the canal was restored and used to transport silk, rice, and salt. The salt merchants in particular built elegant villas and gardens, especially in the 18th century when Yangzhou was part of the imperial inspection tours. Despite development, the city has much to offer, including its several gardens.

**A fruit stall among the historic architecture on Dong Guan Jie**

### 🔲 Daming Si

1 Pingshan Tang Rd. ⬜ *8am–5pm daily.* 🖼

Sitting atop a hill, the Temple of Abundant Light dates to the 5th century AD, but was rebuilt after being destroyed in the Taiping Rebellion *(see p422)*. The central **Jian Zhen Hall** was erected in 1973 in honor of the monk, Jian Zhen, who traveled to Japan in 753. Credited with introducing many aspects of Chinese culture to Japan, he is revered by the Japanese, who funded the main hall's construction, and modeled it on the Tosho-dai Temple in Nara, Japan. Nearby is a natural spring with an adjoining teahouse.

### 🏛 Hanlinyuan Museum

Xiangbie Rd. ⬜ *8:30am–5pm.* 🖼
The magnificent Western Han tomb of Liu Xu, ruler of the Guangling Kingdom, is five levels deep. Its second air-tight layer comprises 840 *nanmu* (cedar) bricks joined by hooks. The third level housed the warehouse, the fourth level

the king's living quarters, and the fifth level, a coffin on wheels. The tomb was equipped with every imaginable luxury, including a bathroom.

### 🌿 Shou Xi Hu

28 Da Hongqiao Rd. ⬜ *7:30am–5pm daily.* 🖼
Yangzhou's most popular sight, the Thin West Lake is a slim version of Hangzhou's famous West Lake *(see pp242–3)*. It winds through a park filled with willow trees, pavilions,

and bridges. The handsome **Wuting Qiao** (Five Pavilion Bridge) is its most famous structure, built by a salt merchant in 1757 to honor the Qianlong emperor's visit to Yangzhou. To the west is Ershisi Qiao (Twenty-Four Bridge), so called because its 24 archways could be appreciated 24 hours a day. **Bai Ta** (White Dagoba) is a Tibetan-style stupa, modeled on the one in Beijing's Beihai Park *(see p90)*. In the Xu Garden, the **Listening to Orioles Pavilion** has fine woodwork, while the **Pinyuan Lou** offers views that supposedly demonstrate the rules of perspective as compiled by the Song artist, Guo Xi. East of the lake, the Imperial Jetty is where Qianlong's barge was moored.

### 🏛 Yangzhou Museum

Near Tianlin Si. **Tel** (0514) 8522 8018. ⬜ *8:30am–11am, 1–5pm daily.*
This museum is housed in a temple that was built in 1772 in memory of a Ming official who refused to surrender the city to the Qing rulers. On display are some splendid items, including an ancient boat salvaged from the Grand Canal, and a burial suit made of jade.

### 🌿 Ge Yuan

10 Yanfu East Rd. ⬜ *7:15am–5pm daily.* 🖼
Yangzhou's most famous garden, Ge Yuan was once owned by the painter Shi Tao, and later by a salt merchant. Its name derives from the leaves of its bamboo plants, that resemble the character *"ge"* meaning "self". Its central feature is its rockeries, but it also has some fine pavilions.

**Wuting Qiao (Five Pavilion Bridge), Shou Xi Hu Gongyuan**

### 🏛 Wang Shi Xiao Yuan

14 Dongquan Men Lishi Jiequ.
⬤ 8am–5pm daily. 📷

Located on a street of historic homes including that of former president Jiang Zemin, the grand Wang Shi Xiao Yuan was the residence of a wealthy salt merchant. Dating to the Qing era, it has nearly 100 rooms. The interior is lavishly furnished, and its main Spring Hall contains a German chandelier and marble wall panels.

### 🏛 Garden Tomb of Puhaddin

17 Jiefang South Rd. ⬤ 8am–5pm daily.

Said to be the 16th descendant of the Prophet Mohammed, Puhaddin was a teacher who lived in Yangzhou until his death in 1275. His grave is enclosed in a building filled with inscriptions from the holy Koran. Other noted Muslim figures from the Song and Ming eras are buried nearby. Puhaddin also built the tiny **Xianhe Mosque**, located southwest on Ganquan Road. Its wall is covered in arabesques, a legacy of the Persian traders who once frequented the city.

**The Tang-dynasty Shi Ta or Stone Pagoda**

### 🍀 He Yuan

66 Xuning Men Jie. ⬤ 7:45am–5pm daily. 📷

This small garden creates an illusion of space and depth by the clever arrangement of its features, including shrubs, trees, and a walkway. Named after one of its 19th-century owners, it is divided in two,

## VISITORS' CHECKLIST

37 miles (60 km) NE of Nanjing.
🚊 4,500,000. 🚌 East Bus Station, West Bus Station.
ℹ 99 Daxue North Rd.

with some pavilions decorated in southern-style lattice work, although northern influences prevail in its overall layout and style. A few teahouses also dot the garden.

### 🏯 Wenchang Ge

The round Wenchang Ge (Promoting Literature Pavilion) is all that remains of the old Confucian Academy. Founded by the first Ming emperor, Hongwu, who believed in education for all, the academy originally had two pavilions. To the north, the **Si Wang Ting** (Pavilion of the Four Views) was a part of the Ming-era Provincial College, and was used as an observatory. Lying west of Wenchang Ge, the Tang-dynasty **Shi Ta** (Stone Pagoda) was once part of a temple located outside the city walls. It was moved here in the Song era.

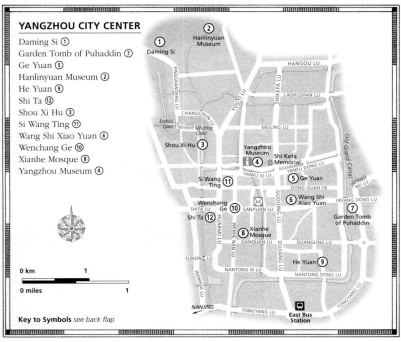

## YANGZHOU CITY CENTER

Daming Si ①
Garden Tomb of Puhaddin ⑦
Ge Yuan ⑤
Hanlinyuan Museum ②
He Yuan ⑨
Shi Ta ⑫
Shou Xi Hu ③
Si Wang Ting ⑪
Wang Shi Xiao Yuan ⑥
Wenchang Ge ⑩
Xianhe Mosque ⑧
Yangzhou Museum ④

0 km          1
0 miles       1

**Key to Symbols** see back flap

# Nanjing ⑩

南京

**Statue, Fuzi Miao**

Of all China's great cities, Nanjing or Nanking, as it was once known, is the most attractive. The capital of Jiangsu province, it is picturesquely set on the banks of the Yangzi, close to the magnificent Purple Mountain. This city of lakes is still enclosed within its grand city wall, and its streets are shaded by plane trees. Meaning "southern capital," it was the capital of several regional kingdoms up to AD 220. Later, it was China's capital under the early Ming. It was also the capital of the 19th-century Taiping Heavenly Kingdom and the first Chinese Republic under Dr. Sun Yat-sen. Today, Nanjing is a fast developing city, with good restaurants and a lively nightlife.

**Garden and pavilions at the Taiping Heavenly Kingdom History Museum**

### Exploring Nanjing

Although the medieval city walls give the impression that Nanjing is a small city, it is in fact fairly spread out. A lot of ground can be covered on foot, but visitors will also need to use the city's local transport, either the comprehensive bus service or taxis, which are plentiful and reasonably priced.

### 🏯 Zhonghua Gate
*See pp224–5.*

### 🏛 Taiping Heavenly Kingdom History Museum
128 Zhanyuan Rd. **Tel** (025) 5220 1849. 🔲 *daily.* 🎟
This museum commemorates the anti-dynastic Taiping Heavenly Kingdom Rebellion of 1851–64 (*see p422*). The building was used by one of the rebellion's leaders, or Heavenly Princes, while one section – the Zhan or Enthusiasm Garden – originally belonged to the first

Ming emperor, Hongwu. Today, the halls are filled with memorabilia and photographs relating to the rebellion, which overran large parts of China. After the rebels claimed Nanjing as their base, they came very close to toppling the Qing dynasty in Beijing, but were eventually defeated by the Qing army under Western leadership in

1864. On display are weapons and uniforms, samples of Taiping currency, and documents explaining the Heavenly ideology, which aimed to change China's feudalistic society into one based on equality. Their aims included the modernization of the education system that was still based on Confucian classics, the redistribution of land, and equality of the sexes.

### ♣ Bailuzhou Park
🔲 *daily.* 🎟
The White Egret Park was once the property of the Ming general Xu Da, and subsequently became the Chinese quarter during the centuries of Manchu rule. The pavilions were all destroyed during the Taiping Rebellion but the park was restored in 1951, and the area still abounds in traditional houses.

### 🏛 Fuzi Miao
Gongyuan Rd. **Tel** (025) 8662 8639. 🔲 *8am–9pm daily.* 🎟
The origins of Fuzi Miao (Temple of Confucius) go back to AD 1034, while the current buildings date to the late 19th century, with later additions. The temple was the seat of Confucian study for more than 1,500 years. Its halls feature a small exhibition of folk arts. The surrounding streets are flanked by houses with long upturned eaves and whitewashed walls – many of which are being restored in typical southern style. Nearby, the attractive canal bank has plenty of boats that ply the short distance to Zhonghua Gate.

**The distinctive double-eaved main hall of the Fuzi Miao**

*For hotels and restaurants in this region see pp561–2 and pp588–9*

### ☗ Chaotian Gong

Mochou Rd. **Tel** (025) 8446 6460. ◻
8am–4:30pm daily. ▨ **Court Rites
Display** 11:15am–12:15pm daily.
The substantial Chaotian Gong
(Heaven Palace) was once a
place of ancestor worship, a
seat of learning, and a Confucian temple. Its mid-19th
century buildings such as
halls, towers, and walkways,
stand on an ancient temple
site dating to AD 390. It now
houses the Municipal Museum,
displaying Shang bronzes and
fragments of the legendary
porcelain pagoda, destroyed
in the Taiping Rebellion. The
pagoda was built in the 15th
century by the Ming Yongle
emperor to honor his mother,
and was covered in glazed
white bricks. There are daily
shows of Ming-dynasty **Court
Rites** in the palace square.

Nearby along Tangzi Jie,
house No. 74 has colorful
paintings dating to the Taiping
occupation that were discovered in 1952. The house was
occupied by a follower of the
Taiping Eastern Prince, Yang
Xiuqing. The paintings – of

**Detail from the Sun Yat Sen Hall,
Tianchao Gong**

animals and birds – are more
interesting for their historical
associations than for their
deft execution.

### ☗ Tianchao Gong & Xu Yuan

292 Changjiang Rd. **Tel** (025) 8454
2362. ◻ 9am–5pm daily. ▨
The Tianchao Gong
(Heavenly Kingdom Palace),
together with the surrounding
classical Xu Yuan Garden

(Balmy Garden), were
originally built by a Ming
prince. Under the Qing
dynasty, it became the seat of
provincial government until
1853, when it was seized by
the leader of the Taiping
Rebellion, Hong Xiuquan, as
his headquarters. Finally, after
the overthrow of the Qing
empire, the palace housed the
Republican Government, from
where both Dr. Sun Yat-sen
and Chiang Kai-shek ruled
China. Inside, there is an
exhibition devoted to the
Taiping Rebellion and to Dr.
Sun Yat-sen. The surrounding
Xu Yuan Garden is a popular
weekend spot with the locals.

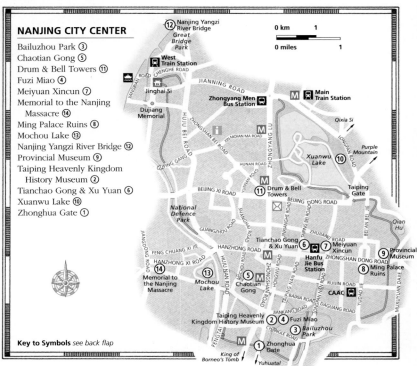

## NANJING CITY CENTER

0 km                              1

0 miles                           1

**Key to Symbols** see back flap

# Zhonghua Gate
中华门

Built under the orders of the first Ming emperor, Hongwu, from 1368–86, the walls surrounding the capital were the most extensive in the world at the time. The 40-ft (12-m) high walls snaked 20 miles (33 km) around the city's natural contours. Given that the city was elsewhere protected by river and mountain, Zhonghua Gate was a key element in Nanjing's southern defences. Its walls were cemented by a super-strong mortar made with glutinous rice. Certainly the Emperor's show of defense was effective – no enemy attempted to breach the walls via Zhonghua Gate. Today the gate's impressive remains are open to visitors and an interesting museum has been built into the battlements.

**Nanjing from the city wall adjacent to Zhonghua Gate**

**Four gatehouses**, sitting above each arched gateway, contained armaments and supplies.

**Portcullises** blocked passage through the gateways. The grooves are still visible.

**★ Inner Citadels**
*Behind the main gate are three courtyards or citadels. During an attack, enemy forces that breached the main gate could be trapped in these courtyards. The cavities in the walls concealed soldiers waiting in ambush.*

## RECONSTRUCTION OF ZHONGHUA GATE
The main gate tower sat adjacent to the top of the wall, with the rest of the citadel protruding into the city. Today, only the brick walls remain – none of the gatehouses has survived.

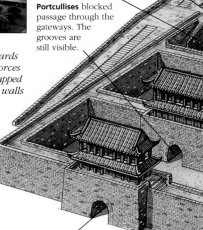

**STAR SIGHTS**
★ Inner Citadels
★ Arched Gateways
★ Signed Bricks

**★ Arched Gateways**
*Four arched tunnels, each as long as 174 feet (53 m), run through the battlements. Each gate had massive double doors and a portcullis.*

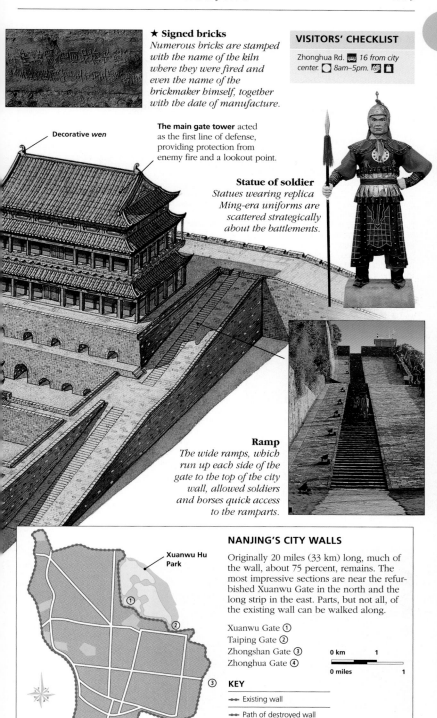

★ **Signed bricks**
*Numerous bricks are stamped with the name of the kiln where they were fired and even the name of the brickmaker himself, together with the date of manufacture.*

**VISITORS' CHECKLIST**

Zhonghua Rd. 16 from city center. 8am–5pm.

Decorative *wen*

**The main gate tower** acted as the first line of defense, providing protection from enemy fire and a lookout point.

**Statue of soldier**
*Statues wearing replica Ming-era uniforms are scattered strategically about the battlements.*

**Ramp**
*The wide ramps, which run up each side of the gate to the top of the city wall, allowed soldiers and horses quick access to the ramparts.*

**NANJING'S CITY WALLS**

Originally 20 miles (33 km) long, much of the wall, about 75 percent, remains. The most impressive sections are near the refurbished Xuanwu Gate in the north and the long strip in the east. Parts, but not all, of the existing wall can be walked along.

Xuanwu Gate ①
Taiping Gate ②
Zhongshan Gate ③
Zhonghua Gate ④

Xuanwu Hu Park

0 km                    1
0 miles                 1

**KEY**

— Existing wall
— Path of destroyed wall

### 🏛 Meiyuan Xincun

🕐 *9am–4:30pm daily.* 📷

The former Chinese Communist Party office was headed in 1946–47 by Zhou Enlai *(see p250)*, who held negotiations with the Kuomintang after the Japanese surrender. The restored building houses a museum commemorating these events.

### 🏯 Ming Palace Ruins

Zhongshan Donglu. 🕐 *daily.* 📷

The old Ming Palace (Ming Gugong) was built in the 14th century for the first Ming emperor, Hongwu, who made Nanjing his capital. Within a century of its construction, this splendid palace was severely damaged by two fires. Later, the Manchus and then the Taiping soldiers completed its destruction. All that remains are ten marble bridges, the old Wu Men or Meridian Gate, and a large number of pillar bases worth examining for their finely sculptured details. The pillars also give an idea of the layout of the palace buildings. Along its main axis, the palace would have had three major courtyards enclosed by enormous halls raised on platforms. These were flanked on either side by altars and temples. Beijing's Forbidden City *(see pp86–9)* is a larger version of this palace complex. The grounds have plenty of trees, which offer shade in the summer months.

**Sculptural detail, Ming Palace Ruins**

**Xuanwu Lake, edged by pavilions and boat piers**

### 🏛 Provincial Museum

4 Chaotiangong Rd. **Tel** *(025) 8480 2119.* 🕐 *8am–4:30pm daily.* 📷

The Provincial Museum, founded in 1933, is one of China's better museums and definitely worth a visit. Its highlights include some wonderful ornate sedan chairs, bronzes from the Zhou dynasty, and model trading ships. The collection of jade and lacquerware includes a jade burial suit consisting of rectangles of jade sewn together with silver thread, dating from the Eastern Han dynasty. Also on display are bricks from the city wall, pictures of the old city, and relics from the Taiping Heavenly Kingdom Rebellion. Many of the exhibits are captioned in English, which makes the museum even more interesting.

### ⛰ Purple Mountain

*See pp228–9.*

### ❧ Xuanwu Lake

Xuanwu Park. 🕐 *daily.* 📷

In the northeast corner of the city an especially fine stretch of the Ming city walls skirts the western shore of the enormous Xuanwu Lake, situated in Xuanwu Park. At well over 1 mile (2.5 km) long, the lake was an important water source for the city, as well as a popular imperial resort for many centuries. During the Song dynasty, it was also used for naval exercises. The park was opened to the public after the fall of the Qing dynasty in 1911.

Xuanwu Lake has five small islands named after the five continents, which are linked by bridges and causeways. They offer a variety of entertainment options with teahouses, restaurants, pavilions, boats of various types, swimming areas, an open-air theater, and even a small zoo. The most scenic is Yingzhou Island, delightfully laid out with lily pads, trees, and flowers. Although the park can get crowded, especially on weekends, it is a charming place to relax. The most convenient entrance is through the triple-arched Xuanwu Gate in the old city wall on Zhongyang Road; tickets are available from the booth on Jiwusi Road.

### 🏯 Drum & Bell Towers

🕐 *daily.*

The much-restored Drum Tower dates back over 600 years to 1382, and is fronted by a traditional gateway. It was built to house several drums that were beaten through the

**Marble pillar bases mark the layout of the palace, Ming Palace Ruins**

night to mark the change of the watch, and occasionally to sound alarms. Today, only one large drum remains. The tower also houses a collection of amateur paintings, and a part of it has been converted into a teahouse. A short distance to the northeast is the Bell Tower (Dazhong Ting), constructed during the Ming dynasty and rebuilt in 1889. The huge bronze bell, cast in 1388, is one of the largest in China.

The area surrounding the towers was the administrative center of the old city. It is now a busy place, full of offices and heavy traffic.

**Traffic on the Nanjing Yangzi River Bridge**

### 🚆 Nanjing Yangzi River Bridge

Daqiao Nanlu. *Tel (025) 5878 5703.*
**Elevator** ◯ *daily.* 📷
This impressive piece of engineering, completed in 1968, is one of the great achievements of the Chinese Communists, who took over the project after the Russians

## NANJING MASSACRE

The Nanjing Massacre, or the Rape of Nanking as it is also known, is still an object of friction between the Chinese and the Japanese. In 1937, when the invading Japanese army succeeded in capturing Nanjing, a large number of civilians stayed behind instead of fleeing, following an appeal made by the Chinese government. While the government fled, the occupying army proceeded to carry out a brutal campaign of murder, pillage, and rape on the civilian population. It is thought that up to 400,000 people were killed in the incident. After Japan's surrender in 1945, the government returned to Nanjing and the city regained its status as the capital of China until the Communists shifted the capital back to Beijing in 1949.

**Monument to the Nanjing Massacre**

marched out in 1960. According to the official Chinese version, the bridge was built from scratch, as the Russians took the original plans with them when they left. The double-decker bridge, designed for road traffic as well as trains, is almost a mile (1.5 km) long, and is one of the longest in China. Before it was built, ferries used to carry entire trains across the river, one carriage at a time. An elevator takes visitors to the top of one of the towers, from where there are excellent views across the river. Also worth noting are the Soviet-style sculptures that decorate the bridge. The best approach to the bridge is through the adjacent Daqiao Gongyuan (Bridge Park).

### 🌿 Mochou Lake

◯ *daily.*
Just outside the city wall in western Nanjing, Mochou Lake (Mochou Hu) is named after the legendary heroine, Mochou. Her name, meaning "Without Sorrow", was bestowed because her singing was so sweet that it banished all sorrow. Surrounding the lake, Mochou Lake Park is especially pretty when the lotus flowers on the water are in full bloom. An open-air stage and a teahouse lie along the water's edge. The **Square Pavilion** contains a statue of Mochou in a small pond, while the **Winning Chess Pavilion** next door was where the first Ming emperor, Hongwu, played an important game of chess with his general.

**Square Pavilion with a statue of the legendary maiden Mochou, Mochou Lake Park**

# Purple Mountain

## 紫金山

**Door handle Ming Xiao Ling**

Overlooking the city, Zijin Shan, or the Purple Mountain, is said to take its name from the color of the rocks. It is a picturesque area of gentle hills shaded by woodland and bamboo groves, dotted with villas. It also contains several of the most important points of interest in Nanjing such as the Mausoleum of Dr. Sun Yat-sen, Ming Xiao Ling, and the Linggu Temple complex. Seeing everything will take a whole day and, although there are food stalls around, visitors are advised to take along a picnic. The energetic can make the long climb to the summit for splendid views over the city; alternatively you can take a cable car from outside the eastern wall.

**Statue of Sun Yat-sen, "Father of Modern China," in his mausoleum**

**Purple Mountain Observatory**
*Alongside more modern equipment, the observatory houses a display of bronze instruments that date back to the 15th century. However, similar pieces were used by the Chinese as long as 3,000 years ago.*

**Cable Car Summit**

**Tomb of Liao Zhongka**

**Botanical Gardens**

**Nanjing City Wall**

**Qian Lake**

**Plum Blossom Hill**

**The cable car** goes to the summit in two stages and is recommended for the views.

| 0 meters | 500 |
|---|---|
| 0 yards | 500 |

## KEY

🚠 Cable car

═ Road

## STAR SIGHTS

★ Ming Xiao Ling

★ Linggu Temple & Beamless Hall

★ Mausoleum of Dr. Sun Yat Sen

**★ Ming Xiao Ling**
*This tomb was completed in 1405 for the first Ming emperor, Hongwu, and his wife. Although much of it was destroyed in the Taiping Rebellion (see p422), enough remains to give a sense of the grandeur of the original.*

## Museum of Dr. Sun Yat-sen
*Set in a pretty building this museum is often overlooked by visitors. Four floors of exhibits chronicle Sun Yat-sen's life with paintings, photographs, and personal effects.*

**The Music Stage** was built in 1933 as part of Sun Yat-sen's mausoleum.

### Linggu Pagoda
*Built in 1929, this 199-ft (61-m) high pagoda was designed by an American, Henry Murphy, at the behest of Chiang Kai-shek, in memory of the soldiers killed in the 1911 revolution (see pp62–3).*

Guanghua Pavilion

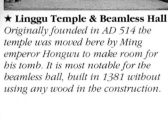

★ **Linggu Temple & Beamless Hall**
*Originally founded in AD 514 the temple was moved here by Ming emperor Hongwu to make room for his tomb. It is most notable for the beamless hall, built in 1381 without using any wood in the construction.*

★ **Mausoleum of Dr. Sun Yat-sen**
*Despite the use of blue tiles, instead of the emperor's yellow ones, this grand mausoleum has imperial resonances. Completed in 1929, the blue and white colors represent the Nationalist Party.*

# Exploring the Purple Mountain

Also known as Zhongshan Mountain, after Sun Yat-sen's Mandarin name, the Purple Mountain (Zijin Shan) is best explored by starting from the easternmost site at the Linggu Temple and slowly working your way west back to the city. To fully explore the area requires a long day, but if time is scarce, half a day will do for visiting Sun Yat Sen's Mausoleum, the most popular site on the mountain, and one other. However, it is also pleasant just to get away from everybody else and wander the network of shady woodland paths that crisscross the hillside, and to visit the many smaller visitor attractions.

**Lake beside the Linggu Temple at the foot of the Purple Mountain**

### Linggu Temple, Beamless Hall, and Pagoda

The Linggu Temple was originally sited where the Ming emperor Hongwu wanted to build his tomb (Ming Xiao Ling), and so he had it moved to this site. The only original building that remains is the Beamless Hall. Built in 1381, it is a brick vaulted edifice constructed without any wooden beams. This was supposed to be the solution to a timber shortage, but, with few exceptions, it failed to be adopted. A small, restored Buddhist temple reputedly houses the remains of the Tang dynasty monk Xuanzang who traveled to India to get Buddhist scriptures (see p487). The nearby Linggu Pagoda is inscribed in the handwriting of Chiang Kai-shek saying "repaying the country with extreme loyalty." The building is meant to combine the future and the past in that it is an old style of building – a pagoda; but built with modern materials –

reinforced concrete. From the top, there is a great view of the thick green leafy carpet that cloaks the mountain.

### Sun Yat-sen's Museum

Slightly off the tourist trail, this museum is inside a beautiful building that once held a Buddhist library. The collection of paintings, black and white photos and artifacts chronicles in detail the life of the "father of the people." The top two floors have captions in English. The Buddhist library of *sutras* is now housed in a separate building out the back.

### Sun Yat-sen's Mausoleum (Zhongshan Ling)

The revolutionary leader died in 1925 and a competition was held to design his tomb. The winner was Y.C. Lu, a graduate of Cornell University School of Architecture. The tomb is approached up a typically long marble stairway

**Stone sculpture from the Xiao Ling sacred way**

of 392 steps and comprises a square hall with a lifesize marble statue of the man leading to a round, domed building that contains his sarcophagus inset in the floor. There are other memorials in the area such as the **Music Stage**, an auditorium popular with picnicking visitors and the Guanghua Pavilion.

### Xiao Ling Tomb

Although much of it is derelict, the site is mainly of interest as the first of the Ming Tombs. The sacred way, an avenue of stone statues of pairs of animals and officials, some sitting, some standing on duty is also impressive. Unusually it does not run south to north but winds its way up the hillside. South of the tomb lies the scenic area of **Plum Blossom Hill**, especially pretty in spring when the trees bloom pink. To the west lie the **Botanical Gardens**, a huge area with colourful planting, lawns, hills, and lakes. Nearby lies the **Tomb of Liao Zhongkai** and his wife He Xiangning, prominent Nationalists who followed Sun Yat-sen.

### Observatory

Built in the 1930s, the observatory is slightly run down these days. The main point of interest for the casual visitor is the small collection of copies of bronze Ming and Qing astronomical instruments.

**Approach to the tomb of the first Ming emperor, Hongwu**

Memorial to the 300,000 victims of the Nanjing Massacre

## Around Nanjing

There are plenty of interesting sites around Nanjing that are worth seeing along with the Purple Mountain. All can easily be reached by taxi or in the case of Qixia Si, by bus.

### 🏛 Memorial to the Nanjing Massacre

418 Shuiximen Rd. **Tel** (025) 8661 2230. ◻ 8:30am–4:30pm daily. 📷
A short distance west of Mochou Park, this site recalls the Japanese atrocities, known as the Nanjing Massacre *(see p227)*, that took place during the city's occupation in World War II. In the garden, shards of bone and piles of skulls are grim mementoes. Amid a photographic chronicle of the events, one room focuses on the post-war reconciliation between the two nations.

### ♣ Yuhuatai

215 Yuhua Rd. **Tel** (025) 5241 1523. ◻ 8:30am–5:30pm daily. 📷
According to legend, Yuhuatai, south of Zhonghua Gate, is where a 5th-century monk gave a sermon that was so moving that flowers rained down from the sky. Chinese visitors still collect the colored pebbles that are found here. Sadly, the park became an execution ground during the Chinese Revolution (1927–49), and thousands lost their lives here. The **Martyrs' Memorial** consists of nine gigantic, 98-ft (30-m) high figures in typical Soviet realist style. Behind it is a pagoda, from where there are good views across the city.

### 🏯 King of Borneo's Tomb

Off Ning Dan Gong Rd. Over 1 mile (2 km) NW of Yuhuatai. ◻ daily.
Situated close to Yuhuatai, the King of Borneo's Tomb was discovered as recently as 1958. The rulers of Borneo had been sending tribute to China since AD 977. In the mid-14th century, the first Ming emperor, Hongwu, greatly expanded the existing tribute system, whereby foreign nations paid "tribute" to China in the form of gifts and precious goods. He sent envoys to all of China's tributary states including Borneo, to ensure that this economic exchange continued. The King of Borneo arrived in Nanjing in 1408, but died during his stay. His tomb is marked with a tortoise stele, and, similar to other tombs of the period, a sacred pathway with statues on either side. The site is not clearly signposted, so it is advisable to have the tomb's name written in Chinese in order to ask for directions.

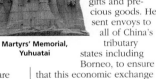

**Martyrs' Memorial, Yuhuatai**

### 🏯 Qixia Si & Thousand Buddha Cliffs

Qixia Shan. 9 miles (15 km) NE of Nanjing. 🚌 bus from opposite the railway station, 1 hr. **Tel** (025) 8576 8152. ◻ 7am–5:30pm daily. 📷
One of the largest Buddhist seminaries in the country, Qixia Si was originally founded in AD 483, but the current building dates from 1908, at the end of the Qing dynasty. It consists of two principal temple halls; one has walls that are extensively covered with flying *apsarases* (celestial maidens), while the other houses a statue of an upright Vairocana Buddha, known as the Cosmic Buddha who is the embodiment of Truth and Knowledge. To the east stands an octagonal stone pagoda built in AD 601, which bears carvings of scenes from the life of the Buddha.

Behind the halls are the **Thousand Buddha Cliffs**. These are in fact just over 500 Buddha statues carved into the cliff face, but "thousand" is often used in China to denote "many." The earliest statues date to the 5th century Qi dynasty, while most were carved during the Song and Tang dynasties. Some statues were badly defaced during the bloody Taiping Rebellion *(see p422)* and again during the Cultural Revolution *(see pp64–5)*, but enough remain to make the visit worthwhile. Visitors can spend a few enjoyable hours walking in the woods behind the cliffs.

Octagonal stone pagoda with carvings of the Buddha's life, Qixia Si

# Traditional Medicine

Medicine in China dates back some 4,000 years and evolved as a result of the search for the elixir of life, research in which many emperors took a keen interest. Over the centuries an approach was adopted that would today be called holistic – the importance of diet, emotional health, and environment was emphasized. Today, treatment is still founded on the use of herbs, diet and acupuncture. Daoist philosophy is an integral ingredient, the most notable aspect being *qi (see pp32–3)*, the vital

**Yin yang symbol**

force of living things. *Qi* gives rise to the opposite and interdependent forces of *yin* and *yang*, signified in the universe and body by wet and dry, cold and heat, etc. Unlike western medicine, where an outside force, such as bacteria or a virus, is assumed to cause disease, in Chinese medicine a medical problem is caused by a *yin-yang* imbalance within the patient. When *yin* and *yang* are out of balance, the flow of *qi* has been depleted or blocked; Chinese medical practitioners seek to return the balance.

**10TH-CENTURY CHANNEL CHART**
*Qi* flows through channels that radiate throughout the body from the vital organs to the extremities. This chart clearly illustrates a channel that runs from the intestines through the arm to the finger tips. Applying pressure to the specified points will moderate the flow of *qi*.

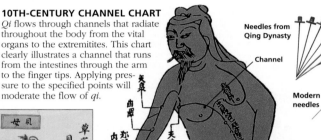

**Needles from Qing Dynasty**

**Channel**

**Modern needles**

**Acupuncture needles** *are inserted just below the skin at pressure points, also called men or gates, along the channels. Acupuncture has even proved an effective anesthetic.*

**The Bencao Gangmu,** *a pharmacopeia of medicine listing all known diseases and their treatments, was compiled by the naturalist Li Shizhen during the 12th century.*

**Pressure point**

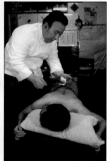

**Moxibustion,** *used in chronic cases, involves burning artemisia leaves to heat up the pressure points. The heat is conveyed by needles, but the moxa is sometimes held so close to the skin that it singes.*

**A mixture of herbs,** *fungus, roots, bark, and sometimes dried animal products, such as ground antler, are carefully combined and dispensed to the patient who boils the ingredients to make a powerful decoction.*

Plaque over the beautifully decorated entrance to the Guangji Si, Wuhu

# Bozhou ⓫
亳州

155 miles (250 km) NW of Hefei. 🚃 🚌

Bozhou's medicinal market – the largest of its kind in the world – attracts over 50,000 traders from China and Southeast Asia. Every conceivable plant, insect, and animal limb, in whole and powdered form, can be found in its hall.

Also of interest is the 17th-century **Flower Theater** with wood and brick carvings and painted friezes around the stage. The town's museum exhibits a Han-dynasty jade burial suit of the father of Cao Cao, the Three Kingdoms warlord, who built the **Underground Tunnel** to conceal the army, if attacked.

🏬 **Medicinal Market**
Zhongyao Shiyang. ◻ Mon–Fri.

🏯 **Underground Tunnel**
Caocao Yunbingdao. ◻ daily. 🎫

# Hefei ⓬
合肥

93 miles (150 km) W of Nanjing. ✈
🚃 🚌 🏨 42 Changjiang Zhong Rd.
**Tel** (0551) 283 0207.

Anhui's provincial capital grew into a flourishing industrial center after 1949, when the new Communist government supported the growth of industry in areas that had been previously impoverished. Although not of very great interest, visitors are likely to pass through this town while exploring the province. The **Provincial Museum** has some interesting exhibits including bricks from Han-dynasty tombs, a cranium belonging to *Homo erectus* discovered in Anhui, and an exhibition on the "Four Treasures of the Study" *(see p219)*, mainly ink sticks, ink stones, brushes, and paper, for which the province is known. Baohe Park, set around a pretty tree flanked by a lake, has a **Memorial Hall** devoted to the great Song dynasty administrator, Lord Bao. The 16th-century **Mingjiao Si** temple stands 16 ft (5 m) above the ground, while nearby **Xiaoyaojin Park** has a 3rd-century well and is a good place for walks.

🏛 **Provincial Museum**
268 Anqing Rd. ◻ Tue–Sun.

🏯 **Lord Bao Memorial Hall**
58 Wuhu Rd. ◻ 8am–5:30pm daily. 🎫

**Mingjiao Si**
Huaihe Rd. ◻ daily. 🎫

# Wuhu ⓭
芜湖

78 miles (125 km) SE of Hefei. 🚃 🚌

The province's main ferry port has little to offer, and its few sights include the **Guangji Si** on Zhe Shan, founded in AD 894, and the nearby **Zhe Pagoda**, from where there are views over the town. Some streets in the town's center are lined with old houses with thatched roofs and mud walls, and make for a pleasant stroll. Wuhu is also a good base for visiting **Li Bai's Tomb** at Caishiji, 4 miles (7 km) from Ma'an Shan, the first stop south of Wuhu on the railway line. Li Bai (AD 701–762), a Tang-dynasty poet, was a famous drunk and is said to have died drowning in the moon's reflection. His tomb stands at the top of a long series of steps behind a Qing-dynasty temple, and overlooks the Yangzi. It may only contain Li Bai's clothes, as his final resting place is still the subject of debate.

🏯 **Li Bai's Tomb**
Caishiji. 🚃 to Ma'an Shan, then bus or taxi. ◻ daily.

Li Bai's Tomb, Caishiji

**Environs:** Located 37 miles (60 km) southeast of Wuhu, **Xuancheng** is the site of the Alligator Breeding Center, which has successfully increased the population of this endangered species. Found only in Anhui, the wild population remains small, but the captive population now runs into thousands, and it may soon be possible to reintroduce these reptiles back into the wild.

Alligators sunning themselves in Xuancheng's breeding center

# Jiuhua Shan
## 九华山

100 miles (160 km) SE of Hefei. 🚌
ℹ️ *135 Baima Xincun, Jiuhua Jie.*

One of the four mountains
holy to Chinese Buddhists,
Jiuhua Shan has been sacred
since the Korean monk Jin
Qiaojue – thought to be a
reincarnation of Bodhisattva
Ksitigarbha – died here in AD
794. It is also an important
place of pilgrimage for the
recently bereaved, who come
to hold services for those
who have passed on.

Over 60 temples linked by
paths from Jiuhua village dot
the mountain. The first is the
Qing-dynasty **Zhiyuan Si**,
with a honeycomb of halls.
Farther up is the oldest temple,
**Huacheng Si**, a part of which
possibly dates to the Tang
era. Beyond, an ornamental
gate marks the path up the
mountain. From here, one
option is an hour-long walk
that passes Ying Ke Song
(Welcoming Pine), and bears
left past a series of temples
until **Baisui Gong**, where the
preserved body of the priest,
Wu Xia, sits at prayer. Visitors
can either walk back or take
the funicular railway. The
other option is the path
leading right at Yingke Song,
which passes **Feng Huang
Song** (Phoenix Pine) to the
summit at **Tiantai Zhengding**
(Heavenly Terrace), where a
huge Buddha statue is due to
be built. The four-hour walk
to the summit can be
curtailed by taking the cable
car from Fenghuang Song,
and returning by taxi.

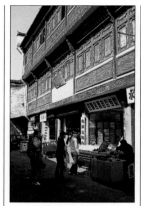

A restored Ming-dynasty shop,
Lao Jie (Old Street), Tunxi

# Tunxi ⑮
## 屯溪

44 miles (70 km) SE of Huang Shan.
✈️ 🚌 🚍 ℹ️ *3/4F, 99 Fushang Rd.*
**Tel** *(0559) 231 0616.*

An important transport hub for
visiting the popular Huang
Shan *(see pp236–7)*, Tunxi has
numerous fine examples of
traditional classical architecture.
In certain areas such as along
**Lao Jie** (Old Street), restored
houses dating to the Ming
dynasty have been converted
into shops selling souvenirs
and antiques, while others
serve as tourist restaurants.
The high standard of restoration gives visitors a clear
picture of a typical Ming-era
town. Many of the houses
bear the decorative "horse
head gables" *(see opposite)*,
which originally had a
practical use as fire baffles.

# Shexian ⑯
## 歙县

16 miles (25 km) E of Tunxi. 🚌 buses
to Tunxi.

Formerly known as Huizhou,
Shexian is renowned for its
wealth of well-preserved Ming-
dynasty houses, once owned
by wealthy salt merchants.
Many of these houses lie
along the lanes off Jiefang Jie
and along Doushan Jie, still
occupied exactly as they were
as far back as the 14th century.

The wealthy Huizhou
tradesmen also erected many
memorial archways *(paifang)*
in Shexian county but the
most famous is the complex
of seven Ming and Qing arches
at **Tangyue**, a village about 4
miles (7 km) west of Shexian.
The arches acknowledge the
political career, filial piety,
chastity, and charity of a
successful local family.

# Yixian ⑰
## 黟县

22 miles (35 km) NW of Tunxi.
🚌 Minibus to Tunxi. **Permit** required,
available at Tunxi.

The UNESCO world heritage
Sites of **Hongcun** and
**Xidi**, known for their Ming
and Qing houses, lie in the
vicinity of Yixian. About 7
miles (11 km) to the northeast, Hongcun dates to 1131.
Picturesquely ringed by mountains, it is known as "a village
in a Chinese painting." The
village is laid out in the shape
of a water-buffalo, and is watered by a network of canals
that feed the Moon Pond and
South Lake, representing the
buffalo's stomach, while the
canals represent its intestines.

Xidi, 5 miles (8 km) north of
Yixian, has a maze of lanes
flanked by over 100 houses,
dating mainly from the late
Ming and early Qing eras.
Some have charming court-
yards, while their interiors are
often decorated with carved
wooden screens and panels.
Some houses feature performances of local arts. **Nanping**,
3 miles (5 km) west of Yixian,
also has fine examples of
classical architecture.

The serene Jiuhua Shan or Nine Glorious Mountains

# Huizhou Architecture

Shexian county is home for the descendants of a group of people who played a key role in the Chinese economy 400 years ago. Today, the people of southern Anhui province are mostly farmers, but from the fourteenth to seventeenth centuries, their forefathers were the wealthy merchants of Huizhou, famous the length and breadth of China for their commercial acumen and integrity.

**Huizhou memorial archway (paifang)**

They used their money to build large family houses, with whitewashed exteriors and beautiful wood interiors. The distinctive features of these houses are a result of social and environmental factors, and are attempts to deal with the weather, earthquakes and the risk of attack by bandits. Many of these houses still remain, sometimes a little run down, but still a testament to the enterprise of the Huizhou traders.

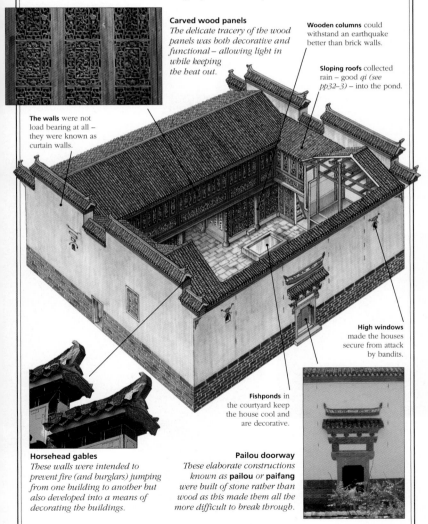

**Carved wood panels**
*The delicate tracery of the wood panels was both decorative and functional – allowing light in while keeping the heat out.*

**Wooden columns** could withstand an earthquake better than brick walls.

**Sloping roofs** collected rain – good *qi (see pp32–3)* – into the pond.

**The walls** were not load bearing at all – they were known as curtain walls.

**High windows** made the houses secure from attack by bandits.

**Fishponds** in the courtyard keep the house cool and are decorative.

**Horsehead gables**
*These walls were intended to prevent fire (and burglars) jumping from one building to another but also developed into a means of decorating the buildings.*

**Pailou doorway**
*These elaborate constructions known as* **pailou** *or* **paifang** *were built of stone rather than wood as this made them all the more difficult to break through.*

# Huang Shan ⑱
黄山

**West gate detail**

Reputed to be the most beautiful mountain range in the country, the startling, cloud-cloaked peaks of Huang Shan (Yellow Mountain) have for centuries been celebrated by poets and painters. Although the main peak is under 6,200 ft (1,900 m), the 70 sheer rock cliffs are spectacular to hike, and the winding concrete steps are usually very crowded. Even when shrouded in mist as is the norm, the scenery of precipitous peaks, bamboo groves, and ancient, twisted pines is unusually beautiful. Accommodation is available in pretty Wenquan or nearby Tangkou. Consider spending a night at the top for spectacular, but not solitary, sunsets and sunrises.

**Qingliang Tai** (Refreshing Terrace) is a popular spot for watching the sunrise.

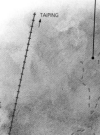

TAIPING

Guangming Ding (Bright Summit Peak) 6035 ft

Lianhua Feng (Lotus Flower Peak) 6145 ft

★ **Feilai Shi**
The "Rock Flown From Afar," a massive, rectangular boulder poised at an unlikely angle, overlooks the "Western Sea," an endless vista of mountain peaks and cascading clouds.

**Western Trail**
This path, more physically demanding than the eastern route, cuts through splendid rock formations, along narrow, and very steep, flights of steps.

Shen Quan Feng 5340 ft

Banshan Si

Ciqua Ge

Wenqua

**Welcoming Guest Pine**
*Huan Ke Song, featured on endless postage stamps, appears to beckon the visitor up the mountain and is said to be over a thousand years old*

## STAR SIGHTS

★ Feilai Shi

★ Shixin Feng

★ Aoyu Bei

**View from the Top**
*The summit with its stunning views takes about three hours to explore. Head to Paiyun Ting, "Cloud Dispelling Pavilion," at the top of the Taiping cable car, for the best views of the sunset.*

## VISITORS' CHECKLIST

125 miles (200 km) S of Hefei. ✈
at Tunxi. 🚍 to Tunxi. 🚍 from
Nanjing or Hefei to Tangkou (5 hr);
from Tunxi to Tangkou (1.5 hr);
bus to main gate. 🔾 daily. 🎫
www.huangshanguide.com

### KEY

| | |
|---|---|
| 🚐 | Minibus stop |
| 🚠 | Cable car |
| 🛕 | Temple |
| – – | Path |
| ═ | Road |

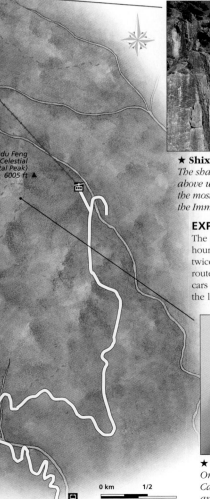

du Feng
*Celestial
al Peak)*
6005 ft ▲

★ **Shixin Feng**
*The shard-like "Beginning to Believe" peaks, rising above woodland and glistening streams, offer one of the most spectacular views at Huang Shan. Access is via the Immortals' Bridge at the eastern end of the summit.*

## EXPLORING HUANG SHAN

The eastern route (5 miles/8 km) takes about three hours; the western route (9 miles/15 km) up to twice that. Some hikers choose to take the eastern route up and the western route down. Two cable cars allow you to bypass much of the walking, but the line-ups are usually very long.

★ **Aoyu Bei**
*On the approach to Tiandu Feng, Aoyu Bei, the Carp's Backbone, is a disconcertingly exposed and narrow 30-ft (9-m) arch with sheer drops down both sides.*

0 km       1/2

0 miles       1/2

TANGKOU

# ZHEJIANG & JIANGXI

Lying immediately to the south of Shanghai, Zhejiang is bordered by Jiangxi to its southwest. Northern Zhejiang is a vast region of fertile farmland, with canal towns such as the provincial capital of Hangzhou, and lovely Shaoxing. Hangzhou and the great port of Ningbo are the region's chief industrial and commercial centers. Just off Zhejiang's coastline are some 18,000 islands, among them the holy shrine of Putuo Shan. The south of the province is rugged and mountainous, with superb scenery at Yandang Shan.

Landlocked Jiangxi is sparsely populated compared to the rest of Central China. Its northern reaches are a fertile plain watered by Poyang Hu, the largest freshwater lake in China, and the rivers that feed it. Nanchang, the provincial capital, prospered in the 7th century, following the construction of the Grand Canal. With the growth of coastal treaty ports in the mid-19th century, Jiangxi's economy declined. Later, in the early 20th century, civil strife forced millions into exile. The rugged Jinggang Shan mountains in southern Jiangxi, where most of the fighting took place, are rich in revolutionary associations. To the province's northeast lie the porcelain town of Jingdezhen and the charming mountain resort of Lu Shan.

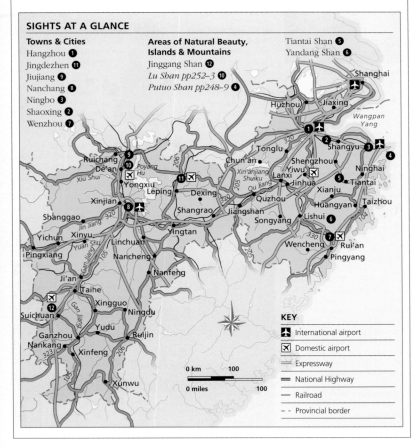

## SIGHTS AT A GLANCE

**Towns & Cities**
Hangzhou ❶
Jingdezhen ⓫
Jiujiang ❾
Nanchang ❽
Ningbo ❸
Shaoxing ❷
Wenzhou ❼

**Areas of Natural Beauty, Islands & Mountains**
Jinggang Shan ⓬
*Lu Shan pp252–3* ❿
*Putuo Shan pp248–9* ❹

Tiantai Shan ❺
Yandang Shan ❻

### KEY

✈ International airport

☒ Domestic airport

═ Expressway

━ National Highway

━ Railroad

-- Provincial border

0 km          100

0 miles          100

◁ **Secluded path up to the Seal Engravers' Society pagoda on Gu Shan Island, West Lake, Hangzhou**

# Hangzhou ❶

## 杭州

**Statue of Yue Fei**

Renowned in medieval China as an earthly paradise, Hangzhou became the splendid capital of the Southern Song dynasty between 1138 and 1279. Later, when the conquering Mongols chose what is now Beijing as their new capital, Hangzhou continued to be a thriving commercial city. Its glories were extolled by Marco Polo, who allegedly visited Hangzhou at the height of its prosperity and described it as "the City of Heaven, the most magnificent in all the world." Although most of the old buildings were destroyed in the Taiping Rebellion, the attractive West Lake and its surrounding area are still worth visiting.

**Entrance archway to Yue Fei Mu (Tomb of Yue Fei)**

### 🛕 Yue Fei Mu

80 Bei Shan Rd. **Tel** (0571) 8796 9670. ⏰ 7:30am–5:30pm daily. 🎟️

Just north of the West Lake lies the tomb of the Song general, Yue Fei, a Chinese hero revered for his patriotism. His campaigns against the invading Jin were so successful that his overlords began to worry that he might turn against them. He was falsely charged with sedition and executed, only to become a martyr.

The Yue Fei Temple is a late 19th-century construction, and the tomb lies beside it. The central tumulus belongs to Yue Fei, while the smaller one is his son's, who was also executed. The kneeling figures in iron represent his tormentors – the prime minister, his wife, a jealous general, and the prison governor. It was customary to spit on them, but this is no longer encouraged.

### 🏛️ Impression West Lake

Bei Shan Rd. **Tel** (0571) 8796 2222. **Light Show** 7:45–8:45pm daily. Every evening, on the lake in front of Yue Fei Mu Temple, is

a water, light, and animation show. It was created by the famous Chinese director Zhang Yimou, who produced the 2008 Olympics opening ceremony, and has music by Zhang Liangying.

### ❀ Huanglong Dong Park & Qixia Shan

North of West Lake (Xi Hu). Huanglong Dong Park, nestling in the hills, is very attractive with its teahouses, ponds, and flowers, and a pavilion where musicians perform traditional music in summer. To the east is **Baoshu Ta**, a 20th-century rebuild of a Song-era pagoda. Looming close by is Qixia Shan (Lingering Clouds Mountain), with the **Baopu Daoist Compound** located halfway up its slopes. This active temple has services on most days.

### 🏛️ Hu Qingyu Tang Museum of Chinese Medicine

95 Dajing Xiang. **Tel** (0571) 8702 7507. ⏰ 8:30am–5pm daily. 🎟️

This interesting museum is housed in a beautiful old apothecary's shop. It was established by the merchant Hu Xueyan during the Qing dynasty and traces the history of traditional Chinese medicine, which goes back thousands of years. It is still an active dispensary and pharmacy.

### ❀ West Lake

See pp242–3.

### 🏛️ Tea Museum

88 Longjing Rd. **Tel** (0571) 8796 4221. ⏰ 8:30am–4:30pm Tue–Sun. 🎟️ www.teamuseum.com

Tracing the history of tea production (see p293), the Tea Museum has lots of interesting information regarding the different varieties of tea, its cultivation, and the development of tea-making and tea-drinking vessels. Fortunately, many of the captions are in English.

**Wood panel carving at Baopu Daoist Temple**

### 🏯 Longjing Village

SW of Tea Museum. 🎟️

The village of Longjing (Dragon Well) produces one of China's most famous varieties of green tea. Visitors can wander around the tea terraces, catching glimpses of the different stages of production – cutting, sorting, and drying – and also buy the tea, which varies in price according to its grade.

**Inside the main hall of the Hu Qingyu Tang Museum of Chinese Medicine**

For hotels and restaurants in this region see pp562–3 and pp589–90

## Lingyin Si

1 Fayun Nong, Lingyin Rd. *Tel* (0571) 8796 8665. ◯ 7am–5pm daily.

The hill area known as Feilai Feng (The Peak that Flew Here) is home to some of the city's main sights, including Lingyin Si. Founded in AD 326, this temple once housed 3,000 monks who worshiped in more than 70 halls. Though now much reduced in size, it is still one of China's largest temples. It was damaged in the 19th-century Taiping Rebellion, and then again by fire in the 20th century. It is said to owe its survival to Zhou Enlai (*see p250*), who prevented its destruction during the Cultural Revolution. Still, some parts of the temple are ancient, such as the stone pagodas on either side of the entrance hall, which date from AD 969. Behind this hall is the **Great Buddha Hall**, with an impressive 66-ft (20-m) statue of the Buddha carved in 1956 from camphor wood.

The **Ligong Pagoda** at the entrance was built in honor of the Indian monk, Hui Li, who gave the mountain its eccentric name. Hui Li thought it was the spitting image of a hill in India and asked whether it had flown here. Feilai Feng is known for the dozens of Buddhist sculptures carved into the rock, many dating from the 10th century.

Buddha sculptures at Feilai Feng

## VISITORS' CHECKLIST

75 miles (120 km) SW of Shanghai. 6,800,000. Train Station, East Train Station. East Bus Station, North Bus Station, West Bus Station, CAAC (buses to airport). (0571) 8505 9039.

## Six Harmonies Pagoda

16 Zhijiang Rd. *Tel* (0571) 8659 1364. ◯ 6:30am–5:30pm daily.

Standing beside the railway bridge on the northern shore of the Qiantang River, Liuhe Ta is all that is left of an octagonal temple first built in AD 970 to placate the tidal bore, a massive wall of water that rushes upstream during high tide. Over 197-ft (60-m) high, it served as a lighthouse up until the Ming dynasty.

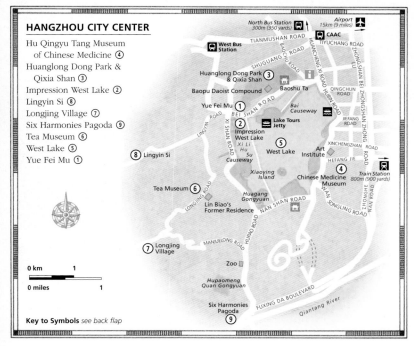

## HANGZHOU CITY CENTER

Hu Qingyu Tang Museum
of Chinese Medicine ④
Huanglong Dong Park &
Qixia Shan ③
Impression West Lake ②
Lingyin Si ⑧
Longjing Village ⑦
Six Harmonies Pagoda ⑨
Tea Museum ⑥
West Lake ⑤
Yue Fei Mu ①

North Bus Station 300m (350 yards)
Airport 15km (9 miles)
West Bus Station
TIANMUSHAN ROAD
TIYUCHANG ROAD
SHUGUANG ROAD
BAO CHU ROAD
HUANCHENG XI ROAD
HUBIN ROAD
ZHONGSHAN BEI ROAD
ZHONGSHAN ZHONG
Huanglong Dong Park & Qixia Shan ③
Baoshu Ta
QINGCHUN ROAD
Baopu Daoist Compound
Yue Fei Mu ①
Bai Causeway
JIEFANG ROAD
BEI SHAN ROAD
Lake Tours Jetty
LINGYIN ROAD
XI SHAN ROAD
② Impression West Lake
Xi Li Hu
Su Causeway
West Lake ⑤
Art Institute
XINCHENGZHAN ROAD
⑧ Lingyin Si
Xiaoying Island
HEFANG JIE
Chinese Medicine Museum
④
Train Station 800m (900 yards)
Tea Museum ⑥
Huagang Gongyuan
Lin Biao's Former Residence
NAN SHAN ROAD
HUPAO ROAD
ZHONGHE NAN ROAD
LONGJING ROAD
⑦ Longjing Village
MANJUELONG ROAD
SONGLING ROAD
Zoo
Hupaomeng Quan Gongyuan
Six Harmonies Pagoda ⑨
FUXING DA BOULEVARD
Qiantang River

0 km 1
0 miles 1

**Key to Symbols** *see back flap*

# West Lake
西湖

**Metal work,
Xiaoying Island**

Long considered one of the scenic wonders of China, covering over three square miles (8 sq km), West Lake (Xi Hu) is situated at the heart of Hangzhou. Surrounded by gentle green hills, the lake's willow-shaded causeways and fragrant cover of lotus blossoms have long been an inspiration for artists. Originally the lake was an inlet off the estuary of the Qiantang River, becoming a lake when the river began to silt up in the 4th century. The lake had a tendency to flood, so several dykes were built, including the Bai and Su Causeways. Hiring a private boat from the eastern shore for an afternoon on the water is highly recommended, as is a leisurely stroll along the shady causeways.

**★ Three Pools Reflecting the Moon**
*Three small stone pagodas rise from the waters near Xiaoying Island. At full moon candles are placed within and their openings are covered in paper to create reflections resembling the moon.*

*XI LI HU*

**Huagang Garden**
*This garden is intended as a place for viewing fish. Designed by a Song-dynasty eunuch, its pools are filled with shimmering goldfish in a restful setting of grasses and trees.*

**STAR FEATURES**

★ Xiaoying Island

★ Three Pools Reflecting the Moon

★ Su Causeway

**★ Xiaoying Island**
*Often called San Tan Yin Yue Island, referring to the three moon-reflecting pagodas off its shores, Xiaoying Island consists of four enclosed pools fringed by pavilions first built in 1611. The zig-zagging Nine Bend Bridge was built in 1727.*

## VISITORS' CHECKLIST

Hangzhou. 🚋 regularly from eastern shore near Hubin Rd. Boats for hire on Gu Shan Island.
**Zhejiang Provincial Museum** 25 Gushan Rd. **Tel** (0571) 8797 1177. 🕐 9am–5pm Tue–Sun. 🖳 www.zhejiangmuseum.com

### ★ Su Causeway

*The longer of the two causeways takes its name from the Song-dynasty poet, Su Dongpo, who also served as governor. Linked by six stone bridges, the causeway is a peaceful thoroughfare running along the lake's western edge.*

**Bridge to Quyuan Garden**
*This bridge leads to a stunning garden surrounded by lotus flowers. It is considered one of the ten prospects from where the lake can be seen to best advantage.*

**The Seal Engravers Society** is open in the summer months.

GU SHAN

**Zhejiang Provincial Museum**

XI HU

BEI LI HU

### MARCO POLO

Whether Marco Polo ever visited China is much disputed. However, according to the book he dictated to a ghost writer who embroidered it substantially, Polo became governor of nearby Yangzhou for three years during the Yuan dynasty. He describes Hangzhou as paradise and the finest city in the world, with fascinating markets, pleasure boats, and prostitutes. Hangzhou was indeed a cosmopolitan city, ever since the Southern Song dynasty made it their capital. *The Travels of Marco Polo*, however, may be based on earlier journeys by his father and uncle, and stories from other merchants.

**Engraving of Marco Polo, 1254– 1324**

### Bai Causeway

*Named after the 9th-century poet-governor Bai Juyi, this dyke leads to Gu Shan, an island first landscaped during the Tang dynasty, and now containing a tea house and the provincial museum.*

Lu Xun's Former Residence, Shaoxing

## Shaoxing ❷
绍兴

47 miles (67 km) SE of Hangzhou.
🏙 4,340,000. 🚉 🚌 🛈 200
Guang Fu Rd, (0571) 8755 3527.
www.sx.gov.cn

Despite the proliferation of new buildings, this canal town has retained its charm, with its narrow streets, arched bridges, and whitewashed houses. Ancient Shaoxing was the capital of the Yue kingdom during 770–221 BC. It remained important over the years even when Hangzhou became the Song capital. Today, it is a scenic place to explore for its waterways.

The **Qing Teng Shu Wu** (Green Vine Study), former home of the 16th-century writer and artist Xu Wei, lies off Dacheng Long, an alley not far from Jiefang Nan Road. Regarded as the best example of traditional domestic architecture in China, the house has a simple ornamental garden, while one of its rooms displays Xu's expressive art.

There are also several houses associated with Lu Xun, perhaps the best known modern Chinese writer, born here in 1881. Most of them are clustered together on Lu Xun Road. The Lu Xun Memorial Hall has no English captions, but **Lu Xun's Former Residence** is a fine example of domestic architecture, with photographs, furniture, and personal items. Opposite is Sanwei Sushi, the school where he studied.

Shaoxing's most famous bridge, the 13th-century **Bazi Qiao**, resembles the Chinese character for number 8, and lies in a charming area of old streets off Baziqiao Zhi Jie, north of Lu Xun Lu.

The town makes a good base for several excursions. The scenic **Dong Hu** (East Lake) is nearby. Visitors can also take a boat to **Yu Ling**, allegedly the tomb of Yu the Great, founder of the Xia kingdom (2200 BC). Farther out is **Lan Ting** (Orchid Pavilion), where China's greatest calligrapher, Wang Xizhi (AD 321–79), threw a party where, so one story goes, guests had to drink cups of wine as they floated past and compose a poem, recorded by the host.

🛕 **Qing Teng Shu Wu**
10 Qian Guan Xiang. ☐ daily. 🎫

🛕 **Lu Xun's Former Residence**
235 Lu Xun Zhong Rd. ☐ daily. 🎫

## Ningbo ❸
宁波

90 miles (145 km) SE of Hangzhou.
🏙 5,500,000. 🚉 🚌 🛳
🛈 221 Jiang Dong Bei Rd, (0574) 8719 9722.

China's greatest port between the Song and Ming eras, Ningbo is located upstream from the coast on the Yong River. It was later eclipsed by Shanghai, but has regained some importance due to its deep natural harbor. The town has had a long association with commerce. When Shanghai and Guangzhou prospered in the 19th and early 20th centuries, Ningbo's residents were employed as "compradors," agents or mediators by the foreign companies.

Ningbo's main sight is the **Tianye Ge**, a 16th-century private library, the oldest in China. It resembles a traditional garden with bamboo groves, rockeries, and pavilions, one of which exhibits ancient books and scrolls. To the southeast off Kaiming Jie, is the 14th-century Tianfeng Pagoda. The former foreign concession lies at the northern end of Xinjiang Bridge, with a 17th-century Portuguese church and a riverside Bund. Outside the city, **Baoguo Si** temple's Mahavira Hall is the oldest surviving wooden building in the Yangzi delta region.

Stone lion, Tianye Ge

🛕 **Tianyi Ge**
5 Tianyi Jie. ☐ 8:30am–5pm daily. 🎫

Charming narrow streets around Tianye Ge, Ningbo

◁ Su Causeway bridge on a misty West Lake, Hangzhou

# Putuo Shan ❹

*See pp248–9.*

The Guoqing Si Monastery, at the foot of Tiantai Shan

# Tiantai Shan ❺

天台山

118 miles (190 km) SE of Hangzhou.

The heavenly terrace Mountain – Tiantai Shan – is the seat of the Tiantai Buddhist sect, which also has strong links with Daoism *(see pp30–31)*. A pilgrimage site since the Eastern Jin, today it is especially popular with Japanese Buddhists, who regard China as the Buddhist motherland. The sect's founder, the monk Zhiyi, spent most of his life on the mountain, where the imperial court helped him to construct a temple. This wonderfully scenic spot, with its paths, streams, and woodlands, is ideal for walking. Several famous plants such as huading cloud, mist tea, the Tiantai mandarin orange, as well as a variety of medicinal plants, were discovered here.

The first of Tiantai Shan's monasteries, **Guoqing Si**, lies at its foot, 2 miles (3 km) from Tiantai village. From here, a road leads to the 3,609 ft (1,100 m) **Huading Peak**. Visitors can then walk to Baijingtai Si (Prayer Terrace Temple) on the summit or to Shiliang (Stone Beam) Waterfall, near the Upper Fangguang Monastery, where there are a number of inscriptions, including one by the famous Song artist, Mi Fu.

The **Zhenjue Si** (Monastery of True Enlightenment) houses Zhiyi's mummified body in a pagoda in its main hall.

**Huading Peak**
daily.

# Yandang Shan ❻

雁荡山

50 miles (80 km) NE of Wenzhou.
*from Wenzhou to terminus at Baixi.*

This is a beautiful area of sheer hills, luxuriant slopes, and monasteries. Its highest peak, Baigang Shan, reaches 3,773 ft (1,150 m). The **Big Dragon Pool Falls** (Dalongqiu Pubu) cascade 623 ft (190 m), making them one of China's highest. The path leading to them weaves among towering columns of rock, where, on the hour, a cyclist performs a high-wire act. The largest area is **Divine Peaks** (Ling Feng), excellent for hiking among caves and strangely shaped peaks. The **Divine Cliffs** area (Ling Yan), reached by cable car, has walkways and a suspension bridge. From the bus terminus at Baixi, there are several walking trails.

**Big Dragon Pool Falls**
daily.

**Divine Peaks**
daily.

# Wenzhou ❼

温州

124 miles (200 km) S of Ningbo.
7,500,000. 107–1 Xiaonan Rd, (0577) 8815 7990.

Located on the southeast coast of Zhejiang province, Wenzhou has always been a seafaring city. It is still a busy port and its booming economy is mainly due to heavy investment in manufacturing and textiles by overseas Chinese. A good base for visiting nearby Yandang Shan, the city also offers a few sights of its own. The most popular, **Jiangxin Park**, is situated on an island in the Ou River and can easily be reached by the regular ferry service from Maxingseng Jie. Completely devoid of traffic, the park's pretty gardens, pavilions, pagodas, and footbridges make it a pleasant place to spend a few hours. It also has a working lighthouse. Stretching between Jiefang Road and Xinhe Road to the south of the Ou River is what is left of the old town. Here and there are a few particular buildings of interest such as the 18th-century British-built Protestant church, the 19th-century Catholic church, and the Miaoguo Temple, whose origins are Tang-dynasty.

**Jiangxin Park**
Jiangxin Dao. from Jiangxin Matou, Wenzhou. 7:30am–10pm daily.

Walkway with panoramic views, Yandang Shan

# Putuo Shan ❹
普陀山

**Detail of an incense burner**

Nestled amongst numerous islands in the Zhou Shan archipelago, Putuo Shan is one of the four sacred Buddhist mountains, having strong associations with the goddess of compassion and mercy, Guanyin. It has been considered holy since the 10th century, and although the temples suffered greatly at the hands of the Red Guards during the Cultural Revolution, they are still impressive and full of fascination. A small, attractive island, fringed with bright blue waters and sandy beaches, Putuo Shan has become a very popular place of pilgrimage. Minibuses ply the roads between the major temples and sights, but the island's hills, caves and beaches are best explored on foot.

**To the summit**
*A cable car links a minibus stop with the summit of Foding Shan from where there are wonderful views across the island and out to sea.*

**★ Puji Si**
*Surrounded by beautiful camphor trees, this extensive temple is located at the island's tourist center. The first temple was built here in the 11th century, although the current temple is far newer.*

**★ Guanyin Colossus**
*At the southern tip of the island a massive 108-ft (33-m) statue of Guanyin stands near the shore. A pavilion at its base exhibits a collection of some 400 statues representing the goddess in her numerous incarnations.*

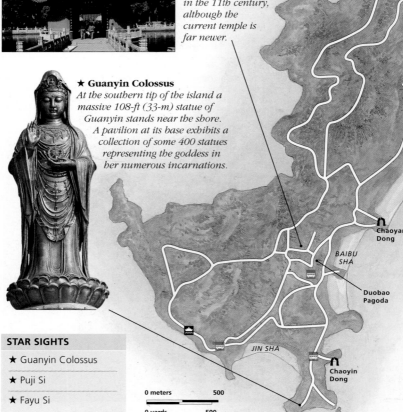

Chaoyang Dong

BAIBU SHA

Duobao Pagoda

JIN SHA

Chaoyin Dong

### STAR SIGHTS

★ Guanyin Colossus

★ Puji Si

★ Fayu Si

| 0 meters | | 500 |
| 0 yards | | 500 |

**Huiji Si**
*Close to the top of Foding Shan, Huiji Temple, dating back to 1793, stands resplendent amid tea bushes and bamboo groves.*

HUO'AI SHA

Gufo Dong

Shancai Dong

Fanyin Dong

## VISITORS' CHECKLIST

50 miles (80 km) east of Ningbo, off coast of Zhejiang. ✈ at Zhou Shan. ⛴ from Shanghai (fast ferry: 4 hrs; slow ferry: 14 hrs), Ningbo (fast ferry: 2.5 hrs; slow ferry: 5 hrs), and Zhou Shan (half hour). 🎫 for island access, plus minimal fees for separate sights. 🎎 Guanyin Festival (early Apr).
**www**.putuoshan.net

## KEY

| | |
|---|---|
| 🚐 | Minibus stop |
| ⛴ | Ferry |
| 🚡 | Cable car |
| ⋂ | Cave |
| – – | Paths |
| ═══ | Road |

**Qian Bu Sha**
*The loveliest of Putuo Shan's beaches, Qian Bu Sha (Thousand Step Beach) stretches along the eastern coast and is separated from Bai Bu Sha (Hundred Step Beach) by a headland and cave, Chaoyang Dong, concealing a teahouse.*

**★ Fayu Si**
*The 200 halls of this charming temple pile up against the flank of a hill overlooking the sea. The Dayuan Hall, unusual for its domed roof and beamless arched ceiling, was brought here from Nanjing in the late 17th century.*

### THE LEGEND OF HUI'E

Hui'e, a Japanese monk who had purloined a Guanyin figure from the holy Buddhist mountain Wutai Shan, was sailing home when his ship was caught in a violent storm. Fearing for his life, he vowed to build a temple to Guanyin if he were saved. The seas suddenly calmed, and the ship floated gently towards the nearby shores of Putuo Shan. Believing that Guanyin was choosing the island, Hui'e built the promised temple and became a devoted hermit spending the rest of his life on Putuo Shan.

**Frieze of Hui'e sailing near Putuo Shan**

# Nanchang ❽
南昌

**Detail of façade, Youmin Si**

Founded during The Han era, this provincial capital flourished under the Ming dynasty as a center of trade. However, it is best remembered as the scene of a significant uprising led by the Communist leader Zhou Enlai, who took control of the city for a few days in 1927. Although Nanchang was soon recaptured by the Nationalists, the incident started a chain of events that ultimately led to the formation of the People's Republic of China. Despite being largely an industrial city, Nanchang has numerous sights including a good museum and several sites with revolutionary associations.

**Offering incense sticks in front of the Youmin Si**

## 🏛 People's Square
**Memorial Hall to the Martyrs of the Revolution** 399 Bayi Dadao. *Tel (0791) 626 2566.* ⬜ *9am–4pm Tue–Sun.* 🅿
The huge, open space of Renmin (People's) Square is surrounded by some impressive, if slightly chilling, examples of Soviet-inspired revolutionary architecture. At the southern end is the **Monument to the Martyrs**, a theatrical sculpture of revolutionary fervor topped by a rifle, while the vast **Exhibition Hall** is decorated with a glittering red star. Just north of the square is the **Memorial Hall to the Martyrs of the Revolution**, which exhibits archival photographs of events in China between the 1920s and 1940s.

## 🏯 Zhu De's Former Residence
2 Dong Ming De Rd. ⬜ *daily.*
This attractive wooden house dates from 1927, when it housed the fledgling revolutionaries, Zhu De and Zhou

Enlai, who led the uprising that briefly captured the city on August 1 of that year. Their army, consisting of about 30,000 rebels, held the city until the Kuomintang forces drove them out. Although the operation was a failure, it is considered a defining moment in 20th-century Chinese history, and celebrated as the day of the birth of the Red Army.

## 🏛 Youmin Si
181 Minde Rd. *Tel (0791) 622 2301.* ⬜ *8am–5pm daily.* 🅿 **Bayi Park** ⬜ *8am–6pm daily.* 🅿
This Buddhist temple founded in the Liang era in the 6th century is one of Jiangxi's principal shrines. It was damaged during the Cultural Revolution, and has now been restored. One of its three halls has a 33-ft (10-m) high Buddha standing on a lotus. The temple also houses a Ming-dynasty bronze bell and another cast during the Tang era in AD 967.
Just south of the temple is **Bayi Park** (August 1st Park), formerly the site of the imperial examination halls. It is a pleasant expanse of water and greenery, with an enclosed garden known as Old Man Su's Vegetable Plot, after its Song-dynasty owner.

## 🏛 Revolutionary Museum
380 Zhongshan Rd. ⬜ *daily.* 🅿
Housed in a striking building that was once a hotel, the August 1 Uprising Museum was the headquarters of the Communist forces led by Zhou Enlai, that captured the city in 1927. Its three floors are filled with period furniture and weaponry.

## 🏯 Teng Wang Pavilion
7 Yanjiang Rd. ⬜ *8am–5pm daily.* 🅿
The impressive Teng Wang Pavilion was first built in 653, during the early Tang era and immortalized by the poet Tang Bo. There have been about 26 versions of the pavilion since then – the latest was erected in 1989 to replace the one

---

### ZHOU ENLAI (1898–1976)

**Premier Zhou Enlai in 1973**

Zhou Enlai, one of the early members of the Chinese Communist Party, became the nation's prime minister in 1949. His pragmatism and diplomacy helped him survive the constant upheavals of Mao Zedong's chairmanship. To the West, he represented the reasonable and affable side of the Chinese people, while to his countrymen, he was the only member of the government to understand their problems. He is credited with curbing some of the excesses of the Cultural Revolution. When he died, the outpouring of grief in China was spontaneous and heartfelt.

---

**The stately Teng Wang Pavilion, on the banks of the Gan Jiang**

## VISITORS' CHECKLIST

312 miles (500 km) SW of Hangzhou. 🚶 4,900,000. ✈ Xiangtan Airport. 🚉 Train Station. 🚌 Long Distance Bus Station, CAAC (buses to airport). ⛴ Ferry Terminal. 🏠 32 Ming De Rd, (0791) 620 0289.

destroyed by fire in 1926. The 197-ft (60-m) high structure is in the Southern Song style. Visitors can take a lift to the top for views of the city. Occasional performances of dance and music or local opera are also held in the tiny theater.

### 🏛 The Provincial Museum

2 Xinzhou Jiangxi Rd. **Tel** (0791) 659 5424. ⏱ 9am–4:30pm Tue–Sun. 🌐 Located near the river in the west of the city, this museum's exhibition space still needs to be filled. However, the existing exhibits are interesting, and include fossils found in Jiangxi, and a range of porcelain from

the kilns at Jingdezhen, dating from the 4th century to the Qing era. There are also several funeral items from the Spring & Autumn period and the Ming era, including statuary, jade belts, and jewelry, some of which was discovered in the tomb of the son of Hongwu, founder of the Ming dynasty.

### 🏯 Shengjin Ta

Zhishi Jie. ⏱ 8am–5pm daily. 🌐 Formerly part of a temple, this 194-ft (59-m) high brick pagoda was first built in the late Tang dynasty, but was entirely rebuilt in the 18th century. Like many

pagodas, its construction was said to avert disaster, while its destruction heralded the fall of the city. The pagoda is located in a quaint neighborhood with a handful of teahouses, barber shops, and grocery stores.

### 🏛 Qingyun Pu

Dingshan Qiao. ⏱ Tue–Sun. 🌐 The Blue Cloud Garden or Ba Da Shan Ren Museum was the retreat of one of China's great painters, Zhu Da, who flourished at the end of the Ming era and the early Qing dynasty. He was a descendant of the Ming imperial family who went into hiding here after their fall, in what was originally designed as a Taoist retreat. His paintings, strikingly spare and direct, are reproduced here.

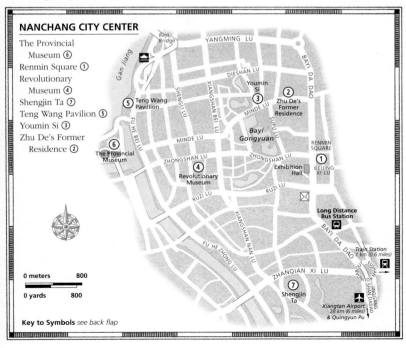

## NANCHANG CITY CENTER

The Provincial
   Museum ⑥
Renmin Square ①
Revolutionary
   Museum ④
Shengjin Ta ⑦
Teng Wang Pavilion ⑤
Youmin Si ③
Zhu De's Former
   Residence ②

0 meters     800
0 yards     800

**Key to Symbols** see back flap

**Xunyang Lou, an impressive re-creation of a Tang-era tavern**

# Jiujiang ❾
九江

115 miles (184 km) N of Nanchang.
🏙 4,380,000. ♒ 🚌 🚕 6 Lufeng Rd, (0792) 856 0600.

The gateway to Lu Shan, the ancient port of Jiujiang, was used for shipping rice and tea and, during the Ming dynasty, porcelain from Jingdezhen. Badly damaged during the Taiping insurrection, it was later opened to foreign trade in 1861 and became noted for its tea bricks.

The older and livelier part of town lies close to the river, separated from the industrial section by two lakes. Yanshui Ting, the Misty Water Pavilion, is located on a small island on Gantang Hu. It was most recently rebuilt in the Qing dynasty and contains a museum showing old photos of Jiujiang. **Nengren Si** was founded in AD 502. Closed during the Cultural Revolution, it now houses a flourishing community of monks.

The **Xunyang Lou** is a modern reincarnation of a Tang-dynasty wooden tavern, which was the setting for a raucous scene in the Chinese classic, *The Water Margin (see pp28–9)*.

🏯 **Nengren Si**
168 Yuliang Nan Rd. ☐ daily. 🈺

🏯 **Xunyang Lou**
908 Binjiang Rd. ☐ 8am–7pm. daily. 🈺

# Lu Shan ❿
庐山

**Circular gateway at Lu Shan**

During the 19th century, this beautiful area of highland scenery was developed by Edward Little, a Methodist minister and property speculator, as a resort area for Europeans. Later it became a favorite retreat among Chinese politicians; Chiang Kai-shek had a summer residence here and from 1949 Lu Shan was popular with Mao and his ministers. Today, despite the summer crowds, Lu Shan remains a refreshing place for walks among lakes, hills, and waterfalls.

**★ Floral Path**
*This walk skirts the edge of the western cliffs, giving marvelous views over the Jinxui Valley. The path leads to the Immortal's Cave, once inhabited by a Daoist monk.*

**★ Dragon's Head Cliff**
*Magnificent views combine with the sound of the wind in the pine forest and the roaring of waterfalls in the Stone Gate Ravine.*

## STAR FEATURES

★ Dragon's Head Cliff

★ Floral Path

★ Meilu Villa

**Suspension Bridge**

Jiangjun He

*For hotels and restaurants in this region see pp562–3 and pp589–90*

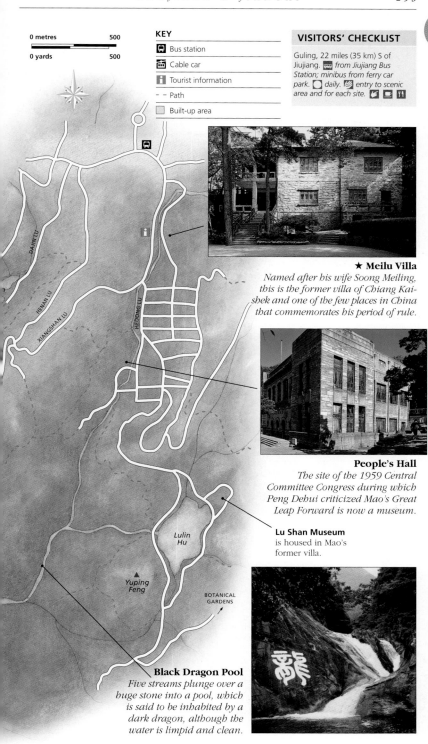

**KEY**

| | Bus station |
|---|---|
| | Cable car |
| | Tourist information |
| – – | Path |
| | Built-up area |

0 metres        500

0 yards         500

DAJHE LU

HENAN LU

XIANGSHAN LU

HEDONG LU

Lulin
Hu

Yuping
Feng

BOTANICAL
GARDENS

★ **Meilu Villa**
*Named after his wife Soong Meiling,
this is the former villa of Chiang Kai-
shek and one of the few places in China
that commemorates his period of rule.*

**People's Hall**
*The site of the 1959 Central
Committee Congress during which
Peng Dehui criticized Mao's Great
Leap Forward is now a museum.*

**Lu Shan Museum**
is housed in Mao's
former villa.

**Black Dragon Pool**
*Five streams plunge over a
huge stone into a pool, which
is said to be inhabited by a
dark dragon, although the
water is limpid and clean.*

# Porcelain

Despite Chinese pottery's long history, it was not until the Bronze Age (between about 1500 and 400 BC) that special clays and hotter kilns resulted in a harder, sometimes glazed stoneware. True porcelain, however, did not appear until the Sui dynasty. A far finer type of ceramic, true porcelain is smooth and polished, and produces an almost crystalline ring when struck; at its most delicate, it is even translucent. Porcelain became popular in Europe during the 16th century, and the Portuguese, and later the Dutch and English, set up a lucrative trade between China and the rest of the world.

**Blue and White Ming** *porcelain is seen by some as the epitome of Chinese style. The elegance of the designs and the depth of color are astounding.*

**Jingdezhen clay** *is the key to the quality of the porcelain and is a mixture of fine white kaolin and "petuntse" (a crushed feldspar rock). The resulting fine powder is washed, strained through silk, and dried.*

**As on a production line**, *each artisan performs a single task in the porcelain-making process. The clay is centered on a wheel and thrown into a rough shape, sculpted into a finer piece with scrapers, and brushed with water to create a smooth surface.*

**A cobalt blue underglaze** *may be added before coating with a clear glaze of limestone ash, the finest petuntse, and water. The glaze absorbs the blue dye and fuses into the original clay to form a hard glassy porcelain.*

**Firing** *is a crucial stage in making porcelain – fluctuations in temperature can ruin thousands of pieces in one go. The best porcelain is fired inside clay "saggars" – cases that protect them from dust and sudden variations in heat.*

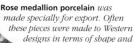

**Rose medallion porcelain** *was made specially for export. Often these pieces were made to Western designs in terms of shape and decoration. Sometimes dinner sets displaying a family or even a royal crest were produced, and designs were sent from Europe to be reproduced by the Chinese.*

**Reign mark starts here and reads top to bottom, right to left**

大明弘治年製

**Reign marks** *show the reign name of the emperor when the piece was made. However, the ease with which they can be faked renders accurate dating the task of experts.*

**Characters for Emperor Hongzhi**

## PORCELAIN TIMELINE

### HAN

A key development during this period was the art of glazing. Simple pots began changing from everyday items to works of art.

### TANG

Technical advances during the Tang dynasty saw the production of new types of porcelain, most famously the *sancai* (tri-colored) pieces illustrating figures from the Silk Road.

### SONG

Beautiful Song porcelain is characterized by simple shapes glazed in a single, rich color. New shapes were developed, as well as the cracked glazing technique.

### YUAN

Porcelain from the Mongol dynasty absorbed foreign influences. Cobalt blue underglaze was introduced, and later perfected during the Ming period.

### MING

The Ming dynasty was the era of imperial patronage of Jingdezhen and large-scale exportation to the West. The kilns flourished and the artisans returned to a richer palette of colors and pictorial design.

### QING

The latter part of this dynasty was often characterized by overly elaborate design and poor quality, but the early part of the Qing saw the production of delicate *famille rose* porcelain.

One of Jingdezhen's many pottery shops

# Jingdezhen ⑪
景德镇

90 miles (145 km) NE of Nanchang. 🚉 1,520,000. ✈ 🚌 🚆 ℹ *CITS, 1 Zhushan Xi Rd, (0798) 862 9999.*

For centuries the ceramic capital of China, Jingdezhen is still one of the country's major porcelain producers. Although pottery kilns were operating here as far back as the Han dynasty, it was the discovery of real porcelain, during the Five Dynasties era (907–79 AD), which depended on locally found clay rich in feldspar, that brought Jingdezhen its pre-eminence. During the Ming dynasty, its location near the imperial capital of Nanjing increased its importance and it became famous for fine porcelain with a blue underglaze. Although the quality of the porcelain is lower than in the past, the main reason for visiting Jingdezhen is still ceramic production. Visiting a factory or one of the ancient kiln sites will need to be arranged though CITS but there are also several places of interest that can be visited independently.

The **Museum of Ceramic History** (Taoci Lishi Bowuguan) is located in a rural setting on the western edge of town. Displays of items taken from ancient kiln sites around Jingdezhen and of potters at work effectively make this museum interactive. It is housed in an elegant Ming house, a rare survivor among the many that would once have graced the town. The

Detail from museum entrance

adjacent **Ancient Pottery Factory** (Guyao Cichang) gives demonstrations of the ancient techniques used in the making of porcelain.

The **Porcelain Museum** (Taoci Guan) houses a collection of beautiful porcelain from the Song, Ming, and Qing dynasties, as well as some of the finer creations produced since the establishment of the PRC in 1949. The main porcelain market is on Jiefang Road. Porcelain in all shapes and sizes is sold here, from classical-period reproductions to garden ornaments and sentimental reproductions of dogs and cats. For a view across the roofs of town, visitors can climb the wooden four-story **Longzhu Ge** (Dragon Pearl Pavilion).

🏛 **Museum of Ceramic History**
Zhonghua Bei Rd. **Tel** *(0798) 822 1390.* ◯ *8:30am–5:30pm daily.* 📷

🏛 **Porcelain Museum**
21 Lianshe Beilu Rd. **Tel** *(0798) 822 8005.* ◯ *8am–5pm daily.* 📷

The wooden Longzhu Ge, with views across Jingdezhen

# The Long March

During the 1920s the outlawed Communist leaders sought refuge from the Kuomintang (KMT) at remote rural bases, or "soviets," in Sichuan, Hunan, and, in Jiangxi province, at Jinggang Shan, the headquarters run by Mao Zedong and Zhu De. In October 1934, with the KMT closing in, the Jiangxi Soviet was forced to break out and join thousands of revolutionaries on a tactical retreat. Covering, largely at night, an average of 20 miles (32 km) a day, the Communists marched 5,900 miles (9,500 km) in a year. The march, however, was not a strategic success and many did not survive it.

**The Red Army** – *outlawed, harried and hungry – had to fight battles, outwit their better equipped enemy, and cross inhospitable terrain in all seasons.*

⑦ **Crossing the** remote, boggy and freezing Aba Grasslands brought enormous losses. A subsequent meeting with rival, Zhang Guotao, firmly established Mao's primacy.

### KEY

= = Long March

0 kilometers 300

0 miles 300

⑧ **Yan'an** *was the end point of the march on 19 October 1935. Mao arrived with 5000 marchers and established the Yan'an Soviet as an independent communist state.*

[map showing Long March route with labels: NINGXIA, Lanzhou, GANSU, SHAANXI, Xi'an, Yellow River, SHAN, ⑧, SICHUAN, HU, Chengdu, ⑥ ⑤ ⑦, CHONGQING, Yangzi, ④ ③, GUIZHOU, Guiyang, Kunming, YUNNAN, GUANG]

⑥ **Daxue Shan,** *the Great Snowy Mountains, are some of the highest in the country. Crossing the passes was the most challenging episode of the Long March, and led to the death, through altitude sickness, exhaustion, and exposure, of many Red Army soldiers.*

④ **At Lu Shan Pass**, the Red Army reached the pass just ahead of the KMT, deceived their pursuers, and gained an unexpected victory.

⑤ **The Luding Chain Bridge** *(see p371) was the only means of crossing the Dadu River. Blocked by KMT troops who had removed most of the bridge's planks, 22 Red Army soldiers took the bridge by crawling along the remaining chains, with the loss of seven men.*

③ **Zunyi** *was taken despite heavy losses in January 1935. Mao emerged from the ensuing conference as leader of the Communist Party and commander of the Red Army; the Soviet-supported general was expelled.*

Many prominent *Long Marchers became China's future leaders, including (from left) Bo Gu (Communist leader until 1935), Zhou Enlai, Zhu De, and Mao Zedong.*

① **Jinggang Shan** *was the base of the Jiangxi Soviet whose position was steadily being eroded by advancing KMT troops. Led by Mao Zedong, the Long March started from here on 16 October 1934.*

② **The crossing of** the Xiang river was the marchers' first major battle. Accounted a disaster, huge amounts of equipment were lost in the waters.

The thickly-wooded slopes of Jinggang Shan

# Jinggang Shan ⑫
井冈山

Ciping, 220 miles (350 km) S of Nanchang. 🚌 🏢 *2 Tianjie Rd, (0792) 655 6788.* 🔲 *for most revolutionary and scenic sights.* **www**.jgstour.com

There are two reasons for visiting Jinggang Shan: its scenery, which has been featured on Chinese bank notes, and its revolutionary associations. The mountain range, of which the main peak is Jinggang Shan, sometimes known as Wuzhi Feng (Five Fingers Peak), reaches to 5,200 ft (1,586 m). There are magnificent views, especially at sunrise, as well as a great variety of plants, birds, butterflies and other insects.

The village of Ciping was completely destroyed during the civil war of the 1930s but was rebuilt after 1949 as a sort of shrine to the communist struggle and to the Long March in particular. There are a number of buildings commemorating the way of life of the early revolutionaries, forced here in the late 1920s by Chiang Kai-shek's obsessive persecution, which culminated in a massacre of striking workers in Shanghai in 1927. It is possible here to gain some idea of what life was like for the revolutionaries, as they developed their strategy before the epic walk to Shaanxi. A short distance away is the watching post at Huangyang Jie, where the

**Monument outside Wulong Tan**

Red Army repulsed Kuomintang troops in 1928.

Located at about 3,300 ft (1,000 m), Ciping was the centre of the Jinggang Shan revolutionary base during the 1920s and 1930s and is now the site of local government. Its location at the center of the mountain range and growing collection of hotels make it a good base for exploring the area. The beauty of the area is a startling contrast with its image as a gritty, revolutionary stronghold. There are the 33-ft (100-m) Shuikou waterfalls, located in a luxuriant valley surrounded by rocks amid bamboo, azaleas and pine forest. Wulong Tan, a few miles north of Ciping, is composed of several limpid pools into which stream a number of rapids and waterfalls. A cable car can take you to the top and give you magnificent views over the whole area, whilst for those with the energy, much of the area can be enjoyed on foot.

**Pearl Pool, one of the five waterfalls at Wulong Tan**

# HUNAN & HUBEI

Hunan and Hubei are central China's westernmost provinces. Hubei is dominated by the mighty Yangzi River, and its capital Wuhan is a great industrial city on the river. The mountainous Three Gorges in western Hubei near Yichang is the site of the world's largest dam, which was completed in 2007. The scenic Shennongjia Forest Reserve, home of the legendary Wild Man, and Wudang Shan, known for its martial arts school, are spectacular sights definitely worth visiting, although remote and difficult to access.

Hunan's fertile farmlands lured millions of migrants during the political upheavals in North China between the 8th and 11th centuries. An important grain producer during the Ming and Qing dynasties, by the 19th century the population had outgrown the land, and the ensuing unrest was exploited by the Taiping Heavenly Kingdom Rebellion (see p422). The region's poverty also had a great impact on China's history in the 20th century. As the birthplace of Mao Zedong, Hunan's revolutionary credentials are still one of its principal attractions, both in Changsha, the capital, and in Mao's birthplace at Shao Shan. Other popular sights include Dongting Hu, China's second-largest lake, in the northeast, the temples at scenic Heng Shan in the south, and the wonderful mountain scenery of Wulingyuan in the northwest.

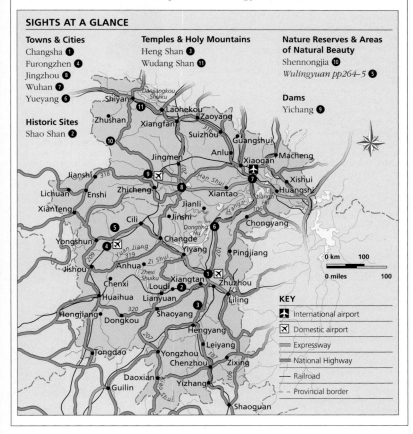

## SIGHTS AT A GLANCE

**Towns & Cities**
Changsha ❶
Furongzhen ❹
Jingzhou ❽
Wuhan ❼
Yueyang ❻

**Historic Sites**
Shao Shan ❷

**Temples & Holy Mountains**
Heng Shan ❸
Wudang Shan ⑪

**Nature Reserves & Areas of Natural Beauty**
Shennongjia ❿
*Wulingyuan pp264–5* ❺

**Dams**
Yichang ❾

### KEY

✈ International airport
☒ Domestic airport
━ Expressway
━ National Highway
━ Railroad
- - Provincial border

◁ **Martial artist practicing in one of the temples on Wudang Shan**

**No. 1 Teachers' Training College, Changsha**

# Changsha ①
长沙

180 miles (290 km) S of Wuhan.
🏯 6,000,000. ✕ 🚉 🚌
ℹ 59, 2 Duan, Furong Zhong Rd.

An important ancient city, Changsha was the capital of the Chu kingdom until the unification of China under the Qin in 280 BC. Much later, the city's profile was raised once more when in 1903 it became a treaty port, open to foreign trade. During the Sino-Japanese war in 1938, it was damaged by the Kuomintang. The town is associated with Mao Zedong, who attended college here from 1912 to 1918.

The excellent **Hunan Provincial Museum** houses many items of interest, including a collection of painted neolithic pottery and bronzes from the Shang and Zhou eras. However, the principal displays were excavated from three Han-dynasty tombs at Mawangdui, to the east of the city. The first tomb belonged to the wife of the Marquis of Dai, the second was that of the Marquis himself, while the third contained their son. The Marquis, Li Cang, became prime minister in 193 BC, and died in 186. The tombs contained a wooden outer coffin, surrounded by a protective layer of clay and charcoal, within which were four other coffins, lacquered and handsomely painted. The bodies had been dressed in several layers of silk. His wife's body (on display in a liquid-filled tank) was so well preserved that her skin retained a certain amount of elasticity.

Amazingly scientists were able to determine that she died at 50, and was suffering from tuberculosis and arthritis. According to the customs at the time, the tombs were filled with foods and furnishings to comfort that part of the soul that remains on earth, and a silk banner that mapped the Han belief system. Close by is the pleasantly landscaped **Martyrs' Park**.

Among the numerous sites related to Mao Zedong, the most interesting is the **Hunan First Normal College**, where he studied from 1913, when he was 19, until 1918. Although he famously failed his art exam, by drawing a circle and calling it an egg, he was declared student of the year in 1917. At college, he devoted much of his time organizing student societies, a useful practise for his future role as leader. Mao returned as a teacher between 1920 and 1922. Visitors can follow a self-guided route through the rebuilt college, which is still active, visiting the dormitories, the well where Mao bathed, and the halls where he held political meetings.

🏛 **Hunan Provincial Museum & Martyrs' Park**
50 Dongfeng Rd. **Tel** (0731) 8451 4630. ⏰ 8:30am–5:30pm daily. ♿

🏛 **Hunan First Normal College**
356 Shuyuan Rd. **Tel** (0731) 8822 8210. ⏰ daily. ♿

**Mao statue, No. 1 Teachers' Training College**

# Shao Shan ②
韶山

80 miles (130 km) SW of Changsha.
🚉 daily from Changsha. 🚌

The birthplace of Mao Zedong, China's leader from 1949 until his death in 1976, Shao Shan is really two towns. The newer one is near the railway station, while the village of Shao Shan Dong, where the "Great Helmsman" spent his early years is 4 miles (6 km) away. At the height of the Mao phenomenon during the Cultural Revolution, special pilgrimage trains, crowded with Red Guards, brought almost 8,000 worshipers a day. Shao Shan is still popular and any buildings connected with Mao are now preserved as museums. **Mao's Family House**, where he was born in 1893, is typically rural, except for its displays of memorabilia. Next to it lies the **Mao Zedong Exhibition Hall** and nearby to that sits the **Mao Ancestral Temple**. Overlooking the village is Shao Peak, accessed by cable car. About 2 miles (3 km) from the village is **Dripping Water Cave**, where, legend has it, Mao pondered over the Cultural Revolution in 1966.

🏛 **Mao's Family House & Mao Zedong Exhibition Hall**
Shao Shan Chong. **Tel** (0732) 5568 5157. ⏰ 8am–5pm daily. ♿

**Stone tablets engraved with Mao's poems, Shao Peak, Shao Shan**

**Grand gateway of the Zhusheng Si Monastery, Nanyue**

# Heng Shan ❸
衡山

75 miles (120 km) S of Changsha.
**Tel** (0734) 567 7801. 🚌 from
Changsha to Nanyue. ◯ daily. 📷

One of the five holy Daoist mountains, Heng Shan at 4,232 ft (1,290 m) is a cluster of wooded peaks, dotted with temples that were established some 1,300 years ago. The gateway to Heng Shan is **Nanyue**, a five-hour bus journey from Changsha. It is a pleasant little town with two main streets, and a couple of significant temples. **Nanyue Damiao** has been a place of worship for both Buddhist and Daoists since the early 8th century AD, although the current buildings, modeled on Beijing's Forbidden City, date from the 19th century. The other, **Zhusheng Si**, is an 8th-century Buddhist monastery, rebuilt in the 18th century.

The mountain can be explored on foot by mini-bus, but it is a 9-mile (15-km) walk to the top. There is a cable car to the summit from about halfway. A number of monasteries and temples lie along the path that meanders through lush countryside before reaching the **Martyrs' Memorial Hall**, honoring those who died in the 1911 revolution. Next is the 7th-century **Xuandu Si**, Hunan's main Daoist temple. The route finally leads to **Shangfeng Si**, also the minibus terminus. Just beyond is the summit marked by **Zhurong Gong**, a tiny stone temple. Visitors can stay at a hotel near the top for views from the **Terrace for Watching the Sunrise**.

# Furongzhen ❹
芙蓉镇

249 miles (400 km) NW of Changsha.
🚌 to Mengdonghe, then bus or boat. 🚌 🚲 from Mengdonghe.

Mengdonghe is the jumping-off point to Furongzhen (Wang Cun), the location of the eponymous 1986 film, *A Small Town Called Hibiscus*. Furongzhen means Hibiscus Town and the film was an adaptation of the novel *A Town Called Hibiscus* by Gu Hua. It was one of the first books to show how the political upheavals of the 1950s and 1960s affected people in rural China. Furongzhen is an attractive town with stone streets and old wooden buildings. Its **Tujia Museum** on Hepan Jie is devoted to the culture of the indigenous Tujia people. Visitors can also go rafting near Furongzhen, on the Yuan Jiang River.

# Wulingyuan ❺

See pp264–5.

# Yueyang ❻
岳阳

62 miles (100 km) N of Changsha.
🚶 5,200,000. 🚌 🚲 at Chenglingji.
🏨 25 Yunmeng Rd, (0730) 828 2222.

Situated on the banks of the Yangzi and the shores of Dongting Hu, China's second largest freshwater lake, Yueyang is an important stopping point for river ferries and trains on the Beijing to Guangzhou line. Its main sight, **Yueyang Tower**, was once part of a Tang-era temple. The current structure, dating from the Qing era, is an impressive sight, with its glazed yellow-tiled roofs overlooking the lake. Nearby are two pavilions, Xianmei Ting and Sanzui Ting; the latter was where Lu Dongbin, one of the Taoist Eight Immortals (see pp30–31), came to drink wine. To the south is **Cishi Ta**, a pagoda built in 1242 to propitiate flood-causing demons.

A 30-minute boat ride from Yueyang is the small island of **Junshan Dao**, a former Daoist retreat that is now famous for its silver needle tea.

🏛 **Yueyang Tower**
Dongting Beilu.
**Tel** (0730) 831 5588. ◯ daily. 📷
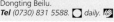

**A river boat at the scenic Junshan Dao (Junshan Island)**

# Cult of Mao

**1960s Mao lapel badge**

When he became Chairman in 1949, Mao Zedong was already a figure of almost mystical stature, having led the Red Army since 1934. He was an ideologue and whilst his impatience at the pace of reform led to decisions that often brought disaster, skillful maneuvering by the party meant that he remained a heroic figurehead. The Cultural Revolution (*see pp64–5*) 1966–76, was, at the expense of millions of lives, a calculated attempt to make Mao a deity. The years after his death saw a diminution of his status, but since the 1990s his popularity has revived. Once again Mao is considered by millions to be *weida* – Great.

**Mao's portrayal**, *not only as a deity but as a man of the people, was part of the ambiguity of the cult. Nonetheless, Mao remains at the center of the image surrounded by adoring women.*

## POSTER ART
In the 1960s the Chinese propaganda machine turned out posters featuring Mao by the million. He was often portrayed as a benevolent avatar, a god come among the people to transform their lives.

**A Mao study group** *discusses Mao's philosophy in the late 1960s. His thought briefly became a modern substitute for the Confucian philosophy that had dominated Chinese intellectual life for millennia.*

**"Celebrate the birth and life of Chairman Mao for 10,000 years."**

**Mao's face** was always a ruddy red, as artists were told to avoid grey and to imbue him with cherub-like youth.

**The thoughts of** *Chairman Mao were collected in 1961 in a volume, known as the "Little Red Book," which was distributed to all Red Guards.*

**Pilgrims at Shao Shan**, *Mao's birthplace (see p260), pay their respects. At the height of the Cultural Revolution, several trains a day pulled into Shao Shan to disgorge thousands of fervent pilgrims. In the 1980s this traffic all but ceased but was revived again in the 1990s.*

**"Chairman Mao is the red sun** *in our hearts", this poster asserts. The uppermost characters say "the East is Red," the name of a piece of music that became an anthem of the Cultural Revolution.*

**Light always** radiates from behind Mao, just as a halo might appear behind a god in a temple.

**Early poster art** *was slightly different in character from later propaganda. Although this poster asks people to march forward under the banner of Mao Zedong, revolutionary Soviet-endorsed communism, rather than Maoism, is celebrated on the flags.*

**Mao memorabilia** *is widely available in China, although many of the pieces on sale at markets today have been produced specifically for the tourist market.*

**Since Mao's death** *the Party has had to tread a delicate line between condemnation of his excesses and praise for his achievements. His portrait still hangs at the north end of Tian'an Men Square and his image is on all Chinese banknotes; perhaps his posthumous function is as a symbol of a united China.*

**Domestic shrines** *with a figure of Mao to whom family members would address their revolutionary prayers started replacing Daoist and Buddhist shrines during the 1960s. Mao shrines are still seen, although the Party disapproves.*

## MAO ATTACKED

In 1994 Mao's private physician, Li Zhisui, wrote *The Private Life of Chairman Mao*, in which Mao is portrayed as vain, cold, and contemptuous of his colleagues and of the suffering of the Chinese people. The book was instantly banned by the Chinese government. At the time of publication, Li was living in the United States and so escaped persecution. The book provides some surprising insights into Mao's habits and opinions. However, many critics, even those unsympathetic to Mao's politics, claim that the book is simply opportunistic.

**The jacket of Li's biography**

# Wulingyuan ➎

武陵源

**Sedan chair for
tired tourists**

Often called Zhangjiajie, this 243-square-mile (391-sq-km) scenic preserve is a karst landscape *(see pp412–13)* of enormous beauty, with rocky pinnacles rising from a coverlet of dense sub-tropical vegetation. Wulingyuan covers three natural reserves – Zhangjiajie, Tianzi Shan, and Suoxi Yu – and contains well over 500 species of tree, including the dawn redwood, which was believed to be extinct until it was re-identified in 1948. It is also a haven for fauna, including giant sala-manders, rhesus monkeys, and a wide variety of birds. The park is often cloaked in fog, adding atmosphere but obscuring most views. Summers are excessively humid.

★ **Xianren Qiao**
*The Bridge of the Immortals
is a spectacular, narrow and
unfenced span of rock over
a deep chasm.*

★ **Huang Shi Zhai**
*At 3,450 ft (1,050 m), Huang Shi Zhai is
the highest area in Wulingyuan. The climb
up the 3,878 steps requires a good two
hours; there is also a cable car if the
stairway sounds too daunting.*

TIANZI SHAN
ZHEN

ZHANGJIAJIE
NATURE PRESERVE

Jinbian Xi

ZHANGJIAJIE
CUN

ZHANGJIAJIE SHI

**Jin Bian Yan**
*This sandstone
peak stands at
1,312 ft (400 m).*

**Kongzhong
Tianyuan**
*The Heavenly Garden
is an isolated outcrop
covered in a mantle
of green and
surrounded by
clusters of slender
pinnacles and
towering peaks.*

## STAR SIGHTS

★ Huang Shi Zhai

★ Xianren Qiao

★ Huanglong Dong

**Tianzi Ge**
*In the northern part of the preserve, the pinnacle of this hill allows views of a valley forested with dozens of fine, splinter-like tors. Numerous underground caverns are found throughout the surrounding area.*

### KEY

| | |
|---|---|
| 🚌 | Bus station |
| 🚡 | Cable car |
| – – | Path |
| ▨ | Built-up area |
| = | Road |

**Yubi Feng**
*The limestone columns of the Emperor's Brushes are featured on Chinese stamps and resemble traditional Chinese calligraphy brushes.*

ANZI SHAN
RE PRESERVE

SUOXI YU
NATURE PRESERVE

*Suo Xi*

SUOXIYU CUN

Baofeng
Hu

| 0 meters | | 1000 |
|---|---|---|
| 0 yards | | 1000 |

**Boat trips on** Baofeng Hu's pristine waters are included in the price of admission.

## EXPLORING WULINGYUAN

The main entrance is just past Zhangjiajie Cun. Follow the left path for a four-hour walk that includes Huang Shi Zhai. The right path presents several options, taking you, eventually, away from the crowds. Accommodations are available in Zhangjiajie Cun, as well as Suoxiyu Cun, which is a good base for exploring the east and north of the park. Simple inns are scattered throughout the reserve.

**★ Huanglong Dong**
*Although illuminated garishly, 7 mile (11 km) Yellow Dragon Cave loses none of its impact. Boat tours drift down its subterranean river.*

# Wuhan

## 武汉

Daoist statue, Changchun Guan

An important port on the Yangzi, Hubei's capital is an amalgamation of three older cities. Wuchang, capital of the State of Wu (770–221 BC), and Hanyang, founded in the Sui era (AD 581–618), are ancient settlements, while Hankou was founded in 1861 when it became a treaty port for foreign trade. As a result the city was a center for early Chinese industrialization, when iron and steel works were built here in the 19th century. It was also the site of the first uprising of the 1911 Revolution that led to the fall of the Qing dynasty and the formation of Republican China.

Ancestral musical instruments at the Hubei Provincial Museum

### 🏛 Hubei Provincial Museum

156 Donghu Rd. *Tel* (027) 8679 4127. ◯ 9am–5pm daily. 📷
Located on the shore of Dong Hu, this is one of China's best museums. Among its highlights are items excavated in 1978 from the tomb of the Marquis of Yi, an eminent figure from the Warring States period. He died in 433 BC and was buried in a lacquered coffin, accompanied by his concubines, his dog, and thousands of bronze, stone, and woodem items. Many of these are on display, but the most impressive is the panoply of bronze bells which produce two notes each when struck.

Ferry rides are available to explore the scenic area around Dong Hu, with its many pavilions and gardens.

### 🏯 Mao's Villa

Donghu Rd. *Tel* (027) 6888 1918. ◯ 8am–5pm daily. 📷
This pleasant villa (Mao Zedong Bieshu) was Mao's hideaway between 1960 and 1974, where he stayed for prolonged periods during the first years of the Cultural Revolution. It is set in a spacious garden, and visitors can see

his living quarters, conference room, bomb shelter, and swimming pool.

### 🏯 Yellow Crane Pavilion

Wuluo Rd. ◯ daily. 📷
The Yellow Crane Pavilion on She Shan, south of the Yangzi in Wuchang district, is a reconstruction of a 3rd-century edifice that burned down in 1884. According to legend, it was built to honor one of the Daoist Eight Immortals, who paid his tavern bills by drawing cranes on the walls. The 164-ft (50-m) high pavilion is a handsome Qing-style building. It can be climbed for fine views across the city. On the eastern part of the hill is **Changchun**

Enormous bronze bell behind the Yellow Crane Pavilion

**Guan**, a Daoist temple with a pharmacy, where a doctor dispenses locally collected herbs. To the south is Hong Ge, a red-brick building that housed the **Former Headquarters of the Hubei Military Government** (Hong Lou) during the 1911 uprising, provoked by Sun Yat-sen *(see p297)*. Behind the Pavilion itself is an enormous bronze temple bell which, for a small fee, visitors may strike. Sun Yat-sen's statue stands in front of the building.

### 🚉 Yangzi Bridge

This impressive 361-ft (110-m) long bridge was built in 1957 by the Communists. Before its construction, all road and rail traffic crossed the river by ferry. A second bridge was built a short way downriver in 1995.

Hankou Train Station 2 km (1.2 miles)

Hankou Bus Station
Zhongshan Gongyuan
HANGKONG ROAD
JIEFANG DA DAO
Chongren Road
Youyi Road
Liji Beilu
CAAC
Qiaokou Road
ZHONGSHAN DA DAO
WUSHENG ROAD
HANKO
YAN HE DA DAO
Jianghan Bridge
Han Shui
Guqin Tai
Gui Shan ⑤
Guishan Gongyuan
GUISHAN ROAD
Hanyang Bus Station
Yangzi Bridge ④
HANYANG DA DAO
Guiyuan Si ⑥
HANYANG
Zho Road Te
Yangzi

**Key to Symbols** *see back flap*

**Daoist priests depicted in a wall painting at Changchun Guan**

### 🛕 Gui Shan

Wuhan's industrial quarter of Hanyang has a few sights of interest, most of which lie on or around Gui Shan or Turtle Hill. This was named after a magic turtle that defeated a threatening water demon and prevented the Han and Yangzi rivers from flooding. The **Guqin Tai** (Lute Terrace) was where the legendary musician, Bo Ya, would come to play his lute. After the death of his friend, the woodcutter who could understand his music, Bo Ya destroyed his lute and vowed never to play again. A couple of tombs survive in the eastern part of the mountain. Near the tomb of **Xiang Jing Yu** (1895– 1928), one of the first women leaders in Communist China, lies that of a semi-mythical hero from a much earlier era – **Lu Su**, a Wu general from the Three Kingdoms period.

**VISITORS' CHECKLIST**

470 miles (750 km) W of Shanghai. 🚊 7,950,000. ✈ 🚉 Hankou Train Station, Wuchang Train Station. 🚌 CAAC (buses to airport), Hankou Bus Station, Hanyang Bus Station, Wuchang Bus Station. 🚢 Yangzi Ferry Terminal. 🛈 6 Baofeng Rd, (027) 8366 9955.

**Buddha statue, Guiyuan Si**

### 🛕 Guiyuan Si

20 Cuiweiheng Rd. **Tel** (027) 8484 4756. ◻ 7:30am– 5:30pm daily. 🈺

This Buddhist temple in western Hanyang was founded in the early Qing era (1644–62), although the current buildings are late Qing and early Republican. It has a few ancient relics including a Northern Wei Buddha statue, but is most famous for its hall of 500 *arhat* statues sculpted in the 1820s, including a statue of Buddha carved from a single piece of jade.

### 🛕 Hankou

From 1861, the district of Hankou was the site of the former foreign concession. This area has several fine examples of European-style colonial architecture. The best are located between the river and Zhongshan Dadao, particularly along Yanjiang Dadao and Jianghan Road. The old **Customs House** looking over the river is a vast Renaissance style building with a striking grey-stone portico and Corinthian capitals.

*(Map of WUCHANG showing: International Airport 5 km (3 miles), DAJIE ROAD, Sanyang Road, Changjiang Bridge, WUHAN CHANG JIANG, Wuchang Bei Train Station, Changjiang Tunnel, Yangzi Ferry Terminal, Customs House, LINJIANG DADAO, HEPING DADAO, YOU YI DA DAO, Sha Hu, ZHONG BEI ROAD, DONGHU ROAD, Dong Hu Gongyuan, Hubei Provincial Museum ①, Mao's Villa ②, Dong Hu, HONGSHAN ROAD, ZHONGSHAN ROAD, Yellow Crane Pavilion, MINZHU ROAD, She Shan Gongyuan ③, Changchun Guan, ZHONG NAN ROAD, Wuchang Bus Station, Wuchang Train Station, Nan Hu, JINGZHOU; 0 meters 100, 0 yards 100)*

**Colorful kites on sale on the Yangzi riverfront**

Jingzhou Museum, part of the
Taoist Kaiyuan Temple

## Jingzhou 8
荆州

Jingzhou Municipality. 150 miles (240
km) W of Wuhan. 🏯 6,500,000.
🚗 🚅 ✈ 🛈 52 Jingding Rd,
(0716) 840 7999.

A worthwhile short stop
if cruising the river, the
ancient town of Jingzhou is
about 8 kms to the west of
its modern counterpart
Shashi. The old town is
ringed by walls 20 ft (7 m)
in height, which were
constructed by General Guan
Yu of the State of Shu (AD
221–63). Within the walls
stands the Jingzhou Museum.
This has a a large collection
of ancient silk and fabrics
and, more notably, finds
from a Western Han tomb of
a court official called Sui
including his gory but well-
preserved corpse complete
with organs.

## Yichang 9
宜昌

Yichang District. 155 miles (250 km)
W of Wuhan. 🚗 ✈ 🚅 🛈 52
Jiefang Rd, (0717) 676 0392.

Yichang, which was once a
treaty port for foreign
traders, is now associated
with the Gezhou Dam,
completed in 1986 and the
huge and controversial
Three Gorges Dam,
completed in 2008. It is
possible to visit the site of
the Three Gorges Dam at
Sandouping, which lies 24
miles (38 km) upstream. The
town is also a starting point
for a visit to Shennongjia
scenic area.

# The Three Gorges Dam
长江三峡

Observation
Station Statue

The construction of the Three Gorges Dam,
at over 600 ft (180 m) high and more than
a mile (2 km) across, was intended to provide
a significant amount of China's energy, curb
the Yangzi's tendency to flood, and channel some of the country's wealth, for long
concentrated along the coastal regions, into
China's heartland. However, creating a 400-
mile (645-km) long reservoir has also meant the relocation
of many thousands of people, the obliteration of important cultural sites, and long-term environmental damage.

Three Gorges Dam seen from the low-water side

## ENVIRONMENTAL ISSUES

Hundreds of miles downstream, the rapidly growing
municipality of Chongqing has been pumping untreated
waste and chemicals into the Yangzi. With the river no
longer able to flush this
away, the fear is that it
could all collect in a 400-
mile (645-km) long
cesspool. Additionally,
the reduced flow of the
water could substantially
increase the silting up of
subsidiary waterways,
further harming the
fragile ecosystem and
closing the migration
routes of many fish
species and rare
freshwater dolphins.

Part of the Three Gorges before the
water levels rose 575 ft (175-m)

### ★ Jar Hill Observation Platform

*This highpoint provides an excellent bird's eye view of the dam as well as a museum showing the history of the construction.*

### VISITORS' CHECKLIST

Sandouping, 22 miles (35 km) W of Yichang. 🏠 CITS, 21 Yunji Rd, (0717) 622 0848. 🚌 4 from Yichang train station or hire a minibus or taxi for a couple of hours. **Visitor Center** 🗓 daily. 🎫

**The Yangzi Sculpture** is a large lump of eroded rock that is said to be from the Yangzi River.

**The Ship Lifting Tower** is simply a large and very powerful elevator for ships less than 80-ft (25-m) long – faster than using the 5-level lock.

### STAR SIGHTS

★ Jar Hill Observation Platform

★ 5-Level Ship Lock

### ★ 5-Level Double Ship Lock

*At over a mile long (1600 m) this lock can raise or lower ships a total vertical distance of 370 ft (113 m) and is, not surprisingly, the largest lock system in the world. It takes nearly three hours to pass through the lock gates.*

Dense virgin forests lining a gorge at Shennongjia

# Shennongjia ⑩
神农架

124 miles (200 km) NW of Yichang.
🚉 from Yichang to entrance at Muyu,
then hire a car. 🏢 100 Yiling Da Dao,
(0717) 690 8026. 🎫 from Yichang
tourist office & Forestry Office Travel
Service, Muyu.

This remote and little-visited
forest reserve has some
remarkable scenery. It is
covered with rare trees and
several hundred species of
plants used in traditional
medicine, samples of which
were introduced to the West
by the botanist Ernest Wilson
in the early 20th century. It is
also home to many of China's
rarest animals, including the
splendid golden monkey.

Inside the reserve, at **Xiaolong Tan**, is a museum dedicated to the legendary Chinese
Wild Man (*ye ren*), who is like
the Himalayan Yeti and just as
hard to find. The first reported
sighting was in 1924. Walking
trails around Xiaolong Tan lead
into the heart of the reserve,
providing an excellent opportunity to see the rare golden
monkeys, giant salamanders,
and golden pheasants. Some
trails follow forest roads, others
meander gently across meadows, while the crudest lead to
mountain tops. Foreign visitors
can explore the Muyu area,
where peaks reach 10,187 ft
(3,105 m). It may be possible
to visit the main town of Song-
bai, but only if accompanied
by a tour guide. An airport will
be completed by 2014.

# Wudang Shan ⑪
武当山

218 miles (350 km) NW of Wuhan. 🚉
from Wuhan or Xiangfan to Wudang
Shan town. 🚌 from Shiyan, Xiangfan
or Liuliping to Wudang Shan town. 🎫

The many peaks of Wudang
Shan – the highest reaching
5,289 ft (1,612 m) at **Tianzhu**
(Heavenly Pillar) **Peak** – have
been associated with Daoism
since the Tang era. Wudang
Shan has also been known for
its martial arts since the Song-
dynasty monk, Zhang Sanfeng,
created a style called Wudang
boxing from which *tai ji quan*
later developed. After years of
neglect, the many temples
here have been refurbished
and are now flourishing. The
entry point is the town of
Wudang Shan, which has little
to offer except the temple
museum of **Tai Shan Miao** and
the ruins of Yuxu Gong temple.

Wudang Shan lies to the
south of town, and there are
several ways of reaching it. A
path near the railway station
takes eight hours to reach the
summit at Tianzhu Peak.
Minibuses go about three-
quarters of the way up, from
where it is another two hours
on foot to the top. Other
options are sedan chairs and
a cable car that runs between
a point called Qiongtai and
the summit. Going up by
minibus, visitors first pass the
**Martial Arts School** and
then the **Zixiao Gong**
(Purple Cloud Palace), an
impressive Ming temple that
has become the busiest in the
area. Inside the main hall is a
beautiful spiral cupola. From
the minibus terminus, a short
diversion leads to the
**Nanyan Gong** temple at the
very edge of the cliff. Nearby
is **Dragon Head Rock** that
projects horizontally from the
edge, and is covered in
sculpted designs. The main
path goes past **Lang Mei
Xian Ci**, a shrine dedicated to
the monk Zhang Sanfeng. The
path eventually divides into
two at Huanglong Dong. Of
the two paths, it is easier to
take the one leading straight
on to the group of temples at
Tianzhu Peak. At the summit,
the peak is surmounted by
**Jindian Gong** (Golden Hall),
built of gilded copper and
bronze in 1416. It has a statue
of the Ming emperor Zhen
Wu, who retreated to Wudang
Shan in the 15th century. The
views from Tianzhu, of razor-
edge cliffs covered in mist,
are magnificent.

The Ming-era Zixiao Gong (Purple Cloud Palace), Wudang Shan

◁ **The Yangzi River at sunset, winding its way through the Three Gorges**

# *Tai Ji Quan* (Tai Chi)

Practiced daily by millions of Chinese, *tai ji quan*, or "Supreme Ultimate Fist," is a slow-moving, graceful form of kung fu *(see p159)*. Developed over a thousand years ago by Daoist recluses and monks, *tai ji quan* is based on the movements of birds and animals and the Daoist concept of *yin* and *yang* or equal opposites. All of the movements, each with their own names and prescribed patterns, have elements of *yin* and *yang*; movements contract and expand, sink and rise, move inwards and outwards. The movements follow one another fluidly and sets can involve anywhere from 12 to 108 moves, and take up to an hour to complete. *Tai ji quan* does have martial aspects, but is utilized chiefly to improve the flow of *qi* *(see pp32–3)*, or vital energy, through the body. The exercises leave the practitioner feeling revitalized and relaxed.

**Daoist bagua**

**Zhang Sanfeng**, *an official, retired in disgust at the Court to Wudang Shan. Inspired by a battle between a crane and a snake, he came up with the basis for* tai ji quan, *combining knowledge of kung fu and Daoist health principles.*

**The Sword set** *involves the use of a weapon to aid balance and concentration. The simple sword form, with some 50 movements, is related to the water element, whilst the sabre is related to fire.*

## MOVEMENTS OF THE *TAI JI QUAN* SET

*Tai ji quan's* numerous schools have different sets and movements. "Whip to one side" is a common move often repeated in a set.

**One arm pushes** forward; the other whips sideways.

**Legs are** in a classic sturdy *tai ji quan* pose, as the weight shifts forward.

**As the body turns to** a 45 degree angle, the feet turn and the weight shifts to the back leg.

**The front leg** slides forward, the body sinking *(yin)* close to the ground in a powerful position ready to sweep upward *(yang)*.

**The trunk** sinks, while the back remains upright. Arms are poised as if to ward off attack.

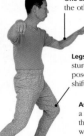

**Exercising in public squares** *is a feature of daily life in China. Early in the morning crowds of mostly elderly people perform* tai ji quan *in large groups executing the movements in graceful unison.*

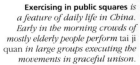

# THE SOUTH

# The South at a Glance

Encompassing the provinces of Fujian, Guangdong, and Hainan, as well as Macau and Hong Kong, the South is China's most familiar region, mainly because millions of immigrants from the area have moved overseas, taking their cooking and traditions with them. Yet, with the exception of Hong Kong and Guangzhou, the area rarely features on travelers' itineraries. There is much to enjoy, however, from the ancient Ming city of Chaozhou and Wuyi Shan's superb scenery, to the historic ports of Quanzhou, Xiamen, and Shantou along the coasts of Guangdong and Fujian, and the tropical beaches of Hainan.

**Fishermen laboring on the beach at Meizhou Island**

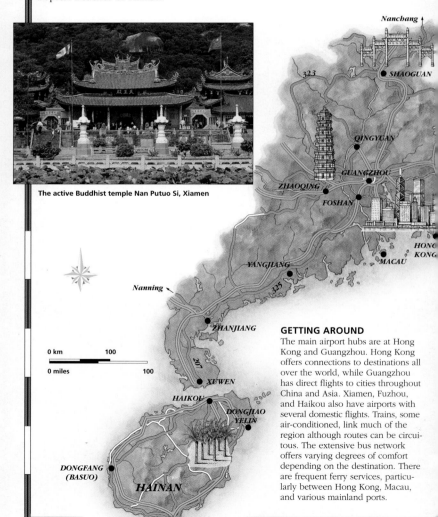

**The active Buddhist temple Nan Putuo Si, Xiamen**

## GETTING AROUND

The main airport hubs are at Hong Kong and Guangzhou. Hong Kong offers connections to destinations all over the world, while Guangzhou has direct flights to cities throughout China and Asia. Xiamen, Fuzhou, and Haikou also have airports with several domestic flights. Trains, some air-conditioned, link much of the region although routes can be circuitous. The extensive bus network offers varying degrees of comfort depending on the destination. There are frequent ferry services, particularly between Hong Kong, Macau, and various mainland ports.

◁ **Houseboats moored in orderly lines at Aberdeen Harbour, Hong Kong Island**

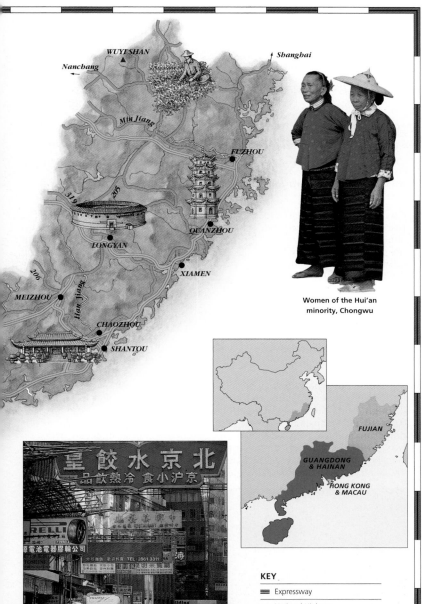

WUYISHAN ▲

Nanchang ←

Min Jiang

Shanghai ↑

FUZHOU

319 205

QUANZHOU

LONGYAN

XIAMEN

206

MEIZHOU

Han Jiang

CHAOZHOU

SHANTOU

Women of the Hui'an
minority, Chongwu

FUJIAN

GUANGDONG
& HAINAN

HONG KONG
& MACAU

Traffic and advertisements along the bustling Gloucester
Road in Wan Chai, Hong Kong

**KEY**

≡ Expressway

― National Highway

= Minor road

▲ Mountain

**SEE ALSO**

• *Where to Stay* pp564–7

• *Where to Eat* pp590–93

# A PORTRAIT OF THE SOUTH

*An enduring maritime tradition has influenced life and culture in the South. The long coastline along the South China Sea gave the ports of Fujian and Guangdong easy access to trade routes leading East and West. Trade also brought the British and Portuguese to the South, ultimately leading to the colonization of Hong Kong and Macau. Only Hainan Island remained isolated from the developments that took place across the sea on mainland China.*

Guangdong and Fujian are particularly mountainous, and although the mountains are not especially high, they have isolated the provinces from the political mainstream of the center and north of the country. Consequently, the South has tended to look outwards, across the sea, and over the centuries has been far more inclined than much of China to deal with foreigners – either by design or default.

**Picking tea leaves, Fujian**

From the 7th century onwards, Arab traders introduced Islam to China through ports such as Guangzhou (Canton) and Quanzhou, and took silk, porcelain, and tea away with them. It was from these ports that China launched its overseas naval expeditons. The Ming emperors sponsored the great voyages of Admiral Zheng He, a Muslim eunuch, who crossed the Indian Ocean from Fuzhou to Africa in the early 1400s. Almost a century later, Portuguese vessels ventured up the Pearl River to Guangzhou; an expedition that eventually led to the colonization of Macau in 1557. The British soon followed, but their nefarious policy of flooding the Chinese market with opium led to the two Opium Wars (1839–42, 1856–60), after which China ceded Hong Kong and the tip of the Kowloon Peninsula to Britain.

Over the centuries, waves of Southern Chinese migrated overseas, first to Southeast Asia, and later westward as far as North America, as indentured labor. Their global presence

Hong Kong Island's glittering skyline, seen from Kowloon across Victoria Harbour

**Tiled-roofs above the harbor at Meizhou Island**

Highlands around Tongshi offer glimpses into their unique culture.

Strong overseas connections have meant that in the last 20 years, money has poured back into the South. China's more flexible modern economy as well as large investments from Hong Kong have also enhanced the region's affluence. Development has been rapid, propelling the growth of new cities, such as Shenzhen, helped

is one of reasons why visitors consider this the most familiar region in China.

The Cantonese culinary tradition is distinct and known the world over. The local cuisine, however, may encompass outlandish ingredients not used in overseas restaurants; it is said, with some justification, that the Cantonese will eat anything.

Teas from the south are exported throughout the world and Fujian produces some of China's finest, including oolong. The area has cultivated the arts of tea brewing and

**A traditional Hakka dwelling**

tasting, and so-called "tea art halls," where resident brew masters demonstrate techniques associated with particular varieties of tea, are still found in Fuzhou, the province's capital.

The South's largely subtropical climate has encouraged a gregarious lifestyle, which tends to manifest itself in an active, open-air streetlife. The local language of Cantonese is quite different from Mandarin, the national language. The sound is distinctive, even to the untrained ear. The region's other major dialect is Fujianese *(Minnan hua)*.

The South is home to several ethnic communities, including the Hakka and the Li. The Hakka migrated to south and central China from the north. The impressive round mansions of the Fujianese Hakka are a highlight of a trip to the interior. The Li are Hainan's original people, who settled here almost 2,000 years ago and lived a primeval existence until the 1930s. The Central

by their status as Special Economic Zones. Inspired by Hong Kong's sleek, contemporary architecture, construction has been frantic and the proliferation of high-rise buildings has transformed the skyline of historic cities.

There are still many hidden gems to explore among the region's skyscrapers and new developments. Chief among these are Guangzhou's Nan Yue Tomb, the rarely-visited Chaozhou with its still-intact Ming city wall, and one of China's oldest mosques in Quanzhou. Some of the finest examples of colonial architecture can be seen in Macau and on the islet of Gulang Yu in Xiamen. Tropical Hainan's main appeal lies in its beaches, but the mountainous center is worth exploring as well. Finally, there is always Hong Kong, a frenetic, cosmopolitan city that vibrates day and night with an energy that is in keeping with its status as a global financial center.

**Women of the Hui'an minority, Chongwu**

# Rice

**A bottle of rice wine**

Rice has long been vital to the Chinese as both a food staple and a cash crop. So intrinsic to life is the grain that *"Chi fan le ma?"* (Have you eaten rice today?) is one of the most common greetings in China. Rice-growing is thought to have its origins in southern China around 10,000 BC, although the flooded-field method that allowed larger yields and required massive irrigation projects was not perfected until thousands of years later. Today, rice is grown throughout much of China and accounts for 35 percent of the world's total.

**Rice plants,** *like most other cereals, produce dense flower-heads, with the grains tightly packed inside protective husks.*

**An endless chain** *of wooden pallets pulls water from a lower source to the fields by the pedaling power of laborers. Although much irrigation is now mechanized, numerous ingenious devices, many of them ancient technology once fashioned from bamboo, are still used to water the fields.*

**Japonica rice**

**Glutinous rice**

**Japonica,** *a sub-species of* Oryza sativa, *is the most common rice in China, and is generally short grained and slightly sticky. Glutinous rice, grown in the south-east, becomes a sticky mass when cooked. It is often served wrapped in bamboo leaves.*

## RICE PRODUCTS

The Chinese have found many uses for their pervasive staple. During the Ming dynasty, builders used water in which glutinous rice had been cooked as mortar mix to strengthen defensive walls. Rice straw, the leaves of the plant left after harvest, is pulped to produce a fine white paper, perfect for paintings and kites. Husks are used as fertilizer, packing material, or simply fed to animals. Rice is ground to produce rice flour which can be rolled and pulled to create a huge range of noodles. Numerous rice wines are sold in China, some of them quite palatable, including sweet Shaoxing, made from glutinous rice.

**Extracting juice from rice to ferment and make into** *jiu* **(wine or spirits)**

**Water buffalo** *pull plows, harrows, and other agricultural implements. These sturdy animals thrive in the waterlogged conditions, produce valuable manure, and require less maintenance than tractors.*

## TERRACED HILLSIDES

Vast areas of China are dominated by rice cultivation, and paddy fields have transformed the landscape, especially in the subtropical regions of the south, where cascades of terraces clothe many hillsides. Low mudbanks trap the water as it trickles down the slopes, creating an attractive sequence of narrow, contour-hugging fields which are worked mainly by hand. Farmers are not completely reliant on rainfall because the water flow is carefully controlled, as is the depth, which is typically 6 in (15 cm). Ever resourceful, some farmers raise edible fish such as grass carp in the paddy waters.

## CULTIVATING RICE

In much of rural China, rice growing is very much a hands-on activity, and traditional methods are still used, especially in hilly country. The work is labor-intensive, but the two or three harvests a year that are possible in the south make the efforts worthwhile.

**Rice seedlings** *are grown in special protected beds. After about 40 days they are transplanted by hand to the paddies.*

**Planting** *is tiring, back-breaking work, and in some areas is now mechanized. Teams of workers wade through the paddy fields planting the seedlings one by one.*

**At harvest** *time, the fields are drained before the rice plants are cut either by hand-held sickle or by machine.*

**To dry** *the rice, mounds of freshly harvested grain are raked out in a thin layer and left to warm in the sun.*

**Winnowing,** *tossing or pouring the rice from a basket, separates the dried rice grains from their husks – the wind carries away the chaff.*

# Regional Food: The South

The southern school of Chinese cooking, called by the generic name Cantonese, is centered around Guangzhou, where the Pearl River delta runs into the South China Sea. Situated at the mouth of this estuary lies Hong Kong, another culinary center of China. Fish, of course, plays a major role in this coastal economy and rice is the dominant food grain. Other food crops include tea, peanuts, sugar cane, and subtropical fruits such as bananas, pineapples, oranges, and lychees. Large-scale emigration from the south has meant that Chinese food served outside China is likely be southern Chinese cooking.

**Bitter melon and water spinach**

**Lush and colorful vegetables on display in the market**

## GUANGZHOU (CANTON)

The epicenter of Chinese cuisine, Guangzhou owes its culinary primacy to its geography. As a port it had a well-off, cosmopolitan merchant class who could afford expensive foods. It also has a subtropical climate and a summer that lasts for almost six months, with the rest of the year divided into autumn and spring: there is no winter. As a result crops grow luxuriantly all year round and supplement the abundance of fish. Despite this fecundity, the size of the population the land has to support means that it has always struggled to provide enough food. Therefore the Cantonese also eat less expensive "delicacies" not popular in other provinces such as frogs' legs, turtles, dogs, snakes, and nearly every kind of animal there is. Food has become almost a religion to the Cantonese and the locals claim that in Guangzhou "there is a restaurant every five steps."

**Pork dumplings**
**Turnip cake**
**BBQ pork buns**
**Prawns in beancurd skin**
**Spring rolls**
**Chicken feet**
**Prawn dumplings**

**A selection of *dim sum* dishes**

## REGIONAL DISHES AND SPECIALTIES

Most people probably associate Cantonese cuisine with *dim sum* (meaning "dot on the heart" or "snack"), delectable, dainty bites of steamed or fried food: dumplings with prawn or pork fillings, miniature spareribs, deep-fried spring rolls, paper-wrapped prawns, chicken feet, or glossy custard-filled tarts. These snacks are to be eaten during the day for lunch with pots of tea, never as dinner. Other famous specialties are the fish and shellfish dishes, and roast meats – duck, *cha shao* (roast pork), and suckling pig. Key to the southern school of cuisine are its various sauces. Although such fresh food is often quickly steamed with a few simple aromatics, sauces such as oyster, hoi sin (sweet soy bean and garlic), mushroom, lemon, black bean and *chu hou* (soy bean, garlic and ginger) are also used to add flavor.

**Soy-cured bacon and sausages**

**Steamed Seabass:** *steamed with scallions and ginger, and seasoned with light soy sauce, rice wine and sesame oil.*

## CHAOZHOU & DONGJIANG

Chaozhou (also known as Teochew) is a richer cuisine than Cantonese. Because this cuisine specializes in shell-fish and seafood, freshness is vital – hence the emphasis on buying live animals or fish, be it at a market or restaurant. They like to use stocks flavoured with fish sauce, hot sauce, or red rice vinegar. Dongjiang is a more rustic and salty cooking – soy-cured bacon and air-dried sausages are a specialty – and it also uses more poultry. This cooking is also sometimes known as Hakka, meaning "family of guests," which refers to the immigrants from

**Fish drying in a shop in Hong Kong**

**Dried vegetable and spices stall**

northern China who settled in the south some time after the invasion by Mongols in the 13th century. Later there were other large-scale migrations overseas, one of the reasons why most Chinese restaurants in the West serve only southern Chinese (Cantonese) food.

## HONG KONG

Although mainly Chinese, Hong Kong is a unique city in China: as an interna-tional port, it has been open to outside influences. So, while most of the restaurants are Cantonese, you will also find all the regional Chinese cuisines here alongside those from other Asian countries and Europe. A gastromomic supermarket, Hong Kong doesn't really have a specialty dish although some claim that "smelly beancurd" (a pungent type of fermented tofu) fulfils that role. Hong Kong is a 24-hour city and, all day ev-ery day, all the food places, from the humble street stands to the luxury banqueting halls, are filled with people eating. The story goes that you could visit a different restaurant each day for a year, and never eat the same dish twice.

### ON THE MENU

**Seafood with Vegetables** A popular dish of prawns, squid, and scallops stir-fried with whatever vegetables are available and noodles.

**"White-cut" Chicken** A whole chicken blanched in boiling water or stock, then left to cool in the liquid under cover for 6–8 hours. Tender and moist.

**Stir-fried Squid with Black Bean Sauce** In fact any seafood such as crab, lobster, or prawns may be substituted for the squid. This can also be made with chilies for a more spicy alternative.

**Eight-treasure Stuffed Beancurd** The stuffing is pork and prawn – vegetarians should stick with the Eight-treasure Buddha's Special (*see p180–1*).

**Steamed Chicken with Dried Mushrooms** Chicken pieces steamed with Chinese mushrooms – simple but great.

**Lobster with Ginger & Scallions:** *lobster braised with aromatics and served on a bed of soft noodles.*

**Oyster Sauce Beef:** *stir-fried beef with mushrooms and vegetables, all cut to the same size, in oyster sauce.*

**Roast Meats:** *choice cuts of suckling pig, duck, pork, and chicken served cold with tasty dipping sauces.*

# FUJIAN

The sea and mountains form the essential features of the province of Fujian. Its major cities thrive as coastal ports, while inland there is the spectacular, rugged beauty of Wuyi Shan.

Fujian's historical importance dates back almost as far as the Warring States period (475–221 BC), when the Yue people, defeated by the State of Chu (today's Hubei and Hunan), migrated southwards to settle in this part of China and Vietnam. Those who came to what is now Fujian were called Min Yue, later known as the Min people. Even today the Fujianese are sometimes referred to as Min and the southern Fujian language as Minnan Hua. The native people who preceded them are thus called the Ancient Min. Very little survives from this period, apart from the mysterious boat-shaped coffins, found lodged high above the river in the Wuyi Mountains. The main attractions are strung along the busy coastline and include the historic ports of Xiamen and Quanzhou, as well as Fuzhou, the capital, which was a major maritime center for over 1,000 years. Other attractions are the stone town of Chongwu, and Meizhou Island, birthplace of the important Goddess of the Sea. Inland, Fujian's hinterland is wild and unspoilt enough to protect the last remaining South China tigers. It is also the home of the Hakka people, whose traditional dwellings can be seen at the rural settlements around Yongding.

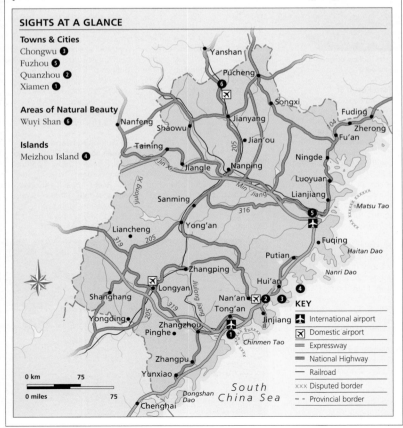

## SIGHTS AT A GLANCE

**Towns & Cities**
Chongwu ❸
Fuzhou ❺
Quanzhou ❷
Xiamen ❶

**Areas of Natural Beauty**
Wuyi Shan ❻

**Islands**
Meizhou Island ❹

KEY

🛬 International airport

✕ Domestic airport

═ Expressway

═ National Highway

─ Railroad

xxx Disputed border

- - Provincial border

◁ Looking out to sea over the gabled rooftops of Meizhou Island

# Xiamen ❶
## 厦门

An attractive city with a bustling nautical atmosphere, Xiamen was known as Amoy in the 19th century. It was first settled in the Song dynasty (960–1279 AD) but did not become a significant port until the Ming dynasty. It also served as an important stronghold against the Manchus when they invaded in the 17th century. The resistance was led by the legendary pirate and Ming loyalist Zheng Chenggong, also known as Koxinga, who is commemorated in the city. Xiamen became an early treaty port in the 19th century, when the foreign community established itself on Gulangyu Island. The city was also declared one of China's first Special Economic Zones in the 1980s.

Cannons guard the ramparts at Huli Shan Fort

Colorful rooftop dragon, Nan Putuo Si

### 🏯 Nan Putuo Si
515 Siming Nan Lu. **Tel** (0592) 208 6586. ◯ 6am–5pm daily. 🖼

This busy temple was founded in the Tang era in the extravagant southern style (see p300). Its three halls hold a wealth of Buddhist statuary. The Heavenly King Hall has an image of Wei Tuo, Protector of Buddhist Doctrine, who holds a stick pointing down to signify that the temple offers lodging to pilgrims.

### 🏯 Huxiyan
A quaint little temple lies high on a rocky outcrop at Huxiyan (Tiger Stream Rock). Another temple, Bailu Dong (White Deer Cave), is located even higher up the hill. Built in the Ming era, its main draw is the fine view across the city.

### ♣ Wanshi Botanical Garden
25 Huyuan Lu. **Tel** (0592) 203 8471. ◯ 6:30am–6pm daily. 🖼

This large scenic area houses over 5,300 species of plants, especially from South China and Southeast Asia. These include eucalyptus, bamboo,

and a redwood tree planted by the former US President Richard Nixon. A bullet-scarred rock marks the spot where Koxinga killed his cousin.

### 🏛 Overseas Chinese Museum
493 Siming Nan Lu. **Tel** (0592) 208 4028. ◯ 9:30am–4:30pm Tue–Sun. 🖼

In this museum of two sections, the first focuses on the history of Fujianese emigration, illustrated by photographs, paintings, and mementoes. The second houses bronzes, pottery, and artworks once owned by non-resident Chinese. The bronze collection is remarkable, spanning the period from the Shang (16th century BC) to the Republican era.

### 🏯 Huli Shan Paotai
Daxue Lu. ◯ daily. 🖼

Situated in the Huli Shan Fort along the coast, this huge cannon was made for the Qing government by a German manufacturer in 1891.

Almost 46-ft (14-m) long and weighing 49 tons (50,000 kg), it had a firing range of 6 miles (10 km). Taiwan's islands are visible from the ramparts – a fascination for locals, who were forbidden entry to the site until 1984.

### 🏯 Jimei School Village
◯ daily. 🖼

Located 9 miles (15 km) north of the city, Jimei School Village was founded by the philanthropist Tan Kah Kee (Chen Jiageng) in 1913. A succesful Singapore businessman, he returned to China in 1950 and held various government posts. Built in Chinese-Gothic style, the college is set in a beautiful park filled with pagodas and close to the sea. Tan Kah Kee's former residence, also here, is open to the public.

### 🏯 Gulangyu Island
Xiamen Seaworld **Tel** (0592) 206 7668. ◯ 8am–5:30pm. 🖼 **Shuzhuang Garden** ◯ daily. 🖼 **Sunlight Rock** ◯ daily. 🖼 **Koxinga Memorial Hall** ◯ 8:40am–5pm.

The tranquil island of Gulangyu lies only a ten-minute boat ride from

Gulangyu Island's tiny streets and elegant colonial houses

Xiamen, with attractive buildings, and no traffic apart from battery-powered buggies. The island first became important in 1842 after the signing of the treaty of Nanking, when the resident representatives of the foreign powers established themselves here. It soon grew into a European-style town with churches, consulates, and spacious villas. In 1903, it was designated an International Settlement for Europeans and Japanese, complete with a municipal council and Sikh police force, and it retained this status until the end of World War II. The island still retains an atmosphere reminiscent of Southern Europe.

Spread over nearly one square mile (2.5 sq km), Gulangyu Island is very pleasant to explore on foot, with its tiny streets and elegant houses, fronted by pretty flower gardens. Close to the ferry terminal is **Xiamen Seaworld**, which houses an interesting collection of sharks, seals, dolphins, penguins, and tropical fish. To the southeast is the **Statue of Koxinga**, which

**Statue of the legendary rebel commander, Koxinga, Gulangyu**

commemorates Xiamen's famous rebel. Koxinga and his fleet held out against the encroaching Manchus for years. He is also credited with ousting the Dutch from Taiwan. Farther south along the coast is **Shuzhuang Garden**. Built in 1931 as a private villa, the garden opened to the public in 1955. Today visitors are enticed by its numerous tropical plants and flowers, as well as its

## VISITORS' CHECKLIST

155 miles (250 km) SW of Fuzhou. 🚩 2,500,000. 🚶 🚲 🚌 Hubin Nan Lu Bus Station, Xiahe Lu Bus Station, Siming Bus Station. 🚢 weekly from Hong Kong to the Heping Ferry Terminal; to Gulangyu Island from the ferry terminal near Lujiang Hotel. 🛈 78 Huajian Building, Xinhua Lu, (0592) 204 6847.

complex of traditional Chinese gardens. Adjacent to the gardens is the attractive, but usually crowded **Gangzaihou Beach**. Close by to its north is **Sunlight Rock**, the island's highest point that can easily be reached by cable car. At the foot of the rock is the **Koxinga Memorial Hall**, which houses a handful of Koxinga's personal possessions, such as his jade belt and parts of his robe, as well as other historical items.

Farther toward the southwestern coast is **Yingxiong Shan**, with an unusual openair aviary at the top of the building. It is filled with colorful parrots, egrets, and tropical pigeons.

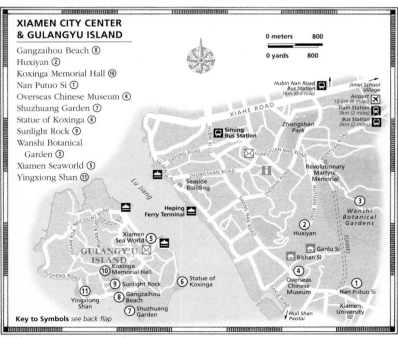

## XIAMEN CITY CENTER & GULANGYU ISLAND

Gangzaihou Beach ⑧
Huxiyan ②
Koxinga Memorial Hall ⑩
Nan Putuo Si ①
Overseas Chinese Museum ④
Shuzhuang Garden ⑦
Statue of Koxinga ⑥
Sunlight Rock ⑨
Wanshi Botanical Garden ③
Xiamen Seaworld ⑤
Yingxiong Shan ⑪

**Key to Symbols** see back flap

# Earthen Dwellings of Yongding

The Hakka people were driven south from the Yellow River plains by war in the late Tang and early Song dynasties. It is perhaps due to their past experiences of persecution, and to their presence in a new land (their official minority name is Kejia, which means "guest people") that they adopted a fortress-like style of rammed earth buildings called *tulou*. Capable of

**Lucky emblem on dwelling**

housing several hundred people, these round or square buildings are constructed around a courtyard, containing a maze of storage sheds and public meeting rooms. Hukeng is one of the more accessible towns in the Yongding area with several Hakka dwellings. The train from Xiamen to Longyan takes one hour (the bus takes four) after which it is a two-hour bus ride to Hukeng.

**Numerous *tulou* are located in the** *countryside surrounding Yongding. Although the round houses are the most celebrated, other styles are found in the vicinity: massive square dwellings similar in scale to the round houses and smaller rammed-earth residences facing onto a central courtyard.*

**Thick fire walls** divide the building into eight segments, echoing the Daoist octagonal symbol, the *bagua* (see pp32–3).

**Grain storage**

**Living quarters**

**Outward-facing windows** are small and trapezoidal and only located in the upper stories for security.

**Outer walls** are thick for defense, often as wide as 5 feet (1.5 m) at the base, tapering towards the top.

**An ancestral hall** at the center of the inner buildings may be used for ceremonies, such as weddings.

**The lower level** *is dedicated to communal Hakka life. Outdoor sculleries for washing and food preparation are located before the kitchens and dining rooms.*

◁ **An enchanting view of the summit of Wuyi Shan, Fujian**

**Entrance to Qingjing Mosque, one of China's oldest extant mosques**

# Quanzhou ❷
泉州

45 miles (72 km) N of Xiamen. 🏯 7,800,000. ✕ 🚉 🚌 ℹ️ Fengze Jie, (0595) 2217 7719.

Located on the Jin Jiang, Quanzhou was China's principal port during the Song and Yuan dynasties. The city's trade with India and elsewhere resulted in a permanent community of foreign residents. It was known to Arab geographers as Zaitun, from which the word "satin" is derived. Although Quanzhou's importance declined during the Ming dynasty, the town still offers insights into its maritime past.

Currently roofless, the **Qingjing Mosque** was first built in 1009, with extensive repairs in 1309, 1350, and 1609. Unlike other mosques in southern China which follow the traditional Chinese architectural style, this one is an elegant stone structure with an obvious Arabian influence. The surviving gate is supposedly modeled on a mosque in medieval Damascus. Its museum details the port's significance as a trade center.

In the north of the city, the **Kaiyuan Si** was built in AD 686 and called Lianhua Si (Lotus Temple), after a lotus miraculously grew on a mulberry bush that still exists to the west of the Great Hall. In the Song period, 1,000 monks worshiped here. Among the temple's three halls, the Sweet Dew Vinaya Hall has a splendid ceiling and a throne on which sits

Bodhisattva Ksitigarbha, Guardian of the Domain of Death. On each side of the halls are two ancient pagodas with carvings. The eastern part of the temple houses the **Museum of Overseas Trade**. One of its highlights is a Song trading vessel dating to 1274. Found in 1973, it was made of cedar wood and would have had sails of bamboo and hemp. At that time, such ships traveled to Arabia, Africa, and Asia, exporting porcelain and silks and importing spices, ivory, and glass. The museum also has stone carvings relating to Nestorian Christianity and to the Arab presence in the city.

North of Kaiyung Si is the **Qingyuan Shan** scenic area with the enormous **Laojun Yan**, a Song-dynasty sculpture of the Daoist Laozi (see p31).

**🄲 Qingjing Mosque**
108–112 Tumen Jie. **Tel** (0595) 2219 3553. ◻ 8:30am–5pm daily. 📷

**🏛 Kaiyuan Si & Museum of Overseas Trade** 176 Xi Jie. **Tel** (0595) 2238 3285. ◻ 8am–5:30 pm daily. 📷

# Chongwu ❸
崇武

20 miles (32 km) E of Quanzhou. 🚌 from Quanzhou to Huian, then minibus to Chongwu.

The Chongwu Peninsula's importance as a defensive stronghold was bolstered by the construction of the stone town of Chongwu in 1387, as

a bastion against pirates. As part of its defense, the granite houses had flat roofs, making them almost invisible from beyond the forbidding 22-foot (6.6-m) high boundary wall. The main inhabitants are the Hui'an people, whose women wear distinctive cropped blue tops and wide black trousers. Fishing and stone carving are the main industries today, but the walls and old streets of Chongwu's fortress days still make a striking impression.

# Meizhou Island ❹
梅州岛

35 miles (56 km) NE of Quanzhou. 🚌 from Putian to Wenjia, then ferry.

**Statue of Mazu, Meizhou Island**

For the Fujianese, this island near Putian is associated with Mazu, Goddess of the Sea and Protector of Sailors (see p149). Mazu is the deification of a 10th-century girl, whose powers enabled her to make maritime predictions, and her birthday is the island's main festival, celebrated on the 23rd day of the third lunar month. Numerous temples to the goddess dot the island, all the way up the hillside where her statue proudly stands on the summit. The main temple, **Mazu Miao**, is a short walk uphill from the pier. Rebuilt many times, it now resembles Beijing's Forbidden City. Due to the effort involved in getting here, it may be worthwhile staying overnight in one of the island's numerous hotels.

**Flat-roofed houses below the level of the wall, Chongwu**

For hotels and restaurants in this region see pp564–5 and pp590–91

European-style architecture on Zhongzhou Island, Fuzhou

# Fuzhou ⑤
福州

155 miles (250 km) N of Xiamen. 🏙
6,750,000. ✈ 🚉 🚌 🚢 121 Dong
Jie, (0591) 8711 9928.

With its scenic location on the
Min Jiang, Fujian's capital was
a major maritime port for more
than 1,000 years. It was the
center of a lucrative trade first
in tea and sugar, and later in
cotton, lacquer, and ceramics.
When the legendary explorer
Marco Polo visited Fuzhou in
the 13th century, he recorded
that the city was garrisoned by
imperial troops. The city still
has large numbers of troops
due to its proximity to Taiwan.

  **Wuyi Square**, with its
statue of Mao Zedong, marks
the city center. Just north is the
10th-century **Bai Ta** (White
Pagoda), while to the west is
**Wu Ta**, a black granite pagoda
from the same era. North of
Wu Ta, the **Lin Zexu Memorial
Hall** commemorates Lin Zexu,
a Qing-dynasty official who
destroyed an opium shipment
in protest at the British trade,
an act that led to the First
Opium War *(see p67)*. Farther
north is the **Kaiyuan Si**, which
has a Tang-dynasty iron
Buddha. To its west lies
Xi Hu Gongyuan (West

Lake Park), where the **Fujian
Museum** contains a
3,500-year-old boat coffin.
  **Cang Shan**, south of the
river, was once the site of the
Foreign Concession Area.
**Zhongzhou Island** (located in
the middle of the river) is a
modern development with
foreign bars and restaurants.
About 6 miles (10 km) east
of the city is **Gu Shan**, a
wooded area with pleasant
walks and the much-restored
**Yongquan Si**, built in AD 908.

🏛 **Fujian Museum**
96 Hutou Jie. **Tel** (0591) 8375 7627.
◯ 9am–4:30pm Tue–Sun.
🏯 **Yongquan Si**
◯ 9am–6pm daily. 🈺

# Wuyi Shan ⑥
武夷山

144 miles (230 km) NW of Fuzhou.
✈ 🚉 to Wuyi Shan City (Wuyi Shan
Shi), then bus 6 to park. 🈺 Shangu Jie
Guolu Da Lou, (0599) 525 0380.
**www**.wbr.cn

Magical Wuyi Shan, a hilly area
renowned for its oolong tea,
offers some of the most
stunning scenery in southern
China. Its sheer, mist-shrouded
sandstone mountains, known
as the Thirty-six Peaks, are
threaded by the Jiuqu Jiang
and covered in lush vegetation.
First visited by the Han
emperor Wudi (r.141–87 BC),
Wuyi Shan came to be regarded as a sacred place by
subsequent emperors.

  The best way to enjoy the
landscape is to take a raft
along the river, as it meanders
through gorges known
collectively as **Jin Qu Xi**
(Nine Bend Creek). Above
the fourth bend, mysterious
3,000-year-old coffins are
lodged high in the cliffs.
Made of *nanmu* (cedar), they
are about 16 ft (5 m) long;
each contains a single
individual wrapped in silk
and hemp. How they got here,
however, remains a mystery.

  Several trails lead to the
summits. The table-top shaped
**Da Wang Feng** is the most
difficult, while an easier climb
is **Tianyou Shan**, the traditional
spot from where to watch the
sunrise. The highest peak is
**Sanyang Feng** at 2,356 ft
(718 m). A path also leads to
the **Shuilian Dong**, with a
teahouse next to a waterfall.

## LACQUERWARE – A CHINESE CRAFT

Made from the sap of the "lac" tree *(Rhus
verniciflua)*, lacquer was used long before
the Han dynasty as a timber preservative
– it hardens easily, even in damp conditions. It was later used in making plates
and cups by applying layers of sap on
wood or cloth, and painting the final
layer. The modern craft, which appeared
in the Yuan dynasty, uses the same basic
method of applying layers on a wooden
base, but before the lacquer completely
hardens, it is deeply and intricately carved.
The surface is then inlaid with gold, silver,
or tortoiseshell, and usually painted red.

A lacquered
screen

# The Story of Tea

Tea *(cha)* is associated with China more than with any other country. Its legendary origins in China date back over 5,000 years although some believe that it was introduced from India about 1,800 years ago. At first it was drunk as a tonic; now it is simply an indispensable part of daily life for almost all Chinese. It is widely grown throughout the warmer and wetter southern areas of China, particularly in Fujian, Yunnan, and Zhejiang. Although tea comes in many

**German ad for tea, 1908**

forms, all tea comes from the same species, *Camellia sinensis*. The most common Chinese teas – green, black, and oolong – have differing appearance and taste due to the process of fermentation, although the flavor of the tea does vary depending on where it is grown, and whether other ingredients have been added such as chrysanthemums in *huacha*. Tea is always drunk clear, never with milk or lemon. Sugar is added only in the north western Muslim areas, while the Tibetans drink theirs with butter.

**Shen Nong** *was the mythological emperor who discovered tea, according to Chinese lore. A wise ruler, he pronounced that all drinking water should be boiled. One day, tea leaves fell from a tree into a pot of boiling water and the resulting brew delighted him.*

**By the Tang dynasty,** *tea was drunk throughout the empire. Before the 8th century, tea merchants commissioned Lu Yu to explain the advantages of the drink. He produced the* Cha Jing, *a compendium of tea, which systemized its production and traditions.*

**The tea trade** *was a key element in Britain's interest in China. The Portuguese were the first Europeans to enjoy tea, and the Dutch the first Europeans to deal in tea commercially, but it was the British who became the greatest tea traders as the fashion for tea spread from Holland to England in the late 17th century.*

**Upscale tea shops** *abound in the larger city centers. Highly prized specialty teas such as the Fujianese oolong tie guanyin can be purchased and sometimes sampled.*

**Tea plantations,** *many of them terraced, cover the hillsides of the southern interior. Up to five harvests can take place in a year. Picking is still done mostly by hand – an experienced picker can harvest 70 lb (32 kg) in a day – but mechanical methods are becoming common.*

# GUANGDONG & HAINAN

Located at the southernmost tip of continental China are the province of Guangdong and the island of Hainan, just off its coast in the South China Sea. Guangdong's capital, the great city and port of Guangzhou (Canton), stands on one of China's longest rivers, the Pearl (Zhu Jiang), while Haikou, the capital of Hainan, is on the island's north coast, about 30 miles (50 km) to the south of the mainland.

Guangdong is perhaps the most familiar part of China, since a large proportion of expatriates around the world are of Cantonese origin. The province also lies very close to Hong Kong, whose inhabitants are mostly Cantonese. Given its long-standing contacts with the outside world, it is not surprising that Guangdong was only fully integrated into China in the 12th century, when large numbers of Han settlers migrated here from the north. Today, it is a key area of China's economic development, most evident in Guangzhou and the cities of Shenzhen and Zhuhai. Despite the recent development, there are several places of historical interest, as well as some beautiful inland countryside.

Formerly administered as part of Guangdong, the tropical island of Hainan is now a separate province. A place of exile for centuries, its superb beaches on the southern coast have been developed as thriving tourist resorts. There are still vestiges of the indigenous Li culture to seek out, and some wild mountains to explore at the island's center.

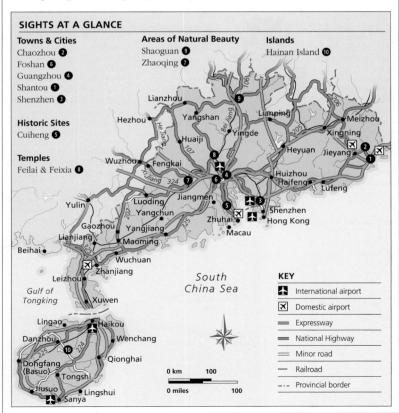

## SIGHTS AT A GLANCE

**Towns & Cities**
Chaozhou ❷
Foshan ❻
Guangzhou ❹
Shantou ❶
Shenzhen ❸

**Historic Sites**
Cuiheng ❺

**Temples**
Feilai & Feixia ❽

**Areas of Natural Beauty**
Shaoguan ❾
Zhaoqing ❼

**Islands**
Hainan Island ❿

**KEY**

| | |
|---|---|
| ✈ | International airport |
| ☒ | Domestic airport |
| ═══ | Expressway |
| ━━ | National Highway |
| ══ | Minor road |
| ── | Railroad |
| --- | Provincial border |

◁ On the beach mending fishing nets, Hainan Island

The dramatic Shipaotai Gongyuan fortress and moat, Shantou

# Shantou ❶
汕头

225 miles (360 km) E of Guangzhou.
🚶 5,000,000. ✈ 🚆 🚌 🛥 42
Shanzhang Lu, (0754) 889 724555.

This city was originally a fishing
village, whose strategic location
on the Han Jiang estuary was
exploited by foreign traders
from 1858. Known then as
Swatow, it soon became
a major center for trade.
In 1980, it was declared
a Special Economic
Zone and today it is
essentially a modern
city. The old quarter
still has a few sights
of interest such as
the restored 1879
**Tianhou Gong**, a
temple with vibrant
carvings. Nearby
along **Anping Lu**
are the remains of
old colonial houses
and warehouses.
East of Anping Lu at the
waterfront is **Shipaotai
Gongyuan**, a fortified gun
emplacement that was built
in the 1870s.

**Guangji Men,
Chaozhou**

🏯 **Shipaotai Gongyuan**
Haibin Lu. **Tel** (0754) 885 43120.
⭕ 8am–6pm daily. 📷

🏯 **Tianhou Gong**
Shengping Lu. **Tel** (0754) 884
54097. ⭕ 7am–5:30pm daily. 📷

# Chaozhou ❷
潮州

220 miles (350 km) E of Guangzhou.
🚶 2,500,000. 🚆 🚌

This ancient city was the
seat of a highly cultured
civilization during the Ming
dynasty. Its fortunes declined
rapidly in the 17th century,

when almost 100,000 people
were massacred for opposing
the Manchu regime. Later,
during the 19th century,
terrible famines and poverty
led to mass emigration.
Today, the remains of the
23-ft (7-m) high **Ming City
Walls** run along the banks of
the Han Jiang, defining the
eastern boundary of the old
city center. Extending up to
Huangcheng Lu in the west,
the old city is Chaozhou's
most fascinating quarter,
where its historic past
is visible on streets
such as Zhongshan
Lu and Jiadi Xiang
with its well-
preserved Qing-
dynasty architec-
ture. To the north
of Jiadi Xiang is
**Kaiyuan Si**, an
active Buddhist
temple founded in
AD 738, with pretty
courtyards and
several colorful halls, one of
which has a gorgeous vaulted
ceiling. The grand **Guangji
Men** along the city wall has
steps leading up to a trail along
the top of the wall. Across
the river is the 10th-century

temple **Hanwen Gong Ci**,
and downstream is the slowly
crumbling Ming dynasty
pagoda **Fenghuang Ta**.

🏯 **Kaiyuan Si**
Kaiyuan Lu. ⭕ daily. 📷

# Shenzhen ❸
深圳

62 miles (100 km) SE of Guangzhou.
🚶 4,000,000. ✈ 🚆 🚌 from
Hong Kong & Macau. 🛈 Jinwei
Building, Jiabin Rd, (0755) 6169 5908.

Shenzhen was one of the first
towns to become a Special
Economic Zone as part of
Deng Xiaoping's economic
reforms of the late 1980s. SEZ
status transformed this tiny
village bordering Hong Kong
into a booming metropolis in
just a few years. Today, it is
an important, although rather
soulless, business center and
transport hub. On its western
outskirts are a host of strange
theme parks. **Splendid
China** and **Window on the
World** have scale models of
famous monuments such as the
Eiffel Tower in Paris and the
Great Wall, as well as plenty of
souvenir shops. The **Folk
Culture Village** displays China's
folk traditions, and has
paintings, pavilions, and shows
of traditional dances. East of
Shenzhen, at Shatoujiao, **Citic
Minsk World** displays an entire
Soviet aircraft carrier, complete
with aircraft.

🎢 **Shenzhen Theme Parks**
Guangshen Expressway, Shenzhen
Bay. ⭕ daily. 🎢 **Citic Minsk
World** ⭕ daily. 📷

Aircraft on the Russian carrier at Minsk World, Shenzhen

# Sun Yat-sen

For many, Sun Yat-sen, who planned the overthrow of the last Chinese dynasty and the establishment of a republic, is the father of modern China. Born in Guangdong in 1866, he studied medicine and was greatly influenced by the leader of the Taiping Rebellion, and fellow Cantonese, Hong Xiuquan *(see p422)*. A failed uprising in Canton in 1895 forced him abroad, where he spent fifteen years raising money in support of his cause (in London he was abducted and held in the Chinese legation). Abroad when the Qing dynasty fell in 1911, he was made president of the new republic in 1912. Power struggles soon forced him from office. He died in 1925 before he was able to establish an independent government, with the aim of uniting the country.

**Sun marries Song Qingling, 1915**

**"The World Belongs to All"** *is a slogan reflecting Sun's democratic notions: the right to vote, the right to recall, and the powers of legislation and amendment.*

**Sun Yat-sen** *working in the office of his Guangzhou headquarters, from where he strove to create the circumstances that would lead to a democratic and united China.*

**Chiang Kai-shek** *(standing), who also married a Soong sister (see p198), used Sun's theories of political tutelage to justify military dictatorship.*

**Discussing the organization** *of a new government in 1911, before Sun Yat-sen (second from left) became president. He then installed Yuan Shikai in his own place, who declared himself emperor in 1913, plunging China back into civil war.*

**Seen here** *as Generalissimo in 1922, Sun Yat-sen established a military government in Guangzhou, the base of the Nationalist Revolution.*

**On National Day** *portraits of Sun Yat-sen are brandished together with those of Marx and Engels in Tian'an Men Square. Sun Yat-sen, despite his Kuomintang connections and his antipathy to class war, is seen as a revolutionary who paved the way for communism.*

# Guangzhou ❹
## 广州

Guangdong's capital, known as Canton to its 19th-century foreign residents, is an ancient and significant port. During the Tang dynasty, the city's trade links throughout Asia gave it a sizable Muslim community. Later, Western merchants made their first contact with China through this port. Today, Guangzhou is an affluent, bustling city, with a handful of interesting sights including the 2,000-year-old tomb and excavated palace gardens of

**Bronze luohan, Hualin Si**

the Nanyue kings. Recent developments have greatly improved the infrastructure, with new metro lines, and the restoration of old buildings. South of the city, Shamian Island was the site of the foreign concession and is filled with charming colonial-style buildings.

**A variety of foodstuffs, grains, and spices on sale, Qingping Market**

## 🛒 Qingping Market
Qingping Lu. M Huang Sha. ⏱ daily.
Just across the road from Shamian Island (see pp300–1) is one of China's largest and most famous markets, devoted to all types of produce. On sale are medicines, spices, vegetables, dried seafood, grains, fish, meat, and live animals, including cats, dogs, and endangered species. Fortunately, the numbers of endangered animals on sale have drastically reduced in recent years. For some visitors, the atmosphere is too gory, while for others it is exhilaratingly Chinese.

## 🏯 Hualin Si
Near Changshou Lu. **Tel** (020) 8139 6228. M Changshou Lu. ⏱ daily.
The city's liveliest Buddhist temple, founded in AD 526, was one of the many shrines visited by Bodhidharma, the Indian founder of Chan Buddhism (see p159). Hualin

Si is notable for its main hall with 500 images of luohan or arhat (those freed from the cycle of rebirth); one of them, sporting a broad-brimmed hat, is supposed to be the merchant Marco Polo.

**Devotees lighting incense sticks, Hualin Si**

## 🏛 Sacred Heart Church
56 Yide Lu. M Haizhu Guangchang.
A Gothic-style Roman Catholic church, the Sacred Heart Church (Shi Shi Jiaotang) was built by the French between 1863 and 1888. The land was granted to France as compensation for its losses during the Second Opium War. The church's twin spires rise to a height of 190 ft (58 m), and its bell tower contains four bronze bells cast in France.

## 🏛 Peasant Movement Institute
42 Zhongshan Lu. **Tel** (020) 8387 3066. M Nongjiang Suo. ⏱ 9am–4pm Tue–Sun.
The city's revolutionary past is on display in this former Ming Confucian temple. In 1924, the building became a training school for peasant revolutionaries, who were taught by leaders such as Mao Zedong and Zhou Enlai (see p250). The school closed in 1927, after the Guandong Communist uprising, when 5,000 people were killed under the orders of General Chiang Kai-shek (see p66).

## 🌿 Nan Yue Palace Gardens
Zhongshan Lu. M Nongjiang Suo.
⏱ 9am–noon & 2:30–5:30pm daily.
This extraordinary site contains the excavated gardens that surrounded the palace of Zhao Tuo, the founder of the ancient Nan Yue Kingdom (see p300). A Qin general from Hebei province, he founded an independent kingdom after the fall of the Qin dynasty. The site is covered by a corrugated roof, and a raised pathway leads past the main sights. To the northeast, a paved lake and an ornamental stream are clearly visible, while in the southwestern corner are the remains of an even older Qin dynasty shipyard. The site's small museum exhibits stone slabs, pillars, and roof-tiles, many of which bear the inscription "Panyu," Guangzhou's original name.

## C Huaisheng Mosque

56 Guangta Lu. **M** *Xi Men Kou.*
**◐** *to Muslims only.*

Said to have been founded
during the Tang dynasty by
Abu Waqas *(see p300)*, this is
one of China's oldest mosques. Although much of the
mosque has been recon-
structed, it contains an
ancient Islamic-style
minaret and numerous
stone stelae.

## 🏯 Guangxiao Si

109 Guangxiao Lu. **Tel**
(020) 8108 9831. **M** *Xi Men
Kou.* **◐** *daily.* 🎟

Thought to have been
founded during the
Western Han
dynasty, the
Guangxiao Si
(Temple of Glorious
Filial Piety) is one of
the city's most attrac-
tive sights. Built
over the palace of the
last Nan Yue king, it
became a temple in the 5th
century and was later visited
by Bodhidarma, the founder
of Chan Buddhism. None of

**Ancient pagoda
Guangxiao Si**

the original buildings survive,
and most of the current halls
date to the 19th century. The
pillared main hall has several
Buddha images, while the
three pagodas behind it are of
great antiquity. Of these, one
was built in AD 676 over a
hair of Hui Neng, the
Sixth Zen Patriarch (AD
638– 713) who came
from Guangzhou, while
the other two are 10th-
century structures.

## 🏯 Liu Rong Si

Liurong Lu. **Tel** (020) 8339
2843. **M** *Gongyuan Qian.*
**◐** *8am–5pm daily.* 🎟

Liu Rong Si, the Six
Banyan Temple,
was established in
AD 537 to house a
portion of the
Buddha's ashes,
which were brought
from India and
enshrined in the
Flower Pagoda (Hua
Ta). Rebuilt in 1097, the 187-ft
(57-m) octagonal pagoda
appears to have nine stories
from the outside, but in fact

has a total of 17 – they are
well worth a climb. The
pagoda's wooden eaves are
covered in intricate carvings
of birds, insects, and lion. At
the top is an enormous
bronze pillar with reliefs of
meditating figures.

Little remains of the original
temple, which was associated
with Hui Neng. The Hall of
the Sixth Patriarch contains a
bronze figure of him, cast in
AD 989. The temple was
named by the exiled Song
dynasty poet Su Dongpo *(see
p304)* in appreciation of the
trees in the temple. His calligraphic characters that read
"Liu Rong" are engraved into
stone over the gateway.

### VISITORS' CHECKLIST

94 miles (150 km) NW of Hong
Kong. 🚇 7,500,000. ✈ 🚆
*Guangzhou Station & East Train
Station.* 🚌 *Provincial Bus
Station, Liuhua Station & Tianhe
Bus Station* 🚢 *to Hong Kong
from Nanhai Port.* 🛈 195 Yan
Jiang Rd, (020) 8333 6888.

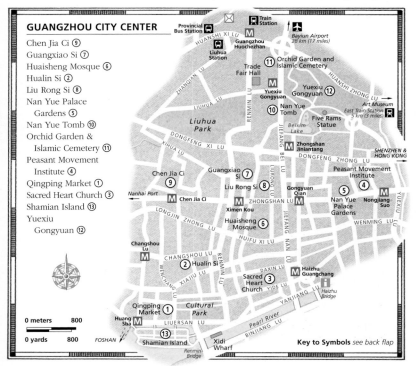

## GUANGZHOU CITY CENTER

**Key to Symbols** *see back flap*

### ▣ Chen Jia Ci

Zhongshan Qi Lu. *Tel (020) 8181
4371.* Ⓜ *Chen Jia Ci.* ◯ *8:30am–
5pm daily.* ▨

This temple, in the gloriously
colorful southern style, was
built in 1890 with funds donated by members of the Chen
clan. It was to act as a temple
of ancestor worship and as a
school. Though obviously
Chinese, these southern temples are quite different from
their northern counterparts.

Less severely classical, their
halls are generally lower and
broader. Roofs, and as in the
case of the first hall here,
façades, are often smothered
in fantastic designs and
sculpted figures from operas.

### ▥ Nan Yue Tomb

867 Jiefang Bei Lu. *Tel (020) 3618
2920.* Ⓜ *Yuexiu Gongyuan.* ◯ *9am–
5:30pm, last entry 4:45pm daily.* ▨

This is the site of the 2,000-
year-old tomb of Zhao Mo,
grandson of Zhao Tuo. Zhao
Tuo, a Qin general from Hebei
province, was sent here in 214
BC to control southern China.
After the fall of the Qin, Zhao
Tuo established the Nan Yue
Kingdom. Shortly after his
grandson's death, it was
reclaimed by the Han kings.

The tomb contains magnif-
icent burial items made of
gold and precious stones,
including a jade burial suit.
Many of the captions are in
English, and a video recounts
the story of the excavation
that took place in 1983.

### ♣ Orchid Garden & Islamic Cemetery

Jiefang Bei Lu. Ⓜ *Yuexiu Gongyuan.*
◯ *6am–9pm daily.* ▨

This charming garden has
bamboo groves and ponds
overhung with palms. The
orchids are in greenhouses,
and the best time to see them
is late winter to early spring.
Along the garden's western
edge, the cemetery contains

Brick relief of a traditional opera on the façade of Chen Jia Ci

# Shamian Island

沙面岛

Leased to the French and British after the Chinese were
defeated during the Second Opium War (1856–60),
this island is really little more than a sandbank about half
a mile (800 m) long. Before being allowed to
settle on Shamian Island, foreigners had
previously been compelled to remain in
their warehouses. Soon after the French
settled at the east end and the British at
the west, the streets filled with
European-style villas, banks, and
churches. Chinese people were long
forbidden to enter the island, so an
exclusively European way of life
prevailed on this strange outpost.

**Christ Church** served
the Protestants among
the British community
at the west end of the
island.

SHAMIAN WU JIE

SHAMIAN SI JIE

SHAN

American Consulate

White Swan Hotel

### Cannon in Shamian Park

*The two cannons found in Shamian Park
were manufactured in the neighboring
city of Foshan for use during the mid-19th
century Opium Wars.*

what is said to be the tomb of Abu Waqas, the uncle of the Prophet, credited with bringing Islam to China. Though closed to non-Muslims, it can be viewed through a screen.

### ♣ Yuexiu Gongyuan

*Jiefang Bei Lu.* M *Yuexiu Gongyuan.*
Spread over 222 acres (90 ha), Yuexiu Park is one of the largest municipal parks in China. It is split into several parts by Huanshi Zhong Lu and Qingyuan Lu. The most striking building, the **Sun Yat-Sen Memorial Hall**, is in the southernmost section off Dongfeng Zhong Lu. Built in 1931 in traditional style with a blue tiled roof, it marks the spot where Dr. Sun Yat-Sen *(see p297)* was proclaimed head of government in 1923.

Most of the other sights lie in the middle of the park, including the **Five Rams Statue** – the city symbol that commemorates the myth that Guangzhou was founded by

**Sun Yat Sen Memorial Hall, Yuexiu Gongyuan**

Five Immortals riding five rams, who planted sheaves of corn to ensure that famine would never strike.

Nearby, the **Municipal Museum** is housed in the Zhenhai Lou, a Ming watchtower. It has 1,200 exhibits dating from 4000 BC to the present, and includes a Christian tract that inspired the Taiping Rebellion *(see p422).*

### 🏛 Art Museum

*13 Luhu Lu.* **Tel** *(020) 8365 9337.* ☐ *9am–5pm Tue–Fri, 9:30am–4:30pm Sat & Sun.* 🈷
This contemporary museum exhibits shows by major Chinese artists. On permanent display is an exhibition of the works of political cartoonist Liao Bingxiong, who was criticized in 1958 for his Rightist leanings.

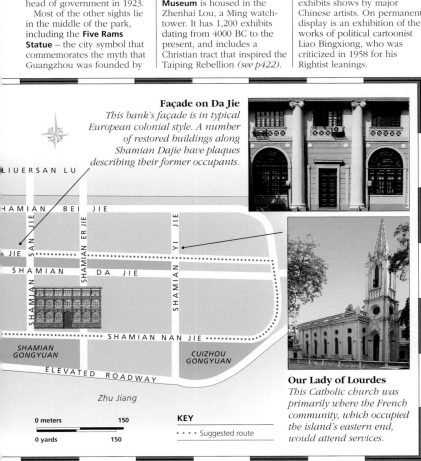

**Façade on Da Jie**
*This bank's façade is in typical European colonial style. A number of restored buildings along Shamian Dajie have plaques describing their former occupants.*

LIUERSAN LU

HAMIAN / BEI JIE

SHAMIAN SAN JIE

SHAMIAN ER JIE

SHAMIAN YI JIE

JIE

SHAMIAN DA JIE

SHAMIAN NAN JIE

SHAMIAN GONGYUAN

CUIZHOU GONGYUAN

ELEVATED ROADWAY

*Zhu Jiang*

0 meters 150
0 yards 150

**KEY**
• • • • Suggested route

**Our Lady of Lourdes**
*This Catholic church was primarily where the French community, which occupied the island's eastern end, would attend services.*

The bedroom at Sun Yat-sen's residence, Cuiheng

## Cuiheng ⑤
翠亨

19 miles (30 km) E of Zhongshan town. 🚌 from Zhongshan & Zhuhai.

Zhongshan county, located 56 miles (90 km) south of Guangzhou, is the birthplace of Sun Yat-sen (see p297), whose name is Sun Zhongshan in Mandarin. This revolutionary leader was born in Cuiheng village on the outskirts of Zhongshan town in 1866. The Portuguese-style house in which he lived with his parents between 1892 and 1895 is now part of a memorial garden devoted to his life. Nearby, other houses belonging to the same period have been restored and are also open to the public.

🏛 **Sun Yat-sen's Residence**
Cuiheng Dadao. **Tel** (0760) 8550 1691. ◯ 9am–5pm daily. ◻

## Foshan ⑥
佛山

17 miles (28 km) SW of Guangzhou. 🚶 3,210,000. 🚉 🚌 minibuses from Guangzhou. 🅸 14 Zumiao Lu, (0757) 8222 3828.

Foshan has been known since the Song dynasty for its fine ceramics, particularly figurines with a pale blue glaze. Visits to factories can be arranged through the tourist office. To view the town's other crafts, it is worth visiting the **Foshan Folk Art Studio**, housed in a former Ming temple, the Renshou Si, in the southern part of town. Nearby, the **Zuci Miao** was founded in AD 1080 as a Daoist temple. It is lavishly decorated with ceramic figures, made in nearby Shiwan, representing scenes from traditional opera and folk stories. Near the entrance is a garden displaying the cannons that were used against the British in the Opium Wars.

Elaborate stone roof of Zuci Miao, Foshan

🏛 **Foshan Folk Art Studio**
Zumiao Lu. **Tel** (0757) 8225 4052. ◯ daily. 🖥 www.fsfolkart.com

🏛 **Zuci Miao**
21 Zumiao Lu. ◯ 8:30am–7:30pm daily. ◻

## Zhaoqing ⑦
肇庆

68 miles (110 km) W of Guangzhou. 🚶 3,900,000. 🚉 🚌 ⛴ to Hong Kong. 🅸 90 Tianming Bei Lu (0758) 222 9908.

This attractive city was the home of the Italian Jesuit priest Matteo Ricci in the late 16th century, before he was summoned to Beijing by the Ming emperor, Wanli. Today, it is famous for the scenery at **Qixing Yan** (Seven Star Crag), 1 mile (2 km) to the north. Located beside a lake, the mist-covered peaks lie in the shape of the Big Bear constellation, and are thought to be fallen stars. They can be explored via a network of bridges and causeways.

The city's sights include the **Chongxi Ta**, a pagoda overlooking the Xi Jiang. Built in the Ming period, it is the tallest pagoda in Guangdong. The old **City Walls** still stand on Jianshe Lu, while in the western suburbs, the **Plum Monastery** is associated with Huineng, the Sixth Chan Buddhist Patriarch.

A short bus ride northeast of the city is the forested reserve of **Dinghu Shan**, which offers numerous scenic walking trails.

🌲 **Qixing Yan**
**Tel** (0758) 223 4728. ◯ 8am–5:30pm daily. ◻

The Piyun Tower perched atop Zhaoqing's ancient city walls

The grand gateway of Feilai Gusi along the banks of Bei Jiang

# Feilai & Feixia ❽
飞来 和 飞霞

52 miles (85 km) NW of Guangzhou.
🚍 to Qingyuan. **Feilai & Feixia Temples** 🚤 depart daily at 8am from Qingyuan.

The busy market town of Qingyuan is the access point for two picturesque temples located at **Feilai** and **Feixia** on Bei Jiang, that can only be reached by ferry. The ferries, which depart early in the morning and return in the afternoon, pass fishermen whose cormorants – trained to fish for them – sit patiently on the prows of sampans. The first temple, Feilai Gusi, was founded about 1,400 years ago and is situated on the steep riverbank of a gorge. Steps lead up from the river to its ornate gateway. Its current buildings are mainly from the Ming dynasty. A short walk through the various buildings leads to a modern pavilion, from where there are superb views along the river.

Located a short distance farther along the gorge is Feixia Gusi comprising two late 19th-century Daoist temples, Feixia and Cangxia. Feixia is much larger than Feilai, and its stone halls and temples are surrounded by a fine set of walls. Cangxia, located up the hillside, is often

being refurbished as a result of regular flooding. There are, however, some impressive frescoes and hiking paths.

# Shaoguan ❾
韶关

125 miles (200 km) N of Guangzhou.
🚉 🚌

Shaoguan town has only a handful of sights such as the Fengcai Lou, a reconstruction of an ancient city gate, and the Dajian Chan Monastery founded in AD 660, but there are three worthwhile places of interest in the vicinity. The **Nanhua Si** (Southern Flower Temple) 16 miles (25 km) to

Statue of a monk walking on "improbable stilts," Nanhua Si

the southeast, was founded in AD 502 and became renowned for its connection with Bodhidarma, the founder of Chan (Zen) Buddhism who meditated here for 36 years. One of the halls contains a statue of him, said to have been cast from his corpse; another has a statue of a monk walking on stilts. The bell tower has a large, 700-year-old bronze bell cast in the Song dynasty.

About 31 miles (50 km) northeast of town, **Danxia Shan** is a 112-sq-mile (290 sq-km) park on the banks of the Jin. It has rocky outcrops in fascinating shapes, with trails leading to their summits. A boat or bus takes visitors farther along the river to Danxia Shan itself. Meaning "Red Cloud," it has brilliant red sandstone cliffs, with paths leading past hillside monasteries.

About 11 miles (18 km) south of Shaoguan is **Shizi Yan**, a cave where the prehistoric remains of *Homo erectus* were found. The museum displays arrowheads, pottery, and artifacts from local prehistoric sites.

🏯 **Nanhua Si**
**Tel** (0751) 650 1223. ⬜ 7am–6pm daily. 🎫
🗻**Danxia Shan**
⬜ daily. 🎫
⛩**Shizi Yan**
⬜ daily. 🎫

# Hainan Island

海南

Although China's largest island became a part of the Chinese empire during the Han dynasty, it remained a backwater and place of exile until the mid-20th century. It was so remote that its ethnic Li people still lived a primitive hunter-gatherer existence until as late as the 1930s. In 1988, it became a Special Economic Zone, but a decline in investments has left behind unfinished construction sites all over. Despite this, Hainan is today an independent province with much to offer. Its attractions include the tropical beaches around the southern city of Sanya, impressive mountain scenery in the southwest, and coffee plantations on its east coast.

**Fish being laid out to dry in Xincun on the East Coast**

## Haikou

175 miles (285 km) N of Sanya. 🏯 1,835,000. ✈ 🚌 🚢 mainland ferries from Xingang pier.

The island's capital is a busy port and transport hub, with the ambience of a tropical Asian city. To its southeast, **Wugong Ci** (Five Officials Memorial Temple) was built during the Ming dynasty (1368–1644) to honor a group of scholars who were banished here during the Tang and Song dynasties for criticizing their government. One of its halls commemorates the Song-era poet, Su Dongpo, who was also exiled here between 1097 and 1100.

To the west of the city center is a massive fortification at **Xiuyang**, constructed by the Chinese in the 19th century to resist the French. Thick stone walls conceal six large cannons, that are connected by subterranean passages. Farther southwest is the tomb of **Hai Rui**, an upright Ming dynasty official who was exiled to Hainan for criticism.

## Tongshi & the Central Highlands

Tongshi 260 miles (416 km) SW of Haikou. 🚌 from Sanya & Haikou.
**Nationality Museum** 🕐 daily. 🎫
The central mountainous region is worth visiting for its spectacular landscape as well as for the chance to explore the island's ethnic culture. The main town is the pleasant **Tongshi**, which is the capital of the autonomous Li & Miao governments. The **Nationality Museum** offers an excellent insight into all aspects of Hainan's history and culture. Tongshi's surrounding countryside has remnants of traditional Li houses and barns. About 31 miles (50 km) northeast of town is the 6,125-ft (1,867-m) high **Wuzhi Shan**, which is sacred to the Li people. It is a pleasant hike to the mountain's summit. Also northeast

of Tongshi, the town of **Qiongzhong** is surrounded by some beautiful scenery, including the impressive 984-ft (300-m) high waterfall at Baihua Shan.

## The East Coast

Wenchang 68 miles (109 km) SE of Haikou. 🚌
**Overseas Chinese Tropical Farm** *Tel* (0898) 6362 2808. 🕐 daily. 🎫
The town of **Wenchang** is the ancestral home of the Soong sisters *(see p198)*, two of whom, Qingling and Meiling, married the revolutionary leaders Sun Yat-sen and Chiang Kai-shek. Its main attractions are the beaches and coconut groves at Dongjiao Yelin. About 62 miles (100 km) south on the outskirts of Wanning town, **Dongshan Ling** has curiously shaped natural rock formations. Farther south, Xinglong is known throughout China for its coffee, and the **Xinglong Tropical Botanical Gardens**, 2 miles (3 km) south of town offer coffee and tea tastings. Xinglong's **Overseas Chinese Tropical Farm** is home to over 20,000 overseas Chinese, who emigrated from Vietnam and other countries in Southeast Asia to make their living through the production of coffee and rubber. South of Xinglong is **Lingshui**, the principal town of the Lingshui Li Autonomous County, that is home to a large number of Li people who have lived on Hainan since 200 BC. The

**Calligraphy at Dongshan Ling Ridge**

The pristine, palm-fringed beach at Yalong Bay

### VISITORS' CHECKLIST

15 miles (25 km) S of Guangdong.
🚶 8,450,000. ✈ 🚆 train-ferry
shuttle from Guangzhou. ⛴
from Beihai, Shenzhen & Guangzhou. ℹ 26 Guomao Da Dao,
Haikou, (0898) 3198 2739. 🎭 Li
People San Yue San Festival (the
3rd day of the 3rd lunar month).

Communist Museum commemorates China's first Communist government that was formed in Hainan in 1928. Many of Lingshui's narrow streets remain unchanged since the early 1900s, and are lined with quaint shops and houses. Just 6 miles (10 km) south of Lingshui is **Xincun** with a large Hakka population (see p290). Close by and accessible only by boat, Monkey Island has a sizable colony of Guangxi macaques, and is a popular day trip from Xincun.

### Sanya & the South Coast

175 miles (285 km) S of Haikou.
🚶 536,000. ✈ 🚆
Hainan's main attractions are the tropical beaches near the town of Sanya. The busiest beach is **Dadonghai**, just south of town, with hotels, restaurants, and shops. The area's best beach is to the east of town at **Yalong Bay**, with a 4-mile (7-km) stretch of pristine sand. The beach at **Tianya Haijiao**, 16 miles

(25 km) northwest, is known for its famous rock that appears on the two-yuan note. The other attraction is **Ximao Zhou Island**, a two-hour boat ride off the coast. It is popular for snorkeling and hiking.

### 🥾 Jianfeng Ling Nature Reserve

65 miles (115 km) NW of Sanya.
🚌 to Dongfang (Basuo) from Sanya, then local bus. 🕐 daily.
Pleasantly situated in the mountains, this highland rainforest, with its huge trees, ferns, and vines as well as species of birds and butterflies, offers great walks and hikes.

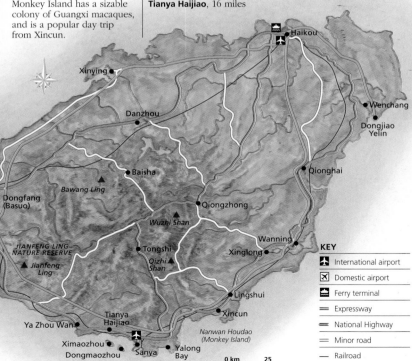

KEY

✈ International airport
☒ Domestic airport
⛴ Ferry terminal
━ Expressway
━ National Highway
━ Minor road
━ Railroad
▲ Mountain peak

# HONG KONG & MACAU

*A*lthough tiny and relatively recently developed, Hong Kong and Macau are rich and fascinating oddities. They owe their unique identities as administrative regions separate from China to the trade that flourished between East and West from the 16th century onwards, and to the British and Portuguese powers that annexed and held them until 1997 and 1999 respectively.

The Portuguese were the first Europeans to settle at "A-Ma Gau" or the Bay of A-Ma – the region's patron goddess – in 1557. Today, Macau, as it came to be known, is a charming haven of pastel-colored colonial mansions and glitzy casinos, the proceeds of which, along with tourism, keep this tiny region financially afloat.

In the 1800s, China's attempt to destroy Britain's lucrative opium trade drove the British to blockade Chinese ports and eventually secure Hong Kong as their own trading enclave in 1841. The area, hitherto inhabited by farmers and fisherfolk, quickly flourished. After World War II and the four-year Japanese occupation, trade resumed and Hong Kong's manufacturing industry boomed. It soon grew into a densely packed, high-rise city built by ambitious colonial administrators and millions of Chinese migrants escaping the turmoil convulsing their Communist homeland. In its final years as a British territory, Hong Kong's status as a major financial center was established. Despite the 1997 Asian financial crisis, it retains its sleek international gloss, its enterprise, and its breathtaking visual impact. Standing in Kowloon and gazing at the skyscrapers scaling Hong Kong Island's hills, writer Pico Iyer's description sums it up succinctly: "a dream of Manhattan, arising from the South China Sea."

Spirals of fragrant incense hanging in Daoist Man Mo Temple, Hong Kong

◁ The Star Ferry dwarfed by Central's modern skyscrapers, Hong Kong

# Exploring Hong Kong & Macau

The bustling heart of Hong Kong is broken in two and divided by Victoria Harbour. Its key sights, cultural attractions, shopping, and eating spots are found along the northern shore of Hong Kong Island, and at, or close to, Kowloon's southern tip. Between Kowloon and the border with the rest of China lie the New Territories, with their rugged mountains and most of Hong Kong's modern, high-rise dormitory towns. The other major islands – Lamma, Cheung Chau, and Lantau – are west of Hong Kong Island, and beyond these is Macau. A passport is necessary to leave or arrive in both Macau and Hong Kong, as they are still administered as autonomous regions of China.

**LOCATOR MAP**
*See Map pp276–7*

## SIGHTS AT A GLANCE

### Historic Sites, Neighborhoods & Towns
Aberdeen **28**
Causeway Bay **3**
Central **1**
The Central-Mid-levels Escalator **8**
Hollywood Road **9**
Lan Kwai Fong **7**
Lung Yeuk Tau Heritage Trail **24**
*Macau pp326–9* **36**
Nathan Road **15**
Stanley **32**
Tsim Sha Tsui Waterfront **13**
Wan Chai **2**

### Museums
Hong Kong Heritage Museum **21**
Hong Kong Museum of Art **14**
Hong Kong Museum of History **17**
Hong Kong Science Museum **16**

### Parks, Gardens & Areas of Natural Beauty
Deep Water & Repulse Bays **30**
Hong Kong Zoological & Botanical Gardens **5**
Kadoorie Farm & Botanic Garden **25**
Maclehose Trail **27**
Mai Po Marshes **26**
Sai Kung Town & Peninsula Beaches **23**
*The Peak pp312–13* **6**

### Temples & Monasteries
10,000 Buddhas Monastery **1**
Hong Kong Life Saving Society **31**
Man Mo Temple **10**
Wong Tai Sin Temple **20**

### Other Attractions
Happy Valley Racecourse **4**
Ocean Park **29**
Star Ferry **12**

### Shops & Markets
Bird & Flower Markets **19**
Sheung Wan's Markets **11**
Temple Street & Jade Markets **18**

### Islands
Cheung Chau Island **34**
Lamma Island **33**
Lantau Island **35**

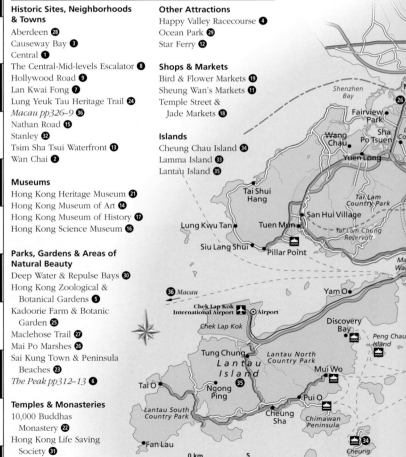

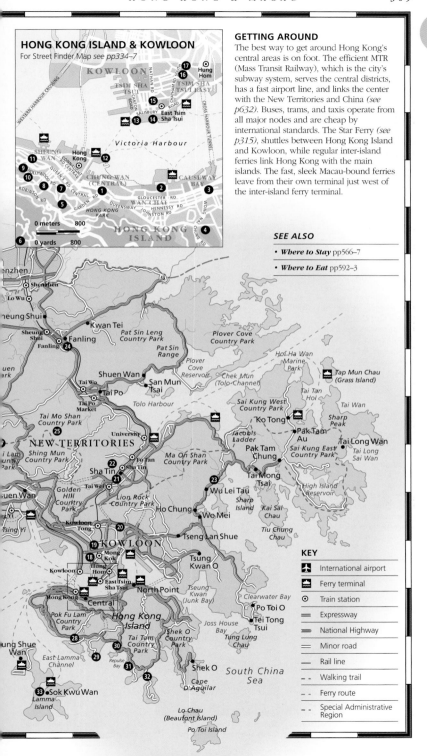

## HONG KONG ISLAND & KOWLOON

For Street Finder Map see pp334–7

KOWLOON

TSIM SHA TSUI

⑰ ⑯ ⊙ Hung Hom

TSIM SHA TSUI EAST

⑮ ⊙ East Tsim Sha Tsui

⑬ ⑭

Victoria Harbour

SHEUNG WAN

Hong Kong ⑫

⑨ ⑪

⑩

⑧ ⑦ ① ②

⑤ CHUNG WAN (CENTRAL)

WAN CHAI

CAUSEWAY BAY

③

HONG KONG PARK

0 meters 800

0 yards 800

⑥

④

HONG KONG ISLAND

## GETTING AROUND

The best way to get around Hong Kong's central areas is on foot. The efficient MTR (Mass Transit Railway), which is the city's subway system, serves the central districts, has a fast airport line, and links the center with the New Territories and China (see p632). Buses, trams, and taxis operate from all major nodes and are cheap by international standards. The Star Ferry (see p315), shuttles between Hong Kong Island and Kowloon, while regular inter-island ferries link Hong Kong with the main islands. The fast, sleek Macau-bound ferries leave from their own terminal just west of the inter-island ferry terminal.

### SEE ALSO

• **Where to Stay** pp566–7

• **Where to Eat** pp592–3

Shenzhen

Lo Wu ⊙ Shenzhen

heung Shui

Sheung Shui ⊙ Fanling

Fanling ㉔

Kwan Tei

Pat Sin Leng Country Park

Plover Cove Country Park

Pat Sin Range

Plover Cove Reservoir

Hoi Ha Wan Marine Park

Tap Mun Chau (Grass Island)

uen ark

Shuen Wan

San Mun Tsai

Chek Mun (Tolo Channel)

Tai Wo Tai Po Tai Po Market

Tolo Harbour

Sai Kung West Country Park

Tai Tan Hoi

Tai Wan

Sharp Peak

Tai Mo Shan Country Park ㉕

University

Ko Tong

Pak Tam Au

Tai Long Wan

i Lam unty ark

NEW TERRITORIES

Shing Mun Country Park

Fo Tan

Ma On Shan Country Park

Jacob's Ladder

Pak Tam Chung

Sai Kung East Country Park

Tai Long Sai Wan

Sha Tin ㉒ ㉑ Sha Tin

Golden Hill Country Park Tai Wai

Lion Rock Country Park

㉓

Tai Mong Tsai

High Island Reservoir

uen Wan ng Yi

Tsing Yi

Kowloon Tong ⑳

Ho Chung

Wu Lei Tau

Sharp Island

Kai Sai Chau

Wo Mei

Tiu Chung Chau

KOWLOON

⑲ Mong ⑱ Kok

Hung Hom

East Tsim Sha Tsui

Tseng Lan Shue

Tsung Kwan O

Kowloon

Hong Kong Central

North Point

Tseung Kwan O (Junk Bay)

Clearwater Bay

Po Toi O

### KEY

| | |
|---|---|
| ✈ | International airport |
| ⛴ | Ferry terminal |
| ⊙ | Train station |
| ═ | Expressway |
| ━ | National Highway |
| — | Minor road |
| — | Rail line |
| - - | Walking trail |
| - - | Ferry route |
| - - | Special Administrative Region |

Pok Fu Lam Country Park ㉘

Hong Kong Island

Tai Tam Country Park

Shek O Country Park

Joss House Bay

Tei Tong Tsui

Tung Lung Chau

ung Shue Wan

East Lamma Channel

Repulse Bay ㉙ ㉚ ㉛ ㉜

Shek O

Cape D'Aguilar

South China Sea

㉝ Sok Kwu Wan

Lamma Island

Lo Chau (Beaufont Island)

Po Toi Island

**The Two IFC Tower near the Star Ferry Terminal**

# Central ❶
中環

Hong Kong Island. **Map** 2 C3. M Central. ⛴ Star Ferry from Kowloon.

The sleek, corporate cathedrals of local banks and businesses tower over the ever-teeming streets of Hong Kong's financial and administrative epicenter. Apart from Statue Square, which is at the heart of the area, there are few cultural sights in Central, as many colonial buildings have long since disappeared, making way for high-rise development. The desire for real estate has always been strong, and land reclamation started almost as soon as the British took over in 1841. This continous reclamation has made Hong Kong Island and Kowloon creep even closer. Central is easily explored on foot, allowing visitors a close view of some of the most interesting buildings, especially in **Statue Square**.

The elegant Neo-Classical **Legislative Building**, surmounted by the blind-folded figure of Themis, the Greek goddess of justice, is the sole surviving colonial structure in the square. Completed in 1911, it originally served as Hong Kong's Supreme Court and today houses the Legislative Council (Legco), the legislative arm of the region's government.

Beyond the Legislative Building, the municipal-style architecture of the square's center is rather disappointing. However, not all the structures lack imagination. The

modernistic, but *feng shui*-friendly girders of the **HSBC (Hong Kong & Shanghai Banking Corporation) Headquarters** loom over the square. Designed by British architect Sir Norman Foster and completed in 1985, it was at that time one of the most expensive buildings, costing more than HK$5 billion. Be sure to take the escalators up to its impressive lobby, and rub the paws of the regal-looking lions outside for luck. The stark spike of the **Bank of China** headquarters rises behind the HSBC Headquarters. Designed by the renowned Chinese-born architect I.M. Pei, its harsh, angular lines go against all *feng shui* guidelines, and it is seen as an aggressive statement that offsets the benign energies of the HSBC Headquarters.

Northwest of Statue Square near the Star Ferry Terminal is Hong Kong's second tallest building, the 88-story, 1,362-ft (415-m) **Two International Finance Centre (IFC)**, built in 2003. Two more hotels and residential towers have also been erected here. The IFC Mall at the tower's base is one of Hong Kong's largest malls, adding to Central's several upmarket shopping malls, such as **The Landmark**.

**HSBC building (right) on Statue Square and Bank of China (left)**

The International Commerce Centre across the water in Kowloon is even taller than the IFC, at 1,587 ft (484 m), and marks a shift away from Hong Kong Island's north shore for competitive hi-tech architecture.

Hong Kong's history is now showcased during the winter holiday season in a sound and light show, where the Victoria Harbour skyline is lit with festive lights that create giant pictures on the buildings.

**The roof of the Convention & Exhibition Centre**

# Wan Chai ❷
灣仔

Hong Kong Island. **Map** 3 F3. M Wan Chai. ⛴ Star Ferry from Kowloon. 🚊 🚌

Made famous in Richard Mason's 1957 novel *The World of Suzy Wong*, Wan Chai's colorful 1950s and 60s red light district has given way to new development, fancy bars, restaurants, and hotels. The Wan Chai MTR is a good starting point for a walking tour. A trip down Lockhart Road, just around the corner from the MTR, reveals the area's few remaining ties with its past in the form of a handful of go-go bars.

A five-minute walk north of the MTR across Gloucester Road is **Central Plaza**, at one time the tallest, and still one of Hong Kong's grandest skyscrapers. There are splendid views from the 46th floor. Facing Central Plaza across Harbour Road is the HK$4.8 billion **Convention & Exhibition Centre**. The sweeping lines of the extension at its northern end are intended to create the impression of a bird taking flight. This was the venue for the 1997 ceremony during which Britain handed Hong Kong back to China. The glass walls offer fine harbor views, and outside are a large promenade and a pleasant sitting area.

## Causeway Bay ❸
銅鑼灣

Hong Kong Island. Ⓜ *Causeway Bay.* 🚋 *Eastbound (to Shau Kei Wan) trams.*

A neon-lit crush of giant department stores, such as Sogo and Times Square, and the ever-present crowds of shoppers is the first view of Causeway Bay when emerging from the MTR. East of the MTR sprawls **Victoria Park**, Hong Kong's largest public park and a serene place to swim, play tennis, or practice *tai ji quan.* Close to the harbor, also known as the typhoon shelter, is the **Noonday Gun**, fired daily since the 1840s and retained as a charity fundraising event. The enclosure housing the gun opens for half an hour after noon, where a small plaque explains the origins of the tradition, celebrated in

The historic Noonday Gun, fired daily at noon, Causeway Bay

Noel Coward's song "Mad Dogs and Englishmen."

Most of the land that Causeway Bay stands on is reclaimed. The old shoreline used to skirt the temple to Tin Hau (Guanyin) near Tin Hau MTR and was edged with British-owned warehouses.

## Happy Valley Racecourse ❹
快活谷馬場 / 跑馬地馬場

Hong Kong Island. 🚋 *Happy Valley.* 🏇 *For race night details, call 1817.* **www**.hkjc.com/english

The racecourse at Happy Valley crackles with nervous energy during the Wednesday race nights, as tens of thousands of eager gamblers shout their way through the evening. Horse racing is a passion in Hong Kong; it's the only legal gambling opportunity available to local people. The industry is carefully controlled, with only the Hong Kong Jockey Club allowed to run the betting.

Formerly a malaria-ridden marsh, Happy Valley was turned into a racecourse as it was the widest stretch of flat land on Hong Kong Island. The first race was held here in 1845. Today, the huge stand holds up to 54,000 spectators. Racing is open all year except in July and August. Happy Valley's small Racing Museum details Hong Kong's racing history.

## Hong Kong Zoological & Botanical Gardens ❺
香港動植物公園

Albany Road. **Map** 2 B4. *Tel* (0852) 2530 0154. Ⓜ *Central.* 🚌 *3B, 12, 12A, 12M.* **Zoo** 🕐 *6am–7pm daily.* **Gardens** 🕐 *6am–10pm daily.* **www**.lcsd.gov.hk

Opposite Hong Kong Park, just across Cotton Tree Drive, lie the Zoological and Botanical Gardens, established in 1864. The gardens house dozens of exotic animals such as lemurs, orangutans, and the world's largest collection of red-cheeked gibbons, while its aviaries have a colorful collection of birds. Hundreds of plants, including some ancient trees, provide welcome shade in this oasis of quiet. There is also a playground, some sculptures and fountains.

### HAPPY VALLEY RACES

Hong Kong's punters are crazy about horse racing. A single race at Happy Valley or at Sha Tin in the New Territories, often attracts more bets than an entire week of racing in Britain, and in 2006/7, the turnover surpassed HK$100 billion for the first time. The government collects significant tax revenues from the races, and although revenue has always been lost to illegal betting syndicates, the advent of internet gambling increased losses by almost 10 percent.

A thrilling finish at Happy Valley Race Course

# The Peak ❻
## 山頂

Cooling sea breezes, shaded woodland walks and spectacular views of the city, harbor and outlying islands make the Peak an unmissable Hong Kong experience. Ever since colonial days, the Peak has been the place to live in the city. Governors and rich merchants built houses here in the mid-1800s to escape the worst of the summer heat and humidity. The Peak's inhabitants were hauled up the sheer slopes in sedan chairs and numerous Chinese had to be employed to lug supplies to the mansions. When the Peak Tram (actually a funicular railway) was built in 1888, the trip was slashed from an hour's slog to a pleasant, if alarmingly steep, 10-minute ride. Despite the new accessibility, Chinese were excluded from buying real estate on the Peak well into modern times. Today, anyone with the means can acquire these properties – among the world's most expensive.

**★ Peak Circuit**
*This flat 2-mile (3-km) circuit offers breathtaking views over Victoria Harbour to the north, and Aberdeen and Lamma Island to the south.*

**Victoria Peak Garden**
*A steep trudge towards the summit leads to these well-manicured gardens, which were once part of the Governor's Lodge (destroyed after World War II). Sadly, the summit is fenced off and houses telephone masts.*

**Governor's Walk** winds from the garden to Harlech Road. It tends to be overgrown and slippery.

LUGARD ROAD

GOVERNOR'S WALK

VICTORIA GARD

HARLECH ROAD

POK FU LAM COUNTRY PARK

POK FU LAM RESERVOIR

**Pok Fu Lam Reservoir**
*This 3 mile (5 km) path descends through the peaceful woods of the Country Park and past the reservoir. It emerges on Pok Fu Lam Road, where frequent buses head back to the city center.*

### STAR SIGHTS

★ Peak Circuit

★ The View

★ The Peak Tram

*For hotels and restaurants in this region see pp566–7 and pp592–3*

**★ The View**
*Equally stunning by day or night, the panorama of harbor activity and high-rises is endlessly fascinating. Clouds and smoggy haze, however, often obscure the views; early mornings tend to be clearer.*

**VISITORS' CHECKLIST**

The Peak Tower, 128 Peak Road.
**Map** 2 A5. **Tel** (0852) 2849 0668.
🚋 *Lower Peak Tram Terminal, Garden Road.* 🚌 *15c at Central Bus Terminal (Pier 7); minibus 1 at Central (Two IFC).*
**www**.thepeak.com.hk

**KEY**

- - To Victoria Peak Garden
- - Peak Circuit
- - To Pok Fu Lam Resevoir
- - Old Peak Road to Central
— Peak Tram

| 0 meters | 300 |
| 0 yards | 300 |

**This old route** to Central is pleasantly shaded but unrelentingly steep. To avoid the busy traffic near the bottom, detour onto Tregunter Path.

OLD PEAK ROAD

MOUNT AUSTIN ROAD

VICTORIA GAP

POK FU LAM RESERVOIR ROAD

**The Peak Tower**
*This imposing mall at the tram terminus contains over 30 shops, Madame Tussauds, many cafés offering good views, and a 360° viewing terrace.*

**Peak Galleria** houses pleasant shops and cafés.

**★ The Peak Tram**
*A commuter line with one of the best safety records in the world, the Peak Tram has been trundling up the hair-raisingly steep 27° incline between St. John's Cathedral and Victoria Gap for over a century.*

## Lan Kwai Fong ❼
蘭桂坊

Central. **Map** 2 B3. **Ⓜ** *Central.*

It is only at night that Lan Kwai Fong ("Orchid Square") really starts to buzz, attracting office workers, including plenty of city suits, to its many bars, clubs, and restaurants. It houses some of the trendiest pubs and entertainment hangouts in Hong Kong, and the street is especially packed with revelers on Fridays and Saturdays, although most places remain open until late throughout the week. The partying spills across D'Aguilar Street to tiny Wing Wah Lane's bars and good-value Thai, Malay, and Indian restaurants, most of which have outdoor dining spaces.

Crowds outside Lan Kwai Fong's many bars and clubs

## The Central–Mid-levels Escalator ❽
中環半山自動扶手電梯

Central. **Map** 2 B3. **Ⓜ** *Central.* **◯** *6am–midnight.*

All the roads between Queen's Road and Conduit Road are linked by a 2,598-ft (792-m) long string of escalators. This is the longest covered outdoor escalator system in the world, and took two-and-a-half years and more than HK$205 million to build. It is the best way to commute between Central, the Mid-Levels, and SoHo (South of Hollywood Road). Several bars, cafés, restaurants, and market stalls

Entrance to the Central–Mid-levels Escalator

cluster round the Escalator. Good Spring Company, on Cochrane Street, sells foul-tasting health tonics from a brass urn. Inside, its herbalist consultants, some of whom speak English, can tailor-make a brew for those who are curious.

Partly as a result of the completion of the Central–Mid-levels Escalator, SoHo has been transformed from a sleepy district into a thriving entertainment area. Elgin, Shelley, and Staunton Streets are excellent places to find food and drink. A plaque on Staunton Street marks the site of the house in which Dr. Sun Yat-sen (*see p297*), seen by many as China's revolutionary forefather, met with fellow members of his society in the late 1890s. It also marks a historical trail of 13 sites connected with him.

## Hollywood Road ❾
荷李活道

Central. **Map** 2 B3. **Ⓜ** *Central, then Escalator.*

The many antique shops here no longer offer the bargains they once did, but Hollywood Road still has shops selling ancient ceramics, mammoth ivory carvings, and delicate snuff bottles. The stalls on Upper Lascar Row are a good hunting ground for antiques, old coins, and kitsch. Haggling is acceptable here. Some home furnishings shops, located at the eastern end, sell traditional items such as teardrop-shaped silk lampshades.

## Man Mo Temple ❿
文武廟

126 Hollywood Rd. **Map** 2 A2. **Tel** *(0852) 2540 0350.* **Ⓜ** *Central, then Escalator.* **◯** *8am–6pm daily.*

Atmospheric Man Mo Temple stands at the corner of Ladder Street. Inside its red and gold interior, smoke curls from giant incense spirals hanging from the ceiling, and flames in large brass urns devour paper offerings to the dead, such as the ubiquitous Hell bank notes. Built in 1847, the temple was dedicated to two deities, Man and Mo (the Gods of Literature and War), believed to be real men – the 3rd-century administrator Cheung Ah Tse and the 3rd-century soldier

Lion, Man Mo Temple

Lighting a joss stick at Man Mo Temple

*For hotels and restaurants in this region see pp566–7 and pp592–3*

**The city's Star Ferry service – an unmistakable sight in Hong Kong**

Kwan Yu – who were deified by the emperors. Their statues can be seen at the back of the main chamber. The temple served as a courthouse and community center to the Chinese in the 19th century, as an alternative to adopting the alien policies followed by the British.

## Sheung Wan's Markets ⓫
上環街市

Hong Kong Island. **Map** 2 A1.
Ⓜ *Sheung Wan.*

The short stroll from Central's slick modernity into the western district of Sheung Wan feels like entering a different city. Beneath the scruffy 1950s tenement blocks, the area around Queen's Road West and Wing Lok Street teems with Chinese medicine and dried seafood wholesalers. This is probably the world's largest center for the shark's fin trade, an exorbitantly priced delicacy, usually used in soups. The piles of fins on view explain why the world shark population is fast declining.

Apart from dried goods, fresh produce is available in the many fruit, vegetable, and "wet" markets dotted between the Central–Mid-levels Escalator and Morrison Street. Live produce, of the feathered, finned or webbed kind, is usually sold in the wet markets, while the fruit and vegetable markets sell a wonderful selection of fruit and typical Chinese fare, including fresh, still-steaming beancurd and tangy "1,000 year eggs," which are not, in fact, that old, but given an aged look by the mineral earth they are stored in. These places are not to be missed, although the squeamish may want to avoid the "wet" markets.

**Fresh fruit piled high at a market in Sheung Wan**

## Star Ferry ⓬
天星小輪

Star Ferry Terminals: Central, Wan Chai & Kowloon. **Map** 2 C2, 3 F3, 3 E1. *Tel* (0852) 2367 7065.
**www.**starferry.com.hk

Few activities in Hong Kong can compete with the sheer excitement and romance of jumping on these old 1960s ferries that chug ponderously between Kowloon and Hong Kong Island. They are by far the best and cheapest way to view the city skyline by day or night. The main route links the Kowloon peninsula (just near the Clock Tower) with the Star Ferry Terminal at Central, but it is also possible to reach the Convention Centre and Wan Chai from Kowloon aboard these jolly green boats. Touted as Hong Kong Island's most dependable sight, the Star Ferry service was started by Mr. Dorabjee Nowrojee, a Parsi gentleman, way back in 1898. At that time, the only people allowed on first-class decks were Europeans, and a collar and tie were obligatory.

Forecourt of the Hong Kong Cultural Centre

# Tsim Sha Tsui Waterfront ⓭
尖沙咀沿岸

Kowloon. **Map** 1 B5. Ⓜ *Tsim Sha Tsui*. 🚢 *Star Ferry*. ℹ *Star Ferry Concourse*. **Hong Kong Cultural Centre** *10 Salisbury Rd, (0852) 2734 2009*. ⏲ *9am–11pm*.

The Tsim Sha Tsui waterfront is a popular tourist destination with some of the ritziest arcades, museums, and hotels in the city. The Star Ferry *(see p315)* docks are also located here. East of the pier is the **Hong Kong Cultural Centre**, which houses halls, theaters, and galleries. Adjacent to the Centre is the Space Museum, ideal for children with its interactive exhibits beneath a golf-ball dome. Other attractions include the Avenue of Stars honoring the city's film greats and an Observation Wheel for views of its skyline.

# Hong Kong Museum of Art ⓮
香港藝術館

*10 Salisbury Road, Tsim Sha Tsui*. **Map** 1 B5. **Tel** *(0852) 2721 0116*. Ⓜ *Tsim Sha Tsui*. 🚢 *Star Ferry*. ⏲ *10am–6pm Fri–Wed (8pm Sat)*. 🎫 *free Wed*. **www**.lcsd.gov.hk

The Museum of Art is renowned for its exhibitions of traditional Chinese watercolors and calligraphy. Exquisite craftware from Southern China and Asia fills the second floor. Also on display are more than 3,000 objects in ceramics, jade, bronze, lacquer, enamel, glass, ivory, as well as furniture and fine porcelain.

# Nathan Road ⓯
彌敦道

Kowloon. **Map** 1 B4. Ⓜ *Tsim Sha Tsui*.

Also known as the Golden Mile on its lower reaches, Nathan Road is Kowloon's main transport artery. Running north through the center of the peninsula, it is bright, busy, and packed with hotels and shops. The term Golden Mile, however, flatters the area – far more glitzier enclaves can be found in Central. Nonetheless, a stroll along Nathan Road is one of the essential

Neon sign, Nathan Road

Hong Kong experiences for its crowds of shoppers and workers, the tangle of neon signage, the ever-present tailoring shops, and the mixture of smart hotels, Cantonese canteens, and grim guesthouse tenement blocks, such as the notorious Chungking Mansions, nightmare of many a backpacker. The road's far northern end offers glimpses of the past. Here, the ramrod-straight Boundary Street still marks the line of the 1860 border, the year Britain forced China to cede Kowloon to accommodate the burgeoning island colony.

# Hong Kong Science Museum ⓰
科學館

*2 Science Museum Rd, Tsim Sha Tsui East*. **Map** 1 C3. **Tel** *(0852) 2732 3232*. Ⓜ *Tsim Sha Tsui*. ⏲ *1– 9pm Mon–Wed & Fri, 10am–9pm Sat, Sun & public hols*. 🎫 *free Wed*. **www**.lcsd.gov.hk

A great destination for children, the Science Museum is packed with fun interactive displays on its four floors that detail basic scientific principles, including electricity and gravity, and how weather systems such as tornados are formed. There are also good displays on technology, which demonstrate the workings of various types of machinery ranging from the combustion engine to computer chips, as well as robotics and virtual reality.

Model of a DNA molecule at the Hong Kong Museum of Science

# Hong Kong Museum of History ⓱
香港歷史博物館

*100 Chatham Road South, Tsim Sha Tsui East*. **Map** 1 C3. **Tel** *(0852) 2724 9042*. Ⓜ *Tsim Sha Tsui*. ⏲ *10am–6pm Mon & Wed–Sat, 10pm–7pm Sun & most public hols*. 🎫 *free Wed*. **www**.lcsd.gov.hk

The pursuit of profit and the resulting change of pace in much of Hong Kong has eroded most of its historical and cultural heritage. The excellent Museum of History shows what the region looked like before the skyscrapers arrived. Walk around replicas of traditional villages, street blocks, and shops or linger over fascinating displays of old photographs. There is also a display of Bronze Age daggers, pottery, and arrowheads found on Lamma and Lantau Islands *(see pp324–5)*, and a fun exhibit on toys made in Hong Kong.

## Temple Street & Jade Markets ⑱
### 廟街及玉石市場

Yau Ma Tei. **Map** 1 B2. Ⓜ *Jordan or Yau Ma Tei.*

Haggling is an essential skill at the Temple Street night market, which only livens up after 8pm. Although cheaper bargains are available elsewhere, the atmosphere and range of items, including fake designer labels, shoes, Mao memorabilia, and pirated DVDs, are unbeatable. Adding to the experience are fortune tellers, Cantonese operas, and food vendors. The market snakes north from Ning Po Street to Man Ming Lane. The daytime Jade Market is a good place to pick up inexpensive trinkets, although cheaper jade can be found in Guangzhou *(see pp298–9)*, and elsewhere in China.

**Caged song birds for sale at the Bird Market in Mong Kok**

## Bird & Flower Markets ⑲
### 雀仔街及花園街

Flower Market Road, Mong Kok, Kowloon. Ⓜ *Prince Edward.*

The Bird and Flower markets are less frenetic and more convenient than Temple Street, and are well worth a visit. Colorful blooms and clever bamboo creations line Flower Market Road, just north of Prince Edward Road West. Located at the end of Flower Market Road is the small Bird Market with a few stalls selling elegant cages, food, and

songbirds. Some bird lovers can be seen feeding their birds grasshoppers through the cage with chopsticks.

## Wong Tai Sin Temple ⑳
### 黃大仙祠

Wong Tai Sin, Kowloon. *Tel (0852) 2328 0270.* Ⓜ *Wong Tai Sin.* ◯ *7am–5:30pm daily.*

The Temple at Wong Tai Sin is one of Hong Kong's largest, busiest, and most interesting places of worship. The complex contains altars and shrines to Buddhist, Confucian, and Daoist deities. It is primarily dedicated to the god Wong Tai Sin, a shepherd reputed to have performed healing miracles. Beside the main temple are fortune tellers, some of whom can reveal your fortune for a hefty fee in English, mostly through palm and face reading. Some worshipers try to divine what lies in store for them by shaking small canisters of bamboo sticks, until one emerges from the stack. Each is marked with a numeral and a corresponding meaning. Also used are *bui* or "Buddha's lips," two pieces of wood shaped like orange-segments. A question is asked, the *bui* are thrown, and the "lips" answer yes or no, depending on which way they land.

**Wong Tai Sin Temple, one of Hong Kong's busiest places of worship**

**Life-size Buddhas, 10,000 Buddhas Monastery**

## Heritage Museum ㉑
### 香港文化博物館

1 Man Lam Rd, Sha Tin, New
Territories. 🚇 *Sha Tin MTR, then free
shuttle bus or bus 68A.* **Tel** *(0852)
2180 8188.* 🕐 *10am–6pm Tue–Sat
(7pm Sun & public hols).* 📷
**www**.*heritagemuseum.gov.hk*

This excellent, modern
museum tells the story of
Hong Kong's 6,000 year-old
human history. The largest of
the city's museums, it has six
permanent exhibitions and
plenty of space for temporary
shows. The New Territories
Heritage Hall illustrates prehistoric human life, the rise of
village society, colonial rule and
the large-scale development of
the New Territories towns.
There is also a display on
Cantonese opera, which
explains the elaborate ritual
and color symbolism involved
and contains exquisitely-
crafted costumes. Beautiful
calligraphy scrolls hang from
the second floor. The Children's
Discovery Gallery on the
ground floor is a fun look at
Hong Kong's natural habitat.

## 10,000 Buddhas
## Monastery ㉒
### 萬佛寺

21 Pai Tau Village, Sha Tin, New
Territories. 🚇 *Sha Tin MTR.* **Tel**
*(0852) 2691 1067.* 🕐 *9am–5pm
daily.*

Ruby-lipped, life-size golden
Buddhas line the steep path up
to the Temple of the 10,000
Buddhas, a 15-minute walk

from the northern exit of the
Sha Tin KCR station. Cross the
road and follow the clear
signposts to the temple, which
is at the top of the wooded
hill. The main temple
houses hundreds of tiny
golden Buddhas which
line shelves reaching up
to the ceiling. There are
more Buddha images
outside, including
one astride a giant
white elephant and
another on top of a
huge dog. Still more
statues peep from the
monastery's bright-
red, nine-story
pagoda. The small
annex above the main
temple contains the embalmed
body of the temple's founding
monk, covered in gold leaf
and placed in a glass case.

**Pagoda,
10,000 Buddhas**

## Sai Kung Town &
## Peninsula Beaches ㉓
### 西貢海灘

New Territories. Ⓜ *to Choi Hung
station then taxi or bus 92 to Sai
Kung Town.*

It may seem incredible,
but just a few miles from
Kowloon's bustling streets,
it is possible to find empty
beaches, clear surf, and
seclusion on the shores of the
rugged Sai Kung Peninsula.
The area is best accessed via
Sai Kung Town, a pleasant
place to wander among the
stalls selling fish near the seafront, and to eat at the profusion of seafood restaurants.
Some of the most
pristine beaches on the
peninsula can be found
at **Tai Long Wan**, where
there is a small village
and a couple of cafés
and shops. The best way
to reach this secluded
spot is to take bus 94
from Sai Kung Town to
Pak Tam Au, part of
the Maclehose Trail
*(see p321)*, and then
hike to Tai Long Wan.
A reasonable level of
fitness is required and
remember to take along a good
map and plenty of fluids.
Much shorter and flatter
woodland walks start at

**The emerald waters and beaches of the Sai Kung Peninsula**

**Pak Tam Chung Visitor Centre.** Maps are available here for numerous walks, including a worthwhile nature trail. Take a taxi or bus 94.

Alternatively, hire a *kaido*, a small ferry, from Sai Kung Town for a tour of the many small islands. It is easy to find eager operators near the jetty, although without speaking Cantonese, travelers will need a map to point out where they would like to go, as most of the operators don't speak English.

**One of the buildings along the Lung Yeuk Tau Heritage Trail**

# Lung Yeuk Tau Heritage Trail ㉔
龍躍頭文物徑

Fanling, New Territories. 🚇 *Fanling MTR, then 54K minibus.*

For a glimpse of pre-colonial times in rural Hong Kong, spend a couple of hours exploring the mile-long Lung Yeuk Tau Heritage Trail near Fanling. This passes five *wais* (walled villages) and six *tsuens* (villages), mostly built by the Tangs, one of the five great New Territory clans. The buildings are in various states of repair, from dilapidated ruins to pristine walled compounds and some modern houses. Most of these are still lived in. Among the best-preserved buildings is the large **Tang Chung Ling Ancestral Hall**, founded in 1525 and still used today by the Tangs to pay respects to their ancestors and to hold celebrations. **Tong Kok**, a *wai*, also has dozens of old houses.

# Kadoorie Farm & Botanic Garden ㉕
嘉道理農場暨植物園

Tai Mo Shan, New Territories. **Tel** *(0852) 2483 7200.* 🚇 *Tai Po Market MTR then 64K bus.* ⏰ *9:30am–5pm daily, but check in advance for irregular closed days.* **www**.kfbg.org.hk

This working organic farm and wildlife refuge is nestled in the wooded foothills of Hong Kong's tallest mountain, 3,140-ft (957-m) high **Tai Mo Shan**. It is a great place to escape the crowds and modernity of downtown, with an easy hike to the top. There are terraced vegetable plots and groves of fruit trees, a small enclosure of orphaned animals, including wildcats, deer, and birds of prey, and a walking trail. You will need a good half-day to see everything the farm has to offer.

# Mai Po Marshes ㉖
米埔自然保護區

New Territories. **Tel** *(0852) 2471 6306.* 🚇 *Sheung Shui MTR then 76K bus or taxi.* **Permits** *deposit & advanced booking required.* 📷 *on weekends.* 📷 **www**.wwf.org.hk; **www**.wetlandpark.com

Wedged between Hong Kong and the urban sprawl of Shenzhen, this globally important wetland is home to a range of wildife species. Pollution has taken its toll elsewhere along the Pearl River Delta, making this 940-acre (380-ha) park the last refuge for many species. Apart from herons and egrets, otters and the very rare black-faced spoonbills can be seen. There are numerous bird hides for keen bird-watchers. Contact HKTB *(see p333)* for details on guided weekend tours. The **Hong Kong Wetland Park**, explores the area's diverse ecosystems and occupies a 150-acre (61-ha) area.

# MacLehose Trail ㉗
麥理浩徑

New Territories. **Tai Mo Shan** *taxi from Tsuen Wan MTR.* **www**.hkwalkers.net

Strung east–west across the middle of the New Territories, this 62-mile (100-km) route takes in huge, wild and high areas from Tuen Mun in the west to the lovely Sai Kung Peninsula in the east. Divided into 10 manageable stages, it is possible to walk for long stretches without seeing a soul. One of the most scenic sections takes in **Tai Mo Shan**, Hong Kong's highest peak with views, on a clear day, down to the distant city. The far eastern stage is also very beautiful, concluding at Tai Long Wan's lovely beaches *(see p320)*. Sturdy shoes, fluids, and maps (from the Government Publications Centre) are essential. The record for completing the trail is under 13 hours as part of the Annual Trailwalker Charity Race.

**A scenic waterway in Mai Po Marshes**

*For hotels and restaurants in this region see pp566–7 and pp592–3*

**A traditional fishing boat moored in Aberdeen's bustling harbor**

## Aberdeen 28
香港仔

Hong Kong Island. 🚌 *7 or 70 from Central.*

Once a quiet fishing village, Aberdeen is today the largest separate town on Hong Kong Island with a population of more than 60,000. Named in 1845 after the British Colonial Secretary, the Earl of Aberdeen, the harbor housed Hong Kong's first dockyard, which was built in the 1860s.

A short bus ride from Central (*see p310*), the Aberdeen district has a rather unattractive town center, edged by massive, high-rise apartment blocks, commercial towers, and factories. What it lacks in aesthetic appeal,

however, it makes up for in bustle and atmosphere. The boat-filled harbor is the big attraction in Aberdeen as it is the center of all activity. Many of the boats found here are actually part-time residences for Hong Kong's fishermen and their families; so much so that the district still has the characteristics of a traditional fishing village. Tiny sampans dodge among the wooden fishing fleet and the large, palatial floating restaurants. Pushy operators on the waterfront offer tours by sampan that take visitors past the fishing boats, the houseboats, and small harbor-side shipyards.

Alternatively, for a quicker (and free) tour, jump aboard the shuttles to the floating restaurants moored here, such as the **Jumbo Floating**

**Restaurant**. The first and most famous of the floating restaurants, it is a massive, palatial hulk that is part Las Vegas-style casino and part Chinese temple. The top deck is a sophisticated seafood restaurant with occasional live jazz.

## Ocean Park 29
海洋公園

180 Wong Chuk Road, Aberdeen. **Tel** (0852) 3923 2323. 🚌 *Ocean Park City Bus from Central's Star Ferry Pier or 6A, 6X, 70, 75, 90, 97, or 260.* 🈳 🕙 *10am–6pm daily.* **www**.oceanpark.com.hk

With the arrival of a mega competitor in the shape of Lantau Island's Disneyland (*see p325*), Ocean Park, Hong Kong's first amusement park, has fought back with more attractions. It is much better than it ever was, although it will be hard pressed to compete with the might of Disney. There is plenty to do for adults and children alike, and it's easy to spend a day exploring the six themed areas of this pleasant complex. The Lowland Gardens area is one of the most enjoyable sections, with a butterfly house, and the theme park's pride, four giant pandas. A scenic cable car skirts the

**The garish Jumbo Floating Restaurant lights up Aberdeen Harbour**

edge of Deepwater Bay, dropping passengers in Marine World. Here, a large and impressive aquarium captivates visitors with close-up views of schools of fish and an underwater tunnel through a tank of sharks. Numerous thrilling rides are found throughout the grounds, including the Space Wheel, the dizzying Mine Train rollercoaster jutting out over the sea, and Raging River, which guarantees a good soaking.

The popular beach at the seaside town of Stanley

## Deep Water & Repulse Bays 30
### 深水灣及淺水灣

Hong Kong Island.
🚍 6, 6A, 61, 260, 262 from Exchange Square bus station.

Several good beaches line these two scenic bays located along the road from Aberdeen to Stanley. Deep Water Bay is a pretty spot favored by the wealthy, with many luxurious houses. The long stretch of beach lined by cypress-like trees is reminiscent of the French Riviera.

**Colossal statue of goddess Guanyin, Repulse Bay**

Upmarket apartment blocks, inhabited by Hong Kong's business elite, surround the long, well-tended beach at Repulse Bay. The beach is a popular summer destination and gets very crowded in season and on weekends. The pricey Verandah Restaurant – the only surviving section of the stately Repulse Bay Hotel, which was torn down in the 1980s – is a good place for a drink or afternoon tea. Just behind the Verandah is a supermarket for picnic supplies, and a few cafés.

## Hong Kong Life Saving Society 31
### 香港拯溺協會

Repulse Bay, Hong Kong Island.
🕐 7am–7pm daily.

At the far southern end of Repulse Bay is the Hong Kong Life Saving Society. The building also serves as a temple, and is a great place for children to explore. Garish statues – a menagerie of gods, animals, and mythical beasts – are scattered across the grounds in amongst the life-saving equipment. Among the gods is a large statue of Guanyin, the Boddhisattva of Mercy, to whom the temple is dedicated. Several other gods are represented, including a number of smiling bronze Buddhas. Rubbing their bald heads is said to bring good luck. Some believe that crossing the Bridge of Longevity also adds three days to a person's life.

## Stanley 32
### 赤柱

Hong Kong Island. 🚍 6, 6A, 6X, 260 from Exchange Square bus station.
🕐 9am–6pm daily.

This pre-colonial fishing village today resembles a British seaside town, complete with English-style pubs. The extensive sprawl of market stalls selling clothes, beachwear, silk, jade, trinkets, and furniture draws weekend crowds. The area also has a good selection of Thai, Italian, Spanish, Vietnamese, and Chinese restaurants.

Beside the square is **Murray House**, a large, Neo-Classical building, housing some fine restaurants with bay views. Dismantled and rebuilt here in 1998, it originally stood on the site now occupied by the Bank of China tower in Central. Next to it **Tin Hau Temple**, built in 1767, is one of the island's oldest and most evocative shrines. The festival of Tin Hau (see p45) is celebrated in late April or early May with dances and boat races.

On the other side of town is the beautifully-kept **Stanley Cemetery**, dating to the earliest colonial days. It contains the gravestones of early residents and soldiers killed in World Wars I and II, including those who died in the Japanese concentration camp built nearby. Stanley Beach, on the other side of the peninsula, is a long stretch of sand and the venue for the local dragon boat races.

Lamma Island, with hilltop views of the sea and Hong Kong Island

# Lamma Island ⬤

南丫島

🚢 from Central (pier 4) and from Aberdeen (via Mo Tat).

Good seafood restaurants and pubs, a relaxed atmosphere, pleasant hilltop walks, and the absence of cars make leafy, low-key Lamma the perfect escape from the city bustle. Its two main villages, **Yung Shue Wan** on the west coast and restaurant-packed **Sok Kwu Wan** on the east coast, are a half-hour ferry ride from Central. Yung Shue Wan is an expat stronghold with two or three English-style pubs and some good restaurants. A steep climb leads to the hills above Yung Shue Wan, where there are fine views of the sea and Hong Kong Island. Visitors can hike on the path between the two villages, but should plan their walk around the infrequent return ferry from Sok Kwu Wan. The harbor here is also home to the **Lamma Fisherfolk's Village**, a fascinating floating exhibition that looks at the life of a fisherman and the skills and traditional techniques of the trade.

# Cheung Chau Island ⬤

長洲

🚢 from Central (pier 5). 🎎 Bun Festival (May).

This charming island, just a half-hour by ferry from Hong Kong Island, has plenty to offer, from paddling near its beaches to exploring the traditional shops and shrines along its narrow lanes and eating at the many seafood places at the harbor's edge on Pak She Praya Road. The squid with shrimp paste is a local speciality. The southern coast offers the best walks, with fine sea views and woodland pathways threading past colonial mansions.

The island's earliest settlers lived here some 2,500 years ago; their only surviving relics are the geometric etchings on the rocks below Warwick Hotel. In the 19th century, the island was a haven for pirates, where the notorious Cheung Po-Tsai supposedly hid plunder. The fishing community is depleted today due to excessive fishing over the past 50 years.

Close to the harbor, the 1783 **Pak Tai Temple** is dedicated to the island's patron deity, who is credited with saving islanders from the plague in 1777. The annual Bun Festival (see p333) is celebrated here in May, when young men scale 26-ft (8-m) towers made entirely of buns.

Colorful sampans and fishing boats in Cheung Chau harbor

# Lantau Island ⬤

大嶼山

🚢 from Central (pier 6) to Mui Wo (Silvermine Bay).

Twice the size of Hong Kong Island, Lantau was ceded to the British in 1898 along with the other islands and the New Territories. Despite the addition of a bridge and the huge Chek Lap Kok airport, large tracts of the island still remain largely uninhabited, including two country parks in which are the peaks that form the island's backbone and numerous hiking trails.

Lantau's seclusion has made it a popular place for religious retreats. The most striking of these is **Po Lin Monastery**, located on a hilltop on the Ngong Ping plateau. The

**Tai O Fishing Village**
*Traditional stilt houses cluster on the muddy banks of the small estuary at this rural fishing settlement.*

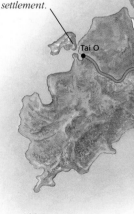

Tai O

0 kilometers    2

0 miles         2

*For hotels and restaurants in this region see pp566–7 and pp592–3*

monastery grounds are grand and colorful, and the over-the-top, gaudy main temple is well worth a visit. **The Big Buddha**, an 85-ft (26-m) statue perched at the top of a 268-step flight of stairs, is the monastery's biggest draw. Since the Buddha's consecration in 1993, the monastery has been overrun with tourists. There are also bauhinia and orchid gardens and basic vegetarian food in two canteens.

The area around Ngong Ping is also a great place for walks and picnics. Keen hikers stay at the SG Davis Youth Hostel before making a predawn hike up **Lantau Peak** to watch the spectacular sunrise.

At the island's western end, the sleepy fishing village of **Tai O** has narrow streets and tiny residences reminiscent of rural China. Once a major salt

**The Big Buddha at Po Lin Monastery**

trading center, today the old saltpans are being used as fish-breeding ponds. Tai O has a few temples and many shops selling live seafood and dried fish, the local speciality.

To the west of the island, **Discovery Bay** is the starting point for a gentle walk to a Trappist Monastery. Its chapel is open to visitors willing to observe the vow of silence taken by the monks.

Lantau's newest attraction, the multi-billion dollar **Hong Kong Disneyland**, is modeled after the original Disneyland in California, and the 311-acre (126-ha) area includes a park featuring Mickey Mouse and his friends, as well as original attractions designed especially for Hong Kong, themed hotels, and a retail and dining center.

**Ngong Ping & The Big Buddha**
*Bus 2. Also taxi or cable car from Tung Chung MTR.*

**Disneyland**
*Yam O MTR to Penny's Bay station.*

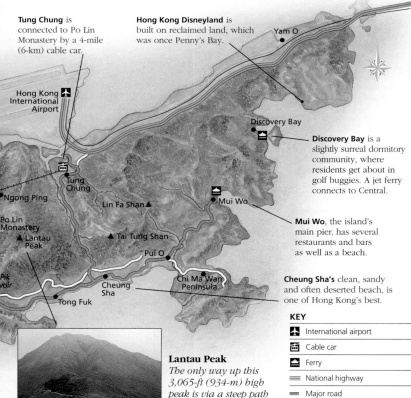

**Tung Chung** is connected to Po Lin Monastery by a 4-mile (6-km) cable car.

**Hong Kong Disneyland** is built on reclaimed land, which was once Penny's Bay.

Yam O

Hong Kong International Airport

Discovery Bay

**Discovery Bay** is a slightly surreal dormitory community, where residents get about in golf buggies. A jet ferry connects to Central.

Ngong Ping

Po Lin Monastery

Tung Chung

Lin Fa Shan

Mui Wo

**Mui Wo**, the island's main pier, has several restaurants and bars as well as a beach.

Lantau Peak

Tai Tung Shan

Pui O

Pik voir

Cheung Sha

Chi Ma Wan Peninsula

**Cheung Sha's** clean, sandy and often deserted beach, is one of Hong Kong's best.

Tong Fuk

**Lantau Peak**
*The only way up this 3,065-ft (934-m) high peak is via a steep path through tea gardens. It is an ideal spot for watching the sunrise.*

**KEY**

| | |
|---|---|
| ✈ | International airport |
| 🚠 | Cable car |
| ⛴ | Ferry |
| ═ | National highway |
| ▬ | Major road |
| ═ | Minor road |
| — | Railroad |

# Macau ㊱
## 澳門

An hour by ferry from Hong Kong, Macau was once seen as principally a sleepy side-trip offering a break from the buzz and bustle of the British enclave. Economically backward, it traded on the preservation of colonial-era buildings and as a gambling weekend resort. But even before the Portuguese colony's return to China in 1999, two years after Hong Kong, a complete restructuring of the tiny territory was underway, with vast public works projects including harbor reclamation, an airport, new bridges, and the fusing of the islands Taipa and Coloane into one. The connecting land, known as the Cotai Strip, is filling up with luxurious hotel-casinos, anchored by a copy of Las Vegas's The Venetian, with sampans floating amongst the gondolas. Macau now out-glitzes neighboring Hong Kong.

Historic cannons on the ramparts of Fortaleza do Monte

### ♜ Fortaleza do Monte
Rua de Monte. ◷ May–Sep: 6am–7pm; Oct–Apr: 7am–6pm daily.
**Macau Museum** Praceta do Museu de Macao, No 112. *Tel* (0853) 2835 7911. ◷ 10am–6pm Tue–Sun. 🎫 (but free on 15th of each month).
Built between 1617 and 1626, this fortress housed the original Portuguese settlement at Macau. Its thick ramparts, surmounted by ancient cannons, still occupy a commanding position and appear as invincible as they did in 1622, when the invading Dutch forces were defeated.

Dug into the hill beneath the fort is the informative **Macau Museum**. Its escalators and stairs are an air-conditioned route to the hill-top fortress passing through re-creations of Portuguese and Chinese life. Beginning with the arrival of Portuguese traders and Jesuit missionaries, the exhibitions compare the two cultures at the time of contact and cover the development of Macau and its unique traditions.

### ♜ Ruinas de São Paulo
Rua de São Paulo. *Tel* (0853) 2835 8444. ◷ 9am–6pm daily.
All that is left of this once grand cathedral, built by the Jesuits and perched precariously atop a steep flight of steps, is its magnificent, crumbling façade. Its most outstanding features are the ornate figures on the façade, comprising a "sermon in stone" that records some of the main events from the Christian scriptures.

The cathedral was built by Japanese Christian converts, who fled to Macau in the 16th century following religious repression. In the 18th century, Macau also expelled the Jesuits, and the building was

Gravestone, Old Protestant Cemetery

converted into barracks until it was destroyed by a fire in 1835. Only extensive structural work in the 1990s stopped the façade from crumbling. The attached museum houses paintings, sculptures, and relics from Macau's churches.

### ♜ The Old Protestant Cemetery
Praca Luis de Camões. ◷ 9am–5:30pm daily.
The gravestones at this cemetery at the corner of the Camões Gardens are crammed with fascinating historical details that give some wonderful insights into the lives led by early colonists. Many of them were Britons, who traded, married, or fought in and around Macau before Hong Kong was established as a British territory. Among the notable people buried here are Robert Morrison, the first Protestant missionary to venture to China, and the artist George Chinnery. The gravestones speak of short but heroic lives, such as that of the brave Lieutenant Fitzgerald killed after "gallantly storming" a gun battery at Canton (now Guangzhou). The inscription on Robert Morrison's tomb states that he produced the first Chinese version of the Old and New Testaments. The adjoining Camões Gardens are named after the renowned Portuguese poet Luis Vaz de Camões, the author of the 16th-century epic *The Lusiads*.

### ♜ Guia Fort & Lighthouse
Estrada de Cacilhas. *Tel* (0853) 2859 5481. ◷ 10am–5pm daily.
The Guia Fort was built between 1622 and 1638, and offers great views over the town. Initially it served as a fort to defend the border with China, but in 1865 a lighthouse was added. A pleasant way to get here is to take the cable car to the hilltop. A small chapel stands next door and there are several gentle walking trails around the hill.

The magnificent façade of the Ruinas de São Paulo

*For hotels and restaurants in this region see pp566–7 and pp592–3*

**Colonial façade on Largo do Senado**

### 🏯 The Venetian
Cotai Strip. **Tel** (0853) 2882 8888.
**www**.venetianmacau.com
Inspired by The Venetian in
Las Vegas, Macau's most
spectacular hotel-casino
recreates a miniature Venice,
complete with campanile,
Rialto Bridge, and gondolas
with singing gondoliers. The
mega-resort is suites-only and
offers themed shopping as
well as a theater seating up
to 1800 people. There is the
usual array of slot machines,

blackjack, baccarat,
roulette, and *keno*
(bingo), as well as
some Chinese games,
including the dice
game *dai sui* and the
*mahjong*-style *pai kao*.
Gambling is Macau's
lifeblood, contributing
more than half the
government's revenue.
Macau also hosts horse
racing, held twice a
week, and greyhound
racing, four times a
week (*see p332*).

### 🏯 Largo do Senado
The symbolic heart of
Macau, the Largo do
Senado or Senate
Square has numerous
stately colonial buildings set
around it, including the Leal
Senado or Loyal Senate, which
now houses the municipal
government, the General Post
Office, and the Santa Casa de
Misericordia, an old refuge for
orphans and prostitutes. There
are also numerous restaurants
and the tourist office. The
striking, wavy black and white
tile patterns snaking across
the square make it a great
place to take photographs by
day or floodlit by night.

### 🏯 Praia Grande
Perhaps the best way to get a
flavor of Macau's colonial
architecture is to take a stroll
on the Avenida de Praia
Grande. Although land
reclamation has encroached
on the waterfront and robbed
the Praia Grande of some of
its elegance, it is still a
charming place with many
grand houses still in excellent
condition. The monument to
Jorge Alvares, the first Portuguese explorer to reach China,
stands near the corner of
Avenida do Dr. Mario Soares.
One of the most handsome
buildings is the old Governor's
Residence. Although it is not
open to the public as it is a
private residence, a good view
can be had from the road.

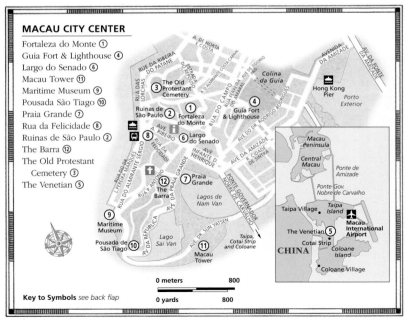

## MACAU CITY CENTER

0 meters 800

0 yards 800

**Key to Symbols** *see back flap*

### ⊞ Rua da Felicidade

A variety of sweet scents waft from the Rua da Felicidade or "Street of Happiness," where tasty and colorful Macanese biscuits and cakes are baked and sold. The area once teemed with brothels, hence its somewhat ironically bestowed name. Today, it is a charming, cobbled street lined with small eateries, which makes it a good place for a quick lunch stop.

### 🏛 Maritime Museum

Largo do Pagode da Barra 1.
**Tel** (0853) 28595 481.
◯ 10am–6pm Wed–Mon. 🈺
**www**.museumaritimo.gov.mo
Small-scale but interesting exhibits make this museum worth a visit for insights into Macau's maritime past upon which its wealth was built. Displays include models of Chinese junks, Portuguese ships and fishing boats, a mock Hakka village *(see p290)*, a dragon boat, and a small aquarium. There are also motorized junk rides around the harbor.

### ⊞ Pousada São Tiago

Avenida da Republica Fortaleza de São Tiago da Barra. **Tel** (0853) 2837 8111. **www**.saotiago.com.mo
Well worth a visit for a drink on the terrace, a night's stay, or a meal at its restaurant, this tiny but enchanting hotel *(see p567)* was once a fortress hewn from the rock on which

A scale model of a Chinese junk, Maritime Museum

it stood in the 17th century. The chapel to São Tiago, Portugal's patron saint of soldiers, remains to this day. The structure is more a rocky grotto than a smart hotel, which only adds to its charm. A natural spring runs through the lobby and the corridors are paved with flagstones. Its rooms are traditionally decorated in Portuguese style. The hotel also runs a good restaurant, La Paloma.

### ⊞ Macau Tower

Largo da Torre de Macau. **Tel** (0853) 2893 3339. ◯ 10am–9pm Mon–Fri, 9am–9pm Sat & Sun.
**www**.macautower.com.mo
The Macau Tower, the peninsula's most visible attraction, is 1,107 ft (338 m) high. The

**The modern Macau Tower**

tower provides a great view; in fact, visitors can see Hong Kong's surrounding islands on a clear day. It is, however, not the ideal place for those who don't like heights. Glass-sided elevators rocket visitors skywards, and the restaurants and viewing galleries at the top are also partially glass-bottomed. For the truly adventurous, it is possible to don overalls and a harness, and explore parts of the tower's exterior with the adventure sports company, A.J. Hackett, which runs a number of activities, including bungy trampolining and a dizzying skywalk around the tower's outer rim at a height of over 764 ft (233 m).

### ⊞ The Barra

Located south of Senado Square, Rua Central and Rua P. Antonio cut through the Barra district, where Macau's first European residents settled. A 40-minute walk through narrow streets sided with old colonial buildings will bring you to the classical bright green front of **Teatro Dom Pedro V** dating back to 1873. Farther down, **São Laurenço** is a plain but beautifully proportioned church set high off the street. Eventually you reach tiny **Largo do Lilau**, a pretty cobbled square with a fountain and the restored **Mandarin's House** dating from 1881. Another 1,640 ft (500 m) along, the finely collonaded **Quartel dos Mouros**, once a Muslim barracks, is now a post office. Beyond lies the **A-Ma Temple**, Macau's oldest.

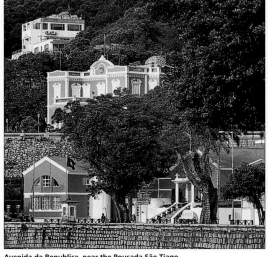
Avenida da Republica, near the Pousada São Tiago

*For hotels and restaurants in this region see pp566–7 and pp592–3*

# Regional Food: Macau

When the Portuguese arrived in Macau 450 years ago, the peninsula was virtually uninhabited. They cooked using Portuguese methods, but with local Chinese ingredients and southeast Asian herbs and spices picked up from their other outposts in Africa, Goa, Malacca, Indonesia, and Japan. As the years went by, and links home were established, some of the grander families stuck with Portuguese recipes made with the traditionally correct ingredients, while the less well-off incorporated more Cantonese-style dishes and ingredients, and over time the two cuisines fused together to form a separate Macanese cuisine.

**Flowering choi sum**

**A selection of Cantonese sweetmeats in a Macau shop**

## PORTUGUESE

Bacalhau is the most famous Portuguese ingredient. This dried and salted cod is integral to Iberian cookery and in Macau is cooked in every way possible. Distinguishing other Portuguese influences is difficult but good signs include the liberal use of olive oil, almonds, *chorizo* (paprika sausage), rabbit, and saffron. Other non-Chinese foods that are available are bread, cakes, cheese, olives, and coffee. Macau is also home to a well-developed wine culture, and naturally almost all the wines on offer are Portuguese. These are generally better quality than on the mainland and even better value.

## OTHER INFLUENCES

The other obvious change to Cantonese cuisine is the more generous use of herbs and spices: coriander and chilies in peri-peri dishes from Africa; fish sauce from SE Asia; hot and spicy curries from Goa; *feijoada* and sweet potatoes from Brazil; tamarind from Malacca.

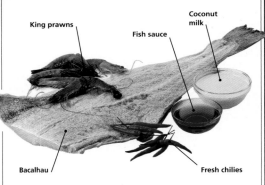

**King prawns**

**Coconut milk**

**Fish sauce**

**Bacalhau**

**Fresh chilies**

**A selection of typical Macanese ingredients**

## REGIONAL DISHES AND SPECIALTIES

There are very few totally Cantonese-inspired dishes in the Macanese cuisine. Tacho – a winter casserole of beef, pork, chicken and Chinese sausage is perhaps the most Cantonese of all Macanese dishes. As expected, *bacalhau* dishes feature prominently. There are *Bacalhau Guisado* (Salted Cod Stew), *Bacalhau a Gomes de Sa* (Salted Cod in Gomes de Sa Style), and *Pasteis de Bacalhau* (Salted Cod Cake) to name just a few. Other popular dishes include *Caril de Camarao* (Shrimp Curry). There are traditional Portuguese dishes like *Caldo Verde* (Cabbage and Potato Stew) and *Carne de Porco a Algarvia* (Braised Pork with Clams). At first sight, *Pasteis de Nata* (Egg Tartlets) look the same as the Cantonese ones in Hong Kong, but they taste quite different.

**Saffron strands**

**Galinha Africana** *(African Chicken) derives from a West African recipe in which char-grilled chicken is coated in a spicy peanut and coconut sauce then roasted.*

# Shopping in Hong Kong & Macau

**Ceramic art, Tsim Sha Tsui**

Label-mad Hong Kong is a paradise for shoppers, and is jammed with opportunities to buy from swanky designer boutiques in modern shopping malls to inexpensive street markets. It is a competitive destination for some electronic and computing items as well as good-quality, custom-made suits, shirts and *cheongsams* – the tight-fitting, traditional Chinese silk dresses. Visitors are unlikely to find good bargains, however, especially if comparing prices with those in China. Hong Kong's main advantage, though, is the sheer, unrivaled profusion of items on sale. Don't be afraid to haggle in markets and smaller stores, though prices are usually fixed in smarter shops and department stores.

## MARKETS

Street markets are one of the best bargain-hunting grounds in Hong Kong, as long as you're prepared to sift through the ever-present fake designer goods. The **Temple Street Night Market** *(see p317)* in Yau Ma Tei is perhaps the most celebrated for its atmosphere, its prices and the range of accessories, clothes, trinkets, and other memorabilia. The **Jade Market**, near the night market, sells exactly what it advertises. The market at **Stanley** *(see p323)*, on Hong Kong Island's southern coast, is as much fun for the trip out on the dramatic winding roads across the island. It is a good place to shop for touristy arts, crafts, clothes, and accessories.

**Western Market** is a more sedate place, located in the western district of Sheung Wan. The handsome colonial-era building outshines the nondescript restaurants on the ground floor, while the middle floor, spilling over with huge bolts of fabric in every color and stripe, offers the best deals on lengths of silk in Hong Kong.

## SHOPPING CENTERS, MALLS & DEPARTMENT STORES

Even seasoned department store junkies can over-dose on the huge variety available in Hong Kong's sprawling shopping malls. **Harbour City**, with its massive extended malls containing hundreds of individual shops, even dwarfes the big liners that dock near the Star Ferry at Tsim Sha Tsui in Kowloon. Across Victoria Harbour on Hong Kong Island, **The Landmark** in Central and **Pacific Place** in Admiralty are the places to go to for designer clothing labels such as Prada, Versace, and Zegna, and super-chic consumables from Vuitton, Bulgari, and Tiffany. **Sogo** at Causeway Bay *(see p311)* is another mammoth department store, while **Island Beverley**, nearby, crams hundreds of small outlets into its dozen or so floors, and sells modish street fashion.

## ANTIQUES & JEWELRY

Hollywood Road *(see p314)* in Central is best for antiques, and is full of emporia selling everything from huge terracotta tomb guards to delicate little snuff bottles. Established names include **Honeychurch Antiques** specializing in wooden carvings, bracelets, and necklaces, **Gorgeous Arts & Crafts**, which stocks reasonable antique furniture, and **Dragon Culture**, offering a good selection of pottery, bamboo carvings, and snuff bottles. **Schoeni** is a good place to find contemporary Chinese art. There are also some good antique shops in Macau *(see pp326–9)*, immediately to the south of the Ruinas de São Paulo.

## ELECTRONICS, CAMERAS & COMPUTERS

Tsim Sha Tsui as well as the rest of Kowloon are generally the places to head to for electronics and gadgetry. Once the bargain basement of international electronics retail, **Nathan Road** is still packed with camera and electronics outlets, but prices aren't as competitive as they once were. Be wary, as there are numerous tales of less-than-honest vendors. If you plan to shop here anyway, do your homework, make sure you compare like for like, ask questions (ensuring that your purchase is compatible with your home country's voltage), and you may find a bargain.

**Star House**, opposite the bus terminal and the Star Ferry at Tsim Sha Tsui, is convenient and contains about 20 computer boutiques on its second floor. Farther north, the **Mongkok Computer Centre** houses more retailers. Its prices are generally lower than other stores, and visitors can try bargaining. However, if you would like to keep your shopping more straight-forward, the **Fortress** chain stores are reasonably-priced and a safe bet for cameras and handhelds. They will provide warranties and guidance on foreign voltages.

## CHINESE ARTS & CRAFTS

There's little doubt that the wares on offer in **Yue Hwa** can be found at a much cheaper price over the border, but it is a convenient place to go to when buying last-minute presents. The store in Jordan is packed with silk goods, carvings, ceramics, jade, and teapots. The **Lok Cha Tea Shop**, just below Hollywood Road in Central, is a cosy, friendly place, where visitors can sample delicate green and jasmine teas and buy some exquisite traditional teapots.

Bargain teapots can also be found at Macau's **Culture Club**. For a modern take on Chinese style, the upmarket **G.O.D.** (Goods of Desire) chain offers smart interior goods at reasonable prices.

## CLOTHES

Needless to say, the malls and department stores are the best places for clothes. However, **Joyce** is also a good destination for shoppers seeking a large range of smart labels under one roof. Great value Gap-style clothing can be found at one of the many **Giordano** stores in town.

**Shanghai Tang** in Central offers traditional Chinese clothes and home decor with a contemporary twist. For Europeans who despair of finding essentials in their size, there is always the well-known British **Marks & Spencer** chain of stores.

Party-goers may want to sift through the stylish, modern and retro street fashion offerings at the independent boutiques in **King Wah Building**. Legendary for its tailors and shirt makers, Hong Kong is still the place to come. Take a chance with the ever-present street stores in Tsim Sha Tsui or go for established names such as **David's Shirts** at the Mandarin Oriental or the renowned **Sam's Tailor**, who has made elegant outfits for an illustrious clientele. For end-of-line designer bargains, the small boutiques at the top of the **Pedder Building** (floors four and above), may yield some big savings.

Hong Kong's markets are awash with fake designer wear, whose quality and cut are often far inferior to the real thing. If looking for authentic labels, it is best to avoid the street markets altogether, and shop only at the larger department stores and boutiques.

# DIRECTORY

## MARKETS

**Jade Market**
Kansu & Shanghai Sts, Yau Ma Tei. **Map** 1 B1.
⬭ 10am–3:30pm daily.

**Stanley Market**
Stanley, Hong Kong Island.
⬭ 9am–6pm daily.

**Temple Street Night Market**
Temple St, Yau Ma Tei.
**Map** 1 B2.
⬭ 6pm–midnight daily.

**Western Market**
Des Voeux Rd Central, Sheung Wan. **Map** 2 A2.
⬭ 10am–7pm daily.

## DEPARTMENT STORES

**Harbour City**
3 Canton Rd, Tsim Sha Tsui. **Map** 1 A4.
**Tel** (0852) 2118 8666.

**Island Beverley**
1 Great George St, Causeway Bay.
Ⓜ Causeway Bay.

**The Landmark**
12–16 Des Voeux Rd Central. **Map** 2 C3.
**Tel** (0852) 2526 4416.

**Pacific Place**
88 Queensway. **Map** 3 D4.
**Tel** (0852) 2844 8988.

**Sogo**
555 Hennessy Rd, Causeway Bay.
**Tel** (0852) 2833 8338.
Ⓜ Causeway Bay.

## ANTIQUES & JEWELRY

**Dragon Culture**
231 Hollywood Rd, Central.
**Map** 2 A2.
**Tel** (0852) 2545 8098.

**Gorgeous Arts & Crafts**
Upper Ground Floor, 30 Hollywood Rd, Central.
**Map** 2 B3. **Tel** (0852) 2973 0034.

**Honeychurch Antiques**
29 Hollywood Rd, Central.
**Map** 2 B3.
**Tel** (0852) 2543 2433.

**Schoeni**
27 Hollywood Rd, Central.
**Map** 2 B3.
**Tel** (0852) 2542 3143.

## ELECTRONICS, CAMERAS & COMPUTERS

**Fortress**
Shop 3320, The Gateway, Harbour City, Canton Rd, Tsim Sha Tsui.
**Map** 1 A4.
**Tel** (0852) 2116 1022.

**Mongkok Computer Centre**
8a Nelson St, Mongkok.
Ⓜ Mongkok.
**Tel** (0852) 2384 6823.

**Star House**
3 Salisbury Rd. **Map** 1 A5.

## TRADITIONAL ARTS & CRAFTS

**Culture Club**
390 & 398 Avenida Almeida Ribeiro, Macau.
**Tel** (0853) 921 811.

**G.O.D.**
Sharp St, Leighton Centre, Causeway Bay.
**Tel** (0852) 2890 5555.
Ⓜ Causeway Bay. Hong Kong Hotel, Harbour City, Canton Rd.
**Map** 1 A4.
**Tel** (0852) 2784 5555.

**Lok Cha Tea Shop**
290b Queen's Rd Central, Sheung Wan. **Map** 2 A2.
**Tel** (0852) 2805 1360.

**Yue Hwa**
301–309 Nathan Rd, Jordan. **Map** 1 B1.
**Tel** (0852) 3511 2222.

## CLOTHES

**David's Shirts**
M17, Mandarin Oriental, Queen's Rd Central.
**Map** 2 C3.
**Tel** (0852) 2524 2979.

**Giordano**
Shop 4, Grd Floor, China Building, 29 Queen's Rd Central.
**Map** 2 C3.
**Tel** (0852) 2921 2028.

**Joyce**
232 Pacific Pl, Admiralty.
**Tel** (0852) 2523 5944.

**King Wah Building**
628 Nathan Rd, Mongkok.
Ⓜ Mongkok.

**Marks & Spencer**
Ocean Terminal, Canton Rd. **Map** 1 A4.
**Tel** (0852) 2926 3331.
Central Tower, 24–28 Queen's Rd Central.
**Map** 2 C3.
**Tel** (0852) 2921 8365.

**Pedder Building**
12 Pedder St, Central.
**Map** 2 C3.

**Sam's Tailor**
Burlington Arcade, Shop K, 94 Nathan Rd, Tsim Sha Tsui.
**Map** 1 B4.
**Tel** (0852) 2367 9423.

**Shanghai Tang**
Pedder Building, 12 Pedder St, Central.
**Map** 2 C3.
**Tel** (0852) 2525 7333.

# Entertainment in Hong Kong & Macau

**Fruity cocktails**

Hong Kong's entertainment options are incredible. There are several good venues attracting local and international musicians, Chinese opera groups, and theater and comedy shows, particularly during the arts festival in February and March. The city's nightlife has begun to boom, and bars, dance venues, pubs, and music clubs are plentiful. The younger crowd have discovered an appetite for house and techno music, although they retain their liking for Cantopop, the older pop genre. Karaoke bars are also a favorite with locals.

Macau, although a lot quieter, is the place to go to for serious gambling or to eat at its excellent restaurants.

## ENTERTAINMENT GUIDES

Visitors will be spoilt for choice in terms of good listings in Hong Kong. Perhaps the best is the free, weekly *HK Magazine*, available in most cafés and bars, that offers a thorough guide to eating, drinking, shopping, and entertainment. The Friday ·edition of the *South China Morning Post* is another good listings guide. The free *BC Magazine* is a glossy fortnightly, with listings of clubs aimed at the young.

## BARS & PUBS

The places to find many of the best clubs, bars and pubs in Hong Kong are in Lan Kwai Fong *(see p314)* near Central, the streets around the Escalator, and SoHo. **Goccia**, in Wyndham Street, is always full of Hong Kong's most beautiful people. **Le Jardin**, around the corner, is less frenetic than nearby Lan Kwai Fong, and quiet enough to have a conver-sation in. If you want to drink with the jet-set, there are a number of super-smart bars including **Felix** above the Peninsula Hotel with sensational harbor views. Alternatively, try the **Rooftop Bar** in Central, or the fashionable **Drop** in SoHo, which turns into a club later in the evening. For a more laid-back drink in a pleasant organic café, go to **Life**, just off the Escalator in SoHo.

## NIGHTCLUBS

Nightclubs vary hugely from down-at-heel, free-to-enter clubs that just play music to slick, cutting edge venues for the rich and famous. Cover prices vary but a typical mid-range fee would be around HK$100. In Lan Kwai Fong, **Club 97** is small and smart with an exclusive reputation. Its disc jockeys spin fine jazz, funk, and house tunes. **Volar** in D'Aguilar Street is a great place for house music. The **Drop, Homebase** and the exclusive **Dragon I** are a few of the other popular clubs.

## MUSIC & ARTS VENUES

There's no shortage of venues for large musical, operatic, and dramatic productions. These include the **Cultural Centre**, that sometimes offers free concerts, the **Hong Kong Convention & Exhibition Centre** in Wan Chai and the **Hong Kong Coliseum** in Hung Hom. Close to the Coliseum, the **Ko Shan Theatre** is the place to go for Chinese opera and orchestral music performances. The **Hong Kong Arts Centre, The Fringe Club**, and **The Hong Kong Academy of the Performing Arts** all offer more intimate venues for an excellent and diverse range of arts from dance to stand-up comedy. **The Wanch** is a tiny place that hosts local folk and indie acts.

The **Macau Cultural Centre** is also worth a visit. It houses art, history and architecture exhibitions and runs a busy calendar of music, theater, opera, and dance, particularly in May during Macau's arts festival.

## SPORTS

Spring heralds the start of the dragon boating season check the HKTB for event details. The Rugby Sevens tournament in March is a huge, boisterous event for Hong Kong's expats, many of whom see its main purpose as an opportunity to drink large quantities of beer. For those interested in the actual game, 50 matches are played by the assembled internationals in 72 hours. Hong Kong is also host to a number of professional tennis tournaments from October to December.

## GAMBLING

Horse racing at the tracks in **Sha Tin** and **Happy Valley** *(see p311)* is the only spectator sport where you can gamble legally in Hong Kong. It is the biggest such spectator event in the region and race days or nights are well worth attending for the sheer atmosphere alone. Macau also has its own, less fevered horse racing nights as well as an excellent greyhound racing track, the rather grandly titled **Canidrome**. Macau, of course, is best known for its glitzy casinos, running all day and night. The most spectacular of them is **The Venetian**, complete with miniature campanile, Rialto Bridge, gondolas, and themed shopping.

## CHILDREN'S ENTERTAINMENT

Hong Kong's favorite attractions are two state-of-the-art amusement parks: **Ocean Park** *(see p322)*, the region's oldest amusement park, and **Disneyland** *(see p325)*, offering a massive range of rides, attractions and entertainment. Up in the New Territories, **Kadoorie Farm & Botanic Garden** *(see p321)* has a small zoo of orphaned native animals, including muntjac deer and wild cats. In a similar vein, but much more central is the enchanting **Edward Youde Aviary** in Hong Kong Park, which is built to resemble a tropical rainforest and has elevated walkways.

## TRADITIONAL FESTIVALS

One of Hong Kong's grandest annual celebrations is the **Chinese New Year**. Victoria Park becomes a huge open-air market and there are spectacular harbor fireworks that rival any display in the world. The **Birthday of Tin Hau**, the Goddess of the Sea, is more low key. Parades and lion dances take place at the larger temples, including the one at Joss House Bay in the New Territories, and temples and fishing boats are decorated all over Hong Kong. The **Cheung Chau Bun Festival** in May is a fun week-long celebration on Cheung Chau Island (see p324). It culminates in the eating of huge piles of buns offered, some say, to the unhappy spirits of victims of the island's pirate past, and a procession of "floating" children, carried aloft on hidden poles. The **Dragon Boat Festival** in June is marked with a great flourish, making it one of the region's most exciting events. Other traditional festivals celebrated in Hong Kong include the **Hungry Ghost Festival** in mid/late August and the **Mid-Autumn Festival** in late September/early October.

# DIRECTORY

## HONG KONG TOURISM BOARD (HKTB)

Hong Kong Island: The Centre, 99 Queen's Road Central. **Map** 2 C3.
Kowloon: Star Ferry Concourse. **Map** 1 5A.
**Tel** (0852) 2508 1234.
**www.**discover hongkong.com

## BARS & PUBS

**Drop**
Basement, On Lok Mansion, 39–43 Hollywood Rd, Central (entrance on Cochrane St). **Map** 3 B3.
**Tel** (0852) 2543 8856.

**Felix**
Peninsula Hotel, Salisbury Road. **Map** 1 B4. **Tel** (0852) 2315 3188.

**Goccia**
Shop 1 & 2, G/F 73 Wyndham St. **Map** 2 B3.
**Tel** (0852) 2167 8181.

**Le Jardin**
10 Wing Wah Lane, Central. **Map** 2 B3.
**Tel** (0852) 2526 2717.

**Life**
10 Shelley Street, SoHo.
**Map** 2 B3.
**Tel** (0852) 2810 9777.

**Rooftop Bar**
Fringe Club, 2 Lower Albert Rd, Central.
**Map** 2 C3.
**Tel** (0852) 2521 7251.
**www.**hkfringe.com.hk

## NIGHTCLUBS

**Club 97**
9 Lan Kwai Fong. **Map** 2 B3. **Tel** (0852) 2810 9333.

**Dragon I**
The Centrium, 60 Wyndham St. **Map** 2 B3.
**Tel** (0852) 3110 1222.
**www.**dragon-i.com.hk

**Homebase**
LG/F Au's Bldg, 17-19 Hollywood Rd, Central.
**Map** 2 B3. **Tel** (0852) 2537 1000.

**Volar**
44 D'Aguilar St, Central.
**Map** 2 B3.
**Tel** (0852) 2810 1510.
**www.**volar.com.hk

## MUSIC & ARTS VENUES

**Hong Kong Cultural Centre**
L5, Auditoria Building, 10 Salisbury Rd. **Map** 1 B5.
**Tel** (0852) 2734 2009.
**www.**lcsd.gov.hk

**The Fringe Club**
2 Lower Albert Rd, Central.
**Map** 2 C3.
**Tel** (0852) 2521 7251.
**www.**hkfringe.com.hk

**Hong Kong Academy for Performing Arts**
1 Gloucester Rd, Wan Chai.
**Map** 3 E3.
**Tel** (0852) 2584 8500.
**www.**hkapa.edu

**Hong Kong Arts Centre**
2 Harbour Rd, Wan Chai.
**Map** 3 E3.
**Tel** (0852) 2582 0200.
**www.**hkac.org.hk

**Hong Kong Coliseum**
9 Cheong Wan Rd, Hung Hom, Kowloon.
**Tel** (0852) 2355 7233.
🚆 Hung Hom KCR.
**www.**lcsd.gov.hk/hkc

**Hong Kong Convention & Exhibition Centre**
1 Expo Drive. **Map** 3 F3.
**Tel** (0852) 2582 8888.
**www.**hkcec.com.hk

**Ko Shan Theatre**
77 Ko Shan Road, Hung Hom.
**Tel** (0852) 2740 9212.
**www.**lcsd.gov.hk/kst

**Macau Cultural Centre**
Av. Xian Xing Hai S/N NAPE, Macau.
**Tel** (0853) 28700 699.
**www.**ccm.gov.mo/

**The Wanch**
54 Jaffe Road, Wan Chai.
**Map** 3 F4.
**Tel** (0852) 2861 1621.
**www.**thewanch.hk

## GAMBLING

**The Canidrome**
Avenida General Castelo Branco, Macau.
**Tel** (0853) 2833 3399.
**www.**macaudog.com

**Happy Valley Racecourse**
Happy Valley, Hong Kong Island.
**Tel** (0853) 1817.
**www.**hkjc.com/english

**Sha Tin Racecourse**
**Tel** (0853) 1817.
**www.**hkjc.com

## CHILDREN'S ENTERTAINMENT

**Disneyland**
Penny's Bay, Lantau Island.
**Tel** (0852) 2203 2000.
Ⓜ Penny's Bay.
**www.**hongkong disneyland.com

**Edward Youde Aviary**
Hong Kong Park, Cotton Tree Drive, Central.
**Map** 2 C4.
**Tel** (0852) 2521 5041.
**www.**lcsd.gov.hk/parks

**Kadoorie Farm & Botanic Garden**
Lam Kam Rd, New Territories.
**Tel** (0852) 2483 7200.
**www.**kfbg.org.hk

# HONG KONG STREET FINDER

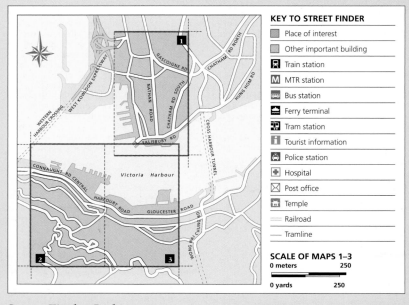

### KEY TO STREET FINDER

- Place of interest
- Other important building
- Train station
- M MTR station
- Bus station
- Ferry terminal
- Tram station
- Tourist information
- Police station
- Hospital
- Post office
- Temple
- Railroad
- Tramline

### SCALE OF MAPS 1–3

| 0 meters | 250 |
| 0 yards | 250 |

## Street Finder Index

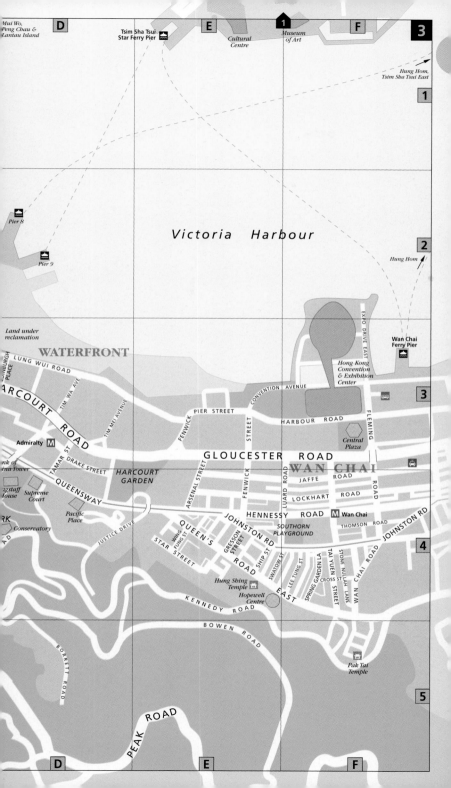

# THE
# SOUTHWEST

# The Southwest at a Glance

Some of China's most evocative landscapes are found in the Southwest: the fertile Red Basin of eastern Sichuan, deep gorges along the Yangzi River, the mountainous fringes of the Tibetan Plateau, Xishuangbanna's tropical forests, and the karst hills of Guizhou and Guangxi. Cultural highlights include the sites of Buddhist art at Le Shan and Dazu, and the remains of Ming city walls at Dali and Songpan. Ethnic minority communities include Tibetans in the west, Miao and Dong in Guizhou and Guangxi, Dali's Bai, Lijiang's Naxi, and the Dai of Xishuangbanna. There are wildlife preserves for giant pandas in Sichuan, waterfowl at Cao Hai, and elephants in Xishuangbanna; and trekking opportunities at Tiger Leaping Gorge, Emei Shan, and along the Lao border in southern Yunnan.

The stepped and calcified Mirror Pools in Huanglong, Sichuan

The Miao village of Xijiang nestled into a terraced valley near Kaili, Guizhou

## GETTING AROUND

The major cities and destinations, such as Chengdu, Chongqing, Kunming, Guiyang, Guilin, Lijiang, and Jinghong, are all served by air. Train lines, though more restricted, offer fairly direct services connecting the provincial capitals with most of the larger cities. A comprehensive network of buses covers much of the region, with comfortable express coaches and surfaced roads linking key sites, though travel through remoter areas on local buses can be rough and slow-going, particularly in Guizhou and Guangxi. It is also possible to spend a few days taking a ferry down the Yangzi from Chongqing, or to take a scenic day trip along the Li River between Guilin and Yangshuo in Guangxi province.

◁ Bizarre karst landscape surrounding Yangshuo, Guangxi

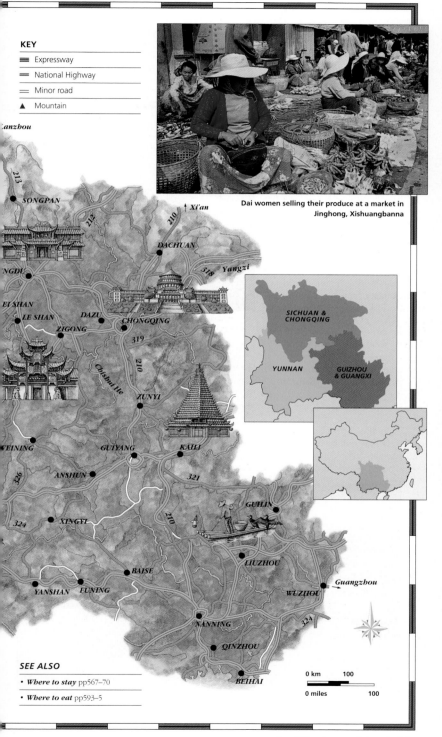

**KEY**

▬ Expressway

▬ National Highway

▭ Minor road

▲ Mountain

*Lanzhou*

Dai women selling their produce at a market in
Jinghong, Xishuangbanna

213

● SONGPAN

212

210 ↑ *Xi'an*

● DACHUAN

318 *Yangzi*

NGDU

EI SHAN

● LE SHAN    ● DAZU

● ZIGONG    ● CHONGQING

*Chishui He*    319

210

● ZUNYI

SICHUAN &
CHONGQING

YUNNAN    GUIZHOU
& GUANGXI

WEINING

● GUIYANG    ● KAILI

● ANSHUN    321

326

324    ● XINGYI    210

● GUILIN

● BAISE    ● LIUZHOU

*Guangzhou* →

● YANSHAN    ● FUNING    ● WUZHOU

324

● NANNING

● QINZHOU

*SEE ALSO*

• *Where to stay* pp567–70    0 km    100

• *Where to eat* pp593–5    ● BEIHAI    0 miles    100

# A PORTRAIT OF THE SOUTHWEST

*The southwest's stunning landscapes, from the impossibly steep limestone hillocks along the Li River, to the deep gorges cut by the upper reaches of the Yangzi, make it one of China's most picturesque regions. The area's ethnic diversity, evident in the traditional culture and lifestyles of its numerous minority communities, also adds to its attraction as an exotic tourist destination.*

The Southwest's isolation has meant that for much of its past it has forged its own path. The area roughly covered by today's Yunnan has always had closer ties with its neighbors to the south and east than with China's traditional dynastic centers. During the period of the Warring States (475–221 BC), Zhuang Qiao, a Chu general, was sent here to subdue the tribes, but after a long campaign, he was impelled to stay, establishing the Kingdom of Dian at what is now Kunming in around 300 BC. For the next 500 years, the kingdom existed as a loose conglomerate of tribute-paying tribal chiefs.

In the 8th century, the Kingdom of Nanzhao emerged in Dali, extending its territory into Vietnam and Myanmar. The dynasty grew wealthy on trade along the

The endangered panda, indigenous to Sichuan

Southern Silk Route, until it was conquered by the Yuan emperor Kublai Khan in the 13th century. Through much of the Ming and Qing eras, the area that is now Yunnan, Guizhou, and Guangxi was ruled as a colonized outpost, dominated by tribal chieftains.

During the 1800s, the dispossessed, ground down by merciless warlords and extra imperial taxes, revolted in two major uprisings: the Muslim Uprising of 1856 (also known as the Du Wenxiu Rebellion) which lasted until 1873 and centered on Kunming, and the Taiping Rebellion (which lasted from 1850–1864) begun in Guangxi (*see p422*). Both uprisings were brutally suppressed by the Qing and colonizing forces, sending the region into a downward spiral of provincial obscurity and abject poverty. The Miao minority

Fishing boats on the banks of peaceful Er Hai (Ear Lake) near Dali

Worshipers wreathed in incense smoke at Chengdu's main Daoist temple, Qingyang Gong

revolted again in 1870. When the Communists marched through during the Long March in 1934, they encountered a population ready for revolution and took on many recruits.

Sichuan, the region's largest province, has long been a part of China – the enigmatic bronze-working Ba culture flourished here around 1000 BC, with its capital at Sanxingdui, north of modern Chengdu. After the fall of the Han dynasty in AD 220, the province's fertile eastern part became the agriculturally self-sufficient Kingdom of Shu during the Three Kingdoms period (AD 221–63), whose wealth sponsored great religious works under the Tang and Song dynasties such as the huge Buddha at Le Shan. Sichuan remained a crucial outpost during the ensuing eras. Chongqing, its major city, was targeted for heavy industry under the Communists and is today the world's largest municipality, breaking away from Sichuan in 1997. It's from Chongqing that the Three Gorges Cruise down the Yangzi begins *(see pp352–4)*, still the main reason to visit the city.

Sichuan's heavily populated eastern plains give way to the sparsely populated foothills and Aba Grasslands plateau,

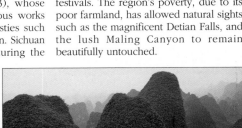

Bai women in traditional dress, Shaping

inhabited mainly by ethnic Tibetans. On the fringes of this frontier, the last few remaining pandas live in what is left of Sichuan's bamboo groves. For a fashionable metropolis, the capital of Chengdu is surprisingly laid-back, a characteristic that is best seen in the many teahouses found in parks, temples, and old courtyards.

Yunnan stretches from the Tibetan foothills in the north, where the headwaters of the Yangzi gather strength, to Xishuangbanna and the Laotian border in the south, through which the Mekong flows. Today, Yunnan is quickly becoming one of the country's foremost tourist destinations. North of Kunming lie the pretty towns of Dali and Lijiang, surrounded by villages inhabited by the indigenous Bai and Naxi peoples. Xishuangbanna's landscape and culture, on the other hand, are reminiscent of Vietnam, Laos, and Myanmar. The regular markets, where minority people gather, are very colorful.

Most tourists head to Guangxi for the stunning karst landscapes surrounding Guilin and Yangshuo. The charms of Guizhou and Guangxi lie, however, in the less visited areas of hilly rural landscape, peppered with wooden villages and inhabited by minority peoples – the Miao in particular are renowned for their ultra-sociable festivals. The region's poverty, due to its poor farmland, has allowed natural sights such as the magnificent Detian Falls, and the lush Maling Canyon to remain beautifully untouched.

Limestone peaks coated in vegetation, Li River area

# The Flora of Southwest China

**Colorful bracts of bougainvillea**

Southwest China has the greatest variety of flora in the whole country, and Yunnan Province in particular can claim the diversity prize, having some 15,000 species of plant, or about half the country's total. Many garden plants originate from this part of China, including the ubiquitous rhododendron and magnolia. The reason for this richness lies in its unique geography: in a very short distance the environment changes from high altitude mountain plateau to moist subtropical jungle on the Tropic of Cancer in the south, with isolated valleys that restrict access and cross-pollination in between.

**A major tourist site,** *the Tropical Botanical Gardens at Xishuangbanna are also where research into tropical forest ecosystems takes place.*

## MOUNTAINS AND VALLEYS

The landscapes of this region are dominated by seemingly endless vistas of mountain ranges and deep valleys. In northern Yunnan, western Sichuan and southwest Tibet lie the headwaters of three of the world's great rivers: from west to east, the Nu Jiang (Salween), the Lancang Jiang (Mekong), and the Jiansha Jiang (Yangzi). All originate high in the mountains of Tibet and Qinghai.

**Magnolia** (Magnolia campbellii), *with its showy pink flowers, is native to the Himalayas and China. It was discovered by George Forrest, a Scottish plant hunter, in 1904 but was not brought into cultivation until 1924.*

Mountain slopes, lush with beautiful plants such as rhododendrons and magnolias.

**Wild rhododendrons** *grow in this region, a center of diversity for many plants. Most of the modern hybrid garden forms originate from wild species introduced from southwest China.*

**Poppy** (Meconopsis integrifolia) *grows high in the mountains of southwest China at 8,850–16,730 ft (2,700–5,100 m), its foliage protected by soft silky hairs. First collected by renowned botanist E.H. Wilson, the poppy is used in traditonal medicine.*

**Many slipper orchid** *species thrive in the alpine meadows of the Sichuan mountains above 7,800 ft (2,400 m) and* Cypripedium tibeticum *is one of the most attractive.*

**Camellias,** *of which there are many beautiful garden species, are grown mainly for their lovely flowers. Also, more than 200 kinds of tea in China are based on* Camellia sinensis.

## TROPICAL FOREST OR JUNGLE

A rare habitat in China, jungle covers only about 0.5 per cent of the country, but it contains 25 per cent of the species. One of the largest remaining areas lies in the southwest, in Xishuangbanna Prefecture, Yunnan Province. Here, there is a rainy season between April and October, the annual rainfall is about 60 in (1,500 mm), and both humidity and temperatures are high. Jungle is also found on Hainan Island, and in southern Guangxi Province.

**Typically dense patch of natural tropical forest in Jinghong, southern Yunnan**

**Pomelo** *or Chinese grapefruit* (Citrus maxima) *has been cultivated in southern China for thousands of years. The flowers are followed by very large fruits with green rind and sweet, juicy flesh.*

**Dragon's blood** (Dracaena cochinchinensis) *plays an important role in traditional Chinese medicine. Its red, blood-like sap is collected and used in a variety of preparations to improve the circulation of the blood. Endangered in the wild, it is now being planted to ensure supplies continue.*

**Musella** (Musella lasiocarpa), *closely related to the banana, is a beautiful but rare plant in Yunnan and Guizhou Provinces. It is low-growing and has a dense yellow flowerhead, reminiscent of a globe artichoke.*

**The jungle floor** *is carpeted with ferns and shrubs while above, lianas and figs drape and strangle tree branches. Mists and monsoon rains constantly dampen the air, so epiphytes (plants growing on trees) flourish.*

**The red dwarf banana,** (Musa coccinea), *is one of the prettiest banana plants and is popular in gardens. About 6.5 ft (2m) tall, it has bright red flowers that last up to two months. It is now scarce because of over-collection and habitat destruction.*

## FAMOUS PLANT HUNTERS

The beginning of the 20th century saw a number of intrepid botanists and explorers set out to discover and bring back new and exotic plants from around the world. Among the most famous were George Forrest (1873–1932), E.H. Wilson (1876–1930), Joseph Rock (1884–1962), and Frank Kingdon Ward (1885–1958). Although only one of the early pioneers, Kingdon Ward achieved renown exploring and collecting botanical specimens in Yunnan Province just before and after World War I, and also later in Tibet. Among his most celebrated discoveries are several rhododendron species. In the 1920s he brought back seeds of the beautiful blue poppy *Meconopsis betonicifolia*, which inspired the title of the most famous of his many books: *The Land of the Blue Poppy*.

**Frank Kingdon Ward, explorer and collector**

# Regional Food: The Southwest

Subject to hot summers and mild winters with plenty of rain, the Southwest enjoys year-round crop growth, making it one of China's "rice bowls." The Sichuan basin also yields a wealth of subtropical products such as fruits, tea, and herbal medicines and its spicy cooking has become the region's dominant cuisine. By contrast, the cooking of Yunnan is underrated despite some wonderful produce; while the cuisines of Guizhou and Guangxi lie somewhere between Sichuanese spiciness and the subtle, delicate flavors of the Cantonese kitchen.

**Eggplants and yard-long beans**

**Fruits and deep-fried snacks on sticks, typical of the Southwest**

not paralyze the tastebuds, but stimulate the palate. Each dish should be a balance of flavors such as sweet, sour, bitter, hot, salty, aromatic, and fragrant. When the palate is stimulated by the heat of the chili, it becomes sensitized and can appreciate even more flavors at the same time.

The most famous regional spice is the Sichuan peppercorn *(hua jiao)*. This dried berry has an aromatic, lemony heat that makes the mouth tingle, even numbing it against the chilies' heat. The final secret of Sichuan food is the purity of the salt collected from the wells of Zigong.

## SICHUAN

The cuisine of Sichuan has the reputation of being richly flavored and peppery hot but, in fact, a lot of Sichuanese dishes are not hot at all. After all, the chili is a relatively recent import from the Americas that was not widely cultivated here until the 19th century. According to Sichuanese chefs, chilies do

**Fresh green & red chilies (sharp, hot)**

**Large dried chilies (smoky, warm)**

**Chili bean paste (rich deep heat)**

**"Red oil" (mild heat)**

**"Towards the sky" chilies (very hot)**

**Sichuan peppercorns (aromatic spicy)**

**Small dried chilies (hot)**

**A selection of Sichuan spices**

## REGIONAL DISHES AND SPECIALTIES

Most visitors to China will at some time come across versions of Kung-Po Chicken and Ma Po Doufu. However, outside Sichuan it is likely to lack the depth of flavors and balance of textures of the original. Each region of China has its own "preserved vegetables" but Sichuan's is among the best – a pickled mustard root in a spicy sauce.

**Fresh water chestnuts**

Yunnan's "Crossing the Bridge Noodles" is said to have been created by the wife of a Qing-dynasty scholar to prevent the noodles cooling on the way to her husband studying in an island pavilion. This consists of a chicken broth with a hot, insulating layer of oil on top served with noodles, slices of ham, vegetables, and egg to be added to it at the table. Another specialty is Steam Pot Chicken cooked with vegetables and often medicinal herbs; as it steams a flavorful broth is created in the pot.

**Kung-Po Chicken:** *the best-known Sichuan dish; Kung-Po was an official from Guizhou, but his chef was Sichuanese.*

## YUNNAN

Yunnan's tropical climate means the province is a haven for vegetable lovers – lotus roots, bamboo shoots, beans and garlic shoots. Several products distinguish Yunnan on the map of gastronomy – firstly the highly-prized *pu'er* tea. Dried into bricks, this is strong and black and often taken as a medicine. Just as famous is Yunnan ham, which rivals the ham from Jinhua in Zhejiang. Unusually for China, Yunnan is also known for its milk products, especially a type of goat's cheese.

When the rain finally stops, a profusion of mushrooms fills the hills and forests of

Stall selling *zongzi*, parcels of sticky rice wrapped in bamboo leaves

**Vegetables on sale in a street market in Guizhou**

the region, sending the locals out to collect these delicacies. Finally, the tropical climate means that all sorts of exotic fruits grow here and many turn up in the area's dishes.

## GUIZHOU & GUANGXI

Relatively poor provinces, Guizhou and Guangxi are known for their famine cuisine especially among the minorities, but despite the stories the average visitor will be hard pressed to find bee grub stir-fries and the like.

Fiery hotpots are a specialty of Guizhou, including those made with dog but these can easily be avoided *(see p399)* if not wanted. The cooking here is spicy and sour. The province's most distinguished product is Maotai. A strong spirit distilled from sorghum and other grains, it is drunk at formal occasions.

Guangxi cuisine includes Cantonese-style sweet and sour dishes along with more rustic Zhuang minority food. *Zongzi* are also a favorite and the pyramids of sticky rice can be savory or sweet.

### ON THE MENU

**Aromatic & Crispy Duck** Quite different to Peking Duck, this is marinated, steamed, and then deep-fried. A special version – Tea Smoked Duck – is created when it is smoked with tea, cypress and camphor wood chips.

**Twice-cooked Pork** Another traditional Sichuan dish that is extremely popular. The secret is that the pork is first boiled, then stir-fried till tender.

**Steamed Beef in a Basket** Spicy beef coated with ground rice and steamed – served in the bamboo steamer basket.

**Toban Fish** A whole fish deep-fried then braised with chilli, garlic, ginger, scallions, soy, sugar, wine, chili bean paste *(toban jiang)*, and vinegar.

**Ants Climbing Trees** Minced pork with rice vermicelli – the minced pork forms the "ants" and the vermicelli the "trees".

**Ma Po Doufu:** *pockmarked tofu – is a classic dish that combines ground meat, tofu, and chilies in a ginger broth.*

**Hot & Sour Soup:** *this dish, when made properly, derives its pungency solely from the use of ground white pepper.*

**Fish-fragrant Aubergine:** *"fish-fragrant" sauces use the same seasonings as traditional fish cookery.*

# SICHUAN & CHONGQING

The province of Sichuan and the neighboring municipality of Chongqing cover 220,078 sq miles (570,000 sq km) and are home to almost 120 million people. This vast region can be divided into three distinct geographical zones. In the east is Chongqing, a municipality based around the heavily industrialized Chongqing city, with a rural strip running east along the Yangzi River and its famous Three Gorges *(see pp352–4)*. In the center lies the hugely fertile Red Basin, whose laid-back capital Chengdu sits surrounded by chequerboard fields and well-irrigated plains.

The wealth generated by this fertile land helped sponsor the temples on Emei Shan's forested slopes and the startling Buddhist sculptures at Dazu and Le Shan. In contrast, Northern and Western Sichuan are covered by the snow-capped foothills of the Himalayan range, rising well over 16,400 ft (5,000 m), a thinly settled region whose culture is predominantly Tibetan. Northwest of Chengdu is the Wanglang Nature Reserve, home to the critically endangered giant panda, while to the far north is the beautiful alpine scenery around Songpan and Jiuzhai Gou.

## SIGHTS AT A GLANCE

### Towns & Cities
Chengdu ④
Chongqing ①
Huanglong Xi ⑩
Kangding ⑲
Songpan ⑭
Zigong ②

### Historic Sites
*Dafo, Le Shan pp364–5* ⑨
Dujiangyan ⑫
Luding ⑰
Sanxingdui Museum ⑦

### Temples & Monasteries
Baoguang Si ⑥

### Mountains, Grottoes & Caves
*Baoding Shan pp356–7* ③
*Emei Shan pp362–3* ⑧
Qingcheng Shan ⑪

### National Parks & Zoos
Huanglong ⑮
*Jiuzhai Gou Tour p370* ⑯
Moxi Xiang & Hailuo Gou
    Glacier ⑱
Panda Breeding Center ⑤
Wanglang Nature Reserve ⑬

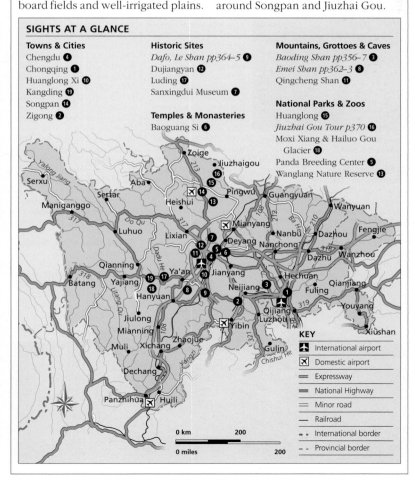

### KEY
✈ International airport
☒ Domestic airport
═ Expressway
═ National Highway
═ Minor road
— Railroad
- - International border
- - Provincial border

◁ The mineral-rich waters and thick forests of Jiuzhai Gou (Nine Stockades Gully)

# Chongqing ❶
重庆

**Calligraphy, Luohan Si**

Believed to have been founded as the capital of the shadowy State of Ba in 1000 BC, this port is situated on a peninsula at the junction of the Yangzi and Jialing rivers. Also known as Shan Cheng (Mountain City), due to the hills covering the peninsula, it is one of the Yangzi valley's "three furnaces" owing to its stifling summer humidity, made even worse by pollution. The main reason to visit Chongqing, a lively, rapidly modernizing city with few historic sights, is to catch a Yangzi ferry downstream through the Three Gorges *(see pp352–4)*. In 1997, Chongqing became the administrative center of the new city-province of Chongqing Shi, which stretches 311 miles (500 km) east to Hubei.

**The Liberation Monument (Jiefangbei) in downtown Chongqing**

**People and goods coming off river-ferries, Chaotian Men Wharf**

## 🚋 Chaotian Men

Chaotian Men (Gate Facing Heaven) is Chongqing's wharf district right at the tip of the peninsula, where cruise boats line the muddy banks, readying themselves for their journey into Eastern China. A viewing platform overlooking the river junction was built in 2000, and offers splendid views on a windy day, though often visibility is impaired by the heavy fogs caused by intense pollution.

## 🏯 Luohan Si

7 Luohansi Jie. ⬜ *daily.*
🔲 🚫

This Ming-era temple is famed for its hall crowded with *luohan* (those freed from the cycle of rebirth). The Indian Buddhist pantheon has just 18 *luohan*, but the Chinese have added hundreds of their own, including Buddhist figures, folk heroes, and even Daoists. The hall has 524 life-sized statues; some sit serenely, while others have grotesque faces. The most easily identifiable figure is Ji Gong, a comic peasant hero near the exit.

## 🚋 Liberation Monument

Situated in the heart of downtown Chongqing, the Liberation Monument is a plain-looking clocktower that commemorates

the Communists' defeat of Kuomintang forces in 1949. It is surrounded by a busy shopping district.

## 🏛 Three Gorges Museum

Opposite Great Hall of the People.
⬜ 9:30am–5pm daily.

This museum, also known as Chongqing Museum, houses a superb collection of Eastern Han tomb relics (AD 25–220) from sites around Sichuan. Peculiar to the region are 20-in (50-cm) long mausoleum bricks, illustrated with figures depicting religious and secular themes. A recurrent image is that of the dragon-bodied sun god, Rishen, associated with Fuxi, legend-ary ancestor of the Chinese. The highlight is a frieze of soldiers and chariots passing a nobleman being entertained. Upstairs is a display of Ba-era boat coffins.

## 🚋 Great Hall of the People

173 Renmin Lu. ⬜ *daily.*
This 213-ft (65-m) high rotunda, seating 4,200 people, was built in 1954 as a conference hall to commemorate Chongqing's important wartime role. Inspired by

**The extravagant Great Hall of the People, now part of the Renmin Hotel**

*For hotels and restaurants in this region see pp567–8 and pp593–4*

Beijing's Temple of Heaven (*see pp96–7*), it is now a part of the Renmin Hotel and is occasionally used for concerts. Its striking exterior, with three tiers of red-pillared eaves beneath a blue canopied roof, stands out from the modern high-rises that are slowly encircling it.

### ⛩ Stilwell Museum

63 Jialing Xin Lu, Liziba, 3 miles (5 km) SE of city center.
🔲 9am–5pm. 🖼
This is the former home of General Stilwell (1883–1946), who was based here between 1942 and 1944 as Commander of the US forces and Chiang Kai Shek's Chief of Staff. The US was instrumental in helping China overthrow the Japanese, and Stilwell led the effort. Exhibits include a display on the legendary Flying Tigers, a volunteer group of US fighter pilots who held off the Japanese along the China-Burma border between 1941 and 1942.

### ⛩ Hongyan Cun

52 Hongyan Cun. 3 miles (5 km) W of Chongqing. 🔲 8:30am–5pm daily. 🖼
This group of whitewashed buildings was the base of the Nationalist-Communist "United Front" government during World War II. Among the prominent people based here were the Communist leader Zhou Enlai and his wife, Deng Yingchao. Chairman Mao briefly visited Hongyan Cun (Red Crag Village) after Japan surrendered in 1945, to attend the US-sponsored talks with the Kuomintang forces led by Chiang Kai-shek. The buildings now house a collection of sparsely-captioned wartime photographs. More appealing is the hilly parkland surrounding the site.

### ⛩ Ciqi Kou

9 miles (14 km) W of Chongqing. 🔲 from Chongqing Hotel.
Founded 1,700 years ago on the banks of Jialing Jiang, Ciqi Kou (Porcelain Port) was a famous porcelain production center during the Ming era, and is something of a museum piece. Its riverfront lanes, preserved in their original flag-stoned state, are flanked by old timber, adobe, and split-stone buildings with carved stonework, latticed windows, and gray-tiled roofs. Teahouses are everywhere, and there are about 100 to choose from. A couple of traditional ones overlook the river and occasionally host opera shows. Busy markets sell food

and local arts and crafts. Porcelain is no longer made here, but Ciqi Kou is now popular with modern and traditional painters.

**A colorful and bustling food market, Ciqi Kou**

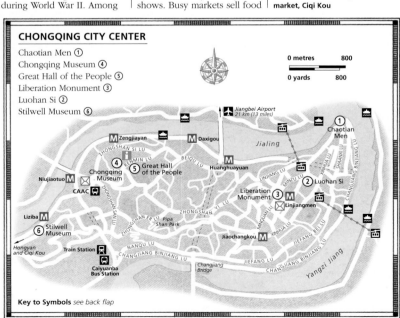

### CHONGQING CITY CENTER

Chaotian Men ①
Chongqing Museum ④
Great Hall of the People ⑤
Liberation Monument ③
Luohan Si ②
Stilwell Museum ⑥

0 metres 800
0 yards 800

Jiangbei Airport 21 km (13 miles)

Jialing

Zengjiayan
Daxigou
Chaotian Men ①
Huanghuayuan
Great Hall of the People ⑤
Chongqing Museum ④
Niujiaotuo
CAAC
Luohan Si ②
Liberation Monument ③
Linjiangmen
Liziba
Pipa Shan Park
Jiaochangkou
Stilwell Museum ⑥
Hongyan and Ciqi Kou
Train Station
Caiyuanba Bus Station
Changjiang Bridge
Yangzi Jiang

ZHONGSHAN SI LU
RENMIN LU
BEIQU LU
LINJIANG LU
MINZU LU
CANGBAI LU
SHAANXI LU
ZHONGSHAN SAN LU
ZHONGSHAN ER LU
ZHONGSHAN YI LU
MINQUAN LU
XINHUA LU
NANQU LU
CHANGJIANG BINJIANG LU
JIEFANG LU
JIEFANG BEI LU
CHANGJIANG BINJIANG LU
CHANGJIANG BINJIANG LU

**Key to Symbols** *see back flap*

# The Yangzi and Three Gorges
长江三峡

Before the 20th century, rugged mountains would have virtually isolated Sichuan from eastern China if it hadn't been for the 400 mile (650 km) stretch of the Yangzi linking Chongqing with Yichang in Hubei Province. The journey was a perilous one, the river tearing through the sheer-sided Three Gorges. Today, with the shoals cleared, the journey makes a popular cruise through spectacular scenery, with regular stops at famous sights. The landscape has been irrevocably changed by the Three Gorges Dam, which filled to its maximum capacity in 2009, making the cruise even more leisurely and extending the cruising season.

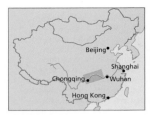

**LOCATOR MAP**

☐ *Area illustrated below*

★ **Shibao Zhai**
*This outstanding monastery (see p354) sits on an island, with Lanruo Dian (Orchid Palace) built into the cliff above.*

**Landscape near Chongqing**
*The gentle farmland around Chongqing, fascinating for its depiction of day-to-day life, does little to prepare you for the wild, spectacular gorge scenery downstream.*

**Ancient Ba Kingdom Tombs** have been inundated by the rising waters.

CHONGQING

Wanxian

Wulingzhen

Zhongxian

YANGZI

CHONGQING

Fuling

Fengdu

**Fengdu** was moved here from the opposite shore.

**Wulong**, a scenic reserve of limestone karst formations.

**KEY**

– – –  Provincial border

**STAR SIGHTS**

★ Shibao Zhai

★ Mini Three Gorges

★ Qutang Xia

**The City of Ghosts**
*Ming Shan, a mountain dedicated to the afterworld and its ruler, Tianzi, is scattered with temples, shrines, and waxworks depicting the gorier sides of hell, including various tortures awaiting sinners.*

**The Three Gorges**
*Though the river is no longer the vicious torrent described by countless travelers, the steep walls and tight channels of Qutang Xia, Wu Xia, and Xiling Xia still present an awesome spectacle.*

## VISITORS' CHECKLIST

Chongqing to Yichang or Wuhan.
🚹 Zourong Plaza Bldg, A/8th
Floor, 151 Zourong Lu, (023)
6387 6537 (CITS For bookings).
📷 excursions extra.
**www**.yzcruises.com

★ **Mini Three Gorges**
*The Mini Three Gorges feature the cliffs of Longmen Xia and troupes of wild monkeys.*

**Baidicheng**, an ancient temple complex, sits on an island linked to the north bank by a bridge.

0 kilometers 30

0 miles 30

Yunyang

New Fengjie

Daning He

QUTANG XIA

New Wushan

WU XIA

Shennong Xi

Guandukou

**Shennong Xi**
*(see p354)* makes a pleasant sidetrip.

XILING XIA

HUBEI

Yichang

WUHAN

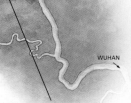

★ **Qutang Xia**
*The first and shortest of the stunning Three Gorges, the once violent waters of Qutang Gorge were described by the Tang poet Li Bai as "a thousand seas poured into a single cup."*

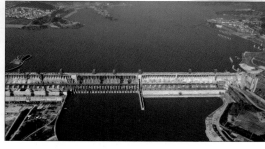

**Three Gorges Dam**
*Before reaching Yichang, there's a chance to witness one of the world's largest construction projects (see pp268–9). Most cruises now end above the dam.*

# Cruising the Yangzi

Planned for more than a century, the Three Gorges Dam was completed in 2009. Its 32 hydroelectric generators will one day produce 10 percent of China's power requirements. Construction required the relocation of millions of people, the rebuilding of several towns above the new waterline, and the loss of some priceless archeological sites. A few key historic buildings were relocated; where this was not possible, protective dikes were built instead. The drama of the landscape has undoubtedly diminished, but the reservoir is so large that the impression of being a river remains.

**Tour sailing up the narrows of Shennong Xi in a sampan**

### Shennong Xi

One of the highlights of the whole Yangzi cruise is detouring up the ever-narrowing waters of Shennong Stream. The cliffs are pocked with post-holes marking the route of a Han-dynasty plank road, built for military access. There are also at least three hanging coffins here, which the now-vanished Bai people mortised into the gorge walls over 1,000 years ago. Burial goods and cliffside paintings link the Bai with both Sichuan's earliest known civilization, the Ba, and also the local Tujia nationality *(see pp24–5)*.

If the waters are too low to navigate this stream, most cruises include a trip up Daning He instead *(see p353)*.

### Wulong

*from Wulong town.* 9am–6:30pm daily (last ticket sold 4pm). *(fee includes bus within reserve areas).* About 62 miles (100 km) south of the Yangzi port of Fengdu, Wulong is a scenic reserve of limestone karst formations *(see pp412–13)* scattered in the countryside around Wulong town. The key area is **Tiansheng Sanqiao**, the "Natural Three Bridges", where a

former underground river system has collapsed, leaving a complex of vast sinkholes and soaring stone archways, all overgrown with luxuriant vegetation. **Tianlong Tiankeng**, the largest sinkhole, is 1,804 ft (550 m) wide and 890 ft (270 m) deep. Around 2 miles (3 km) of well-formed paths and an outdoor elevator provide access around the site.

### Shibao Zhai

The most striking aspect of Shibao Zhai (meaning Precious Stone Fortress) is the beautiful 12-story Lanruo Dian, whose curly eaves are said to resemble an orchid, built in 1750 and rising 184 feet (56 m) up the rock wall above the small temple. The "Precious Stone" of the name relates to a legend about a rock in the monastery with a hole, through which every day trickled just enough rice to feed all the monks. But when one of them greedily enlarged the hole, hoping to sell the surplus, the rice stopped flowing. Shibao Zhai has been protected from rising waters by a large dike, but sadly, the medieval village at its base has been drowned.

## TRACKERS

Before the rapids were cleared in the 1950s, boats could only make it upstream with the help of trackers, teams of barely-paid men who were harnessed together to literally pull the boat, inch by inch, through the Three Gorges' torrents. Paths cut into the bank to make their work easier and slightly less hazardous – or copies of them above the new maximum waterline – can be seen in several places through the gorges.

**Towing a barge on Shennong Xi, a tributary of the Yangtze River**

Gateway to a teahouse in former Guildhall

# Zigong ❷
## 自贡

106 miles (170 km) SW of Chongqing. 🚗 477,000. 🚉 🚌 🚉
*Xiongfei Holiday Hotel, (0813) 211
8899.*

Salt has been mined in
Sichuan for at least 2,500
years, and for much of that
time Zigong has been at the
center of its production,
luring traders from all over
China. Brine is drawn from
artesian wells beneath the
city, along with natural gas
used in the evaporation
process. Chinese well-drilling
techniques, mainly the use of
bamboo cables and heavy
iron drill-bits, were borrowed
by the West during the 1850s,
and later adapted for mining
oil reserves. Until the 1960s,
Zigong was full of bamboo
pipelines and 328-ft (100-m)
high wooden derricks. Even
today one can visit some of
these older mines and vintage
architecture built to display
the salt-merchants' wealth.

The **Zigong Salt Museum**
was built in 1736 as the
Xiqing Guildhall, a meeting
place for salt merchants from
Shaanxi province. This lavish
building features elaborate
flying eaves, and a gilded,
wood-carved interior based
around a large galleried atrium, where plays were once
performed. Exhibits cover the
entire history of salt mining,

from Han dynasty
illustrations, to
huge metal drill-bits
and cutaways
showing the drilling
process. Other contemporary buildings
of interest are two
teahouses with
charming antique
interiors, where
locals sit and chat.
The most attractive
of these is the
19th-century
Wangye Miao, a
smaller version of
the Xiqing
Guildhall, which
perches castle-like
on a rocky outcrop
overlooking the
Fuxi Jiang on
Binjiang Lu. The other is a
former City Storekeepers'
Guildhall on Zhonghua
Road, whose carved entranceway opens into a sloping
courtyard surrounded by
private wood-paneled booths.

The **Shenhai Well**, just east
of the center, was easily the
deepest in the world when
drilling reached a depth of
3,285 ft (1,001 m) in 1835,
producing a daily output of
494 cubic ft (14 cubic m) of
brine and 300,175 cubic ft
(8,500 cubic m) of natural
gas. The 59-ft (18-m) high
timber derrick, bamboo pipes,
cables, and buffalo-powered
winches used in the drilling
and retrieving processes are
on show, along with gaspowered evaporation pans
used to refine salt, which is

still produced and packed on
site. Zigong's other forms of
subterranean wealth are its
fossils, found at a major
Jurassic site in the northeastern suburb of Dashanpu,
that has now been roofed
over as a **Dinosaur Museum**.
In 1985, extensive excavations
were carried out with British
assistance, unearthing hundreds of skeletons, including
the stegosaur-like *Gigantspinosaurus sichuanensis*,
and the 30-ft (9-m) long,
carnivorous *Yangchuanosaurus hepingensis*. Assembled skeletons are displayed
in the main hall, along with
partially excavated remains in
the original diggings.

🏛 **Zigong Salt Museum**
107 Jiefang Lu. *Tel (0813) 220
8581.* ⬜ 8:30am–5pm daily. 📷

🚰 **Shenhai Well**
Da'an Jie. ⬜ 8am–6pm daily. 📷

🏛 **Dinosaur Museum**
Dashanpu. *Tel (0813) 580 1234.*
⬜ 9am–5pm daily. 📷

The main entrance of the Zigong
Salt Museum

## MINING SALT IN SICHUAN

An essential part of imperial tax since the Western Han era,
salt was extracted from salt-water pools on the coasts. In
Sichuan, however, mining from briny grounds (using an
ingenious method that far pre-dated
Western techniques), was cheaper than
importing heavily taxed salt from the
coast. With deep drilling and the
installation of bamboo pipes in the
11th century, production peaked.
Entrepreneurs opened up mines and
workers flocked to the area, leading a
bureaucracy alarmed at the tax losses to
ban deep drilling – although they were
soon opened again. By the 17th century,
the Sichuanese had devised a method
of capturing the natural gas that escapes
from briny deposits to fuel their stoves.

Salt mine model,
Xiqing Guildhall

# Carvings of Dazu

**Figure in meditation**

Combining elements from Confucianism, Daoism, and Indian Tantric Buddhism, the carvings at Baoding Shan, Dazu are a unique example of the harmonious synthesis of these philosophies and religions. Though most are religious in theme, the carvings vary greatly in style. A few are naturalistic depictions of daily life, but most of them are monumental and even surreal, with fanged guardian gods and serene Buddhas at the point of Enlightenment surrounded by cartoon-like details of Buddhist parables. The main colors used are reds, blues, and greens.

**Wheel of Transmigration ③**
*A giant, toothy demon holds a segmented disc depicting the possible states of reincarnation, from Buddhahood down to animals and ghosts.*

**1000-armed Guanyin ⑧** *In fact it has 1007 gilded arms that seem to flicker like flames from the central figure of Guanyin, each palm holding a different symbol of the bodhisattva.*

**Reclining Buddha ⑪** *This 50-ft (15-m) long Buddha lies on his side, his stylized face making the life-like busts of officials and donors arranged in front appear even more striking. The adjacent Nine-dragon Spring refers to the legend of Buddha being washed at birth by dragons.*

**Filial Duty ⑰** *A Confucian theme of honoring parents for the sacrifices they make for their children illustrates the flexible nature of Chinese belief at this predominantly Buddhist site.*

**Buddhist Hell ⑳**
*Buddha and bodhisattvas gaze down at drunken sinners, while animal-headed demons mutilate others on Knife Mountain and in Knee-chopping Hall.*

**Dao Sages ㉔** *These ancient figures of wise old men appear to be representatives of Daoist philosophy.*

**Stone Lion ㉘** *The lion is assigned to Wenshu, the incarnation of Wisdom in Buddhist teaching. Here, this twice life-sized statue guards the entrance to the Cave of Full Enlightenment.*

**The Three Sages** ④ *Three serene figures sit in eternal contemplation of life, the infinite, and everything. The Chinese characters declare the site as Baoding Shan.*

**Parental Care** ⑮ *This expression of the Confucian theme of the duty of parental love at this Buddhist site is an illustration of how religious philosophies could co-exist during the Tang dynasty.*

**Enlightenment Buddha** ㉙ *The centerpiece of Baoding Shan's only true cave, this represents the reward of perfecting the self through cycles of reincarnation.*

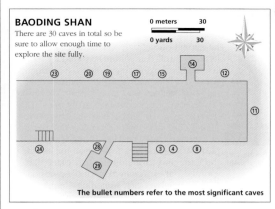

**BAODING SHAN**
There are 30 caves in total so be sure to allow enough time to explore the site fully.

0 meters 30
0 yards 30

㉓ ⑳ ⑲ ⑰ ⑮ ⑭ ⑫
⑪
⑬
㉔ ㉘ ③ ④ ⑧
㉙

**The bullet numbers refer to the most significant caves**

## Baoding Shan, Dazu ❸
### 宝顶山

9 miles (15 km) NE of Dazu. 🚌 *from Caiyuanba Station, Chongqing (2hrs) to Dazu; minibus to caves (half hr).* 🕗 *8:30am–5pm.* 🎫 *includes Bei Shan.* 📷 *fee required for video.*

The hills around Dazu are riddled with caves and grottoes decorated with more than 50,000 carvings dating as far back as the Tang dynasty in the 7th century. The best collection of statuary with the finest craftsmanship and richest content can be found at Baoding Shan; the monk Zhao Zhifeng oversaw the work between 1179 and 1245. The bulk of these carvings decorate thirty separate niches carved into the soft limestone walls of a 28-ft (8-m) high, horseshoe-shaped gully known as Dafo Wan (Big Buddha Bend) after the large sculpture of the reclining Sakyamuni Buddha.

Other carvings worth noting at Baoding Shan are the pastoral scenes of buffalo herding in Cave 5, a whole tableau of activity that stands as a beautiful allegory of the search for enlightenment. The Cat and Mouse between Caves 3 and 4 is a light-hearted carving with a wonderfully naturalistic cat looking up at a mouse climbing a bamboo stalk. The Dazu grottoes are more secular and real to life

than other grottoes – that is to say, they relate the abstract Buddhist doctrines through the lives of ordinary people. The realistic carvings include not only the statues of Buddha and bodhisattvas, but also monarchs, ministers, military officers, officials, monks, the rich, and even the poor.

The site has been listed as a World Cultural Heritage Site by UNESCO since 1999.

**Environs:** Bei Shan, situated just over a mile (2 km) north of Dazu, was originally a military camp whose carvings were commissioned by the general Wei Junjing in AD 892. The caves are somewhat dark and few sculptures stand out. The most outstanding sculpture is in Cave 136 which houses a Wheel of Life carving, Puxian the patron Saint of Emei Shan, and the androgynous Sun and Moon Guanyin.

**One of the sculptures Bei Shan grottoes, Dazu**

# Chengdu ➍
成都

**Statue, Liu Bei's Tomb**

The capital of Sichuan, Chengdu is a modern city with a relaxed culture, typified by its pleasant gardens and teahouses. A distinct part of city life, teahouses are found in parks and other spaces, and are often no more than a collection of rickety chairs and tables. The city's roots go as far back as the enigmatic Ba-Shu era *(see p360)*, though it first became a capital during the Three Kingdoms (AD 221), later gaining a reputation for its silk brocade and for being the first place that printed paper money. By Chinese standards, Chengdu is a fairly compact city, stretching 4 miles (6 km) across, with most sights within its central area.

**Business as usual at the bustling teahouse in Wenshu Yuan**

## 🏯 Wenshu Yuan
Wenshu Yuan Jie. ◯ 8am–6pm daily. 📷
This busy Chan Buddhist temple is dedicated to Wenshu, the incarnation of Wisdom, whose lion is depicted in sculptures and paintings in the monastery's elegantly austere halls. The small gilded pagoda to one side is said to contain the skull of Xuanzang, a famous Tang dynasty pilgrim and star of TV series *Monkey*. After a visit, relax at the teahouse or restaurant.
 Adjacent to the temple, **Wenshu Fang** is an area of antique alleys and restored period buildings, thick with snack stalls and shops.

**Incense for sale at Wenshu Yuan**

## 🏛 Yong Ling Museum
10 Yong Ling Lu. 🚌 42, 48, 54. ◯ 8am–5:30pm daily. 📷
A large mound in the north-west of town was excavated in 1942 to uncover Yong Ling, the Tomb of Wang Jian, self-appointed emperor of Sichuan, who fought his way to power in AD 907 and died in 918. The relics include a 20-ft (6-m) long stone platform which formed the base for a multi-layered wooden sarcophagus, carved with a 22-figure female orchestra. Life-sized busts of warriors, sunk up to their waists in the floor, support the platform. A simple statue of Wang Jian enforces the impression of a cultured, modest man, though his self-indulgent son lost the empire to the Late Tang in AD 925.

## 🏛 Du Fu's Thatched Cottage
38 Qinghua Lu. ◯ daily. 📷
The Tang dynasty's most celebrated poet, Du Fu, arrived in Chengdu during a nationwide uprising in AD 759. He spent the next five years living in poverty in a tumble-down thatched cottage on the outskirts of the city, where he wrote around 240 soulful poems contrasting the forces of nature with the turmoil of contemporary life. Admirers first founded gardens here in the 10th century, although the traditional arrangement of pools, bridges, trees, and pavilions dates from 1811. Simple whitewashed halls display antique collections of Du Fu's poems, and a museum gives an outline of his life in models and paintings.

## 🏯 Qingyang Gong
9 Xi Er Duan. ◯ daily.
The name of this sprawling Daoist temple, meaning Green Goat, refers to the obscure final words of Daoism's mythical founder, Laozi, that those who understood his teachings could find him at the Green Goat market. The story is commemorated at the Bagua Pavilion, where a life-sized statue of Laozi riding his buffalo is surrounded by coiled dragons and also at the Three Purities Hall, where there are two bronze statues of what are supposedly goats, although the right-hand animal has tiger paws, a unicorn's horn, a snake's tail, and other attributes of animals in the Chinese zodiac.

## ♣ Renmin Park
12 Xiao Cheng Lu. ◯ 7am–9pm daily. 📷
This is the best of Chengdu's parks, with year-round floral displays, ponds, terraces draped in wisteria, and a hall hosting weekend shows of shadow-puppetry. The Martyrs' Monument, commemorates the 1911 rail dispute that mobilized opposition to the Qing and eventually led to their demise.

**Worshipers outside the Daoist Qingyang Gong**

*For hotels and restaurants in this region see pp567–8 and pp593–4*

## ⛩ Wuhou Ci

231 Wuhou Ci Dajie. ⏰ *8am–6pm daily.* 📷

Meaning "Shrine to the Minister of War," Wuhou Ci commemorates Zhuge Liang (AD 181–234), a brilliant military strategist from the Three Kingdoms period. In 1672, the complex was expanded to include its series of temple-like halls, filled with statuary of Three Kingdoms' characters, all guarding **Liu Bei's Tomb**. The Three Kingdoms Hall has statues of Liu Bei, robed in gold along with his grandson, while another room has statues of Zhuge Liang. The last hall is used for Sichuan theater.

East of Wuhou Ci, **Jin Li** alley has colorful Song-style houses, shops and stalls, and is a good place to sample Chengdu's famous street food.

## ⛩ Sichuan Museum

251 Hanhua Nan Lu. **Tel** *(028) 8522 6723.* 🚌 *19, 35, 47, 82 to Songxian Qiao stop.* ⏰ *9am–5pm Tue–Sun.*

A trove of ethnographic and cultural artifacts on three levels, this museum's lower floor is full of animated Han dynasty pottery models of musicians, court figures,

acrobats, and warriors; while the upper two stories focus on bronze sculptures and Tibetan Buddhist artifacts. A wing at the rear features silk brocade.

Across the road, **Songxian Qiao Curio Market** is a wonderful place to browse among porcelain, wooden screens, and Cultural Revolution momentos.

## ⛩ Jinsha Museum

227 Qingyang Dadao. 🚌 *47, 901.* ⏰ *8am–6pm daily.* 📷

This museum occupies the site of a previously undocumented Shang dynasty settlement, which was discovered during building work in 2000. Thousands of

artifacts, animal bones, graves, and house foundations indicate that Jinsha was a major center for the later Ba-Sha culture. The glass-sided **Exhibit Hall** is built over the excavations, exposing sacrificial pits where valuables were ceremonially buried.

**A striking moon gate at Wuhou Ci**

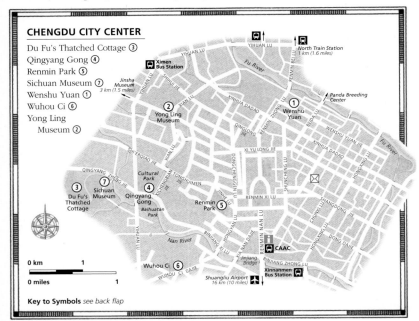

**CHENGDU CITY CENTER**

Du Fu's Thatched Cottage ③
Qingyang Gong ④
Renmin Park ⑤
Sichuan Museum ⑦
Wenshu Yuan ①
Wuhou Ci ⑥
Yong Ling Museum ②

YIHUAN LU
YIHUAN LU
Ximen Bus Station
Fu River
North Train Station
1 km (1.6 miles)
Jinsha Museum
3 km (1.5 miles)
YIHUAN LU
SHIHU JIE
XIAN LU
XINHUA DADAO
RENMIN BEI LU
Panda Breeding Center
Yong Ling Museum ②
RENMIN ZHONG LU
Wenshu Yuan ①
QINGLONG JIE
WENSHU YUAN JIE
BEIDA JIE
XINHUA DADAO
Fu River
XI YU LONG JIE
SHUNCHENG LU
QINGYANG ZHONG JIE
SHIERQIAO JIE
KECHENGBIAN TONGHUIMEN JIE
DONGCHENGGEN LU
HONGXING LU
SHANGDONG JIE
QINGYANG ZHONG JIE
Cultural Park
Du Fu's Thatched Cottage ③
Sichuan Museum ⑦
Qingyang Gong ④
Baihuatan Park
RENMIN XI LU
Renmin Park ⑤
JINHE LU
CHUNXI LU
DONG DAJIE
YIHUAN LU
Nan River
BINJIANG XI LU
RENMIN NAN LU
Jinjiang Bridge
CAAC
ℹ
BINJIANG ZHONG LU
HONGXING LU
Wuhou Ci ⑥
WUHOU CI DAJIE
Shuangliu Airport
16 km (10 miles)
Xinnanmen Bus Station

0 km — 1
0 miles — 1

**Key to Symbols** *see back flap*

A bizarre yet exquisitely crafted Sanxingdui mask

# Panda Breeding Center ❺

熊猫繁殖中心

6 miles (10 km) NE of Chengdu. 🚌 or taxi. ⏺ 8am–6pm daily. 🎫
**www**.panda.org.cn

This research base set up in 1987 has bred and raised over 88 giant panda cubs, scoring well over the usual captive survival rate. While so far this has been for the benefit of zoos, the center's main aim is to start returning pandas to the wild. One of the best places to see pandas in China, the center currently displays around 30 red and 83 giant pandas. Mostly inactive, they can be seen chewing piles of arrow bamboo or sleeping.

# Baoguang Si ❻

宝光寺

12 miles (19 km) NE of Chengdu. 🚌 or taxi. ⏺ 8am–5pm daily. 🎫

A place of worship since the Han dynasty, Baoguang Si owes its current name and reputation to the Tang emperor Xizong, who took refuge here in AD 881, during a rebellion. He called the temple Baoguang, or Shining Treasure, after he saw a light underneath a wooden pagoda in the temple, which was supposedly emanating from the buried holy relics. The pagoda, which he ordered to be rebuilt in stone, still stands as the 13-story, 98-ft (30-m) high **Sheli Ta**, just inside the entrance. Its top, however, broke off during an earth-quake. The temple has well-tended gardens planted with ginkgos, besides a dozen or more halls filled with holy relics, including a room dedicated to the Tsongkhapa sect of Tibetan lamaism, and a stone stele carved with Buddha images from AD 540. Baoguang Si's biggest draw is its Qing-era **Luohan Hall**, where 518 brightly painted, life-sized sculptures of Buddhist saints are joined by 59 Buddhas and Bodhidarma – the Indian founder of Zen Buddhism – along with a huge phoenix statue. Among the statues are the emperors Kangxi and Qianlong, with their distinctive beards, boots, and capes. Also within the compound is a little vegetarian restaurant.

# Sanxingdui Museum ❼

三星堆博物馆

15 miles (24 km) N of Chengdu in Guanghan. **Tel** (0838) 550 0349. 🚌 from Chengdu to Guanghan. ⏺ 8:30am–5pm daily. 🎫

In the 1980s archeologists began excavating at Sanxingdui, where farmers had been finding ancient pieces since 1929. They unexpectedly uncovered traces of an ancient city, over 3,000 years old, tentatively believed to have been the capital of the Ba-Shu culture. Numerous sacrificial pits were found containing an extraordinary trove of bronze, gold, and jade artifacts. Key pieces in the museum include a 7-ft (2-m) high bronze figure with huge, coiled hands, a giant "spirit tree" hung with mystical animals, and several leering, 3-ft (1-m) wide masks whose eyes protrude on stalks. Also on display are smaller, finely detailed pieces, along with accounts of the excavations. Highly individual in style, though evoking the contemporary Shang bronzes of eastern China, the Sanxingdui artifacts reveal a very high degree of craftsmanship. The finds perhaps challenge the popular theory that China evolved from a single culture living by the Yellow River.

## SICHUAN OPERA

Elaborately costumed actors at an opera performance

Sung in the Sichuanese dialect, this 300-year-old tradition is immensely popular. Lacking the formality of Beijing Opera, but filled with wit and dynamism, the Sichuan style portrays local legends, while its high-pitched singing is accompanied by percussion and wind instruments. Acrobatics are a major part of the performance. *Bianlian*, the Sichuanese trick of face-changing, allows each actor to portray many characters; with a swift move of the hand, makeup is added, or a layer of mask removed. Sichuan Opera is usually performed in small, casual theaters, even teahouses. In Chengdu, tickets are available at Jinjiang Theater on Xianliong Jie and Shudu Theater down Yushuang Lu. Many tour operators run excursions to theaters, giving an explanation of the plot and a fascinating glimpse backstage.

# Giant Pandas

The famously rare giant panda occurs only in China, and, according to genetic tests, is distantly related to the bear. The wild panda population of around 1,600 is increasing, though with perhaps only another 370 in zoos worldwide, they remain seriously endangered. There is added concern following the 2008 Sichuan earthquake, which seriously affected the panda population and habitat. Pandas feed primarily on bamboo. They have developed large molars for grinding

**Hard Rock Café logo**

up the stalks, but are not well adapted to digesting them and so spend almost all their waking hours eating. Bamboo flowers and dies off simultaneously over huge areas, periodically depriving giant pandas of their food source. In the past, they could travel to other regions to find more bamboo to eat, but now their habitat has been carved up by development. Some 49 reserves are dedicated to panda preservation in China, including the Wanglang reserve in North Sichuan (*see p369*).

**Pandas eat** *between 35 and 65 pounds (15 and 30 kg) of bamboo a day, despite having a carnivore's digestive tract. They only digest 20 per cent of the nutrients, so spend the rest of the day asleep, conserving energy.*

**The panda's paw** *is adapted to its special diet. The wrist is modified into a sort of opposable "thumb" that helps it to grasp delicate bamboo stems.*

**Pandas are not prolific breeders,** *even in the best equipped zoos, as they only have a brief breeding window (for only a few days in spring) and they are extremely choosy about whom they mate with.*

**Pandas in the wild** *are occasionally seen in family groups, but mostly they live a solitary existence for much of their 25 years in a clearly defined territory marked out by scent. One theory for their striking coloration is that it helps them recognize each other in the forests.*

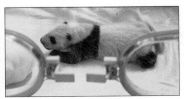

**Breeding programs** *in Sichuan saw 32 births (with 29 survivors) in 2008. Artificial insemination is usually used. Incubators reduce the high infant mortality found in the wild.*

**A panda baby** *weighs just 3½ oz (100 g) at birth – compared to the adult's 440 lb (200 kg). The cub is carried by the mother for 90 days and stays on with her for up to three years.*

# Emei Shan ⓼

峨眉山

Puxian on his
elephant

Rising to 10,167 feet (3,099 m), Emei Shan has been considered holy by both Daoists and Buddhists since the Eastern Han dynasty. Many of the temples nestled on the mountain's lush slopes are dedicated to the Bodhisattva of Universal Benevolence, Puxian, who is said to have ascended the mountain during the 6th century atop a six-tusked elephant. Emei Shan is also a storehouse of botanic diversity, with over 3,200 plant species found on the mountain – 10 per cent of China's total. Many can be seen in monastery gardens, including the white-petalled handkerchief tree; the ginkgo, which is extinct in the wild; and the straight-trunked *nanmu*, a favored wood for temple pillars. The most visible of Emei's animals are the aggressive monkeys, who pester hikers for handouts – keep food packed away.

★ **The summit**

*Emei's three main peaks are the crests of an undulating ridge, with a sheer drop of over 3,000 feet (1,000 m) on the front face.*

### Hikers

*Hawkers hoist sedan chairs for those who have had enough of walking. To cut down some of the trekking, take a bus from Baoguo to the cable car leading to Wannian Si, or, easiest of all, to the cable car going all the way to the summit at Jieyin Dian.*

Hong Cl
Ping

### Baoguo Si

*One of the most important temples on Emei, Baoguo Si contains a massive bronze bell. Cast during the Ming dynasty, it is rung with a large swinging tree trunk and is said to be audible for 10 miles (16 km).*

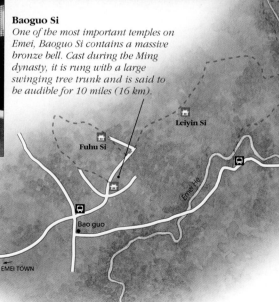

Leiyin Si

Fuhu Si

0 kilometers　3

0 miles　　　　3

Emei He

Bao guo

## STAR SIGHTS

★ The summit

★ Wannian Si

★ Qingyin Ge

EMEI TOWN

**Jin Ding Si**
*The terrace in front of this temple is a favorite spot for watching the sunrise, cloud seas, and other atmospheric phenomena.*

Jianfo Ding
67 ft

Dianfo Ding
9,990 ft

Jin Ding
▲ 10,095

Jieyin Dian

Xianfeng Si

**Xixiang Chi** (Elephant Bathing Pool) is at the spot where Puxian is said to have stopped to wash his elephant.

**★ Wannian Si**
*The oldest surviving building on Emei dates to 1611 and houses a famed golden statue of Puxian.*

**VISITORS' CHECKLIST**

89 miles (143 km) SW of Chengdu. 🏠 near Baoguo Si, (0833) 552 0444. 🚌 to Emei Town. 🚌 from Chengdu or Le Shan to Emei Town or Baoguo; Emei Town to Baoguo (20 min). ◯ daily. 📷

**KEY**

| | |
|---|---|
| 🚌 | Bus stop |
| 🚡 | Cable car |
| 🏛 | Temple |
| = = | Path |
| = | Road |

THE SUMMIT

**EXPLORING EMEI SHAN**
It takes about three days to climb and descend Emei Shan; basic accommodations and food are available at numerous temples. Pack rain gear and wear stout footwear as the flagstone paths can be slippery, particularly from October to April when hawkers sell straw soles and metal crampons to attach to boots. Warm clothing is essential at the summit year round.

**★ Qingyin Ge**
*Reached over a pair of arched bridges, the Pure Music Pavilion is set in lowland forest at the junction of two streams. The nearby temple is the most romantic place to spend a night on Emei Shan.*

# Dafo, Le Shan ❾

乐山

**Heavenly King, Dafo Temple**

The enormous 230-ft (71-m) high Dafo (Great Buddha) is carved into the red sandstone face of Lingyun Hill overlooking the treacherous confluence of the Min, Dadu, and Qingyi rivers below. In AD 713 a monk, Haitong, decided to safeguard passing boats by creating a protective icon in the cliffs – though he was also practical enough to realize that the resultant rubble would fill in the shoals. By the time Dafo was completed, other temples had been built around it and on the adjacent Wuyou Hill, and today a network of paths links this UNESCO World Heritage site.

**Jiazhou Huayuan**
*This museum, located in a pretty temple, gives a full account of Dafo's history and construction, with interesting models.*

**★ Dafo (Great Buddha)**
*Up close, the remains of a drainage system can be seen. The statue must be restored every decade to survive plant invasion and pollution.*

**Nine Turns Staircase**
is a steep, narrow set of steps down to the toes.

## STAR SIGHTS

★ Buddha's Feet

★ Dafo (Great Buddha)

★ Haoshang Bridge

**★ Buddha's Feet**
*At his huge 26-ft (8-m) feet you can really appreciate one of the world's biggest Buddhas. His other statistics are equally impressive: each ear droops 23 ft (7 m), his shoulders span 92 ft (28 m), while his nose measures 18 ft (5.6m).*

## HAITONG, SCULPTOR AND MONK

When Haitong's idea was accepted, funds were raised by public subscription and regional government contributions from the salt revenue (*see p355*). The monk lived in a cave behind Dafo's head and when a local official threatened to blind Haitong unless he could take a cut of the funds, the monk gouged his own eyes out to prove his sincerity. However, the project was only completed in AD 803 after his death, and after Wei Gao, the regional governor, donated his own salary to finish off the legs and feet.

**Haitong, a pious monk devoted to his project**

**VISITORS' CHECKLIST**

Le Shan, 96 miles (154 km) SW of Chengdu. 🚌 from Chengdu Bus Station to Le Shan, then bus no. 3 to Dafo. 🚢 from Le Shan to Wuyou Si, then walk to Dafo. ⏰ 7:30am–7:30pm May–Sep; 8am–6pm Oct–Apr. 🎫 📷

**Ancient shrines and temples close by**

**★ Haoshang Bridge**
*This elegant, part-covered structure is built in an "antique" style and links the Great Buddha with outlying temples on the adjacent hills.*

**Guardian figures flank the Buddha**

**Wuyou Hill**
was cut off from Lingyun Hill around 250 BC to reduce the river's currents. Wuyou's Buddhist temple was founded in AD 742.

**Mahao Cave Tombs**
*Dating from the Eastern Han dynasty (AD 25–220), these grottoes were built to house the remains of local nobles, with carved scenes of cavalry and some early Buddha figures.*

**Dafo or Great Buddha, best seen from a river boat, hired from Le Shan**

Qingcheng Shan's ornate front gateway, with sharply upturned eaves

# Huanglong Xi ⑩
黄龙溪

31 miles (50 km) SW of Chengdu. 🚌

Consisting of just seven narrow lanes on a quiet riverbank surrounded by fields, the delightfully dated village of Huanglong Xi served as one of the sets in the martial-arts romance, *Crouching Tiger, Hidden Dragon*. Most of its timber-framed, stone buildings date from the Ming or Qing eras. Of its three temples, **Gulong Si** is the largest, with a few slightly shabby halls and a low entrance guarded by two stone lions, above which is a theater stage used during temple fairs. At the other end of the village, **Nanwu Chaoxi Si** is a tiny nunnery with a painted stone carving of the dragon spirit Nanwu in human form, with red hair and a

mustache. **Zhenjiang Si** is mostly closed to the public, but does have a pleasant, relaxed riverfront teahouse.

# Qingcheng Shan ⑪
青城山

43 miles (70 km) NW of Chengdu. 🚌 from Chengdu. 🚃 to Dujiangyan then taxi. 🎫

As its name "Green City Mountain" suggests, this renowned Daoist retreat is beautifully forested. Its two separate sections are dotted with Daoist temples linked by stone paths, ideal for rambling. The front face is reached from the main entrance in town, while the wilder rear face, with steeper gradients and narrower paths, lies 9 miles (15 km) farther west. **Jianfu Gong**, outside the entrance, is the best-preserved shrine. The

main temple on the mountain's front face lies halfway up at **Tianshi Dong**. Ming-dynasty panels decorate its main hall, where the Han-era Daoist master Zhang Daolin once taught. Situated on the 4,134-ft (1,260-m) summit, two hours on foot and accessible by cable car, **Shangqing Gong** was first built in the 4th century AD and houses a tea-room. From here, it is a short climb to the **Laojun Pavilion**. On the lower slopes of the peak's rear face is the huge **Tai'an Temple**.

# Dujiangyan ⑫
都江堰

37 miles (60 km) NW of Chengdu. 🚌 from Chengdu. 🚃 from Xi Men Station, Chengdu. 🕐 8am–5pm daily. 🎫 for Irrigation Scheme Area.

The vast town of Dujiangyan is primarily known for the Dujiangyan Irrigation Scheme, built in 256 BC by the Sichuanese governor Li Bing. He organized the building of an artificial island to tame and divide the flood-prone Min Jiang into two channels which could be regulated and tapped to provide a steady flow for crop irrigation. Li Bing's project is still fully functional and was made a UNESCO World Heritage site in 2000, but it was affected by the construction of Zipingpu Dam, 9 miles (15 km) north. During the 2008 Sichuan earthquake, the dam cracked causing extensive damage to the town. Some scientists have

A ferry on the scenic Yuechang Hu (Moon Wall Lake) at Qingcheng Shan

◁ Crowds viewing Le Shan's Dafo (Great Buddha) from Nine Turn Staircase and upper platforms

**Songpan's east gate and impressive stone wall**

suggested that building work at the dam may have triggered the earthquake. **Erwang Miao** (Two Kings Temple) collapsed and is being rebuilt.

## Wanglang Nature Reserve ⑬
王朗自然保护区

186 miles (300 km) N of Chengdu. *Access via hired minibus from Pingwu.* **Tel** *(0816) 882 5312.* **http://** slack.net/~rd/wanglang/home.htm

Set in the heart of the Min Shan Mountains is this high-altitude nature reserve. Wanglang is remote and difficult to access, but there is a good chance of seeing rare animals here, including takin, musk deer, and serow, along with abundant birdlife. A few **pandas** inhabit the reserve, but unless you are extraordinarily lucky you are unlikely to encounter these elusive animals since they generally stay hidden deep inside Wanglang's impenetrable bamboo thickets.

From the research base and accommodation center (where rooms must be booked in advance), the 7-mile (12-km) long **Baisha Gou** road passes through old-growth pine forest and boggy moorlands to a scree-strewn alpine gully dotted with rhododendron thickets and splashes of hardy flowers. Alternatively, **Baixong Gou** is 6 miles (9 km) from camp via high ridges where goat-like serow and takin are sometimes seen. At the end of the road, there are board-walks through dense stands of bamboo and juniper.

## Songpan ⑭
松潘

137 miles (220 km) N of Chengdu. 🚌 *from Xi Men Station, Chengdu.*

Founded as a Ming-dynasty garrison post to guard a 8,200-ft (2,500-m) mountain pass, Songpan is an administrative center and busy marketplace for nearby Tibetan, Qiang, and Hui communities. It derives its ancient character from the surviving original cross-shaped street plan with high stone walls and its north, south, and east gates. Walled-in courtyards in front of the South Gate were once the "customs area" for searching caravans coming into town. Min Jiang, bisecting Songpan's center, is crossed by the covered **Gusong Qiao**, the Ancient Pine Bridge whose two-tiered roof is decorated with carved animals. Songpan's two large mosques, one in the center of town and the

**Lantern at the east gate, Songpan**

other along the river outside the north gate, resemble standard Chinese temples except in their use of green and yellow paint and the Arabic script over their doors. Shops sell beaten copper pots, turquoise jewelry, sheepskin coats, yak butter, and wind-dried yak meat. Just outside the north gate, two tour companies organize overnight guided horse treks to nearby villages. Sleeping arrangements are out in the open air or in tents and food is basic. Trekkers should have the itinerary and fees agreed, in writing, before setting off to avoid argument.

## Huanglong ⑮
黄龙

40 miles (65 km) W of Songpan. 🚌 *from Chengdu or Songpan.* 🎫 *Huanglong Temple Fair (Jul/Aug).*

Huanglong is a 5-mile (7.5-km) long valley, 9,845 ft (3,000 m) above sea level in the foothills of the snowcapped Min mountain range. Deposited minerals from the river descending the valley have created 12 terraced pools and calcified cascades, whose yellow rocks give Huanglong (Yellow Dragon) its name. Of the four nearly-ruined temples, the **Huanglong Temple**, at the valley's upper end, has a statue of Huanglong's patron saint, and hosts an annual temple fair featuring a horse race.

**Calcified terraces in Huanglong**

*For hotels and restaurants in this region see pp567–8 and pp593–4*

# Jiuzhai Gou Tour ⑯
## 九寨沟

**Mandarin duck**

One of China's most scenic reserves and a UNESCO World Heritage site, Jiuzhai Gou (Nine Stockades Gully) covers 280 sq miles (720 sq km) of mountain valleys dotted with Tibetan villages. Beneath the snow-capped mountains, the valley floors are strung with extraordinarily blue lakes, said to be the broken slivers of the Tibetan goddess Semo's mirror. Broad waterfalls, heavily encrusted with lime deposits, connect many of the lakes. Aside from herds of yaks, birds are the most evident wildlife, including rare mandarin ducks; a panda sighting is unlikely.

### Zharu Temple ①
This small temple, its interior adorned with bright murals, is looked after by just two monks.

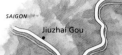

SAIGON
Jiuzhai Gou

### Nuorilang Falls ③
Jiuzhai Gou's most renowned cataract is best seen in full flood in late spring, when the water foams wildly in multiple ribbons over its stony outcrops.

### Pearl-Beach Falls ④
Water tumbles down a calcified slope, spraying pearl-like drops on its rocky ridges.

### Primeval Forest ⑤
An atmospheric coniferous forest at the far end of the reserve is far from crowds.

### Shuzheng Zhai ②
A Tibetan stockaded village, replete with Buddhist shrines and water-powered mills, sits halfway along a string of deep blue pools and reed beds.

```
0 kilometers    4
0 miles         4
```

**KEY**

▬▬ Tour route

═══ Other road

### Long Lake ⑦
This pool is not only the largest, but also the highest in the park, sitting at 10,170 feet (3,100 m).

### Five-colored Pool ⑥
Surrounded by a fringe of ferns and dark woods, this pool's kingfisher-blue depths are enhanced by green algae in the shallows, and milky-white swirls that seep in after rain.

The debris-laden Hailuo Gou Glacier descending the southeastern slopes of Gongga Shan

# Luding ⓲
泸定

143 miles (230 km) W of Chengdu.

The small market town of Luding is surrounded by mountains above the banks of Dadu Jiang. The 328-ft (100-m) **Luding Chain Bridge** over the Dadu, comprising 13 iron chains spanned by wooden planks, was built in 1705 to improve transportation through the region. The Luding Chain Bridge became a national icon in May 1935 due to an incident during the Long March (see p256). The Nationalist forces had removed the bridge's planks to trap the Red Army on the south side of the river, but "22 Heroes" clambered along the chains and managed to capture a Nationalist camp on the opposite side. The

The historic Luding Bridge, flanked by two gateways

bridge is flanked on either side by gateways, while a museum on the river's far side exhibits contemporary photos.

# Moxi Xiang & Hailuo Gou Glacier ⓲
磨西和海螺沟

28 miles (45 km) SW of Luding.
Treks organized by hotels.

The tiny town of Moxi Xiang, with its large Qiang population, is a staging post for trekking up the adjacent Hailou Gou (Conch Valley) to the Hailou Gou Glacier, whose tongue, at 12,205 ft (3,720 m), makes it the lowest and most accessible glacier in Asia. Moxi's wooden church sheltered the Red Army in 1935, before they attempted crossing the passes over Daxue Shan – Great Snow Mountain – during which a third of the army died (see p256). The glacier descends the southeastern side of Sichuan's highest peak, the 24,790-ft (7,556-m) Gongga Shan. The three-day return trek passes rhododendron forests before reaching the glacier's snout, blackened by debris. Its upper reaches comprise tumbled blocks of blue-green ice, while a hot spring mixes with icy glacial streams to provide pools for bathing.

Moxi's early 20th-century church

# Kangding ⓲
康定

31 miles (50 km) W of Luding.
from Xin Nan Men Station, Chengdu.

Lying between China and Tibet, Kangding is a bustling trading depot situated in a valley on the Zhepuo River. During the Qing era, the town developed on the tea trade between Tibet and China and was the place where porters would exchange bricks of tea for Tibetan goods such as wool and copperware. Ethnically, the region is inhabited largely by the Khampa, a Tibetan people whose heavy turquoise jewelry, forward manners, and habit of carrying knives match their reputation for toughness. The central **Anjue Lamasery** is a focus for the Khampa community. The town also has a handful of Qiang, Hui, and Han Chinese. To the southeast, Paoma Shan (Horse Race Mountain) is the venue for the Walking Around the Mountain festival, which takes place in the 4th calendar month of the Chinese year, and where the Khampa demonstrate their equestrian skills during horse races. Heading west from Kangding, it is 311 miles (500 km) to the fringes of Tibet, with a worthwhile stop at Dege town and its Scripture Printing Lamasery.

# YUNNAN

Located along China's southwest frontier, Yunnan offers an unmatched diversity of landscapes, climate, and people. The Tibetan highland frames its northwestern fringes; tropical rainforests and volcanic plains lie to its south. In the center are plains and hills, crisscrossed by some of Asia's great rivers – the Yangzi, Salween, and Mekong.

The seat of the pastoral Dian Kingdom founded in the 3rd century BC, Yunnan was for centuries an isolated frontier region that resisted Han influences and upheld local identities. Even today, the province is home to a third of China's ethnic minorities and has much in common with neighboring Myanmar, Laos, and Vietnam.

The province's capital, Kunming, is one of the more relaxed cities in China; nearby are the astonishing rock formations of the Stone Forest (Shi Lin). Several minority villages dot the tropical forests of Xishuangbanna, while in the north, Dali is home to the indigenous Bai people. Farther north is the UNESCO World Heritage Site of Lijiang, capital of the Naxi Kingdom, with cobbled streets and ancient architecture. Tiger Leaping Gorge, an impressive, steep-sided ravine, offers superb, accessible two-day hikes.

Kunming is well connected to the rest of China, but the bulk of the province has only limited train services. Bus travel is necessary to access most of Yunnan.

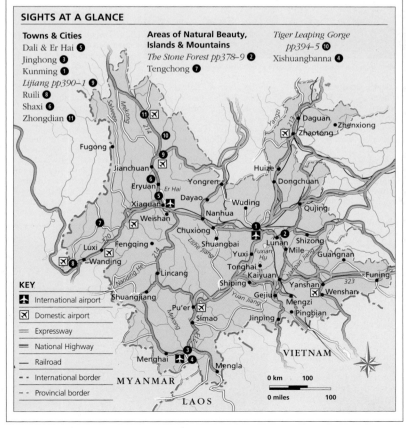

## SIGHTS AT A GLANCE

**Towns & Cities**
Dali & Er Hai ⑤
Jinghong ③
Kunming ①
*Lijiang pp390–1* ⑨
Ruili ⑧
Shaxi ⑥
Zhongdian ⑪

**Areas of Natural Beauty, Islands & Mountains**
*The Stone Forest pp378–9* ②
Tengchong ⑦

*Tiger Leaping Gorge pp394–5* ⑩
Xishuangbanna ④

**KEY**

| ✈ | International airport |
| ✕ | Domestic airport |
| = | Expressway |
| = | National Highway |
| — | Railroad |
| - - | International border |
| - - | Provincial border |

0 km          100

0 miles          100

◁ **9th-century Qianxun Ta** *(right)*, **the oldest of the three elegant pagodas (San Ta) on the outskirts of Dali**

# Kunming ❶

昆明

**Sutra Pillar, City Museum**

The capital of Yunnan province, Kunming rests at 6,500 ft (2,000 m) above sea level. Its clement weather and floral wealth have earned it the nickname "City of Eternal Spring." An ancient city that first came to prominence as part of the Nanzhao Kingdom *(see p388)*, Kunming had grown into a thriving city with a cosmopolitan character by the 13th century. Kunming is fast becoming indistinguishable from the redeveloped metropolises found throughout the country, but it is still considered one of China's more laid-back cities, with lakeside vistas just to the south.

**Modern high-rise architecture has come to dominate Kunming's center**

### ❧ Cui Hu Gongyuan

67 Cui Hu Nan Lu. ◯ *daily.*
Northwest of the city, this park has pavilions and bridges, and its lotus-filled ponds are visited by migrant red-beaked gulls in winter. Just west of the park, the old **French Legation** now holds temporary exhibitions. To the northwest is the university district, with its student cafés.

### ⛩ Yuantong Si

30 Yuantong Jie. **Tel** (0871) 519 3762.
◯ *8am–5:20pm daily.*
At the foot of Yuantong Hill lies Yunnan's largest Buddhist complex and a popular pilgrimage spot. Renovated and rebuilt many times, it has an imposing Ming gateway, while a bridge over the central pond crosses through a Qing-era pavilion. Enshrined here is a 6-ft (3-m) golden statue of Maitreya Buddha. Behind the pavilion, the Ming-dynasty Great Hall of the Buddha has two wooden dragons on its main pillars, referring to a legend that the temple was built to pacify a dragon living

in the pond. A Thai-style hall behind holds a marble statue of Sakyamuni, donated by the King of Thailand. At the back of the temple is a cliff cut with steps allowing a view of religious poems and sayings carved into the rock.

### 🛕 Bird & Flower Market

The many stalls lining the crammed alleyways off Jingxing Jie sell an eclectic variety

of goods. Splayed out in colorful rows at the huge pet market are a wealth of bird, fish, and animal species, while the antique and curio booths sell souvenirs such as *tai ji quan* swords, jewelry, old coins, bamboo pipes, and Cultural Revolution mementos.

### ⛩ Provincial Museum

Corner of Dongfeng Xi Lu & Wuyi Lu.
**Tel** (0871) 617 9535. ◯ *9:30am–5pm Tue–Sun.* **www**.ynbwg.cn
The second floor of this museum houses splendid bronze drums *(see p423)* excavated from tombs on the shore of Lake Dian and dating back more than 2,000 years to the Warring States and Western Han periods. The drums are embellished with relief dioramas, largely showing typical scenes of rural life, although there are also wrestling scenes, a dramatic image of an ox battling a tiger, and a strange picture of a bamboo house transformed into a coffin. The most ornate of the drums were used to store cowry shells, then a form of currency. The others served as musical instruments or elements in sacrificial rites. Even today, bronze drums play an important role at weddings, festivals, and funerals for some of Yunnan's minority groups. Another hall holds bronze and wooden Buddhist statues from various periods. Upstairs, an exhibition on pre-history displays human remains and plaster models of armored fish.

**Pavilions on the fish-filled waters of Cui Hu Gongyuan**

### Zhenqing Guan

Cnr of Tuodong Lu & Chuncheng Lu.
8:30am–5pm.

Located near the City Museum, this restored complex of stone courtyards and smartly painted halls was founded in 1419 to honor the Taoist warrior deity Zhen Wu. Today it is full of friendly monks in black, blue, and white robes, their hair pinned up in buns. The largest temple in Kunming, Zhenqing Guan has five entrances and three courtyards. The gateway is guarded by a fierce golden statue of three-eyed Wan Ling Guan, the protector spirit, wearing a severed demon's head as a belt buckle and brandishing an iron pagoda to scare off evil. Inside, the main hall features an intricately bracketed domed ceiling and murals of the Taoist pantheon, while the adjacent Dulei mansion is dominated by a statue of the Thunder God and a model of the globe wrapped in animals of the zodiac. The complex sometimes hosts musicians, including a full traditional Chinese orchestra.

### Xi Si Ta

Dong Si Jie. 7am–8pm.

The 13-storied Tang-era Xi Si Ta (Western Pagoda) has statues in the niches of each story. Close by, Dong Si Ta (Eastern Pagoda) is a more attractive replica standing in a garden. Although visitors cannot enter the temples associated with both pagodas, a small fee permits entry into Xi Si Ta's courtyard, where people come to relax on sunny afternoons. Both pagodas are surrounded by small parks, with the Eastern park offering more greenery.

### City Museum

71 Tuodong Lu. **Tel** (0871) 315 3256.
10am–5pm Tue–Sun.

Though less interesting than the Provincial Museum, this museum houses a few relevant artifacts. The most striking is the Song-dynasty **Dali Sutra Pillar**, a 20-ft (7-m) sculpture in pink sandstone, commissioned by the Dali king, Yuan Douguang, in honor of General Gao Ming.

Seven tiers swarm with lively images of guardian gods and captive demons, and at the top is a ring of Buddhas holding up the universe. On the upper floors are bronze drums, a display on Kunming, and five locally-found dinosaur skeletons, including an allosaur and a *Yunnanosaurus robustus*.

Skeleton of *Dilophosaurus*, City Museum

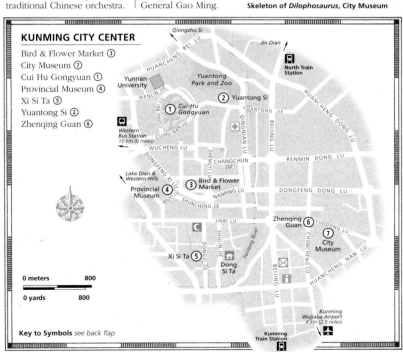

## KUNMING CITY CENTER

Bird & Flower Market ③
City Museum ⑦
Cui Hu Gongyuan ①
Provincial Museum ④
Xi Si Ta ⑤
Yuantong Si ②
Zhenqing Guan ⑥

Qiongzhu Si
Jin Dian
North Train Station
HUANCHENG BEI LU
Yuantong Park and Zoo
Yunnan University
WENLIN JIE
② Yuantong Si
YUANTONG JIE
① Cui Hu Gongyuan
CUIHU BEI LU
CUIHU NAN LU
QINGNIAN LU
BEIJING LU
HUANCHENG DONG LU
Western Bus Station 10 km (6 miles)
WUCHENG LU
ZHENGYILU
RENMIN DONG LU
Lake Dian & Western Hills
DONGFENG XI LU
CHANGCHUN LU
Provincial Museum ④
③ Bird & Flower Market
NANPING LU
DONGFENG DONG LU
WUYI LU
SHUNCHENG JIE
JINBI LU
Panlong River
Zhenqing Guan ⑥
TUODONG LU
⑦ City Museum
CHUNCHENG LU
SHULIN JIE
DONGSI JIE
BEIJING LU
HUANCHENG NAN LU
Xi Si Ta ⑤
Dong Si Ta

0 meters 800
0 yards 800

Kunming Wujiaba Airport 4 km (2.5 miles)
Kunming Train Station

**Key to Symbols** see back flap

The double-eaved Jin Dian, entirely made of bronze

## Jin Dian

7 miles (12 km) NE of Kunming.
No. 10, 6, 71, 76 from Kunming's North Train Station. daily.

Well-kept flower gardens and leafy pine woods are reason enough to visit this secluded spot in the city's northeastern suburbs. However, the park's ostensible focus is the Jin Dian (Golden Temple) located on top of its central hill. Originally built in 1602 during the Ming Dynasty, and rebuilt in 1671 as the summer residence of the Qing rebel general, Wu Sangui, this unusual two-tiered shrine is made entirely of bronze. Its overall construction imitates the more conventional wooden temples, with screens, columns, and flying eaves. Just over 20-ft (6-m) high and weighing nearly 300 tons (272,155 kg), the temple sits atop a base of Dali marble and is almost completely black with the patina of age. In the courtyard stand ancient camellia trees, one of which is 600 years old. The main hall, with bronze lattices, beams, and statues, houses two magical swords used by Daoist warriors. Fragrant with camellias, the gardens here serve as popular picnic spots. Visitors can either take a bus or hire a bike to reach the base of the hill, from where it's an easy hike uphill to the temple.

Situated on the hill behind Jin Dian is another Daoist shrine with a tower that houses a 14-ton (12,700-kg) bronze bell. Dating to 1423, it was retrieved from Kunming's demolished southern gates.

## Qiongzhu Si

7 miles (12 km) NW of Kunming.
from K.ming's Western bus station. 8am–5pm daily.

The Tang-era Qiongzhu Si (Bamboo Temple) was burned down and subsequently rebuilt in the 15th century. Today, this elegant Buddhist structure, with fine black and red woodwork, stands on Yuan-dynasty foundations. Besides housing three impressive Buddha statues, the temple is famous for its dazzling array of life-size clay sculptures, created over ten years toward the end of the 19th century by a supremely talented Sichuan sculptor, Li Guangxiu. The sculptor and his five assistants were commissioned to produce clay figures of the 500 *arhat* or *luo han* (those freed from the cycle of birth and death) for the main building. Today, these sculptures are the highlight of the temple, though at that time they were regarded as so distressing that Li Guangxiu was forbidden from ever working again. Along one wall a set of snarling, outlandish figures – one with arms longer than his body, another with eyebrows to his knees – ride foaming waves swarming with sea creatures. Elsewhere, three shelves of figures depict Buddhist virtues and faults. Many aspects of human life and folly are depicted in these beautiful characters: reaching for the moon, playing with a pet monster, yawning, debating, and eating a peach. While Li Guangxiu's skill at rendering facial expressions and gestures makes these figures unique, many are thought to be caricatures of his contemporaries, probably the reason they were so disliked at the time.

Also worth a glance is a 14th-century stone tablet, housed in the main hall. It records imperial China's dealings with Yunnan in Chinese and Mongolian scripts. A good vegetarian restaurant lies within the temple grounds.

An aerial view of the extensive Qiongzhu Si (Bamboo Temple)

*For hotels and restaurants in this region see pp568–9 and pp594–5*

Haigeng Park viewed against the expanse of Lake Dian

## Lake Dian & the Western Hills

from Kunming. daily.

The 25-mile (40-km) long Lake Dian (Dian Chi), just south of Kunming, is lined with fishing villages and is very pretty. Plying the waters of the elongated lake are *fanchuan*, traditional junks with bamboo masts and square canvas sails, used for fishing. **Daguan Pavilion** on the north shore has good views of the area, while a few miles south is **Haigeng Park** with green willows and eucalyptuses.

The most rewarding way to see the lake is from the Western Hills (Xi Shan), about 10 miles (16 km) southwest of Kunming. The undulating contours of the "Sleeping Beauty Hills" are said to resemble a reclining woman with tresses flowing into the lake. The path leading to the summit holds a treasury of temples. Visitors can either climb up or take a minibus. The first temple, a mile (2 km) from the entrance, is **Huating Si**. Designed originally as a country retreat for Gao Zhishen, who ruled Kunming in the 11th century, it has been rebuilt several times. The attractive gardens, dotted with stupas and ponds, contain interesting figures, including the four fierce-looking Guardians of the Directions, the gilded, blue-haired Buddhas, and a set of 500 *arhat*.

From Huating Si, a steep, winding road leads deep into the forest for 1 mile (2 km) to **Taihua Si**, established by Xuan Jian, a wandering Chan (Zen) Buddhist monk in 1306, and dedicated to Guanyin, the Goddess of Compassion. It is

well known for its garden of camellias and magnolias, and excellent views. Another 20-minute walk up the hill leads to **Sanqing Si**, a complex of temples, halls, and pavilions, which formerly served as a summer palace for a

A picturesque pavilion with a pond and garden, Taihua Si

14th-century Mongolian prince. It was converted to a Daoist shrine in the 18th century.

Just half a mile away is the **Dragon Gate Grotto**, a set of chambers, steps, and tunnels excavated from the mountain. The mammoth construction task, which involved swinging from ropes and hacking at the rock with chisels, was begun by the late 18th century monk Wu Laiqing, and took 70 years to complete. Worth exploring along the way are niches with several fantastic statues, including those of Guanyin and the Gods of Study and Virtue. A cable car runs from near Sanqing Si to the summit at **Grand Dragon Gate**, a balcony perched at 8,200 ft (2,500 m), from where there are fine views over Lake Dian.

### THE BURMA ROAD

For 1,500 years, the southern Silk Route ran through Yunnan, across Burma, and into India, traversing thick jungle and bandit-ridden mountains. In the 1930s, the Chinese government, driven west by the invading Japanese, reopened the route to use as a supply line into China from Burma. The 684-mile (1,100-km) road was built by 300,000 laborers, with primitive tools, and connected Kunming with the British railhead at Lashio in Burma. After the beginning of World War II, it became a strategic lifeline for the Allied troops, bringing in food, arms, and medical supplies. Provisions arrived by rail from Rangoon, and were then trucked to China on this route. After the Japanese occupied Lashio in 1942, another road, built under the command of US General Stilwell (*see p351*), linked Ledo in India to the Burma Road at Bhamo.

The Burma Road in the 1930s, snaking through the hills

# The Stone Forest ❷
石林

Celebrated as a natural wonder, the limestone pillars
of the Stone Forest (Shi Lin) are Yunnan's most
visited sight. The bizarre, tightly-packed formations, some
as tall as 100 feet (30 m), have been given imaginative
names such as "Rhinoceros Gazing at the Moon" and
"Everlasting Fungus." Resembling a petrified forest, the
area is shot through with winding pathways, ponds, and
look-out points. So popular is this place that the central
paths can get clogged with tour groups. Head to the
edges of the forest to find a quiet corner, but keep in
mind that it is easy to get lost in this otherworldly
landscape. For a more ethereal experience, spend the
night and explore when it's deserted and eerily lit.

★ **Wangfeng Ting** ③
*Many of the paths lead to the
central Peak Viewing Pavilion, a good meeting point,
with views over the forest to
help you gain your bearings.*

**Xiao Shi Lin** ①
*The Minor Stone Forest, a smaller rock cluster to the north
of the main forest, is a little quieter. Each evening Sami
minority dances are performed at an amphitheater here.*

Fluted shape created
by retreating water

**Ode to Plum Blossom** ②
*Many of the rocks are cut
with calligraphy, including
one of Mao Zedong's most
loved poems, executed in his
elegant flowing script.*

## SHI LIN'S FORMATION
Fossils found in the area
reveal that Shi Lin was
underwater during the
Permian period, 270 million
years ago. The retreating sea
left a limestone seabed that
has been eroded since by
wind and rain into today's
weird, twisted shapes.

## THE SANI

The area around Shi Lin is home to
the Sani, one of the many subgroups
of the Yi minority. Spread throughout
the Southwest, the Yi have their own
written language, with six dialects,
and numerous tracts on medicine,
history, and the genealogy of ruling
families. Much of Yi society was
feudal well into the 20th century, and
some groups still practice shamanism.
The Sani are known for their embroidery, widely available at Shi Lin,
and many local Sani work at the
forest as tour guides and dancers.

A Sani tour guide,
posing at Shi Lin

### STAR SIGHTS

★ Wangfeng Ting

★ Jianfeng Chi

**★ Jianfeng Chi ④**
*This ornamental pool is ringed by jagged ridges. A narrow walkway runs from here across the top of the forest.*

**Wife Waiting for Husband ⑤**
*This formation, reminiscent of a woman waiting impatiently, sits in the quiet area right at the back of the forest, on the route of the overhead walkway.*

**The wavy shapes** and thin edges were created by chemicals in standing water dissolving the limestone.

Sharp edge or *karren*

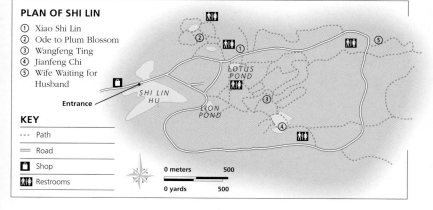

**PLAN OF SHI LIN**

① Xiao Shi Lin
② Ode to Plum Blossom
③ Wangfeng Ting
④ Jianfeng Chi
⑤ Wife Waiting for Husband

Entrance

LOTUS POND

SHI LIN HU

LION POND

**KEY**

--- Path

═ Road

🔲 Shop

🚻 Restrooms

0 meters    500
0 yards     500

Dai women selling vegetables in a busy market, Jinghong

# Jinghong ❸
景洪

420 miles (690 km) SW of Kunming. 🚹 363,000. ✈ 🚌 ℹ️ *Luandian Lu, (0691) 212 4479.*

The tropical region of Xishuangbanna, in the far south of Yunnan, resembles its neighbors, Myanmar and Laos, more than dynamic modern China. Jinghong, its sleepy capital, was founded in the 12th century by the Dai warlord Dazhen. It is today an incongruous mix of concrete architecture and palm-lined streets. With an attractively torpid pace of life, it is an ideal introduction to the region and its indigenous Dai culture *(see opposite)*.

**Manting Wat**, situated southeast of the city center, is Xishuangbanna's largest Buddhist temple. Built entirely of wood and raised off the ground on stilts, it has a simple interior, with vivid frescoes illustrating Buddhist themes. Next door is a school where Dai boys learn Buddhist lore. Behind the temple, **Chunhuan Park**, once the quarters for royal slaves, is a lush place with numerous resident peacocks. There are several paths leading across the tiny river to replicas of temples and pagodas. A shop here sells live fish for people to release into the river and thus gain merit.

**Budding plant, Tropical Flower & Plant Garden**

Located in the west of town, off Jinghong Xi Lu, is the lovely **Tropical Flower & Plant Garden**, a must-see for anyone interested in the incredibly diverse flora of the region. It is bursting with a wealth of tropical plants – over 1,000 species – quite a few with labels in English. In the early afternoon, tour groups are entertained by vibrant displays of traditional Dai dancing. A prominent statue of Zhou Enlai *(see p250)* commemorates a summit he held here with the Burmese leader U Nu in 1961 to defuse border tensions.

### 🏯 Manting Wat
Manting Lu. ⭕ *8am–7pm daily.* 📷

### 🌸 Tropical Flower & Plant Garden
28 Jinghong Xi Lu. ⭕ *daily.* 📷

**Environs:** Located 20 miles (30 km) southeast of Jinghong, **Ganlanba** makes a good base for exploring the surrounding area. In the southeast of town, the **Dai Minority Park** is a collection of refurbished Dai villages, with traditional bamboo and wood houses raised on stilts. Near the park's center stands the 700-year-old, gilded **Wat Ben Pagoda**. The town's main attraction, however, is its picturesque setting in lush jungle beside the Mekong River. Several cafés here offer advice on walks and bike rental.

The popular **Sanchahe Elephant Reserve**, 30 miles (50 km) north of Jinghong, is home to a herd of 50-or-so wild elephants. Visitors are not allowed to wander off the paths without a guide. Raised treetop walkways allow for observing the wild elephants, while a chairlift provides a real bird's-eye view. Near the southern entrance is a bird and butterfly zoo. The reserve's frequent elephant displays are best avoided, since the animals are coaxed into performing with spears.

A visit to **Banla Village**, 24 miles (38 km) west of Jinghong, is the most accessible way to experience Hani culture (one of the four subgroups of Xishuangbanna Dai). The village is attractive with typical Dai houses overlooking rice terraces and tea plantations. Besides dance recitals held at the village hall, visitors can also see the distinctive Hani dress, with embroidered tunics, silver breastplates, and ornate headdresses.

The lush Tropical Flower & Plant Garden, Jinghong

◁ Pavilion in the midst of Black Dragon Pool backed by majestic Jade Dragon Snow Mountain, Lijiang

# The Dai

**Silver elephant-shaped brooch**

In China, the Dai people live in the lush lands of Xishuangbanna. Once spread as far north as the Yangzi Valley, the Dai were driven south during the 13th century by Mongol expansion, and are now found throughout Thailand, Laos, Myanmar, and Vietnam. The Dai in all of these countries share a similar culture, following Theravada Buddhism rather than Mahayana, the Buddhist school practiced in much of the rest of China, and speaking their own language with its own script.

Known as skillful farmers, the Dai have always flourished in fertile river basins, growing rice, sugar cane, rubber trees, and bananas. Dai cuisine is well worth trying, with sweet flavors not found elsewhere in China. Rice is steamed inside bamboo or pineapple, and exotic specialties include ant eggs and fried moss.

**Traditional Dai homes** *are made of bamboo and raised on stilts, with the livestock penned underneath and generations of the same family living above. The well outside will likely have a shrine over it, water being sacred to Dai culture.*

**Dai women** *traditionally wear a sarong or long skirt, a bodice, and a jacket. Hair is tied up, fixed with a comb, and often ornamented with flowers. Gold-capped teeth are considered attractive and married women wear silver wrist bands.*

**Many Dai men** *have impressive tattoos of animals, flowers, geometric patterns, or Dai script. Traditionally, when a boy reaches 12 years, he has his torso and limbs decorated. This rite of passage has largely died out in mainstream Dai culture, but it is still undertaken in some very rural areas.*

**Markets in rural** *Dai homelands offer the only opportunity for some to buy products they can not produce themselves. Huge social occasions usually held on a Monday, they attract villagers for miles around. A lot of hard bargaining – as well as gossip and flirting – goes on.*

## WATER SPLASHING FESTIVAL

Originally a solemn Buddhist rite celebrating the defeat of a demon, Poshui Jie, the Water Splashing Festival, is today a joyous and hedonistic carnival. Water is liberally hurled at friend and stranger alike, and becoming thoroughly drenched is seen as fortuitous. The festival also features a massive market on the first day; dragon boat racing, fireworks, elephant and peacock displays on the second; and the biggest drenching of all, along with much singing and dancing on the third.

**Yunnan's Water Splashing Festival a celebration in mid-April, usually the 13th to the 16th**

# Xishuangbanna 4

## 西双版纳

**Bai woman at market**

In climate and culture, the subtropical far south of Yunnan, Xishuangbanna, feels a part of southeast Asia. Much of the area is primeval rainforest, the last left in the country, and home to a huge diversity of flora and fauna, including a third of China's bird population. A third of the population is Dai (*see p383*); another third is made up of the numerous other minorities. Most of the population lives in small villages and the area's appeal lies in the opportunity to hop between towns, explore the countryside by bike, and trek through the jungle.

**Pillar-like palm trees at Menglun's Botanic Gardens**

## EAST TO LAOS

This route travels through cultivated flat lands and then highland forest to the Laotian border, which you can cross, provided you have the required visa.

The small settlement of **Manting**, a few miles east of Ganlanba (*see p382*) is full of traditional wooden Dai houses. The town's **Fo Si** and **Du Ta** are excellent reconstructions of 12th-century temples destroyed in the Cultural Revolution.

Three hours east by bus lies **Menglun**, a dusty couple of streets beside the Luosuo Jiang. The superb **Botanic Gardens**, across a suspension bridge on the opposite bank, were set up to research medicinal uses of local plants. With over 3,000 different species, there's plenty to see, even for the not-so-botanically minded, including the celebrated Dragons' Blood Trees whose sap is used to

heal wounds, as well as bamboo and ancient cycad groves. Stay the night, in the small hotel within the gardens.

Leaving the farms behind, the road to **Mengla** travels through a great tract of thick tropical jungle, the largest of Xishuangbanna's five wildlife preserves, which gives way to rubber plantations. Mengla itself is a rather drab and unattractive town.

A short taxi ride north of Mengla, the **Bupan Aerial Walkway**, a chain of slender bridges 130 feet (40 m) in the tree canopy, allows for unrivaled views of the jungle below. It's another 9 miles (15 km) to the Yao minority village of **Yaoqu**. There's a hostel, and from here it is possible to trek into some very remote regions – you're advised to hire a guide.

**Shangyong** is the last village before the Laos border and though not really worthy of a

trip in itself, it's interesting as Xishuangbanna's Miao center (*see pp406–7*).

🌿 **Botanic Gardens**
Menglun. ⬜ 8:30am–6pm daily. 🅿️

🌿 **Bupan Aerial Walkway**
19 miles (30 km) N of Mengla.
⬜ 8:30am–6pm daily. 🅿️

## WEST TO MYANMAR

Western Xishuangbanna is less developed than the east, with rougher roads and sketchier transport. The many fascinating villages inhabited entirely by minorities, however, make the rigors of travel worthwhile.

Sprawling **Menghai** is unremarkable, but useful as a base for exploring villages and the countryside by bike. It's renowned for its *pu'er* tea and hosts a lively Sunday market.

The monastery at **Jingzhen** is known for its *busu*, an octagonal pavilion for delivering sermons. The main temple has beautiful decorative wall paintings. A bit farther on at **Mengzhe**, the hilltop **Manlei Si** is a bizarre-looking, frilly octagon built in the 18th century, which holds an important collection of *sutras* written on palm fiber. **Xiding**, an attractive Hani village, holds a large Thursday market.

**Gelanghe** is dominated by the Hani, whose women wear elaborate silver headdresses. A sub-group, the Ake, who wear

**Picking *pu'er* tea, outside Menghai**

**Life of the Buddha wallpaintings, Jingzhen monastic complex**

**Manfeilong Ta, supposed to resemble emerging bamboo shoots**

their long hair in braids, live in a settlement just north of town on the way to the lake.

Heading south towards the border, **Menghun** is a sleepy town with a huge Sunday market, beginning at dawn and over by noon. Most participants are Dai, but you will also see Hani and Bulang. There's also a rather run-down 19th-century monastery in town.

The border town of **Daluo** is the end of the line for westerners who are not allowed to travel to Myanmar, unless

being met at the border as part of an official tour. The cross-border market, which attracts hill tribes and Burmese traders, makes the trip to this outpost worth it.

## DAMENGLONG TO BULANG SHAN

**Damenglong**, 44 miles (70 km) south of Jinghong, comes alive on market days and is a popular spot for trekking and temple hopping. On the way, it's worth stopping at **Gasa** to explore **Manguanglong Si**, a monastery with a lovely dragon-shaped stairway.

**Manfeilong Ta** is a half-hour walk north of Damenglong and its nine graceful spires make it the most impressive of the local temples. Built in 1204 to enshrine what is purported to be Buddha's footprint, it is popular with Buddhist pilgrims and is the center of festivities during the Tan Ta Festival in late October or early November. Another Buddhist monument, **Hei Ta**, is rather run-down, but set in a very pleasant location.

The **walk to Bulang Shan** is a simple, well-established three-day walk along the Nana Jiang and its tributaries, passing through dense jungle

and villages of the Dai, Hani, Bulang, and Lahu minorities. Hire a guide and be careful not to stray off the path into Myanmar. From Damenglong it's 6 miles (10 km) to the Dai village of **Manguanghan**, then a further 8 miles (13 km) to the Bulang village of **Manpo**, which makes a good place to spend the night. The next day is a 14-mile (22-km) tramp through heavy jungle on winding paths to **Weidong**, and the following day is an easy hike of 6 miles (10 km) along the road to Bulang Shan, which offers rudimentary accommodations and a daily bus to Menghai.

### TIPS FOR EXPLORERS

*Getting around:* Cars with drivers are available in Jinghong. Local buses are frequent along main roads. Bikes can be hired from cafés in the touristed areas.
*Trekking:* Numerous trekking organizations are based in Jinghong. A guide is recommended for jungle treks. This is a sensitive border region – do not walk unguided near the Myanmar border. Take plenty of water, sunscreen, a raincoat, a hat, and a first aid kit.
*Accommodation:* Basic accommodation is available in most villages, sometimes in locals' homes.

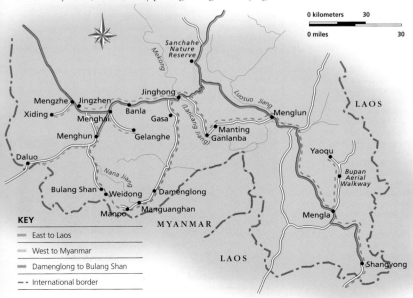

# Dali & Er Hai ❺

大理 和 洱海湖

"Dali" inscribed at
South Gate

Sandwiched between Er Hai to the east and the Cang Shan range to the west, the picturesque little town of Dali draws innumerable visitors. The old town, surrounded by the remains of the Ming city walls, is characterized by cobbled lanes and stone houses. In the nearby countryside, numerous Bai villages offer a glimpse into traditional culture, and are particularly interesting on market days. Other activities include hiking in the mountains, and watching traditional cormorant fishing on Er Hai. The best time to visit is during the Spring Fair, when hundreds of Bai come for five days of bare-back horse racing, wrestling, dancing, and singing.

Looking north over the city's rooftops from Nancheng Men

## Exploring Dali

Dali's old town center, just 1.5 sq miles (4 sq km) across, can be explored in a single morning. It takes about half an hour to walk from the South Gate to the North Gate across town. There is plenty to interest visitors, from small souvenir shops to teahouses and traditional masseurs. Crowds of shoppers and farmers also arrive here for the weekly Friday market. The best vantage point is at the top of Nancheng Men (South Gate), from where there are views to Er Hai and Cang Shan.

## Huguo Lu & Fuxing Lu

Running east-west through the center of town, Huguo Lu, nicknamed Foreigners' Street, is full of guesthouses and cafés that serve pizzas and cappuccinos. Most of the old town's sights lie along the main north-south artery, Fuxing Lu. The Drum Tower, lying close

to the Dali Museum, once signalled the close of the city gates each evening. Farther north along Fuxing Lu, the square outside the library is a popular venue for a game of cards or dominoes. Still farther is the quiet Yu'er Park, full of fruit trees and ponds, while tucked away in the streets to its north is Dali's Catholic church, with a Tang-era tiled roof and painted gables.

## 🏛 Dali Museum

8 Erhe Nan Lu. *Tel* (0872) 267 0196.
⬭ 8:30am–5pm daily.
Just inside Nancheng Men, the Dali Museum was originally the mansion of the Qing governor, and later served as the headquarters of Du Wen Xiu, leader of the 1856–1873 Muslim Uprising. It is worth visiting for its tranquil courtyards, filled with bougainvillea and lantana. The huge bronze bell hanging outside in a pavilion came from the old Bell Tower. Inside, the most interesting relics are a collection of Buddhist figurines from the Nanzhao Kingdom (*see p388*), and statues of serving girls and an orchestra excavated from a Ming-dynasty tomb. A hall at the back houses copies of scroll paintings, including one depicting the founding of the Nanzhao Kingdom.

## 🏯 San Ta

1 mile (2 km) NW of Dali. *Tel* (0872) 2666 6107. 🖥 www.dalisanta.net
The distinctive San Ta (Three Pagodas) that symbolize Dali stand within the monastery of Chongwen Si, which was destroyed during the Qing dynasty and rebuilt in 2005. A 20-minute walk or short bus ride north of town, the pagodas are best visited early. The 16-tiered, square-based **Qianxun Ta** is the tallest of the three at 230 ft (70 m), and is also the oldest, dating to around AD 800. Each tier is embellished with fine marble figures. Buddhist relics including *sutras* (scriptures), copper mirrors, and gold ornaments were found during a renovation in 1979, and are displayed in a museum behind

The Dali Museum, set in picturesque grounds

*For hotels and restaurants in this region see pp568–9 and pp594–5*

The splendid San Ta just north of town

the pagodas. The two smaller octagonal pagodas were built in the 11th century, and are 138 ft (42 m) high. As well as serving as reliquaries, they were built to appease the gods and thus gain protection against natural disasters. The characters inscribed in front of the Qianxun Ta read "subdue forever mountains and rivers."

### Zhonghe Si
W of Dali. 🚠
Situated an hour's walk from town, Zhonghe Si can be reached by heading past the small bridge to the north of Dali into the cedar and eucalyptus woods at the foothills of Zhonghe Feng. From here, zigzag paths lead up the mountain to the temple. An easier approach is via the chairlift from the main road. Originally built in the Ming-era, the temple has been reconstructed and serves both Daoists and Buddhists. The views from here over the lake and town are superb. Locals offer horse trips farther up the mountain, and for the ambitious, there is a 6-mile (9-km) hike along a stone path to **Wuwei Si**, where monks study *tai ji quan*. Visitors can stay the night before heading back.

### Guanyin Si & Gantong Si
Approx 3 miles (5 km) S of Dali.
Dedicated to the Buddhist Goddess of Compassion, Guanyin Si sits at the foot of Foding Shan. It has a colorful entrance, and within the grounds are fine wood and stone carvings. At the back of the temple, a 2-mile (3-km) path leads uphill to Gantong Si. Alternatively, you can hike the spectacular 7-mile (11-km) Jade Belt trail from Zhonghe Si. Once, Gantong Si was the largest shrine in the area. Today, despite only two partially-restored halls surviving, the temple remains impressive.

*Map showing the Er Hai region with locations including Lijiang, Shaping, Zhoucheng, Xizhou, Wase, Xia Putuo, Er Hai, Wuwei Si, San Ta, Caicun, Haidong, Zhonghe Si, Dali Old Town, Jinsuo Dao, Xiadui, Yinsuo Dao, Zhonghe Feng, Guanyin Si, Cang Shan, Gantong Si, Foding Feng, Xiaguan Airport, Er Hai Park, Xiaguan (Dali New City), Baoshan, Kunming, Lincang*

0 km    5
0 miles    5

### KEY
- - Hiking trail
🚠 Cable car
🛕 Temple

A bustling market at one of the many towns around Dali

A fisherman and his cormorants in Er Hai's jade waters, Dali

### Er Hai

*daily.*

Located 2 miles (3 km) east of Dali, Er Hai (Ear Lake), a symbol of natural fecundity to the Bai, is named after its shape. The 25-mile (40-km) long lake has numerous ferry services and is home to 50-odd species of fish. Any café in Dali can arrange a tour on the lake; most trips usually involve visits to small temples, or excursions to scenic spots on the eastern shore. Visitors can also accompany a cormorant fisherman *(see p418)* and watch the trained birds catch fish. A variety of tour boats, from big, virtual floating pagodas for large groups, to smaller craft, leave from Caicun on Er Hai's western shore.

Tours usually take in **Jinsuo Dao**, across the lake near its eastern shore. Once a summer retreat for Nanzhao royalty, it is now home to a fishing village. Farther north lies **Xia Putao**, a tiny rocky crag with a Buddhist temple.

At the southern tip of the lake, **Er Hai Park** was once a royal deer ranch during the Nanzhao Kingdom. A lush path leads up to a peak, which offers splendid views.

### Surrounding Villages

Dotting the shore of Er Hai are several villages worth exploring, especially on market days. One of the

numerous minibuses, which congregate just outside Dali's North Gate, can easily be flagged down as they hop from village to village.

Lying 12 miles (20 km) north of Dali, **Xizhou** was an important military outpost during the Nanzhao period. Today, it has about 90 significant Bai mansions with rooms arranged around a courtyard. Most lie northeast of the central square, and one of them has been converted into the pleasant Tianzhuang Hotel.

A few miles northeast of Xizhou is **Zhoucheng**, the largest lakeside Bai village with several tie-dye cottage industries. Just north of here, **Shaping** is a sleepy village that transforms into an indigenous metropolis every Monday, when it hosts a huge market. On sale are a

A Bai woman from Shaping

variety of local produce and livestock, besides delicious wild honey, condiments, and traditional Bai clothing. The scale, bustle, and color make this one of the great highlights of the area.

On the eastern side of the lake, **Wase** village is a maze of narrow back lanes. It has a simple government guesthouse and its own Monday market, which is less touristy than the one at Shaping. Boats return to Dali from **Haidong**, 6 miles (10 km) south of Shaping.

## Shaxi ⑥
沙溪

56 miles (90 km) N of Dali. *from Dali or Lijiang via Jianchuan.* *to enter the village.*

Tiny mud-brick Shaxi, a traditional Bai village set in the bowl of a river valley, is a relic of Yunan's **old tea-horse road**. This is the trade route along which tea and other goods such as salt were once ferried between China and Tibet. The Chinese sought sturdy Tibetan ponies for military uses while the Tibetans wanted coarse *pu'er* tea from southern Yunnan, which was steamed into compressed "bricks" for the journey.

Shaxi's handful of lanes all lead to **Sideng**, the old town square, where **Xingjiao Temple** dates from 1451. Its famous Buddhist frescoes are protected by two fierce gate guardians. The square hosts a market each Friday, when the usually sedate village fills

### THE NANZHAO KINGDOM

In the 8th century, the Bai unified under a ruthless prince, Pileguo, who vanquished his rivals by inviting them to a banquet and setting fire to the tent. He then founded the Nanzhao Kingdom, with Dali as its capital. The city's strategic location, in a valley shielded by mountains, helped protect it against two attacks by invading Tang armies, and established its control over the southern Silk Road trade. At its zenith, the kingdom stretched across Southwest China and into Burma and parts of Vietnam. It survived until the 13th century, when the Great Mongol Kublai Khan founded the Yuan dynasty.

Nanzhao figurine

A historic bridge in Shaxi Valley

with the noise and bustle of farmers from the hills.

About 6 miles (9 km) from Shaxi, **Shibao Shan** is a wooded hillside that offers pleasant walks. On its upper ridge, **Shizhong Si**, the Stone Bell Temple, dates back more than 1,300 years.

## Tengchong ⑦
腾冲

105 miles (168 km) W of Baoshan.

A thriving settlement during the Han era, Tengchong prospered from the Silk Road trade. Today a remote backwater, it has preserved more of its traditional wooden architecture than neighboring Baoshan. Set amidst jungle, volcanoes, and hot springs, Tengchong is also a major seismic zone, having experienced 70 earthquakes since records began in the 16th century.

In the north of town, on **Guanghua Lu**, stands the imposing British consulate established in 1899. A mix of Victorian and Chinese architecture, the derelict structure has been converted into a museum. Along western Guanghua Lu is the main market, held every morning. Tengchong's most charismatic alleys run west off **Yinjiang Xi Lu**, where Burmese traders, distinctive in their sarongs and sandals, frequent the Burmese Teahouse. Most are involved in the gem and jade trade, but be wary of their goods unless you are an expert. Just west of town, **Laifeng Shan Park** is a pine forest criss-crossed

with paths. Near the top of the hill, **Laifeng Monastery** is now a museum and holds exhibits on local history.

🌳 **Laifeng Shan Park**
⬜ 8am–7pm daily. 🎫

**Environs:** The sights out of town are best visited on a tour, which can be arranged by any large hotel in Tengchong. **Heshun**, 2 miles (4 km) west of town, was founded in the Ming dynasty and is as pretty as a postcard. Funds from thousands of former residents now living abroad have kept the traditional courtyard houses, ornate pavilions, and gardens in an excellent state of repair. One of the finest buildings is the wooden library, which was built in 1928.

As a result of its fragile faultlines, the entire region is dotted with volcanoes, dry lava beds, geysers, and hot springs. The most impressive of the 100-odd small volcanoes lie 12 miles (20 km) north of town. **Dakong Shan** is 820-ft (250-m) high,

and beside it is the smaller **Heikong Shan**, only 262-ft (80-m) high, but over 328-ft (100-m) deep. Steps cut into the rock lead into the crater. Just 7 miles (12 km) southwest of Tongcheng, **Rehai** or "Hot Sea" is an area of geothermal springs, popular among the Chinese who throng here for a bath in the mineral-rich water.

🏔 **Dakong & Heikong Shan**
⬜ daily. 🎫
🏔 **Rehai**
⬜ 24 hr daily. 🎫

## Ruili ⑧
瑞丽

80 miles (125 km) SW of Tengchong.
✈ from Kunming. 🚌

Ruili, on the Myanmar border, is in every way a frontier town – slightly exotic, with a touch of the illicit. Although much Burmese heroin passes through here, and gambling and prostitution are rife, the town should not necessarily be avoided as the presence of Burmese traders, and Dai and Jingpo minorities make it one of the most intriguing places in southwest China. An interesting jade and gem market lies in the north of town, parallel to **Nanmao Jie**. The town really comes to life at night, when gambling and food stalls are set up in the back streets. Numerous hotels advertise tours into Myanmar, often to watch transvestite shows, but the frontier is closed to all foreign visitors, except those being met by Burmese officials for a pre-arranged tour.

Lush Tengchong countryside, with hills in the background

# Street-by-Street: Lijiang ❾
丽江

Maize drying

Set in a picturesque valley with a stunning mountain backdrop, Lijiang's Old Town, Dayan, is a labyrinth of cobbled alleys lined with wooden houses, cafés, and the workshops of traditional craftsmen. Home to the Naxi people, Dayan is one of the most pleasant urban scenes in China. Lijiang came to international attention in 1996 when an earthquake killed over 300 people and devastated the city. Money poured into Dayan's relatively sensitive reconstruction, and numerous hotels as well as an airport were built. Lijiang has been a UNESCO World Heritage Site since 1999.

A typical narrow street in the center of the Old Town

**Heilong Tan Gongyuan**

**Water Wheels**
*Heralding the entrance to the Old Town, these water wheels are ornamental. Lijiang once had numerous mills.*

**Nightly performances** of Naxi music are held at the Naxi Music Academy.

**Kegong Fang**
*This distinctive tower is the center of celebrations during the Sanduo Festival which honors the Naxi's protector deity Sanduo.*

DONG DAJIE

YU HE

XINHUA JIE

## JOSEPH ROCK

An eccentric Austrian botanist, Joseph Rock lived in Lijiang between 1922 and 1949. He gathered over 80,000 plant specimens, pioneered the use of photography in the field, and wrote reports for *National Geographic*. He was a defender of Naxi culture and compiled the first dictionary of the language. His entourage was huge, and included cooks, hundreds of mercenaries, and servants to carry such dubious necessities as his gramophone, gold dinner service, and collapsible bathtub.

**Joseph Rock (right) with the Prince of Choni, 1925**

| 0 meters | | 100 |
| 0 yards | | 100 |

**KEY**

– – – Suggested route

**STAR SIGHTS**

★ Mishi Xiang

★ Sifang Jie

**View of the rooftops of Dayan from Wangu Lou**

**The canals** are helpful if you get lost. Walk against the current to head towards the water wheels.

★ **Mishi Xiang**
*With a canal bubbling beside it, this is one of Dayan's most charming streets. Locals stop for a drink from the well here, outside the Blue Page Vegetarian restaurant.*

## OLD TOWN CENTER

The old town is a cobweb of narrow cobbled alleyways, criss-crossed with canals, and free of traffic. It's extremely pretty, and very popular. If you want to escape the crowds head off into the alleys away from the major tourist routes, where local people still live.

★ **Sifang Jie**
*Though it's always busy with tourists, Market Square is still at the heart of Lijiang. Naxi gather here to play cards and chat. Local men who enjoy falconry often display their hawks.*

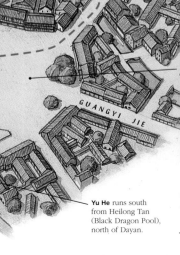

**Yu He** runs south from Heilong Tan (Black Dragon Pool), north of Dayan.

Fu
ngu Lou

# Exploring Lijiang and Beyond

Shizi Shan (Lion Hill) divides the Old Town (Dayan) from the New Town, where most hotels and other amenities can be found. There are a few sights just south of Dayan, on Shizi Shan, and clustered around Heilong Tan (Black Dragon Pool), north of Dayan. The countryside surrounding Lijiang is dotted with Naxi hamlets, many of which have interesting temples. Some of these can be reached by bicycle; otherwise by a short bus trip.

**Wangu Lou, a perfect vantage point for viewing Dayan**

## Wangu Lou

Shizi Shan. ☐ 7:30am–7pm daily.
Standing at the highest point in Lijiang, this 108-ft (33-m) pavilion is accessible from either the old town or from Minzu Lu on the west side of the hill. A four-story edifice with huge wooden pillars, it offers superb views overlooking the old town.

## Mu Fu

SW of the Old Town. ☐ daily.
The Mu were Lijiang's ruling family up to 1723 and the mansion they built for themselves at the south end of the Old Town contained over 100 buildings. Destroyed by the Qing, the residence was built after the earthquake on the ruins of traditional housing in Han, Naxi, Bai, and Tibetan architectural styles.

## Heilong Tan Gongyuan

Xin Dajie. ☐ 7:30am–6pm daily.
On the northern edge of town, Black Dragon Pool Park is stunningly picturesque with the elegant Deyue Lou placed at the center of a carp-filled pool, and backdropped by the peak of Yulong Xue Shan (Jade Dragon Snow Mountain). The

**Dongba Research Institute**, in the southwest corner of the park, is an academic institution for the preservation of Naxi culture – there are about thirty dongba shamans here, studying and translating Naxi religious texts. In the north of the park stands a set of halls transported during the 1970s from what was once Lijiang's biggest monastery, **Fuguo Si**. The grandest is the 66-ft (20-m), triple-roofed Wufeng Lou (Five Phoenix Hall), built in 1601. The **Museum of Naxi Culture**, by the park's north gate, holds exhibitions on Naxi dress and customs.

**Environs: Baisha**, a sleepy village 6 miles (10 km) north of Lijiang, was, until Kublai Khan's invasion, the capital of the Naxi Kingdom. Today there's little evidence of its past importance except for two grand temples. The first, at the village entrance, stands neglected, but the second, the Liuli, just north of it, holds some well-preserved 14th-century frescoes that exhibit a

**Red chilies drying**

promiscuous pantheism. Baisha is home to the Daoist physician Dr Ho, made famous by travel writer Bruce Chatwin. He will doubtless track you down and offer his tonic herb tea in exchange for a small donation.

**Beiyue Si** in the village of Yulong, a couple of miles north of Baisha, is dedicated to the protector deity Sanduo, depicted with a white hat and spear. The temple has been managed by the same family for almost 1,000 years.

Built in 1756, the small lamasery **Yufeng Si** is 8 miles (13 km) northwest of Lijiang at the foot of Snow Mountain. A huge ancient camellia tree produces thousands of flowers each spring and is cared for with impressive dedication by the monks. A Naxi orchestra often practice here in the afternoon. The magnificent mountain range **Yulong Xue Shan** dominates the countryside surrounding Lijiang. To access this mountain that was first scaled in the 1960s, you'll need to either join an organized tour or hire a taxi. From the entrance of the main scenic area there are two chairlifts to points above the snow line. The first takes you to the gruesomely named Love Suicide Hill; the second, Asia's highest, takes you 14,750 ft (4,506 m) up to a ridge with amazing views of glaciers. Watch out for altitude sickness, and don't bother if it's foggy.

**The jagged peaks of Yulong Xue Shan (Jade Dragon Snow Mountain)**

*For hotels and restaurants in this region see pp568–9 and pp594–5*

# The Naxi

The Naxi Minority, numbering about 278,000, live in Sichuan and Yunnan, with Lijiang as their spiritual capital. Descended from Tibetan nomads, the Naxi lived until recently in matriarchal families, though local rulers were always male. There are strong matriarchal influences throughout Naxi society and in particular in the Naxi language. For example, nouns become superlative when the word "female" is added and diminutive with the addition of "male." A "female stone," therefore, is

**Dongba pictogram**

a boulder; a "male stone" a pebble. The script, called Dongba, consists of about 1,400 pictograms and is the only hieroglyphic writing system still in use. The Naxi religion, also called Dongba, is polytheistic, and mixes elements of Daoism and Tibetan Lamaism with older animist beliefs. The main Naxi deity is Sanduo, a protector war god depicted in white, carrying a white spear and riding a white horse. He is celebrated twice a year with the sacrifice of a goat and, of course, much singing and dancing.

*Naxi society's matriarchal nature results in the women controlling businesses, but also doing most of the work. Inheritance passes through the female line to the eldest daughter. Naxi men are expected to while away their time as gardeners or musicians.*

**Traditional shawls** *have an upper blue segment which represents night, a lower sheepskin band to represent daylight, and small circles recalling the stars. Two circles on the shoulder areas depict the eyes of a frog, an ancient Naxi deity.*

**Dongba** *sorcerers, are invited to chant scriptures at weddings, funerals, on New Year Day, and at festivals. A few of these shaman survived the purges of the Cultural Revolution and are training a new generation in ancient Naxi ritual.*

**Naxi music** *is unique – a combination of Daoist rite, Confucian ceremony, and literary lyrics, played on venerable instruments such as the flute, reed pipes, lute, and zither.*

**This page of** *pictographic Dongba script is from the Naxi manuscript "Sacrifices to the High Deity." It is one of numerous Dongba documents translated by Joseph Rock (see p390).*

# Tiger Leaping Gorge ❿
### 虎跳峡

**Arrows mark the upper path**

This popular trek follows the roaring Jinsha Jiang's route through one of China's deepest gorges, supposedly named after a tiger escaped hunters by leaping it at its narrowest point. With peaks on either side reaching an average of 13,000 ft (4,000 m), the gorge makes for a thrilling trek. The 18-mile (30-km) trail along the ridge is well marked, though at times arduous, and passes through rustic hamlets which allow visitors to rest up amid beautiful countryside. The walk can easily be completed in two days, but many hikers decide to stay an extra night. If time is tight, daylong bus tours from Lijiang head into the gorge along the lower road, which currently runs as far as Walnut Grove.

**Bendiwan**
*A tiny village with superb views, Bendiwan has numerous guesthouses and is a convenient place to overnight 10 miles (16 km) from Qiaotou.*

**★ Views of the Gorge**
*Starting at the Qiaotou end of the gorge provides magnificent views right from the start. The peaks of Jade Dragon Snow Mountain rise far above Jinsha Jiang, the River of Golden Sands.*

**A short** diversion down a steep, winding trail leads to Longdong Waterfall.

**The 24 Bends**
*When coming from Qiaotou, the 24 Bends are the toughest part of the trail and consist of rather more than 24 gruelling switchbacks. Some hire horses at Nuoyu for this part of the trip.*

Jinsha Jiang

Yongsheng ●

Qiaotou ●

**Relatively new lower road**

**Farms at Nuoyu**
*The lovely village of Nuoyu is just two hours from Qiaotou. A few guesthouses here offer dorm beds and meals, as well as horses.*

### STAR SIGHTS

★ Views of the Gorge

★ Walnut Grove

**Goat**
*Flocks of goats have
stripped much of
the slopes clean
of flora.*

The "new" ferry
crossing is
sometimes closed.
Check at Walnut
Grove or Daju
before departing.

**Original
ferry
crossing**

● Daju

Dabai

**Traditional Tibetan buildings at
Ganden Sumtseling Gompa**

# Zhongdian ⑪
中旬

119 miles (198 km) NW of Lijiang.
✈ 🚌 3 to 5 hrs from Lijiang.
🛈 Changzheng Lu, (0887) 822 5657.

## WALKING
## THE GORGE

The upper trail follows the
peaks between Qiaotou and
Daju, either of which can be
used as a starting point. Both
Bendiwan and Walnut Grove are about
a day's walk from either end, so make
good spots to overnight. Don't attempt
the trek on your own, or in heavy rain or thick
mist. Landslides occur in the area so be wary,
especially after the rains in July or August.

0 kilometres          3

0 miles               3

**KEY**

🚢 Ferry crossing

▬ Major road

▬ Minor road

– – Path

**Follow the path** down to
the Jinsha Jiang to judge for
yourself whether any animal
could have made this jump.

Touted as the true Shangri-la
(the city's name was officially
changed to Xianggelila in
2002), Zhongdian is the
capital of Diqing Tibetan
Autonomous Region and
worth visiting if you're not
able to visit Tibet. The
ramshackle town filled with
blocky architecture does not
quite live up to the paradise
billing, but there is an interesting section of traditional
Tibetan buildings to the south
of town. Just north is the
largest Tibetan monastery in
the Southwest, Ganden Sumtseling Gompa (Songzanlin
Si), home to over 600 monks.
It was built by the fifth Dalai
Lama almost 400 years ago,
destroyed during the Cultural
Revolution, and re-opened in
1981. Head to the roof for
stunning views over
Zhongdian.

**Environs:** There are plenty of
possible trips out into the
countryside – geographically,
part of the Tibetan plateau –
to **Baishui Tai**, for example,
a set of limestone terraces,
or to **Bita Hai**, an emerald
lake and home to many
endangered species. These
trips are best arranged with
local agencies, who can also
set up a trip into Tibet – it
takes about a week to reach
Lhasa by four-by-four.

**★ Walnut Grove**
*This quiet village of terraced fields, walnut trees, and stone
and timber houses is 14 miles (23 km) from Qiaotou and
a great place to rest up. The views of the gorge's narrowest
section are not to be missed.*

# GUIZHOU & GUANGXI

Guizhou and Guangxi share a dramatic mountainous landscape of weathered limestone (karst) pinnacles, which hide some of China's largest cave systems. Despite the abundant rainfall, the region possesses poor soil, which discouraged Han settlement until the late Ming period. As a result, the area saw little development, and many indigenous groups, especially the Miao and Dong, have retained their traditional customs, including several festivals. Guangxi is also home to the Zhuang, China's largest ethnic minority, and became the Guangxi Zhuang Autonomous Region in 1958.

Still among China's least devel-

oped regions, Guizhou and Guangxi do have a few sights that are well-touristed and easily accessible. The city of Guilin in eastern Guangxi is fa-mous for the Li River cruise through astonishing karst landscape, and ending at the backpacker haven of Yangshuo. Kaili, a convenient base for exploring sociable Miao villages, is becoming more accessible and popular with tourists. For determined travelers with time on their hands, long bus journeys are rewarded with beautiful Detian Falls, stunning scenery near the Vietnamese border, the wooden Dong villages around Zhaoxing, and the calm waters of bird sanctuary Cao Hai.

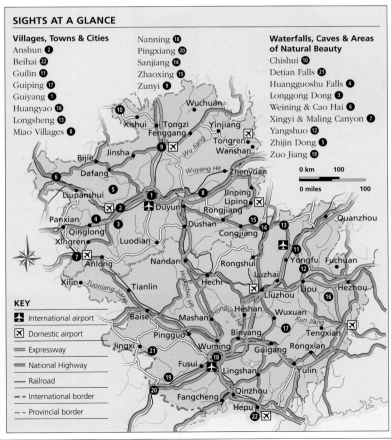

## SIGHTS AT A GLANCE

**Villages, Towns & Cities**

Anshun ❷
Beihai ㉒
Guilin ⓫
Guiping ⓱
Guiyang ❶
Huangyao ⓰
Longsheng ⓭
Miao Villages ❽

Nanning ⓲
Pingxiang ⓴
Sanjiang ⓮
Zhaoxing ⓯
Zunyi ❾

**Waterfalls, Caves & Areas of Natural Beauty**

Chishui ❿
Detian Falls ㉑
Huangguoshu Falls ❹
Longgong Dong ❸
Weining & Cao Hai ❻
Xingyi & Maling Canyon ❼
Yangshuo ⓬
Zhijin Dong ❺
Zuo Jiang ⓳

### KEY

✈ International airport

⊠ Domestic airport

━━ Expressway

━━ National Highway

─── Railroad

- - International border

- - Provincial border

◁ **Women of the Bunu ethnic minority with drying chilies, Guizhou**

# Guiyang ❶
贵阳

Ornamental window, Cuiwei Yuan

Founded during the Han era, Guiyang remained a minor provincial center until it became the capital of Guizhou in the early 20th century. The city is situated in a valley along the little Nanming River, protected from the unlucky northern direction by high hills. Guiyang means "Precious Sun," which reflects the general Chinese opinion of the province's damp climate. An easy-going place, Guiyang is a steadily modernizing city surrounded by parklands, with a couple of historic relics dotted among its tower blocks. The Huaxi District to its south includes rural parks, a few villages inhabited by the Bouyi minority *(see p400)*, and a well-preserved Ming-era town.

Jiaxiu Lou & the arched Fuyu Qiao over Nanming He

Traditional temple buildings in Cuiwei Yuan

### 🏯 Jiaxiu Lou & Cuiwei Yuan

2 Cuiwei Xian Nanming Lu. ⬜ daily. 📷
The small Jiaxiu Pavilion was constructed in 1598 on a tortoise-shaped rock jutting out of Nanming He. It was built as an inspirational meeting place for scholars studying for the imperial civil service examinations. The pavilion is now a teahouse decorated with antique poetry scrolls. Its upper floor offers views of Guiyang's modern downtown district. The 95-ft (29-m) high, three-storied wooden tower is connected to the banks by the arched, Fuyu Qiao (Floating Jade Bridge), made of solid stone. On the bridge's southern side, adjacent to Jiaxiu Lou, Cuiwei Garden was originally part of a temple dedicated to Guanyin, the Buddhist Goddess of Compassion. It was founded around 1500, although all that remain today are late Qing-era buildings.

### 🏯 Qianming Si, Jue Yuan, & Wenchang Ge

City center, N of the river. ⬜ daily. 📷
A few examples of Guiyang's classic architecture survive around the city center. The most interesting is Qianming Si, located on Yangming Lane on the north bank of the river. Its main point of interest is the street market outside, selling bonsai trees, pets, fishing gear, and Cultural Revolution memorabilia. Jue Yuan on Fushui Nan Lu is another temple, whose main attraction is the excellent vegetarian restaurant out front, which uses generous quantities of chilies to spice up the tofu, vegetable, and gluten dishes. Just off Wengchang Bei Lu, Wenchang Ge features an elegant three-story tower with flared and pointed eaves built between 1609 and 1669. It was originally part of the east city wall.

### 🏛 Provincial Museum

168 Beijing Lu. **Tel** (0851) 682 2214.
⬜ 9am–5pm Tue–Sun.
The second floor of this dusty building houses an interesting collection of local finds, though there are few captions. The pride of the collection is a 3-ft (1-m) high Han-era bronze horse and chariot, and some glazed clay figurines from a Ming tomb near Zunyi. A document on one wall refers to the 19th-century Miao Uprisings, a series of conflicts against increased taxation in Guizhou. Ethnological displays include silverware, batiks, and embroideries from Guizhou's many minorities.

Vermilion-red joss sticks & trinkets on sale outside Qianming Si

**Stone steps leading up a thickly-forested hill, Qianling Shan Park**

♣ **Qianling Shan Park**

187 Zhaoshan Lu. ☐ *daily.* 🚫

This scenic park comprises an unexpected patch of forested hills to the north of the city. A flagstoned path leads uphill past several shrines, trees hung with red ribbons, and groups of monkeys to **Hongfu Si**, the main attraction. Entry to the temple is past a 33-ft (10-m) marble stupa and a tiled screen depicting the infant Buddha being washed by nine colorful dragons. The temple was originally founded in 1672, although its present buildings were constructed later, including a Luohan Hall with several hundred painted statues of Buddhist saints. On the hilltop above, Kanzhu Pavilion offers fine views of the city.

🏯 **Huaxi District**

11 miles (17 km) S of Guiyang. 🚌 *16, 25, 47.*

The small town of Huaxi is the location of Guizhou University and the attractive Huaxi Park, a 2-sq-mile (5-sq-km) stretch of woodland, river, and ornamental gardens. A handful of Bouyi villages lie close by, including **Zhenshan**, built entirely in stone. The village is known for its Ground Opera, derived from local animistic rituals, where dancers wear stylized wooden masks. Just 8 miles (12 km) to the south is **Qingyang**, a garrison outpost founded in 1373. Its 33-ft (10-m) high city walls, dating to the 18th century, are still intact, along with watchtowers, stone gateways and 17 temples.

**VISITORS' CHECKLIST**

865 miles (1,394 km) NW of Guangzhou. 🚶 *1,600,000.* ✈ *Longdong Bao Airport.* 🚌 *Guiyang Bus Station, CAAC (buses to airport), Tiyu Guan Bus Station.* ℹ *Floor 7, Longquan Building, 1 Hequan Rd, (0851) 690 1575.*

**DOG MEAT**

One thing to look out for in Guizhou is the locals' fondness for eating dog meat, a habit shared by people in parts of Guangxi and other Southeast Asian countries. Rather like chilies, dog meat is considered "warming" in Chinese medicine, and also a remedy for male impotence. The meat is often served as a hot pot. However, visitors shouldn't worry about being served dog meat by accident, as restaurants specializing in such dishes usually make it very clear by displaying the carcasses outside their establishments.

**Characters for "dog meat" on a restaurant sign**

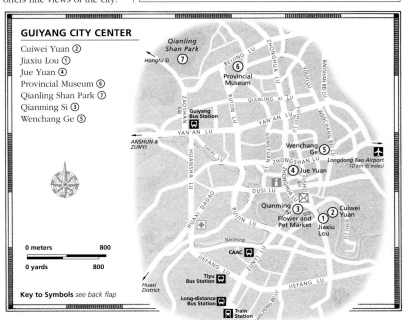

**GUIYANG CITY CENTER**

Cuiwei Yuan ②
Jiaxiu Lou ①
Jue Yuan ④
Provincial Museum ⑥
Qianling Shan Park ⑦
Qianming Si ③
Wenchang Ge ⑤

Traditional houses of the Bouyi community near Anshun

# Anshun ❷
安顺

62 miles (100 km) SW of Guiyang.
🚫 🚉 🚌

Founded as a garrison town in the 13th century, Anshun grew into a prosperous trading post, mainly because of its strategic position along the overland trade routes between central and southwestern China. Today's city survives on tourism, subsistence farming, and its traditional batik industry, which capitalizes on the highly-developed textile skills of the local Bouyi minority. The Bouyi number around 3 million and live throughout western Guizhou. A writing system for the Bouyi language was devised in the 1950s and is used to record their rich folk literature.

Surrounded by karst hills, Anshun has one of Guizhou's most scenic landscapes, despite the frequent gusts of coal dust from nearby mines. It also has numerous bustling street markets, and offers easy access to several of the surrounding traditional villages. The busy town center lies at the intersection of Nanhua Lu and Tashan Lu. The **Bai Ta** (White Pagoda), one of Anshun's two surviving Ming structures, overlooks the center from Xixiu Hill. The other, **Wen Miao**, is a Confucian temple and lies in the town's northeastern backstreets. The 600-year-old temple was once embellished with superb stone carvings. Today, what survives are its front pillars covered in beautiful spiraling dragons and considered to be the finest in the country.

The area around the city center bustles with rural commerce. Rows and rows of shops selling beautiful batik

Fruit sellers at the Sunday market, Anshun

products, including wall hangings and colorful banners, are displayed outside the **Batik Factory** on Nanhua Lu.

**Environs:** Lying about 9 miles (15 km) east of Anshun, **Yunshan** is a fortified village, founded by Ming-dynasty troops. It contains a scattering of old structures, including the elegant Qiyan Qiao, a seven-arch bridge. **Tiantai Shan,** 16 miles (25 km) northeast of town, is a 1,300-ft (400-m) hill with a cluster of thickly-forested crags, whose summit is crowned by a Buddhist temple dating from 1616. Another 16 miles (25 km) southwest of Anshun, **Zhenning County** has a concentration of traditional Bouyi villages. The houses are built of skillfully-laid drystone walls, with roofs tiled in hand-cut slates, overlapping like fish scales. The village of **Shishao**, built almost entirely in stone, is known for its Ground Opera, a regional variation of traditional Han opera, brought here by soldiers from Nanjing during the Ming era.

# Longgong Dong ❸
龙宫洞

17 miles (27 km) SW of Anshun.
🚌 from Anshun. ⏰ 8am–6pm daily. 🎫

Longgong Dong (Dragon Palace Caves) comprise a 9-mile (15-km) long complex of 90 or more caves,

A strikingly designed, contemporary batik, filled out in red and orange

## ANSHUN BATIK

Several ethnic groups across southwestern China have been traditionally involved in creating batik. For almost 1,000 years, the Bouyi around Anshun have been using batik as a background to embroidery on clothing, and since the establishment of a factory in Anshun in the 1950s, have come to monopolize the indigenous textile market. The designs, which were originally of abstract plants and animals, are drawn with wax on cloth. The cloth is then dyed in indigo before being boiled to remove all traces of the wax, leaving the pattern in white on a blue background. The earlier monochromatic batiks have now given way to multi-colored, mass-produced designs, which include stylized representations of zodiac animals, scenes from Bouyi legends, and mythical creatures. Today, Anshun's batik is in great demand across China.

**Tour boats used to explore the watery Longgong Dong**

connected by an underground river. Only six caves, covering 2,800 ft (854 m), are open to exploration, accessed by boat through the flooded entrance, Tian Chi (Heaven's Pool), which is partially concealed by a 130-ft (40-m) high waterfall. Inside, the largest cavern is about 260-ft (80-m) high. The caves are filled with colorfully-lit stalactites and stalagmites, and numerous oddly-shaped rock formations. During the rainy season, the boat ride ends at **Tiger Lair**, a broad platform from where visitors hike out of the caves and walk back to the entrance through an attractive stone forest of weathered karst spikes.

# Huangguoshu Falls ❹
## 黄果树瀑布

31 miles (50 km) SW of Anshun. 🚌
🕐 7am–6pm daily. 🌐
**www.hgscn.com**

Immensely popular in China, the Huangguoshu Da Pubu (Yellow Fruit Tree Falls) on the Sanche River rise to a height of 223 ft (68 m). During the summer rains in June and July the river becomes a torrent, and the 266-ft (81-m) broad curtain of water creates an awesome spectacle as it hits the Rhinoceros Pool below. It does not, however, rank as China's largest cataract; in fact, during drier months, its flow shrinks to a pretty network of streams pouring over the rock face. Low water levels during this time of the year make it

possible to wade across the streams. Staircases and bridges connect viewing areas opposite the falls. **Shuilian Dong**, a 440-ft (134-m) long tunnel, runs behind the falls, where natural "windows" look out through the curtain of water. Visitors should be prepared to get wet.

Of the remaining dozen-or-so water features along the Sanche, the pick of the crop lies upstream at **Doupotang Falls**, which though only a quarter of the height of Huangguoshu, are a staggering 340-ft (105-m) wide. About 3 miles (5 km) downstream at **Tianxing** are a series of small caves, some karst spires rising 66 ft (20 m), and the Yinlianzhuitan (Silver Chain Cascades), where water tumbles into a network of streams between rocky islets.

# Zhijin Dong ❺
## 织金洞

81 miles (130 km) N of Anshun. **Tel** (0857) 781 2015. 🚌 from Anshun, via Zhijin town. Taxis also available.
🎦 compulsory. 🕐 daily. 📷
**www.gzzjd.com**

Extending for over 7 miles (12 km) into limestone hills, these 492-ft (150-m) high caves are ranked as the largest in China, and are also among the biggest in the world. They are located 16 miles (25 km) northeast of old, but rather unattractive, Zhijin town, which has a few guesthouses. Paths and stairways link the caves between fossilized waterfalls and elephantine stalactites and stalagmites. The imposing rock formations have each been given descriptive names, such as "Puxian Riding the Elephant," "Goddess and Snake," and the aptly named and impressive "Old Woman and Daughter-in-Law."

The largest cavern, **Guanghan Dong** is about 1,312-ft (400-m) long. It contains the immensely elegant, 56-ft (17-m) stalagmite, known as the "Silver Rain Tree." The obligatory guided tour, which lasts for more than 2 hours, requires a minimum of 10 people, so smaller groups may have to wait for more sightseers to arrive.

**The Huangguoshu Falls, spectacular even during drier periods**

**Punting on Cao Hai, with low mountains on the horizon**

# Weining & Cao Hai ⑥
威宁 / 草海

171 miles (275 km) W of Guiyang. 🚌 to Weining, or to Liupanshui, then bus. 🚌 🎎 Yi Torch Festival (Jun/Jul).

A destitute area with coal mining as the main industry, western Guizhou has a rugged mountain landscape of karst hills and jungle. In the far west, bordering Yunnan, is the 7,200-ft (2,195-m) high Weining Plateau, whose main town is the small, chaotic, and ugly Weining, inhabited by Hui, Yi, and Da Hua Miao. The Muslim Hui, scattered throughout China, are descendants of Arab and Persian traders who came to China along the Silk Road during the Tang and Yuan dynasties. The Yi community number around 6.6 million and are spread through southwestern China. Their torch festival is a major annual event featuring archery contests, bonfires, and wrestling. The Da Hua Miao (*see pp406–7*) differ from the Miao near Kaili in both language and embroidery patterns, which feature the stylized flower motif, inspired by their name Da Hua, meaning "Big Flower."

Immediately southwest of Weining is Cao Hai, known throughout China as one of the prominent spots for bird-watching. The 17-sq mile (45-sq km) nature reserve was set up in 1992. The shallow, blue, oval-shaped lake is ringed with low mountains and fringed with reedbeds that attract tens of thousands of wintering birds between November and March. Its most important annual visitors include a large flock of 400 endangered black-necked cranes, along with Eurasian cranes, barheaded geese, and several duck species.

It is possible to observe the abundant birdlife by either walking around the shore where the cranes congregate, or hiring a punt to approach flocks of wild fowl out on the lake. Boats can also be rented for a tour of the lake.

# Xingyi & Maling Canyon ⑦
兴义 和 马岭河峡谷

186 miles (300 km) SW of Guiyang. 🚌 to Xingyi. **Maling Canyon** White-water rafting arranged by hotels. 📷

In the far southwestern corner of Guizhou, the small and remote market town of Xingyi is surrounded by low, rounded limestone hills and flat paddy fields. Northeast of Xingyi, just outside the suburbs, lies the 9-mile (15-km) long slash of Maling Canyon. About 330-ft (100-m) deep in places, the canyon has been carved by a fast-flowing river. Ground-level springs gush down mossy cliffs in miniature waterfalls. The river's currents and cataracts make for exciting white-water rafting trips from Maling's upper section, 16 miles (25 km) northeast of town. The canyon's lower section features several walking tracks and bridges which zigzag down to the water level and then follow the river, sometimes through natural tunnels, for some distance upstream.

**River running through the lower section of Maling Canyon**

# Chinese Cranes

The lakes and marshes of China are vital to the survival of eight of the world's 15 species of crane, many of which are highly endangered. Most breed in northern China, in particular at Zhalong Nature Reserve in Heilongjiang province. All are migratory, but several species – including the tropical sarus and China's sole endemic variety, the black-necked crane – occur only in the central and south-western parts of the country. Aside from being naturally elegant birds, cranes have spectacular mating "dances," where they energetically leap and flap around to attract their lifelong partners. As a result of this display, the crane is a Chinese symbol of fidelity and longevity. The Daoist god of longevity, Shou Lao (also known as Shao Xing), is often depicted riding a crane.

*Sarus – world's tallest crane*

**Courting cranes** *pair for life. They cement the bond with elaborate courtship displays, during which the couple loop necks, toss their heads back, throw around twigs and pebbles, and leap high into the air, parachuting down with wings spread.*

**The crane** *is a symbol of good fortune, wisdom, and the quest for spiritual improvement, as well as fidelity – so it is often seen on official and imperial clothing.*

**Trailing legs**

**Cranes migrate great** *distances, with some species covering up to 2,500 miles (4,000 km) between their summer breeding grounds and winter quarters. The younger birds learn the routes in a V-formation behind their elders.*

**Cruising speed** of up to 44 miles per hour (70 km/ hour)

**Demoiselle cranes** *are gregarious and have been recorded in flocks several thousand strong. Their diet is mostly frogs, fish, and insects, though they can also eat grain and carrion.*

**Common cranes** *are a very vocal species, and their deep booms, loud honks, and raucous croaks are produced by a specially adapted windpipe or trachea.*

# Miao Festivals and Crafts

**Geometric embroidery**

The Miao people, or Hmong as they call themselves, believe they originated on the Himalayan plateau, migrating over the last few thousand years to their current homelands in southwestern China, Laos, Cambodia, Vietnam, and Myanmar. As Miao communities tend to exist in remote mountainous areas, each village has developed its own customs, and can be identified by their distinct ornamentation, such as the fine silverwork and embroidery made and worn by unmarried girls. These are displayed at the many Miao social festivals where mass dancing is featured.

**MIAO COMMUNITIES OF ASIA**

☐ *Miao population*

**Huge horns** adorn these fabulous headdresses.

**Miao People** *in the Kaili area call themselves Hei Miao, or Black Hmong, irrespective of their color-ful clothing, which identifies the wearer's village or region. This woman is from the Leigong Shan area.*

**Da Hua Miao,** *or Big Flower Miao, from western Guizhou, wear wax-resist (batik) dyed skirts, and for festivals, bright red headgear.*

**This Gejia headpiece** *with orange tassels shows that this Gejia girl is unmarried. These people's designs are unusual in that they embellish their batik work with embroidery.*

### SISTERS' MEAL FESTIVAL
Amid three days of drinking and dancing at this important festival, teenage girls choose their husbands. The man offers a packet of sticky rice; she returns it with two chopsticks buried inside if she agrees, or chilies if she refuses.

**The Changjiao,** *or Long-horned, Miao of western Guizhou bundle several pounds of their own and ancestors' hair around horn-like headpieces for festivals.*

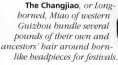

◁ **The intricately layered rice terraces of Longji Titian (Dragon's Backbone Terraces), near Ping An, Guangxi**

**Embroidery** *is an integral Miao skill, and girls learn it from an early age. They create elaborate panels for sewing on to their clothes. The finer the design, the better a girl's marriage prospects.*

**This jacket** *is typical of dark geometric Gejia pieces. It is heavily embroidered and incorporates batik work of abstract buffalo and plant motifs.*

**Elaborate** silverwork, including headpieces, breastplates, and necklaces, are collected by families of Hei Miao girls from the time they are born.

**Miao silverwork** *ranges from simple earrings to twisted, weighty necklace chains and fantastic headpieces with bells, horns, and animal figurines.*

**Dragon-boat races** *are held in the Kaili region at least twice a year, celebrating a local victory over invading Chinese armies. Villages send a team of rowers and a long, narrow boat with carved wooden dragon-head prows.*

**Traditional long pleated skirt**

**Two buffalo going head-to-head** *is a feature of Miao festivals, but buffalo are cherished creatures, and there is usually no bloodshed.*

**Only men play the lusheng**, *usually at festivals. This instrument is made from a gourd with a mouthpiece and a dozen or so bamboo pipes. It produces a nasal humming sound.*

# Miao Villages

## 凯里苗寨

**Window in pagoda, Kaili**

China's Miao *(see pp406–7)* look to the area around Kaili and the ancient town of Zhenyuan as their homeland. In between, the terrain rises to rough hills, planted with pine trees and split by river valleys. A few villages maintain traditional wooden houses and cobbled streets; others are not so pretty, but host large festivals. Markets come close to a festival atmosphere and operate on a five-day cycle. Numerous buses run from Kaili, but to reach remoter places, hiring a taxi – or hiking – is necessary.

The traditional village of Langde tucked into a steep valley

## Kaili

105 miles (170 km) E of Guiyang. 🚉 🚌 ℹ️ *Yingpanpo Hotel, 53 Yingpan Dong Lu, (0855) 822 2506.*

Kaili is a large town of busy streets and unremarkable architecture. Back-street markets add a bit of color, and there's also a dusty **Minorities Museum**, displaying local silver and embroidery. Hilltop Dage Park is crowned by a wooden pagoda, unusual in its Daoist iconography and statues ritualistically smeared with bloody chicken feathers.

🏛 **Minorities Museum**
5 Guangchang Lu. ⬜ *daily.* 📷

## LANGDE & XIJIANG

This route includes the most accessible traditional villages covered by buses from Kaili. Possible as a day-trip if you hire a taxi, otherwise, plan to overnight at Xijiang.

**Langde** is an easy 20-minute walk from the main road. It is entirely traditional, with 50 wooden houses knotted into a fold in the hillside. At Langde's center is a pond and a dancing ground cobbled in concentric rings around a wooden pole adorned with buffalo horns and painted dragons.

**Lei Shan** is a down-at-heel collection of concrete buildings at the foot of **Leigong Shan** (7,150 feet, 2,178 m). Some of the region's remotest villages are found on the mountain and it's possible to organize hiking trips between them. From Lei Shan, it's another 18 miles (30 km) on a dirt road to **Xijiang**, the largest Miao village at around 1,200 wooden homes. The best times to visit are during the autumn New Rice Tasting Festival, or Miao New Year celebrations.

## EASTERN ROUTE

There are several buses daily from Kaili via Taijiang and Shidong through to Zhenyuan. Both towns host major festivals, with extra transport during festival events. Each can be done as a daytrip, but Taijiang does have several hotels, and there's a basic guesthouse in Shidong.

**Taijiang** is an untidy market town 34 miles (55 km) from Kaili. It transforms during Sisters' Meal Festival, when thousands of villagers descend to watch Miao girls choose their husbands. At other times, the old village of **Fanpai** is a more photogenic place to spend a day.

**Shidong** is a partially wooden riverside village of half a dozen lanes. You can shop for beautifully designed silverwork and embroideries on market days, or see them worn during dragon-boat races, held at least twice a year. Afternoon races are accompanied by furious drumming, and the day winds down with a dance in which everyone present – sometimes 10,000 people – joins in.

The terraced slopes of Leigong Shan

## WESTERN ROUTE

Frequent buses ply the route from Kaili to Shibing; change here for connections to Zhenyuan. There's some basic accommodations in Chong'an and hotels in Shibing.

Pleasantly rural **Matang** is home to the majority of Gejia, a Miao sub-group. The road passes close by, but you'll need to hire a taxi from Kaili if you don't want to walk the last 3 miles (5 km). About 6 miles (10 km) west of Matang, **Xianglu Shan** (4,265 feet/1,300 m) is where Zhang Xiumei, one of the leaders of the Miao Rebellion, was defeated by government troops in 1873. An annual Hill Climbing festival is held here in his honor.

The riverside town of **Chong'an** uses its old core of wooden shops for a lively market, somewhere to

A battery of old stone water-powered mills, Chong'an

**Miao woman with baby**

experience crowds bargaining for everything from ducklings to home-made spirits.

Right on the roadside, **Feiyun Dong** is a curious Daoist shrine founded in 1443, whose few moss-covered halls (one contains a museum of Miao artifacts) are built right into a natural arrangement of grottoes and vegetation.

From **Shibing**, another nondescript place on the south bank of Wuyang

He, it's possible to arrange rafting trips down Shanmu Jiang, or to hike up Yuntai Shan, which features the ruins of a Ming-dynasty temple.

### Zhenyuan

62 miles (100 km) NE of Kaili. *26 Ximen Jie, Wuyangzhen.*

An old garrison town, Zhenyuan is squeezed by flanking cliffs into two long streets either side of Wuyang He. In the old town on the north bank, Qing-dynasty buildings with wavy eaves and ornate stonework have been carefully restored. East of the old town, a stone Ming bridge leads to Heilong Dong (Black Dragon Cave). This Daoist complex is built right into the overhanging cliffs, where water seeps onto shrines dedicated to numerous deities. It's also possible to cruise a stretch of the Wuyang He east of Zhenyuan, through a series of limestone gorges.

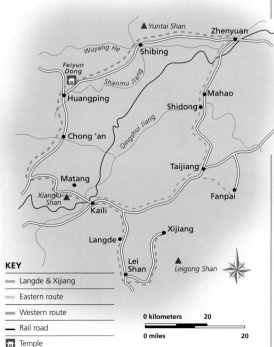

### FESTIVALS

*Jan:* Drum festival, Gaowu, near Taijiang
*Feb/Mar:* Lusheng Festivals across region
*Apr/May:* Sisters' Meal, Taijiang & Shidong
*Jun/Jul:* Dragonboat Races at many riverside villages and towns
*Jul/Aug:* Festival at Xianglu Shan
*Aug/Sep:* New Rice Tasting Festival in villages around Kaili & Lei Shan; Lusheng Festival, Chong'an
*Oct/Nov:* Lusheng Festival and horse races, Yongxi, near Zhenyuan
Dec: Miao New Year, Xijiang & villages around Kaili

### KEY

- ▬ Langde & Xijiang
- ▬ Eastern route
- ▬ Western route
- ▬ Rail road
- 🏠 Temple

*Map labels:* Yuntai Shan, Zhenyuan, Wuyang He, Shibing, Feiyun Dong, Shanmu Jiang, Huangping, Mahao, Shidong, Qinghui Jiang, Chong 'an, Taijiang, Matang, Fanpai, Xianglu Shan, Kaili, Xijiang, Langde, Lei Shan, Leigong Shan

0 kilometers 20
0 miles 20

Steps leading up to the Monument to the Red Army Martyrs, Zunyi

# Zunyi ❾
遵义

---

150 km N of Guiyang. ✈ 🚆 🚌

The largest city in northern Guizhou, Zunyi is encircled by a gray mass of cement factories and bustling transport terminals that conceal a quiet and clean older quarter, north across the river. The city holds a special place in the history of the Chinese Communist Party (CCP). In January 1935, Zunyi was invaded by the Red Army during the Long March *(see p256)*. Having suffered major defeats at the hands of the Nationalists, Communist leaders including Mao, Zhou Enlai, and Otto Braun, the Soviet advisor, convened the Zunyi Conference. During the three-day meeting, Mao emerged as the party leader and severed

Carved detail, Monument to the Red Army Martyrs

ties with the Russians, a vital step that helped the CCP defeat the Nationalists and eventually emerge as China's ruling party. The **Conference Site**, a sparsely-designed, gray brick house, displays CCP memorabilia. A similar building, in the lane behind, housed the China Soviet Republic State Bank and Commission of Expropriation & Collection, which printed banknotes and redistributed captured wealth among the peasantry. The adjacent **Long March Museum**, a former Catholic Church, displays CCP mementos. Up the river, in Fenghuang Shan Park, the **Monument to the Red Army Martyrs** commemorates the heroes of the Long March.

🏛 **Conference Site**
80 Hongqi Lu.
🕗 8:30am–5pm daily.

**Environs:** About 6 miles (10 km) south of Zunyi, **Yang Can Mu** is the final resting place of the local military official, Yang Can, who died around 1250. The stone reliefs of this well-preserved Song-era mausoleum are beautiful, depicting plants, guardian figures, and dragons curling around an ornamental gateway. There is also a portrait of Yang Can in court robes.

# Chishui ❿
赤水

---

112 miles (180 km) NW of Zunyi. 🚌

On the banks of Chishui Jiang in northwestern Guizhou on the Sichuan border, Chishui is encircled by limestone hills. The subtropical forests covering these hills are divided into nature reserves, reached by minibus from town. The finest is **Shizhang Dong**, 23 miles (37 km) south of town, with a 236-ft (72-m) waterfall. Some 10 miles (16 km) southwest, **Sidong Gou** is a valley whose red-silted river gives Chishui its name, "Red Water." It runs over four waterfalls and through a forest thick with bamboo. Locals harvest the edible bamboo shoots, and the mature stems are split and woven into matting. The region is also world famous for its *baijiu*, an alcoholic drink produced in **Maotai**, 50 miles (80 km) southeast in Xishui county *(see p581)*.

🌿 **Nature Reserves**
🚌 minibus from Chishui. 🕗 daily. 🎟

Façade of the elegant Song-dynasty mausoleum, Yang Can Mu

# Bamboo

A fast-growing, long-lived type of grass found throughout central and southern China, bamboo is put to a huge array of uses. The culms (stems) are turned into pipes, hats, furniture, mats, and cooking utensils, while the shoots of certain varieties are cooked and eaten. The body of the plant is a rhizome (a horizontal, underground stem) that, according to type, clumps or runs, putting out regularly-spaced shoots that grow nearly 2 feet (60 cm) per day until they reach full height. Plants might flower only every few decades, or even just once per century, after which they die back. The plant has become part of the religion, philosophy, and culture of the Chinese: it represents Confucian values of devotion and righteousness; the segments on its straight stem symbolize the steps along the straight path to enlightenment; and its strength, grace, and longevity have made it the subject of a great many poems and paintings.

**Versatile bamboo stems**

**In the wild**, *bamboo covers the hillsides in tall, dense, waving green forests, a sight often called a "bamboo sea." In gardens smaller plants are often used as symbolic elements (see p179).*

**Bamboo painting** – *or mozhu – is an esteemed art considered to be on a par with calligraphy (see p219). Using a monochrome ink the painter attempts to convey the bamboo's spirit rather than its exact form in just a few fluid and almost abstract brush strokes.*

**Split bamboo** *can be woven into many useful objects such as lattice screens and blinds for use around the home as well as baskets such as these, used for carrying chickens to market.*

**Whole bamboo stems** *are versatile enough to be sawn, drilled, bent or spliced, while keeping their strength. Items of furniture like these teahouse chairs can be made by a skilled craftsman in a matter of minutes.*

**The strength** *of bamboo is such that, in the south of the country where it is easily available, bamboo is preferred over steel poles as scaffolding even for high-rises. China's urban boom is being built on the back of this giant grass.*

# Karst

Huge areas of China's Southwest comprise visually spectacular landscapes featuring karst – weathered limestone formations. In China, limestone has been created from fossilized prehistoric sea floor sediments, brought to the surface by geological upheavals. The exposed alkaline limestone is then eroded by naturally-occurring acidic rain. Above ground, this results in anything from closely packed "stone forests," poking a few meters skywards, to the huge conical hills covering half of Guizhou, and the tall, elegant pinnacles around Guilin. Underground, percolating water and subterranean rivers carve out long, interlinked caverns, hung with oddly shaped rock formations.

**Stone forests,** *such as Shi Lin outside Kunming* (see pp378–9), *are karst formations created by the retreating waters of ancient seas, and wind and rain erosion.*

## KARST FORMATION

Southwest China's thick and fractured pure limestone has led to a dramatically eroded landscape. The warm wet climate speeds up the weathering of limestone by acid rainwater and chemicals in rotting plants.

**1 Surface streams** *lose water to cave systems developing in the limestone. Surface drainage is diverted down sink holes to below the water table.*

**2 Peaks develop** *from the land left after erosion by the streams. The cave system gets larger as fast-moving subsurface streams bore through the limestone, and the water table drops.*

**3 Much of the limestone** *has eroded past the caves down to a layer of shale. Limestone peaks remain, many fractured with small, waterless caves.*

**Sinkholes, or tiankeng** (*heavenly pits*), *are formed by repeated cave-ins of thinning layers of limestone. The holes can be disturbingly massive. This one at Xiaozhai, Chongqing, is almost as wide as it is deep – 2,200 ft (666 m).*

**The limest one** of southern China's crust is exceptionally thick and extensive, enabling the creation of spectacular karst.

## KARST LANDSCAPE

This cut-away artwork shows an idealized karst landscape, with all the features shown together. Karst topographies usually have a thick layer of cave-ridden limestone, and then, depending on the area's geology and the age of the formation, a few of the features shown here.

**The Li River** (see pp416–17) *cuts through an impressive variety of karst hills. Cruises start in Guilin with* fenglin, *which gradually give way to dense* fengcong.

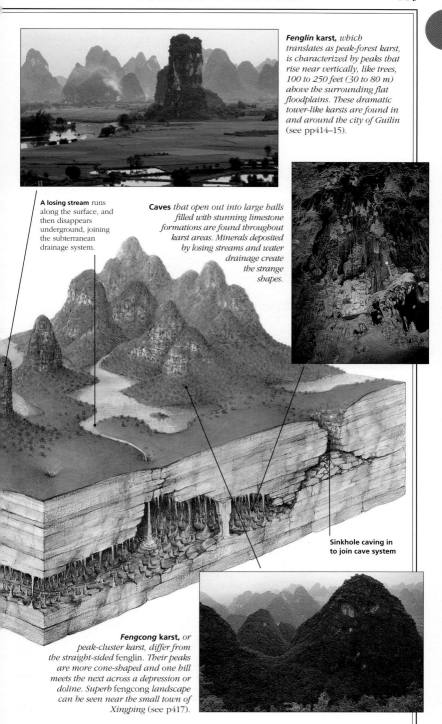

**Fenglin** karst, *which translates as peak-forest karst, is characterized by peaks that rise near vertically, like trees, 100 to 250 feet (30 to 80 m) above the surrounding flat floodplains. These dramatic tower-like karsts are found in and around the city of Guilin (see pp414–15).*

**A losing stream** runs along the surface, and then disappears underground, joining the subterranean drainage system.

**Caves** *that open out into large halls filled with stunning limestone formations are found throughout karst areas. Minerals deposited by losing streams and water drainage create the strange shapes.*

**Sinkhole caving in to join cave system**

**Fengcong** karst, *or peak-cluster karst, differ from the straight-sided fenglin. Their peaks are more cone-shaped and one hill meets the next across a depression or doline. Superb fengcong landscape can be seen near the small town of Xingping (see p417).*

# Guilin ⑪
## 桂林

Guilin is renowned for its karst peaks, most under 650 ft (198 m) high. Dotted throughout the city, they are particularly concentrated along the Li River *(see pp416–7)* to the south of town. Guilin dates back to the Qin era, and by the 6th century AD, its hills were already inspiring poets. Under the Ming, it emerged as a provincial capital, a position it lost in 1914 to Nanning. Guilin today is a tidy tourist city, with about 10 parks enclosing some fine peaks and limestone caves. Guilin means "Osmanthus Forest," and has an avenue of these sweet-scented trees along the riverside Binjiang Lu.

**Tai ji quan in the park**

Karst hills rise amongst apartment blocks in the center of town

### 🌸 Rong Hu & Shan Hu
Rong Hu Bei Lu & Shan Hu Bei Lu. **Pagodas** ⬜ *daily.* 🖼

The conjoined Rong and Shan Lakes lie on either side of Zhongshan Lu, which runs through the heart of town. Originally a part of the Ming city's moats, the lakeshores have been paved and pleasantly planted with shady banyan and willow trees. On the shore of the westerly Rong Hu stands an 800-year-old banyan tree, which gives the lake its name. On the lake's northern shore lies **Gu Nan Men**, Guilin's old South Gate, the only remains of the Ming city walls. Several classical-style arched bridges join the two banks. Shan Hu, on the eastern side of Zhongshan Lu, is overlooked by the twin 130-ft (40-m) pagodas, **Riyue Shuang Ta**, built in an antique style.

**One of the two Riyue Shuang Ta**

### 🗻 Xiangbi Shan
Off Minzhu Lu. 🚌 2, 58. 🚤 *from Nanhuan Lu.* ⬜ *7am–6pm daily.* 🖼

The most famous of the city's rock formations, the 328-ft (100-m) high Xiangbi Shan (Elephant Trunk Hill), with a hole through one end, resembles the stylized form of an elephant taking a drink from the adjacent Li River. According to a local legend, a baggage elephant in an imperial convoy was abandoned by the riverside by an uncaring emperor after it became sick. Nursed back to health by an elderly couple, the elephant refused to rejoin the returning convoy and was killed by the emperor and turned into a hill, the one that stands here to this day. The small stupa at the summit is said to be the hilt of the emperor's sword sticking out of the elephant's

back. Ferries can be taken from Nanhuan Lu to the hill. Along the path to the summit stands an old, crumbling pagoda.

### 🌸 Qixing Gongyuan
Qixing Lu. ⬜ *7am–8pm daily.* 🖼

The pleasant and lush Qixing Gongyuan (Seven Stars Park) covers an area of 1 sq mile (2 sq km) along the eastern shore of the Li River. It is named after the four peaks on Putuo Hill, and three on Crescent Hill. Seen together, the peaks form the shape of the Great Bear or Big Dipper constellation, which governs fate in Chinese mythology. Covered in thick scrub, they provide shelter to about 100 half-wild monkeys. There are several trails and pathways ascending to viewing pavilions.

Guilin's crags are renowned for their graffiti and caves. Crescent Hill is known for the 200-odd poems and commentaries carved into its overhangs, some of which are believed to date back to the Tang dynasty. Putuo Hill, which houses the 22-story high Putuo Si, is hollowed out by Qixing Yan (Seven Stars Cave), a broad cavern with a small subterranean waterfall and surprisingly few rock formations. The 246-ft (75-m) Luotuo Shan (Camel Hill), standing on its own to the north of the park, resembles a seated single-humped camel. From its summit, there are views of Chuan Shan (Hill with a Mole), and the adjacent Ta Shan (Pagoda Hill) with a Ming-dynasty pagoda.

The pleasant Qixing Gongyuan (Seven Stars Park)

Colorfully illuminated formations inside Ludi Yan (Reed Flute Cave)

### 🏯 Jinjiang Prince's Palace & Duxiu Feng

Off Xihua Lu. ◯ *daily.* 🌐

Complete with its own encircling wall and four gates, this palace resembles a miniature Forbidden City. It was originally built for the Ming prince Zhou Shouqian in 1372, predating Beijing's palace by 34 years. Having housed 14 successive Ming princes, it later served as Sun Yat-sen's headquarters in the 1920s. Today, it houses the Guangxi Teacher Training College. A sloping marble slab, carved with clouds at the entrance, indicates an imperial residence, while the absence of the usual dragons indicates that the palace was for a prince, not an emperor.

Within the palace grounds lies **Duxiu Feng** (Solitary Beauty Peak), whose 707-ft (216-m) spike protects the palace from the unlucky northern direction. At its foot is a tag carved by the 5th-century governor Yan Yanzhi, extolling Guilin's charms. Steps lead to the summit, offering splendid views.

## VISITORS' CHECKLIST

260 miles (420 km) NE of Nanning. 🏠 *620,000.* ✈ *Liangjiang International Airport.* 🚉 *Guilin Train Station.* 🚌 *Guilin Bus Station, CAAC (buses to airport), Minibus Station (to Yangshuo).* ℹ *11 Binjiang Lu, (0773) 288 6393.*

### 🏔 Fubo Shan

Binjiang Lu. ◯ *daily.* 🌐

A tall, yellow-gray rock rising from the river, Fubo Shan is believed to calm the rough waters below, hence its name, "Wave-Subduing Hill." A crumbling temple on the peak houses a huge bronze bell and several hundred Buddha images from the Song era.

### 🕳 Ludi Yan

3 miles (5 km) NW of city center. 🚌 3, 58. ◯ *daily.* 🌐

Used as a hideout by Guilin's residents during the Japanese invasion in the 1940s, Ludi Yan (Reed Flute Cave) has 33-ft (10-m) tunnels winding for 1,640 ft (500 m) through Guangming Hill. Inside, its numerous rock formations are lit with neon lights.

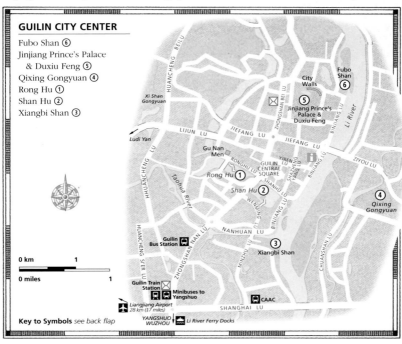

## GUILIN CITY CENTER

Fubo Shan ⑥
Jinjiang Prince's Palace & Duxiu Feng ⑤
Qixing Gongyuan ④
Rong Hu ①
Shan Hu ②
Xiangbi Shan ③

0 km                    1

0 miles                1

**Key to Symbols** *see back flap*

# Li River Cruise
漓江

The cruise along the Li River (Li Jiang) from Guilin south to Yangshuo passes through landscape that seems lifted straight out of a Chinese scroll painting. The shallow river weaves between sheer-sided, 980-foot (300-m) karst peaks, all weathered into intriguing shapes and interspersed with the villages and bamboo groves so typical of southern China's rural areas. People here still travel the river on low bamboo rafts, often

**Fisher and cormorant**

using trained cormorants to catch fish *(see p418)*. Cruises take about six hours and usually include a buffet lunch. Foreign visitors sail in boats with English-speaking guides, although this costs more.

**Bamboo rafts, for navigating the river during winter's low waters**

*GUILIN*

Zhu Jiang Dock

## ★ Elephant Trunk Hill

*Located on the riverside in downtown Guilin, Elephant Trunk Hill (Xiangbi Shan) is an endearing symbol of the city (see p414). It resembles an elephant who has placed its trunk in the Li River waters for a drink.*

**The pier at** Zhu Jiang is where many tours begin.

0 km        3

0 miles      3

### KEY

═══ Minor road

▢ Built-up area

### STAR SIGHTS

★ Elephant Trunk Hill

★ Penholder Peak

★ Scenery at Xingping

## Daxu

*Downstream from Guilin, Daxu is a Song-era market town, whose cobbled main street still retains many timber and stone houses over a century old, as well as an attractive Qing bridge, just outside town.*

Pointed *fengcong* karst formations near Yangdi

## VISITORS' CHECKLIST

Guilin to Yangshuo 52 miles (85 km), 6hrs. **🛈** *11 Binjiang Lu, Guilin, (0773) 288 6393 (CITS for booking).* **🚌** *to starting point and from Yangshuo provided.* 🚢

★ **Penholder Peak**
*Just past Yangdi and facing Writing-brush Mountain, this sharp, vertical outcrop does indeed resemble a traditional Chinese penholder. This section of hills is the beginning of the most spectacular mountain ranges.*

**Fish Tail Peak**

**Nine Horse Fresco Hill** is a cliff face stained brown by minerals creating a mural resembling galloping horses.

★ **Scenery at Xingping**
*Xingping, an old, wooden town and ferry port, marks the start of a spectacular 12-mile (20-km) stretch of scenery. Pick of the peaks are Five Fingers Hill and swirly-patterned Snail Hill.*

**Five Fingers Hill**

**Yellow Cloth Shoal**, a shallow patch of yellow riverstones, is easily seen even during high water.

**Snail Hill**

ping

Yangdi

Xingping

**In winter**, tours start at Yangdi, as water levels are too low upstream.

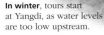

*YANGSHUO*

**Dragon Head Hill**
*Visitors to Yangshuo are greeted by this imposing peak, said to resemble the head of a dragon with its gaping jaws wide open.*

# Yangshuo ⑫

阳朔

A small highway town at the end of the Li River Cruise (*see pp416–17*), Yangshuo is surrounded by some spectacular karst hills interspersed with green paddy fields. It was nothing more than a rural marketplace until the late 1980s, when it became popular with visitors taking the cruise from Guilin. Not as tranquil as it used to be, Yangshuo remains a good base to explore the surrounding peaks and river, as well as a few caves and outlying villages. Hiring a bicycle is one of the easiest ways to explore the area. Local specialties include grapefruit-like pomelos and "beer fish" – served at most restaurants in town. Yangshuo has become one of Asia's favorite rock-climbing centers, with more than 200 short routes mapped out.

The forested Bilian Feng (Green Lotus Peak), overlooking the river

Ferries moored along the Li River, with karst hills rising in the distance

### 🏯 Xi Jie

An 820-ft (250-m) long cobbled street running between the highway and the Li River, Xi Jie (West Street) is lined with restored rural architecture dating from the Qing dynasty. Today, it has a glut of friendly restaurants, cafés, guesthouses, and souvenir shops aimed at foreign visitors. Restaurants serve western cuisine such as wood-fire pizzas and steak as well as local specialties including a variety of fresh fish dishes. Shops sell a range of inexpensive Chinese souvenirs, from Mao memorabilia and wooden theater masks to antique wooden panels, batiks, silk T-shirts, scroll paintings, modern and traditional clothes, and pirated Western music CDs. A few shops also sell factory-reject designer wear at bargain prices. The Hongfu Hotel, located about halfway down the street, was built in the 19th century as an

inn for merchants from Jiangxi. The docks area at the river end, where ferries pull in from Guilin, is covered in ornamental paving and offers good views of the angular peaks upstream. In the area north of the highway are some lovely back alleys, and a lively produce market where locals shop.

### 🏯 Bilian Feng & Yangshuo Gongyuan

🕐 daily.

Situated close to the center of town are two 328-ft (100-m) high peaks which can be climbed. To the southeast of town, overlooking the river, is the towering Bilian Feng (Green Lotus Peak), with a steep track to the summit. The second peak, Xilang Shan (Man Hill), is situated in Yangshuo Gongyuan to the west of town. It has an easier set of steps that lead to a viewing pavilion. The park is also a pleasant place to stroll and watch sessions of early-morning *tai ji quan*.

### 🏯 Jianshan Si & Underground Caves

3 miles (5 km) S of Yangshuo.

🚌 or cycle. 🕐 8:30am–5pm daily.

The only temple in the area around Yangshuo, Jianshan Si is built in a simple, late Qing-dynasty style, with wing-like horsehead gables protecting

---

### CORMORANT FISHING

The Chinese have used tame cormorants to fish for thousands of years, and this unusual technique is still practiced in southern areas. Fishermen set off on bamboo rafts after dark, with cormorants wearing collars to prevent them from swallowing

Cormorant fishing at night using lanterns

their catches. The birds swim just below the surface alongside the raft towards a light hanging from the bow. When a bird has made a catch, the fisherman pulls it from the water and retrieves the fish from the bird's beak. Hour-long viewing trips can be organized during the summer months through most hotels.

its doorway. Located nearby, the Black Buddha, Assembled Dragons, and New Water Caves are a series of underground caverns discovered in the 1990s. Locals show people around the cool, damp, and muddy caves using hand-held flashlights. Although visitors have to negotiate tall bamboo ladders and scramble over rocks, the lack of well-laid paths and garish colored lights that usually illuminate subterranean rivers and waterfalls is refreshing.

**Pomelos on sale at market**

### 🐾 Yueliang Shan

4 miles (7 km) S of Yangshuo.
🚌 or cycle. ⭕ daily. 🎫
The distinctive crescent-shaped arch that pierces Yueliang Shan (Moon Hill) has made it the most famous of Yangshuo's peaks. Stone steps, steep in places, lead to the base of the arch, a half-hour climb through bamboo thickets and bushes. The view of the Li River valley from the far side of the arch is magnificent, with fields laid out below, encircling the jagged karst pinnacles. The best time to visit is during the summer rains, when the fields are bright green. If traveling by bicycle, visitors should

take the main road south of town toward the river and turn right about 220 yards (200 m) before the bridge. From here, it's an hour to Yueliang Shan. Close by, **Longtan Village** has several unrestored old buildings, with whitewashed brick walls, wooden doors, and tiled roofs supporting intricate "flying eaves" drawn out into points.

### 🚌 Fuli Village

5 miles (8 km) E of Yangshuo. 🚌 or cycle.
🚌 🚲
The pretty village of Fuli is a quiet rural center except when it hosts a busy produce market on days

ending in 1, 4, or 7. One of the best in the region, it is visited by throngs of villagers who bargain for livestock, seasonal fruit, plastic buckets, wooden pipes, all kinds of vegetables, and bamboo fans – a famous local product. To the north is Donglang Shan, a narrow hill often paired with Yangshuo's Xilang Shan in local legends.

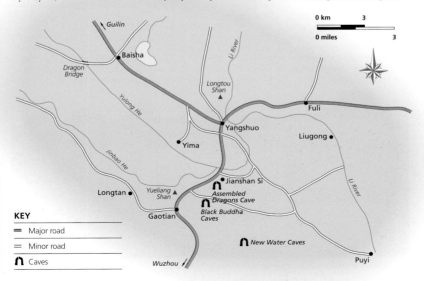

**The pretty countryside surrounding Assembled Dragons Cave, Yangshuo**

**KEY**

━━ Major road

══ Minor road

∩ Caves

A view of the complex terracing on Longji Titian, Longsheng

# Longsheng ⑬
龙胜

56 miles (90 km) NW of Guilin.
🚶 170,000. 🚐 minibuses from
Longsheng to Ping An.

The high ridges of the
Rongshui River Valley
surround the township of
Longsheng, which serves as a
good base for exploring the
adjoining countryside dotted
with Zhuang and Yao villages.
To the southwest is a steep
range of 3,280-ft (1,000-m)
high hills, known as **Longji
Titian** (Dragon Backbone
Terraces), whose lower and
middle reaches have been
covered in rice terracing by
the Zhuang people (see p424).
The Zhuang, who form the
majority of Longsheng's
population, live in traditional
wooden houses. On the hill-
tops lie a few villages, inhabited by the Yao, an ethnic
community that consists of
numerous sub-groups, some
of whom still depend on
hunting rather than farming.
They are also especially skilled
in embroidery, weaving, and
dyeing. The Zhuang village of
**Ping An** sits near the top of a
ridge in the heart of Longji
Titian. It offers basic accommodations in traditional
wooden buildings, as well as
walking trails leading to other
settlements in the area.

# Sanjiang ⑭
三江 程杨

109 miles (175 km) NW of
Guilin. 🚶 330,000. 🚐 🚍
ℹ Wind & Rain Bridge Travel
Service (0772) 861 8448.

Bamboo shoots for
sale, Sanjiang

Situated on the
Rongshui River,
Sanjiang was the base of
resistance against the
Japanese during World War II,
when Danzhou, the former
regional capital located 22
miles (35 km) south, was
captured. Today, Sanjiang is
the main town of a region
central to the indigo-clad
Dong community, which has
a population of around 2.5
million. Typical Dong
architecture, consisting of
wooden houses, towers, and
bridges, can be found in
several villages up in the hills
to the north. The hospitable
Dong usually offer visitors
their favorite *douxie cha* or
oil tea, a bitter soup made
with rice and fried tea leaves.

On the south bank of the
river is an 11-story **Drum
Tower**, the largest in the
region. It was built in 2003,
using entirely traditional
techniques. The structure is
supported by four 154-ft
(47-m) pillars, each carved
from separate tree trunks.
The third story of the tower
houses a large drum.

The small **Fulu Buddhist
Nunnery**, situated on the hill
behind, is a little unusual,
since the Dong community is
mainly Daoist. The
nunnery's three
halls contain a
mix of statuary
representing
both religions.
Situated to the
north of the river,
the County
Museum stands next
to the Government
Guesthouse. The
museum exhibits
several scale models
of traditional Dong architecture, photographs, and maps
displaying Sanjiang's strategic
wartime role. Also displayed
here are a number of colorful
costumes worn by the Dong,
Zhuang, and Yao communities
during festivals.

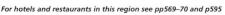
The intricately-crafted *fengyu qiao*, wind-and-rain bridge, Chengyang

*For hotels and restaurants in this region see pp569–70 and p595*

## DONG ARCHITECTURE

The Dong, who dwell in forested hill country where stone is of poor quality, make efficient use of timber. Nails are avoided, and even the largest structures are skillfully pegged together. As incomes rise in the region, there's been a resurgence of traditional building with villages competing with one another to sponsor the construction of bridges and towers. Drum towers are usually square-based, with multiple octagonal eaves. Originally they served as watchtowers and rallying places for the village, many with adjoining theater stages for use during festivals. Elaborate, covered wind-and-rain bridges are also places for villagers to meet, and are believed to ward off inauspicious energy.

**Traditional drum tower in one of Chengyang's pretty rural hamlets**

**Environs:** The most accessible Dong villages lie 11 miles (18 km) north of Sanjiang at **Chengyang**, a group of hamlets on the far side of the Linxi River, accessible by bus or minivan taxi from Sanjiang. Connecting Chengyang to the main road are over 100 bridges. One of the most exquisite is a *fengyu qiao*, a wind-and-rain bridge, dating from 1916. The 256-ft (78-m) long bridge, built from pegged cedar – no nails are said to have been used – took 12 years to complete. The roof is especially elaborate, with five raised pavilions, each built in a different regional style. These beautifully-built bridges not only served a practical function, but acted as shrines to river spirits as well. Most of the altars have now been moved to the riverbank, as the incense is considered a fire hazard.

Basic accommodations are available for visitors interested in exploring the ethnic villages and surrounding countryside. Each hamlet in Chengyang houses a small drum tower, while the surrounding fields are irrigated by bamboo pipes fed by huge, spindly water-wheels, also made from plaited bamboo.

The highland market town of **Dutong** lies two hours by bus north of Sanjiang, on a separate road past numerous Dong villages. Situated near the Hunanese border, it provides basic accommodations for visitors. A cobbled walking track leads uphill to **Gaoding**, a cluster of six drum towers and 100-or-so dark-roofed wooden houses.

# Zhaoxing ⑮
肇兴

75 miles (120 km) NW of Sanjiang. ☐ *from Sanjiang.*

One of the most attractive Dong villages, sprinkled with fish ponds and bisected by a stream, Zhaoxing sits in a wide, flat valley and is famed throughout China for its impressive collection of traditional architecture (although there are a few modern buildings found on its outskirts). The town is divided into five sections, each inhabited by a different clan, and each possessing its own drum tower, theater, and wind-and-rain bridge. The original structures were destroyed during the Cultural Revolution, and although they

have been rebuilt since, they are charmingly well-worn and impressively intricate. The bridges and theaters are embellished with mirror fragments and detailed moldings.

The Dong community here still makes and wears traditional dark-blue clothing, which is hand-beaten with wooden mallets until soft, and then varnished with eggwhite to ward off mosquitoes.

Numerous muddy tracks lead through the surrounding rice terraces. One trail leads 4 miles (7 km) uphill to the small village of **Tang An**, packed with wooden buildings. **Jitang**, 2 miles (3 km) south of Zhaoxing, is also worth the steep climb. It has some old drum towers that survived the vandalism of the early 1970s.

**A cluster of Dong wooden houses, Zhaoxing**

# Huangyao ⑯
黄姚

68 miles (110 km) SE of Yangshuo.
🏯 3,000. 🚌 from Yangshuo or Guilin.

This sizeable rural village survives almost completely intact from Qing times. Its atmospheric cobbled streets, stone bridges, and old houses are laid out along a small river beneath a ring of limestone peaks. Many houses have heavy wooden doors and elaborate "fire-baffle" end walls – to direct heat and flames in a certain direction – drawn up into a decorative oval shape, while the village gates are guarded by short brick watchtowers with gun slits at the front, left over from days of banditry. The most impressive building is an **ancestral hall** built in the southern Chinese style, with atriums separated by carved wooden screens.

Huangyao's rural Chinese setting and beautiful scenery draws artists and photo-graphers, and has been used as a location in such films as *The Painted Veil* (2006). Huangyao is neither as developed for tourism as many other old villages in China, nor does it attract the same volume of tourists. By late afternoon, the streets are generally empty except for a few chickens and dogs. At night the back lanes are hung with attractive red lanterns.

Xi Shan's tea plantation surrounded by mist-covered forest, Guiping

# Guiping ⑰
桂平

137 miles (220 km) S of Guilin. 🚌

Located at the confluence of Yu and Xun rivers, Guiping is an unremarkable city surrounded by lush mountain scenery. Its importance as a regional center has declined, due to the cessation of river traffic during the 1990s. Its main industry is now sugar cane.

Guiping is renowned for its high-quality green tea, *xi shan cha*, which grows on **Xi Shan** (West Mountain), on the outskirts of town. The long leaves of tea are

**Lion statute from Longhua Si, Guiping**

processed and rolled into what look like miniature black cheroots. They are steeped one at a time to produce a faintly bitter, yet refreshing brew.

Xi Shan itself can be easily ascended from town. The 2-hour hike, past tea plantations and through bamboo groves, passes a number of Tang-era Buddhist temples. Longhua Si, deep in the forest on the upper slopes of the mountain, was built during the Song dynasty and heavily renovated during the 1980s. It contains numerous Buddhist statues. The temples sell Xi Shan *cha*, which is said to be superior to that sold in

**A depiction of imperial forces recapturing Nanjing from the Taiping rebels in 1864**

### THE TAIPING REBELLION

After being defeated in the 1840–42 Opium Wars, China was forced to pay a huge indemnity to Britain. Taxation was increased, causing great hardship in poor rural areas such as southern Guangxi. People's discontent with the weak Qing rule was fuelled by Hong Xiuquan, who formed a 10,000-strong militia, known as Taiping Tianguo (Kingdom of Heavenly Peace), at Jintian village in January 1851. Marching north, the Taiping captured Nanjing, making it their capital in March 1853. Influenced by Hong's personal interpretation of Christianity, the Taiping initially planned the overthrow of the Qing dynasty along with traditional religions, aiming to establish an egalitarian society. However, poor military planning and Hong's paranoia saw the movement falter. In July 1864, imperial forces wrested back Nanjing after a siege in which Hong died. It is thought that 20 million people were killed during the 13-year-long Taiping Uprising, one of the world's bloodiest civil conflicts.

Guiping shops. The summit offers splendid views of the river plains.

**Environs:** A 40-minute journey by bus from Guiping, the hamlet of **Jintian** lies 16 miles (25 km) north of town. From the bus stop, it's a 3-mile (5-km) walk across rural fields to the location of the first headquarters of Hong Xiuquan's Taiping Army. A museum here houses weapons, paintings, and maps recording the main events of the Taiping Uprising.

**Waterfall pouring down a Xi Shan rock face, Guiping**

# Nanning ⑱
南宁

218 miles (350 km) SE of Guilin.
👥 2,450,000. ✈ 🚌 🚃
ℹ 40 Xinmin Lu, (0771) 280 4960.

Nestled in the southern half of the province, only 120 miles (200 km) from the Vietnamese border, the

---

## DONGSON DRUM

Named for an archeological site in Vietnam, the oldest Dongson Drums are over 2,200 years old. They appear to have originated in Thailand or Vietnam, from where their use spread across Southeast Asia. The characteristic narrow-waisted drums are made from bronze, and reach up to 3 ft (1 m) in height, in styles that vary greatly from region to region. In Guangxi, timpani are marked with a 12-pointed star, and are often decorated with frog figurines,

**Bronze drum from Nanning**

while their middles are finely chased in stylized designs of warriors in boats wearing feathered headdresses. Originally used as storage vessels, later, as Ming historians observed, they came to symbolize chiefly authority amongst the Zhuang. They were played during agricultural ceremonies, and still feature as percussion instruments in some festivals amongst Guizhou's Miao community.

---

Guangxi capital of Nanning is somewhat removed from the rest of the province. Founded in the Song dynasty, Nanning became the provincial capital in 1912, until it was occupied by the Japanese forces during World War II. Reinstated as the capital in 1949, Nanning later served as an important center for supplies going to North Vietnam during the Vietnam War in the 1960s. In 1979, relations with Vietnam soured, and China went to war with its southern neighbor; Nanning once more became a military stronghold. Today, the city is expanding rapidly, partly as a consequence of cross-border traffic, which resumed in the 1990s.

Nanning makes a useful transit point for those heading to Vietnam or towards sights located in the southwestern corner of the province, such as Detian Falls and the Zuo Jiang (see pp424–5). Nanning itself has only a handful of monuments and sights, but is a nice enough place with a laid-back atmosphere and many bustling markets. It is also the main city of the Zhuang minority (see p424), who make up over 60 percent of the population.

The busy shopping district of **Xingning Lu**, with its well-restored European-style buildings, is a reminder that Nanning was opened to foreign trade in 1907. The **Provincial Museum** on Minzu Dadao has a display of over 50 antique bronze "Dongson" drums in many different styles, some of which are about 2,000 years old.

On Renmin Dong Lu, **Renmin Park** is planted with a variety of tropical plants such as giant taro, heliconias, bird-nest ferns, and philodendrons. To the east of the city on Chahua Yuan Lu, **Jinhua Cha Gardens** exhibits the rare Golden Camellia, only found in the mountains of Guangxi and quite possibly now extinct in the wild. Unusual for a camellia, its petals are large and rather tough.

**🏛 Provincial Museum**
Minzu Dadao. **Tel** (0771) 281 0907.
⏰ 9am–5pm Tue–Sun.

**🌺 Renmin Park**
1 Renmin Dong Lu. ⏰ daily.

**Vegetable vendors with their baskets at an outdoor market, Nanning**

Ancient rock art on the cliff of Hua Shan along the Zuo Jiang

# Zuo Jiang ⑲
左江

62 miles (100 km) SW of Nanning.
🚃 to Ningming. 🚌 to Ningming.
⛵ sampan to Hua Shan from
Ningming. 📷 📷 contact the Nanning tourist office for river tours.
**Longrui Reserve** 📷

A river tour up the peaceful
Zuo Jiang in a sampan
hired from Ningming, a small
settlement on the railroad
between Nanning and Ping-
xiang, takes visitors past prehistoric rock art and towering
karst scenery. Produced almost
2,000 years ago between the
Warring States and the late
Han period, the paintings of
over 2,600 human figures are
scattered across 70 locations
along the river. Painted in
red-brown ferrous oxide, they
mainly depict mass shamanistic
ceremonies. The designs show
marked similarities to those on
bronze Dongson drums (see

*p423)* that were found in
Vietnam and southern China.
It is believed that the artists
were the Luo Yue, ancestors
of the indigenous Zhuang.
    The first paintings are about
12 miles (20 km) upstream
from Ningming, but the largest
concentration is situated at
**Hua Shan** (Flower Mountain),
about three hours or so along
the river. A steep cliff rising
33 ft (10 m) above the water
is covered in as many as 1,200
stick figures, mostly male,
engaged in what appears to
be a ritual dance. A frequently
recurring symbol is a small
circle, thought to represent a
bronze drum, around which
several figures seem to dance
with their arms raised as if to
invoke the gods. A few carry
swords or ride on the back of
beasts. Only two of them are
clearly women, depicted with
long, flowing hair. Other
figures include dogs, a horse,
farmers, and rowers in a

dragon-boat race. A shaman,
identifiable by his elaborate
headdress, appears at the
center of all this activity.
    **Panlong,** a tiny hamlet on
the river between Ningming
and Hua Shan, has gorgeous
views of the rural peaked
landscape. Lodging is available
here in a handful of pretty
wooden buildings. Paths lead
from Panlong through the
**Longrui Nature Preserve**,
meant to protect the very rare
white-headed leaf monkey.
A sighting of these black-and-
white primates amongst the
dense forest and undergrowth
is unlikely, but its rugged paths
are well worth exploring.

Gatetower along the Vietnamese
border, Pingxiang

# Pingxiang ⑳
凭祥

93 miles (150 km) SW of Nanning.
🚃 🚌

Surrounded by vast fields of
sugar cane and the jagged
hills so typical of this region,
Pingxiang is a busy market

---

A group of Zhuang women in
traditional clothes

## THE ZHUANG COMMUNITY

With a population of around 18 million, the Zhuang form China's
largest ethnic minority. Most live in the Guangxi Zhuang Autonomous Region, although there are also communities in adjoining
provinces and Vietnam. They speak their own language, which
uses the Roman alphabet instead of Chinese characters. Visitors will
see bilingual road signs all across the region, particularly in Guilin
and Nanning. Apart from their language, it is hard to distinguish
urban Zhuang from the Han Chinese, although in the country the
men often dress in turbans and black pyjamas, while the women
wear blue embroidered jackets. The Zhuang are mainly animistic,
which explains the lack of Buddhist and Daoist temples in Guangxi.
One of their most famous festivals is Buffalo Soul Day, held in
honor of the Buffalo King's birthday on the eighth day of the fourth
lunar month (Apr/May). On this day, all buffalos are washed and
groomed, fed a special rice dish, and given the day off work.

The magnificent Detian Falls surrounded by spectacular karst hills

town and the railhead for the crossing into Vietnam. Visitors require a valid visa to enter Vietnam at the border crossing, **Youyi Guan** (Friendship Pass), another 9 miles (15-km) away. The current border was demarcated as early as the Ming era, and a good stretch of the original 33-ft (10-m) stone wall still stands, along with a restored watchtower and gateway under which visitors pass. The tower's second floor houses a diorama of the area and offers views into Vietnam. An early 20th-century European-style building on the Chinese side was built by the French when they controlled this region, known then as Indo-China. For those crossing into Vietnam, the rail line for Hanoi resumes 3 miles (5 km) away on the far side at Dong Dang.

## Detian Falls ㉑
德天瀑布

93 miles (150 km) W of Nanning. 🚌
via Daxin to Shuolong, minibus from
Shuolong to falls, 10 miles (16 km). 🎫

A spectacular set of broad cataracts dividing China from Vietnam, Detian is the second largest transnational waterfall in the world, after Niagara Falls on the US-Canada border. The two attractions, however, have little else in common. Detian

does not possess the sheer force of Niagara, but is more gently beautiful, falling in stages, and surrounded by an emerald karst landscape of jagged hills and plowed fields. It is possible to swim in the broad pool beneath the falls, and to take a bamboo raft into the spray near its base. Remember that a border runs through the center of the river – do not stray too far across. A road running along the top of the falls leads to a stone tablet from the 1950s that marks out the border.

## Beihai ㉒
北海

93 miles (150 km) S of Nanning.
✈ 🚊 🚌 ⛴ to Hainan Island.

A tropical port city of about 400,000 people, Beihai is one of the departure points for ferries to Hainan Island (see pp304–5). Many of the city's residents are ethnic Chinese from Vietnam, whose expulsion from that country in the late 1970s sparked a brief attempt by China to invade its neighbor.

Established over 2,000 years ago, the city prospered during the Han era, when it was a busy port. The old Colonial Quarter, on the northern seafront along Zhongshan Lu, is a 1.2-mile (2-km) stretch of narrow lanes and disintegrating

1920s plasterwork, at least one former church, and several colonnaded shopfronts.

About 2 miles (3 km) west of the center farther down Zhongshan Lu is the **Hainan Ferry Port**. Lying beyond is a small harbor crammed with motorized junks, rusty cargo ships, and battered trawlers.

Beihai's other attraction, **Yin Tan** (Silver Beach), lies 6 miles (10 km) south of town, but it does not compare with the lovely beaches of Hainan.

Located about 36 miles (58 km) southeast of Beihai, volcanic **Wiezhou Island** offers beautiful scenery and good opportunities for diving. It also has a Gothic church built by French churchmen in 1882.

Façade of an old colonial church on Weizhou Island

# THE
# NORTHEAST

# The Northeast at a Glance

Lying in the peripheral corner of China, the Northeast (Dongbei) abounds in raw beauty and mineral wealth, and was inhabited for centuries by indomitable tribes including the Khitan, Mongols, and Jurchen (Manchu), the latter ruling China for over 250 years. Today, the region's three provinces of Liaoning, Jilin, and Heilongjiang form China's industrial heartland, although the many lakes, mountains, and rugged borderlands offer scenic getaways. In Liaoning, Shenyang's palaces are testament to its great Manchu past, while Dalian is a fast-moving city with architectural marvels. The city of Jilin, once the capital of Manchukuo (1933–45), the puppet state installed by the Japanese, has stunning winter landscapes. Changchun, the capital of Jilin province, has a thriving automobile industry, while Heilongjiang is famed for its Harbin Ice Festival.

The ornate *paifang* or gateway to the rugged scenery of Bingyu Valley (Bingyu Gou), Liaoning

## SIGHTS AT A GLANCE

**Towns & Cities**

Changchun ❻
Dalian ❺
Dandong ❸
Harbin ❾
Jilin ❼
Jinzhou ❷
Shenyang ❶

**Nature Reserves, Mountains & Areas of Natural Beauty**

Bingyu Valley ❹
*Changbai Shan pp448–9* ❽
Mudanjiang Jingpo Hu ❿
Wu Da Lian Chi & the River Border ⓬
Zhalong Nature Reserve ⓫

◁ The Nen Jiang, a tributary of the Amur River winding through Heilongjiang's frozen landscape

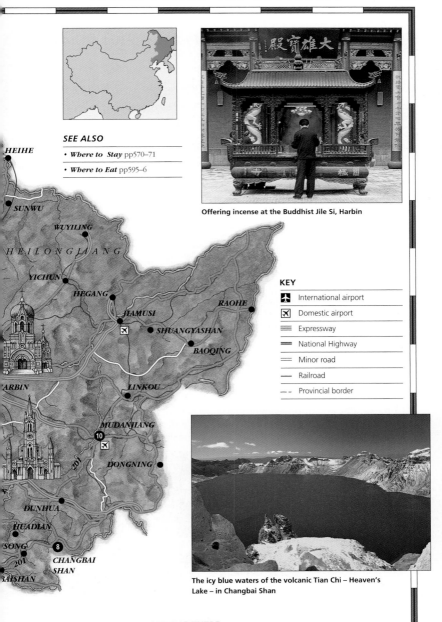

**HEIHE**

Offering incense at the Buddhist Jile Si, Harbin

**SUNWU**

**WUYILING**

**HEILONGJIANG**

**YICHUN**

**HEGANG**

**JIAMUSI**

**RAOHE**

**SHUANGYASHAN**

**BAOQING**

**KEY**

| | |
|---|---|
| ✈ | International airport |
| ⊠ | Domestic airport |
| ≡ | Expressway |
| ▬ | National Highway |
| ═ | Minor road |
| — | Railroad |
| -- | Provincial border |

**LINKOU**

**ARBIN**

**MUDANJIANG**

**10**

**DONGNING**

**201**

**DUNHUA**

**HUADIAN**

**SONG**

**8**

**201**

**CHANGBAI SHAN**

**BAISHAN**

The icy blue waters of the volcanic Tian Chi – Heaven's Lake – in Changbai Shan

| 0 km | 100 |
|---|---|
| 0 mile | 100 |

## GETTING THERE

The major cities – Shenyang, Dalian, Changchun, Harbin, and Jilin – are connected to Beijing by air and rail. There are express buses from Beijing to Shenyang, Dalian, and Changchun. Regular trains and buses also ply within the region. A few flights operate between the major cities, including Harbin and Dalian. In winter, popular destinations such as Jilin and Harbin are relatively easy to reach, while remoter areas such as Jingpo Hu and Changbai Shan are more difficult to access. Within cities, taxis are the best option.

# A PORTRAIT OF THE NORTHEAST

*Sandwiched between Russia, Korea, and Inner Mongolia, the three northeastern provinces constitute China's easternmost extent. Even though the prevalent culture is Han Chinese, the Northeast's geography, history, and extended external boundaries have shaped a distinct regional identity. The region's attractions range from the bustling sprawl of its big cities to the rugged, and sublime terrain beyond, and the cultural mix of its border towns.*

It is hard to categorize the Northeast (Dongbei) – it enjoys hot summers but glacial winters, and while heavy industry and socialist planning blight some cityscapes, others sport elegant pockets of colonial architecture. And while parts of the region have been revelling in China's economic boom, others have suffered from chronic unemployment.

**Statue of twin Buddhas, Bei Ta, Shenyang**

Encompassing the three provinces of Liaoning, Jilin, and Heilongjiang, the Northeast was a latecomer to the Chinese empire and is sometimes considered as little more than an appendix to the rest of the country. As part of former Manchuria, however, it was the cradle of the magnificent civilization that ruled China from 1644 until 1912. Shenyang, Liaoning's present capital, became the Manchu capital in 1625, and the site of the Imperial Palace. Here they perfected their Eight Banner system of color-coded hereditary social and administrative divisions *(see pp432–3)*. Taking advantage of the overthrow of the Ming dynasty in 1644, they moved their capital to the Forbidden City in Beijing. Even today, the region's Manchu population take great pride in their heritage and still adhere to the Eight Banners.

Stately Russian architecture in Daliqu district, Harbin

**Façade of the Puppet Emperor's Palace, Changchun**

southern cousins, they speak Mandarin with a coarse, albeit intelligible accent. Unlike the sophisticated cuisine of Hong Kong and Shanghai, the local food – including *jiaozi* (dumplings), *dun* (stews), and *tudou* (potatoes) – is hearty and filling. The temperament of the people matches the vigorous landscapes that range from dense forest to volcanic regions

In more recent time, the Northeast attracted the attentions of Russia and Japan, both of which have helped shape the region's destiny. At the end of the 19th century the Russians, interested in the ice-free port of Lushun, tried to annexe parts of Manchuria and built part of the Trans-Siberian Railway line, before being humiliated by Japan. The area suffered again during the Japanese occupation of the 1930s and 40s, when it was renamed Manchukuo and Pu Yi was installed as Puppet Emperor. The brutal occupation left deep scars on the region's psyche along with some pitiful sights, such as the Japanese Germ Warfare Experimental Base near Harbin.

**Door handle Confucius Temple**

Japanese occupation came to an end after World War II, ushering in a period of industrialization under Chairman Mao. His camaraderie with Russia in the 1950s resulted in the installation of a Stalinist state-sector economy. The peaceful relationship was shortlived and conflicts soon flared along the border.

The Northeast's rich mineral wealth has made it China's industrial heartland. However, underinvestment and ruthless downsizing with huge state-sector layoffs have resulted in high unemployment.

Centuries of hardship have molded the character of the *Dongbeiren* (Northeasterners). Resolute, unaffected, forthright, and hospitable, they are looked upon by their compatriots as a hardy, stalwart people, prone to hard drinking. Taller and stockier than their

and the tough terrain along the Russian and North Korean borders. These areas offer plenty of outdoor options including trekking and bird-watching, particularly in Zhalong Nature Reserve.

The border town of Dandong has a thriving tourist industry, catering mainly to North Korean visitors.

Despite the unfortunate effects of industrialization, there is much worth seeing. The onion domes and Byzantine ornamentation visible in Harbin's buildings are distinctly Russian, a legacy of the city's cross-cultural links. Dalian, on the Yellow Sea, is a dynamic and progressive city that has enjoyed the same economic success as Shanghai. Known as the "Hong Kong of the North," it adds an affluent touch to the Northeastern rustbelt.

**A secluded bay by the blue waters of the volcanic Jingpo Hu, Heilongjiang**

# The Manchu Dynasty

Carving from Manchu palace

The final overlords of the Middle Kingdom, the Manchus from the Northeast, took advantage of a China weakened by peasant rebellion to invade and establish the Qing or "pure" dynasty in 1644. This foreign Manchu court preserved much of China's governing apparatus and over time absorbed local ways. Despite providing some of China's most illustrious emperors, including Kangxi (see p122) and Qianlong, the Qing declined into an ineffectual torpor. Coupled with the seizure of territories by foreign powers, the Qing failure to modernize led to the collapse of Manchu legitimacy and the final downfall of the dynasty.

**The queue,** *a long plaited hairstyle that has come to symbolize Chinese traditions, was a Manchu import imposed on Han Chinese men.*

## THE COURT AT THE FORBIDDEN CITY

Like the Ming before them, the Manchu Qing established their court in Beijing. The Manchus were the last dynastic occupants of the Forbidden City. Served by as many as 3,000 eunuchs, they were immersed in a court life of arcane ceremony and ritual until the dynasty was unseated by the founding of the Republic of China in 1912.

**Nurhachi (1559–1626),** *the first Manchu emperor, organized the scattered tribes of the northeast into eight banner units in the early 17th century. He moved his capital to Shenyang, but did not live to see the subjugation of China. After his death, his son Ababai established the Qing dynasty in 1636 and proceeded to invade China.*

**The Manchu Imperial Palace** *in Shenyang was begun during Nurhachi's reign and completed by Ababai. In 1644, when the Manchus toppled the Ming, the Shenyang complex became a "travelling palace", used by the emperor during tours of inspection.*

**Elaborate summer camping trips** *in Inner Mongolia were undertaken by the early Qing rulers, as a break from Confucian court life. They hunted, practiced archery, and slept in yurts, in order to preserve their Manchu vigor.*

**Qianlong (r. 1735–1796),** *the fourth Qing emperor, was a generous patron of the arts. His lengthy reign was also marked by territorial expansion, including the absorption of Xinjiang, and was largely a period of Chinese prosperity.*

**Yuanming Yuan,** *the Garden of Perfect Brightness (see p103), was designed by Jesuits for the Qianlong emperor. Much of its grandiose architecture was destroyed by French and English troops in 1860.*

萬國來朝

**Jesuit missionary** *Adam Schall von Bell (1591–1666) impressed the Manchu court with his knowledge of astronomy. The Jesuits realized that having influence in China required mastering the Confucian Classics and Mandarin.*

**In 1793, Lord Macartney** *arrived with elaborate gifts from King George III, seeking to establish trade between Britain and China. Macartney was rebuffed by the Qianlong emperor, who refused Britain a single concession.*

## THE BOXER REBELLION

The Boxers, a band of xenophobic rebels from north China who rose up to rid China of the "foreign devils," drew from superstitious rituals that they believed made them invulnerable. Cixi, seeking an opportunity to strike back at the foreign powers, allied herself to their cause. The rebels laid waste to Beijing's Legation Quarter in 1900, while besieging the district's foreign population. The siege was finally lifted by an eight-power allied force. The Qing government was forced to sign The Boxer Protocol which, among other conditions, allowed the stationing of foreign troops in Beijing.

**Boxer massacre of Chinese Christians**

**The Empress Dowager,** *Cixi (see p101), was deeply conservative and a shrewd manipulator. Dismissive of foreign powers, she appointed pro-Boxer Prince Duan as Minister of Foreign Affairs.*

# Trans-Siberian Railway

The term Trans-Siberian Railway refers to three services: the Trans-Siberian, the Trans-Mongolian, and the Trans-Manchurian. In 1891 Russia decided to join the extremities of her empire by rail. A short cut through Manchuria was negotiated with China and the line was completed in 1903. War with Japan forced the Russians to cede the railroad to them in 1905 and build a new line skirting Manchuria – the Trans-Siberian route was finished in 1916. The Trans-Mongolian route was added in the 1940s and 50s. In an era of jet travel, this epic week-long journey is an experience not to be missed.

**Conductor and train on the Trans-Siberian Railway**

**Orthodox priest** *running a mobile religious service in Manchuria at the turn of the 20th century. Today the historic Russian presence in the Northeast can still be seen in Harbin, Lushun, and border towns like Manzhouli.*

**Steam trains** *were finally replaced in 2002, although electrification began in 1939. Because of differences in the track widths of Chinese and Russian lines, huge cranes lift the carriages up onto the correct width "bogeys" when crossing the border.*

**This 1907 poster** *advertises the romance of a winter trip on the Trans-Siberian Railway. The poster's distinct Japanese feel derives from Japan's occupation of Manchuria and Korea at the time.*

**The train** carves its way through the grasslands of the north Manchurian plain.

**The standard of luxury** *is reasonable. (The Chinese deluxe carriage has showers.) If the dining car doesn't appeal, at each stop there's a throng of vendors on the platforms selling goods.*

**The longest railway service** *in the world at nearly 6,000 miles (9,500 km), it takes up to 7 days to cover the journey.*

**KEY**

— Trans-Siberian
— Trans-Mongolian
— Trans-Manchurian

RUSSIAN FEDERATION

Yekaterinburg
Moscow • Omsk • Lake Bykal
Irkutsk • Ulan-Ude
KAZAKHSTAN    MONGOLIA    Harbin
Vladivostok
CHINA    Beijing

## TRANS-MANCHURIAN RAILWAY

The *Vostok* makes the six-day trip once a week from Beijing through Shanhaiguan and Harbin, before heading through the spectacular Manchurian plain, the huge expanse of Russia, and back.

*The Trans-Mongolian is probably the most interesting route of the three: it goes through China – past the Great Wall and Datong, site of the Yungang Caves; via Mongolia and its grasslands; and finally through the expanse of Russia. However, it also requires three visas.*

**Lake Baykal's** *cliffs proved problematic for the builders. They had to chisel miles of tunnels out of solid rock and construct many bridges. It was worth it in the end because the southern end of the lake provides all three lines with some of the most picturesque scenery of the trip.*

### TRAVELERS' TIPS

- You can book tickets through Seat 61 – see **www.**seat61.com
- Summer is the peak season; Fall is quieter; the train is heated, but Winter can be very cold outside.
- Bring dried noodle snacks, hot chocolate, a bowl, and cutlery as there is boiling water on tap.
- Arrange for at least one or two stops on the way – separate ticket required for each stop.
- Be prepared to drink vodka.

**Looking out** the window occupies most of your time on the trip – when not meeting other travelers.

**Moscow** *is the end (or indeed start) for the three Trans-Siberian Railway services. It is possible to go on to St. Petersburg and the Baltic Sea. However, Moscow has plenty of museums, churches, and grand architecture to see, and deserves a few days of exploration.*

# LIAONING, JILIN & HEILONGJIANG

*S*tretching from Shanhaiguan – the Great Wall's terminus at the
Yellow Sea – to the Siberian borders in the north, the provinces of
Liaoning, Jilin, and Heilongjiang cover 309,000 sq miles
(800,000 sq km), an area larger than Spain and Portugal. With a
population of over 100 million, they offer a variety of landscapes
from seaside ports to expanses of uninhabited forests and mountains.

The region was once part of erstwhile Manchuria, and the lavish palace of the Manchu kings at Shenyang in the heart of Liaoning stands testament to their might. On Liaoning's balmier southern coast, Dalian features scenic coastal drives and fine, sandy beaches. As the only ice-free port in the area, it was coveted by both Japan and Russia, and occupied continuously by one or the other between 1895 and 1955.

Japan's imperialist stamp also survives in Jilin's capital, Changchun, from where China's last emperor, Pu Yi, ruled the Japanese state of Manchukuo as a mere puppet. In Heilongjiang, the city of Harbin has heavy Russian overtones, clearly evident in its buildings and restaurants, while strong Korean influences color Dandong town, situated along the North Korean border. Also straddling the border is the rugged, spectacular Changbai Shan Reserve, which abounds in lush, jagged peaks and hiking opportunities. Its volcanic lake, Tian Chi, is China's deepest, rumored to be home to a mysterious aquatic beast.

Other natural attractions include Liaoning's Bingyu Valley with its towering rock formations, Heilongjiang's volcanic lakes – Wu Da Lian Chi and Jingpo Hu, and the huge bird sanctuary at Zhalong Nature Reserve, whose marshy expanse supports hundreds of species of birds during the summer breeding season.

A secluded sandy cove in the Bangchuidao Scenic Area, Dalian

◁ Pleasureboats on the Songhua River, near Jilin

# Shenyang
沈阳

**Colossal
Mao statue**

Capital of Liaoning province and the largest city in the Northeast, Shenyang may lack the panache of Dalian, but it serves as an important transport and industrial hub at the heart of the province. Of strategic importance in the state of Yan during the Warring States period (475–221 BC), the town was first called Shenyang during the Mongol Yuan dynasty, before rising to prominence as the first Manchu capital in 1625, when it was known as Mukden and was chosen as the setting for the Imperial Palace, a splendid rival to Beijing's Forbidden City.

A throng of visitors outside the Dazheng Hall, Imperial Palace

### 🏯 Imperial Palace

171 Shenyang Lu. **Tel** *(024) 2484 4192.*
◯ *summer: 8:30am–5pm, winter: 9am–4:30pm.* 🖼 🚫 *interiors.*

Second only in scale to the Forbidden City in Beijing, the Imperial Palace, also called Shenyang Gugong, is Shenyang's premier historical sight, situated in what was the center of the old city. Its construction began in 1625, during the reign of Nurhachi (1559–1626), leader of the Manchus. In 1644, Manchu troops breached the Great Wall at Shanhaiguan *(see p128)* and swarmed into China to establish the Qing dynasty. Serving as the imperial residence of both Nurhachi and his son and heir Abahai, the palace is composed of 300 rooms. While its features reflect a pronounced Manchu and Mongol influence, the palace was obviously an attempt to emulate its Ming counterpart, the Forbidden City, Beijing. The palace

divides into three sections. The dominating feature of the central section is the **Chongzheng Hall**, from where Abahai oversaw political affairs and received envoys from vassal lands and border territories. In the courtyard behind the hall, the **Qingning Palace** is where the emperor and his concubines resided. The Phoenix Tower, the tallest structure in the imperial grounds can be found here too.

In the western section, the Wensu Pavilion formerly housed one of seven copies of the 36,078-volume *Siku Quanshu* (Complete Library of the Four Treasures), an encyclopedic collection of Chinese literature compiled in the Qing era, of which only four sets survive. The **Dazheng Hall** is the central

feature of the eastern section, fronted by pillars emblazoned with sinuous dragons. It was here that Shunzhi (Aisin Gioro Fulin) was crowned as the first Qing emperor, before he conquered China in 1644. In front of the hall stand the Ten King Pavilions, once used as offices by the chieftains of the "Eight Banners" – the Manchu system of land and hereditary divisions. The palace has been undergoing extensive restoration and some halls that are usually open may be closed. It achieved UNESCO World Heritage Site status in 2004.

### 🏯 Mao Statue

Zhongshan Square.
The statue of Mao Zedong situated in Zhongshan Square in downtown Shenyang stands as a reminder of a vanished era. Mao statues tower over public squares across China, including such far-flung outposts as Lijiang *(see pp390–91)* in Yunnan and Kashgar *(see pp510–11)* in Xinjiang, but this example is perhaps the most histrionic, depicting Mao's giant monolithic figure as a superman in an overcoat.

### 🏯 North Pagoda

27 Beita Jie. ◯ *summer: 8:30am–5pm, winter: 9am–4:30pm.* 🖼
Built in 1643, Bei Ta is the only one of four temples and pagodas situated on the city boundaries in a decent state of repair. The surviving features of the original pagoda are the Great Hall and Falun Temple.

### 🏛 18 September Museum

46 Wanghua Nanjie.
◯ *as above.* 🖼 🚫
The Jiuyiba Lishi Bowuguan commemorates the occupation of Shenyang on September 18, 1931, by Japanese troops. Its exhibits make up the most comprehensive chronicle of Japanese aggression in Manchuria. Like other museums with a similar theme, some of the displays can be rather gruesome.

Wei Tuo Buddha, North Pagoda

**North Tomb's ornate west wall and gateway**

## VISITORS' CHECKLIST

440 miles (700 km) NE of Beijing. 5,000,000. Shenyang Airport. South Train Station or North Train Station. South Bus Station, Express Bus Station, CAAC (buses to airport). Bldg 4, 290 Shi Fu Lu (024) 2295 8888.

### 🏯 North Tomb

12 Taishan Lu, Beiling Gongyuan, North Shenyang. 7am–6pm daily. interiors.

The huge Beiling Park houses the tomb of Abahai (1592–1643), the son of Nurhachi, and his wife, Empress Borjijit. One of the largest and best-preserved of China's imperial mausoleums, the North Tomb (Bei Ling) was built in 1643, the year of the emperor's death. The layout of the complex is typical of imperial Chinese tombs (see pp104–5), and is accessed through Zhenghong Gate to the south. Of the pavilions lying on either side of the gate, the easternmost pavilion was used as a dressing room for visiting emperors, while the westernmost was the site for sacrificing animals. A spirit way (shendao), lined with animal statues, leads to the Hall of Eminent Favor (Ling'en Dian). Right behind the hall lie the tree-covered imperial burial mounds, formally called Zhao Ling (the Luminous Tomb), and an exquisite dragon screen.

**Mythical animal, North Tomb**

### 🏯 East Tomb

3 miles (5 km) E of Shenyang. 8am–4pm daily. interiors.

The impressive East Tomb (Dong Ling), the final resting place of Nurhachi and his wife Yehenala, was completed in 1651. Arranged attractively on the slopes of Mount Tianzhu near the Hun River, the three-storied tomb has a flight of 108 steps leading to its main gate. The number 108 is sacred to the Chinese; in the Daoist celestial order, 108 represents the 36 stars of heaven and the 72 stars of hell. The number is also sacred to Buddhists, reflected in the 108 beads on Buddhist rosaries and the number of luohan in certain Buddhist sects.

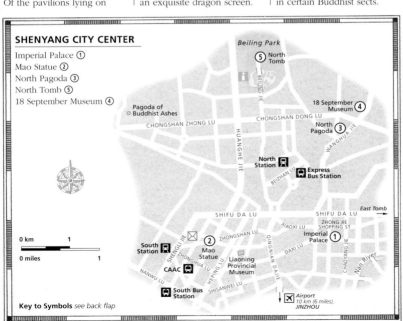

### SHENYANG CITY CENTER

Imperial Palace ①
Mao Statue ②
North Pagoda ③
North Tomb ⑤
18 September Museum ④

Beiling Park

North Tomb ⑤

Pagoda of Buddhist Ashes

18 September Museum ④

CHONGSHAN ZHONG LU
CHONGSHAN DONG LU

North Pagoda ③

BEILING JIE
HUANGHE JIE
NANGHUA JIE

North Station
BEIZHAN LU
Express Bus Station

East Tomb →

SHIFU DA LU
SHIFU DA LU
ZHONG JIE SHOPPING ST

TIAOXI LU
Imperial Palace ①

QINGNIAN DAJIE

0 km 1
0 miles 1

South Station
SHENGLI JIE
ZHONGSHAN LU
Mao Statue ②
ZHONGSHAN LU
HEPING LU
CAAC
DAXI LU

Liaoning Provincial Museum

CHAOYANG JIE
Nan River

NANWU LU
South Bus Station
SHISANWEI LU

Airport
10 km (6 miles),
JINZHOU

**Key to Symbols** see back flap

**The impressive Bijia Shan, connected to the mainland by an isthmus at low tide**

# Jinzhou ❷
锦州

125 miles (200 km) SW of Shenyang.
☒ ☒ ☒

An industrial city on the eastern shores of the Liaoning Gulf, Jinzhou is visited mainly for its storehouse of Jurassic period fossils, of which more than 300 are housed in the private **Wenya Museum** (Bowuguan). Set up by the amateur collector Du Wenya, this unremarkable three-story building stands on Heping Lu although there is talk of relocating it in the near future. The star attraction is a specimen of *dushi kongzi niao*

(*Confuciusornis dui hou*), a winged, avian dinosaur with feathered features, that was unearthed in 1998 in western Liaoning, a region rich in dinosaur remains. Other exhibits include another dinosaur with bird-like features known as *Sinosauropteryx*, a 120-million-year-old and 29-ft (9-m) fossilized tree, and fossilized dinosaur eggs from the Jurassic period. Jutting out of Jinzhou Bay, 21 miles (34 km) south of town, is **Bijia Shan** (Pen-holder Mount). It is connected to the mainland by an isthmus that emerges from the sea at low tide. The island's peaks – which resemble a Chinese pen rest – support several Buddhist temples and offer magnificent views over the bay. Visitors who wish to walk to Bijia Shan along the isthmus should check the timings of low-tide before planning a trip. An alternative way of reaching the island is by taking a fishing boat.

🏛 **Wenya Museum**
33–13 Erduan, Heping Lu. **Tel** *(0416) 234 3999.* ◯ *8:30am–5pm daily.*

🎇 **Bijia Shan**
◯ *8:30am–5pm daily.* 📷

# Dandong ❸
丹东

172 miles (277 km) SE of Shenyang.
🏯 *7,500,000.* ☒ ☒ ☒
ℹ *20 Shiwei Lu, (0415) 213 7493.*

Presided over by a statue of Mao Zedong in the heart of town, Dandong is located along the Yalu Jiang (Yalu River) in the eastern part of Liaoning province. It would have been little more than an obscure outpost, ignored by travelers, if it were not for its proximity to North Korea. Today, the largest border town in China, Dandong has an unmistakable Korean stamp, from the *shaokao* (barbecue) dishes, to the signs in *hangul* (the Korean script), and the Korean shops and souvenirs.

Within reach of Dandong are several other interesting sights, and the town acts as a useful launch pad to Changbai Shan *(see pp448–9)* and the stunning mountain lake of Tian Chi. Dandong's trademark sight is the **Yalu Jiang Duan Qiao** (Yalu River Bridge) that reaches out into the river alongside the bridge connecting China with North Korea – this railway line runs all the way from Beijing to Pyongyang. The steel bridge ends halfway along its full span, the remainder having been dismantled by the Koreans. The surviving half in Chinese territory bears the

**The Yalu Jiang Duan Qiao, that once connected China with North Korea**

**Dramatic karst hills rising up from the river, Bingyu Valley**

scars of combat, having been strafed in 1950 by US fighter planes during the Korean War. The ruin serves as a monument to the **Kang Mei Yuan Chao Zhanzheng** (War to Resist US Aggression & Aid Korea), as the Chinese refer to their part in the conflict. Boats and speedboats offer cruises along the Yalu River, for visitors who want to get within two or three feet of the hermit kingdom. It is permitted to take photographs of North Korea, though there are few photogenic features – just factories, civilians, and Stalinist housing. Those who wish to learn more about China's contribution to the Korean War can visit the **Museum to Commemorate Aiding Korea & Resisting America**, with a plethora of exhibits on the war. Even though the captions are almost exclusively in Chinese, the nationalistic refrain is clearly evident.

Located 31 miles (50 km) northwest of town, the 2,760-ft (840-m) **Fenghuang Shan** (Phoenix Emperor Mountain) is associated with Daoist mythology. It supports a crop of temples and caves, besides offering some excellent hiking trails. A good time to visit is during the temple fair (*miaohui*), held every April. The **Hushan Great Wall**, a

**A traffic policewoman on duty**

little-visited and restored vestige of the Great Wall, is located 20 km (12 miles) northeast of Dandong, near Jiuliancheng town, overlooking the Yalu River and the North Korean border. This section of the wall, dating from the reign of the Ming Wanli emperor, is its easternmost point. In 2003, the **Great Wall Museum** opened at the site, displaying relics associated with the defensive barrier.

Since the North Korean border is not always clearly marked, hiking around this area is inadvisable, in case visitors inadvertently cross over into North Korea.

🔲 **Yalu Jiang Duan Qiao**
*Tel* (0415) 212 2145. ⬜ *daily.* 🖾

🔲 **Fenghuang Shan**
Fengchen City. ⬜ *daily.* 🖾

# Bingyu Valley ❹
冰峪沟

149 miles (240 km) NE of Dalian.
🔲 *from Dalian to Zhuanghe, then bus.* 🔲 *from Dalian to Zhuanghe, then bus to Bingyu Fengjingqu.*

A picturesque river valley, Bingyu Gou lies sprawled across 42 sq miles (110 sq km). It offers long riverside walks and hikes in fabulous trekking terrain overlooked by jagged peaks, karst rock formations, temples, and cliffs hollowed out by numerous caves. Opportunities for climbing, fishing, and rafting are also available. The valley can be reached via the town of Zhuanghe, northeast of Dalian. Accommodations are available for those who wish to stay overnight. It is best to avoid the holiday periods as well as weekends during summer, when the valley receives crowds of visitors.

**Steps leading to a Daoist temple on Fenghuang Shan**

# Dalian ⑤

大连

**Giant football, Labor Park**

Sparkling with self-assurance and confidence, Dalian is Northeast China's most dynamic and attractive city. It is famed throughout China for its top-notch hotels, progressive economy, modern and European-style architecture, football team, and cleanliness. The city resembles Shanghai in its port setting, cosmopolitanism, Special Economic Zone status, and history of foreign control, but has the added attraction of a coastline dotted with scenic beaches and lawns. Located at the southernmost point of Northeast China near the tip of the Liaodong peninsula, Dalian enjoys sea breezes and a warmer winter than other parts of the region.

**Colonial architecture and modern highrises around Zhongshan Square**

## Exploring Dalian

The city of Dalian has few temples or monuments of note, but most visitors come for its beaches, seafood, shopping, and striking modernity. Serving as a dazzling hub from which major streets radiate, **Zhongshan Square** (Zhongshan Guangchang) is laid out with lawns and encircled by a ring of colonial buildings dating from the Russian and Japanese eras. At night, locals gather here to dance and listen to music, and to watch the occasional cultural performances that are held. The most interesting buildings along the square's periphery are the Dalian Hotel (Dalian Binguan) at No. 4 to the south, and the Bank of China (Zhongguo Yinhang) on the northern rim at No. 9.

Dalian's main shopping area is **Tianjin Jie**, a pedestrianized stretch of shops northwest of Zhongshan Square. Beneath Shengli Square to the west is a huge underground shopping center, while the

Friendship Store lies farther east on Renmin Lu.

Dotting Dalian are several tree-lined streets and spacious parks. Southwest of Zhongshan Square is **Labor Park** (Laodong Gongyuan), with its hallmark giant football at the center. It is known for hosting the Locust Flower Festival each spring. Farther southwest is Dalian's other main square, **Renmin Square**. Formerly known as Stalin Square, it was originally overlooked by a large statue

of a Russian soldier, that now stands in nearby Lushun. The square is pleasantly laid out with grass and is lit at night.

Dalian is famous for its beaches and these can easily be reached by bus or taxi. In the northeast of the Dalian peninsula, just off Binhai Lu near the Eighteen Bends, is the scenic **Donghai Park**. Covering 1,112 acres (450 ha), this seaside park has a 3,937-ft (1,200-m) long coastline. It was founded to celebrate Dalian's centennial anniversary, and has striking statues of oversized sea-creatures, including a giant octopus and a shark. There are fine sea views, and the water is clean though rather cold until mid-July for swimming. The pebble beach is popular with visitors, who often bring tents and beach towels and spend the whole day here.

Farther south along the coastal Binhai Lu, the **Bangchuidao Scenic Area** (Bangchuidao Jingqu) has the best beaches on China's east coast, once reserved for party officials and now open to all. Binhai Lu makes for a marvelous walk with fantastic views over the cliffs across the Yellow Sea. The next stop is the more touristy **Tiger Beach Scenic Area** (Laohutan Jingqu), which sports an amusement park and an aquarium. Several miles farther west, the **Fujiazhuang Scenic Area** (Fujiazhuang Jingqu) is also rather boisterous and crowded, and farther still is the Xinghai Beach Scenic Area, housing the immensely popular **Sun Asia Ocean World**. This aquarium has a 381-ft (116-m) long

**Statue of a rowing team in midstroke, Xinghai Square**

◁ **Impressive ice sculptures being made in preparation for the Harbin Ice Festival**

underwater tunnel and several tanks filled with sea-life that attract children in droves. Just off the coast, Xinghai Square was built to commemorate the return of Hong Kong to China in 1997.

🌺 **Donghai Park**
Binhai Lu. ○ 8am–5pm daily. 🎫

🎋 **Bangchuidao Scenic Area**
○ daily. 🎫

🐟 **Sun Asia Ocean World**
○ 9am–5pm daily. 🎫

**Environs:** Lying 22 miles (35 km) southwest of Dalian, **Lushun** enjoys an excellent strategic position, its harbor benefiting from the perennial ice-free waters. Known as Port Arthur, it was the chief naval base for the Chinese Beiyang fleet from the mid-19th century, and was seized by the Japanese during the Sino-Japanese War (1894–95). Returned to China soon after, the port fell to the Russians in 1897, who developed the base for their Pacific fleet, but Japan wrested Lushun back in

**Barber attending to a customer**

## VISITORS' CHECKLIST

180 miles (300 km) S of Shenyang. 🚆 3,400,000. ✈ Dalian Airport. 🚌 🚉 Dalian Bus Station, CAAC (buses to airport), Heishijiao Bus Station. ⛴ from Yantai & Weihai. 🎭 Locust Flower Festival (Spring). ℹ 9 Jie Fang Road, (0411) 836 91165.

1905, forfeiting it only at the end of World War II. Among the surviving Russian architecture is the **Railway Station**, built in 1898 as the terminus of the South Manchuria Railway (see pp434–5). The **Japanese-Russian Prison**, which incarcerated Russian, Japanese, and Chinese prisoners, also has a gory torture room and gallows. Tours take in the compound and photographs on display. North of the bay and near the station, **Baiyu Hill** is topped with rows of cannons and a tower, plus great views.

Visitors must check with the Public Security Bureau just off Zhongshan Square for permission to visit, since Lushun is a closed military zone.

🏯 **Japanese-Russian Prison**
139 Xiangyong Jie. ○ daily. 🎫 🚩

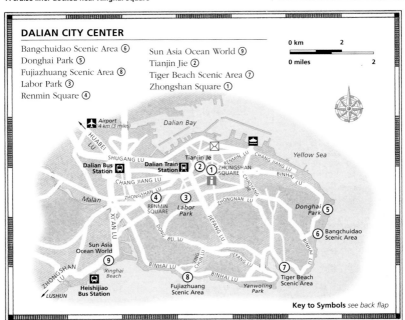
A cruise liner docked near Xinghai Square

## DALIAN CITY CENTER

Bangchuidao Scenic Area ⑥
Donghai Park ⑤
Fujiazhuang Scenic Area ⑧
Labor Park ③
Renmin Square ④

Sun Asia Ocean World ⑨
Tianjin Jie ②
Tiger Beach Scenic Area ⑦
Zhongshan Square ①

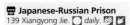

0 km     2
0 miles     2

**Living quarters at the Puppet Emperor's Palace, Changchun**

# Changchun ❻
长春

185 miles (300 km) NE of Shenyang.
🚶 2,200,000. ✈ Xiangtan Airport.
🚉 🚌 to Dalian, Shanghai &
Tianjin. 🛈 1323 Xi'an Da Rd, (0431)
8892 9311.

The sprawling modern capital of Jilin province is cheerfully known as "Eternal Spring" despite its brutal winter. The city was badly damaged at the end of World War II, which ended its ignominious phase as the capital of the Japanese-controlled state of Manchukuo, when it was known as Hsin-Ching. Industrialized after the war, Changchun today has emerged as an attractive, green city in China's northeastern "rustbelt," famed for its car production.

Changchun's only major sight of interest is the **Puppet Emperor's Palace**, the residence of the "Last Emperor," Pu Yi, whom the Japanese installed as the Emperor of Manchukuo. Located in the city's northeast, the palace, with its period

furnishings and old photographs, serves as an apt epitaph to the tragic folly of Pu Yi's life. The palace lacks the majesty of the Forbidden City, and instead is suggestive of the sanctuary of an exiled monarch. Renovations have, however, restored much of its former grandeur. It is now a fascinating museum of artifacts relating to the 13 powerless years that Pu Yi spent here. Scenes from Bertolucci's 1987 epic film *The Last Emperor* were filmed here. Other period buildings include the Manchukuo State Council Building on Xinmin Dajie in the southeast of town, a further relic of the Japanese occupation. Open to the public, the

building is a government structure that features a brass Otis elevator that once ferried Pu Yi aloft.

In the northeast corner of People's Square on the main street of Renmin Dajie stands **Banruo Temple**, an active Buddhist temple dating to 1921. Inside the main hall is a statue of Sakyamuni with attendant *arhat (see pp30–31)*. Changchun is also famous for its cinematic output and the city's film studio can be visited, although it is only really of interest to specialist film buffs.

🏛 **Puppet Emperor's Palace**
5 Guangfu Lu. ◷ 8:30am–4:40pm.
🖥 **www**.wmhg.com.cn

**Official buildings at the Puppet Emperor's Palace, Changchun**

---

### THE LAST EMPEROR

Aisin Gioro or Pu Yi ascended the Qing throne at the age of three in 1908 after the death of his uncle, the Guangxu emperor. His brief reign as the Xuantong emperor was brought to an end on February 12, 1912, when he abdicated the throne in the Forbidden City to make way for the new Republican government. The powerless Pu Yi continued to live in the palace until 1924, before furtively escaping to live in the Japanese concession in Tianjin. He was later installed as the Japanese puppet emperor of Manchukuo, residing in his palace in Changchun. At the end of World War II, he was arrested and handed over to the Chinese Communists, who imprisoned him in 1950. In 1959, Mao granted him amnesty. Pu Yi never returned to the Forbidden City, and he died of cancer, childless and anonymous, in 1967, after working for seven years as a gardener at the Beijing Botanical Gardens.

**Pu Yi (1905–1967), China's "Last Emperor"**

# Jilin ❼
吉林

60 miles (100 km) E of Changchun.
🏯 2,000,000. ✈ 🚇 🏢 🚌 to
Shanghai Dalian, Tianjin. 🚇 Shi Ji
Cheng Building, Song Jiang Dong Rd,
(0432) 6244 5707.

Known as Kirin during the Japanese occupation between 1931 and 1945, the city of Jilin is a little-visited industrial settlement on either side of the Songhua or Sungari River. Like many other cities in the northeast, Jilin has a short history and was a small village until the 17th century when it was fortified. It was heavily industrialized during the Japanese occupation, when the huge hydro-electric power station at Fengman on the Songhua River was constructed. The station generates one of Jilin's major winter attractions – *shugua* or needle-like white frost which covers the branches of the riverside pine and willow trees. As warm water from the power station flows into the Songhua, its temperature rises and it remains unfrozen. Evaporating water droplets from the river condense along the branches of trees and freeze, producing a sparkling display of ice-rimmed branches, resembling pieces of coral. As with Harbin, winter is the main tourist

Statues at the scholars' altar,
Confucius Temple, Jilin

season, and Jilin also stages an ice festival from January to the end of February.

Pleasant walks along paths, and past shrines and pavilions are possible in hilly **Beishan Park** in the west of town. The park has an array of Daoist and Buddhist temples that are worth investigating, including the Guandi Temple (Guandi Miao), the Three King Temple (Sanwang Miao), and the Jade Emperor's Temple (Yuhuang Ge), with a gaggle of fortune tellers in front.

Locals are proud of the city's attractive **Catholic Church**, built by the French in the early 19th century. It rises west of Jilin's main bridge on Songjiang Lu, the road along the north bank of the river. Vandalized during the Cultural Revolution, the church became the city's emblem after it reopened in 1980. East of the church is the **Confucius Temple** (Wen Miao), dedicated to the great sage. Candidates of the imperial civil service examinations came here to pray for his help and blessings. The sedate temple provides an escape from Jilin's modern face.

In the south of the city, the **Meteorite Shower Museum** houses a scattering of rock fragments that rained down around Jilin in 1976, including a vast specimen weighing nearly two tons (1,770 kg).

Catholic Church, Jilin

🌺 **Beishan Park**
◯ daily. 📷

✝ **Catholic Church**
3 Songjiang Lu. ◯ daily during service hours only.

🏯 **Confucius Temple**
2 Nanchang Lu. ◯ daily. 📷

**Environs:** Not far from Jilin, **Zhuque Shan** (Rosefinch Mountain) has earned a reputation for its ski slopes. Formerly known for its temples and hiking opportunities, it now offers two slopes for sledding and skiing. Its restaurant, which stands on a heated platform, provides panoramic views over the hills.

About 15 miles (24 km) southeast of Jilin is the picturesque **Songhua Lake** (Songhua Hu), covering a vast and panoramic area surrounded by peaks. It provides an excellent getaway from town, offering hiking and boating in a huge forested park setting. Every winter, an expensive, state-of-the-art ski resort operates on the slopes around the lake, attracting crowds of cross-country fans. At the lake's southern end is the Fengman Dam, the site of the city's hydro-electric power station. Due to the river's annual flooding, four sluice gates are opened to keep Jilin from being submerged.

⛷ **Zhuque Shan**
Taxi from Jilin train station. ◯ daily.
📷 Ski gear available.

⛷ **Songhua Lake**
🚌 No. 338 from Jilin to Fengman. then taxi to ski resorts.

**The delicate frost that covers Jilin's trees each year**

# Changbai Shan ❽

长白山

**Korean minorities in ethnic dress**

Listed as a UNESCO Biosphere Reserve, Changbai Shan (Ever-White Mountains) is the largest of China's nature reserves at 760 sq miles (1,965 sq km) with a rich abundance of fauna and flora. Thick belts of deciduous and coniferous forest harbor important medicinal plants like ginseng, and endangered animals like the Siberian (or Manchurian) Tiger, while above the treeline lies the only alpine tundra in East Asia. The highlight of any visit to Changbai Shan is Tian Chi (Heaven's Lake), a glittering volcanic crater that straddles the mountainous border with North Korea. This is China at its wildest and most spectacular, with opportunities for hiking amid dramatic scenery, although the area is only open to exploration during summer and early autumn.

**White birch**
*Despite heavy deforestation, there are still healthy numbers of over 80 species of tree such as these white birch.*

**★ Changbai Waterfall**
*Tian Chi releases huge quantities of water (the mountains are capped with snow between October and June) creating the dramatic 225-ft (68-m) high waterfall near the volcanic crater.*

BEIHE

Tianwe Feng

Longmei Feng

Jinping Feng

## GINSENG

The root of the ginseng *(Panax ginseng)* plant has been valued in China for thousands of years for its healing and rejuvenating properties. Native to Korea and Northeast China, ginseng is a slow-growing herbaceous perennial that is widely farmed (although wild specimens are most highly prized). Ginseng from Northeast China is especially esteemed and was once protected under imperial edict to prevent overharvesting. Its efficacy does not develop until the plant is around six years of age. Premium quality wild ginseng is very expensive costing between US$150–450 per gram. However, buyer beware; the market is awash with fake produce.

**The root and leaves of the ginseng plant**

0 kilometers 1

0 miles 1

**KEY**

– · – International Border

– – – Path

**STAR SIGHTS**

★ Changbai Waterfall

★ Tianchi – Heaven's Lake

**★ Tian Chi – Heaven's Lake**
*The volcano last erupted in
1702, wiping out most of the
surrounding forest. The deep
waters of Tian Chi (China's
deepest lake) are said to harbor
an aquatic beast similar to
the Loch Ness Monster.*

**NORTH
KOREA**

**Hot springs near Tian Chi**
*Many springs reach temperatures of over
176° F (80° C) – hot enough for local
hawkers to boil eggs and for visitors to
take therapeutic dips in steamy pools.*

▲
*Bai Yun
Feng*

### CLIMBING CHANGBAI SHAN
Due to heavy snowfall, Changbai Shan is
only open to trekking from June to October.
Although a tempting 8 miles (13 km) in
circumference, Tian Chi cannot be circum-
navigated as it overlaps with North Korea.
Prepare for unpredictable weather conditions
as it can get very cold (and carry plenty of
food and water.) The more sedentary can
hire a 4-wheel-drive taxi all the way to the
main peak. Visitors can overnight in one of
the hotels on Changbai Shan or in tents on
the lake shore. Tours are easy to find and
usually include two nights in a hotel.

**Trekking opportunities**
*Even at peak periods, it is easy to enjoy
and explore the wilderness and beauty
of Changbai Shan at leisure – however,
do not stray into North Korea.*

# Harbin ❾
哈尔滨

Situated in the far north of China close to the vast sub-Siberian plains, Harbin is the pleasant capital of Heilongjiang province. It was a simple fishing hamlet on the Songhua River until the Russians linked it to both Vladivostok and Dalian (see pp444–5) by rail at the close of the 19th century. The railway and the Bolshevik Revolution brought large numbers of Russians to the city, prompting a change in Harbin's fortunes. Once called "Little Moscow" for its charming pockets of Russian architecture, Harbin still vaguely resembles an outpost of Imperial Russia. While the city's summer is quite pleasant, its winter temperatures dip below –22°F (–30°C), perfect weather for its spectacular Ice Festival.

**People walking and relaxing along Harbin's riverbank**

### Exploring Harbin

Harbin's most pleasurable aspects lie within the Daoli district (Daoli Qu), the area stretching from the main railway station to the Songhua River. The district's downtown area is lined with several upmarket boutiques, fur shops, and department stores. Visitors can walk north along the pedestrianized shopping street of **Zhongyang Dajie** to explore the picturesque cobbled alleys and architectural legacies of the grand Russian era. Numerous shops and buildings on Zhongyang Dajie have been restored, and their histories recorded in English on exterior plaques. The lanes leading off Zhongyang Dajie are ideal for a leisurely stroll, while along its length are several good bars and restaurants. Lined with ice sculptures in winter, the streets here are alive with the bustle of pavement cafés during summer.

**A motorcycle taxi in Harbin**

East of Zhongyang Dajie is the **Church of St. Sofia**, the city's most spectacular Russian edifice. Dating from 1907, it is also the largest Russian Orthodox church in the Far East. This Byzantine-style red-brick cathedral is topped with a green, onion-shaped dome. It houses the Architecture and Arts Centre, a rewarding photographic exhibition of the Russian influence on Harbin.

To the north, **Zhaolin Park** is the setting for many of the ice sculptures of the annual Ice Festival (Bingdeng Jie), officially held every year from January 5 to February 25. In winter, the park is transformed into a glistening wonderland of brightly-lit ice sculptures, ranging from simple statues to buildings, monuments, and temples.

Close by, Harbin's riverfront is dotted with a number of interesting sights. The **Flood Control Monument** at the northern end of Zhongyang Dajie was erected in 1958 to commemorate the river's flood-prone history. Stretching 26 miles (42 km) along the riverbank is **Stalin Park**, China's last public memorial to Joseph Stalin. It is an engaging riverside promenade and meeting place for Harbin locals. In summer, boat trips can be taken along the river and across to **Sun Island Park** on the northern bank. The park has a variety of recreational attractions and can also be reached by cable car. In winter, the river freezes over completely, and visitors can hire go-carts or simply walk across. An annual snow sculpture exhibition is held on Sun Island, which is also home to the Siberian Tiger Park, where the endangered Manchurian tiger is currently being bred. Visitors may want to give this rather dismal place a miss, as the fenced-off area seems much too small for the big cats, who are constantly being teased with live chickens by noisy busloads of tourists.

Southeast of the main railway station, the **Provincial Museum** has a rather uninspiring collection of exhibits with no English captions. Farther east along Dong

**The splendid Byzantine-style Church of St. Sofia**

Tiger at the Siberian Tiger Park, Harbin

🏛 **Church of St Sofia**
Diduan Jie. ⬜ *daily.* 📷
🌿 **Sun Island Park**
3 Jingbei Lu. ⬜ *daily.* 📷
🏛 **Jile Si**
9 Dong Dazhi Jie. ⬜ *daily.*
🌿 **Harbin Northern Forest Zoo**
Gezidong. ⬜ *daily.* 📷

**VISITORS' CHECKLIST**

340 miles (550 km) N of Shenyang. ✈ *4,750,000.* 🚉
🚌 🚌 *Harbin Bus Station,* *CAAC (buses to airport).* ℹ *14 Songhuajiang Jie, (0451) 5360 1717.* 🎫 *Ice Festival (Jan 5–Feb 25), Harbin Music Festival (Jul).*

Dazhi Jie are some of Harbin's Buddhist temples, all of which were damaged during the Cultural Revolution. The quiet **Jile Si** is home to an active Buddhist community. The complex follows a typical Buddhist temple layout with Drum and Bell Towers, Hall of Heavenly Kings, and a main hall, adorned with statues of Sakyamuni (the Historical Buddha) and various bodhisattvas. Adjacent is the seven-tiered **Qiji Futu Pagoda**, standing within the largest temple complex in the province. Nearby on Wenmiao Jie, the Confucian Temple is a sizeable shrine also worth visiting. Harbin's zoo has been moved 25 miles (41 km) away from the city center, renamed **Harbin Northern Forest Zoo**, and is now one of the largest zoos in China.

**Environs:** 12 miles (20 km) southwest of Harbin in the small village of Pingfang, the **Japanese Germ Warfare Experimental Base** is the city's most notorious sight. Formerly

The elegant, seven-tiered Qiji Futu Pagoda in the northeast of town

operated by the Japanese army's 731 Division, the gruesome remains of the experimental base are now open to the public. It housed a top-secret research unit that subjected thousands of Chinese, Korean, British, Mongolian, and Russian prisoners to some truly horrendous experiments. The Japanese destroyed the base at the end of World War II, and it was only after the dogged efforts of a Japanese journalist in the 1980s that the existence of the base was exposed. The museum is largely limited to photographs and all captions are in Chinese, but the site survives as a somber monument to the atrocities of World War II.

🏛 **Japanese Germ Warfare Experimental Base**
Pingfang. ⬜ *daily.* 📷

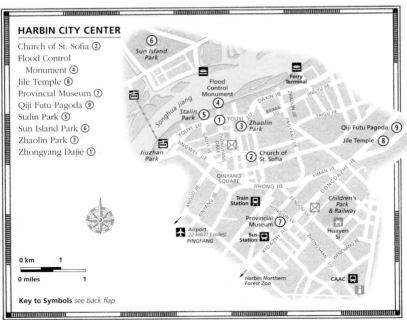

**HARBIN CITY CENTER**

0 km          1
0 miles          1

**Key to Symbols** *see back flap*

**Diving off the edge of Diaoshuilou Pubu (Diaoshuilou Waterfall), Jingpo Hu**

# Jingpo Hu ⑩
镜泊湖

62 miles (100 km) SW of Mudanjiang.
🚌 from Mudanjiang to Dongjing,
then minibus to Jingpo Hu in summer
only; in winter via taxi. 🚌 from
Harbin & Mudanjiang. 🅘 34
Jingfu Jie, Mudanjiang, (0453)
691 1944. ◯ daily. 📷

An attractive,
31-mile (50-km)
long winding strip
of water, Jingpo Hu
was carved from the
Mudan River by
volcanic eruptions
thousands of years ago. The
surrounding forested slopes
are clearly reflected in the
lake's waters, hence its name,
"Mirror Lake." In summer,
busloads of visitors – largely
Chinese and Russian – gather
at Jingpo Shanzhuang, a
village on the northern shore
equiped with abundant resort
facilities. Although tourism
has spoiled some of the lake's
natural beauty, much of its
huge body of water and the
luxuriant wooded hills are still
tranquil and worth exploring.
The 131-ft (40-m) wide waterfall **Diaoshuilou Pubu** lies at
the northern end of the lake.
Its cascade is most impressive
in the wetter summer months,
while in winter, it freezes into
a spectacular curtain of ice.
Visiting the lake is possible in
winter, although temperatures

can also dip well below
freezing point through to
April, with fewer transport
and accommodations
options. July and August
are the wettest and busiest
months, and booking
ahead at lakeside hotels
is recommended. An
alternative is to stay in
Mudanjiang city to the
north, from where buses
depart for Jingpo Hu.
Activities include boating,
fishing, and hiking and
boat tours around the lake
can also be arranged. Not
far from the waterfall is a
Korean minority village.
    Several volcanic features
dot the surrounding area,
including lava caves and
the **Dixia Senlin** (Underground Forest), 31 miles
(50 km) northwest of
Jingpo Hu. Not actually
subterranean, the forest has
grown spectacularly in the
fertile soil of ten dormant
volcanic craters. The delicate
ecosystem here supports
a varied animal and
plant population
including black
bears, leopards,
purple pines,
firs, and drag-
on spruces.
Taxis and buses
leave regularly
from Jingpo
Hu's main gate
to Dixia Senlin.
It is also worth looking out
for tour buses to the lake that
include trips to Dixia Senlin.

**A visitor enjoying a ride
on a jet ski at Jingpo Hu**

🏞 **Dixia Senlin**
50 km NW of Jingpo Hu. ◯ daily. 📷

# Zhalong Nature Reserve ⑪
扎龙自然保护区

17 miles (27 km) SE of Qiqiha'er. 🚌 to
Qiqiha'er, then bus. 🚌 ◯ daily. 📷

China's largest wetland
reserve, the 518,700-acre
(210,000-ha) Zhalong Nature
Reserve lies in the Songhua-
Nen River plain, along a major
bird migratory route from the
Arctic to Southeast Asia.
Zhalong's reedbeds, ponds,
and marshland provide an
ideal home to almost 300
species of birds, including
swans, storks, ducks, geese,
egret, white ibis, and other
waterfowl. Established in
1979, the reserve is one of the
few breeding grounds in the
Far East for the marsh
grassbird (*Megalurus pryeri*).
Six of the world's 15 varieties
of crane are also found here.
The most famous are the
endangered red-crowned
crane (*Grus japonensis*), a tall
bird with black and white
plumage and a red crest that
is the symbol of longevity in
China, and the white-naped
crane (*Grus vipio*), both of
which are bred at a research
center here. Other rare bird
species that visit Zhalong
include the swan goose (*Anser
cygnoides*), and the Siberian
crane (*Grus leucogeranus*).
Birds arrive in spring, and
begin breeding in summer.
The best time to visit the
reserve is from April to June.
It is advisable to take binocu-
lars, as Zhalong's population
of waterfowl can be elusive.

**The marshlands at Zhalong Nature Reserve, important to migrating birds**

# Fossils of Northeast China

China has long been an excellent hunting ground for fossil collectors. Over 130 million years ago much of northern China was volcanic, richly forested and teeming with life. As the volcanoes erupted they covered the land with dust, hot ash, and mud, and for many years fossils of all kinds have been uncovered, from simple, shellfish-like ammonites through to complete skeletons of large dinosaurs. More recently, the area of northeast China

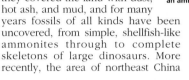

**Coiled shell of an ammonite**

has captured the imagination because of the discovery of at least five feathered species of dinosaurs. The feathers were not only used for flight, but also for insulation and perhaps decoration. Such has been the excitement – and indeed money – generated by these discoveries that fossils have become big business in the area. Locals are discovering and illegally selling what they find, and even going so far as to create fake fossils that have fooled the scientists.

**Dragonfly** *fossils like this reveal even the delicate tracery of the insect's wings. This amazing detail was retained thanks to a thin dusting of fine volcanic ash that was followed by a thick layer of mud, preventing oxidation and rapid decay.*

**Paleontology** *has become a booming business in China and placed the country at the heart of important debates about evolution. Therefore the government has been keen to sponsor further research and museums.*

**This Dicynodont** *was a plant-eating reptile the size of a pig, with two large front teeth – its name means "two dog teeth." One of the most common dinosaur fossils, it has been found all over the world.*

**Dinosaur eggs** *are classified by size and shell type because it is difficult to tell what species they were laid by. Some are very similar to birds' eggs, further strengthening the theory that birds descended from a specific group of dinosaurs.*

**Microraptor gui** *was a four-winged creature – its legs were feathered too – that glided from tree to tree. The outline of the feathers can clearly be seen, and some think that it might represent an intermediate stage between dinosaurs and birds.*

One of the five volcanic lakes at Wu Da Lian Chi

# Wu Da Lian Chi & the River Border ⑫
五大连池

232 miles (375 km) N of Harbin. ☐ from Harbin or Qiqiha'er to Beian, then bus to Wu Da Lian Chi. ☐ from Harbin.

A large and popular nature reserve situated in a volcanic field, Wu Da Lian Chi lies in a region in western Heilongjiang inhabited by the ancient Daur minority. Its name, meaning "Five Big Connected Lakes," is derived from the five bodies of water created by a succession of volcanic eruptions, the most recent occurring in the 18th century. The resulting lava, which blocked the Bei River and created the lakes, has turned Wu Da Lian Chi into a volcanic spa, with geothermal springs and sulphurous waters that have a reputation throughout China for their curative powers.

The 14 volcanoes at Wu Da Lian Chi add a measure of drama and character to the region's flat terrain. To the west of Number 3 Lake are the two principal volcanic vents, **Lao Hei Shan** (Old Black Hill) and **Huoshao Shan** (Fire Burn Hill). The sites of the most recent eruptions, which took place between 1719–21, both volcanoes are popular with visitors and can be climbed for panoramic views of the area. Surrounded by fields of lava, Laohei

Shan generated most of the magma that spilled out into the surrounding area. However, like all the volcanoes at Wu Da Lian Chi, it is now dormant. Visitors can also bathe in the area's pungent hot water springs and taste the local mineral water. Apparently bursting with dissolved minerals and curative powers, the waters are sought by a devoted band of the ill and infirm, as well as elderly Chinese, who flock to Wu Da Lian Chi to avail of treatment in the numerous sanatoriums that have opened here. The waters are also the star attraction of the annual Water Drinking Festival of the local Daur people, held every May.

Underground caverns dot the area, including the freezing **Crystal Palace** and **Bai Long Dong** (White Dragon Cave), subterranean ice caves decorated with ice sculptures and crowded with visitors in summer. The nearest settle-

ment is the village of Wu Da Lian Chi, which has several hotels. Since the guided tours available often make costly and needless diversions, visitors may find it more efficient to travel independently by regular taxi or motorcycle cab.

## 🎫 Bai Long Dong
⬜ daily. 📷

**Environs:** The **Heilong Jiang** (Black Dragon River, known as the Amur in Russia), that lends its name to this province, demarcates a long section of the border between China and Siberia. Several of Northeast China's ethnic tribes traditionally settled in this region, making their living from the river, although many have now been assimilated into the larger Han Chinese population. It is possible to see Siberian forests and small settlements along the border. Since most parts of this region require a permit, it is advisable to check with Harbin's Public Security Bureau.

Connected to Harbin by train, the large border town of **Heihe** sees a healthy cross-border trade with the Russian port town of Blagoveshchensk, which can be visited with a tourist visa for Russia, arranged in Beijing. Hour-long cruises along the Heilong Jiang are also available. At the northern tip of Heilongjiang is **Mohe**, whose main attraction is the spectacular aurora borealis (northern lights) in winter. The town records almost 22 hours of daylight in June.

The frozen Heilong Jiang, used for traveling through the heavily forested terrain

# River Border Minorities

Although the majority of the population in Heilongjiang is Han Chinese, the River Border is home to several minorities, including the Oroqen, Hezhen, and Ewenki. Traditionally these nomadic peoples eke out a living in this inhospitable environment. They rely on animal furs for clothes and local plants for medicines, and, when on the move, even construct tents out of birch bark. The Oroqen are hunters, descended from Khitan nomads. They speak an Altaic language and are noted for their

**Medicinal berries of the Huaqiu tree**

shaman and animistic customs and rituals. Numbering a few thousand, the Hezhen are one of China's least populous tribes but their skill at fishing is legendary. The Ewenki supplement their fishing and hunting mainly through breeding reindeer. For all these peoples, however, this way of life is slowly dying out: hunting has been banned in some of the mountain reserves, forcing the nomads to settle down as farmers, while others have left for the cities in search of an easier life.

**The Ewenki** *are dependant on reindeer which are well adapted to survive in the cold climate. However this nomadic and traditional way of life is slowly disappearing.*

**Ewenki tents** *traditionally have a frame made out of birch poles that are covered with birch bark in summer and with animal skins in winter. Practical* feng shui *means that the entrance is usually south-facing to avoid the wind from the north.*

**The Oroqen** *are expert hunters who even make clothes from the animals that they kill for food. Subsidies are now enticing some of them to settle down as farmers.*

**The Hezhen** *are legendary for their fish-skin shirts, trousers and even shoes. The dried skins of carp, pike and salmon are stitched together to make waterproof items that are highly prized.*

**The Oroqen's traditional hunting grounds** *have suffered from encroachment by industry as well as general deforestation and finally by China's newfound enthusiasm for wildlife preserves that have closed off large areas of the wilderness from hunting.*

# INNER MONGOLIA & THE SILK ROADS

# Inner Mongolia & The Silk Roads

This massive region, forming a giant northwesterly arc linking Siberia with Central Asia, takes up a third of China's area. Geographically it ranges from forest to sandy desert to grassland, whilst ethnically these lands are home to several Chinese minorities, notably Mongolians, Uighur, and Hui, as well as, among others, Russians, Kazakhs, and Kyrgyz. Three provinces – Inner Mongolia, Ningxia, and Xinjiang – are officially designated autonomous regions. The main attractions in Xinjiang and Gansu are the dusty oasis towns of the Silk Road, replete with Buddhist cave paintings, evocative ruins, and chaotic markets, whilst elsewhere the appeal is the beauty of China's last great wildernesses.

**A monk prays at the Gao Miao, Zhongwei**

ALTAI

YINING

URUMQI

TURPAN

KUQA

KASHGAR

*KARAKORAM HIGHWAY*

*TAKLAMAKAN DESERT*

HOTAN    QIEMO    RUOQIANG

MINFENG

*Shigatse*

DUNHUANG    JIAYUGUA

AKSAY

LENGHUZHEN

GOLMUD    DU

217    216

314

315

315

109

214

**Buddha sculpture at Bingling Si, Gansu, still retaining some of its original color**

## GETTING AROUND

There are airports in the major towns and cities, whilst the rail network is confined to trunk routes linking major centers. Independent travelers will need to use local bus services, which are comprehensive but crowded and uncomfortable. Because of the distances involved, visitors are likely to focus on one area at a time – the Silk Road, or the Mongolian grasslands, for example.

◁ **Bactrian camels grazing near the Karakoram Highway, Kashgar**

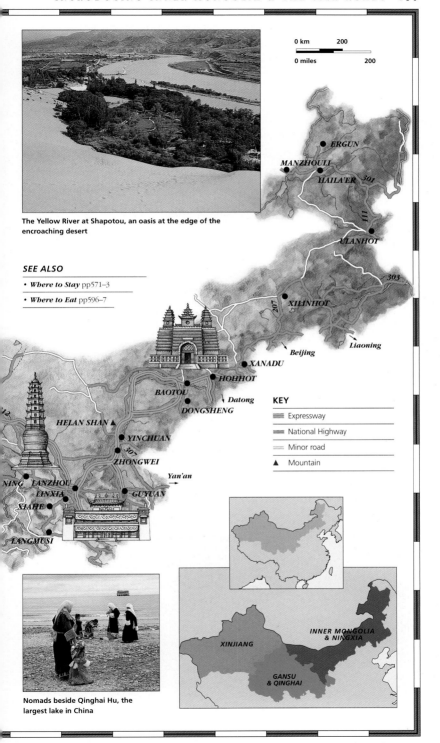

The Yellow River at Shapotou, an oasis at the edge of the encroaching desert

**SEE ALSO**

- *Where to Stay* pp571–3
- *Where to Eat* pp596–7

0 km    200
0 miles    200

ERGUN
MANZHOULI
HAILA'ER    301
111
ULANHOT
303
XILINHOT
207
Beijing
Liaoning
XANADU
HOHHOT
BAOTOU
DONGSHENG
Datong
HELAN SHAN ▲
YINCHUAN
307
ZHONGWEI
Yan'an
NING  LANZHOU
LINXIA  GUYUAN
XIAHE
LANGMUSI

**KEY**

▨ Expressway
▨ National Highway
═ Minor road
▲ Mountain

INNER MONGOLIA
& NINGXIA
XINJIANG
GANSU
& QINGHAI

Nomads beside Qinghai Hu, the largest lake in China

# A PORTRAIT OF INNER MONGOLIA & THE SILK ROADS

T*his vast region, comprising Inner Mongolia, Ningxia, Gansu, Qinghai, and Xinjiang, covers a significant proportion of the total area of China. Although sparsely populated, the area's appeal lies in its magnificent landscape, the distinctive lifestyles of its indigenous peoples, and its Silk Road past. This fabled route's legacies are visible everywhere, from historic sights to the Islamic religion.*

Bordering the Mongolian Republic and Russia to the north, the Central Asian states to the west, and the Indian subcontinent to the south, this region is now indissolubly attached to China, as a result of vigorously pursued Chinese hegemony. Today, although the local population is largely Han, they have little in common with the area's indigenous peoples. Only the eastern portion of Gansu seems naturally to form part of China proper. Gansu to the west of Lanzhou and the other provinces are at best indifferent to and at worst in uneasy thrall to the government in Beijing, which has often ruled with callous disregard for local sentiments. For the Chinese, there still lingers a historic suspicion of the barbarians living beyond the frontier marked by the course of the Great Wall.

**Tiled decoration Praying Hall, Ta'er Si**

However, historic cultural identities have been retained, and this, together with the region's distinctive geography, means that Inner Mongolia and the northwest have a different character to most of China. Because of this, these three areas – Ningxia, Xinjiang, and Inner Mongolia – are not officially provinces but so-called Autonomous Regions, where the Hui, Uighur, and Mongolian peoples theoretically have a measure of self-government. In practice, any autonomy is superficial, though local languages are spoken and religions practised reasonably freely.

Although the communities are united by their ethnic minority status, the region is by no means an organic entity. For example, the Mongolians and Uighur are only connected by the fact of their inclusion within the

Dramatic sand dunes near Crescent Moon Lake, Dunhuang

Incense burner in the inner courtyard of the Gao Miao, a multi-denominational temple in Zhongwei

the Yellow River. Inner Mongolia, composed of grassland, steppe, desert, and mountain, has short, pleasant summers but cold, windswept winters.

Historically, this area's most significant period was during the great days of the Silk Road, when caravans carrying silk, spices, and tea crossed the inhospitable terrain, stopping at oasis towns along the way. Centuries later, this region became the domain of Genghis Khan, the Mongol warlord *(see p471)*. These desert gardens are still markets where local products, from raisins to saddles and daggers, are traded just as they have been for centuries.

The most significant Silk Road monuments are the Mogao Caves in Dunhuang, perhaps the greatest repository of Buddhist murals, sculpture, and manuscripts. Other Buddhist sites such as the Labrang monastery in Gansu and Ta'er Si in Qinghai owe their origins to the influence of Tibetan Buddhism.

political borders of China. Mongolia's grasslands are inhabited by a traditionally nomadic people who obtain their livelihood through the grazing of sheep and horses. Xinjiang, the homeland of the Turkic-speaking Uighur, on the other hand, is a stony desert relieved by oases dependent upon an ancient but sophisticated system of underground irrigation channels. The one feature that links the region is the extreme nature of its climate and terrain. Whilst much of Xinjiang is flat and featureless, it is fringed by some of the world's highest mountains, including the Pamirs to the southwest and Tian Shan to the northwest. At its center sits the Taklamakan Desert, an immense tract of sand dunes characterized by its name, which means "Go in not come out." Summers here are unbearably hot, and its winters are dry and very cold. Qinghai is a mountain plateau whilst arid Ningxia and Gansu are rendered habitable only by the presence of

Statue inside the Fuxi Miao, Tianshui

Besides visiting caravanserais, grottoes, and monasteries, it is worth exploring the grasslands, mountains, and lakes such as Qinghai Hu, as some of China's last great wilderness areas can be seen here. While it is true that some of China's prosperity has begun to trickle west, it will take some time before the nomads and traders give up their ingrained habits and culture. Thus, despite its size, there are only a few large cities, in particular Lanzhou, provincial capital of Gansu, and Ürümqi, capital of Xinjiang.

Tibetan nuns gathering outside their nunnery in Xiahe, Qinghai

# Mongols of the Steppe

In the 13th century Genghis Khan *(see p471)* united the steppe-land tribes into a confederation that briefly ruled the civilized world. Today, the Mongolian nation is divided into two parts: the Mongolian Republic to the north, and the Inner Mongolia Autonomous Region in China. Traditionally, Mongols are nomadic herders who travel and work on horseback, mostly on the vast, grass-rich steppe. Their diet consists largely of meat and many dairy products, including fermented mare's milk, the intoxicating *airaq*. In Inner Mongolia, most of the Mongolian minority now lead a sedentary life of farming. They are striving, however, to keep their traditions alive, by staging the annual Nadaam Festival, for example.

**Motorbike** *travel has replaced the horse for many families and it is not unusual to see an entire family astride a bike which is just as likely to be seen parked outside a ger as a horse.*

### EQUESTRIAN SKILL
The key to the Yuan Empire's success was the Mongolians' horse-riding prowess. Horsemanship is still valued, and many learn to ride before they can walk. The sturdy Mongolian pony remains an integral feature of life in the countryside for nomadic herders.

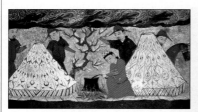

**The name Mongol,** *first used during the Tang dynasty, referred to several tribes. This illumination from 1350 shows that the essential lifestyle of Mongolians changed little up to the 20th century.*

**Gers** (yurts) *are the traditional felt homes of the nomads. They are found in the rural grasslands. Permanent encampments of gers are found closer to Hohhot.*

**Tied down skillfully** *to withstand fierce winds, the outer and inner skins are made of canvas, with an insulating layer of felt between.*

**The frame** *comes apart for easy transportation. The wooden poles (orange like the sun) are called uni, between ten and fifteen of which support each of the khanas, or sections of wall.*

**The principal traditional** *garment, the* deel, *is a long gown tied with a brilliant sash at the waist. It is worn by both women and men and comes in different weights – lined with sheepskin for winter, quilted for spring, and made of light cloth for summer.*

**Colorful banners** are carried by riders at the competitive Nadaam Festival.

**Mongolian wrestling**, *a favorite event at the Nadaam Festival along with equestrianism and archery, has no weight classes and no time limits. The winner is the one who throws or trips his opponent in such a way that some part of his body touches the ground.*

**Buddhism** *is the main religion among Mongols. Tibetan influence became very strong at the Mongolian court of Kublai Khan and by the 16th century Lamaist Buddhist images found a place in every ger.*

**Leather saddles** have replaced the less comfortable traditional wooden version.

**Hardy Mongolian pony**

## DESERTIFICATION

The incursion of dry soil into fertile lands, desertification, is caused by overworking the soil and inappropriate irrigation, a major problem in China. In Inner Mongolia, it is severely affecting the traditional way of life, as it destroys grazing pastures. Poor farmers swarm to the area to harvest *facai* or "get rich" grasses removing the topsoil's anchoring root-structure. Mongols have been encouraged to abandon the pastoral life and settle as farmers and so increase the pressures on the land.

**Once-rich grassland reduced to infertile sand**

*Inside is warm and comfortable. A stove sits in the center of the ger, whilst the back is reserved for the family altar and is the place for elders and honored guests.*

# The Silk Road

In reality several ancient trading routes between China and eastern Europe, the Silk Road – the term was coined in the 19th century by Baron von Richthofen – first became busy in the Han dynasty, exposing the Chinese capital Chang'an (Xi'an) and ultimately all of China to the influences and styles of an alien world. Technologically advanced, with a large workforce, and a monopoly on some highly valued products, China was well placed to benefit from a massive expansion in trade.

A foreign – big-nosed – trader

Camel caravan crossing the daunting Silk Road dunes

## SILK ROAD COMMERCE

The merchants who used the Silk Road dealt not only in spices, silk, porcelain and jade but also in gold and silver, wool, Arab horses, and many other commodities. However, it was silk (*see pp208–9*), a mysterious Chinese invention, that particularly captivated the west.

**This piece of silk** *dating from 1500 BC was discovered in what was Bactria, today's Afghanistan, indicating that a network of trading routes had been established long before the heyday of the Silk Road under the Tang.*

**Rome** *was a major importer of silk and knew China as "Seres" – the land of silk. This gold Roman coin was found along the Silk Road in Xinjiang.*

## EMPEROR WU & GENERAL ZHANG QIAN

In the second century BC the Han emperor Wudi saw that his cavalry's horses – better suited to pulling carts – were struggling against the fast horses of his enemy, the Xiongnu. Therefore he sent Zhang Qian, his general, to Sogdiana and Ferghana to obtain some of their legendary horses. Although the mission failed, the information Zhang Qian brought back about the riches he saw led to the development of trade along the Silk Road, and the Ferghana horses did eventually make it to China.

**Statue of one of Ferghana's "heavenly horses"**

**Gold and silver** *were not highly prized in China until after contact with the West. These precious metals became fashionable in the Tang dynasty, as shown by this gold teacup with Middle Eastern styling.*

**This Chinese incense burner** *shows that silverworking techniques must have made it to China along with the vogue for precious metals.*

**The Silk Road** *was a series of routes linking China in the east with the Roman Empire to the west. The principal routes looped south and north of the Taklamakan Desert, to join with other branches from Siberia and India, as they headed through Central Asia and Persia as far as the Mediterranean. The route flourished in periods of calm and declined in times of war.*

## FOREIGN IDEAS AND RELIGIONS

Contact with foreigners meant traders brought back religions such as Buddhism, which eventually became the national religion, as well as philosophies and artistic styles.

**Most artistic influences** *came from Gandhara, a center of Buddhism. The area's unique artistic styles developed after its conquest by Alexander the Great in the 4th century BC. This Gandharan-inspired Chinese bust recalls the graceful sculptures of Classical Greece.*

**DETAIL FROM THE CATALAN MAP**
Made in the 14th century for Charles V of France, this map gives an indication of the extent of geographical knowledge as it stood during the later Middle Ages. The inclusion of China was helped by Marco Polo's account.

**This cross** *is evidence of Nestorianism in China around the 8th century BC. Other religions to make it to China include Islam, Judaism, and Manicheanism, a Babylonian religion based on the opposing principles of Light and Darkness.*

**The period of unrest** *after the demise of the Tang led to a decline in trade. The Silk Road prospered again during the Yuan dynasty when the region came under the control of the Mongol Empire. Silk was no longer a Chinese monopoly, but their porcelain was clearly the finest pottery in the world.*

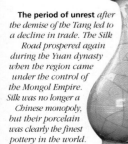

**The final decline** *came with the large ships of the 15th century that could travel with less cost, harassment, and danger. Dwindling use saw the gradual abandonment of the caravanserais that had been the merchants' refuges.*

# INNER MONGOLIA & NINGXIA

This area comprises two autonomous regions, Inner Mongolia, stretching across northern China in an enormous arc, and Ningxia, China's Smallest province after the island of Hainan. The region's main attractions are its great landscapes and the unique cultures of its minority people.

Much of Inner Mongolia consists of rolling grasslands dotted with the traditional tents (*gers* or *yurts*) of the nomadic Mongols. The capital of Hohhot is the most convenient place to join a tour and experience their traditional way of life, while the more adventurous can head north to the towns of Xilinhot and Haila'er, where vast tracts of untouched wilderness lie waiting to be explored. The historic Mongolian homeland was made up of the independent Republic of Mongolia, Inner Mongolia (now in China), and parts of Siberia. Bordering Inner Mongolia to the south, Ningxia was first established in 1928. In the 1950s, it became part of Gansu, and in 1958 was designated an autonomous region for the indigenous Hui *(see p475)*. Living in pockets throughout China, the Muslim Hui descended from Arab Silk Road traders, but are now largely assimilated with the Han culture. Despite some industrialization, Ningxia is a largely undeveloped region with a smattering of interesting sights. At the foot of the scenic Helan mountains near the capital of Yinchuan stand the crumbling tombs of the Western Xia dynasty. The Xumi Shan Caves near Guyuan are another key sight with a wealth of Buddhist carvings.

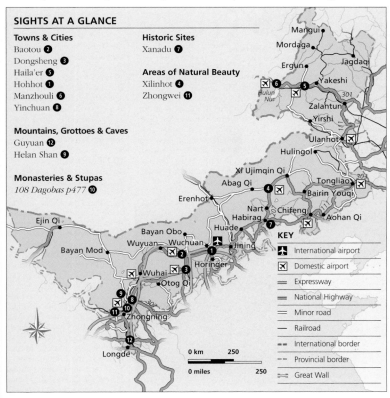

## SIGHTS AT A GLANCE

**Towns & Cities**
Baotou ❷
Dongsheng ❸
Haila'er ❺
Hohhot ❶
Manzhouli ❻
Yinchuan ❽

**Historic Sites**
Xanadu ❼

**Areas of Natural Beauty**
Xilinhot ❹
Zhongwei ⓫

**Mountains, Grottoes & Caves**
Guyuan ⓬
Helan Shan ❾

**Monasteries & Stupas**
*108 Dagobas p477* ❿

**KEY**

| | |
|---|---|
| ✈ | International airport |
| ⊠ | Domestic airport |
| ═ | Expressway |
| ═ | National Highway |
| ═ | Minor road |
| — | Railroad |
| ▬▬ | International border |
| ▬ ▬ | Provincial border |
| ⌇⌇ | Great Wall |

◁ Traditional Mongolian tent or *ger* on the steppes of Inner Mongolia

# Hohhot ❶
## 呼和浩特

255 miles (410 km) W of Beijing.
🏙 2,580,000. ✈ 10 miles (16 km) E
of town. 🚉 🚌 ℹ Hohhot Travel
Agency, (0471) 460 7395.

A small Buddhist settlement
since the Ming era, Hohhot
became the capital of Inner
Mongolia in 1952. Although it
has expanded considerably,
the city has kept some of its
charm, visible in traditional
mud-brick houses in the
south, as well as a few
temples and an excellent
museum. However, the
surrounding grasslands and
the traditional way of life they
support are probably the main
interest. The greenery in
summer makes it the
best time to visit the
city. Hohhot is largely
inhabited by Han
Chinese, with a
small Mongol and
Hui population.

### 🏛 Inner
### Mongolia
### Museum
Hulunbei'er Lu.
🕐 9:30am–5pm daily. 📷

**Local fruit stall being
carried on a bicycle**

Situated in the center of the
new part of town, the Inner
Mongolia Museum is defi-
nitely worth visiting for an
insight into the history and
traditions of the Mongolian
people. The museum's
ground floor exhibits the
paraphernalia used by the
nomadic Mongols, including
saddles, costumes, archery

**Dinosaur skeletons on display at the Inner Mongolia Museum**

and polo equipment, and a
*ger* (portable tent used by
Central Asian nomads). The
museum also has an excellent
collection of fossils discovered in Inner and Outer
Mongolia, including
the complete
skeleton of
a woolly
rhinoceros
unearthed
from a coal
mine in
Manzhouli
(see p474), as
well as several
impressive dinosaur skeletons. The museum's upper
floor is dedicated to the life
of Genghis Khan, who, in the
13th century, united the disparate Mongol tribes and
established arguably the
largest land empire in human
history. Some of the maps
and objects on display have
English captions.

### ☪ Great Mosque
28 Tongdao Nan Jie. 🕐 daily.
In the old southwestern part
of the city, the attractive Great
Mosque (Qingzhen Da Si) is
best known for its fusion of
both Chinese and Arab
architectural influences. The
main building, dating from the
Qing dynasty, is constructed in
black brick, while its minaret
has a Chinese-style pagoda
roof. It is an active place of
worship, which permits non-
Muslim visitors, especially if
they are accompanied by a
local Hui worshiper. The
mosque's prayer area, however, is reserved for Muslims.
The surrounding Muslim area
is well worth exploring, with
its narrow alleys lined with
restaurants selling delicious
noodles and kabobs.

### ☸ Xilitu Zhao
Tongdao Nan Jie. 🕐 daily. 📷
A short walk south of the
Great Mosque in the old city,
the Xilitu Zhao (Xilitu Temple)
started off as a small Ming-
dynasty temple and is one of
Hohhot's oldest shrines. This
Tibetan-Buddhist temple
became the spiritual home of
the 11th Grand Living Buddha
in 1735. Since then, it has
served as the official residence
of successive reincarnations
of the Grand Living Buddha,
who presides over Buddhist
affairs in the city. This version
of the temple was built in the
19th century, after its prede-
cessor burned down. Xilitu
Zhao was also badly damaged
during the Cultural Revolution,
but has since been heavily
restored. It is essentially

**Main prayer hall at the Tibetan-Buddhist Xilitu Zhao**

Chinese in style, with a few Tibetan elements. Its dagoba (Tibetan-style stupa), for example, features Sanskrit writing, Chinese dragons, and tantric Tibetan murals that vividly depict the horrors of hell in gory detail. The temple is still active and the monks here are friendly and speak English. They are usually happy to show visitors around.

### Da Zhao

Tongdao Nan Jie. ◻ *daily*. 🖼

The largest Buddhist temple in the city, the Da Zhao is located in a narrow alley just west of Tongdao Nan Jie. Similar in style and layout to the Xilitu Zhao, it was originally built in 1579, and renovated during the 1990s. The shrine was dedicated to the renowned Qing emperor, Kangxi, in the late 17th century, and murals in the main hall commemorate his visit. An astounding 10-ft (3-m) silver Sakyamuni Buddha is amongst the temple's many treasures. Da Zhao also boasts an extensive collection of musical instruments and dragon sculptures, and is the venue for Buddhist festivals held through the year.

**Wusutu Zhao, Hohhot's Mongolian temple**

### Wu Ta Si

◻ *9am–7pm daily*. 🖼

Just south of Qingcheng Park, amidst the remains of the old city, the Indian-style Wu Ta Si (Five Towers Temple) is one of Hohhot's most attractive buildings. It was constructed in 1727, as part of another temple that has now disappeared. The distinctive five pagodas surmount a solid-looking base that contains a smallish temple with 1,563 images of the Buddha carved into its walls, each differing slightly from the others. Inside is a rare Mongolian cosmological map carved onto a large stone, which illustrates a zodiac and the positions of numerous stars.

**Guardian, Wusutu Zhao**

### Wusutu Zhao

7 miles (12 km) NW of Hohhot. ◻ *9:30am–4:30pm daily*. 🖼

Founded in 1606, the predominantly Mongolian-styled Wusutu Zhao includes some Chinese and Tibetan features. Inside the monastery there are Ming-dynasty murals on display as well as some intricate woodcarvings with imperial dragon motifs. The name "wusutu" means "near to water" in Mongolian. The nearby grasslands and Daqing mountains make pleasant day-trips from town.

### Bai Ta

9 miles (15km) east of Hohhot
◻ *8am–5:30pm daily*.

Bai Ta (White Pagoda) is a seven-storied, octagonal structure. It was first built in the 10th century to house Buddhist scriptures dating from the Liao dynasty *(see pp50–51)*. Over 164 ft (50 m) high, and made of wood and brick, it has some striking carvings inspired by Chinese mythology and nature, including coiled dragons, flowers, and birds. A winding staircase leads to the top, from where there are panoramic views. Bai Ta is best reached by taking a taxi from town.

**The open grasslands, traditional home to nomadic Mongols**

## THE GRASSLANDS

Mongolia's history is linked to its grasslands, and for many people, the classic image of the Mongolian landscape is unbroken grassy steppe spreading to the horizon. The steppe provides fodder for the horses and sheep that support the Mongolians' nomadic lifestyle. The three grassland areas accessible from Hohhot are Xilamuren, 50 miles (80 km) north; Huitengxile, 75 miles (120 km) west; and Gegentela, 93 miles (150 km) north. The easiest way to explore them is by taking a tour, which includes a stay in a village of traditional tents *(gers)*, where visitors attend a banquet and watch Mongolian sports. Though obviously stage-managed, they do show something of Mongolian culture. One can also travel independently by hiring a horse, or negotiating an overnight stay in a *ger* belonging to a local.

**Buddhist mural outside a hall at Wudang Zhao monastery, Baotou**

# Baotou ②
包头

105 miles (170 km) W of Hohhot.
🚶 2,460,000. ✈ 🚌 from Beijing.
🚍 🚕 33 Gang Tie Da Jie, (0472)
536 9029.

The largest city in Inner
Mongolia, Baotou was
once an arid and undevel-
oped region, inhabited by
Mongolian herders of sheep
and horses. Today, it is an
industrial community, made
up largely of Han Chinese,
with a visible Mongol presence.
The town is divided into three
principal areas – **Donghe**, the
oldest part lies to the east,
while the western area consists
of **Qingshan**, the main shopping
district, and **Kundulun**, the
industrial hub. While Qingshan
resembles any modern Chinese
town, with its tower blocks
and array of shops, Kundulun
is a depressing leftover from
the Communist era, with large,
bleak squares, and no sign of
greenery. Donghe, a pleasant
quarter of streets lined with
mud-brick houses and their
cluttered courtyards, lends
color to this fairly drab city.

**Environs:** The region's best-
preserved Lamaist monastery,
**Wudang Zhao** lies 43 miles
(70 km) northeast of Baotou
in a tranquil valley. Built in
1749 in the Tibetan flat-roofed
style, it quickly became an
important place of pilgrimage,
and was home to several
hundred monks belonging to
the Yellow Hat Sect. It houses
a collection of Buddhist
murals from the Qing era.

Just 6 miles (10 km) south of
Baotou lies a section of the
**Yellow River** that inscribes a
huge northerly loop enclosing
an area called the Ordos,
which was not conquered by
the Chinese until the Qing era.
The irrigation projects
made possible by the
Yellow River have
made this area a
fertile oasis. There is
little to see besides
the river, but its
sluggish progress
through the flat,
cultivated landscape
is impressive.

**Plaque in four
scripts, Wudang Zhao**

South of Baotou is
the great Gobi, a desert that
stretches across the northern
reaches of Inner Mongolia and
the Republic of Mongolia. The
**Resonant Sand Gorge**,
37 miles (60 km) south of
Baotou, is filled with sand
dunes, some of which soar 295
ft (90 m) high. Visitors slip and
slide on the dunes, and its
name refers to the sound made
by the falling sand. Paragliding
and camel rides are also
available, and a chairlift shuttles
visitors from the main road.

🏯 **Wudang Zhao**
⏱ daily. 🎫
🏜 **Resonant Sand Gorge**
⏱ daily. 🎫

# Dongsheng ③
东胜

62 miles (100 km) S of Baotou.
🚶 160,000. 🚌

Reasonably attractive, the
small town of Dongsheng
serves mainly as a base for
visiting **Genghis Khan's
Mausoleum** (Ejin Horo Qi),
a rather uncomfortable bus
trip 30 miles (50 km) to the
south. It is almost certain that
Genghis Khan is not buried
here, as his real tomb is
thought to lie in the Hentei
Mountains near Ulan Batur in
the Republic of Mongolia.
However, scholars believe
that this site
contains a few relics
of the Great Khan,
and it has grown
into a place of
pilgrimage for many
Mongolians. The
mausoleum consists
of three conjoined
halls, each echoing
the shape of a *ger*
(Mongolian tent)
decorated with murals. The
middle hall has a large statue
of Genghis with a map of his
empire. Some of the halls are
bedecked with hangings, and
contain *gers*, altars, and other
religious paraphernalia. Special
ceremonies are held here four
times a year to honor Genghis
Khan, attracting pilgrims from
all over Mongolia.

🏛 **Genghis Khan's
Mausoleum**
⏱ 8am–7:30pm daily. 🎫

**Genghis Khan's Mausoleum, a place of pilgrimage for Mongolians**

*For hotels and restaurants in this region see p571 and p596*

# Genghis Khan

Born in 1162 to the head of the Kiyat-Borjigen tribe, Genghis Khan (or Chinggis Khan) was given the name Temujin. A born fighter, as a teenager he killed his half-brother and in 1206 he was proclaimed Genghis Khan (meaning universal king). He unified Mongolia's warring fiefdoms into a huge army of up to 200,000 warriors that invaded China and much of Asia, and eventually created one of the greatest land empires in history.

**Genghis Khan's statue from his mausoleum**

The secret of his success was the skilful use of cavalry and the toughness of the Mongolians who could survive on very little. Their dietary needs were met either from their horses or from the countryside. Genghis died in 1227, before the capture of Peking, after falling from his horse. In fact it was after his death that the Mongol armies made most of their conquests, but it was thanks to his organization and determination in the first place.

**The empire of Genghis Khan's successors at its greatest extent shown on a modern map**

*Mongol Empire*

**Genghis Khan** *was a supreme organizer and tactician. He also created the first Mongolian code of law, the "Yasak," and promoted the growth of trade between China and Europe.*

**Mongolian bow's** unique shape gave it a better range than standard bows.

**Lance for close-quarters fighting**

## THE MONGOLIAN WARRIOR

This Persian picture, painted 100 years after Genghis Khan's death, shows him fighting the Tartars. The key to Mongolian success was their horsemen. They were disciplined, mobile, and heavily armed, and their ferocity and skill were unmatched at the time.

**Mongolian horses were small but sturdy.**

**The cavalry** were supreme horsemen and able to fight on the move.

**Genghis Khan's Mausoleum** *is perhaps reminiscent of a Mongolian ger or tent. After his death his body was carried by thousands of his followers and taken back to Mongolia. The site of his burial is unknown.*

The vast expanse of the Hulunbuir grasslands around Haila'er

# Xilinhot ❹
锡林浩特

310 miles (500 km) NE of Hohhot. ✈ *from Beijing.* 🚆 *to Erlianhot, then bus.* 🚌 *from Hohhot, check with PSB if a* **permit** *is required.* ℹ️ *Xilinhot Travel Agency, (0479) 824 9165.*

Situated right in the heart of the province's grasslands, Xilinhot's main draw is a visit to the Mongolian wilderness, inhabited by nomadic sheep herders in their *muchang jia* (pastureland homes). The tours available here are quieter and cheaper than the ones around Hohhot. Independent trips can also be organized through private tour agents.

# Haila'er ❺
海拉尔

219 miles (350 km) NE of Xilinhot. ✈ *from Beijing & Hohhot.* 🚆 *from Harbin, Qiqihar & Beijing.* 🚌 ℹ️ *Ali He Lu, (0470) 822 4017.*

Close to the Russian border, Haila'er is Inner Mongolia's northernmost town. This small settlement on the banks of the Amur River is a good base for visiting the grasslands in summer. The town's main sight is the network of tunnels used by the Japanese army during World War II. Built by Chinese prisoners, they were used as defensive bunkers along Haila'er's northwestern ridge, which marked the western boundary of Japan's advance into China. Beyond Haila'er lie the **Hulunbuir Grasslands**,

an expanse of rolling plains threaded by rivers and inhabited by herds of sheep and horses. Tours are arranged by the tourist office.

# Manzhouli ❻
满洲里

116 miles (186 km) W of Haila'er. 🚆 *from Haila'er & Harbin.* 🚌 *from Haila'er.* ℹ️ *Lantian Travel, (0470) 622 3003.*

For long inhabited only by nomads, the border town of Manzhouli became a permanent settlement in 1901, as a stop on the Trans-Manchurian and Trans-Siberian railways. Steam locomotives can still be seen in the shunting yards at Zalainuo'er. Russian influences are still apparent in the architecture, mainly the wooden cottages with painted shutters and stucco buildings in pre-Revolutionary style. The main attraction, however, is **Dalai Hu** or Hulun Nur to the south. Surrounded by marshy grasslands, it is one of China's largest lakes, where migratory

swans, geese, and cranes come to nest. The tourist office organizes grassland tours, where visitors can stay in *gers* (tents).

# Xanadu ❼
夏那都

280 miles (450 km) NE of Hohhot. 🚐 *arranged by Xilinhot Travel Agency, (0479) 824 9165.*

Close to inner Mongolia's border near Duolun lie the remains of Yuanshangdu or Xanadu, the site of the legendary palace of Kublai Khan, grandson of Genghis Khan (*see p471*). One of China's greatest emperors, Kublai Khan and his magnificent summer palace were exalted in Samuel Taylor Coleridge's poem which begins with the lines "In Xanadu did Kubla Khan a stately pleasure-dome decree." The palace was abandoned by the Khan during his lifetime, and eventually crumbled. There is little left to see, but those who wish to visit can contact Xilinhot's tourist office.

Manzhouli, the last stop in China on the Trans-Manchurian railway line

◁ Repetition of Buddha images on the walls of Wuta Si, Hohhot

# Yinchuan ⑧
## 银川

326 miles (525 km) SW of Hohhot.
🚹 1,200,000. ✈ 15 miles (25 km) SE
of Yinchuan. 🚃 🚌 ℹ️ (0951) 672
7898.

Situated in the north of
Ningxia, in the lee of the
Helan mountains, Yinchuan is
well protected from the harsh
desert climate, and makes a
good base from which to
explore the surrounding
sights. Watered by the Yellow
River, this lush and leafy city
was the capital of the little-
known Western Xia Kingdom
from around the 11th century
onward, which has left few
traces of its short existence
except for a set of dagobas,
and a handful of imperial
tombs located 12 miles (20
km) outside the city (see
p476). This mysterious
dynasty materialized in the
early 11th century, in the area
north of Han China. Following a period of expansion
from AD 982 to the 1030s, the
Western Xia empire included
all of modern-
day Ningxia, as
well as parts of
Shaanxi, Gansu,
Qinghai, and
Inner Mongolia.
Although the
Chinese consid-
ered them bar-
barians, they
achieved a considerable level
of sophistication, partly
through the assimilation of
Tang culture, until their kingdom was sacked by the
invading Mongols in 1227.

Today, Yinchuan is a
pleasant and lively city, with
a handful of interesting things
to see. It consists of two
parts, the new town (Xin
Cheng) to the west near the
railway station, and the old
town (Lao Cheng), 4 miles
(7 km) east, where the city's
main bus station and most of
the sights are located.

Jiefang Jie, the old town's
main thoroughfare, has two
well-restored, traditional
Chinese towers. One is the
large **Gulou** (Drum Tower),
while farther east lies the
**Yuhuang Ge** (Yuhuang
Pavilion), which dates back to

The stately Gulou (Drum Tower) in Yinchuan's old town

the Ming dynasty. Just south
of the Drum Tower, Gulou Jie
is the heart of the city's busy
shopping district and is lined
with department stores.
West of Gulou Jie stands
the 13-story, octagonal **Xi Ta**
(West Pagoda), built within the
grounds of the Chetian Temple.
Originally built in the 11th
century, the temple houses
the **Ningxia Provincial Museum**
which has a
large collection of
Western Xia
artifacts. The muse-
um also displays
splendid items
from the Silk Road
era, and has a
section on the
indigenous Hui
people. Followers of Islam, the
Hui originally descended from
Arab and Persian traders from
the Middle East, who came to
China during the Tang and
Yuan eras.

Southeast of the museum,
close to the bus station, is the
**South Gate** (Nan Men) which
resembles a miniature version
of Beijing's Tian'an Men. A
short walk southwest of Nan
Men, **Nanguan Mosque** is a
modern building constructed in
1981 to replace the original
1915 shrine. It is an active
place of worship that caters to
Yinchuan's Hui population.
Unlike most mosques in China,
it has hardly any Chinese
features, and is built in a
distinct Middle-Eastern style. In
the northern reaches of the old
town, the ancient **Haibao Ta**
stands in the grounds of an

**Sign advertising a fortune
teller outside Haibao Ta**

active monastery. According
to records, the 177-ft (54-m)
tower, also known as the
Northern Pagoda (Bei Ta), was
first built in the 5th century AD.
It was rebuilt in the 18th
century in the original style,
after an earthquake destroyed
it in 1739. It is an unusually
angular structure, with ledges
and niches at every level. It is
worth making the climb to the
top of its nine stories, as there
are terrific views across the city
to the Yellow River and Helan
mountains.

🏯 **Gulou & Yuhuang Ge**
Jiefang Jie. ⏰ 8:30am–5pm daily. 🎫

🏛 **Ningxia Provincial
Museum & Xi Ta**
2 Jinning Nan Jie. ⏰ 9am–5pm
daily. 🎫 separate fees for the
temple grounds, pagoda, & museum.

🕌 **Nanguan Mosque**
Yuhuangge Nan Jie. ⏰ daily. 🎫

The 1,500-year-old Haibao Ta in
northern Yinchuan

The striking Xi Xia Wang Ling (Western Xia Tombs) in Helan Shan

# Helan Shan ❾
贺兰山

12 miles (20 km) W of Yinchuan. 🚌 or taxi. ℹ Yinchuan Tourist Office, 116 Jiefang Xijie, (0951) 688 9276.

Looming over Yinchuan, about 12 miles (20 km) to the west, the 11,667-ft (3,556-m) high mountain range, Helan Shan, has some interesting historical places to visit. At the foot of its eastern slopes lie the **Xi Xia Wang Ling**, the royal tombs of the Western Xia dynasty (1038–1227). Spread over a large area, these crumbling but still impressive mounds commemorate the 12 Xia kings. The **Gunzhong Pass**, farther west, makes for pleasant hikes in the surrounding hills if the weather is kind. Located 5 miles (8 km) north of the pass are the 39-ft (12-m) twin pagodas, **Baisikou Shuang Ta**, decorated with Buddha statues. Nearby, at **Suyu Kou**, are hundreds of rock paintings, of uncertain age, depicting animals and human figures. These sights can all be visited in a day by hiring a minibus or car from Yinchuan.

🏯 **Xi Xia Wang Ling**
22 miles (35 km) W of Yinchuan.
◯ 8am–7pm. 📷

# 108 Dagobas ❿

See p477.

# Zhongwei ⓫
中卫

106 miles (170 km) SW of Yinchuan.
🚌 🚆 ℹ Zhongwei Travel Service, 33 Gu Lou Xi Jie, (0995) 701 4880.

The pleasant town of Zhongwei lies between the Tengger Desert to the north and the Yellow River to the south. This small settlement can easily be explored on foot or by cycle-rickshaw. At its center lies a traditional **Drum Tower** (Gulou) dating to the Ming era. Zhongwei's main sight is the 15th-century **Gao Miao**, a rather bizarre temple which serves Buddhists, Daoists, Confucianists, and Christians alike. It was

**Painting on upper pavilion, Gao Miao**

Carved entrance of the multi-denominational Gao Miao, Zhongwei

originally built for Buddhists, but somehow developed ecumenically, which is reflected in the welter of well over 200 chapels and rooms. Rebuilt several times, the temple, in its present form, is an interesting amalgamation of architectural styles.

**Environs:** About 9 miles (15 km) west of Zhongwei, the spectacular resort of **Shapotou** lies on the banks of the Yellow River, between riverbank vegetation on one side, and the striking sand dunes of the desert, on the other. Accessed by minibus from Zhongwei, the Shapotou Desert Research Center was founded in 1956 to reclaim fertile land from the desert. It has met with some success, as seen in the groves of trees and surrounding cultivation. It is now a resort, offering camel rides and trips down river on traditional rafts that are kept afloat with inflated sheep skins. Sand sleds are available to rent for those who wish to speed down the sand dune slopes.

🏯 **Gao Miao**
Gulou Bei Jie. ◯ 8am–6pm daily. 📷
🏞 **Shapotou**
◯ 8:30am–5pm daily. 📷

# Guyuan ⓬
固原

286 miles (460 km) NW of Yinchuan.
🚌 🚆 Xumi Shan Caves 🚌 from Guyuan to Sanying, then taxi.

In the southern part of Ningxia, Guyuan serves as a base for visiting the **Xumi Shan** (Treasure Mountain) **Caves**, 31 miles (50 km) to the northwest. Set in dramatic sandstone hills, these Buddhist grottoes – numbering well over a hundred – are relics from the greatest era of the Silk Road, mostly the period covering the Northern Wei, Sui, and Tang dynasties. They contain more than 300 well-preserved Buddhist statues, the most famous being a colossal Maitreya (Future) Buddha, which stands 62 ft (19 m) high in Cave 5.

# 108 Dagobas ❿
108塔

Set in the desert near the town of Qingtongxia Zhen, the 108 Dagobas stand in twelve gleaming rows, spread out in a perfect triangular formation overlooking the Yellow River. A Buddhist monument, it is not clear exactly what their purpose is. Traditionally it has been thought that they were placed here during the Yuan Dynasty (1279–1368) but there may be some link to the Western Xia Empire. The number 108 is significant in Chinese numerology: there are 108 prayer beads in a Buddhist rosary – the same number of possible sins or worries.

## VISITORS' CHECKLIST

50 miles (85 km) S of Yinchuan. 🚃 or 🚌 from Yinchuan to Qingtongxia Zhen, then minibus or taxi. 🔲 daily. 🎦

Parasol protects from evil

The highest reality

The thirteen steps to enlightenment

Main part represents the primeval mound

Sometimes hollow – used to store relics

Base represents the earth

### ★ The Dagobas
*Like the Indian stupa, the dagoba is a deeply symbolic icon. In early Buddhist art, Buddha was never shown in human form, instead a stupa became his symbol.*

### ★ Hillside Location
*Impressive as the dagobas are, a good reason for visiting them is to get out in the quiet surrounding hills and do a bit of walking. Here you can find quiet temples at the top of some testing steps as well as some inspirational graffiti.*

## VIEWING THE DAGOBAS
The best view is from a boat on the river – if the water level is high enough. The site is in excellent condition as a result of an over-zealous restoration.

## STAR FEATURES

★ Hillside Location

★ The Dagobas

## WESTERN XIA EMPIRE

**Western Xia Coin**

This mysterious dynasty materialized in the early 11th century when they established the Great Xia empire in the area north of what was Han China. Known as Tanguts – and probably from Tibet – they were briefly strong enough to build up a small empire and force tribute from the Song rulers in China. However, they were so thoroughly defeated by the Mongols in 1227 that little evidence of their existence remains except for some coins, books, and a famous stele covered in their feathery script (now in Xi'an).

# GANSU & QINGHAI

For centuries, Gansu and Qinghai were regarded as frontier provinces that marked the outer limits of ancient China. A harsh and rugged region, Gansu connects the Chinese heartland with the vast desert regions to the northwest. The Hexi Corridor, running 750 miles (1,200 km) between two mountain ranges and dotted with oases, formed a link between China and the West. The Silk Road passed through here, as did the Great Wall, and later, the region's only railway line. The Yellow River flows through Lanzhou, for centuries a major stop along the Silk Road. To the southwest lies the Tibetan town of Xiahe and its splendid Labrang Monastery. In the desert landscape northwest of Lanzhou are two great historical relics – the mighty Ming fortress of Jiayuguan and the cave art at Dunhuang.

Lying between Gansu and Tibet, Qinghai is a vast mountain plateau inhabited by a mere 5.5 million people. In every respect – culturally, historically, and geographically – it is part of the Tibetan Plateau, and was once the Tibetan province of Amdo, becoming a province of China only in 1928. Due to its remoteness, it has been used as the site for several prison camps for political dissidents. The province, however, abounds in natural beauty, with lush valleys around the capital of Xining, and miles of unspoilt wilderness around Qinghai Hu, China's largest lake. It also houses one of the country's greatest Tibetan lamaseries, Ta'er Si, and provides access into Tibet from Golmud and Xining across some of the highest mountains in the world.

QINGHAI GANSU

## SIGHTS AT A GLANCE

### Towns & Cities
Dunhuang ⑫
Golmud ⑱
Langmusi ❸
Lanzhou ❻
Linxia ❺
Pingliang ❽
Tongren ⑬
Wuwei ❾
Xining ⑮
Zhangye ❿

### Historic Sites
Jiayuguan Fort
  pp492–3 ⑪

### Mountains, Caves & Lakes
Bingling Si ❼
Luomen ❷
Maiji Shan pp480–1 ❶
Mengda Tian Chi ⑯
Qinghai Hu ⑰

### Monasteries & Temples
Ta'er Si pp500–1 ⑭
Xiahe ❹

### KEY
☒ Domestic airport
  Expressway
  National Highway
  Minor road
  Railroad
  International border
  Provincial border
  Great Wall

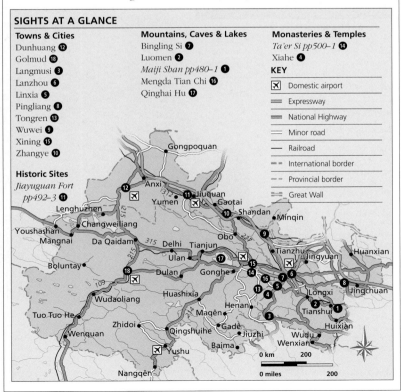

0 km 200
0 miles 200

◁ Colossal statue of the Maitreya Buddha, also known as Jampa, at Ta'er Si, Qinghai

# Maiji Shan ❶

## 麦积山

**Buddha's disciple**

The site of one of China's most important groups of Buddhist carvings, 465-ft (142-m) high Maiji Shan (Corn Rick Mountain) rises up spectacularly like Sumeru, the holy mountain of Buddhist myth. It is likely that the first sculptures were made around the end of the 4th century AD, and work continued up to the Qing dynasty. It provides an invaluable insight into the development of Chinese Buddhist artistic style. Almost 200 caves survive and are reached by a series of precipitous stairways. However, many of the best caves are closed and the gloomy interiors have to be viewed through grilles, so bring a flashlight.

**Maiji Shan, said to resemble a corn rick or haystack from afar**

Cave 5, Calf Hall

Cave 135, Cave of Heaven

★ **Colossal Buddha: Cave 98**
*This finely worked 53-ft (16-m) high statue of Amitabha Buddha is portrayed attended by two smaller statues of Avalokitesvara. The move away from classical Indian-style Buddha sculptures is clearly evident here.*

## WORKING WITH CLAY

Because of the friable nature of the stone at Maiji Shan, many of the statues were not hewn out of the rock but modeled from clay stuck onto a wooden frame. Although they are not as well preserved as a result, they are more lively and with more detail than similar carvings in the Buddhist caves at, for example, Dunhuang. There are a few stone statues at Maiji Shan, but these have been carved from specially imported rock.

**Statue showing details of dress and hairstyle**

**Cave 133** is actually a tomb and home to many sculptures and engravings. It is considered one of the most exquisite holy caves.

### STAR SIGHTS

★ Colossal Buddhas

★ Gallery Views

**Upper Seven Buddhas: Cave 4**
*The upper gallery of Buddhas includes this magnificent Song-dynasty guardian. The cave complex itself is said to have been built by the local governor Li Yunxin, as early as the sixth century.*

Cave 3, Thousand Buddha Corridor

**★ Colossal Buddhas: Cave 13**
*These huge statues originally date from the Sui dynasty and were then repaired during the Ming dynasty. The myriad holes around the statues were probably used to support a protective framework.*

**Middle Seven Buddhas: Cave 9**
*These figures show a transitional phase between Indian-influenced sculpture and later Song-era figures, with pure Chinese characteristics. The statues are well-proportioned and slim in stature, with realistic drapes to their clothes.*

**Cave 43**, is the tomb of a Wei-dynasty empress.

**★ Gallery Views**
*There are excellent views across the countryside from the network of walkways on the cliff face of Maiji Shan. If time allows, a hike around the Botanical Garden at the foot of the cliff is recommended.*

Rock carvings at Lashao Si, Luomen, depicting Sakyamuni Buddha

# Luomen **❷**
洛门

155 miles (250 km) SE of Lanzhou. 🚌 🚆 **Water Curtain Thousand Buddha Caves** 🚌 minibus from Luomen. 📷

The small town of Luomen serves as a base for visiting the **Water Curtain Thousand Buddha Caves**, situated in a spectacular gorge in the nearby mountains. Remote and accessible only by a rough road, which is actually a riverbed, the caves cannot be reached in bad weather as the road becomes unusable. The main attractions are a 98-ft (30-m) Sakyamuni (the Historical Buddha), carved into a rock face, and Lashao Si, a temple built into a cave in the mountainside that has paintings and carvings dating from the Northern Wei dynasty (AD 386–534). Visitors can reach Luomen by bus or train from Tianshui, or from Lanzhou.

# Langmusi **❸**
郎木寺

236 miles (380 km) S of Lanzhou. 🚌 from Lanzhou, Linxia or Xiahe to Hezuo, then direct bus to Langmusi.

Remarkable for its unhurried pace, the remote mountain town of Langmusi is inhabited by a mix of Tibetan, Hui, and Han Chinese. While the hills offer miles of unspoilt country with trails for walking and riding, several active temples dot the town. Built in 1413, the **Dacheng Lamo Kerti Gompa** is the place of worship for several hundred monks, who study astrology and medicine, apart from Tibetan Buddhist theology. Traditional sky-burials, where the dead are left for birds of prey, also take place here. However, visitors are not permitted to view the last rites.

🏯 **Dacheng Lamo Kerti Gompa**
🔲 daily. 📷

# Xiahe **❹**
夏河

175 miles (280 km) SW of Lanzhou. 🚌 🎪 Monlam (Great Prayer) Festival (Feb/Mar).

Perched at a height of 9,514 ft (2,900 m) in a mountain valley at the edge of the Tibetan plateau – that is now a part of Gansu – Xiahe is a significant Tibetan monastery town that attracts many devout Buddhist pilgrims to its **Labrang Monastery** every year. As a result the town's population is a mix of Hui, Tibetan, and Han Chinese.

Xiahe's location offers many opportunities to explore the surrounding grasslands preferably on horseback, although cycling is an option for some. The town itself comprises a single street, running along the Daxia River. The commercial part of town is at the eastern end; the Labrang Monastery is in the center; while the Tibetan quarter is at the western end, offering glimpses of the Tibetan way of life. This town is worth a visit, especially for those not going to Tibet.

**Environs:** Lying near **Sangke** village, 5 miles (10 km) west of Xiahe, is a lake surrounded by the Sangke grasslands, used by nomads for grazing their yaks. This huge area of grass and flowers can be accessed by road, although a fee is charged. Another 19 miles (30 km) north lie the even more vast and picturesque **Ganjia Grasslands.**

Breathtaking alpine scenery around Langmusi

# Labrang Monastery
拉卜楞寺

**Labrang monk**

The most important center of the Yellow Hat Sect (Gelugpa) outside Tibet, the Labrang Monastery (Labuleng Si) attracts Tibetan pilgrims in their thousands. As a result of the Cultural Revolution the monastery was closed until 1980 and the number of monks reduced from 4,000 to about 1,500. Set in an auspicious location with the Dragon mountains to the north and the Daxia river to the south, the impressive monastery buildings are joined by a haphazard maze of alleyways that makes it a fascinating place to wander around.

**VISITORS' CHECKLIST**

Xiahe 175 miles (280 km) SW of Lanzhou. **Tel** (0941) 712 1095.
🚌 Linxia, Lanzhou or Tongren.
🕐 8am–noon, 2–6pm daily.
🚫 Nov–Feb. 🎫 📷 required for the main temple. 🎎 Monlam Festival (see p44).

**Main prayer hall, Labrang Monastery**

## Exploring the Labrang Monastery

This monastery was founded in 1709 during the forty-eighth year of the reign of the Qing Kangxi emperor by a local monk, E'Ang Zongzhe. He became the first generation Living Buddha, or Jiemuyang, who ranks third in the Tibetan hierarchy after the Dalai and Panchen Lamas. The monastery's buildings came through the Cultural Revolution relatively unscathed, but in 1985 a fire seriously damaged the Grand Sutra Hall, which has subsequently been fully restored. Today the sprawling monastery complex dominates the town. It is actually impossible to see where the town stops and the monastery begins, they are so inextricably woven together.

The monastery is built in a typical Tibetan style and consists of six grand halls for the study of scriptures or *sutras*, eighteen Buddha temples, offices for the Living Buddha and many hundreds of residences for the monks. The monastery is also an academic institution and holds an assortment of around 60,000 *sutras* and specialized books. The large halls are colleges for the monks to study a variety of degrees such as mathematics, astronomy, medicine and other more esoteric subjects.

**The Grand Sutra Hall** is the most impressive of the buildings and can hold up to 4,000 monks. It is an eerily impressive sight to see the monks chanting here each morning as they wait to go in and pray. Labrang also has a multitude of prayer wheels set in a long line that encircles the monastery. Spinning these was, and still is, a way for the largely illiterate Tibetan people to pray.

Within the prayer wheels stands the **Gongtang Pagoda**, south of the main road. At nearly 100-ft high (31-m) it comprises five levels topped with a gold colored stupa containing thousands of *sutras* and Buddha statues. You can climb up to the upper level and get an oustanding view over the monastery and town. Parts of Labrang can only be visited as a member of a tour group, although much of the monastery can be freely explored. There are a couple of tours in English each day. Visitors, of course, should be sensitive to the religious nature of the site.

Xiahe is also famous for its Monlam festival. Witnessed by thousands who have come from all over the country, a huge *thangka* of Buddha is unfurled and sanctified on a screen to the south of the Daxia River. There follows several days of festivities including processions, musical performances, and dances.

**Senior Yellow Hat monk**

**View over the monastery with the gleaming Gongtang Pagoda to the left**

Bunches of noodles tied up and ready for sale, Linxia

# Linxia ❺
## 临夏

62 miles (100 km) SW of Lanzhou.
🚶 *200,000.* 🚌 *from Lanzhou, Xining, and Xiahe.* ⛴

A pleasant place for ambling leisurely through streets bustling with locals, Linxia has a predominantly Muslim character, defined by the resident Hui minority. It was once a stopover for travelers passing between Lanzhou and the South Pass along the Silk Road. The town is still a good place to break the journey between Lanzhou and Xiahe. However, it offers very few attractions aside from its numerous mosques. The most prominent is the large and impressive **Nanguan Mosque**, just off the main square.

Linxia's appeal lies in its colorful markets and teahouses. The markets are lined with shops selling carved gourds, carpets, and saddlery. Most interesting are the local spectacles, made from ground crystal lenses, which many elderly men can be seen wearing. At the top end of Jiefang Nan Lu in the south of town is the great night market with numerous stalls stocked with aromatic curry-flavored breads *(bing)* and huge piles of noodles – fresh and dried.

Linxia is popular with the Dongxiang minority, who speak their own Altaic language, and are supposedly descendants of 13th-century immigrants, who moved here after Kublai Khan invaded their homelands in Central Asia.

# Lanzhou ❻
## 兰州

Elephant drum

A large industrial city and Gansu's capital, Lanzhou has for long been the key transport link between the Chinese heartlands and the Northwest. It was an important stop on the Silk Road at the beginning of the Hexi Corridor, and is thus culturally closer to the Northwest than to Central China. The Yellow River flows through the center of the city, and for centuries Lanzhou was the principal point for crossing the river. In fact, until the 19th century, a bridge created by chaining together a flotilla of boats was used. The first iron bridge was built in 1907. Although most of the attractions lie well away from the center, Lanzhou offers good food, shopping, and an excellent museum.

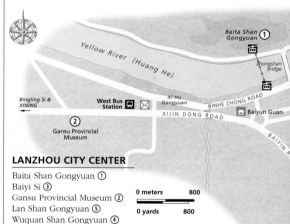

## LANZHOU CITY CENTER

Baita Shan Gongyuan ①
Baiyi Si ③
Gansu Provincial Museum ②
Lan Shan Gongyuan ⑤
Wuquan Shan Gongyuan ④

| 0 meters | 800 |
| 0 yards | 800 |

Yellow River flanked by the lush Baita Shan Gongyuan & Lanzhou city

### 🌿 Baita Shan Gongyuan
🕐 *6:30am–8.30pm daily.* 🎫
To the north of the river, near Zhongshan Bridge, is Baita Shan Gongyuan (White Pagoda Hill Park). It takes its name from the 13th-century pagoda, Bai Ta, which was built as part of a temple at the

hill's summit. Steps have been carved into the steep slopes, while the walkways are dotted with teahouses, mosques, a plant nursery, and assorted pavilions. Chairlifts take visitors to the top from inside the park, or from town, on the other side of the river.

## 🏛 Gansu Provincial Museum

3 Xijin Xi Lu. ◯ *9am–5pm Tue–Sun.* 🖼

This museum is set in an old Soviet-style building west of town. The ground floor has a natural history section with a mammoth skeleton found in the Yellow River in 1973. Captioned in English, the history section upstairs is best known for the striking 2,000-year-old bronze Flying Horse, with its hoof resting on the back of a swallow, that was discovered in an Eastern Han tomb in Wuwei.

**Flying Horse statue at Lanzhou's train station**

Also worth seeing are the bronze chariots, with horses and attendants, from a tomb in the same area, as well as a fine collection of Yangshao pottery dating from the late Neolithic period. Other relics include Silk Road carvings, wooden spills, statuary, and writing tablets. In the garden, a mock tomb recreates burials in the Jiayuguan area in the late 3rd and early 4th centuries. Finally, a large exhibit commemorates the Long March.

### VISITORS' CHECKLIST

425 miles (680 km) W of Xi'an. 🚶 3,000,000. ✈ Lanzhou Airport, 56 miles (90 km) N of city. 🚆 Lanzhou Train Station. 🚌 CAAC (buses to airport), East Bus Station, Private Bus Depots, Main Bus Station, West Bus Station. ℹ 2nd Floor, Tourism Building, Nong-min Xiang, (0931) 881 3222.

## Wuquan Shan Gongyuan

◯ *6am–5pm daily.* 🖼

Also set in the south of town, the Wuquan Shan Gongyuan (Five Springs Hill Park) resembles a traditional garden, with its weathered rocks, cascading streams, elaborate-shaped doorways, and myriad pavilions, and is pleasant enough to wander around in for a while. The hill is said to be the place where the Han general, Huo Qubin, quartered his cavalry as he mounted an

[Map showing Lanzhou with roads including Binhe Road, Yellow River (Huang He), Zhangye Road, Jinning Road, Jinchang Road, Ping Liang Road, Nanchang Road, Tianshui Bei Road, Qingyang Road, Dong Gang Xi Road, Gaolan Road, Zhongshan Road, Jiuquan Road, Minzhu Xi Road, Hongshangen Road, Ding Bei Road, Tianshui Road. Marked locations: Lanzhou Airport, Baiyi Si ③, CAAC, East Bus Station, Chongqing Si, Main Bus Station, Lanzhou Train Station, Wuquan Shan Gongyuan ④, Lan Shan Gongyuan ⑤]

**Key to Symbols** *see back flap*

**Gateway designed as a quatrefoil moon in Wuquan Shan Gongyuan**

## 🏛 Baiyi Si

Baiyi Si, with its temple and accompanying stupa, was built during the Ming dynasty (1368–1644) just a few hundred feet to the east of busy Jinchang Lu, on the north side of Qingyang Lu. The small temple's unusual location, dwarfed by the department stores of Lanzhou's main shopping district, makes it appear strikingly out of place, and worth a visit for this alone.

**Ornamental door knob, Rui Yuan Si, Wuquan Shan**

## 🌿 Lan Shan Gongyuan

◯ *8am–8pm daily.* 🖼

South of the city, Lan Shan Gongyuan (Lan Shan Park) can be reached by chairlift from Wuquan Shan Gongyuan. The 20-minute ride to the top is a pleasant way to escape the summer heat. It is a great spot to watch the sunsets and the city lights at night. An amusement park and several eateries are also located here. A trail leads to Wuquan Shan Gongyuan.

expedition to the northwest. According to one legend, he cut at the rocks until the water he needed for his horses and men gushed forth. Of the several temples on the site, **Chongqing Si** dates back to 1372, and houses an iron bell cast in 1202. Despite its venerable origins, modern materials like concrete have been used several times in building the temple, and it is now an artistic blend of Soviet and traditional Chinese design. Another one of the oldest buildings in the park, the Ming-dynasty **Jingang Palace** houses an impressive, 16-ft (5-m) bronze Buddha, reputedly cast in 1370.

The enormous seated Buddha carved into a cliff, Cave 172, Bingling Si

# Bingling Si ❼
炳灵寺

56 miles (90 km) SW of Lanzhou. 🚌 to Liujia Xia Reservoir, then boat to caves. 🚤 in season, when the water level in reservoir is high. 🎫 🎒 from Lanzhou.

The magnificent group of Buddhist caves at Bingling Si (Bright Spirit Temple) is one of the most intriguing sights in Gansu. Buddhism arrived in China along the Silk Road, and these caves are among the earliest significant Buddhist monuments in the country. Carved into sheer cliffs, the caves stretch for about a mile (1.6 km) along a 196-ft (60-m) high gorge. Isolated by the waters of the Liujiaxia Reservoir on the Yellow River, the splendid sculptures and paintings were saved from damage during the Cultural Revolution, and remain in surprisingly good condition. Known as the Thousand Buddha Caves, there are in fact, only 183 of them, of which 149 can be more appropriately described as niches.

The caves were created about 1,600 years ago during the Northern Wei and Western Jin dynasties. It is believed that the artists hung down the cliffs on ropes, and chiseled out sculptures into the rock-face. The style of work is similar to the Buddhist caves at Datong and Luoyang. Most of the caves contain rock-cut statues, clay sculptures, and colorful frescoes. One of the earliest caves, No. 169, dates to AD 420, and contains a Buddha and two Bodhisattvas

that are among the oldest and best preserved in China. Most of the other caves were completed during the Tang era. The most impressive cave, No. 172, has an 89-ft (27-m) high seated statue of Maitreya (the Future Buddha). There are also four clay pagodas and another one carved from stone.

Work on the sculptures continued long after the Silk Road had lost its importance, and there are examples of work from the Song, Ming, and Qing dynasties. The paintings reached their height during the Song and Ming dynasties, although there are some older and comparatively cruder paintings dating back to the Tang period.

Getting to the caves can be slightly uncertain, as access depends on the water level in

Carved stele, Kongtong Shan, Pingliang

the reservoir. Autumn is usually the best time of year to visit Bingling Si, but it is best to check with other travelers before arranging a trip. It is a two-hour bus journey from Lanzhou to the reservoir and dam, followed by a three-hour boat trip to the caves, passing through some beautiful countryside with fishermen busy at work, and wheat and rice being cultivated on the riverbanks.

# Pingliang ❽
平凉

155 miles (250 km) SE of Lanzhou. 🚌 🏨

Hidden in the hills in a mountainous region near the Gansu-Ningxia border is the sleepy town of Pingliang. Surrounded by beautiful peaks, some of which rise to heights of 6,890 ft (2,100 m), it remains one of the least-visited parts of the province, and is mostly used as a convenient base for exploring **Kongtong Shan**, a Daoist monastery, 6 miles (10 km) west of town. Perched dramatically on a clifftop of the same name, the monastery lies close to a glittering lake and a few other temples scattered across the landscape. The surrounding area is excellent for taking long walks across the lush green hills.

Kongtong Shan's lush north peak, Pingliang

*For hotels and restaurants in this region see pp571–2 and pp596–7*

# The Spread of Buddhism

Buddhism's establishment in China was a long process and the date of its arrival is uncertain. The earliest sign of the religion in China is associated with the foundation of the White Horse Temple *(see p152)* during the Han dynasty near the imperial capital of Luoyang. Based on the teachings of Buddha who lived in northern India during the 6th century BC, Buddhism was probably disseminated along the Silk Route by immigrants from Central Asia from the 1st century onwards. In China, Buddhism surged in popularity during periods of instability, when Confucianism's veneration for authority did not sit well with the populace *(see p30)*, and it was eventually adopted by China's rulers. The Mahayana School *(see p31)* took hold in China, breaking into different sects, such as the Chan sect, which gained a large following in Japan as Zen Buddhism.

**Stone Buddha statue**

**Mahayana Buddhism** *started in India in the first century AD, finally spreading to Japan, via China, around AD 600.*

**The Great Goose Pagoda** *in Xi'an was built for the monk Xuanzang in AD 652 to house the* sutras *he brought back from India, a pilgrimage immortalized in* Journey to the West (see p29). *He spent the remainder of his life translating the* sutras, *aiding the spread of Buddhism.*

**The caves** *at Dunhuang* (see pp496–7), *served as the last stop on the Silk Road for pilgrim monks on their way to India. The frescoes and carvings, which celebrate the spread of Buddhism and date from the 4th to the 11th century, are amongst the most important early Buddhist works in China.*

**Guanyin**, *the female Bodhisattva of Compassion, was originally the male deity Avalokitesvara. This sex change is one way the Chinese adapted Buddhism to suit their needs. Guanyin became the patron of motherhood and is the most worshiped figure in China.*

**The early Tang dynasty** *was a time of Buddhist renaissance, with the religion gaining imperial patronage. In the 9th century, however, rebellions provoked a period of Buddhist suppression.*

# Wuwei ⑨
武威

140 miles (225 km) NW of Lanzhou.

Lying between Lanzhou and Zhangye, this small town is where Gansu's most celebrated relic, the bronze Flying Horse, was discovered in 1969. Found in an Eastern Han tomb in the grounds of **Leitai Si**, a few miles north of town, the Flying Horse is now in the **Provincial Museum** in Lanzhou, and its symbol can be seen all over Wuwei. The tomb, a series of empty passageways, houses replicas of its original relics and is open to visitors.

Other sights are the brick **Luoshi Ta**, off Bei Dajie, and farther east, the old **Bell Tower** with pleasant gardens. To the south is **Wen Miao**, a museum set in the grounds of a temple. The South Gate (Nan Men) has been reconstructed and adds a little old-world grandeur to a rapidly-changing town.

**🏛 Wen Miao**
🕐 8:30am–6pm daily. 📷

# Zhangye ⑩
张掖

280 miles (450 km) NW of Lanzhou.

Once a stopover on the Silk Road, Zhangye has several sights of interest. At its center is a Ming-era **Gulou** (Drum Tower), with a large bell. To the east, **Daode Guan** is an active Daoist shrine also dating to the

A traditional incense burner in the grounds of Dafo Si, Zhangye

Ming era. South along Nan Jie lies **Tu Ta**, a former Buddhist monastery featuring a large stupa. Also nearby is the **Dafo Si**, which houses the largest reclining Buddha in China in its hall.

Lying 37 miles (60 km) south of Zhangye, in the Tibetan town of Mati, is **Mati Si**, a fascinating complex of Buddhist caves carved into a cliff.

**A view of the stupa at Dafo Si**

# Jiayuguan ⑪
嘉峪关

475 miles (765 km) NW of Lanzhou.
📷 from Dunhuang.

Traditionally regarded as China's final outpost, the last point of civilization before the desert, Jiayuguan is visited mainly for its Ming-era fort *(see pp492–3)*. Within town, the **Great Wall Museum** documents the history of the wall from the Han to the Ming eras. Exhibits include photographs of remote sections of the wall as well as scale models.

Several other sights lie around Jiayuguan. About 4 miles (6 km) north of the fort is **Xuanbi Changcheng** (Overhanging Wall), a restored section of the wall dating to the 16th century, that once linked the fort to the mountains. In the same area, the Hei Shan rock carvings depict scenes from daily life during the Warring States period. Situated 4 miles (6 km) south of town is the **First Beacon Tower**, a desolate outpost that marks the start (or end) of the western part of the Ming-dynasty Great Wall. About 12 miles (20 km) east of town are tombs from the Wei and Jin eras (220–420 AD), whose bricks are painted with celebratory scenes. The **Qilian Shan** peaks, 75 miles (120 km) to the south, cradle the 14,110 ft (4,300 m) Qiyi Bingchuan (July 1st Glacier), reached by a combination of train, taxi, and foot.

**🏛 Great Wall Museum**
24 Xinhua Nan Lu. 🕐 daily. 📷

The 16th-century ramparts of Xuanbi Changcheng (Overhanging Wall), Jiayuguan

◁ Jiayuguan Fort, the farthest outpost safeguarding the civilized world of the Ming dynasty

# The Great Game

The "Great Game" was the name, popularized by Rudyard Kipling in *Kim*, of the covert war fought by the Russian and British empires for influence in the deserts and mountains of Central Asia at the end of the 19th century. Afghanistan was the first target for these two great empires and both sides vied for influence, with the British eventually succeeding in establishing a sympathetic regime in 1880. Meanwhile in Chinese Turkestan (Xinjiang) the Muslims broke free of China and set up the state of Kashgaria in 1863 under Yakub Beg. The Russians invaded the Ili Valley and, when China took Xinjiang back in 1877, negotiated to establish consulates in the area. The British response was to set up a trade mission in Kashgar and take a more aggressive approach in Tibet. In 1907 the stand-off ended with the Anglo-Russian Convention, which clearly defined territorial limits.

**Rudyard Kipling**

**Central Asia** *was where the Russian, British and Chinese empires touched. The British, fearful of the Russian threat to India, wanted to cultivate a buffer zone around its frontier, using Afghanistan, Kashgaria and Tibet.*

**Sher Ali** *(1825–79), the son of Dost Mohammed who fought the British in the first Anglo-Afghan War, allowed entry to a Russian diplomatic mission, but turned back a British one. This sparked the second Anglo-Afghan War, after which the British placed Abdur Rahman on the throne in 1880.*

**The Pamir Mountains** *held the passes that Alexander the Great and Timur (Tamerlane) had used to invade India. Russian advances here in 1885 and 1896 led to the mobilization of British troops, but treaties establishing new frontiers prevented war both times.*

**The Open Mouth (1899)**, *a Punch cartoon, shows the British Lion and Russian Bear trying to get their hands on a scared Chinaman. China, weakened by internal strife, was repeatedly forced to sign unfair treaties handing over land and allowing the superpowers to establish trade missions that were used to spy on the other side.*

**Tibet** *became involved when Britain placed it in China's sphere of influence. In response Tibet refused to acknowledge British attempts to set up a trade mission, resulting in the attack on Gyantse in 1903 (see p543) by Younghusband.*

# Jiayuguan Fort ⓫
嘉峪关

**Corner wall tower**

At the western extremity of the Great Wall stands the Jiayuguan Fort, dominating the stony plain that separates two mountain ranges. Built of tamped earth in 1372, in the distinctive, embattled Ming-dynasty style, it was dubbed the "Impregnable Defile Under Heaven." It was of enormous strategic importance as it controlled the only military and trade link between China and the deserts of Central Asia. The frontier lay some way further west, but for the Chinese Jiayuguan was the last outpost of civilisation, beyond which lay barbarian country, a place of perdition, fit only for exiled officials and banished criminals.

**Detail inside tower**
*As shown by these wooden doors, the interiors of the towers were beautifully painted in typical Ming style.*

**Trap Court**
*This was used to lure the enemy into a place from where they could be attacked from above. It also served as a holding bay for caravans.*

**Jiayuguan Men** is three stories high with typical Ming-style upturned eaves.

**"Gate of Sighs"** was once inscribed with the sorrowful graffiti of those leaving China.

**Rou Yuan Men or Gate of Conciliation**

**Corner Towers** gave protection to archers while they fired on the attacking troops.

**★ Fort Walls**
*Built of tamped earth and bricks, the mighty 35-ft (10-m) high walls were designed to be accessed by horses via ramps that lead from the gates to the battlements. The total length of the walls is about half a mile (750 m).*

## STAR SIGHTS

★ Fort Walls

★ Guanghua Men

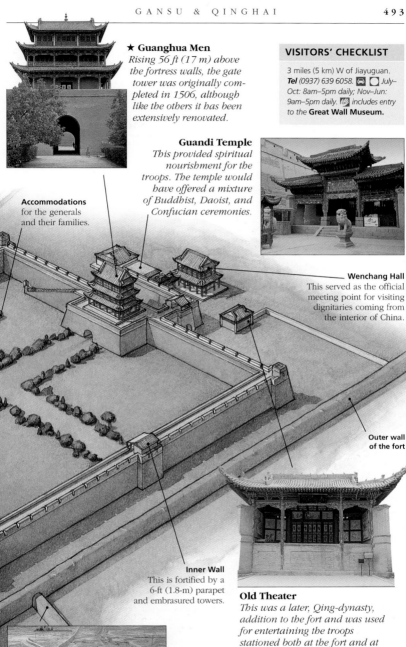

**★ Guanghua Men**
*Rising 56 ft (17 m) above the fortress walls, the gate tower was originally completed in 1506, although like the others it has been extensively renovated.*

**VISITORS' CHECKLIST**

3 miles (5 km) W of Jiayuguan.
**Tel** (0937) 639 6058. 🚌 ⬜ July–Oct: 8am–5pm daily; Nov–Jun: 9am–5pm daily. 🎟 includes entry to the **Great Wall Museum.**

**Guandi Temple**
*This provided spiritual nourishment for the troops. The temple would have offered a mixture of Buddhist, Daoist, and Confucian ceremonies.*

**Accommodations**
for the generals and their families.

**Wenchang Hall**
This served as the official meeting point for visiting dignitaries coming from the interior of China.

**Outer wall of the fort**

**Inner Wall**
This is fortified by a 6-ft (1.8-m) parapet and embrasured towers.

**Old Theater**
*This was a later, Qing-dynasty, addition to the fort and was used for entertaining the troops stationed both at the fort and at garrisons along the Great Wall.*

**End of the Great Wall of China**
*The wall stretches out either side of the fort closing off the plain. The wall is made of tamped earth, a raw material in ready supply in the desert.*

A camel ride across the dunes at Mingsha Shan, Dunhuang

# Dunhuang ⑫
敦煌

⊠ 🚉 *Liuyuan, 80 miles (130 km) to the north, then bus.* 🚌 🚶 *33 Ming Shan Rd, (0937) 883 7021.*

A small oasis town, Dunhuang once prospered as the last stop on the Silk Road before it split north and south to skirt the Taklamakan Desert. It is a pleasant settlement that has achieved a certain level of prosperity, primarily through acting as a base for visiting the famous grottoes at Mogao (see pp496–7), a short distance away. The town caters for its foreign visitors and has several restaurants and budget hotels. The only items of interest at the **Dunhuang County Museum** (Xian Bowuguan) are a few Chinese and Tibetan manuscripts, from Mogao's famous Cave 17, which escaped the looting of explorers and archeologists. The museum also has examples of traditional silks and domestic items found near the beacon towers that were once part of China's outermost line of defense. There is a souvenir night market every summer evening along the town's main thoroughfare, Dong Dajie. The range of items on sale includes leather shadow puppets, Chinese scroll paintings, jade items, coins, Tibetan horns, and Buddha statues.

**Printed textiles, Dunhuang market**

Just 3 miles (5 km) south of Dunhuang is **Yueya Quan** (Crescent Moon Lake), a small freshwater lake that has been a vital source of water here for thousands of years. It lies adjacent to the Mingsha Shan (Singing Sand Mountains), which tower several hundred feet high. The dunes were named after the sound of sand being crunched under foot. For some remarkable views, visitors can climb the dunes – preferably in the cool of the evening. There is also a range of activities, including paragliding, sand tobogganing, and camel rides. A small folk art museum lies nearby.

Situated in the middle of fields about 2 miles (4 km) west of Dunhuang is the nine-story **Baima Ta** (White Horse Pagoda). This Tibetan-style pagoda was built in memory of a horse belonging to the monk, Kumarajiva, who came from the Silk Road kingdom of Kuqa (see p509). The horse died here in AD 384.

🏛 **Dunhuang County Museum**
8 Yangguan Dong Lu.
**Tel** (0937) 882 2981.
⏰ 9am–6pm daily (closed winter). 🎟

🐫 **Yueya Quan**
⏰ 8am–5:50pm daily.

**Environs:** About 12 miles (20 km) southwest of Dunhuang lies **Dunhuang Gucheng** (Dunhuang Ancient City), a film set built in the 1990s that was never dismantled. Its location and panoramic views are impressive, but it is rather dog-eared on closer inspection. However, the set has become a regular tourist stop with souvenir stores and even accommodations in yurts.

Lying 50 miles (80 km) west of Dunhuang are two Han-dynasty gates, **Yu Men Guan** (Jade Gate Pass) and **Yang Guan** (South Pass). Separated by 3 miles (5 km) of desert, they were once linked by the Great Wall. Abandoned over 1,000 years ago and under constant attack by the desert, the two towers remain quite impressive. The huge cube of the Yu Men Guan with its 33-ft (10-m) walls is the only discernible man-made structure in sight.

Yueya Quan and Mingsha Shan dunes, Dunhuang

*For hotels and restaurants in this region see pp571–2 and pp596–7*

# Race for the Silk Road Oases

A scholarly reflection of the political rivalry between the great powers at the end of the 19th century was the race between a group of explorer-archeologists to locate (and plunder) the lost towns of the Silk Road. Between them, they succeeded in uncovering a huge number of long-forgotten, desert-scoured towns. These pioneers furthered the knowledge of life along the Silk Road and saved many items from further degradation.

Tang musician, Dunhuang

However, they did remove vast quantities of priceless works of art, to the eventual annoyance of the Chinese government. These are now scattered in museums around the globe. Initial interest in the region by the British was based on strategic considerations *(see p491)*; then, as stories of lost cities emerged, the interest of antiquarians around the world was aroused. Controversial though they were, their excavations captured the world's imagination.

**Tales of buried cities** *being uncovered by sandstorms emerged at the end of the 19th century. The Gaochang Ruins, discovered by von Le Coq, were found to have been a major Buddhist and Nestorian center (see p465).*

**Sven Hedin** *(1865–1952), from Sweden, was the first of many government-sponsored adventurers to explore these isolated regions. The others were Albert von Le Coq from Germany, Count Otani of Japan, Paul Pelliot of France, Sir Aurel Stein from Great Britain, and Langdon Warner from the USA.*

**This Buddha's head** *came from the Bezeklik Caves, discovered by von Le Coq in 1904. These caves held some beautiful murals protected over the years by the encroaching sand. Von Le Coq simply cut them from the walls and sent them home to Germany. Unfortunately, the murals were destroyed by bombing during World War II.*

**This silk painting** *is from the Mogao Caves, which were reached by Aurel Stein in 1907. He befriended the Abbot, Wang, and gained access to the newly discovered silks and manuscripts of Cave 17.*

**This fresco** *of a bodhisattva and other wall paintings at the Mogao Caves were considered sacred, so the collectors could not remove them (see p496). But Stein and the others negotiated with Abbot Wang to carry off thousands of historic items.*

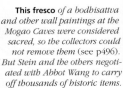

# The Cave Paintings of Dunhuang

Protected by their relative isolation, the cave paintings at Dunhuang form the most fascinating repository of Buddhist art in China. For over 700 years, between the 4th and 11th centuries AD, Buddhist monks excavated and painted these caves, until invasion and the encroachment of Islam brought work to a halt. The paintings were all but forgotten until 1907, when the explorer Sir Aurel Stein stumbled across the caves and the Daoist priest who guarded them, Wang Yuanlu. Among the many thousands of items uncovered by Stein is the Diamond Sutra, the world's earliest printed book (in scroll form), and many of the patterns used by the monks to reproduce paintings at will.

**Cave 275: Sixteen Kingdoms 366–439** *This early cave of the Northern Liang Period is dedicated to the Maitreya or Future Buddha, who is depicted in wall paintings and statues.*

**Cave 272: Sixteen Kingdoms 366–439** *These Devas (Buddhist angels) are in rapture as they listen to the Buddha's teaching.*

**Cave 254: Northern Wei 439–534** *This cave shows stories of Buddha's early life, including the Sacrifice of the Prince. The murals are richer in content than in earlier caves and the artwork has become more accomplished.*

**Cave 249: Western Wei 535–556** *On the north wall there is a wonderfully lively hunting scene showing the backward-shooting hunter – a feat only made possible with the invention of the stirrup.*

**Cave 428: Northern Zhou 557–580** *Stories of the good prince, an earlier incarnation of Buddha, abound. Here he offers himself to a starving tigress so she may feed her cubs.*

**Cave 419: Sui 581–618** *Under the short-lived Sui dynasty, China was reunified with both the north and south adopting Buddhism as their religion. This harmony allowed the development of a more Chinese artistic style and was a highly fruitful time for Dunhuang. This cave portrays the good prince on a hunting trip with his brothers.*

**Cave 420: Sui 581–618** *This fresco portrays a journey on the Silk Road, the route via which Buddhism came to China, as well as pictures of buildings in a style of which no real example survives.*

**Cave 220: Early Tang
618–704** *Rich patrons would
often feature in murals. This
cave portrays ten generations
of the wealthy Zhai family.*

**Cave 217: Early to High
Tang 618–780** *Detail of the
Western Paradise of Amitabha
Buddha. This cave contains
some wonderful, unfinished
paintings of Bodhisattvas.*

**Cave 17: Late Tang 848–906**
*A detail from the famous cave
where the massive library of
sutras was first found by
Abbot Wang.*

**Cave 263: Western Xia
1036–1226** *Under the Western
Xia dynasty a lot of older
caves were simply redecorated.
This was originally a cave of
Northern Wei origin.*

The Dunhuang cliff face, home to 1,000 years of Buddhist history

# Mogao Caves
# 敦煌石窟

*Mogao, 15 miles (25 km) SE of
Dunhuang, Gansu Province.* **Tel** *(0937)
886 9071.* 🚌 🚗 ⬜ *8am–6pm.* 📷
📹 🚫

The caves at Mogao were
dug into cliffs that rise
out of an otherwise
largely flat and
featureless
desert landscape.
Getting there is
relatively easy, if
you are travelling
independently, as
Dunhuang is
crawling with
minibuses. As
usual, the drivers
wait until every
seat is taken before
setting off, but the
half-hour journey is
cheap. Remember that the
caves are closed between
11:30am and 2:30pm.

Of the six hundred
surviving caves, only about
twenty are open to the
public. The entrance fee
includes a Chinese-speaking
guide, although it is
worthwhile, for an additional
fee, engaging an English-
speaking guide, since the tour
party is likely to be smaller
and the choice of caves less
rigidly laid down. The caves
that include portrayals of
tantric sex can also sometimes
be opened for a
supplementary payment. The
guides are generally fairly
knowledgeable about the
history of the caves and the
paintings and sculptures
within. You are, however,

Statue from pagoda
at Mogao caves

recommended to take your
own flashlight and to
remember that photography
is not allowed in the caves
(unless you have a very
expensive permit), a rule
that is strenuously enforced.
The standard tour lasts half
a day, and includes about
fifteen of the caves, as
well as the museum,
which exhibits some of
the ancient manuscripts
found here. It is
also worth visiting the
Research and Exhibition
Center, where seven of
the caves have been
reproduced, permitting
far closer scrutiny of
the paintings than is
possible in the
original caves, albeit
without the same
atmosphere of
antiquity. There is a
simple guesthouse
for those wishing to stay
overnight; otherwise, the
return journey to Dunhuang
is by minibus, the last one
leaving around 6pm.

Façade of Cave 96, covering a
100-ft (30-m) statue of Buddha

The beautifully decorated door of Longwu Si's prayer hall, Tongren

# Tongren ⑬
同仁

66 miles (107 km) W of Xiahe. 🚍
🎭 Lurol Festival (6th lunar month),
Buddhist Festival (1st lunar month).

Known as Repkong in Tibetan, Tongren is a transit point between Xiahe and Xining. This small Tibetan town offers fascinating insights into the life of the Tibetan people. On the outskirts of town lies the colorfully decorated lamasery, **Longwu Si**, containing fine relics in its many halls. Initially built in 1301 during the Yuan dynasty, today's modern reconstruction houses three colleges and an assortment of lamaseries belonging to the Yellow Hat sect – a branch of Tibetan Buddhism *(see pp522–3).* At dusk, visitors can watch the resident monks debating, using elaborate formalized body language to make a point. Sometimes, if you're lucky, they can also be seen making sand paintings. Behind the monastery, a stream flows into the grassland for about a mile, leading to a pretty Tibetan village. Situated in another village, Sengeshong, 4 miles (7 km) from the city center, the **Wutun** and **Gomar** monasteries are home to some of the best Tibetan artists in the world. Both monasteries are magnificently decorated, with every surface of their assembly halls carved and painted with traditional Repkong designs. The residents of this village speak a mixture of Tibetan, Mongolian, and other dialects.

# Ta'er Si ⑭

*See pp500–1.*

# Xining ⑮
西宁

144 miles (232 km) W of Lanzhou.
🏙 2,130,000. ✈ 🚍 🚉 🛈
*Qinghai Tourism Bureau, (0971) 820 3271.*

Although blessed with very few sights, Qinghai's capital, Xining, is home to an intriguing mix of minority peoples, mostly Hui Muslims and Tibetans with a sprinkling of Kazakhs and Mongols. It is the starting point of the railway to Lhasa, and trains depart daily.

From the 16th century, it served as a stopover on the Silk Road's lesser-used southern route, and is now a good base for exploring Qinghai. Xining lies in a remote valley, and, at 7,464 ft (2,275 m), experiences a cool summer and freezing winter.

The **Great Mosque**, one of the largest and most impressive in northwest China, is situated on Dongguan Dajie, close to the city center. It was originally built in the 14th century, and is thoroughly Chinese in design, with elements such as flying eaves and vividly-colored arches. Enclosed within is a public square, that is usually bustling with thousands of worshipers.

A devotee in the Great Mosque

In the far north of town, across the Huangshui River, the Daoist **Bei Shan Si** sits atop a hill and is the focus for a pleasant afternoon's hike. The route, via stone steps and across wooden walkways, passes numerous cave shrines.

Xining's ethnic mix is best appreciated at **Shuijing Xiang Market**, in the west of town off Xi Dajie, where over 3,000 stalls sell all manner of provisions and food, especially hot breads, mutton dishes, and kabobs. It is also a good place to stock up on snacks before heading off on a trip to Qinghai Hu, to the west of town.

The grand Chinese-style architecture of the 14th-century Great Mosque, Xining

*For hotels and restaurants in this region see pp571–2 and pp596–7*

Mengda Tian Chi nature reserve along the banks of the Yellow River

# Mengda Tian Chi ⑯
孟达天池

124 miles (200 km) SE of Xining. ☒ to Guanting or Xunhua, then taxi. ▨

The remarkably beautiful Tian Chi, or "Heavenly Lake," forms the core of the Mengda Nature Reserve, situated along the Yellow River. In contrast to most other parts of the province, the land here is fertile and abounds with vegetation. Most of the reserve is woodland, offering opportunities for scenic walks and birdwatching. Accommodations are available at the reserve, while trips can be arranged through Xining's Tourist Office. The trip to Mengda Tian Chi from Xunhua is spectacular, winding along a precipitous road that cuts into the cliffs along the Yellow River. Xunhua is home to the Turkic-speaking Salar people, who have been here for centuries but originate from modern day Uzbekistan.

**A medallion with Tibetan calligraphy**

# Qinghai Hu ⑰
青海湖

93 miles (150 km) W of Xining. **Bird Island** ⬤ Nov–Feb. ▨ ▨

The largest lake in China, Qinghai Hu covers a vast area of over 1,740 sq miles (4,500 sq km). Its location on the Tibetan plateau, at a height of 10,500 ft (3,200 m) above sea level, makes it extremely remote, accessible only with the help of a tour agency. The lake is home to many Tibetan nomads, who graze their yaks and sheep near the lake, and in summer, numerous herds can be spotted grazing.

The lake's icy salt water is home to large quantities of fish, which feed a thriving bird population. Most trips to the lake center around a visit to **Bird Island**, a rocky outcrop on the western side where colonies of swans, cormorants, bar-headed geese, and rare black-necked cranes, among others, flourish during the breeding season.

On the southern shore, the Qinghai Lake Tourist Center offers opportunities for boating, fishing, horse riding, and trekking. Accommodations are available at the tourist center.

# Golmud ⑱
格尔木

474 miles (762 km) W of Xining. ☒ ▨ ▨ ⓘ 60 Ba Yi Rd, (0979) 849 5123.

In the far west of Qinghai, Golmud is perched at 9,186 ft (2,800 m) in the forlorn Tibetan plateau. The only sizable town for several hundred miles, it is the second largest city in the province after Xining, with a largely Han Chinese population.

The town's bus service, which runs to Lhasa in Tibet, is not particularly cheap and very few people use it now that the 625-mile (1,000-km) railway line to Lhasa has been built, which is the highest railway in the world and has pressurized carriages and oxygen supplies on board. Train journeys to Lhasa do not originate in Golmud, however, contrary to popular belief, but pass through it only. Xining is now the starting point for journeys to Lhasa from Qinghai Province.

One route out of Golmud is to take a land-cruiser tour into some of the remoter parts of Xinjiang.

Golmud itself is largely unappealing, although the surrounding lunar-looking landscape has a rugged charm best appreciated on the way out.

Colorful Tibetan prayer flags on the shore of Qinghai Hu

# Ta'er Si ⑭

塔尔寺

**Prayer wheels each containing a scroll**

Nestled into a hillside, this walled temple complex, also known as Kumbum Monastery is one of the most important Tibetan Buddhist sites in China. Tsongkhapa, founder of the Gelugpa sect *(see p522)*, was born here in 1357, and the first temple was built in his honor in 1577. The monastery was closed for a period under Communist rule, although the buildings were afforded protection during the Cultural Revolution, and reopened in 1979. A major restoration project has been undertaken since an earthquake rocked the complex in 1990. Ta'er Si is easily accessible from Xining, and so is popular with both tourists and pilgrims.

**★ Great Golden Roof Hall**
*This temple was built at the spot where Tsongkhapa was born and a tree is said to have grown with an image of the Buddha on each leaf. It contains a silver stupa holding his image.*

**Nine Room Hall**

**Dinkejing Hall**

**Pilgrim**
*Turning a hand-held prayer wheel and fingering prayer beads, the devout walk clockwise around the perimeter of the complex.*

**Prayer Hall**

**Grand Kitchen**

**★ Hall of Butter Sculpture**
*This strongly fragrant exhibition is packed with intricately carved yak butter sculptures. The gaudily painted figures depict scenes from Buddhist lore.*

**STAR SIGHTS**

- ★ Great Hall of Meditation
- ★ Hall of Butter Sculpture
- ★ Great Golden Roof Hall

**★ Great Hall of Meditation**
*This evocative chamber, where up to 2,000 monks could gather to chant sutras, is hung with silken thangkas. The flat roof rests on grand pillars, each wrapped in an exquisite carpet.*

### Local monk
*Ta'er Si is a working monastery and houses over 650 monks, who spend their life studying Buddhist teachings. There were once as many as 3,500 resident monks.*

## VISITORS' CHECKLIST

Huangzhong. 17 miles (28 km) S of Xining. 🚌 from Xining (depart just west of Xi Men). ◐ 8:30am–6pm. 🎫 🏛 Monlam: 8th–15th of 1st lunar month; Saka Dawa: 8th–15th of 4th month; Tsong-khapa: 20th–26th of 9th month.

**Visitors who climb** these steps are rewarded with views across the valley.

**Dafangzhang Hall**

### Chorten
*A towering chorten of 46 ft (13 m) marks the monastery's entrance. The square base symbolizes earth, the dome water, the steps fire, and the parasol wind, all of which is topped by a crown representing the ethereal sphere.*

**Lesser Golden Roof Hall**
*A truly bizarre pavilion, this temple is dedicated to animals. Stuffed deer, sheep, and goats, draped in ceremonial scarves, peer down from the upper story.*

**Prayer Hall**
*This time-worn temple is still used for religious tutelage. The external murals are new, however, and show a mix of Chinese and Tibetan influences.*

# XINJIANG

Although technically an autonomous region, Xinjiang is the largest of China's provinces, and shares borders with eight countries. This isolated region is largely desert and grassland fringed by some of the highest mountains in the world.

Two thousand years ago a string of oasis towns were established along the Silk Roads that skirted the northern and southern edges of the scorching Taklamakan Desert. Trade attracted merchants from India and Europe, and Xinjiang became the meeting point of east and west, with Christian churches and Buddhist temples. At the end of the Tang era, Turkic tribes repeatedly overran the region, and by the 15th century Islam was established as the main religion. In the 18th century, the Chinese took control of what was then Kashgaria, and despite several revolts, have maintained their rule ever since. Almost fifty percent of the population is comprised of ethnic minorities, and in 1955, in deference to the large Uighur population, the area became the Xinjiang Uighur Autonomous Region, with its capital at Ürümqi. Today, highlights of a visit include the Tian Shan range and the rich pastures around Tian Chi (Heaven Lake) outside Ürümqi, and Silk Road towns such as Turpan and Kashgar, shaded by palm trees and set against a backdrop of desert and mountain. It is also possible to travel southwest over the Karakoram mountains into Pakistan or west into Kazakhstan along the ancient trade routes.

## SIGHTS AT A GLANCE

### Towns & Cities
Ghost City **5**
Hotan **14**
Karghilik **13**
Kashgar **9**
Kuqa **8**
Turpan **1**
Ürümqi **2**
Yarkand **12**
Yengisar **11**

### Lakes, Mountains & Areas of Natural Beauty
Altai **4**
Tian Chi **3**
Karakoram Highway **10**
Sayram Lake **6**
Yining & Ili Valley **7**

### KEY
|  |  |
|---|---|
| ✈ | International airport |
| ✈ | Domestic airport |
| ═ | Expressway |
| ═ | National Highway |
| ═ | Minor road |
| — | Railroad |
| – – | International border |
| - - | Provincial border |
| xxxx | Disputed border |

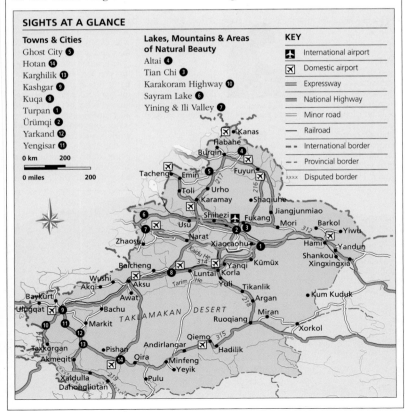

◁ **Valley in the Pamir Mountains at the westernmost edge of China**

The graceful Imin Ta and Iranian-style mosque

# Turpan ❶
吐鲁番

116 miles (187 km) SE of Ürümqi.
🚶 255,000. 🚉 Daheyan, 33 miles
(54 km) N of Turpan, then minibus.
🚌 ℹ Turpan Bing Guan, (0995)
852 1352.

This oasis town on the
northern Silk Road
lies in the Turpan
depression – one
of the lowest areas
on earth – and is
largely an Uighur
settlement. The
Uighur descended from
nomadic Siberian tribes who
united in the 7th century and
settled in the region in the 9th
century. They later converted
to Islam as it spread
across Central Asia.
It is an easy-going
place, famous for
its grapes, with
mud-brick houses
and dusty streets
often covered with
trellised vines. The
original Silk Road
settlements of Jiaohe
and Gaochang lie
outside town along
with other sights. In
summer, the heat is
intense, and it is
best to use donkey
carts as taxis.

Dried fruit on sale,
Turfan bazaar

### 🅲 Imin Ta
1.5 miles (2.5 km) E of
town. 🕐 8am–9pm. 🗹
This is perhaps the
most interesting of Turpan's
numerous mosques because
of its old minaret (Imin Ta),
constructed in 1778, that rises
like a stout but graceful chim-
ney beside it. Built by Prince
Suleiman in honor of his
father, Prince Emin, the
minaret is broad at
the base and tapers
toward the top.
Designed in the
Iranian style with
some elaborately
decorative brick-
work, its staircase
was closed in 1989.

### 🅰 Bazaar
Laocheng Lu. 🕐 daily.
The small Turpan market is
an interesting place to browse
for local products including a
variety of medicinal potions,
decorated knives, clothing,
fabric, nuts, and fruit (especially raisins).

### 🏛 Turpan Museum
Gaochang Lu. 🕐 9am–8pm daily. 🗹
This small museum has a few
worthwhile exhibits. The
main points of interest are
items excavated from the now
empty Tang-dynasty Astana
tombs located outside town.
These include ancient silks,
clothes, food items, and even
some preserved corpses.

### 🏯 Jiaohe Ruins
6 miles (10 km) W of Turpan. 🚌 minibus or cycle. 🕐 9am–6pm. 🗹 🗹
Although less important and
smaller than Gaochang, the
ruins of Jiaohe are better
defined. Jiaohe was founded
as a garrison town but came
under Uighur jurisdiction in
the 6th century. It was finally
abandoned during the Yuan
era, perhaps due to failing
water supplies. The ancient
city occupies a spectacular
position on a steep plateau,
with its street plan clearly visible, and is well worth a visit.

Returning from Jiaohe, visitors can stop off to see the
*karez* irrigation site. Used
throughout Xinjiang, this ingenious system of irrigation taps
into natural underground
water sources by using a network of subterranean tunnels
which channel water to the
fields. Wells, dug at intervals
along the length of the tunnels,
bring water to the surface.

The ruined city of Jiaohe set against a backdrop of hills on a steep plateau

The dramatic Flaming Mountains near Turpan

### Grape Valley

*minibus from town.* *daily.*

A surprisingly attractive desert oasis to the north of Turpan, Grape Valley (Putao Gou) is best visited in the height of summer. With vines and trellises bulging with grapes, it is a pleasant place to stop for lunch, with plenty of grapes and raisins to eat (for a fee). There is a winery nearby, as well as brick silos for drying the grapes.

### Flaming Mountains

*minibus from town.*

The road east to Bezeklik leads past these sandstone mountains, made famous in the novel *Journey to the West*, a fictionalized account of the journey of the pilgrim monk, Xuanzang, to India. In the book, the mountains (Huoyan Shan) are described as being on fire, and at certain times of day, a combination of sun and shadows turns them a brilliant red and makes them seem to flicker as though glowing red-hot.

### Bezeklik Caves

31 miles (50 km) NE of town. *minibus from town.* *dawn–dusk.*

Picturesquely situated in a desert gorge high above the Sengim River, the Bezeklik Caves once formed part of a Buddhist monastery between the 6th and 14th centuries.

Buddha mural in the Bezeklik Caves

The caves originally stored a collection of Buddhist murals in the Indo-Iranian style, which showed unusually marked western influences. Unfortunately, only fragments remain, as after centuries of neglect, they were all removed in the early 1900s by the German explorers, von Le Coq and Grunwedel, and placed in a Berlin museum, where they were later destroyed by Allied bombs during World War II.

### Astana

25 miles (40 km) SE of Turpan. *minibus from town.* *dawn–dusk.*

The cemetery of the ancient city of Gaochang is located at Astana, a few miles northwest of Gaochang. The tombs, dating from between the 3rd and 8th centuries AD, were systematically excavated from 1959, and revealed several corpses, naturally mummified by the dry desert air. They had been wrapped in silks, and buried with many everyday items, including pottery, wooden carvings, coins, and documents relating to military and domestic transactions such as land tenures. Unfortunately, most items are now on display at museums in Turpan and Ürümqi, but the three tombs that are open to visitors display Tang-era paintings and a few preserved corpses.

### Gaochang Ruins

29 miles (46 km) SE of Turpan. *minibus From town.* *8am–5pm.*

Southeast of the Astana tombs lie the impressive ruins of Gaochang city, surrounded by 33-ft (10-m) high walls. Gaochang was founded as a garrison town in the 1st century AD, and by the 4th century it had become the capital of the western Han empire. A cosmopolitan city with traces of Nestorian Christianity and Manichaeism (a Persian dualistic religion), it was visited by the monk Xuanzang in AD 630, on his journey to India in search of Buddhist *sutras*. From the 9th to the 13th centuries, the city became the Uighur capital, but was abandoned during the early Ming era. The ruins are extensive, but little is recognizable, apart from a Buddhist temple outside the southwest walls.

The Bezeklik Caves situated in a spectacular river gorge

# Ürümqi ❷
乌鲁木齐

911 miles (1470 km) NE of Kashgar.
🚆 🚌 📷 ℹ️ 33 Renmin Lu, (0991)
281 7006.

Capital of Xinjiang since the 19th century, Ürümqi sits amidst beautiful scenery, with the snow-laden Tian Shan to the east. It served as the base for a succession of warlords well into the 20th century, including the infamous Yang Zengxin who, in 1916, invited all his enemies to dinner and then beheaded them. Today a growing metropolis with a population of one million, Ürümqi is a modern Chinese city, with designer stores and high-rises. Many Han Chinese have settled here since 1949, and the population is now half-Han and half-ethnic minorities including Uighur, Manchu, Kazakh, Mongolian, and Tajik.

No longer a remote outpost, Ürümqi was finally connected to Central Asia and Europe after the Ürümqi-Almaty rail line was built in 1991. Most visitors come to see Tian Chi (Heaven Lake) but the city has other attractions such as its lively markets and the fascinating mix of ethnic peoples. The fine **Xinjiang Provincial Museum** devotes a section to archeological finds, especially from around Turpan, including some preserved corpses, silk paintings, and lovely brocades. A section dedicated to local peoples includes *gers*, jewelry, and traditional clothes. In the north of the city, the scenic **Hong Shan Park** has a small 18th-century pagoda, and offers wonderful views.

Tian Shan peaks surrounding the deep-blue waters of Tian Chi

**Pagoda in Hongshan Park, Ürümqi**

🏛 **Xinjiang Provincial Museum**
Xibei Lu. 🕐 8:30am–5pm daily.

# Tian Chi ❸
天池

62 miles (100 km) E of Ürümqi.
ℹ️ (0994) 323 1238. 🚌 from Ürümqi. ⬤ in winter. 🐎 Horses available for exploring lake area.

A refreshing break from the arid deserts of northwestern China, Tian Chi (Heaven Lake) is a beautiful stretch of water, surrounded by luxuriant meadows and dense pine forests. It lies at an elevation of 6,500 ft (1,980 m), enclosed by snow-capped peaks including the majestic Bogda Feng, that reaches a height of almost 20,000 ft (6,000 m). A wonderful place for spending a day, or indeed several, Tian Chi offers many opportunities for leisurely walks and hikes in the lake area and through the neighboring countryside dotted with Kazakh *gers*.

The local Kazakhs are mostly nomadic, living off sheep-breeding, and more recently, tourism. Very friendly and hospitable, they can arrange guides and horse treks around the lake and into the hills.

Tian Chi can only be visited during summer (May–September), as it is not accessible during the winter months. There are usually plenty of accommodations available in local Kazakh *gers* around the lake. Staying overnight can be far more fun and interesting than the day-tours which are sometimes a bit tacky.

---

### GRAPES & WINE

Nearly every household in the region is involved in grape production, either in cultivation, or in drying inside ventilated barns. In Xinjiang, the use of grapes for making wine was first recorded by a Chinese emissary in 138 BC, although grapes were possibly cultivated here as early as the Shang era. In fact, all wine-making in China was learned from the peoples of the western regions. By the Yuan era, wine production, based in Xinjiang, was substantial, and by the Ming period, varieties such as the crystal, the purple, and the seedless green rabbit-eye grape were grown. Today, wine production is thriving in China, and most of these varieties are still grown.

**Fruit vendor weighing grapes at the marketplace in Ürümqi**

*For hotels and restaurants in this region see pp572–3 and p597*

# Islam in China

Islam probably came to Xinjiang via the Silk Road in the ninth century, some 200 years after Arab sailors had landed in southern China. By the Ming Dynasty, Muslims had flourished and become fully integrated into Han society without losing their dress and dietary customs. Despite hostile regimes and upheavals there is now a significant Muslim population of about 13 million. These comprise the Xinjiang nationalities –

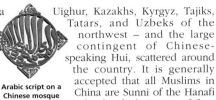

**Arabic script on a Chinese mosque**

Uighur, Kazakhs, Kyrgyz, Tajiks, Tatars, and Uzbeks of the northwest – and the large contingent of Chinese-speaking Hui, scattered around the country. It is generally accepted that all Muslims in China are Sunni of the Hanafi School, which is one of four "schools of Islamic law." It is considered the oldest and most liberal school and is traditionally tolerant of differences within Muslim communities.

**Mosques in China** *retain most traditional Islamic features but the pagodas and upturned eaves are clear signs of Chinese architectural influences.*

**The muezzin**, *as in all Muslim communities, calls the faithful to prayer five times a day. Today, the call is usually recorded and broadcast by loudspeaker.*

**Inside the mosque** *the congregation members, usually men, prostrate themselves before the* mihrab, *a niche in the wall indicating the direction of Mecca. The main hall is reserved for Friday prayers.*

**Dongxiang Muslims** *hail from Gansu province and speak Mongolian. They have left pastoral herding in favor of a sedentary farming life.*

**The Hui** *are said to be the descendants of the Arab and Persian traders who arrived in the Tang dynasty and married into Chinese families. They are the biggest Muslim minority.*

**The Koran** *was first translated into Chinese in 1927. Through the interpretations of the scholars, the Koran is a vital part of Islamic life.*

**The breathtaking alpine scenery of Hanas Lake Nature Reserve, Altai**

## Altai ❹
阿勒泰

404 miles (650 km) N of Ürümqi.
✈ *Altai, then bus.* 🚌 *from Ürümqi to Burqin, then 93 miles (150 km) N via bus or car to reserve.* ℹ *(0906) 652 4464.*

In contrast to the arid deserts of southern Xinjiang, the far north is covered in forests, lakes, and streams, overlooked by high mountains. The Altai region, bordering Mongolia, Russia, and Kazakhstan, is famous for its natural beauty, best seen in the **Hanas Lake Nature Reserve** (can be visited from Burqin). Centered around an alpine lake set at 4,490 ft (1,370 m) in the glorious Altai mountains, the reserve supports a diversity of wildlife. The area is wonderful for walking, and boat trips are available on the lake. Tours from Ürümqi operate all year.

## Ghost City ❺
魔鬼城

Near Urho, 62 miles (100 km) N of Karamay. 🚶 *13,000.* ℹ *(0906) 652 4464.* ✈ *Karamay, then bus.* 🚌 *from Karamay.* 🌐

Rising above the ocean of oil rigs, along the Dsungar Basin, is a collection of wind-shaped rock formations, known as the Ghost City. Made famous by the movies filmed there, including *Crouching Tiger, Hidden Dragon*, it is now a popular destination. Camel rides, mountain bikes, and four-wheel vehicles can be hired.

## Sayram Lake ❻
塞里木湖

75 miles (120 km) N of Yining. 🚌

The jewel-like Sayram Lake, or Sailimu Hu, is a vast stretch of water set amidst magnificent mountain scenery and flowering meadows. Located at 6,560 ft (2,000 m), the lake area is chilly for most of the year, and only warm in summer when it is also covered in flowers. Reached by bus from Yining, it is a beautiful spot, barely touched by tourism, although it is possible to stay in simple lakeside guesthouses or gers (yurts).

## Yining ❼
伊宁

242 miles (390 km) W of Ürümqi. 🚶 *216,600.* ✈ 🚌 *from Ürümqi.* **Ili Valley** 🚌 *from Yining.*

Close to the border with Kazakhstan, Yining is the

**Woman tending her sheep in a flower-covered meadow on the shores of Sayram Lake**

*For hotels and restaurants in this region see pp572–3 and p597*

**A traditional shop in one of Yining's Uighur bazaars**

capital of the Ili Kazakh Autonomous Prefecture. In recent centuries, Russia has noticeably influenced Yining as it was occupied by Russians in 1872 when Yakub Beg ruled the region (then known as Kashgaria) and later, during the period of Sino-Soviet friendship in the 1950s, a number of Russians resided here. After relations between China and the USSR broke down in the early 1960s, there were violent border clashes along the Ili River. More recently, Yining has been the scene of several Uighur uprisings, which were quelled.

Small, but pleasant and friendly with tree-lined streets, Yining is known for its local honey beer, and hard cheese. Its main draws are the lively Uighur bazaars with their range of street food in the old city, south of Qingnian Park. In summer, the town comes alive with bustling night markets and food stalls.

About 3 miles (5 km) south of town, the **Ili Valley** (Ili Gu) is a scenic farm area of fields and meadows. Home to the Xibo people, a tiny minority, whose capital is at Chapuch-a'er. Related to the Manchus, the Xibo were sent here during the Qing era to maintain sovereignty in the region. They have kept themselves separate from the Han and other local communities, and retain their own language and script.

# Kuqa ❽
库车

186 miles (300 km) SW of Ürümqi.
🏯 75,000. ✈ 🚇 🚌 ⛴ Kuqa
Travel Agency, (0997) 712
9558. 🚲 every Fri.

A small oasis town, Kuqa is essentially an Uighur settlement and has an interesting history. An independent state until the 8th century, when it fell under Chinese

**Grapes for sale on the street, Yining**

rule, the kingdom had strong links with India. Its significance as a Buddhist center dates back to the 4th century, when the Buddhist scholar Kumarajiva flourished. Born here, he went to school in Kashmir, northern India, and came back to China as a teacher and linguist, translating Sanskrit texts into Chinese. The town became a focal point from where Buddhism, which reached its zenith during the Tang era, was disseminated throughout China.

Several large monasteries were founded on the vast wealth generated by the Silk Road trade. In the 7th century, the monk Xuanzang passed through Kuqa and claimed to have defeated its ruler in a philosophical debate. With the arrival of Islam in the 9th century, however, most traces of its Buddhist past disappeared.

Mainly a stopover on the long journey to Kashgar, Kuqa is effectively two towns – New Kuqa and Old Kuqa. The old town has a bustling bazaar atmosphere, and a few dusty, narrow lanes lined with traditional mud houses have been preserved. Built in 1923, the attractive green-tiled **Great Mosque** bears no traces of Chinese influences in its traditional arabesque design.

One of the main reasons to visit Kuqa are the **Thousand Buddha Caves**, located at Kizil, 43 miles (70 km) west of town. The caves date to between AD 500–700 and the frescoes, in a mixture of Indo-Iranian and Greek styles, are fascinating for their total absence of Chinese influence. Unfortunately, the caves were looted at the beginning of the 20th century by archeological explorers. While most of the caves have been stripped of their frescoes, some of the cave decoration has survived, notably the musicians in Cave 38, and the domestic and agricultural scenes in Cave 175.

About 19 miles (30 km) north of Kuqa lies the ruins of the ancient city of **Subashi**.

🏛 **Thousand Buddha Caves**
Hired car or taxi. 🔲 daily. 📷
🎫 arranged by the Kuqa tourist office.

**The Thousand Buddha Caves at Kizil, outside Kuqa**

# Kashgar

喀什

**Market caps, Old Town**

In the far west of Xinjiang, the Silk Road town of Kashgar lies at the foot of the Pamir mountains, with the Taklamakan Desert to the east. As the meeting point of the northern and southern Silk Roads and the gateway to the West, it was once a place of great significance. A Chinese garrison was established here in AD 78, but the area succumbed to the spread of Islam in the 9th century, and Kashgar did not become part of the Chinese empire again until the 18th century. Later, a Central Asian warlord, Yakub Beg, proclaimed himself Khan of the state of Kashgaria but he died in 1877 and China annexed the province. Today, Kashgar is once more a busy market town and transport hub, and despite rampant modernization retains much of its old charm.

**Farmers waiting to trade livestock at market, Kashgar**

## ▣ Sunday Market

Near Ayziret Lu. ○ daily.
**Livestock Market** ○ Sun.
One of China's most famous weekly markets, the Sunday Market lies in the northeast suburbs, just beyond the river. Despite now being split into two markets – the livestock market is a few miles southeast of town – thousands of traders flood in from all directions on horseback, in donkey-drawn carts, on foot, and in every form of motorized vehicle. In the crush, stall holders sell blankets, garish fabrics, carpets, and fruit. However, the main attraction is the bustling livestock market. (Carts shuttle between the two.) Here horses are road-tested at a gallop and small herds of sheep are kept in order while waiting to be sold. It is a dusty, noisy, and photogenic place, which comes to life at dawn, and lasts into the evening.

## ▣ Id Kah Mosque

Idi Kah Square. ○ 8:50am–10pm daily (closed during services). 📷
The largest mosque in Xinjiang, and one of the largest in China, Id Kah Mosque (Aitika Qingzhen Si) was probably founded in 1738, although it possibly stands on the site of a smaller mosque, built in the 15th century. Built in the Central Asian style and altered over the centuries, the mosque's current structure dates back only as far as 1838, and was badly damaged during the Cultural Revolution (see pp64–5). The main gate, flanked by a pair of small minarets, is a confection of marzipan-like yellow brick and tiling. Inside the gate is an octagonal pavilion and a pool, as well as a 100-columned space which can accommodate as many as 7,000 worshipers. Although women are generally not permitted to enter the mosque, all modestly dressed foreign visitors should have no problem, although there are times – such as during services – when non-believers are not allowed. Visitors are advised to remove their shoes when entering carpeted areas.

## 🏛 Old Town

Area to the NE of Id Kah Mosque.
Northeast of Id Kah Square is the sprawling Uighur bazaar area. Split into different sections, each specializes in particular items such as hats, musical instruments, carpets, and hardware. The main attractions are the locally-produced Kashgar *kilims* (carpets) and colorful Central Asian hats. Part of the area is a network of mud-brick walls and courtyards, with local teahouses and tiny restaurants selling flat breads, noodles, lamb stews, and kabobs. A 10-ft (3-m) section of the old city walls can be seen at the end of Seman Lu, east of the mosque, and on Yunmulakxia Lu, southwest of the mosque.

**The Id Kah Mosque, with Kashgar city and the Pamirs on the horizon**

*For hotels and restaurants in this region see pp572–3 and p597*

One of many old alleyways lined with mud-brick houses, Kashgar

## Tomb of Yusup Hazi Hajup

daily.

This favorite son of Kashgar was an 11th-century Uighur thinker and poet, renowned for his epic poem *The Knowledge of Happiness*. He was originally buried outside the city, but his tomb was relocated close to Kashgar's main square, when threatened by a flooding river. Although it has a plain interior, the external structure is impressive. Topped with a blue dome and a cluster of minarets, the tomb is encased in blue-and-white tiles with Arabic motifs.

## Aba Khoja Mausoleum

See pp512–13.

## Caves of the Three Immortals

11 miles (18 km) N of Kashgar.

Among the earliest Buddhist cave carvings in China, the Caves of the Three Immortals (Sanxian Dong) possibly date back to the 2nd century. The grottoes are not always accessible as they are perched high on a sandstone cliff. Poor attempts at restoration and embellishment over the years have destroyed many of the paintings and statues. However, a handful of small Buddha figurines remain, which can only be seen with the permission of the Kashgar tourist office. If permitted, visitors will have to take the official guided tour.

### VISITORS' CHECKLIST

920 miles (1,473 km) SW of Ürümqi. 350,000. International Bus Station, CAAC (buses to airport). 144 Se Man Rd, (0998) 298 4836. Sun.

## Ruins of Ha Noi

22 miles (35 km) NE of Kashgar.

The remains of the Tang-era town of Ha Noi lie in an atmospheric desert setting northeast of Kashgar. Abandoned in the 12th century, the ruined 7th-century town offers little besides the **Mor Pagoda**, a large stupa said to have been visited by the monk Xuanzang on his historic journey to India.

## Opal

18 miles (30 km) W of Kashgar.

Opal or Wupoer is the site of the renovated tomb of Mohammed Kashgari – an eminent 11th-century scholar and philologist, credited with compiling the first Turkic-Arabic dictionary. A museum devoted to his life and works is also situated here, and every Monday there is also a colorful local market.

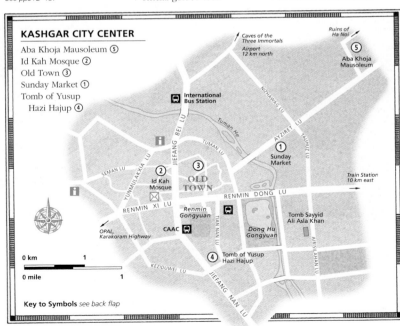

### KASHGAR CITY CENTER

Aba Khoja Mausoleum ⑤
Id Kah Mosque ②
Old Town ③
Sunday Market ①
Tomb of Yusup Hazi Hajup ④

Caves of the Three Immortals
Airport 12 km north

Ruins of Ha Noi

Aba Khoja Mausoleum ⑤

International Bus Station

NIZHAWAG LU
AYZIRET LU
TAIHUZI LU
JIEFANG BEI LU
Tuman He
TUMAN LU
SEMAN LU
YUNMULAKXIA LU

Sunday Market ①

Train Station 10 km east

Id Kah Mosque ②

OLD TOWN ③

RENMIN DONG LU

RENMIN XI LU

Renmin Gongyuan

TIAN NAN LU

CAAC

Dong Hu Gongyuan

Tomb Sayyid Ali Asla Khan

AIKSILAHAN LU

OPAL, Karakoram Highway

KEZIDUWEI LU

Tomb of Yusup Hazi Hajup ④

JIEFANG NAN LU

0 km 1

0 mile 1

**Key to Symbols** see back flap

# Aba Khoja Mausoleum
## 阿巴克霍加 – 香妃墓

Built in the 17th century, the Aba Khoja Mausoleum and nearby buildings form one of the best examples of Islamic architecture in China. The mausoleum is the burial place of the family of Aba Khoja, a celebrated Islamic missionary. However, the monument is also known as Xiangfei's Tomb, as it may be the burial place of one of Aba Khoja's descendants, Ikparhan, said to be the legendary "fragrant concubine" Xiangfei. The wife of a defeated rebel leader, she was captured by the Qianlong emperor and taken back to Beijing to be his imperial concubine. Refusing to submit to him she was, depending on which story you believe, either murdered or driven to suicide by the emperor's mother. Others claim she died of old age.

**The entrance to the Aba Khoja complex lined with plane trees**

**The dome** is 56 ft (17 m) in diameter. Almost half the tiles have now fallen from the dome.

**The casket of Ikparhan** is labelled inside the tomb hall. The carriage which supposedly carried her body back from Beijing is also on display.

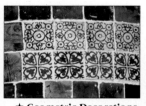

**★ Geometric Decorations**
*Floral and geometric patterns are common in Islamic art because creating animate objects was considered to be in God's realm (flowers were considered inanimate).*

**Minarets**
*The four corner towers lack the slender grace of most other minarets. Instead their charm derives from the colorful striping of the tiles and the exquisite detailing of Islamic motifs and patterns.*

**★ Tombs**
*Decorated with blue-glazed tiles, the tombs of the Aba Khoja family lie on a raised platform, draped in colorful silks.*

**STAR FEATURES**

★ Geometric Decorations

★ Tombs

*For hotels and restaurants in this region see pp572–3 and p597*

**Cemetery**
*The cemetery, still in use by the local Uighur population, is filled with many hundreds of distinctively-peaked, mud and brick tombs. The bodies of the dead are washed and prepared for burial in the adjacent mosque.*

**VISITORS' CHECKLIST**

Just over 2 miles (4 km) NE of Old Town center. 🚌 or 🚕 *from People's Square. Also possible to cycle or walk.* **Mauoleum** ◻ *9am–5pm daily.* 💷 **Mosque** ◻ *daily (prayer day Fri).* 💷

**Minaret decoration**
*Each of the windows are screened in a different geometric pattern. The surrounds are adorned with graceful arabesques while the turret is topped with an inverted lotus dome, scalloped edges, and finial.*

**Graceful minarets flanking the entrance**

**Arabesques** are beautiful floral patterns where a main stem branches into a series of secondary stems that may either branch again or rejoin the main stem, and so on.

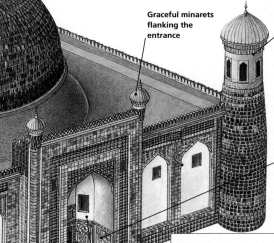

**Mausoleum Entrance**
*The impressive façade of the mausoleum has a tiled iwan niche-style entrance typical of mosques in Central Asia.*

## THE ABA KHOJA COMPLEX

Although Islam came to Xinjiang via Arab traders on the Silk Road in the 9th and 10th centuries, it was not until the 15th century that it became the dominant religion of the area, and Kashgar became an important Islamic center. The Aba Khoja complex is a significant architectural ensemble comprising a mausoleum, four prayer halls, a lecture hall, and a cemetery. There is also a gateway covered in decorative, blue-glazed tiles and a pond in the courtyard for worshipers to cleanse themselves before entering the mosque. The halls are graced by exquisitely painted wooden beams supported by pillars with delightful *muqarnas* – an Islamic feature of projecting niches – on the capitals.

**Arabic *muqarnas* on mosque pillar**

Truck passing a checkpoint on the Karakoram Highway, with the Pamir mountains in the background

# Karakoram Highway ⑩
中巴友谊公路

SW from Kashgar into Pakistan. 🚌

Once a spur of the Silk Road, the Karakoram Highway (Zhongba Gonglu) was the only route over the Karakoram Mountains, to and from India. During the 1970s and 1980s, a road was built across the mountains following the old caravan route, to link China and Pakistan. The 808-mile (1,300-km) route from Kashgar to Islamabad in Pakistan, which stretches across the Pamir mountains over peaks reaching 26,250 ft (8,000 m), is one of awe-inspiring beauty. Camels and yaks, tended by Tajik herdsmen, graze in the highland pastures. Lakes with mirror-like surfaces, such as Lake Karakul, reflect the majesty of the mountains, while the remains of the occasional caravanserai stand crumbling at the side of the road.

The last town in China is **Tashkurgan**, a bleak outpost, with the remains of an ancient fort. Beyond it is the 15,750-ft (4,800-m) high **Khunjerab Pass**, the gateway to Pakistan. The Pakistan border post lies just beyond at Sost. Visitors should note that the border is closed in winter, and that visas

are required – issued in Beijing or Hong Kong – to cross into Pakistan. The highway took nearly 20 years to build. The journey along it is fairly arduous, and although traveling conditions are improving, it is best to carry warm clothing, food, and drink for the trip, which takes about four days.

# Yengisar ⑪
英吉沙

37 miles (60 km) S of Kashgar. 🚌

The small, sleepy town of Yengisar on the southern arm of the Silk Road is renowned for its locally produced knives. For centuries, the town has been manufac-

turing hand-crafted knives for Uighur men, who carry them as traditional accoutrements. Knives of all shapes and sizes are sold in dozens of shops. While most of the knives produced are factory-made, traditional knife-making skills are still practiced by artisans in the center of town. Using basic tools, the workers at the **Yengisar Country Small Knife Factory** produce exquisite designs fashioned from fine woods, their handles inlaid with silver or horn. It is sometimes possible to visit the factory, even though a big board outside bears a "No Entrance" sign. The knives, which make attractive gifts, require special arrangements to be taken home.

Polished knives displayed at a stall in the Sunday Market, Yengisar

## JADE

Jade, or nephrite, has been carved and polished by the Chinese for several thousand years, along with jadeite, soapstone, and chalcedony. While the latter are known as *yu*, nephrite is *zhen yu*, or true jade. Initially used as a tool, jade came to be widely used as jewelry during the Han era. By the Qing period, carvers were producing a variety of decorative pieces including intricate jade animals.

**Uncut nephrite or true jade**

Always thought of as being green, jade can in fact be brown, black, or the prized cloudy white. To the Chinese, it symbolizes longevity and purity, and is worn as an amulet to ward off disease. The country's only source of nephrite is Xinjiang, particularly around Hotan, so a sophisticated supply system must have existed even in neolithic times.

# Yarkand ⑫
莎车

106 miles (170 km) SE of Kashgar. 🚌

For centuries an important commercial center on the southern arm of the Silk Road, Yarkand was, like Kashgar, prominent in the Great Game – the power struggle between China, Russia and Britain *(see p490)*. The old town, with its adobe walls and narrow streets, has a few interesting sights. The **Altyn Mosque** has beautifully painted ceilings, and in its courtyard is the newly-built **Tomb of Aman Isa Khan** (1526–60) – the poet wife of one of the local Khans. Behind the mosque is a sprawling cemetery housing the tombs of the Khans of Yarkand. There is also a lively Sunday market.

**A vendor pulls a cart of radishes, Yarkand**

# Karghilik ⑬
椰城

144 miles (230 km) SE of Kashgar. 🚌

This town was a convenient stop between Hotan and Kashgar on the southern arm of the Silk Road. The colorful old Uighur town is definitely worth exploring, while the town's main attraction, the 15th-century **Jama Masjid**, sits amidst the arcaded bazaar.

# Hotan ⑭
和田

249 miles (400 km) SE of Kashgar. 🚶 100,000. ✈ 🚌 ℹ *Hotan Travel, (0903) 251 5660.* 🚰

The oasis town of Hotan, or Hetian, was an early center for the spread of Buddhism before Islam arrived in the 9th century. Formerly the capital of the Yutian kingdom, it has been, like most Silk Road cities, periodically subsumed into the Chinese empire. For centuries, the town's jade, carpets, and silk have been considered the finest in China, and are still produced in factories across town. According to legend, the secret of silk was first introduced to the region by a Chinese princess betrothed to a local prince, who smuggled silk moth eggs in her hair in AD 440. Craftsmen carve fine jade items at the Jade Factory on Tanai Lu, while the Carpet Factory across the river is a friendly place also worth a visit, especially for those wishing to buy a carpet, as they are available here at bargain prices. Visitors interested in silk production can stop by the **Hetian Silk Factory** in the northeast of town.

Sections of the old city walls still stand on both sides of Nuerwake Lu. The chaotic local market takes place on Fridays and Sundays in the northeast of town. Though not as large as its famous counterpart in Kashgar, it is a colorful affair with livestock, fruit, silks, and carpets on sale.

At the end of the 19th century, the first rumors of the region's lost cities – which inspired several expeditions – emanated from here. A detailed map, indicating the location of the buried cities, lies in the small **Hetian Cultural Museum**. Items of interest include fragments of silk, wooden utensils, and jewelry excavated from nearby lost cities, as well as the mummified corpses of a 10-year-old girl and a 35-year-old man with Indo-European features, which are 1,500 years old. The ruined city of **Melikawat** lies over 18 miles (30 km) south of town. All that remains of this once significant Buddhist center are crumbling walls, and shards of glass and pottery.

🏛 **Hetian Cultural Museum**
Tanai Lu. ⬜ *daily.* 📷

**Craftsmen at the open-air market in Hotan**

# TIBET

# Tibet At a Glance

Bordered on three sides by some of the world's highest mountain ranges – the Himalayas, the Karakoram, and the Kulun – Tibet has remained in relative isolation. Sheltered first by its inaccessibility and then, in the age of air travel, by Chinese occupation, the "Roof of the World" is now open to foreign visitors. Its one major city, Lhasa, retains its spiritual core: the Jokhang; the venerable palace of the Dalai Lamas, the Potala; and great monasteries such as Drepung and Sera. Wherever you go, Tibet offers panoramic vistas of high-altitude desert fringed by peaks, but the turquoise depths of Lake Namtso and the sky-scraping peaks of Mount Everest are particularly worth visiting.

Thangka hanging on a door at the Jokhang Temple, Lhasa

Yamdrok Lake, the largest lake in south Tibet, seen from the Kamba-la Pass

## SIGHTS AT A GLANCE

**Towns & Cities**
Gyantse ⑤
Lhasa ①
The Nepal Border ⑨

**Areas of Natural Beauty**
Everest Base Camp ⑧

Namtso Lake ④

**Temples & Monasteries**
Sakya Monastery ⑦
*Samye Monastery pp540–41* ②
Shigatse & Tashilunpo ⑥
Tsurphu Monastery ③

◁ The snow-blown majesty of Mount Everest, known as Chomolungma to the Tibetans

The Potala Palace seen from the rooftop of the Jokhang, Lhasa's holiest temple

### SEE ALSO

- *Where to Stay* p573
- *Where to Eat* p597

**KEY**

✈ International airport

═ National Highway

═ Minor road

━ Railroad

## GETTING THERE

Visitors arrive mostly by air from Chengdu, the capital of Sichuan, or Kathmandu, Nepal. An overland route also connects Kathmandu and Lhasa, but while individual travelers can leave, only tour groups may enter this way. The bus route from Golmud in Qinghai has been superseded by a high-speed railway line, and most people take the train to Lhasa from Xining or Chengdu. A permit from the Tibetan Tourism Bureau (TTB) – (86) 0891 691 2080 – is required. No independent travel is allowed for foreigners in Tibet. The best option is to arrange a tour with an agency in Lhasa, who will also handle permits.

# A PORTRAIT OF TIBET

*ibet's reputation as a land of exotic mystery is due to centuries of geographic isolation and a unique theocratic culture, based on Buddhism but influenced by an older shamanistic faith called Bon. In 1950, China marched into Tibet and annexed the country. Despite this upheaval, the traditional culture and values of the Tibetans remain strong and continue to lure and enchant visitors.*

Since the introduction of Buddhism in the 7th century, the religion has permeated all aspects of Tibetan life, with monasteries acting as palaces, administrative centers, and schools. Ruled by priests, Tibet was feudal in outlook and resisted all modernization. The country thus entered the modern world without an army, lay education, or roads, and with few technologies more sophisticated than the prayer wheel.

**Buddha mural, Jokhang Temple**

Buddhism was introduced in Tibet by Songsten Gampo (AD 608–50). A remarkable ruler who also unified the country, Songsten Gampo was converted to Buddhism by his Chinese and Nepalese wives. The next religious king, Trisong Detsen (742–803) consolidated the Buddhist faith, inviting the Indian teacher Padmasambhava (Guru Rinpoche) to Tibet and founding Samye Monastery. A revival of the native Bon religion in the 8th century led to Buddhist persecution, and though the religion re-emerged later, the kingdom disintegrated into several principalities.

In the 13th century, Tibet submitted to the all-conquering Mongols, and in 1247 the head lama of Sakya Monastery visited their court and was appointed Tibet's ruler. Subsequently, Tsongkhapa (1357–1419) established the Gelugpa or Yellow Hat sect. His disciples became the Dalai Lamas, rulers of Tibet for 500 years. Each new Dalai Lama is seen as a reincarnation of the previous one.

Sprawling Ganden Monastery, built in the early 15th century

**Buddha's all-seeing eyes on the Kumbum, Gyantse**

In 1950, the Chinese took advantage of a tenuous claim to the territory and invaded, calling it "liberation." In the uprising that followed in 1959, the 14th Dalai Lama (b.1935) fled to India, where he still heads the Tibetan Government-in-Exile. By 1970 more than a million Tibetans had died either directly at the hands of the Chinese or through famine caused by incompetent agricultural policies. Tibet's cultural heritage was razed, and over 6,000 monasteries destroyed.

Some monasteries that were ravaged during the Cultural Revolution are now being re-paired and returned to their former roles, but creating or owning an image of the Dalai Lama is still illegal.

**A Tibetan mandala, a ritual tantric diagram**

The ancient city of Lhasa is the heart of Tibet, though Han Chinese immigrants now outnumber ethnic Tibetans. A spectacular railway line linking Golmud in Qinghai to Lhasa means that immigrant numbers will continue to grow. However, the old quarter, home of the Potala Palace and the Jokhang Temple, illustrates the determination with which Tibetans have held onto their cultural traditions. A common sight here are the pious and cheerful pilgrims, swinging prayer wheels and performing energetic prostrations as they make *kora* – holy circuits – around the temple.

Most of Tibet is desert and the average altitude is over 13,000 ft (4,000 m) with temperatures well below freezing in winter. Many customs arose as response to life in this harsh environment. Sky burials, for example, in which the dead are left in the open for vultures, are practical in a land where firewood is scarce and the earth too hard to dig. Polyandry (the practice of having more than one husband at a time) and celibacy of the clergy were necessary forms of population control.

Almost a quarter of the people are nomads, keeping herds of *dzo* (a cross between a yak and a cow) and living in tents. Their livestock provide products vital for everyday Tibetan life – yak butter is used in the ubiquitous bitter butter tea and burnt in smoky chapel lamps.

Tibet's roads are few, and journeys are always time-consuming. The busiest route is the Friendship Highway between Lhasa and the Nepalese border, which passes through Shigatse, Gyantse, and the dramatic Sakya Monastery. It is a long, bumpy but rewarding diversion from here to the Everest base camp, which offers great views of the forbidding peak. Lhasa, too, can be a good base for exploring some of the other isolated destinations. The monasteries of Drepung, Sera, Ganden, and Tsurphu are easily accessible, while Lake Namtso and Samye are farther away.

**Monks debating under a tree, a common sight at Sera Monastery**

# Tibetan Buddhism

The Mahayana school of Buddhism, which emphasizes compassion and self-sacrifice, came to Tibet from India in the 7th century. As it spread it took on many aspects of the native, shamanistic Bon religion, incorporating Bon rituals and deities. Like most Buddhists, Tibetans believe in reincarnation – consecutive lives that are better or worse depending on the karma, or merit, accrued in the previous life. For many Tibetans, Buddhism suffuses daily life so completely that the concept of a religion separate from day to day occurences, is completely foreign – there is no word for religion in Tibetan.

**A guardian deity or** *dharmapala*

*Chortens hold the ashes of spiritual teachers. The square base symbolizes earth; the pinnacle crown represents the ethereal sphere.*

**A soul can** take one of two paths: the light path leads to auspicious rebirths until final liberation, the dark to poor rebirths and hell.

## MONKS AND MONASTERIES

At the height of monastic power there were some 6,000 monasteries in Tibet, and numerous Buddhist sects. Most families sent a son to become a monk and live a life of celibacy and meditation.

**The Gelugpa** *or Yellow Hat sect was founded in the 1300s by the reformist Tsongkhapa. Dominant in Tibetan politics for centuries, the sect is led by the Dalai Lama and Panchen Lama (see p520, p544).*

**The Nyingma** *order is the oldest and most traditional of all the sects. It was founded during the 600s by Guru Rinpoche.*

## BON – TIBET'S PRE-BUDDHIST FAITH

Bon, an animistic faith with emphasis on magic and spirits and the taming of demons, was Tibet's native religious tradition before the arrival of Buddhism. Many Tibetan legends concern the taming of local gods and their conversion to the new faith. Much of today's Buddhist iconography, rituals, and symbols, including prayer flags and sky burials – where the deceased is chopped to pieces and left on a mountainside for vultures – are Bon in origin. The ancient faith has been revived by a handful of Bon monasteries in Tibet.

**A 19th-century bronze figure of a Bon deity**

**At the axle** the three evils, a snake (anger), a pig (ignorance), and a cockerel (desire), eternally chase each other's tails.

## WHEEL OF LIFE

The continuous cycle of existence and re-birth is represented by the Wheel of Life, clutched in the jaws of the Lord of Death, Yama. Achieving enlightenment is the only way to transcend the incessant turning of the wheel.

**Spinning a prayer wheel** *clockwise sends a prayer written on coiled paper to heaven. The largest wheels contain thousands of prayers and are turned by crank or water power.*

## PRAYER AND RITUAL

Worship in Tibet is replete with ritual objects and customs, many of which help with the accrual of merit. *Koras*, which are always followed clockwise, can be short circuits of holy sites or fully-fledged pilgrimages. The most auspicious *kora* is around Mount Kailash, considered the center of the universe; nirvana is guaranteed on the 108th circuit.

**The outer ring** illustrates the 12 factors that determine karma, including spiritual awareness (a blind man with a stick) and acts of volition (a potter molding pots).

**This ritual drum,** *made from the upper part of two skulls, has extra potency as a tool of prayer, because it is fashioned from human remains.*

**The inner wheel** depicts the six realms into which beings can be reborn – gods, demigods, humans, animals, ghosts, and demons.

**A worshiper** *spins a hand-held prayer wheel, rings a Tibetan bell called a* drilbu *and holds offerings of banknotes, all in aid of prayer.*

**Mani stones** *are carved with the Sanskrit mantra "om mani padme hum" (hail to the jewel in the lotus), a powerful Buddhist chant.*

## THE TIBETAN PANTHEON

An overwhelming plethora of deities, buddhas, and demons, many of them re-incarnations or evil aspects of each other, make up the Tibetan pantheon. Buddhas, "awakened ones," have achieved enlightenment and reached nirvana. Bodhisattvas have postponed the pursuit of nirvana to help others achieve enlightenment.

**Jampalyang** *(Manjusri) represents knowledge and learning. He raises a sword of discriminating wisdom in his right hand.*

### BUDDHIST DEITIES

**Jowo Sakyamuni:** the present Buddha
**Jampa (the Maitreya):** the future Buddha
**Dipamkara (Marmedze):** the past Buddha
**Guru Rinpoche (Padmasambhava):** earthly manifestation of Buddha who spread Buddhism throughout Tibet
**Chenresig (Avalokitesvara):** multi-armed bodhisattva of compassion
**Drolma (Tara):** female aspect of compassion

**Dharmapalas**, *defenders of the law, fight against the enemies of Buddhism. Originally demons, they were tamed by Guru Rinpoche, who bound them to the faith. Mahakala, one of the most common dharmapalas, is a wrathful manifestation of Chenresig.*

# Nomadic life

**Young nomad and *dzo***

The Chang Tang, a high plateau covering almost 70 percent of Tibet, is home to about a quarter of Tibetans, many of whom are nomads, or *drokba*, as the harsh, arid climate precludes farming. Their existence has barely been touched by modern life, and they still herd sheep, goats, and *dzo* (a cross between a yak and a domesticated cow), as they have for centuries. The animals are adapted to high altitude, having larger lungs and more hemoglobin than lowland animals. The nomad's culture is also adapted to the harsh, arid climate.

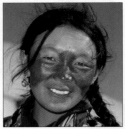

**Dried yogurt** *is thought to protect the skin from the sun, but men don't use it at all; women smear it on with a tuft of wool as a cosmetic.*

**These men enjoy** *cups of salted tea made with yak butter, a popular drink throughout Tibet. The salt combats dehydration and the fat gives much-needed energy. They wear knee-length* lokbars, *with a black strip at the edge, the traditional dress for male nomads.*

**Traditionally**, *nomads wear belted robes made out of goatskin called* lokbars *that double as blankets at night. The fleece is worn on the inside, while the sturdy hide is exposed to wind and snow. The sleeves are extra long to keep hands warm. Women braid their hair and wear their wealth as jewelry. Coral, in particular, is highly valued.*

## THE HERD

Nomads rely totally on their herds for food, clothing, shelter, and sometimes income, so no part of any animal goes to waste. Goats, for example, provide milk for yogurt, skins for clothing, wool for trading, and dung for fuel.

**Each household** *has a home tent, four-sided and made out of the coarse hairs found on a yak's belly. Often, the tent is pitched in a pit and surrounded by stone windbreaks. Another cloth tent may be used for traveling.*

**A woman** *spreads yak dung over a windbreak wall. Once it has dried, she will scrape the dung off the wall and use it to fuel fires for cooking. Such tasks are strictly demarcated by gender; women do all the milking, churning, cooking, weaving, and fuel gathering, and so work harder than the men for most of the year.*

**A nomad pours** *yak butter from a churn for adding to strong, salty tea. The nomadic diet is basic; the staple is* tsampa, *roasted barley flour, which, often eaten dry and on its own, provides about half of a nomad's calories. Goat's milk yogurt, radishes, and occasional meat stews supplement the diet.*

**The wool of the yaks**, *sheep, and goats in the nomad's herd is woven using a loom, creating robust textiles for tent walls, blankets, and clothing. The incomes of many nomads have been augmented by the popularity of cashmere wool, which is the soft down on a goat's underbelly.*

## MOVING THE HERDS

Nomads on the Chang Tang do not move continuously, nor do they move far – only around 10 to 40 miles (15 to 65 km), as the growing season is the same all over the plateau. Indeed, they try to minimize travel, declaring that it weakens livestock. Some families even build a house at their main encampment. In the fall, after the herds have eaten most of the vegetation at the main encampment and the growing season has ended, the nomads move their livestock to a secondary plain for grazing. Here livestock must forage for eight to nine months on dead vegetation. Later the nomads may move some of their herds farther up the hills. They then return to their original encampment.

**A herder driving his yaks over a snowy mountain pass**

# TIBET

The enormous Tibetan plateau stretches across an awesome 463,323 sq miles (1,200,000 sq km). Its northern expanse is the Chang Tang, a vast, uninhabited high-altitude desert, dotted with enormous, brackish lakes. Nearly all the main sights and cities, as well as half of Tibet's population of 2.8 million people, are concentrated in the less harsh southern region.

The fertile valley created by the Yarlung Tsangpo river is bordered by the Himalayas along Tibet's southern boundary. A mere 14 million years old, the Himalayas are the youngest mountains on earth, and also the highest, with over 70 peaks reaching elevations of 23,000 ft (7,000 m), including Mount Everest, the world's highest at 29,029 ft (8,848 m). The spectacle of these snow-clad peaks is perhaps what led to Tibet being called the "Land of Snows." In reality, at an average altitude of over 13,000 ft (4,000 m), the thin air intensifies the sunshine making acclimatization and sun screen essential.

Tibet's eastern reaches are riddled with gorges carved out by the three of China's rivers – the mighty Yangzi, the Salween, and the Mekong. The wide, open spaces of northern Tibet are home to nomads who live a hardy pastoral existence. These wilderness areas are slowly shrinking as a result of the encroaching industrial world.

However, despite rapid development and more than 50 years of Chinese occupation, Tibet still clings strongly to its cultural heritage, most visible in the revitalized monasteries. Tourism too, is a growing industry as more areas are opening up, allowing visitors tantalizing glimpses of a once-forbidden world.

Main prayer hall at Ganden Monastery, the first Gelugpa monastery in Tibet

◁ Monk peering from behind a magnificent door at Labrang Monastery

# Lhasa ●

拉萨

**Statue, Tsepak Lhakhang**

Tibet's capital since the 7th century, Lhasa is an intoxicating introduction to Tibet. The Dalai Lamas' splendid but poignantly empty seat, the Potala Palace, dominates the city from its site on top of Marpo Hill. The old Tibetan quarter to the east is Lhasa's most interesting area; its center-piece is the revered Jokhang Temple. Around it is the Barkhor, which retains its medieval character with smoky temples and cobbled alleys. Most Tibetans come here as pilgrims. The additions of concrete buildings and internet cafés show how the city has changed over recent decades.

## LHASA CITY CENTER

Ani Tsankhung Nunnery ④
Jokhang Temple ⑤
Lukhang ②
Norbulingka ⑦
Potala Palace ①
Ramoche ③
Tibet Museum ⑥

### KEY

▨ Street-by-Street area: see pp530–1

0 meters          500

0 yards          500

**Key to Symbols** see back flap

**Strikingly-colored mural at the Lukhang Temple**

## Potala Palace

See pp534–5.

## Lukhang

Ching Drol Chi Ling Park.
Picturesquely located on an island in the lake behind the Potala, and cloaked by willows in summer, this temple is dedicated to the king of the water spirits (*lu*), who is depicted riding an elephant at the back of the main hall. The upper floors are decorated with striking 18th-century murals, representing the Buddhist Path to Enlightenment. Their great attention to detail and vivid stories offered visual guidance to the Dalai Lamas (*see p520*), who retired here for periods of spiritual retreat.

Buddhist myths dominate the walls on the second floor, while the top-floor murals depict the esoteric yogic practises of the Indian tantric masters. They also illustrate episodes in the life of Pema Lingpa, ancestor of the 6th Dalai Lama who is credited with the Lukhang's original design in the 17th century.

## Ramoche

○ 9am–5pm daily. 🎦 ⭕ fee.
The three-story Ramoche, just north of the Barkhor area (*see pp530–31*), is the sister temple to the Jokhang. It was built in the 7th century by Songtsen Gampo (*see p520*) to house the statue of Jowo Sakyamuni (Tibet's most venerated Buddha image), brought by his Chinese wife Wencheng. According to legend, the threat of Chinese invasion after the king's death compelled his family to hide the statue inside the Jokhang.

It was replaced by a bronze statue of an eight-year-old Sakyamuni (*see pp30–31*), part of the dowry of another of his wives, the Nepalese Princess Bhrikuti.

The reconstructed temple features some huge prayer wheels, and is not as busy as the Jokhang. Next door is the **Tsepak Lhakhang**, a chapel with an image of Jampa, the Tibetan name for the Future Buddha (*see p523*).

**Prayer wheels at the Ramoche Temple**

The Summer Palace of the Dalai Lamas in the Norbulingka

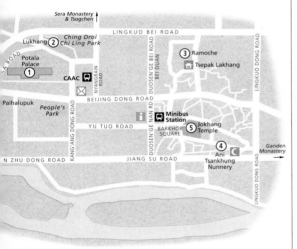

**VISITORS' CHECKLIST**

520,000. Lhasa Airport at Gongkhar, 40 miles (65 km) from Lhasa, then bus. Lhasa Station. Main Bus Station, CAAC, Minibus Station. 4WD vehicle. Tibet Tourism Bureau, (0891) 691 2080.

is a charming place for a leisurely afternoon visit. The path west from the entrance leads to the oldest palace, the **Kelsang Potrang**, used by the 8th to the 13th Dalai Lamas. Its main hall has a wealth of *thangkas (see p536)* and a throne. More diverting is the **Summer Palace**, just north of here, which was built for the present Dalai Lama in 1954. Its audience chamber holds bright murals depicting events from Tibetan history, from the tilling of the first field to the building of the great monasteries, including the Norbulingka. Next to the chamber are the Dalai Lama's meditation room and bedroom, preserved exactly as he left them in 1959, when he escaped from this palace disguised as a Tibetan soldier and began his journey to India. The Assembly Hall where he held state has a golden throne and colorful murals depicting scenes from the Dalai Lama's court, and episodes from the lives of Sakya Thukpa (Sakyamuni, the Historical Buddha) and Tsongkhapa, founder of the Gelugpa order of monks *(see p520)*.

### Ani Tsankhung Nunnery
*daily.*
Situated in the old Tibetan quarter, the Ani Tsankhung Nunnery is difficult to find. Wandering through the busy back alleys south of the Barkhor area in search of the place, can, however, be a wonderful experience. It is located in a yellow building on the street running parallel and north of Chingdol Dong Lu. The nunnery's main hall contains a beautiful image of Chenresig, the multi-armed Bodhisattva of Compassion *(see p523)*, and behind it lies a meditation chamber used by Songtsen Gampo in the 7th century. An air of quiet serenity pervades this quaint place, with its flower bushes and spotless compound. The nunnery's main attraction is the warm welcome the curious nuns give to the visitors that come here.

### Jokhang Temple
*See pp532–3.*

### Tibet Museum
**Tel** (0891) 683 5244. *summer: 9am–6:30pm, winter: 10:30am–5pm.*
This impressive building presents a rather one-sided version of Tibetan history. If the propaganda is ignored, however, the over 30,000 relics are worth a visit. The most interesting displays are of rare Tibetan musical instruments and medical tools.

### Norbulingka
*9:30am–6pm daily.*
Today a pleasantly scrubby park, the Norbulingka (Jewel Park) was once the summer palace of the Dalai Lamas. Founded by the 7th Dalai Lama in 1755 and expanded by his successors, the park contains several palaces, chapels, and buildings, and

Brightly painted doorway, Norbulingka

# Street-by-Street: The Barkhor

匐

Lhasa's liveliest neighborhood, the fascinating Barkhor bustles with pilgrims, locals, and tourists eager to visit the Jokhang *(see pp532–3)* – by dusk the crowds are enormous. The pilgrimage circuit or *kora* that runs clockwise around the Jokhang is Tibet's holiest and has been since the 7th century; market stalls have always lined the route to serve the pilgrims staying in the area. Many of the buildings in the Barkhor are ancient, some dating back to the 8th century.

**Roof ornament, Jokhang Temple**

Despite the efforts of conservationists, some important buildings have been demolished and replaced with less attractive traditional architecture. Still, the Barkhor's cobbled alleyways maintain a unique, archaic character.

**Butter stall**
*A stall selling yak butter for burning candles. Widely available, it gives Jokhang its distinctive smell.*

BARKHOR TROMSHUN

**★ Jokhang Temple**
*The magnificent Jokhang, Tibet's most important religious structure, sits at the heart of the Barkhor, and is the structure around which the rest of Lhasa developed.*

**Prayer flags**
*Two poles laden with flags stand outside the Jokhang. Vertical flag poles originated in the Amdo region, and represent battle flags that have become signs of peace.*

**KEY**

- - - - *Kora* (holy route)

**STAR SIGHTS**

★ Jokhang

★ Meru Nyingba

**Incense burner**
*Juniper bushes are burnt in the four stone incense burners, or sangkang, which mark the route of the kora.*

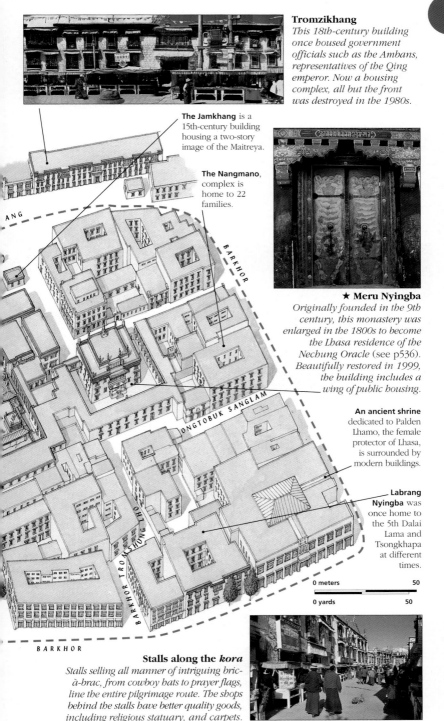

**Tromzikhang**
*This 18th-century building once housed government officials such as the Ambans, representatives of the Qing emperor. Now a housing complex, all but the front was destroyed in the 1980s.*

**The Jamkhang** is a 15th-century building housing a two-story image of the Maitreya.

**The Nangmano,** complex is home to 22 families.

★ **Meru Nyingba**
*Originally founded in the 9th century, this monastery was enlarged in the 1800s to become the Lhasa residence of the Nechung Oracle (see p536). Beautifully restored in 1999, the building includes a wing of public housing.*

**An ancient shrine** dedicated to Palden Lhamo, the female protector of Lhasa, is surrounded by modern buildings.

**Labrang Nyingba** was once home to the 5th Dalai Lama and Tsongkhapa at different times.

| 0 meters | 50 |
| 0 yards | 50 |

**Stalls along the *kora***
*Stalls selling all manner of intriguing bric-à-brac, from cowboy hats to prayer flags, line the entire pilgrimage route. The shops behind the stalls have better quality goods, including religious statuary, and carpets.*

# Jokhang Temple

大昭寺

**Roof detail of fierce creature**

The constant bustle, gaudy paraphernalia of worship, flickering butter lamps, and wreaths of heady incense make the Jokhang Temple one of Tibet's most memorable experiences. The Jokhang was founded in AD 639 to house an image of the Buddha brought as dowry by the Nepali Princess Bhrikuti on her marriage to King Songtsen Gampo. Its location was chosen by another wife of the king, the Chinese consort Princess Wencheng. She declared that a giant female demon slumbered beneath the site and a temple must be built over her heart to subdue her. After the king's death, Wencheng's own dowry image of Jowo Sakyamuni was moved from the Ramoche (see p528) to the Jokhang, where it was thought to be safer from invading forces.

**Prostrating pilgrim**
The Jokhang is Tibet's most venerated site. Pilgrims bow and pray on the flagstones just outside the temple doors.

**Courtyard**
This open courtyard, or dukhang, is the focus for ceremonies during festivals. The long altar holding hundreds of butter lamps marks the entrance to the interior.

**Just inside the entrance** are the four Guardian Kings, the Chokyong, one for each cardinal direction.

**This stele** is inscribed with the terms of the Sino-Tibetan treaty of AD 822, guaranteeing mutual respect for the borders of the two nations.

**Roof ornament**
The spokes of the wheel of law represent the eight paths to enlightenment.

**Alternative entrance**

## STAR SIGHTS

★ Chapel of Chenresig

★ Chapel of Jowo Sakyamuni

★ Inner Sanctum

**The chapel of Tsongkhapa** has an impressive and accurate image of the founder of the Gelugpa order.

**The chapel of Songtsen Gampo**, where the king is flanked by Wencheng on the right and Bhrikuti on the left.

**VISITORS' CHECKLIST**

The Barkhor, Lhasa. ⬭ 9am–6pm daily. Visit from left to right clockwise. Inner Chapels ⬭ 8am–noon. 📷 ♿ Monlam, during the first lunar month.

★ **Chapel of Chenresig**
*A large statue of Chenresig, the Bodhisattva of compassion, dominates this room. The doors and frames, crafted by Nepalis in the 7th century, are among the few remains of the original temple.*

★ **Chapel of Jowo Sakyamuni**
*Pilgrims crowd around this impassive statue of the 12-year-old Sakyamuni to make offerings and pray. Part of Princess Wencheng's dowry, it is the most revered image in Tibet.*

**The Jampa** enshrined here is a copy of the one brought to Tibet by Princess Bhrikuti.

**Prayer Wheels**
*Pilgrims spin the wheels on a route that surrounds the inner chapel called the Nangkor, one of the three sacred circuits of Lhasa.*

★ **Inner Sanctum**
*This houses some of the Jokhang's most important statues, including images of Guru Rinpoche, the Jampa and a thousand-armed Chenresig. The chapels lining the walls are visited clockwise, and there's a line for the holiest, with monks at hand to enforce crowd discipline.*

# Potala Palace
布达拉宫

**Bronze roof statue**

Built on Lhasa's highest point, Marpo Hill, the Potala Palace is the greatest monumental structure in Tibet. Thirteen stories high, with over a thousand rooms, it was once the residence of Tibet's chief monk and leader, the Dalai Lama, and therefore the center for both spiritual and temporal power. These days, after the present Dalai Lama's escape to India in 1959, it is a vast museum, serving as a reminder of Tibet's rich and devoutly religious culture, although major political events and religious ceremonies are still held here. The first palace was built by Songtsen Gampo in 631, and this was merged into the larger building that stands today. There are two main sections – the White Palace, built in 1645 under orders from the 5th Dalai Lama, and the Red Palace, completed in 1693.

**★ Golden Roofs**
*Seeming to float above the palace, the gilded roofs (actually copper) cover funerary chapels dedicated to previous Dalai Lamas.*

**The Chapel of the 5th Dalai Lama** contains a stupa gilded with around 6,600 lb (3,700 kg) of gold.

**★ Chapel of the 13th Dalai Lama**
*Decorated with gold and jewels, the stupa of the 13th Dalai Lama, containing his mummified remains, is nearly 13 m (43 ft) high.*

**Red Palace Courtyard**

**The base** is purely structural, holding the palaces onto the steep hill.

*Thangka Storehouse*

**★ 3D Mandalaw**
*This intricate mandala of a palace, covered in precious metals and jewels, embodies aspects of the path to enlightenment.*

---

**STAR SIGHTS**

★ Chapel of the 13th Dalai Lama

★ Golden Roofs

★ 3D Mandala

---

### View from the Roof of the Red Palace
*On a clear day the view over the valley and on to the mountains beyond is unequaled, although the newer parts of Lhasa are less impressive.*

**Maitreya Chapel**

**East Sunshine Apartment**

### White Palace
*The entrance to the main building has a triple stairway – the middle set of stairs is for the sole use of the Dalai Lama.*

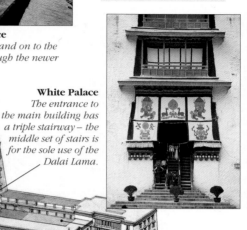

**The Eastern Courtyard**

**School of Religious Officials**

**Defensive Eastern Bastion**

### Heavenly King Murals
*The East Entrance has sumptuous images of the Four Heavenly Kings, Buddhist guardian figures.*

### The Western Hall
*Located on the first floor of the Red Palace, the largest hall inside the Potala contains the holy throne of the 6th Dalai Lama.*

# Exploring Around Lhasa

Lhasa's environs are dotted with the major monasteries of Drepung, Nechung, Sera, and Ganden. Easily accessible from Lhasa by bus, minibus, or hired vehicle, these are ideal for day-trips, especially for those unable to venture farther afield in Tibet. Agencies in Lhasa hire out landcruisers along with a driver and guide. Vehicles can take up to five people – if looking to share the cost with others, check the bulletin boards in backpacker hotels. A Tibet Travel Permit is needed before you enter Lhasa.

**A typically gory tantric painting at Nechung Monastery**

### ▣ Drepung Monastery

5 miles (8 km) W of Lhasa.
⬤ *8am–4pm daily (chapels close between noon–3pm).* 🖼

Drepung, meaning "rice heap," was founded in 1416 by Jamyang Choje, a disciple of Tsongkhapa, the founder of the Gelugpa or Yellow Hat order of monks *(see p520)*. In its heyday in the 17th-century, it was Tibet's richest monastery, with four colleges and 10,000 monks; today there are around 500 to 600.

The site is vast and the easiest way to get around is to follow the pilgrims, who circle the complex clockwise. From the entrance, turn left to the **Ganden Palace**, built in 1530 as a residence by the 2nd Dalai Lama. His rather plain apartments are upstairs on the seventh floor. The courtyard is usually busy with woodcarvers and block-printers creating prayer prints at great speed. Next is the **Tsogchen** or Main Assembly Hall, the most atmospheric building in the complex. About 180 pillars hold up the roof, and the room is draped with *thangkas* and hangings and decorated with suits of armor.

There is plenty of statuary, with the finest images in the **Chapel of the Three Ages** at the back of the Main Assembly Hall.

At the hall's entrance, stairs lead to the upper floor from where it is possible to see the massive head and shoulders of the **Maitreya Buddha**, the future Buddha or Jampa, rising up three stories. Pilgrims prostrate before it

and drink from a holy conch shell. The **Tara Chapel** next door contains wooden racks of scriptures and a statue of Prajnaparamita, the Mother of Buddhas and an aspect of the goddess Tara; the amulet on her lap contains a tooth said to belong to Tsongkhapa. Behind the Tsogchen, the little **Manjusri Temple** has a relief image of the Bodhisattva of Wisdom, Jampalyang, chiseled out of rock. The circuit continues north to the Ngagpa College, then to various colleges toward the southeast.

Each building contains fine sculptures, though some might prefer to skip them and rest in the courtyard outside the Tsogchen. Those who are acclimatized can walk round the Drepung *kora* or pilgrim circuit, which passes rock paintings and the cave dwellings of nuns, and offers great views.

### ▣ Nechung Monastery

4 miles (7 km) W of Lhasa.
⬤ *8am–4pm daily (chapels close between noon–3pm).* 🖼

A fifteen-minute walk southeast from Drepung, Nechung Monastery was the seat of the Tibetan Oracle. The Oracle not only predicted the future, but also protected the Buddha's teachings and his followers. During consultations with the Dalai Lama, the Oracle, dressed in an elaborate and weighty costume,

---

### *THANGKAS* AND MANDALAS

*Thangkas* are religious paintings mounted on brocade that carry painted or embroidered images inside a colored border. Seen in temples, monasteries, and homes, they depict Subjects as diverse as the lives of Buddhas, Tibetan theology and astrology, and mandalas or geometric representations of the cosmos. The Tashilunpo Monastery *(see p544)* displays gigantic *thangkas* during its festivals each year. Mandalas are often used as meditation aids by Buddhists and are based on a pattern of circles and squares around a central focal point. The Potala Palace in Lhasa *(see pp534–5)* has a splendid three-dimensional mandala made of precious metal. Monks spend days creating mandalas of colored sand that are swept away on completion to signify the transient nature of life.

**Mandala symbolizing the universe**

Monks engaged in group debates at Sera Monastery

would go into a trance before making his pronouncements, concluding the session in a dead faint. Tibet's last Oracle fled to India in 1959, and now the monastery has only a few caretaker monks. Nechung's decor is startling as the courtyard outside is filled with gory paintings and demon torturers. Within the chapels, leering sculptures of skulls loom out of the gloom. The airy Audience Chamber on the second floor is a welcome respite. Here, the Dalai Lama used to consult the Oracle. The roof-level chapel is dedicated to Padmasambhava, the Tantric Buddha, also known as Guru Rinpoche.

### 🏛 Sera Monastery
2 miles (4 km) N of Lhasa. ☐ *3–5pm daily.* 🖼

Founded in 1419 by disciples of the Gelugpa order, Sera Monastery was famous for its warrior monks, the Dob-Doa. Once home to 5,000 monks, today there are less than one-tenth that number, although the energetic renovation suggests that this may improve.

Activity centers around its three colleges, visited in a clockwise circuit. Turn left from the main path to reach the first college, Sera Me, that was used for instruction in Buddhist basics. Sera Ngag-Pa, a little farther up the hill, was for tantric studies and Sera Je, next to it, was for teaching visiting monks. Each building has a dimly lit main hall and chapels toward the back that are full of sculptures. The largest and most striking building in the complex is the **Tsogchen** located farthest up the hill. It features wall-length *thangkas*, a throne that was used by the 13th Dalai Lama, and images of him and of Sakya Yeshe, the founder of Sera monastery. At the top of the path stands the open-air debating courtyard. The monks assemble here for debates and their ritualized gestures – clapping hands and stamping when a point is made – which are fascinating to watch. The Sera *kora*, or pilgrim circuit which heads

Rock painting, Sera Monastery

west from the main entrance, takes about an hour to complete and passes some beautiful rock reliefs.

### 🏛 Ganden Monastery
28 miles (45 km) E of Lhasa. 🚌 *Shuttle from the square at Jokhang Temple.* ☐ *8:50am–4pm daily.* 🖼

The farthest of the monasteries from Lhasa, Ganden is probably the one most worth visiting, with its scenic setting high on the Gokpori Ridge. To get a feel of the place, it is best to travel with the excited pilgrims on the bus that leaves from Lhasa's Barkhor area every morning at 6:30am, returning at 2pm. The monastery was founded in 1410 by Tsongkhapa, and its main building, the **Serdung Lhakhang**, has as its centerpiece a huge gold and silver *chorten* (stupa or funerary mound) with Tsongkhapa's remains. However, the buildings are not its main appeal. Its highlight is the *kora*, which takes an hour to walk. The circuit offers fine views of the landscape and a *chorten* or two that pilgrims (and visitors if they wish) must hop around on one leg.

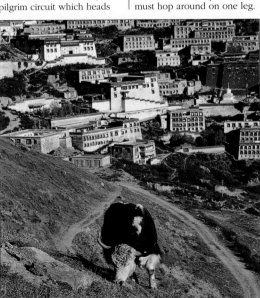
A domestic yak on the steep hills surrounding Ganden Monastery

# Samye Monastery ❷

桑耶寺

**Tantric protector in Gongkhan**

With its ordered design, wealth of religious treasures, and stunning location, Samye makes a deep impression on visitors. Tibet's first monastery, Samye was founded in the 8th century during Trisong Detsen's reign with the input of the great Buddhist teacher, Guru Rinpoche. Indian and Chinese scholars, invited to Samye to translate Buddhist scriptures into Tibetan, argued over the interpretation of doctrine, and so Trisong Detsen held a public debate to decide which form of Buddhism should be followed in Tibet. The Indian school won out and Chinese-religious influence gradually waned. Today the monastery has a well-worn and eclectic feel, having been influenced by numerous sects over the years.

**★ Jowo Sakyamuni Chapel**
*Samye's most revered chapel centers on an image of Sakyamuni at age 38. He is flanked by two protector deities and ten Bodhisattvas.*

**★ Chenresig Chapel**
*This chapel centers on a stunning statue of Chenresig, with an eye painstakingly painted on each of its thousand hands.*

**Monks** live in quarters on the upper level of the outer wall.

## EXPLORING THE ÜTSE

The Ütse is dimly lit, so take a flashlight to explore. The entrance leads directly into the Main Hall, with the Chenrisig Chapel to the left and the Gongkhan Chapel to the right. The Jowo Sakyamuni Chapel is at the far end of the Main Hall. Numerous chapels and the Dalai Lama's quarters are located on the second story. The third story has an open gallery lined with impressive murals.

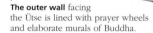

**The outer wall** facing the Ütse is lined with prayer wheels and elaborate murals of Buddha.

### STAR SIGHTS

★ Jowo Sakyamuni Chapel

★ Chenresig Chapel

**View of Samye Monastery**
*A superb view of the monastery can be had from the surrounding hills. From here it is easy to see that the monastery is laid out as a 3-D mandala (see p536).*

◁ Flags hung on the hills around Ganden Monastery to infuse the wind with prayers

## Guru Rinpoche

*An 8th-century monk-king from Swat in modern-day Pakistan, he is said to have subdued evil demons and established Buddhism in Tibet. Images of him carrying a thunderbolt are found throughout the complex.*

### VISITORS' CHECKLIST

93 miles (150 km) SE of Lhasa.
🚌 *Travel to Samye must be arranged by a travel agency.* 📷 📹 *unless fee paid.* 🎭 *Samye Festival, 15th day of fifth lunar month.*

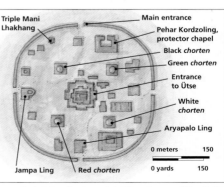

**The mural** to the left of the entrance on the third story depicts the 5th Dalai Lama receiving the Mongol Khan Gushri and his retinue.

### Quarters of the Dalai Lama

*This simple apartment, consisting of anteroom, bedroom and throne room, is full of relics, including Guru Rinpoche's hair and walking stick.*

**Gongkhan Chapel** is packed with draped statues of fierce demons. A stuffed snake guards the exit.

**Main entrance**

**The inscription** on this stone stele (779 AD) declares that King Trisong Detsen has proclaimed Buddhism as the state religion.

**The main hall** houses images and statues of Guru Rinpoche and the Buddhist kings, Trisong Detsen and Songtsen Gampo.

---

### PLAN OF SAMYE COMPLEX

Samye's design echoes Tibetan Buddhism's cosmology of the universe. Many of the 108 buildings have been destroyed, but the four *ling* chapels representing the island continents that surround Mount Sumeru (the Ütse) are still intact. Jampa Ling holds an impressive mural of the complex as it once was. The circular monastery wall is topped with 1,008 *chortens* that represent Chakravla, the ring of 1,008 mountains that surrounds the universe.

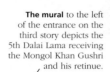

Triple Mani Lhakhang

Main entrance

Pehar Kordzoling, protector chapel

Black *chorten*

Green *chorten*

Entrance to Ütse

White *chorten*

Aryapalo Ling

Jampa Ling

Red *chorten*

0 meters    150
0 yards     150

Nomad tents, at the edge of the breathtaking Namtso Lake

# Tsurphu Monastery ❸

楚布寺

Tolung Valley. 45 miles (70 km) W of Lhasa. 🚌 daily from Barkhor Square in Lhasa. Last bus back to Lhasa, 3pm. 🚗 4WD rented from Lhasa, 2–3 hrs. ⬤ 9am–2pm daily. 📷

Situated at an altitude of 14,700 ft (4,480 m), this monastery was founded in the 12th century by the Karmapa or Black Hats order and is important as the home of the Karmapa Lama, the third most important religious leader in Tibet after the Dalai and Panchen Lamas (see p544). The present incumbent, the 17th Karmapa, fled to India in 1999 at the age of 14. His departure was significant as he was the only senior Tibetan Buddhist official recognized

One of the many brightly-colored murals at Tsurphu Monastery

by both the Chinese authorities and the Dalai Lama. The flood of daily pilgrims who came for blessings has now stopped and the monastery is rather quiet, though several hundred monks still reside here.

The Karmapa's throne, an object of great veneration, is in the audience chamber of the main hall. Here, a *chorten* (stupa or funerary mound) contains the relics of the 16th Karmapa, who died in Chicago in 1981. The *kora* from behind the monastery takes three hours, and provides magnificent views but beware – visitors must be acclimatized.

# Namtso Lake ❹

纳木错湖

125 miles (200 km) NW of Lhasa. 🚗 4WD rented from Lhasa, 2–3 day round-trip. ⬤ daily. 📷

Beautiful Namtso Lake, with its classic Tibetan scenery of azure water beneath snowcapped peaks and grasslands dotted with herds of yak, has made it the most popular overnight jeep trip from Lhasa. About 45 miles (70 km) long and 19 miles (30 km) wide, it is the second largest saltwater lake in China after Qinghai Hu

## THE EIGHT AUSPICIOUS SYMBOLS

The Eight Auspicious Symbols represent the offerings that were presented to Sakyamuni Buddha, after he attained Enlightenment. Born as Siddhartha Gautama, prince of the kingdom of Kapilavastu, he renounced his princely life at the age of 30, and went in search of answers to the meaning of human suffering and existence. After years of penance, Siddhartha attained Enlightenment after meditating under a Bodhi tree in Bodh Gaya, India. Tibetans regard the symbols as protective motifs and use them to decorate flags and medallions as well as tiles in Buddhist temples, monasteries, and homes. The Conch Shell is blown to celebrate Sakyamuni's Enlightenment; the Endless Knot represents harmony, and the never-ending passage of time; and the Wheel of Law symbolizes the Buddha's eightfold path to Enlightenment. Other symbols include the Golden Fish, representing liberation from the Wheel of Life, and the Lotus Flower that represents purity.

**Conch Shell**

**Endless Knot**

**Wheel of Law**

*(see p499).* The flat land around it offers good grazing, and is ususally ringed with nomad encampments in summer. From November to May, the lake freezes over and is impossible to reach. Most people stay a night at **Tashi Dor**, a monastery on a lakeside hill. Bring a flashlight and a warm sleeping bag. The lake is situated at the incredible height of 15,500 ft (4,718 m), so visitors must be thoroughly acclimatized.

**Highly decorated doorway to the main chapel, Kumbum, Gyantse**

# Gyantse **❺**
江孜

158 miles (255 km) SW of Lhasa. *Minibus: alternate days from Lhasa bus station.* 🚗 *4WD from Lhasa.* **Travel Permits** *required (see p519).*

An attractive, if dusty, small town, Gyantse is the sixth largest town in Tibet, famous for its carpets and usually visited en route to Nepal *(see p547).* Often called "Heroic City," it was originally capital of a 14th-century kingdom, and the remnants of its old **Dzong**, or fort watches over the town. Heavily bombarded during the British invasion in 1904, when it was captured at great loss of life to the Tibetans, it is today a dramatic ruin with a small museum. Here, Chinese propaganda describes the "heroic battle fought to defend the Chinese motherland," although at that time China had no authority over Tibet. The Dzong offers good views from its roof.

About 650 ft (200 m) northwest is a compound housing the **Kumbum** and **Pelkor Chode Monastery**.

The Kumbum, constructed around 1440, is a magnificent six-story and 115-ft (35-m) high *chorten*, honeycombed with little chapels. It is built in an architectural style unique to Tibet and this is the finest extant example. A clockwise route leads up past chapels full of statuary and decorated with 14th-century murals – *kumbum* means "a hundred thousand images." On the fourth floor, painted pairs of eyes, signifying the all-seeing eyes of Buddha, look out in each of the cardinal directions. The staircase in the eastern chapel leads into the *chorten's* dome. There are dramatic views from the top.

Built 20 years after Kumbum, the Pelkor Chode Monastery was designed for all the local Buddhist sects to use; its murky Assembly Hall has two thrones, one for the Dalai Lama and one for the Sakya Lama. The main chapel at the back of the hall has a statue of Sakyamuni, the Historical Buddha, and some impressive wooden roof decorations. At the very top, the Shalyekhang Chapel has some fine mandalas *(see p536).*

On the way to Gyantse it is worth taking a detour to see beautiful **Yamdrok Lake**, one of the four holy Tibetan lakes.

🏯 **Dzong**
⬜ *Mon–Sat.* 📷
🏛 **Kumbum & Pelkor Chode Monastery**
⬜ *9am–7pm Mon–Sat (closed noon–3pm).* 📷 🎟 *for a fee.*

**Kumbum, Gyantse, a three-dimensional mandala**

# Shigatse & Tashilunpo ❻

## 日喀则

**Striped cloth woven on loom**

Capital of the Tsang region, Shigatse sits at an elevation of 12,800 ft (3,900 m). To its north, the Drolma Ridge rises steeply, topped by the ruins of the ancient Dzong, once home to the kings of Tsang. Shigatse holds a powerful position in Tibet, and was the capital for a spell during the early 17th century. After Lhasa regained its status, Shigatse continued to hold sway as the home of the Panchen Lama, Tibet's second most important religious ruler, whose seat is located at Tashilunpo Monastery, the town's grandest sight. Worth exploring for a day or two, Shigatse is the most comfortable place in Tibet after Lhasa, with decent food and accommodations on offer.

**A group of carpet makers tying richly colored wool into intricate knots**

come if you are in the market for a Tibetan carpet. The process is sufficiently interesting to warrant a visit even if you have no intention of buying. A project initiated by the 10th Panchen Lama in 1987, the business is part-owned by the monastery. Shipping can be arranged on the premises.

### 🏠 Gang Gyen Carpet Factory
9 Zhu Feng Rd. *Tel (0892) 882 6192.*
⬭ *9am–12:30pm & 2:30–7pm Mon–Fri.* **www**.tibetgang-gyencarpet.com
This factory, where local women produce beautiful carpets, first skeining the wool then weaving it, is the place to

### 🏠 Night Market
A small cluster of street food stalls can be found at the corner of Qomolangma Lu and Jiefang Zhong Lu. Chairs and tables, and even the odd sofa, line the sidewalks next to the stalls. Enjoy a large bowl of noodles or a kabob.

---

### THE 11TH PANCHEN LAMA

The death of the 10th Panchen Lama in 1989 brought Tibet's leaders and the Chinese government into conflict over succession. Like the seat of the Dalai Lama, the Panchen Lama's position is passed on through reincarnation. Traditionally, upon the death of either of these leaders, top monks scour the land hoping to identify the new incarnate. In 1995, after an extensive search, the Dalai Lama named a six-year-old boy, Gedhun Choeki Nyima, as the 11th Panchen Lama. The chosen boy and his family soon disappeared and have not been seen since. Keen to handpick the next Dalai Lama's teacher, the Chinese authorities sanctioned a clandestine ceremony which ordained Gyancain Norbu as the "official Panchen Lama" and immediately whisked him off to Beijing.

**Young Gyancain Norbu, the China-sanctioned 11th Panchen Lama**

### 🏛 Dzong
The leaders of Tsang once ruled from the mighty fortress of **Shigatse Dzong**, in the north of town, built in the 14th century by Karma Phuntso Namgyel, a powerful Tsang king. It once resembled a small Potala but was destroyed by the Chinese in 1959 during the Tibetan uprising, and little remains today except the stumps of a few burned walls. You can walk around the Dzong but you can't enter it. A *kora* or holy route, marked by prayer flags and *mani* stones, leads here from the west side of Tashilunpo. Keep your distance from the packs of stray dogs.

### 🏠 Tibetan Market
At the Dzong's southern base on Tomzigang Lu stands a small Tibetan market selling souvenirs, such as prayer wheels and incense, and a few Tibetan necessities – medicine, legs of lamb, and large knives. Just to the west of the market is an old traditionally Tibetan neighborhood of narrow lanes and tall whitewashed walls.

**Stall selling religious regalia at the Tibetan Market**

### 🏛 Tashilunpo Monastery
*Tel (0892) 882 2114.* ⬭ *Summer: 9am–12:30pm & 4–6pm Mon–Sat; Winter: 10am–noon & 3–6pm Mon–Sat.* 📷
A huge monastic compound of golden-roofed venerable buildings and cobbled lanes, Tashilunpo would take several days to explore fully. It was founded in 1447 by Genden Drup, retrospectively titled the 1st Dalai Lama. It

**Majestic Tashilunpo Monastery with Drolma Ridge rising behind**

## VISITORS' CHECKLIST

172 miles (278 km) W of Lhasa.
🏯 75,000. 🚌 *Only through
travel agency in Lhasa.* 🎭
*Tashilunpo: 2nd week of 5th
lunar month.*

grew suddenly important in 1642, when the 5th Dalai Lama declared his teacher, the monastery's abbot, to be a reincarnation of the Amithaba Buddha and the fourth reincarnation of the Panchen Lama, or great teacher. Ever since it has been the seat of the Panchen Lamas, who are second in authority to the Dalai Lama.

**The Wheel of Law, an auspicious symbol**

Head up the main path to the back of the compound for the most impressive sights. The gold and silver *chorten* straight ahead holds the remains of the 4th Panchen Lama. Built in 1662, it was the only funeral *chorten* in the monastery to escape destruction during the Cultural Revolution. The larger, jewel studded *chorten* just to the west holds the remains of the 10th Panchen Lama, who died in 1989; it was constructed in 1994 at a cost of eight million US dollars.

Continue west for the Chapel of Jampa, which holds the monastery's most impressive artifact, an 85-ft (26-m) golden image of Jampa, the future Buddha, made in 1914. It took almost a thousand artisans four years to complete using more than 600 pounds (275 kg) of gold.

The complex of buildings on the east side is the Kelsang. It centers around a courtyard where monks can be observed praying, debating, and relaxing. The 15th-century Assembly Hall on the west side holds the imposing throne of the Panchen Lamas.

Those with energy left can follow the monastery *kora*, which takes about an hour. It runs clockwise around the outside of the walls before heading up to the Dzong. You'll pass colorful rock reliefs, some of Guru Rinpoche, and the huge white wall where a *thangka* of Buddha is exposed to the sun during the three-day long Tashilunpo Festival.

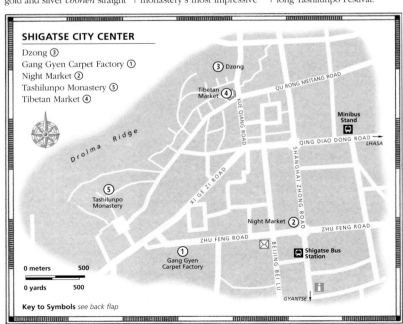

## SHIGATSE CITY CENTER

Dzong ③
Gang Gyen Carpet Factory ①
Night Market ②
Tashilunpo Monastery ⑤
Tibetan Market ④

③ Dzong

④ Tibetan Market

Minibus Stand

QU RONG MEITANG ROAD

XUE QIANG ROAD

QING DIAO DONG ROAD

*LHASA*

SHANGHAI ZHONG ROAD

XI GE ZI ROAD

Drolma Ridge

⑤ Tashilunpo Monastery

Night Market ②

ZHU FENG ROAD

ZHU FENG ROAD

BEIJING BEI LU

Shigatse Bus Station

① Gang Gyen Carpet Factory

GYANTSE ↓

0 meters 500
0 yards 500

**Key to Symbols** *see back flap*

## Sakya Monastery ❼
### 萨迦寺

311 miles (500 km) SW of Lhasa.
🚌 *Only through a travel agency in Lhasa.* ◷ *9am–6:30pm Mon–Sat.*
📷 📷 *fee.* **Travel Permit** *required* (see p519).

The town of Sakya is dominated by the huge, fortress-like monastery, that looms up from the gray plains. Sakya, or "Gray Soil" in Tibetan, was the capital of all Tibet in the 13th century, when monks of the Sakyapa order formed an extraordinary alliance with the Mongols. In 1247, the head of the Sakyapa order, Sakya Pandita, traveled to Mongolia and made a pact, whereby the Mongols were the overlords, while the Sakya monks ruled as their regents – the first time a lama was also head of state. His nephew, Phagpa, later became the spiritual guide to the conqueror of China, Kublai Khan. In 1354, Mongol power waned, and in-fighting among the religious sects led to a decline in Sakya's influence.

Originally, there were two monasteries on either side of the Trum River, but the northern one was destroyed during the Cultural Revolution *(see pp64–5)*. The mid-13th century **Southern Monastery**, built by Phagpa, is a typical Mongol structure, with thick walls and watchtowers. The entrance leads to a courtyard with an enormous prayer pole in the center. To the left is the **Puntsok Palace**, the traditional home of one of the two head

**Detail from wall painting at Sakya Monastery**

lamas, who now lives overseas. Apart from the statue-filled chapel, its rooms are mainly empty. Moving clockwise, the next chapel, the **Purkhang**, holds images of Jowo Sakyamuni and Jampalyang among others, while wall murals depict tantric deities. The **Main Assembly Hall** has 40 huge wooden pillars, one of which was said to have been gifted by Kublai Khan, while another is said to have come from India on the back of a tiger. The elaborately decorated hall has rich brocades, statues, and butter lamps and holds thousands of religious texts *(sutras)*. The fine central Buddha image enshrines the remains of Phagpa. The chapel to the north has 11 silver *chortens* containing the remains of previous Sakya lamas. Sakya houses are

traditionally painted gray with red and white vertical stripes; the colors are supposed to symbolize the Bodhisattvas Channa Dorje, Jampalyang, and Chenresig respectively.

## Everest Base Camp ❽
### 珠峰大本营

**Rongphu** 336 miles (610 km) SW of Lhasa. 🚌 *From Lhasa, 2 days; must be arranged through a travel agency in Lhasa.* **Travel Permits** *required* (see p519).

Despite the spine-jarring, four-hour trip off the Friendship Highway – that connects Lhasa to the Nepal border at Zhangmu – the craggy lunar landscape en route to Everest is enchanting. Rongphu is a good place for a stop and at 16,500 ft (4,980 m) is the highest monastery in the world. Although it has some good murals, the interior is not as riveting as its stunning location in front of Everest's forbidding north face in the Rongphu valley. The monastery was founded in 1902 on a site that had been used by nuns as a meditation retreat for centuries, and is now home to some 30 monks.

Everest Base Camp lies 5 miles (8 km) to the south. The trip across the glacial plain takes about 15 minutes by vehicle or two hours on foot. It is just a jumble of tents, with a makeshift teahouse and the world's highest post box, but the views of Mount Everest, the world's highest mountain at a staggering 29,029 ft (8,848 m), are absolutely unforgettable.

The entire Rongphu and Everest area has been designated a nature reserve that covers 13,100 sq miles (34,000 sq km), and borders three national parks in Nepal. There is a spectacular viewpoint at the Pangla Pass, from which you can see Everest (known as Chomolungma in Tibetan), Cho Oyo, Lhotse, Makalu, and Gyachung. Most people try to

**Houses at Sakya Village, painted gray with red and white stripes**

**Everest Base Camp, with magnificent views of the world's highest mountain**

arrive at this pass either to see the sun rise or the sun set over the Himalayas.

The rarefied air at this altitude (17,000 ft/5,150 m) makes any strenuous activity impossible, however, so unless visitors are properly acclimatized, it is best to go all the way back to the Friendship Highway and carry on to the town of Shegar to spend the night.

## The Nepal Border ❾
尼泊尔边境

**Zhangmu** *Nepal border. 466 miles (750 km) SW of Lhasa.* 🚙 *4WD from Lhasa, 2 days (direct), or 5–6 days (via Gyantse, Shigatse & Everest Base Camp). Travel must be arranged through a travel agency in Lhasa.* **Travel Permit** *for all places (between Shigatze and border) required (see p519).*

The Friendship Highway connecting Lhasa to the Nepal border is one of Tibet's most popular link routes. From the Rongphu turn-off along the highway, it is another 31 miles (50 km) west to **Tingri**, on what is a surprisingly good road. This is a small, traditional Tibetan town with good views of the Everest range. After climbing for 56 miles (90 km) the road

begins a steep, winding descent through mountains that are densely wooded; the change of scenery is startling after the desert landscape of the high, arid plateau. It is only another 20 miles (33 km) to the border town of **Zhangmu**, which is relatively low and oxygen-rich at 7,200 ft (2,200 m). Although much of Zhangmu consists of slightly dilapidated shacks, perched

above one another on the mountainside, this frontier town has a gaudy vibrance. Border formalities to get into Nepal are fairly cursory. The Nepalese immigration post, 6 miles (10 km) farther down at **Kodari**, will issue a single-entry visa, though visitors have to pay in US dollars and provide a passport photo. From here, it is a four-hour trip to Kathmandu.

---

### THE FRIENDSHIP HIGHWAY

The 466-mile (750-km) route between Lhasa and the Nepal border, known as the Friendship Highway, is probably the most popular journey for visitors to Tibet and includes some important sightseeing detours along the way. Many agencies in Lhasa and in Kathmandu in Nepal can arrange the trip, sort out the necessary permits, and provide an appropriate four-wheel drive vehicle, a driver, and guide. Depending on the itinerary, which usually includes the towns of Shigatse and Gyantse, the trip can take up to a week. Visitors must ensure that the contract specifies exactly what they want and what they are paying for.

**Friendship Highway, winding across the plateau to Nepal**

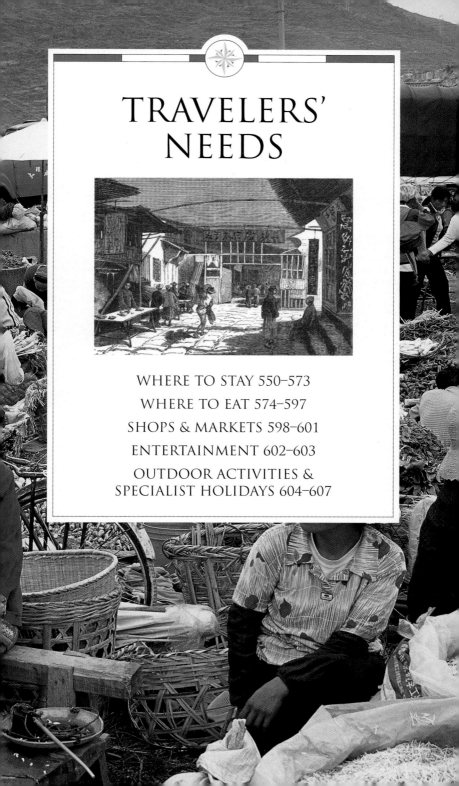

# TRAVELERS' NEEDS

# WHERE TO STAY

An abundance of accommodations is available in China for most of the year, despite the rapid growth in domestic travel. Four- and five-star hotels, sometimes run by foreign hotel chains, are plentiful in the major cities and tourist destinations. In other cities and towns, there are numerous mid-range hotels and budget options with basic facilities to choose from. Generally, there is no

Logo of the White
Swan Hotel

need to book in advance, unless you are traveling during one of the high seasons – the first week of May and October, and the Chinese New Year (Spring Festival). Although you may want to book some of your stay (the first few nights, for example, to ease your arrival), it is perfectly feasible to turn up at your hotel of choice, bargain cheerfully, and book yourself a room at a sizable discount.

## DIFFERENT KINDS OF HOTELS

Visitors in search of international standards of comfort and service should stick either to five-star hotels managed by familiar Western chains, or the Singapore- and Hong Kong-based luxury companies. Several international chains such as Ritz-Carlton, Starwood, Hyatt, Shangri-La, Marriott, and Hilton all have hotels based in the major cities; check their websites for details.

Chinese-run hotels do their best to emulate Western operations and are rapidly raising their standards, design, and service. The published rack rates of Chinese four- and five-star hotels are indeed comparable, although the level of service does not match their Western counterparts, and many do not accept international credit cards. Standards are fast improving, however, and there is a willingness to

please, especially away from the main tourist areas.

The Chinese star system of grading hotels is meaningless. Although authorities have devised a checklist of facilities that hotels must provide within each grade, there is no proper system of monitoring the standards of these services. Therefore, no matter how poorly these facilities may be maintained, no star is ever lost once it has been given. Rather than be involved in this system, some international hotels choose to go starless. These unrated hotels can be far superior to Chinese-run, five-star properties, which may not have been renovated in years. As a general rule for Chinese-run hotels, the newer the hotel, the better the facilities.

For the best deals, and to check out the location and prices of new hotels and make online bookings, www.ctrip.com and www.elong.com are excellent.

The plant-laden lobby of the White Swan Hotel, Guangzhou

## BUDGET HOTELS & OTHER TYPES OF ACCOMMODATIONS

Budget travelers will find a choice of basic and inexpensive accommodations all across the mainland and in Hong Kong. Dormitory beds for around ¥25–30 are common, especially away from the larger cities. Youth hostels with spotless facilities and beds costing about ¥50 are beginning to open up in some metropolises. Many universities will rent out vacant rooms in their "foreign residents wings."

At the upper end of the budget spectrum, the Motel 168 and Jinjiang Inn chains offer excellent rooms, free Internet, private bathrooms, and televisions for an affordable rate. Home Inns and Green Tree are good budget brands with free Internet.

Camping is not an option in China. Pitching a tent, except

The grand Xinhao Ying Hotel on Xinhao Shan, Qingdao

◁ Bai-minority vendors at the Shaping market, near Dali in Yunnan

**The slick stairway at the Novotel Peace hotel, Beijing**

in the most far-flung places, is certain to attract attention, and you are likely to get a visit from the police. Stays in a *ger*, the round portable homes of the nomadic Mongols and Kazakhs, can be arranged in Inner Mongolia and Xinjiang. These overnight camps are firmly targeted at tourists, so may not be an authentic experience. Some monasteries and lamaseries have pilgrims' inns where you are welcome to stay for a minimal fee, but conditions can be very austere. On holy mountains, such as Emei Shan, you will find many temples offering basic but atmospheric accommodations.

## BOOKING A HOTEL

In China, the real price of a hotel room is what the customer is willing to pay. Locals always ask for a discount and you should too. The days of official surcharges for non-Chinese customers are long gone. Although many hotels still quote higher prices to foreign visitors, they are amenable to hard bargaining and will bring their rates down drastically, especially if the rooms in question will otherwise go empty.

For most foreign-run hotels, the best available price will be on the hotel's own website. Unless demand is very high, the price will tend to drop nearer to the planned day of stay.

Some websites for Chinese hotels will quote a wildly inflated rack rate. Only foreigners who try to book in advance from overseas will ever pay this price. Specialist websites often claim to offer huge discounts but, while they can sometimes offer good prices for advance bookings, you should be able to get a better price by a considerable margin if you turn up to book in person. Discounts of 10 to 20 percent are standard, 30 to 40 percent very common, 50 percent not unusual. You can even try for larger discounts, especially in locations with strong seasonal demand.

The introduction of double beds of various sizes in Chinese-run hotels (rather than the standard twin single beds) has led to some confusion. Older hotels and a few newer ones do indeed have regular "single rooms," with a single bed in a relatively small space for a cheaper price. However, rooms described as "single" usually refer to those with a double bed, and can be occupied by two people, although they usually cost slightly less than twin-bed rooms of the same size.

The display of certain credit card symbols at hotels does not guarantee that the hotel will accept the international versions of these cards. It is therefore important to confirm that your international card will be accepted before checking in. You cannot pay directly with travelers' checks, and though most tourist hotels now have foreign exchange facilities, the staff will probably send you to a local bank to exchange your checks. In most places, be prepared to pay in *renminbi*.

## HIDDEN COSTS

The prices quoted by major international hotels do not include their service charges or local bed taxes, although the latter are rarely levied. Many Chinese-run, upper-end hotels have begun to levy service charges of between 5 and 15 percent. Since this is a new practice, most Chinese customers refuse to pay the charges, and hotels rarely insist. Foreign visitors should check their bills carefully before paying, as specialty restaurants in hotels often try to sneak service charges on to their bills. Note that minibar contents are as overpriced in China as they are elsewhere in the world. Costs for phone calls from even modest hotels are computer monitored, and no more than a modest service charge will be added on top of the actual cost of the call.

**Charming rural lodgings in Ping An, near Longsheng, Guangxi**

## SEASONAL DEMAND

While rooms are readily available in China for most of the year, the busiest travel periods are during the week-long national holidays, principally around the Chinese New Year (January or February) and October 1. Unlike the West, very few people in China have discretionary holidays, so almost everyone in the country seems to be traveling at the same time. Another time to avoid traveling is during the Spring Festival, when accommodation is almost impossible to find. The exact dates are not fixed far in advance, but as soon as the dates are declared transport and accommodation costs shoot up.

Spring and autumn, with their milder temperatures and lower humidity, are more popular seasons for traveling than summer or winter, which are both extreme. In summer, some of the cooler destinations within reasonable reach of large cities – such as the island of Putuo Shan, served by short flights and ferries from Shanghai – can be very crowded and expensive during weekends, but very cheap during the week. Other events that affect transport costs and room availability are the festivals of ethnic minorities, particularly in the southwest, and trade events such as the biannual fair in Guangzhou.

The Grand Hyatt Hotel at the Oriental Plaza Shopping Center

The lobby at Dalian Hotel, Harbin

## CHOOSING A HOTEL

When looking for a hotel, keep in mind that the newest hotels are always the best, as most owners seem to resist carrying out repairs and maintenance unless they are absolutely necessary. New hotels, which are constantly springing up in various parts of the country, are mostly one-off operations started by private businesses in the hope of benefiting from the growth in domestic tourism. Hotels run by the police, banks, post offices, tobacco companies, and other businesses, are aspiring to compete with long-standing establishments run by local governments. Any hotel with a decent website or the word "business" in the title is likely to be relatively new and offer good services.

In general, hotels whose names begin with the province or city to which they belong, followed by one of the many Chinese words for hotel such as *dajiudian*, *jiudian*, *fandian*, and *binguan*, are more likely to be owned by local governments. These hotels are best avoided, as most seem to be trapped in an era of guaranteed employment, with shabby, dilapidated rooms, and a rather indifferent staff to whom the Communist motto, "Serve the people," doesn't necessarily extend to the person in front of them.

## GENERAL OBSERVATIONS & PRECAUTIONS

Check-out time is usually noon, but visitors can pay half the nightly rate to keep the room until 6pm. Chinese regulations require all non-residents to be out of hotel rooms by 11pm, but this is widely ignored. Although foreign exchange facilities are usually open seven days a week at most of the better hotels, these facilities can only be used by registered guests.

In most parts of China, hotels which provide accommodations to foreign visitors must have a license to do so. Some hotels without licenses may turn you away, although this is becoming increasingly rare. Beijing and Yunnan have already done away with the licensing system, and more regions can be expected to follow soon.

Many hotels in China, including some establishments with foreign management, advertise facilities such as night clubs, hair and beauty salons, and karaoke bars, but these are often fronts for prostitution. Be wary of unexpected telephone calls to your room offering "*anmo*" or massage. It is best to disconnect your phone if you wish to avoid being solicited.

It is nearly always a mistake to arrange transport services through your hotel, as they often cost as much as four times what they would if you found a taxi on your own. It is wiser to simply walk onto the street and flag down a passing vehicle. Taxis hovering near the doors of hotels in popular tourist destinations should also be approached with caution.

When surveying hotels, remember that the pictures you see on brochures and websites almost always date to the time of opening, and are unlikely to represent the current condition of rooms. You should also not be swayed by the promise of saunas, fitness centers, swimming pools, or jacuzzis, especially in Chinese-run hotels in remote areas, as the presence of these in brochures does not indicate that they are still working or fit for use. Most importantly, the rates mentioned are not fixed.

## FACILITIES FOR CHILDREN & THE DISABLED

Children are welcome everywhere in China, although special facilities for them in hotels are rare. Most hotels allow children below 12 years to stay with their parents free of charge. Most

hotels will also add an extra bed for an older child for a nominal (and usually negotiable) fee. Groups of four, including two children over 12, can sometimes share a room, but may be required to pay for two rooms. However, many older, Chinese-run hotels have three- and four-bed rooms, ideal for families.

In general, China is not a suitable destination for the disabled. Only the newest and best international hotels make any serious effort to provide wheelchair access, or fully adapted rooms. Most places have standard suites

with inconveniently placed light switches, although some have wider bathroom doors to allow wheelchairs. However, most hotels have elevators, so booking a ground-floor room is not necessary.

## TIPPING

As tipping is not very common in China, hotel staff don't usually expect to be tipped. The international hotels will already be charging you a 5 to 15 percent service charge on top of your bill. Some Chinese hotels have started to add these charges as well.

The Yunjincheng Folk Custom Hotel in Pingyao, Shanxi

# DIRECTORY

## HOTEL CHAINS

### ACCOR
**Tel** 1-800 515 5679 (US).
**Tel** 0871 702 9469 (UK).
**www**.accorhotels.com

### Crowne Plaza
**Tel** 1-800 227 6963 (US).
**Tel** 0800 8222 8222 (UK).
**www**.ichotelsgroup.com

### Grand Hyatt
**Tel** 1-888 591 1234 (US).
**Tel** 0845 888 1234 (UK).
**www**.hyatt.com

### Harbour Plaza
**Tel** (212) 253 9606 (US).
**Tel** (0871) 662 7108 (UK).
**www**.harbour-plaza.com

### Hilton
**Tel** 1-800 445 8667 (US).
**Tel** 08705 909 090 (UK).
**www**.hilton.com

### Holiday Inn
**Tel** 1-800 465 4329 (US).
**Tel** 0800 405 060 (UK).
**www**.ichotelsgroup.com

### Howard Johnson
**Tel** 1-800 406 1411 (US).
**Tel** 0845 602 1532 (UK).
**www**.hojo.com

### Hyatt Regency
**Tel** 1-888 591 1234 (US).
**Tel** 0845 888 1234 (UK).
**www**.hyatt.com

### Ibis
**www**.ibishotel.com

### InterContinental
**Tel** 1-800 424 6835 (US).
**Tel** 0800 1800 1800 (UK).
**www**.ichotelsgroup.com

### Jinjiang Inn
**Tel** 400 820 9999.
**www**.jinjianginns.com

### Kempinski
**Tel** 1-800 426 3135 (US).
**Tel** 0800 426 31355 (UK).
**www**.kempinski.com

### Marco Polo
**Tel** 400 120 1481.
**www**.marcopolohotels.com

### Marriott
**Tel** 1-888 236 2427 (US).
**Tel** 0800 221 222 (UK).
**www**.marriott.com

### Motel 168
**Tel** 400 820 7168.
**www**.motel168.com

### Novotel
**Tel** 1-800 668 0835 (US).
**Tel** 08706 090 962 (UK).
**www**.novotel.com

### Park Hyatt
**Tel** 1-888 591 1234 (US).
**Tel** 0845 888 1234 (UK).
**www**.parkhyatt.com

### Peninsula
**Tel** 1-866 382 8388 (US).
**Tel** 0800 2828 3888 (UK).
**www**.peninsula.com

### Radisson Blu
**Tel** 1-800 333 3333 (US).
**Tel** 0800 333 3333 (UK).
**www**.radissonblu.com

### Ritz Carlton
**Tel** 1-800 542 8680 (US).
**Tel** 0800 2413 3333 (UK).
**www**.ritzcarlton.com

### Shangri-La
**Tel** 1-866 565 5050 (US).
**Tel** 0800 028 3337 (UK).
**www**.shangri-la.com

### Sheraton
**Tel** 1-800 325 3535 (US).
**Tel** 0800 3253 5353 (UK).
**www**.starwood.com

### W Hotels
**Tel** 1-877 946 8357 (US).
**Tel** 0800 3252 5252 (UK).
**www**.starwood.com

### Westin
**Tel** 1-800 228 3000 (US).
**Tel** 0800 3259 5959 (UK).
**www**.starwood.com

# Choosing a Hotel

The hotels in this guide have been selected across a wide range of price categories for the excellence of their facilities, location, or character. The chart below lists the hotels in price categories within each chapter of the book. Many hotels have business facilities, gyms, and swimming pools, but only those worth mentioning are listed.

**PRICE CATEGORIES**
The following price ranges are for a standard double room (or single dorm bed) and taxes per night during the high season. Breakfast is not included.
¥ Under ¥200
¥¥ ¥200–¥400
¥¥¥ ¥400–¥800
¥¥¥¥ ¥800–¥1400
¥¥¥¥¥ Over ¥1400

## BEIJING

### Beijing City Youth Hostel Beijing (Chengshi Guoji Qingnian Lüshe)    ¥
*Beijing Zhan Qian Jie 1–5, Dongcheng* **Tel** *(010) 6525 8066* **Fax** *(010) 6525 9066* **Rooms** *200*    **Map** *4 F1*

Among the best value in budget accommodations, this hostel is extremely convenient – located next to the Beijing Railway for those with early morning trains to catch. There's the option of very reasonably priced twin rooms for shoestringers who want a bit of privacy, and YHA members get discounts. Fax and Internet available. **www**.centralhostel.com

### Far East International Youth Hostel (Yuan Dong Qingnian Lüshe)    ¥
*Tieshuxie Jie 90, Xuanwu* **Tel** *(010) 5195 8811* **Fax** *(010) 6318 0324* **Rooms** *160*    **Map** *3 B2*

The city's most charming YHA hostel, with dorms and private rooms available in a pleasantly decorated conventional hotel building and a courtyard house across the street. The surrounding area was an Imperial-era red light district and maintains its lively atmosphere. Walking distance to the subway and Tian'an Men Square. **www**.fareastyh.com

### Red Hotel (Ruixiu Binguan)    ¥¥
*Chunxiu Lu 10* **Tel** *(010) 6416 7810* **Fax** *(010) 6416 7600* **Rooms** *36*

This establishment was formerly a hostel, but has been transformed into a budget boutique hotel. Rooms feature dark wooden floors, faux-antique furnishings, and multi-jet capsule showers. Accommodation is available on a short- and long-term basis. **www**.red-hotel.com

### Templeside House Hostel (Guangji Lin Guoji Qingnian Lüshe)    ¥¥
*Liu He Er Tiao, Fucheng Men Nei Dajie, Xicheng* **Tel** *&* **Fax** *(010) 6617 2571* **Rooms** *9*    **Map** *1 A4*

This spruced-up traditional courtyard house in the hush of the hutong is within walking distance of the White Dagoba Temple and other sights, major Xi Dan shopping, and a subway station. Dorm beds to double rooms share modern shower facilities, laundromat, and a courtyard bar. **www**.templeside.com

### Guxiang 20    ¥¥¥
*Nanluoguxiang 20, Dongcheng* **Tel** *(010) 6400 5566* **Fax** *(010) 6400 3658* **Rooms** *28*

The highlight of this small boutique hotel is its setting, along one of the city's most interesting hutong alleys. From the outside the hotel looks like a traditional, comfy old house but the interior is modern and stylish, and the rooms have excellent bathrooms. However, staff do not speak great English. **www**.guxiang20.com

### Hotel Kapok    ¥¥¥
*Donghuamen Dajie 16, Dongcheng* **Tel** *(010) 6525 9988* **Fax** *(010) 6528 9512* **Rooms** *89*

A stone's throw away from the Forbidden City and Tian'an Men Square, Hotel Kapok's grid-like exterior is eye-catching, as is the bamboo-filled reception area. Rooms, especially those in the courtyard, are equally as stylish. The hotel opened in 2006 and was designed by renowned architect Zhu Pei. **www**.kapokhotelbeijing.com

### Lu Song Yuan Binguan    ¥¥¥
*Banchang Hutong 22, Dongcheng* **Tel** *(010) 6404 0436* **Fax** *(010) 6403 0418* **Rooms** *50*    **Map** *2 D3*

The details – paper lamps mounted over the beds, beautifully painted ceilings, antique door fixtures – are similar to those you'd find in other courtyard hotels, but here they add up to a more comfy, lived-in atmosphere, although unfortunately over-zealous modernisation has stripped the hotel of some of its charm. **www**.the-silk-road.com

### Commune by the Great Wall Kempinski (Changcheng Jiaoxia de Gongshe)    ¥¥¥¥
*The Great Wall, exit 16, Shuiguan Badaling Highway* **Tel** *(010) 8118 1888* **Fax** *(010) 8118 1866* **Rooms** *57*

An hour from Beijing, the Commune enjoys a privileged location nestled in a private grove beneath the Great Wall. Choose from eleven stunning villa designs by different Asian architects and enjoy butler service, private access to the Wall, and a clubhouse. Service can be indifferent. **www**.commune.com.cn/en/

### Hotel Cote Cour    ¥¥¥¥
*Yan Yue Hutong 70, Dongcheng* **Tel** *(010) 6512 8020* **Rooms** *14*

This small courtyard hotel blends traditional Chinese design with antique furniture and provides a wonderful retreat. Breakfast is complimentary and served in the garden in summer, and there is a stylish, contemporary residents' only bar. The staff speaks excellent English. **www**.hotelcotecourbj.com

**Key to Symbols** *see back cover flap*

## Hotel G

*A7 Gongti Xi Lu, Chaoyang* **Tel** *(010) 6552 3600* **Fax** *(010) 6552 3606* **Rooms** *110*

Located at the center of the action in Sanlitun, Beijing's entertainment district, Hotel G is a stylish, well-priced boutique hotel with retro 1960s-style decor and a glamorous vibe. Rooms come with high-speed Wi-Fi, iPod docks, and plasma TVs, and there's a complimentary buffet breakfast. Excellent service. **www**.hotel-g.com

## Traders Hotel Beijing (Guomao Fandian)

*Jianguo Men Wai Dajie 1, Chaoyang* **Tel** *(010) 6505 2277* **Fax** *(010) 6504 3144* **Rooms** *570*

Perfect for business travelers in a hurry – slightly small and dated rooms are stocked with copious office supplies and have complimentary broadband. Service is speedy, and a nicely prepared buffet is constantly replenished. Access to five-star health club facilities in the China World Hotel is offered. Excellent value. **www**.shangri-la.com

## Westin Beijing Chaoyang

*Xinyuan Nan Lu 1, Chaoyang* **Tel** *(010) 5922 8888* **Fax** *(010) 5922 8999* **Rooms** *550*

This is the second Westin in Beijing and is very popular. Suites are worth the extra money, and have televisions that move up and down in front of the bed. Service is extremely friendly and helpful, and feels very personal, despite the size of the hotel. The spa and swimming pool are stunning. **www**.starwoodhotels.com

## Aman at Summer Palace

*Gongmenqian Jie 15* **Tel** *(010) 5987 9008* **Fax** *(010) 5987 9900* **Rooms** *34*

The Aman brand's first property in China is stunning to look at, with guests feeling that they are on the set of a film. Many of the buildings date back 100 years, yet newer buildings reflect traditional Chinese architecture. There are beautiful grounds, private access to the Summer Palace, and three good restaurants. **www**.amanresorts.com

## China World Hotel (Zhongguo Dafandian)

*Jianguo Men Wai Dajie 1* **Tel** *(010) 6505 2266* **Fax** *(010) 6505 3165* **Rooms** *716*

This is the most comprehensively luxurious hotel in Beijing, and one of the top hotels nationwide. The lavish lobby has quickly become a favorite gathering spot for the rich and powerful. Boasts a very fine fusion restaurant and a state-of-the-art health facility. Excellent staff. **www**.shangri-la.com

## China World Summit Wing

*Jianguo Men Wai Dajie 1* **Tel** *(010) 6505 2299* **Fax** *(010) 6505 8811* **Rooms** *278*

Located on the upper floors of the landmark China World Tower, this hotel in the Central Business District guarantees stunning views. Luxurious, over-sized rooms combine elegance with contemporary practicality, and facilities include four excellent restaurants and a great spa. Staff have very high standards. **www**.shangri-la.com

## Grand Hyatt Beijing (Beijing Dongfang Junyue)

*Dong Chang'an Jie 1, Dongcheng* **Tel** *(010) 8518 1234* **Fax** *(010) 8518 0000* **Rooms** *825*          **Map** *4 E1*

In the glimmering Oriental Plaza complex that dominates the central shopping district, no other hotel in Beijing is better located, and few are as well equipped. A few structural glitches predate Hyatt's stewardship, but this is otherwise among the city's finest. Close to the Forbidden City and Tian'an Men Square. **www**.grand.hyatt.com

## Hilton Beijing Wangfujing

*Wangfujing Dajie 8, Dongcheng* **Tel** *(010) 5812 8888* **Fax** *(010) 5812 8886* **Rooms** *255*          **Map** *2 D5*

This large, modern hotel with a rooftop pool is popular with both business and leisure travelers, who are attracted by its excellent executive services and location near the Forbidden City respectively. Rooms and reception areas are modern and open-plan in design. The hotel's Flames Bar is popular with both guests and locals. **www**.hilton.com

## The Opposite House

*Sanlitun Lu 11, Chaoyang* **Tel** *(010) 6417 6688* **Fax** *(010) 6417 7799* **Rooms** *99*

In the heart of lively Sanlitun with its bars and restaurants, The Opposite House combines contemporary Asian design (the exterior is by renowned Japanese architect Kengo Kuma) with attractive but wonderfully functional rooms. It offers great bars and restaurants, and the excellent service is another plus. **www**.theoppositehouse.com

## Park Hyatt Beijing

*Jianguomen Wai Dajie 2, Chaoyang* **Tel** *(010) 8567 1234* **Fax** *(010) 8567 1000* **Rooms** *237*          **Map** *3 A1*

The luxury arm of the Hyatt group opened this hotel in 2008 and immediately won praise for its grown-up ambience and stylish bar and restaurant, which has superb views over the city. The rooms are equally glamorous, with espresso machines and marble baths. Business facilities are excellent. **www**.beijing.park.hyatt.com

## Peninsula Beijing (Wangfu Fandian)

*Jinyu Hutong 8, Dongcheng* **Tel** *(010) 8516 2888* **Fax** *(010) 6510 6311* **Rooms** *530*          **Map** *2 E5*

Combines excellent location with the most distinctive luxuries of any of Beijing's large-scale upmarket hotels, thanks due to management shared with the famed Peninsula Hotel in Hong Kong. Unique are the "Peninsula Academy" courses in subjects like food and antique shopping, and the stunning spa. Close to the subway. **www**.peninsula.com

## Raffles Beijing Hotel (Beijing Fandian Laifoshi)

*Dong Chang'an Jie 33, Dongcheng* **Tel** *(010) 6526 3388* **Fax** *(010) 6527 3838* **Rooms** *171*          **Map** *4 D1*

Sections of the Beijing Hotel have been revamped and re-staffed by the Singapore Raffles group to produce one of Beijing's best addresses. The large old rooms in the original building combine early 1900s charm, four-poster beds, and all modern conveniences, along with views of the capital's main thoroughfare. **www**.beijing.raffles.com

### Shangri-la Hotel Beijing (Beijing Xiangggelila Fandian)

*Zizhuyuan Lu 29, Haidian,* **Tel** *(010) 6841 2211* **Fax***(010) 6481 8003* **Rooms** *670*

Shangri-la's first property in Beijing, inconveniently but peacefully located in the western part of the city. Rooms have top-flight amenities and a pleasantly sleek decor. The excellent garden is also home to a koi pond and various pavilions, and makes the hotel feel more like a retreat. There is also a spa. **www**.shangri-la.com

## HEBEI, TIANJIN, & SHANXI

### CHENGDE Mountain Villa Hotel (Shanzhuang Binguan)

*Xiao Nanmen 127* **Tel** *(0314) 209 5511* **Fax** *(0314) 203 4143* **Rooms** *370*

Six buildings offer a wide range of accommodations from budget traveler basic rooms to well-appointed four-star luxury in high-ceilinged rooms, and multiple restaurants. Basic business facilities available. The hotel complex is located directly opposite the main entrance to the mountain resort. Some guests have complained that the rooms smell of smoke.

### CHENGDE Qi Wang Lou

*Bi Feng Men Dong Lu Bei 1 (just left of main park entrance)* **Tel** *(0314) 202 4385* **Fax** *(0314) 202 1904* **Rooms** *80*

Splendid 18th-century buildings in a courtyard setting on the edge of the mountain resort, once favored by the Qianlong emperor. Fitted with every modern convenience, it is the first choice of Communist Party bigwigs. Reasonably small, the setting and facilities provide an intimate, comfortable stay. Closed for winter (Nov–Mar).

### DATONG Yungang International Hotel (Yungang Guoji Jiudian)

*Daxi Jie 38* **Tel** *(0352) 586 9999* **Fax** *(0352) 586 9666* **Rooms** *236*

Located in the very center of town but off a quiet alleyway. This is a four-star hotel run by experienced management from Beijing's long-established Jianguo Hotel, who know how to look after foreign clientele. Rooms are good value and the hotel has two restaurants. Conveniently located. **www**.ygih.com

### DATONG Datong Binguan

*Yingbin Xi Lu 37* **Tel** *(0352) 586 8666* **Fax** *(0352) 586 8200* **Rooms** *221*

A large, stately building with an audacious formal lobby and meeting rooms on every floor. Cavernous hallways lead to rooms blessed with balconies and sufficiently furnished to warrant a four-star rating. This large complex also provides reasonably substantial business facilities. Room discounts are available online. **www**.datonghotel.com

### PINGYAO Deju Yuan Folk-Style Guesthouse (Deju Yuan Minfeng Binguan)

*Xi Da Jie 43* **Tel** *(0354) 568 5266* **Fax** *(0354) 5685366* **Rooms** *19*

A travelers' rest since the Ming dynasty, when merchants would come to do business at the bank across the street, it now attracts foreigners such as former French president Valéry Giscard d'Estaing. Rooms of various sizes are located around a beautiful courtyard and provide some respite from the busy streets of Pingyao. **www**.pydjy.net

### PINGYAO Tian Yuan Kui Hotel (Tian Yuan Kui Ke Zhan)

*Nan Da Jie 73* **Tel** *(0354) 568 0069* **Fax** *(0354) 568 3052* **Rooms** *25*

Delightfully minimal rooms – black stone floors, simple bathrooms, and antique beds and furnishings – set in a 300-year-old courtyard mansion. Modern conveniences such as air-con, wireless internet and 24-hour hot water are on offer for the less austerely inclined. The limited number of rooms ensures a more intimate stay. **www**.pytyk.com

### SHANHAIGUAN Friendly Cooperate Hotel (Yihe Jiudian)

*Nan Hai Xi Lu 4* **Tel** *(0335) 593 9069* **Fax** *(0335) 507 0351* **Rooms** *37*

Simple two-star hotel with three-star standards of larger bathrooms and decent furnishings, as good as it gets in Shanhaiguan. Conveniently located just one block from the railway station and close to the main south entrance to the old city. The hotel provides one restaurant but no bar. The free breakfast is not particularly recommended.

### SHIJIAZHUANG Yanchun Garden Hotel (Yanchun Huayuan Jiudian)

*Zhongshan Dong Lu 195* **Tel** *(0311) 8667 1188* **Fax** *(0311) 8604 8689* **Rooms** *185*

An escape from the ubiquitous L-shaped rooms of Chinese hotels, interior spaces here fit with this five-star hotel's unusual rippling frontage. It's well located two blocks east of the railway station and next to a park. Children and adults alike will be entertained by its unusual restaurants. **www**.gardenhotel.com.cn

### SHIJIAZHUANG Hebei Century Hotel (Hebei Shiji Dafandian)

*Zhongshan Xi Lu 145* **Tel** *(0311) 8703 6699* **Fax** *(0311) 8703 8866* **Rooms** *439*

Above average service, sizeable rooms with slightly more adventurous decor than the average Chinese five-star hotel. Commendable facilities are all housed in a shiny glass tower west of the city center. Among the leisure facilities provided, the hotel boasts no less than four restaurants and two bars. **www**.hebei-centuryhotel.com

### TAIYUAN Jingang Hotel (Jingang Dajiudian)

*Binzhou Bei Lu 37* **Tel** *(0351) 472 8888* **Fax** *(0351) 472 8333* **Rooms** *300*

Located in the city center, featuring light and airy rooms with rounded windows and friendly staff under local management. Free broadband, indoor swimming pool, and central location near Yingze Park and Wuyi Place. Half-day prices are available for travelers in transit. **www**.jgjt.net/ jgjt-jdjj.htm

**Key to Price Guide** *see p554* **Key to Symbols** *see back cover flap*

## TAIYUAN World Trade Hotel (Shanxi Guomao Dafandian) 🛰️ 🍴 🍷 Ⓦ ¥¥¥

*Fuxi Jie 69* **Tel** *(0351) 868 8888* **Fax** *(0351) 868 8000* **Rooms** *398*

Occupying the 23rd to 41st floors of the 42-story Shanxi World Trade Center, the tallest building in the province. Large rooms have even larger multi-mirrored bathrooms featuring both shower and bath. Helpful touch-screen computer guide located on 1st floor. Choice of four restaurants available. **www**.sxwtc.com

## TIANJIN Hyatt Regency (Kaiyue Fandian) 🛰️ 🍴 🍷 Ⓦ ¥¥¥

*Jiefang Bei Lu 219* **Tel** *(022) 2330 1234* **Fax** *(022) 2331 1234* **Rooms** *360*

A riverside tower with standard business hotel furnishings, well-served on the catering front with both southern and northern style Chinese restaurants, plus Japanese and Western. However, the rooms and lobby are a little dark. The hotel is just across the river from the European architecture of the former foreign concessions. **www**.tianjin.regency.hyatt.com

## TIANJIN Sheraton Tianjin (Xilaideng Dajiudian) 🛰️ 🍴 🍷 Ⓦ ¥¥¥

*Zijin Shan Lu, Hexi* **Tel** *(022) 2334 3388* **Fax** *(022) 2335 8740* **Rooms** *296*

Set in gardens on the edge of a large park, the Sheraton offers some escape from the noise of the city, with classically furnished rooms and top class service. There are Chinese, Western, and Japanese restaurants. Rooms with a garden view are the most pleasant. No in-room Wi-Fi. **www**.starwoodhotels.com

## WUTAI SHAN Guangren Temple (Guangren Si) 📧 🍴 ¥

*Taihuai Zhen* **Tel** *(0350) 654 5352* **Rooms** *20*

Experience life in a monastery, fall asleep to the scent of incense wafting through the air, and wake up to the low moan of chanting Tibetan monks. Rooms are appropriately ascetic, though many have en suite bathrooms. Guests are invited to share breakfast with resident monks. Preferable for hardy travelers. Payment by donation rather than a specific price.

## WUTAI SHAN Wolong Binguan 📧 🍴 ¥¥

*Taihuai Zhen Jiayou Zhan Duimian (opp. filling station)* **Tel** *(0350) 654 5037* **Fax** *(0350) 654 5688* **Rooms** *100*

The largest hotel in Wutai Shan gives travelers a rest from the slightly impersonal government-owned places. The owners do their best to make up for the smallish rooms. One of the few hotels located on the east side of the Qingshui River, you can dine in the hotel restaurant, though you will need to go elsewhere for a bar.

## WUTAI SHAN Yinhai Shanzhuang 📧 🍴 🍷 Ⓦ ¥¥¥

*Wutaishan Yinhai Shanzhuang* **Tel** *(0350) 654 3676* **Fax** *(0350) 654 3679* **Rooms** *83*

Though rated a three-star, this is the classiest place in the valley. Rooms are clean, and bathrooms look as though they belong in a five-star hotel. Located south of town, many rooms have mountain views. Basic business facilities are available and a restaurant and bar will provide for those happy to stay put.

# SHANDONG & HENAN

## JI'NAN Crowne Plaza Ji'nan (Ji'nan Guihe Huangguan Jiari Jiudian) 🛰️ 🍴 🍷 Ⓦ 🏊 ¥¥¥

*Tian Di Tan Lu 3* **Tel** *(0531) 8602 9999* **Fax** *(0531) 8602 3333* **Rooms** *306*

Fully-equipped upmarket hotel with Ji'nan's largest rooms, some with views of Daming Lake and, on a clear day, the Yellow River. Others offer views to the mountains across the city center. Rooms are beginning to show their age, but bonuses include a swimming pool, travel agent desk, and free broadband in rooms. **www**.ichotelsgroup.com

## KAIFENG Dongjing Hotel (Dongjing Dafandian) 📧 Ⓦ 🔧 🏊 ¥¥

*Yingbin Lu 99,* **Tel** *(0378) 398 9388* **Fax** *(0378) 393 8861* **Rooms** *245*

A well-worn "garden style" hotel located around a sizeable goldfish-stocked pond within the city walls. Very popular and often booked up, despite the number of rooms. Numerous staff stand at every corner, ready to assist with guests' every need. Several rooms have balconies. Substantial business services (including translation and secretarial) also provided.

## KAIFENG Kaifeng Binguan 📧 🍴 🍷 Ⓦ ¥¥¥

*Ziyou Lu Zhongduan 66* **Tel** *(0378) 595 5589* **Fax** *(0378) 595 3086* **Rooms** *184*

Enormous hotel built in the Neo-classical Chinese style. Comfortable, but dark, rooms are furnished with traditional Chinese furniture, complete with large bathrooms with bathtub. Noticeably quieter than one would expect given the noise of the street. Built around a large rock garden. Offers three restaurants and a separate café, plus it's near the night market.

## LUOYANG Jing'an Peony Plaza (Jing'an Mudan Cheng) 📧 🛰️ 🍴 🍷 Ⓦ 🔧 ¥¥¥

*Nanchang Lu 2* **Tel** *(0379) 6468 1111* **Fax** *(0379) 6493 0303* **Rooms** *200*

This four-star hotel is situated close to the Development Zone. Rooms are typical well-appointed business standard, although the beds can be hard. Rotating restaurant located on 25th floor, art gallery featured in the lobby. Staff are very friendly and helpful. Good business facilities available. **www**.jingan-peonyplaza.com

## LUOYANG Peony Hotel (Mudan Dajiudian) 🛰️ 🍴 🍷 Ⓦ 🔧 ¥¥¥

*Zhongzhou Xi Lu 15* **Tel** *(0379) 6468 0000* **Fax** *(0379) 6485 6999* **Rooms** *165*

This Chinese-Hong Kong joint venture hotel is located opposite Wangcheng Park. Spacious rooms are decorated with leopard skin carpet and equipped with shower and/or bath. A shopping arcade featuring local souvenirs is located in the spacious lobby. Staff excel at being friendly. Good business facilities available. **www**.peonyhotel.net

### QINGDAO Crowne Plaza Qingdao

🖥 🍴 🍸 �🅦     ¥¥¥

*Xianggang Zhong Lu 76* **Tel** *(0532) 8571 8888* **Fax** *(0532) 8571 6666* **Rooms** *388*

The busiest international hotel in town, with the best location and services to match, including an excellent Brazilian BBQ and pastry counter. Justly popular with both visiting business people and discerning holidaymakers – golf clubs can often be spotted about the lobby. **www**.ichotelsgroup.com

### QINGDAO Grand Regency Hotel Qingdao (Qingdao Lijing Dajiudian)

🖥 🍴 🍸 �Ⓦ     ¥¥¥¥

*Xianggang Zhong Lu 110* **Tel** *(0532) 8588 1818* **Fax** *(0532) 8588 1888* **Rooms** *393*

The first five-star hotel in Qingdao, the Grand Regency has excellent staff and even better facilities, including a health club, billiards room, squash courts, a swimming pool, tennis center, and a bowling alley. Excellent location at the edge of the city, quick access to both recreational and business venues. **www**.grandregencyqd.com

### QUFU Queli Hotel (Queli Binshe)

🍴 🍸 �Ⓦ     ¥¥¥

*Queli Jie 1* **Tel** *(0537) 486 6523* **Fax** *(0537) 486 6524* **Rooms** *165*

Conveniently located Neo-classical Chinese style hotel, a bit worn but comfortable. Rooms have views of the Confucian Temple and Confucian Mansion. Service is straight-faced but there have been incidents of overcharging foreign tourists in the restaurant. This is former Chinese president Jiang Zemin's choice of Qufu accommodations. **www**.quelihotel.com

### QUFU Kong's West Graden Hotel (Kongfu Xiyuan)

🍴 Ⓦ     ¥¥¥

*Ban Bi Jie 8* **Tel** *(0537) 442 3666* **Fax** *(0537) 422 3888* **Rooms** *35*

Perhaps the finest classical Chinese hotel in China. Gorgeous five-star accommodation built in ancient designs with sliding wooden doors and glass hallways. The stunning, spacious rooms are furnished with traditional, yet functional, furnishings. Bathrooms are immaculate, as is the service. Offers two restaurants but no bar. Closes in winter (Nov–Feb).

### TAI'AN Tai Shan Overseas Chinese Hotel (Tai Shan Huaqiao Dasha)

🖥 🍴 🍸 Ⓦ     ¥¥¥

*Dongyue Dajie 15* **Tel** *(0538) 822 0001* **Fax** *(0538) 822 8171* **Rooms** *209*

Rooms provide comfortable furnishings, and computer access, but more importantly offer views of Tai Shan. Bathrooms are only adequate and cheaper rooms are definitely a step down in quality. Leisure facilities like mini-golf and a spa are available. Staff is attentive. **www**.huaqiaohotel.com

### WEIHAI Golden Bay Hotel (Jinhaiwan Guoji Fandian)

🖥 🍴 🍸 Ⓦ 🏊     ¥¥¥

*Beihuanhai Lu 128* **Tel** *(0631) 568 8777* **Fax** *(0631) 568 8796* **Rooms** *154*

The Golden Bay Hotel's location along the quiet, golden sand Jinhai Wan certainly makes up for its distance from the town center. Rooms are spacious, and most have ocean views. The views from the restaurants are reason enough to stay here. Heated saltwater swimming pool and private beach. Free broadband. **www**.gbhotel.com.ch

### YANTAI Golden Gulf Hotel (Jinhaiwan Jiudian)

🖥 🍴 🍸 Ⓦ     ¥¥¥

*Haian Lu 34* **Tel** *(0535) 663 6999* **Fax** *(0535) 663 2699* **Rooms** *285*

The finest hotel in Yantai with a terrific position between the foot of the Yantai Shan park and the Bohai Sea. Large copies of Renaissance paintings in the lobby lend an air of graciousness which extends to the well appointed rooms. The hotel also has no less than five restaurants. Free broadband in rooms. **www**.yantaigoldengulfhotel.com

### ZHENGZHOU Crowne Plaza Zhengzhou

🖥 🍴 🍸 Ⓦ 🛒 🏊     ¥¥¥¥

*Jinshui Lu 115* **Tel** *(0371) 6595 0055* **Fax** *(0371) 6599 0770* **Rooms** *449*

Large columns and a grand staircase in the lobby give this hotel a majestic opera house feel. Well-appointed rooms have wood paneling and bay windows. Swimming pool and fitness facility free for guests. Unsurprisingly for a hotel of this scale, three restaurants are provided and service is outstanding. **www**.ichotelsgroup.com

### ZHENGZHOU Sofitel Zhengzhou

🖥 🍴 🍸 Ⓦ 🏊     ¥¥¥¥

*Chengdong Lu 289* **Tel** *(0371) 6595 0088* **Fax** *(0371) 6595 0080* **Rooms** *240*

This five-star hotel has tastefully decorated rooms and spacious bathrooms. The three-story glass atrium in the lobby features a huge glass flower suspended from the ceiling. There are three bars and two restaurants. Service is everything one would expect from an international upmarket hotel. **www**.sofitel.com

## SHAANXI

### HUA SHAN Xiyue Binguan

🏠 🍴     ¥¥

*Yuquan Lu Zhong Duan* **Tel** *(0913) 436 8299* **Fax** *(0913) 436 8222* **Rooms** *55*

Rooms in this plain hotel with a traditional-style roof tend to be dark and poky, though service is warm. But unlike the rooms at top of the mountain, these come with showers. Get one of the brighter south-facing rooms on the second floor. Located downhill from the entrance to Yuquan Temple at the base of the mountain.

### XI'AN Xi'an Shuyuan Youth Hostel

🏠 🍴 🍸 Ⓦ     ¥

*Nan Dajie Xi Shun Cheng Xiang 2A* **Tel** *(029) 8728 7720* **Fax** *(029) 8728 7720* **Rooms** *40*

Laid out around three large courtyards inside the city wall, attention to detail is evident in the Ming-style decorations of this beautifully restored traditional residence. Tradition means no carpets and simple facilities, but chances to stay in accomodation of this atmosphere and antiquity are few. Free pick up from the railway and coach stations. **www**.hostelxian.com

**Key to Price Guide** *see p554* **Key to Symbols** *see back cover flap*

### XI'AN Jiefang Fandian 🖥️ 🛏️ 🍴 w ⓨⓨ

*Jiefang Lu 181* **Tel** *(029) 8769 8888* **Fax** *(029) 8769 8666* **Rooms** *368*

For those short of time, this hotel is conveniently located opposite both the railway and coach stations. Coaches for the Terracotta Warriors, Famen Si, and Hua Shan leave from outside the hotel. Prices can vary but with some bartering, rates can be reduced by 50% with little fuss.

### XI'AN Xi'an Melody Hotel (Xi'an Meilun Jiudian) 🛏️ 🍴 Y w ⓨⓨ

*Xi Dajie 86* **Tel** *(029) 8728 8888* **Fax** *(029) 8727 3601* **Rooms** *140*

Simply furnished rooms in this new hotel are kept spotless, though service at reception can be abrupt or even non-existent. Enjoy the great bathing facilities which are state-of-the-art, and try to secure one of the rooms with a view of the Drum Tower, directly north of the hotel. Close to the lively Muslim quarter. Airport shuttle stops outside.

### XI'AN Hyatt Regency Xi'an (Kaiyue Fandian) 🛏️ 🍴 Y w ⓨⓨⓨ

*Dong Dajie 158* **Tel** *(029) 8769 1234* **Fax** *(029) 8769 6799* **Rooms** *404*

The most centrally-located of Xi'an's luxury hotels inside the city wall, the Hyatt provides effective, unobtrusive service and smallish but comfortably furnished rooms. Excellent Cantonese cuisine is available at The Pavilion restaurant. Just over a mile (2 km) south of railway and coach stations. **www**.xian.regency.hyatt.com

### YAN'AN Silver Seas International Hotel (Yinhai Guoji Dajiudian) 🛏️ 🍴 Y w 🏊 🛗 ⓨⓨⓨ

*Daqiao Street* **Tel** *(0911) 213 9999* **Fax** *(0911) 213 9666* **Rooms** *212*

One of Yan'an's best four star hotels, offering views of the nearby Bao Pagoda and surrounding hills. The hotel provides broadband access in each room, and has a large swimming pool and gym, and banquet rooms. 10 minutes from the airport, and 5 minutes from the railway station. **www**.yinhaihotel.cn

## SHANGHAI

### Mingtown Hiker Youth Hostel 🖥️ 🛏️ 🍴 Y w ⓨ

*Jiangxi Middle Rd 450* **Tel** *(021) 6329 7889* **Fax** *(021) 6329 8099* **Rooms** *80*

Perfectly located between The Bund, Nanjing Road, and Suzhou Creek, Mingtown is typical of hostel accommodation with noticeboards full of scrawled tips and backpackers waiting on laundry. Poky in places but generally clean, Mingtown offers air conditioned dorms and private rooms, bikes for hire, and a pub.

### Motel 168 (Motai Liansuo Lüdian) 🛏️ 🍴 Y w 🛗 ⓨⓨ

*Yan'an Xi Rd 1119* **Tel** *(021) 5117 7777* **Rooms** *510*

Part of a budget chain, Motel 168 offers no-frills accommodation with clean, compact rooms, and feature walls in funky colours. There are currently more than a dozen branches in Shanghai, but the Yan'an Xi Road location, near Jing'an Temple, is the best placed for sightseeing. **www**.motel168.com

### Okura Garden Hotel Shanghai (Hua Yuan Fandian) 🛏️ 🍴 Y w 🏊 🛗 🛗 ⓨⓨⓨ

*Maoming South Rd 58* **Tel** *(021) 6415 1111* **Fax** *(021) 6415 8866* **Rooms** *492*

This Japanese-managed luxury hotel has an almost unsurpassed location, close to the subway, the French Concession and vibrant Maoming Lu. Lush, pleasant gardens, drinkable tap water in marble bathrooms, and staff with excellent language ability complete the plush picture. Business center available. **www**.gardenhotelshanghai.com

### Old House Inn (Lao Shiguang) 🛏️ 🍴 Y w 🛗 ⓨⓨⓨ

*No. 16, Lane 351 Huashan Rd* **Tel** *(021) 6248 6118* **Fax** *(021) 6249 6869* **Rooms** *12*

Perhaps the best of Shanghai's few boutique hotels, the Old House Inn is central yet peaceful with the creaking of wooden floors likely to be all you will hear. Delightful old furniture highlights the dozen unique rooms; shuttered windows open onto a courtyard. There is an innovative Western restaurant downstairs. **www**.oldhouse.cn

### Tai Yuan Villa (Tai Yuan Bieshu) 🛏️ 🍴 Y w 🛗 ⓨⓨⓨ

*Taiyuan Rd 160, near Yongjia Rd* **Tel** *(021) 6472 5222* **Fax** *(021) 6473 2277* **Rooms** *19*

Perfect for history buffs, this 1920s mansion has housed Ho Chi Minh and Kim Il Sung, and was home to Jiang Qing (Mao's last wife). Inside, polished wood and curios abound while outside is a delightful garden in which to relax.

### Dong Hu Hotel 🛏️ 🍴 Y w 🏊 🛗 🛗 ⓨⓨⓨⓨ

*Dong Hu Rd 70* **Tel** *(021) 6415 8158* **Fax** *(021) 6415 7759* **Rooms** *280*

A stone's throw from bustling Huaihai Road, this lush garden hotel is encircled with high walls that make it a haven and help emphasize its long history. The newer sections lack character so aim for Building 1, with its traditional Chinese furniture. **www**.donghuhotel.com

### Hotel Equatorial Shanghai (Shanghai Guoji Guidu Dajiudian) 🛏️ 🍴 Y w 🏊 🛗 🛗 ⓨⓨⓨⓨ

*Yan'an West Rd 65* **Tel** *(021) 6248 1688* **Fax** *(021) 6248 1773* **Rooms** *509*

Possibly the best value four-star option in town, perfectly located opposite leafy Jing'an Park and a five-minute walk to Jing'an Temple and the nearby subway station. Rooms are quiet, despite the proximity to the Yan'an overpass. Convenient business center with wireless high-speed Internet. **www**.equatorial.com

## Jia Shanghai

*West Nanjing Rd 931* **Tel** *(021) 6217 9000* **Fax** *(021) 6287 9001* **Rooms** *55*

With just 55 rooms – plus Issimo, one of Shanghai's best Italian restaurants – this is the city's most deluxe boutique hotel. The hotel is a renovated 1930s townhouse and rooms are styled in blond wood with leather sofas and hi-tech in-room entertainment. The two penthouse suites have over-the-top theatrical designs. **www**.jiashanghai.com

## Jin Jiang Hotel

*Maoming South Rd 59* **Tel** *(021) 6258 2582* **Fax** *(021) 6472 5588* **Rooms** *515*

Once known as the Cathay Mansions and the scene of some important political events, this famous garden hotel in the French Concession has restyled itself for the 21st century. Rooms are elegant, facilities numerous, and the surrounding area has superb restaurants. **www**.jinjianghotels.com

## Pudong Shangri-La Shanghai (Pudong Xianggelila Dajiudian)

*Fucheng Rd 33, Pudong* **Tel** *(021) 6882 8888* **Fax** *(021) 6882 6688* **Rooms** *957*

This glamorous hotel with its elegant lobby, and the modern addition of the Grand Tower, provides the best of both worlds. Shangri-La is justly famed for its service standards, and many rooms have fine views over the river to the European architecture of the Bund. Basement nightclub is popular with expats. **www**.shangri-la.com

## Fairmont Peace Hotel

*East Nanjing Rd 20* **Tel** *(021) 6321 6888* **Fax** *(021) 6329 1888* **Rooms** *270*

Historically, Shanghai's most famous heritage hotel, located in Sir Victor Sassoon's Art Deco style building overlooking the Bund. The Fairmont has been sensitively renovated, evoking the 1930s whilst offering chic, modern comforts and stylish restaurants and facilities, including the famous Jazz Bar. **www**.fairmont.com/peacehotel

## Grand Hyatt Shanghai (Shanghai Jinmao Junyue Dajiudian)

*Jinmao Dasha, Century Ave 88* **Tel** *(021) 5049 1234* **Fax** *(021) 5049 1111* **Rooms** *555*

The Jinmao Dasha's spike is visible for miles – the hotel begins at the 53rd of 88 storys in one of China's tallest buildings. Large, ultra-modern rooms with big bathrooms and separate showers have bird's-eye views over the Bund and Pudong. Provides a variety of excellent restaurants and plenty of nightlife. **www**.shanghai.grand.hyatt.com

## Hilton Hotel (Xierdun Dajiudian)

*Huashan Rd 250* **Tel** *(021) 6248 0000* **Fax** *(021) 6248 3848* **Rooms** *772*

A favorite of business travelers since 1987, the Hilton's number one status seems to be under threat as newer hotels emerge. Still, service is first rate and the spa's luxury treatments and opulent setting are superb. The top-floor bar commands enviable views of the French Concession. Near Jing'an Park and Temple. **www**.hilton.com

## JW Marriott Hotel Tomorrow Square Shanghai

*Nanjing West Rd 399* **Tel** *(021) 5359 4969* **Fax** *(021) 6375 5988* **Rooms** *342*

Wood-panelled doors, exceptional service and remarkable 360 degree views of People's Square and central Shanghai. Just checking in on the 38th floor with its floor-to-wall windows is an exhilarating experience. A contender for Shanghai's best hotel. Also close to all main attractions. **www**.marriott.com

## Le Royal Méridien Shanghai

*Nanjing East Rd 789* **Tel** *(021) 3318 9999* **Fax** *(021) 6361 3388* **Rooms** *770*

Each room in the chic Méridien on People's Square offers a wonderful panorama (for when you tire of the plasma screen) and a vast bathroom. Elsewhere in this labyrinthine hotel are noteworthy dining options (the French and Italian restaurants are splendid), and an indoor pool bathed in natural light. **www**.lemeridien.com/royalshanghai

## Park Hyatt Shanghai

*Century Avenue 100, Pudong* **Tel** *(021) 6888 1234* **Fax** *(021) 6888 3400* **Rooms** *174*

Designed by Hong Kong-based designer Tony Chi as a "modern Chinese" residence. The lobby is on the 86th floor and an incredibly high bar and restaurant are on floors 91–93. All rooms have world-class facilities, and the views (from public areas too) are jaw-dropping. **www**.parkhyattshanghai.com

## The Peninsula Shanghai

*The Bund 32* **Tel** *(021) 2327 2888* **Fax** *(021) 2327 2000* **Rooms** *62*

One of Shanghai's finest hotels, offering superlative luxury and fabulous views of the river and Pudong skyline from its rooms, restaurants, bars, and most notably from the extensive open-air terrace of Sir Elly's Bar & Restaurant. Rooms offer cutting-edge technology and service standards are exquisite. Mini mall of luxury stores. **www**.peninsula.com

## Portman Ritz-Carlton Shanghai (Shanghai Poteman Lijia Jiudian)

*Nanjing West Rd 1376* **Tel** *(021) 6279 8888* **Fax** *(021) 6279 8800* **Rooms** *590*

The Ritz-Carlton forgoes a grand lobby for in-room check-in. Thoughtful and attentive service intelligently anticipates guests' needs, with discretion when required. The tower stands amidst a sea of top-notch shopping, banking, ticket agencies, and other conveniences. Comfortable rooms and expansive views. **www**.ritzcarlton.com

## St. Regis Shanghai (Shanghai Ruiji Hongta Dajiudian)

*Dong Fang Rd 889, Pudong* **Tel** *(021) 5050 4567* **Fax** *(021) 6875 6789* **Rooms** *328*

Modern, stylish, and beautifully furnished rooms with large bathrooms and proper shower cubicles. 24-hour butler service at the push of a button. Free daily cocktails and canapés and other VIP services available to all guests, including clothes pressing on arrival. Not surprisingly, this hotel is very popular. **www**.stregis.com/shanghai

**Key to Price Guide** *see p554* **Key to Symbols** *see back cover flap*

### The Westin Shanghai (Shanghai Weisiting Dafandian)

*Henan Zhong Rd 88* **Tel** *(021) 6335 1888* **Fax** *(021) 6335 2888* **Rooms** *550*

The Westin's lotus-topped tower is a Shanghai landmark in the heart of downtown shopping. The colorful lobby, with its internally-lit glass staircase, extends to the stylish modernity of the rooms. Bathrooms have torrential overhead showers and pampering is available at a branch of the famous Banyan Tree Spa. **www**.westin.com/shanghai

## JIANGSU & ANHUI

### HEFEI Hilton Hefei

*Shengli Rd 198* **Tel** *(0551) 280 8888* **Fax** *(0551) 280 8889* **Rooms** *561*

Well-located near the city center and the train station, this is one of the city's most popular hotels with business travelers. It has plenty to offer the leisure traveler too, with clean, comfortable rooms, excellent dining, and a spacious pool and fitness center. **www**.hilton.com

### HEFEI Holiday Inn Hefei (Hefei Gujing Jiari Jiudian)

*Changjiang Dong Rd 1104* **Tel** *(0551) 220 6666* **Fax** *(0551) 220 1166* **Rooms** *388*

The first international hotel in Anhui's capital and still the best option in downtown Hefei. Some rooms enjoy a panoramic sweep of the city and Xiaoyaojin Park, as does the revolving restaurant on the 29th floor. Runs a complimentary airport shuttle service, and just 2 miles (3 km) from the railway station. **www**.holidayinn.com

### NANJING Central Hotel (Nanjing Zhongxin Dajiudian)

*Zhongshan Rd 75* **Tel** *(025) 8473 3888* **Fax** *(025) 8473 3999* **Rooms** *360*

A good choice for the budget-conscious wishing to have a more "local" experience as it caters to a largely Chinese clientele, with plentiful eating options, meeting rooms, and business facilities. The outdoor pool allows for a spot of city sunbathing. The hotel is conveniently located for the business and shopping districts. **www**.njcentralhotel.com

### NANJING Crowne Plaza Hotel and Suites Nanjing

*Han Zhong Rd 89* **Tel** *025 8471 8888* **Fax** *025 8471 9999* **Rooms** *290*

A convenient hotel for both business and leisure travelers located in the center with the best views in the city; considerable business facilities plus a variety of dining options. Health club with indoor pool and sauna, department stores, and an art exhibition hall housed in the same building. **www**.crowneplaza.com

### NANJING Parkview Dingshan Hotel (Dingshan Huayuan Dajiudian)

*Cha Er Rd 90* **Tel** *(025) 5880 2888* **Fax** *(025) 5882 1729* **Rooms** *555*

A secluded hillside hotel divided into various sections; the main five-star hotel, a four-star wing popular with families, serviced apartments, and a separate 14-bedroom villa. Has a pleasant tree-shaded outdoor swimming pool and a busy Chinese restaurant serving Huaiyang dishes. **www**.nanjing-dingshan.com

### NANJING Westin Nanjing

*Zhongyang Rd 201* **Tel** *(025) 8556 8888* **Fax** *(025) 8556 9999* **Rooms** *234*

The Westin has raised five-star hotel standards in Nanjing with its modern hotel located in the city's business district and overlooking Xuanwu Lake. Rooms and suites are decorated in contemporary style and feature high-technology amenities. Business facilities are excellent, as are the restaurants, pool, and spa. **www**.starwood.com/westin

### NANJING Metro Park Hotel (Nanjing Weijing Guoji Dajiudian)

*Zhongshan Dong Rd 319* **Tel** *(025) 8480 8888* **Fax** *(025) 8480 9999* **Rooms** *530*

A reliable five-star option in a quieter end of town near the ancient city wall, with views over the nearby lake and mountains plus a good range of restaurants from Italian to local Chinese. Also features a deli serving fresh bread, health club with indoor swimming pool, tennis courts, and a golf simulator. **www**.metroparkhotels.com

### NANJING Sheraton Nanjing Kingsley Hotel and Towers

*Han Zhong Rd 169* **Tel** *(025) 8666 8888* **Fax** *(025) 8666 9999* **Rooms** *350*

A central location, impressive exterior and seamless service make this the best five-star option in town. The interior is both elegant and cozy without being gaudy, while high-level restaurants and bars guarantee good dining and drinking options and fantastic views over the city – try the top floor jazz bar. **www**.sheraton.com

### SUZHOU Shangri-La Hotel Suzhou

*Ta Yuan Rd 168* **Tel** *(0512) 6808 0168* **Fax** *(0512) 6808 1168* **Rooms** *390*

Just ten minutes from most of the Suzhou's best-known sights, the Shangri-La sits atop one of the tallest buildings in the entire province, offering both panoramic views and easy access to the shops and restaurants of Suzhou's commercial district. Excellent facilities. **www**.shangri-la.com

### SUZHOU Garden Hotel Suzhou

*Daicheng Qiao Road 99* **Tel** *(0512) 6778 6778* **Fax** *(0512) 6778 6159* **Rooms** *235*

This famous state guesthouse, established in 1952, has been restyled as a deluxe retreat, featuring an excellent zen spa, leafy garden, and several restaurants, and bars. All buildings are low-rise and in whitewashed, traditional Suzhou style. The hotel has hosted major international politicians and world leaders. **www**.gardenhotelsz.com

## SUZHOU Pan Pacific Suzhou

*Xinshi Rd 259* **Tel** *(0512) 6510 3388* **Fax** *(0512) 6510 0888* **Rooms** *400*

The architecture of this impeccable hotel reflects the heritage of old Suzhou. Canals wind through the quiet, elegant gardens, and the luxurious rooms feature spacious marble bathrooms. Design is memorable from the traditional lobby to the rustic indoor swimming pool. Another tower was added in 2009. **www**.panpacific.com

## SUZHOU Regalia Resort & Spa

*Ligongdi 2* **Tel** *(0512) 6295 0888* **Fax** *(0512) 6895 0260* **Rooms** *50*

This Thai-styled boutique retreat is located a 30-minute cab ride from the city center, and the beautifully styled rooms, terraces, and spa make this a popular weekend getaway for people who live in the region. At night, the views across the lake and surrounding districts are superb. **www**.regalia.com.cn

## TUNXI Best Western Huang Shan Resort & Spa

*Huang Shan Hot Springs Scenic Area* **Tel** *(0559) 251 1818* **Fax** *(0559) 253 8288* **Rooms** *70*

Located in the heart of Huang Shan's famed hot springs area, this hotel in a peaceful setting makes a good base from which to explore the area. Rooms are clean and basic, and staff are friendly. Although the nearby hot springs are not luxurious, they offer welcome relaxation after a day of hiking. **www**.bestwestern.com.cn

## TUNXI Huang Shan Hongta Jiudian

*Huangkou Luyou Dujia Qu* **Tel** *(0559) 232 6666* **Fax** *(0559) 231 3009* **Rooms** *108*

The Hongta has superior facilities, although service is somewhat lacking, and its location in the suburban resort area makes it less convenient for those without a car and driver. The hotel, however, does have two restaurants, and the resort area itself is pleasingly scenic. Broadband available in rooms. **www**.hshongta.com

## TUNXI Huangshan Pine Golf Hotel (Huang Shan Gaoerfu Jiudian)

*Longging 78, Jichang Dadao* **Tel** *(0559) 256 8000* **Fax** *(0559) 256 8111* **Rooms** *293*

This is the best hotel in Huang Shan and the only one with five-star status. Although the service is improving, it lags behind more sophisticated cities on the eastern seaboard. However, the hotel does offer extensive conference facilities and is conveniently located close to Huang Shan's airport. **www**.chinahsgolf.com

# ZHEJIANG & JIANGXI

## HANGZHOU Hyatt Regency Hangzhou

*Hu Bin Rd 28* **Tel** *(0571) 8779 1234* **Fax** *(0571) 8779 1818* **Rooms** *390*

A smarter-than-average horseshoe-shaped mansion, with a vast lobby incorporating cafés and extensive shopping. Many rooms have lake views, and others have private terraces with miniature gardens. The marble bathrooms have separate shower cubicles. Hotel also has a childcare center and large pool. **www**.hangzhou.regency.hyatt.com

## HANGZHOU Radisson Plaza Hotel Hangzhou

*Tiyu Chang Rd 333* **Tel** *(0571) 8515 8888* **Fax** *(0571) 8515 7777* **Rooms** *284*

This slickly-managed shiny tower in the city center, close to West Lake, is so well-equipped with entertainment, fitness, and dining options that you may not want to leave. Large, well-furnished rooms and bathrooms with proper shower cubicles and baths. Personal valet service available on executive floors. **www**.radisson.com

## HANGZHOU Shangri-la Hotel Hangzhou

*Bei Shan Rd 78* **Tel** *(0571) 8797 7951* **Fax** *(0571) 8707 3545* **Rooms** *383*

Two hotels originally reserved for top officials and built in the extensive grounds of a now-vanished temple are now fused into one. Many of their large high-ceilinged rooms overlook West Lake. Quite simply one of the most pleasant hotels in China. Good conference and business facilities. **www**.shangri-la.com

## HANGZHOU Fuchun Resort (Fuchun Shanju)

*Jiangbin 339, Dong Da Dao, Dong Shu Jie* **Tel** *(0571) 6346 1111* **Fax** *(0571) 6346 1222* **Rooms** *110, plus 5 villas*

Probably the Yangzi delta's best resort matching traditional architecture with advanced facilities. The hotel is impressive but Fuchun's cluster of fully-serviced villas is its crowning glory; each with an indoor swimming pavilion and sweeping views of tea-laden terraces. World-class, 18-hole golf course. **www**.fuchunresort.com

## HANGZHOU Sofitel Westlake Hangzhou

*Xi Hu Dadao 333* **Tel** *(0571) 8707 5858* **Fax** *(0571) 8707 8383* **Rooms** *200*

Perched at the end of West Lake, the Sofitel offers smart, colorful interior decor and sharp service. Relatively small scale, this is a deservedly popular choice, with its central, lakeside position, handy for the burgeoning Xi Hu Tiandi bar and restaurant area. Be sure to make a trip to the rooftop bar with splendid lake views. **www**.sofitel.com

## JINGDEZHEN Jinye Hotel (Jinye Dajiudian)

*Cidu Da Dao 1168* **Tel** *(0798) 858 8888* **Fax** *(0798) 856 2233* **Rooms** *228*

Rating three-stars, but the only choice in a city full of tired budget premises, this hotel has clean and comfortable guest rooms. It caters for business too, with basic conference facilities and ADSL broadband available in the more deluxe rooms. A good restaurant serves local specialties as well as pan-China favorites.

**Key to Price Guide** *see p554* **Key to Symbols** *see back cover flap*

### LU SHAN Chevalier Hotel 🖪 🚹 W | ¥¥¥

*Binjiang Rd 68* **Tel** *(0792) 898 8111* **Fax** *(0792) 898 8000* **Rooms** *232*

Lifeless hotel in Jiujiang on the banks of the Yangzi and in need of brightening, but still better than the battered accommodations on Lu Shan itself. Many rooms have views of the river sliding by, and foreign residents gloomily ponder business deals in the unexpectedly good Chinese and Western restaurants.

### NANCHANG Gloria Plaza (Kailai Dajiudian) 🖪 🚹 Y W 🖀 🛅 | ¥¥¥¥

*Yanjiang Bei Dadao 39* **Tel** *(0791) 673 8855* **Fax** *(0791) 673 8533* **Rooms** *327*

Hong Kong-managed four-star hotel right on the Gan River, close to the Tang Wang Ge. Many of the well-maintained rooms have excellent river views. The palatial lobby is an odd mixture of Egyptian, Mexican, and American Indian themes. Broadband Internet access is available in the rooms. **www**.gloriahotels.com

### NANCHANG Regal Hotel (Fuhao Jiudian) 🖪 🚹 Y W 🖀 🛅 | ¥¥¥¥

*Hongcheng Rd 160* **Tel** *(0791) 640 8888* **Fax** *(0791) 640 7777* **Rooms** *234*

Just south of the city center, this sparkling, four-star tower, opened in 2001, is glitzier than the Gloria Plaza but not as well located. Room decor is muted and tasteful in contrast to the extremely busy carpets of the restaurants and other public areas. Amongst other imaginative touches is an accommodation floor for women only.

### PUTUO SHAN Xilei Xiao Zhuang 🖪 🚹 Y W 🛅 | ¥¥¥¥

*Xianghua Jie 1* **Tel** *(0580) 609 1512* **Fax** *(0580) 609 1023* **Rooms** *160*

Next to Puji Si, and a short walk from one of the island's main beaches, the hotel provides varying grades of comfort up to four-star, all better value for money than competitors. The hotel also boasts two restaurants and two bars and extensive business facilities for mixed clientele. **www**.xlxzhotel.com

### WENZHOU Shangri-La Wenzhou 🚹 Y W 🛅 🖀 🛅 | ¥¥¥¥

*Xiangyuan Rd 1* **Tel** *(0577) 8998 8888* **Fax** *(0577) 8998 8899* **Rooms** *409*

In the heart of the business district, this deluxe hotel occupies a city skytower. The Shang Palace Cantonese restaurant serves both Cantonese and local Huaiyang cuisines and there is also a bar, swimming pool, and fitness center. Rooms have all modern facilities such as WiFi, and plasma TV screens. **www**.shangri-la.com

### WENZHOU Wanhao Grand Hotel (Wanhao Shangwu Dajiudian) 🖪 🚹 Y W | ¥¥¥¥

*Wenzhou Dadao* **Tel** *(0577) 8808 9888* **Fax** *(0577) 8808 9222* **Rooms** *200*

Although a fair distance from the center of town and even further from the river, this four-star hotel is far glossier then any of its longer-standing competitors, with modern decor and furniture in comfortable rooms, and staff who try far harder to please. It's also handy for the railway station and the long-distance coach stations.

## HUNAN & HUBEI

### CHANGSHA Hunan Bestride Hotel (Hunan Jiacheng Jiudian) 🖪 🚹 Y W 🛅 | ¥¥¥

*Laodong Xi Rd 215* **Tel** *(0731) 8511 8888* **Fax** *(0731) 8515 3721* **Rooms** *238*

Conveniently closer to the airport than most, this efficient Hong Kong-managed five-star hotel lies a little south of the city center, with conventional rooms rather larger than most. Full facilities include several Western and Chinese restaurants. A lack of other towers in the vicinity means spectacular views are guaranteed. **www**.hnbrhotel.com

### CHANGSHA Dolton Hotel Changsha (Tongcheng Guoji Dajiudian) 🖪 🚹 Y W 🖀 🛅 | ¥¥¥¥

*Shaoshan Bei Rd 159* **Tel** *(0731) 8416 8888* **Fax** *(0731) 8416 9999* **Rooms** *450*

The luxurious Dolton has everything: fresh, comfortably furnished rooms with marble-floored entrances, and every modern facility you could need, plus friendly, courteous staff. The restaurants are popular and it even boasts the largest hotel pool in the province. **www**.dolton-hotel.com

### CHANGSHA Huatian Dajiudian 🖪 🚹 Y W 🖀 🛅 | ¥¥¥¥

*Jiefang Dong Rd 300* **Tel** *(0731) 8444 2888* **Fax** *(0731) 8444 2270* **Rooms** *700*

The unconventionally shaped rooms in the tower are arguably the best in the city, furnished with stylish, comfortable modernity and practicality. Above average bathrooms have proper shower cubicles with massage heads. Staff maintain high standards of English. **www**.huatian-hotel.com

### WUHAN Wuhan Shangri-La Hotel (Wuhan Xianggelila Jiudian) 🖪 🚹 Y W 🖀 🛅 🛅 | ¥¥¥

*Jianshe Dadao 700, Hankou* **Tel** *(027) 8580 6868* **Fax** *(027) 8577 6868* **Rooms** *448*

An efficient and well-run hotel in an otherwise run-down city. The bustling lobby is the favored meeting place of tourists, business travelers, and resident expats alike. The hotel has large, comfortable rooms with spacious, well-fitted bathrooms, and there's a choice of Chinese, Western, and Japanese restaurants. **www**.shangri-la.com

### WUHAN Best Western Premier Mayflowers Hotel 🖪 🚹 Y W 🖀 🛅 | ¥¥¥¥

*Wuluo Rd 385, Wuchang* **Tel** *(027) 6887 1588* **Fax** *(027) 6887 1599* **Rooms** *280*

This hotel is on a par with the best hotels in Hankou and has by far the most comfortable rooms in Wuchang. The well-equipped health club and spacious indoor pool create an enjoyable environment for a workout or swim. Central location to most Wuchang sites. **www**.bwmayflowers.com.cn

### WUHAN Holiday Inn Tian'an Wuhan City Center

*Jiefang Dadao 868, Hankou* **Tel** *(027) 8586 7888* **Fax** *(027) 8584 5353* **Rooms** *355*

A solid choice located in the heart of downtown Wuhan, close to Zhongshan Park, shopping areas, and the former colonial concession district. One of the city's busier upmarket hotels. Recreational facilities include an outdoor pool and tennis court. A cheap airport shuttle is available. **www**.holidayinn.com.cn

### WUHAN Marco Polo Wuhan

*Yanjiang Avenue 159, Hankou* **Tel** *(027) 8277 8888* **Fax** *(027) 8277 8866* **Rooms** *380*

This luxury five-star hotel has well-appointed, contemporary-style rooms; the river-facing rooms are particularly recommended. Popular with business travelers, both for its location and the facilities. There are three restaurants, serving Cantonese and pan-Chinese cuisines, and an excellent buffet restaurant. **www**.marcopolohotels.com

### WULINGYUAN Minnan International Hotel (Minnan Guoji Jiudian)

*Ziwu Xi Rd 18* **Tel** *(0744) 822 8888* **Fax** *(021) 822 9888* **Rooms** *417*

Slightly tired rooms fail to live up to the promise of the shiny lobby in the only four-star hotel in town. It is, however, the best in town, with well-meaning service, not far from the airport (the best choice for those with early morning flights). Convenient for business meetings, there are also two restaurants.

### WULINGYUAN Xiangdian International Hotel

*Senlin Gongyuan* **Tel** *(0744) 571 2999* **Fax** *(0744) 571 2666* **Rooms** *156*

Other hotels' rooms may have the edge over those here, but otherwise there's a genuine four-star level of decor, and very good service. The hotel is close to the Senlin Gongyuan park entrance. The rooms – many with balconies – are arranged around pleasant courtyards, and have sweeping views. **www**.xiangdianhotel.com.cn

# FUJIAN

### FUZHOU Ramada Plaza (Meilun Huameida Guangchang Jiudian)

*Bei Huan Xi Lu 118* **Tel** *(0591) 8788 3999* **Fax** *(0591) 8786 9613* **Rooms** *328*

A fully equipped and spotless if otherwise standard hotel. Situated on the north ring road, it is ideally situated to give quick access to most corners of the city. Good Western and Cantonese restaurants are located within and a business center with Internet, computer, fax, and secretarial service is available. **www**.ramada.com

### FUZHOU Shangri-La

*Xin Quan Nan Lu 9* **Tel** *(0591) 8798 8888* **Fax** *(0591) 9798 8222* **Rooms** *414*

Centrally located and head and shoulders above its competitors in terms of standards of comfort and service. Fuzhou's Shangri-La is utterly luxurious and offers an impressive array of facilities including a large pool. The local restaurants are superb. Provincial room rates make this hotel excellent value for money. **www**.shangri-la.com

### QUANZHOU Quanzhou Jiudian

*Zhuangfu Xiang 22* **Tel** *(0595) 222 89958* **Fax** *(0595) 221 82128* **Rooms** *377*

This is a three-, four-, and five-star hotel, with three separate buildings of different periods all on one site. One wing is sumptuously furnished, but all rooms are in good condition, some offering views of the twin pagodas of the nearby Kaiyuan Si. Extensive conference facilities. **www**.quanzhouhotel.com

### QUANZHOU Xiamen Airlines Quanzhou Hotel

*Fengze Jie 339* **Tel** *(0595) 2216 4888* **Fax** *(0595) 2216 4777* **Rooms** *175*

Nominally a three-star hotel but above average in service and decor, running to higher-end luxuries such as video-on-demand and broadband Internet on some floors. Convenient free shuttle bus to Xiamen Airport. Located in a commercial area slightly west of the older center. **www**.qzair-hotel.com

### WUYI SHAN Wuyi Mountain Villa (Wuyi Shan Zhuang)

*Wuyi Gong* **Tel** *(0599) 525 1888* **Fax** *(0599) 525 2567* **Rooms** *220*

In competition with a local Ramada, but visiting bigwigs have long been happy with this collection of low-rise buildings with hints of local style. Located across the Chongyang Xi river and set in quiet greenery on the edge of the scenic area itself. Rooms vary from the cheap and simple to the four-star; large and well-maintained. **www**.513villa.com

### XIAMEN Crowne Plaza Hotel Harbourview Xiamen

*Zhen Hai Lu 12-8* **Tel** *(0592) 202 3333* **Fax** *(0592) 203 6666* **Rooms** *352*

On the edge of the old town, close to the Hong Kong ferry terminal, and a short walk from the pier for Gulang Yu ferries, this 22-story tower has many rooms with marvellous sea views. An Amex office is located within the hotel and there is broadband Internet access in-room. Good business facilities. **www**.millenniumhotels.com

### XIAMEN Marco Polo Xiamen (Xiamen Mageboluo)

*Jianye Lu 8* **Tel** *(0592) 509 1888* **Fax** *(0592) 509 2888* **Rooms** *318*

A smoothly-run hotel with full four-star amenities, including an open-air pool with poolside bar and views across the Yuandang Lake to the city. The eight-story atrium lobby often echoes to live piano. The hotel caters for large groups with several function rooms and a well-equipped business center. **www**.marcopolohotels.com

**Key to Price Guide** *see p554* **Key to Symbols** *see back cover flap*

### XIAMEN Sheraton Xiamen Hotel

*Jiahe Lu 386-1* **Tel** *(0592) 552 5888* **Fax** *(0592) 553 9088* **Rooms** *360*

Although a little far from the main historic and cultural attractions, one of Xiamen's luxury hotels comes replete with five-star facilities that include an ultra-modern fitness center, sizeable swimming pool, and Xiamen's first spa. Glitzy and modern in design. **www**.starwoodhotels.com

## GUANGDONG & HAINAN

### GUANGZHOU Customs Hotel

*Shamian Dajie 35, Shamian Island* **Tel** *(020) 8110 2388* **Fax** *(020) 8121 8552* **Rooms** *65*

With a Neo-classical front of uncertain date (and uncertain purpose) amongst century-old foreign buildings, this small hotel offers bright and fresh rooms arranged around a central five-story atrium. Set in quiet, leafy Shamian, this offers excellent value for money in otherwise pricey Guangzhou.

### GUANGZHOU Guangdong Victory Hotel

*Shamian Bei Jie 54, Shamian Island* **Tel** *(020) 8121 6688* **Fax** *(020) 8121 6062* **Rooms** *330*

Two colonial-era buildings located on lovely Shamian Island. One is an above average three-star and the other four-star, with a vast choice of food and drink served from twenty restaurants. Service is friendly and efficient. Basic business center with fax and computer access, Internet is available via TV in the rooms. **www**.vhotel.com

### GUANGZHOU Lido Hotel (Lidu Dajiudian)

*Beijing Road 182, Guangzhou* **Tel** *(020) 8332 1988* **Fax** *(020) 8332 3413* **Rooms** *300*

Location at entrance to Beijing Road pedestrian mall sets this mid-range, and otherwise unremarkable hotel apart. Standard two-star features in 30-story building with quick access to city center, nearby subway, and express bus to Hong Kong. Offers business center and executive suite. **www**.lido-hotel.cn

### GUANGZHOU White Swan Hotel (Bai Tian'e Binguan)

*Shamian Nan Jie 1* **Tel** *(020) 8188 6968* **Fax** *(020) 8186 1188* **Rooms** *843*

This hotel is perennially popular, and pleasantly located on Shamian Island. A favorite with tour groups and those in China for adoptions, hence the extensive children's facilities. The hotel offers several dining options, including Chinese, Japanese, and western restaurants. Overlooking the Pearl River. **www**.whiteswanhotel.com

### GUANGZHOU Hotel Canton (Guangzhou Dasha)

*Beijing Road 374* **Tel** *(020) 8318 9888* **Fax** *(020) 8330 1230* **Rooms** *465*

Among the finest of Guangzhou's hotels, with chandeliers, polished stone, and impeccable service. 38 storys of sky-blue glass situated at the top of Beijing Road in the historic city center. Full-service business center and conference rooms. Luxury options include a motor yacht on the Pearl River. **www**.hotel-canton.com

### GUANGZHOU Asia International Hotel (Yazhou Guoji Dajiudian)

*Huan Shi Dong Lu 326, Duan 1* **Tel** *(020) 6128 8888* **Fax** *(020) 6120 6666* **Rooms** *442*

Polished Guangdong marble and granite grace the walls of this 442-room hotel and keep the neon-lit noise outside. Convenient city-center location near club scene. Rooms are spacious and comfortable, and service professional in Guangzhou's most elegant hotel. Great fitness facilities. Dine at the sky-revolving restaurant. **www**.aihotel.com

### GUANGZHOU Garden Hotel (Huayuan Jiudian)

*Huanshi Dong Lu 368* **Tel** *(020) 8333 8989* **Fax** *(020) 8335 0467* **Rooms** *828*

A gargantuan hotel with every facility you can think of. Other mega-hotels may have more restaurants, but the Garden has better service, and its rooms are more comfortable. The facilities include a children's playground, tennis and squash courts, and a shopping arcade. **www**.thegardenhotel.com.cn

### HAINAN Sheraton Sanya Resort (Sanya Xilaideng Dujia Jiudian)

*Yalong Bay National Resort District* **Tel** *(0898) 8855 8855* **Fax** *(0898) 8855 8866* **Rooms** *511*

On a private stretch of beautiful Yalong Bay, this tropical retreat – twice home of the Miss World Finals – is arguably the best beach resort on China's mainland. The enormous open-air teak lobby sets an impressive tone. Equipped with first-rate swimming pools, lagoons and a full program of water sports. **www**.starwoodhotels.com

### HAINAN Sofitel Boao (Hainan Boao Suofeite Dajiudian)

*Boao, Dongyu Island* **Tel** *(0898) 6296 6888* **Fax** *(0898) 6296 6999* **Rooms** *437*

Transformed from a swamp to a world class conference venue, the Sofitel boasts rooms with excellent views which can be enjoyed from balconies or from a freestanding tub in one of the open-plan bathrooms. A one-hour drive from Haikou airport, and 90 minutes from Sanya airport. **www**.accorhotels.com/asia or **www**.sofitel.com

### SHENZHEN Crowne Plaza Shenzhen

*Shennan Dadao 9026, Overseas Chinese Town* **Tel** *(0755) 2693 6888* **Fax** *(0755) 2693 6999* **Rooms** *375*

Shenzhen's first five-star hotel, the grand Venetian exterior finds echoes inside, from the swimming pool adorned with Mediterranean motifs to the highly regarded Italian restaurant, Blue. Nearby theme parks, including the China Folk Cultural Village, make this an attractive location for families, yet the business facilities are also good. **www**.crowneplaza.com

**SHENZHEN Shangri-La Shenzhen (Xianggelila Dajiudian)** 🖼️📶🍴🅦🚄🍽️   ⑨⑨⑨⑨

*Jianshe Lu 1002* **Tel** *(0755) 8233 0888* **Fax** *(0755) 8233 9878* **Rooms** *552*

Despite keen competition, the Shangri-La still has the edge on location (visible from the main border crossing from Hong Kong) and service standards, from lavish lobby to tower-top rotating restaurant, with excellent fitness facilities and Cantonese, Japanese, and American restaurants. **www**.shangri-la.com

# HONG KONG & MACAU

**HONG KONG Mount Davis Youth Hostel** 🖼️   ⑨⑨

*Mt Davis Path, Mt Davis, Hong Kong Island* **Tel** *(852) 2817 5715* **Fax** *(852) 2788 3105* **Rooms** *130 beds*

It's a long trek from the center (by hostel shuttle bus or taxi) and offers barrack-like dorms, but where else can you escape the city bustle, get such great sea views and find such relaxing woodland surroundings for these prices? If you are in need of peace and quiet, this is an ideal, if basic solution. **www**.yha.org.hk

**HONG KONG Caritas Bianchi Lodge** 🖼️   ⑨⑨⑨

*4 Cliff Road, Yau Ma Tei* **Tel** *(852) 2388 1111* **Fax** *(852) 2770 6669* **Rooms** *160*    **Map** *1 B1*

A rather soulless and very basic place that happens to be cheap and well located just off Nathan Road. The old-fashioned rooms are spacious and spotless, and this is an ideal destination for the budget traveler. Located near the Ya Ma Tei subway – handy as the hotel offers no extra facilities and has no restaurant or bar. **www**.caritas-chs.org.hk

**HONG KONG Garden View International House** 🖼️📶🍴   ⑨⑨⑨

*1 MacDonnell Road, Central, Hong Kong Island* **Tel** *(852) 2877 3737* **Fax** *(852) 2845 6263* **Rooms** *130*    **Map** *2 B4*

A good-value option close to the center on Hong Kong Island. The rooms are functional rather than luxurious, the decor is slightly old-fashioned but there is a pool and you are only a short stroll from the Peak tram, Hong Kong Park, and the Botanical Gardens – of which there are views from some of the rooms. **www**.ywca.org.hk

**HONG KONG The Wesley** 🖼️📶🍴🅦   ⑨⑨⑨

*22 Hennessy Road, Wan Chai, Hong Kong Island* **Tel** *(852) 2866 6688* **Fax** *(852) 2866 6633* **Rooms** *251*    **Map** *3 E4*

This is a good no-frills, budget bet, located close to the hubbub of Wan Chai's pubs, bars, and restaurants. The rooms are good value given their relatively generous size and the location. There is a restaurant and a bar in the hotel, though you may as well take advantage of the location and venture out. **www**.hanglung.com

**HONG KONG YMCA - The Salisbury** 🖼️📶🍴🅦   ⑨⑨⑨

*41 Salisbury Road, Tsim Sha Tsui, Kowloon* **Tel** *(852) 2268 7000* **Fax** *(852) 2739 9315* **Rooms** *363*    **Map** *1 B4*

You may not find better value anywhere else in Hong Kong. The harborside setting is spectacular, many rooms boast fine views and all are reasonably spacious. A great option for families (large family suites are excellent value and there's a leisure center attached) and budget travelers. **www**.ymcahk.org.hk

**HONG KONG The Fleming** 🖼️📶🍴🅦🛏️   ⑨⑨⑨⑨

*41 Fleming Road, Wan Chai* **Tel** *(852) 3607 2288* **Fax** *(852) 3607 2299* **Rooms** *66*    **Map** *3 F3*

Well executed conversion of serviced apartments into smart, practical, comfortable, and reasonably-priced rooms. Many of the rooms have kitchenettes and are well suited to families. Handy for the conference and exhibition center, ferries to Kowloon, and Wan Chai's shopping and nightlife. **www**.thefleming.com.hk

**HONG KONG Island Shangri-La** 🖼️📶🍴🅦🚄🍽️🛏️🍷   ⑨⑨⑨⑨⑨

*Pacific Place, Supreme Court Road, Central* **Tel** *(852) 2877 3838* **Fax** *(852) 2521 8742* **Rooms** *565*    **Map** *3 D4*

One of the best hotels in Hong Kong, the Island Shangri-La is efficient, superbly staffed, and with some of the territory's largest rooms. Conveniently situated directly over Admiralty MTR station and some of Hong Kong's smartest shopping. Choose a Peak View room for spectacular views. **www**.shangri-la.com

**HONG KONG JIA Boutique Hotel** 🖼️📶🍴🅦🍽️🛏️   ⑨⑨⑨⑨⑨

*1–5 Irving Street, Causeway Bay* **Tel** *(852) 3196 9000* **Fax** *(852) 3196 9001* **Rooms** *54*

Discreetly tucked away in the midst of Causeway Bay shopping, JIA (Mandarin for "home") features cozy studios and one-bedroom suites with marble kitchenettes and bathrooms. The accommodation is furnished and decorated with outlandish imagination by French designer Philippe Starck. Comfortable and full of surprises. **www**.jiahongkong.com

**HONG KONG The Landmark Mandarin Oriental** 🖼️📶🍴🅦🚄🍽️🛏️🍷   ⑨⑨⑨⑨⑨

*15 Queens Road Central, Central* **Tel** *(852) 2132 0188* **Fax** *(852) 2132 0199* **Rooms** *113*    **Map** *2 C3*

Intelligent conversion of former offices into some of the largest hotel rooms in Hong Kong. The curved walls of the glass and marble bathrooms divide the remaining spaces into living and sleeping areas, all equipped with high-definition TV, circular sunken bathtubs, and wireless broadband. Perfect city location. **www**.mandarinoriental.com

**HONG KONG The Luxe Manor** 🖼️📶🍴🅦🍽️🛏️🍷   ⑨⑨⑨⑨⑨

*39 Kimberley Road, Tsim Sha Tsui, Kowloon* **Tel** *(852) 3763 8880* **Fax** *(852) 3763 8899* **Rooms** *159*    **Map** *1 C3*

The eclectic mix of Oriental, Post-modern and European decor is designed to give guests a "surreal" experience. Accommodation is a choice of deluxe and garden suites, as well as six uniquely-themed suites – the Suite Liason has a circular bed and padded walls. High-tech features and bathrooms with rain showers. **www**.theluxemanor.com

**Key to Price Guide** *see p554* **Key to Symbols** *see back cover flap*

## HONG KONG Mandarin Oriental

*5 Connaught Road, Central* **Tel** *(852) 2522 0111* **Fax** *(852) 2903 1626* **Rooms** *502*

**Map** *2 C3*

The Mandarin Oriental is triumphantly still one of Hong Kong's favorite hotels. The bustling public areas are among the territory's most popular meeting places, as are the clubby atmosphere of the rooms, and the hotel boasts fresh, modern design, including every conceivable high-tech convenience. **www**.mandarinoriental.com

## HONG KONG The Peninsula Hong Kong

*Salisbury Rd, Tsim Sha Tsui, Kowloon* **Tel** *(852) 2920 2888* **Fax** *(852) 2722 4170* *Rooms 300*

**Map** *1 B4*

A fleet of Rolls-Royces awaits to whisk you from the airport to this luxurious hotel. The Peninsula blends marble-clad opulence and old world colonial charm while its modern rooms offer unrivalled harbour views. The hotel is also home to some of Hong Kong's best restaurants and an award-winning spa. **www**.peninsula.com

## MACAU Mandarin Oriental

*Avenida da Amizade, Outer Harbour, Macau* **Tel** *(853) 8805 8888* **Rooms** *416*

The casino-hotels may have glitz but they are no match for the old-world service standards of the Mandarin. The hotel is an oasis of calm away from the newly reinvented Macau. Enjoy views down to a palm-fringed pool and relax in the sumptuous spa with some of the best masseurs in Asia. Excellent restaurants. **www**.mandarinoriental.com/macau

## MACAU Pousada de São Tiago

*Fortaleza de S. Tiago da Barra, Ave. da Republica, Macau* **Tel** *(853) 2837 8111* **Fax** *(853) 2855 2170* **Rooms** *12*

Occupying an old fort hewn into the rocks of a hill in western Macau, this hotel oozes Old-World colonial atmosphere, and comes with charming service. The rooms are beautifully if heavily decorated with dark wood period furniture and Portugese-style tiles. Small pool and decent restaurant. **www**.saotiago.com.mo

## MACAU The Venetian

*Cotai Strip, Macau* **Tel** *(853) 2883 7788* **Fax** *(853) 2882 8855* **Rooms** *2908*

Macau's most glamorous hotel-casino is a repeat of the Las Vegas dream of Italy, complete with miniature campanile, Rialto Bridge, and sampans amongst the 51 gondolas. The mega-resort is suites-only, with themed shopping and an 1800-seat theater featuring a show by Cirque du Soleil. **www**.venetianmacau.com

## MACAU Wynn Macau

*Rua Cidade de Sintra, Nape* **Tel** *(853) 2888 9966* **Fax** *(853) 2832 9966* **Rooms** *600*

This extravagant resort and casino offers a wide range of facilities including three restaurants and a deluxe spa. The rooms are tastefully decorated with high ceilings, sweeping views and electronic controls for everything. All accommodation and restaurants can be entered without passing through the casino. **www**.wynnmacau.com

# SICHUAN & CHONGQING

## CHENGDU California Garden Hotel (Jiazhou Huayuan Jiudian)

*Shawan Lu 258, Intl. Exhibition & Convention Center* **Tel** *(028) 8764 9999* **Fax** *(028) 8764 0988* **Rooms** *419*

Part of a huge complex of retail shops, cinema, and convention center, the hotel's expansive lobby is adorned with pieces of sculpture and paintings. The hotel complex also boasts an opera house and ice-skating rink. A VIP tower offers high-end accommodations alongside the standard three-star rooms.

## CHENGDU Holiday Inn Crowne Plaza Chengdu

*Zong Fu Lu 31* **Tel** *(028) 8678 6666* **Fax** *(028) 8678 9789* **Rooms** *434*

The Holiday Inn has possibly the best location in the city, across from the fashion district mall of Chunxi Street. Unfortunately service fails to live up to the grandeur of the lobby. However, facilities are good and extensive dining is available in four different restaurants. Bank and Post Office available. **www**.crowneplaza.com

## CHENGDU Kempinski Hotel Chengdu (Kaibin Siji Fandian)

*Renmin Nan Lu, Duan 4, #42* **Tel** *(028) 8526 9999* **Rooms** *483*

Another of Chengdu's modern hotels, the Kempinski has a spacious lobby and even bigger spa, with a 26-yard (24-m) pool, mineral water baths, an assortment of massage options, and a gymnasium. Take time out in the cigar room or tea lounges. **www**.kempinski.com/en/hotel/index.html

## CHENGDU Sofitel Wanda Chengdu (Suo Fei Te Wangda Dajiudian)

*Binjiang Zhong Lu 15* **Tel** *(028) 6666 9999* **Fax** *(028) 6666 3333* **Rooms** *262*

This Sofitel hotel could be Chengdu's finest, with its top quality service and pleasant contemporary feel. Overlooks the Nan River and Park, which are nicely lit at night. An English Corner, held on Tuesday and Friday nights attracts hundreds. Large-capacity meeting rooms also make this a convenient meeting venue. **www**.sofitel.com

## CHENGDU Sheraton Chengdu Lido Hotel

*Renmin Zhong Lu, Duan 1, #15* **Tel** *(028) 8676 8999* **Rooms** *404*

The Sheraton Hotel is just a five-minute walk north of Tianfu Square, with some of the best service in Chengdu. Some rooms have views of the nearby sports stadium and Panda Mall. There are impressive business facilities for work, while the health club has amenities for rest. **www**.sheraton.com

### CHONGQING JW Marriott Hotel (Chongqing Wanhao Jiudian)

*Qingnian Road 77, Yu Zhong District* **Tel** *(023) 6388 8888* **Fax** *(023) 6399 9999* **Rooms** *462*

Located in a bustling commercial district, this high-rise boasts an impressive lobby, 45 floors of guestrooms, and a top-floor lounge with a panoramic view of the city. Considered by many to be the place to stay in Chongqing, its multitude of features and well-trained staff help guests forget the dinginess of the exterior. **www**.marriott.com

### CHONGQING Chongqing Carlton Hotel (Nanfang Junlin Jiudian)

*Ke Yuan Si Lu 259, High-Tech Industry Development* **Tel** *(023) 6806 6806* **Fax** *(023) 6806 6666* **Rooms** *330*

A massive two tower affair in the High Technology Development Zone, a short drive from the popular Liberation Monument area. The neighborhood is rather soulless but the impressive lobby and responsive service may help you forget that. A ballroom, disco, fitness center, and sauna will keep you happy. **www**.cqcarltonhotel.com

### CHONGQING Hilton Chongqing (Chongqing Xi'erdun Jiudian)

*Zhong Shan San Lu 139, Yuzhong District* **Tel** *(023) 8903 9999* **Fax** *(023) 8903 8700* **Rooms** *434*

Set in a recreational area just over 2 miles (4 km) from the city center, overlooking the confluence of the Yangzi and Jailing Rivers, the Hilton has fine art throughout and a spectacular spa appropriately called Cloud 9. Well-appointed lobby, top-notch service and diverse leisure facilities. **www**.chongqing.hilton.com

### EMEI SHAN Emei Shan Dajiudian

*Baoguo Si* **Tel** *(0833) 559 5166* **Rooms** *458*

Well situated for those who wish to visit Emei Shan. Located at the base of Emei in a forested area and next to the Baoguo Temple. Service is better than expected for such an out of the way place. Ample nightlife, together with health and beauty salon options, ensure that guests will not feel isolated. **www**.emshotel.com.cn

### LE SHAN Jinhaitang Dajiudian

*Hai Tao Lu 99* **Tel** *(0833) 212 8888* **Rooms** *141*

Located just a few minutes from the city center but tucked away from noisier streets, the hotel spreads out over expansive well-maintained grounds, a few minutes' drive to the boat docks with frequent departures to view the Big Buddha. Wander through the pretty gardens and relish the peaceful location. Basic business amenities. **www**.jht-hotel.com

### ZIGONG Huidong Dajiudian

*Huidong Dong Lu 16* **Tel** *(0813) 828 8888* **Fax** *(0813) 828 8625* **Rooms** *220*

Located in the east of this mountainous city with a view of downtown, the hotel has an impressive lobby but service lets things down a bit and the rooms could do with a little maintenance. Plenty of leisure activities are provided however, and a ticketing office. Boasts a beauty salon, pool room, and sauna. **www**.huidonghotel.com

## YUNNAN

### DALI Landscape Hotel (Lan Lin Ge Jiudian)

*Yu Er Lu 96* **Tel** *(0872) 266 6188* **Fax** *(0872) 266 6189* **Rooms** *284*

Opened in 2002 and formerly a Bai residence, the hotel has the nicest standard rooms in the city – completely modern and with all the amenities. The grounds feature carved screen walls, marbled courtyards, flowers, stone benches, and even a small bubbling stream. Very quiet with good location at the north end of the Old City. **www**.lanlinge.com

### DALI Asia Star Hotel (Yaxing Dafandian)

*Gucheng Nanjiao* **Tel** *(0872) 267 9999* **Fax** *(0872) 267 0399* **Rooms** *310*

Perched on a small hill, all rooms have a lake or mountain view. The six-story lobby mural is just one of many touches that incorporate hints of local ethnic minority culture throughout. There is an organic vegetarian restaurant on the second floor. A free hotel shuttle operates to/from the center of the Old City every half-hour at night. **www**.asiastargroup.com

### KUNMING Grand Park Hotel

*Hong Hua Qiao 20* **Tel** *(0871) 538 6688* **Fax** *(0871) 538 1189* **Rooms** *300*

Popular with business travelers, its quiet, leafy location northwest of the city center makes one forget it is only five minutes from the hustle-bustle of downtown, and a stone's throw from the beautiful Green Lake Park. Ample dining is provided by three restaurants, and guests can lounge in two bars. **www**.parkhotelgroup.com

### KUNMING Zhen Zhuang Ying Binguan

*Beijing Lu 514* **Tel** *(0871) 316 5869* **Fax** *(0871) 313 9756* **Rooms** *86*

Set in the stunning surroundings of a vast traditional garden, and originally the family home of the first governor of modern Yunnan, this unique hotel is where the president, premier, and high-ranking officials of China stay while in Yunnan. The only drawback is the level of English spoken. Picturesque is an understatement. **www**.ynzzhotel.com

### KUNMING Horizon Hotel (Tianheng Dajiudian)

*Qingnian Lu 432* **Tel** *(0871) 318 6666* **Fax** *(0871) 318 6888* **Rooms** *436*

Very popular with Chinese business and tourist guests, its central location and very clean and well-equipped rooms make it a favorite for international travelers as well. The Horizon Lounge, on the revolving top floor, is a popular night spot. Also has a bowling alley on the third floor. **www**.horizonhotel.net

**Key to Price Guide** *see p554* **Key to Symbols** *see back cover flap*

## KUNMING Green Lake Hotel (Cui Hu Binguan)

*Cui Hu Nan Lu 6* **Tel** *(0871) 515 8888* **Fax** *(0871) 515 7867* **Rooms** *302*

This hotel is clearly the most beautiful of the five-stars in Kunming. The mezzanine-level bar affords a panoramic view of nearby Green Lake Park. Private tours of the area by car (with the driver provided) is another service offered by this thoughtful, modern hotel. **www**.greenlakehotel.com

## KUNMING Kai Wah Plaza International Hotel

*Beijing Lu 157* **Tel** *(0871) 356 2828* **Fax** *(0871) 356 1818* **Rooms** *525*

From the overpowering glass lobby to the spectacular views of the city and surrounding mountains, this large, elegant hotel has everything one expects from an international five-star property. A five-storey shopping center is in the same complex and there are plenty of outlets for leisurely pursuits and relaxation. **www**.kaiwahplaza.com

## LIJIANG Guan Fang Garden Villas (Guanfang Huayuan Bieshu)

*Shangri-La Dadao* **Tel** *(0888) 518 8888* **Fax** *(0888) 518 1999* **Rooms** *904*

This large property has two accommodation styles: modern courtyard and "village" style (two and three-floor villas in small cul-de-sacs). The villas have four non-smoking bedrooms sharing a communal living room and complete kitchen. Almost in the countryside and close to Jade Spring Park. **www**.gfhotel-lijiang.com.cn

## LIJIANG Guanfang Hotel Lijiang (Guanfang Dajiudian)

*Xiange Lila Dadao* **Tel** *(0888) 518 8888* **Fax** *(0888) 518 1999* **Rooms** *289*

This large, modern five-star hotel boasts rooms with views across the old city and the surrounding countryside. The VIP Executive Building, at the back of the 30-storey main hotel, offers upgraded standard rooms. The hotel notably provides disabled access and non-smoking rooms with humidifiers. **www**.gfhotel-lijiang.com.cn

## LIJIANG Crowne Plaza Hotel

*Xianghe Lu 276, Lijiang Old Town* **Tel** *(0888) 558 8888* **Fax** *(0888) 531 4999* **Rooms** *270*

In the center of Lijiang's Old Town is this tastefully designed hotel with a modern take on traditional Naxi style. The rooms are built in local stone and timber, with low tiled roofs. Views look out onto courtyards with trees, shrubs, and pot plants. Although it is close to the town center, the hotel has a private, relaxed feel. **www**.ichotelsgroup.com

## SHAXI Shaxi Laomadian Lodge

*Sideng, Shaxi Old Town* **Tel** *(0872) 472 2666* **Rooms** *9*

In a converted old building around a central stone-flagged courtyard, like those seen in period Chinese films, sit nine rooms with beautifully restored wooden screens, four-poster beds, and modern bathrooms. There are dorm rooms too. The friendly service and superb Yunnanese food are a bonus in a remote location. **www**.yourantai.com

# GUIZHOU & GUANGXI

## GUILIN Guilin Lijiang Waterfall Hotel

*Shanhu Beilu 1* **Tel** *(0773) 282 2881* **Fax** *(0773) 282 2891* **Rooms** *646*

This Chinese-managed hotel, with its cavernous lobby, is one of the best in Guilin, and famous for the largest artificial waterfall in the world – 150 ft (45m) high – rushing down the side of the building. There are five restaurants to choose from, and extensive facilities for business clientele. **www**.waterfallguilin.com

## GUILIN Sheraton Guilin Hotel (Guilin Dayu Da Fandian)

*Binjian Nanlu 15* **Tel** *(0773) 282 5588* **Fax** *(0773) 282 5598* **Rooms** *430*

This five-star hotel, conveniently situated on the Li River amongst extensive shopping and dining, offers the best service in town, although the property itself is getting a little long in the tooth. Business facilities are provided and Internet access is available in all rooms. There are two restaurants and a bar. **www**.sheraton.com/guilin

## GUIYANG Nenghui Jiudian

*Ruijin Nan Lu 38* **Tel** *(0851) 589 8888* **Fax** *(0851) 692 8622* **Rooms** *149*

Willing staff and comfortable rooms – usually heavily discounted – make this centrally located four-star a convenient choice. Situated on the airport bus route with two bars and two restaurants, and basic business facilities with free in-room broadband. This is an ideal spot to convene for business.

## GUIYANG Sheraton Guiyang

*Zhonghua Lu 49* **Tel** *(0851) 588 8280* **Rooms** *346*

Located right in the city center, within a short walk of many of Guiyang's sights, is this upscale chain hotel. Rooms are larger than average and many offer city or river views. The hotel has good facilities for both business and leisure travelers, and there's a comprehensive breakfast buffet. **www**.sheraton.com/guiyang

## NANNING Nanning Fandian

*Minsheng Lu 38* **Tel** *(0771) 210 38888* **Fax** *(0771) 210 3105* **Rooms** *450*

Situated in the old city center and commercial district, and close to the train station, this is one of Nanning's most established hotels. Rooms are clean and spacious, and offer good value for money. There are extensive business facilities and a great choice of restaurants, although there are no menus in English. Staff speak basic English.

### NANNING Trans Century Hotel (Kua Shiji Dajiudian)

*Minzu Avenue 111* **Tel** *(0771) 551 9200* **Rooms** *206*

On an intimate scale and with high levels of service, the Kua Shiji is only a short walk from Nan Hu and about five minutes by taxi from the convention center. It has its own extensive business facilities, together with scope for leisure activities. Located close to the financial district, it is an ideal location for business matters. **www**.ksjhotel.com

### YANGSHUO Magnolia

*Diecui Lu 7* **Tel** *(0773) 881 9288* **Rooms** *30*

Located in the old village center, near the river, this contemporary guesthouse-style hotel offers spacious rooms with modern tiled bathrooms. The popular restaurant next door is run by the same management and serves superb vegetarian cuisine. Friendly staff. **www**.magnoliahotelyangshuo.com

### YANGSHUO Snow Lion

*Mushan Village* **Tel** *(0773) 882 6689* **Rooms** *30*

In a small village 1.5 miles (2.5 km) downstream from Yangshuo, this rural hotel run by a friendly English-speaking couple offers plain but comfortable rooms with private balconies and great views. A good base for easy walks nearby. The owners also run a popular local restaurant serving excellent food. **www**.yangshuosnowlionresort.com

## LIAONING, JILIN & HEILONGJIANG

### CHANGCHUN Paradise Hotel (Yuefu Dajiudian)

*Renmin Dajie 1078* **Tel** *(0431) 8209 0999* **Fax** *(0431) 8271 5709* **Rooms** *217*

A four-star at three-star prices and one of the finest mid-range options, not just in the city, but in the entire northeastern region. Rooms are cramped but well decorated and maintained. The staff, too, are uncommonly professional and friendly. Ample culinary fare provided within the three restaurants. **www**.ccyuefuhotel.com

### CHANGCHUN Shangri-la Changchun

*Xi'an Dalu 569* **Tel** *(0431) 8898 1818* **Fax** *(0431) 8898 1919* **Rooms** *458*

The city's oldest luxury hotel is still its best, thanks in large measure to standards of service that no other local hotel can match. Walking distance to People's Square and the main shopping district. If you are hankering after Western food, nothing in the city beats the Coffee Garden. Beer garden also available. **www**.shangri-la.com

### DALIAN Dalian Hotel (Dalian Binguan)

*Zhongshan Guangchang 4* **Tel** *(0411) 8263 3111 ext. 1101* **Fax** *(0411) 8263 4363* **Rooms** *63*

Situated on the architecturally splendid Zhongshan Square, history and location are the attractions here. The hotel was built in 1909 and considered the finest in Manchuria. It languished under the Communists until restoration in the late 1990s. The small number of rooms ensures a unique stay. **www**.chinadalianhotel.com

### DALIAN Swish-Hotel Dalian (Dalian Ruishi Jiudian)

*Wuhui Lu 21* **Tel** *(0411) 8230 3388* **Fax** *(0411) 8230 2266* **Rooms** *327*

The most centrally located luxury hotel in the city, with some of its best service and a nice vista from higher rooms on the park side. Rooms are smallish but impeccable. Connection to a popular mall enables easy shopping. Excellent local seafood buffet, and occasional "international" BBQs. **www**.swishhotel.com.cn

### DANDONG Zhonglian Dajiudian

*Binjiang Zhong Lu 62* **Tel** *(0415) 233 3333* **Fax** *(0415) 233 3888* **Rooms** *165*

The finest lodgings in Dandong, with unbeatable views. Rooms are tasteful and comfortable, and the service pleasantly professional. Peer out at North Korea through the windows of the café. If you are at a loose end, go bowling, venture into the cigar room, or feast on the extensive Western buffet. **www**.zlhotel.com

### HARBIN Modern Hotel (Madie'er Binguan)

*Zhongyang Dajie 89, Daoli* **Tel** *(0451) 8488 4000* **Fax** *(0451) 8461 4997* **Rooms** *141*

Built in 1913 and dripping with character. This was the city's most illustrious hotel in the pre-Communist era and a meeting point for several of the protagonists in the revolutionary struggle. Some evidence of this history still remains within the hotel. Unbeatable location at the heart of historic Zhongyang Dajie. **http**://hotel.hrbmodern.com

### HARBIN Harbin Shangri-la (Ha'erbin Xianggelila Dafandian)

*Youyi Lu 555, Daoli* **Tel** *(0451) 8485 8888* **Fax** *(0451) 8462 1777* **Rooms** *404*

By its own admission this is the least impressive of the many Shangri-La hotels in the northeast, but still the city's best luxury option. It's a bit far from the main sights, but ideal in winter, when the Sungari River freezes over and the Ice and Snow Palace is built. The modern exercise room has views of the river. **www**.shangri-la.com

### JILIN Crystal Hotel (Wusong Binguan)

*Longtian Dajie 29* **Tel** *(0432) 6398 6200* **Fax** *(0432) 6398 6501* **Rooms** *223*

Far from the sights, but beautifully situated to appreciate the famous scenery of the Jilin River in winter. This is the city's oldest luxury hotel and it is evident from the exterior. Rooms are nicely sized and clean, and staff are familiar with foreigners. Enjoy the spa with a view of the river, notably beautiful in winter. **www**.crystal-hotel.com.cn

**Key to Price Guide** *see p554* **Key to Symbols** *see back cover flap*

### MUDANJIANG Jialin Fandian ⬛ ⬛ ⬛ ⓨⓨ
*Xinhua Lu 48* **Tel** *(0453) 653 0888* **Fax** *(0453) 656 0088* **Rooms** *58*

The single exception in a city of grim hotels – it is a charming and friendly little place, with clean and comfortable rooms. Facilities are basic and functional. Can't ask for much more in this area. Fax and Internet facilities are available. A restaurant and bar are located within this small hotel.

### QIQIHA'ER Guomai Dasha ⬛ ⬛ ⬛ ⬛ ⬛ ⓨⓨ
*Junjiao Jie 1* **Tel** *(0452) 241 0000* **Fax** *(0452) 242 0638* **Rooms** *218*

Situated in the city's tallest building on the main east-west road, with an odd space-age antenna visible from the train station, this is the city's best hotel. Not as luxurious as its four-star rating might suggest, it is nevertheless clean and comfortable. Walking distance to city center and convenient for the railway station.

### SHENYANG Liaoning Hotel (Liaoning Binguan) ⬛ ⬛ ⬛ ⬛ ⓨⓨⓨ
*Zhongshan Lu 97* **Tel** *(024) 2383 9166* **Fax** *(024) 2383 9103* **Rooms** *80*

This beautiful historic hotel this was originally part of a famous chain of Japanese-owned WW II-era hotels. The green tile lobby floor and grand marble staircase with brass handrail are original. Rooms feel their age but are comfortable. Conveniently located near the city center, it has two restaurants.

### SHENYANG Sheraton Shenyang Lido (Lidu Xilaideng Fandian) ⬛ ⬛ ⬛ ⬛ ⬛ ⓨⓨⓨⓨ
*Qingnian Dajie 386* **Tel** *(024) 2318 8888* **Fax** *(024) 2318 8000* **Rooms** *590*

The city's most tasteful luxury hotel opened in late 2002 with investment from Hong Kong shipping magnate Li Ka-Shing. Rooms are palatial and nicely decorated with decent artwork. Far from the sights, but with a high standard of service. Health club with gym, and cigar room with live music. **www**.sheraton.com/shenyang

## INNER MONGOLIA & NINGXIA

### HOHHOT Xincheng Binguan ⬛ ⬛ ⬛ ⬛ ⬛ ⬛ ⓨⓨⓨ
*Hulun Nan Lu 40* **Tel** *(0471) 666 1888* **Fax** *(0471) 693 1141* **Rooms** *320*

Originally opened in 1959, this monster hotel houses several restaurants and bars. There are plentiful rooms which are large, albeit a bit worn. The hotel has been updated and rooms have free broadband Internet connections. On-site leisure facilities include pool, tennis courts, and a bowling alley. **www**.xincheng-hotel.com.cn

### HOHHOT Hohhot Holiday Inn (Huhehaote Jiari Jiudian) ⬛ ⬛ ⬛ ⬛ ⬛ ⓨⓨⓨⓨ
*Zhongshan Xi Lu 33* **Tel** *(0471) 635 1888* **Fax** *(0471) 635 0888* **Rooms** *198*

This hotel's rooms and bathrooms are both stylish and huge. Located on exclusive Zhongshan Xi Lu, the main business artery of the city. There are two bars and two restaurants within the hotel, and a convenient airport bus shuttles guests to and from flights. **www**.ichotelsgroup.com

### HOHHOT Phoenix Hotel (Neimenggu Guohang Dasha) ⬛ ⬛ ⬛ ⬛ ⬛ ⬛ ⓨⓨⓨⓨ
*Zhelimu Lu 96* **Tel** *(0471) 660 8888* **Fax** *(0471) 623 0959* **Rooms** *280*

Rooms are elegant and staff very eager to assist, and there are thoughtful extras like fruit plates for guests with reserved rooms and in-house boarding pass arrangements for travelers flying out of Hohhot. The Western restaurant on the top floor serves French cuisine at a dizzying height. Close to to the railway station. **www**.ni-phoenix.com.cn

### XILINHOT Wuhua Hotel ⬛ ⬛ ⬛ ⬛ ⓨⓨ
*Xining Da Jie 43* **Tel** *(0471) 881 8055* **Fax** *(0471) 881 8035* **Rooms** *230*

This modern hotel opened in 2008 and is perfectly located in the city center, close to many stores, restaurants, and public transport links. The hotel has a respectable three star status and the decor, and furnishings are fresh and bright. The in-room Internet access is particularly useful.

### YINCHUAN Rainbow Bridge Hotel (Hong Qiao Dajiudian) ⬛ ⬛ ⬛ ⬛ ⬛ ⬛ ⓨⓨⓨⓨ
*Jiefang Xi Jie 38, Laocheng Qu* **Tel** *(0951) 691 8888* **Fax** *(0951) 691 8788* **Rooms** *231*

An ugly three-star tower with some pretension to better things, this is still this quiet provincial capital's best and most successful hotel. Service is modest but tries to please, and rooms are straightforward but clean enough, many with city-wide views. The basic business center makes a convenient base, a few blocks from the old town center.

## GANSU & QINGHAI

### DUNHUANG The Silk Road Dunhuang Hotel (Dunhuang Shanzhuang) ⬛ ⬛ ⬛ ⬛ ⬛ ⓨⓨⓨⓨ
*Dunyue Lu* **Tel** *(0937) 888 2088* **Fax** *(0937) 888 3245* **Rooms** *269*

This hotel is the best in Gansu and set in the middle of the desert en route to the Mingsha Dunes; the earthy buildings contain spotless, well-furnished rooms which fit in with, rather than exclude, the wild surroundings. Cheaper rooms are available in the attached "youth hostel." Free shuttle service into town. **www**.the-silk-road.com

### GOLMUD Golmud Mansion (Ge'ermu Dasha)

*Yingbin Lu 33* **Tel** *(0979) 845 2208* **Fax** *(0979) 8455 1378* **Rooms** *65*

This is a pleasant hotel located near the train station in downtown Golmud. There are three types of rooms – single, double or triple beds, and all are clean and comfortable. The hotel has a friendly and helpful travel agency that can arrange tours to the salt flats surrounding Golmud.

### JIAYUGUAN Jinye Binguan

*Lanxin Xi Lu 12* **Tel** *(0937) 620 1333* **Rooms** *56*

Large discounts are offered on standard rooms, even in the summer, at this clean and basic hotel located near the bus station. Some rooms are en suite, and all have televisions. There is no restaurant but the Liuyan restaurant next door is a good place to dine.

### LANZHOU Lanzhou JJ Sun Hotel (Jinjiang Yangguang Jiudian)

*Donggang Xi Lu 589* **Tel** *(0931) 880 5511* **Fax** *(0931) 885 4700* **Rooms** *236*

The midsize rooms in this four-star outpost of the Accor empire are four-star standard and offer hairdryers, safety boxes, fridges, and in-room broadband. The enthusiastic staff speak good English, and will offer substantial discounts to those canny enough not to book in advance. **www**.jjsunhotel.com

### LANZHOU Sunshine Plaza (Yangguang Dasha)

*Qingyang Lu 428* **Tel** *(0931) 460 8888* **Fax** *(0931) 460 8889* **Rooms** *223*

This Chinese five-star hotel maintains excellent levels of service. Owned by a local petroleum conglomerate, there's no shortage of funds for renovations, which are continuous. Massage showers in every room are a novel touch, as is the child-friendly games room with every toy imaginable. Restaurant serves non-Chinese food. **www**.soluxe.com.cn

### TIANSHUI Maiji Dajiudian

*Tianshui Huoche Zhan Guangchang Xice* **Tel** *(0938) 492 0000* **Fax** *(0938) 492 9323* **Rooms** *108*

Efficient service and very clean rooms are the main attractions in this otherwise utterly standard two-star hotel. There are some renovated rooms on the top floor. The location in the same square as the railway station may be convenient, but can be noisy, so choose a room facing away from the station for a better night's sleep.

### TONGREN Telecom Hotel (Dianxin Binguan)

*Zhongshan Lu 38* **Tel** *(0973) 872 6888* **Fax** *(0973) 872 2666* **Rooms** *33*

This white-tiled building is in surprisingly good condition for a two-star establishment. For the price, guest rooms are well-appointed and boast sparkling blue bathrooms. Service is as good as it gets in Tongren, which isn't a big claim. The hotel also has a three lane bowling alley which some may find a bonus.

### XIAHE Overseas Tibetan Hotel (Huaqiao Fandian)

*Renmin Xijie 77* **Tel** *(0941) 712 2642* **Fax** *(0941) 712 1872* **Rooms** *35*

The energetic manager of this once dire hotel has slowly turned it into the best in town. Small, with a moderate number of rooms – those on the third floor are fitted with Tibetan-style furnishings and comfortable beds. The Everest Café serves delicious Nepali cuisine and a decent Western breakfast. There is a travel agency in the summer.

### XINING Lete Youth Hostel

*Guo Ji Cun Gong Yu, Building 5* **Tel** *(0971) 820 2090* **Fax** *(0971) 820 3271* **Rooms** *25*

Xining's youth hostel is located on the 16th floor of a tall building and offers great views of the city. The English-speaking staff are helpful, and the in-house travel agency can arrange tours across Qinghai and Tibet. Double rooms have private bathrooms and there are clean budget dorm rooms. Bike rentals are available.

# XINJIANG

### HOTAN Tianhai Binguan

*Beijing Xi Lu 49* **Tel** *(0903) 202 6666* **Fax** *(0903) 202 2000* **Rooms** *180*

Located just west of the post office is Hotan's most luxurious hotel, which has a well-deserved three-star rating. Mid-sized rooms are cozily furnished and the bathrooms are kept in immaculate condition. The refrigerators provided in every room are a nice touch and can be a lifesaver in the heat of summer. Restaurant serves non-Chinese food.

### KASHGAR Chini Bagh Hotel (Qiniwake Binguan)

*Seman Lu 144* **Tel** *(0998) 298 0671* **Fax** *(0998) 298 2299* **Rooms** *258*

Situated on the edge of the Old Town, the original early-20th century British Consulate building still stands behind the modern hotel buildings. The afternoon teas and carefully tended lawns of the Great Game era may have gone, but the Chini Bagh is nonetheless a decently-run hotel with a variety of rooms to suit every budget.

### KASHGAR Seman Binguan

*Seman Lu 337* **Tel** *(0998) 258 2150* **Fax** *(0998) 258 2861* **Rooms** *222*

This sprawling two-star hotel offers a rare opportunity to stay in an old colonial consulate building (Russian) behind the main accommodation block. There are some small, oddly-shaped rooms with simple bathrooms. Common areas feature high ceilings and military-themed oil paintings. Dorms in the main building are basic, but dirt cheap.

### KUQA Jiaotong Binguan
*Tian Shan Dong Lu 87* **Tel** *(0997) 712 2682* **Fax** *(0997) 712 7230* **Rooms** *56*

The spartan rooms of this inexpensive inn were renovated in 2001, and the staff are notably embarrassed about the hotel's previous incarnation as a decrepit flophouse. If you are leaving early in the morning, be warned you may miss the hot showers. Rooms at the back are quieter and the hotel is convenient for the coach station.

### TURPAN Grand Turpan Hotel (Tulufan Dafandian)
*Gaochang Lu 422* **Tel** *(0995) 855 3918* **Fax** *(0995) 855 3919* **Rooms** *154*

This sleepy hotel is part of a Hong Kong chain and sports two wings. The more modern wing has four-star rooms; standard rooms are large and clean, and rates are discounted by 60% in the off-season. Comfortable dorm beds in the older wing come with bathrooms and showers – the best budget deal in town. **www**.xjturpanhotel.com

### URUMQI Urumqi City Hotel (Chengshi Dajiudian)
*Hong Qi Lu 27* **Tel** *(0991) 220 7666* **Fax** *(0991) 230 5321* **Rooms** *226*

This three-star hotel is located in Urumqi's city center, near the People's Square and close to bus and train stations. Though it looks small it has a large number of rooms. Rooms are clean and affordable and have refrigerators, television with cable, and Western toilets. If you are on a very tight budget ask for a room without windows.

### URUMQI Hoi-tak Hotel (Haide Jiudian)
*Dongfeng Lu 1* **Tel** *(0991) 232 2828* **Fax** *(0991) 232 1818* **Rooms** *318*

The 36-story Hoi-tak Hotel has an excellent location in the center of town. Fitted to five-star standards, rooms are modern and comfortable with large beds. On clear days, marvellous views of Tian Shan may be enjoyed from upper floors. Substantial discounts (up to 70%) are offered all year round. **www**.hoitakhotel.com

### YINING Yili Binguan
*Yingbin Lu 8* **Tel** *(0999) 802 3799* **Fax** *(0999) 802 4964* **Rooms** *240*

This hotel greets you with a bust of Lenin and a map. You will need the latter as the grounds are extensive. The hotel has "received Li Peng", but non-cadres are bundled out of the luxurious Building 5 before reaching the marble staircase. Buildings 2, 3, and 4 are for civilians; cheap rooms are located in the charming but dilapidated Building 4.

## TIBET

### GYANTSE Jiang Zang Fandian
*Yingxiong Nan Rd 14* **Tel** *(0892) 817 3720* **Rooms** *40*

The Tibetan-run Jian Zang hotel is the best option in Gyantse, and is located a five minute walk from the Gyantse Fort entrance. The rooms are all clean and spacious; standard rooms are equipped with 24 hour hot water. Newer rooms have wooden floors and Tibetan decor. The restaurant offers well-priced Tibetan and Western food.

### LHASA Oh Dan Guesthouse (Oudan Binguan)
*Close to the Ramoche Monastery, Xiaozhao Si Road 15* **Tel** *(0891) 634 4999* **Fax** *(0891) 636 3992* **Rooms** *40*

Located on an atmospheric Lhasa backstreet, this guesthouse is a short walk from the Barkhor and has views of the Potala Palace and the Ramoche Monastery. Rooms are clean and pleasant and there are both dorm beds and private rooms available. The standard doubles with en suite bathrooms are excellent value for money.

### LHASA Kyichu Hotel (Jiqu Fandian)
*Beijing Dong Rd 149* **Tel** *(0891) 633 1541* **Fax** *(0891) 633 5728* **Rooms** *50*

For once it may be worth reserving your room in advance since the cozy rooms in this Tibetan-run hotel are often booked out. Service is exceptionally friendly. Rooms in the south wing, overlooking a sunny courtyard, are worth the extra outlay. Only a short walk from the heart of Lhasa, the Barkhor. **www**.kyichuhotel.com

### SHIGATSE Hotel Mansarovar (Shenhu Jiudian)
*Qingdao Dong Rd 14* **Tel** *(0892) 883 9999* **Fax** *(0892) 882 8111* **Rooms** *82*

Standard rooms are simply but elegantly appointed, and dorm rooms are spotless, if overpriced. Staff are generally friendly and professional, despite the management's close ties with Tibet's FIT (Foreign Individual Travel) tourism monopoly. A bonus feature are the delicious Nepali curries in the attached restaurant. **www**.hotelmansarovartibet.com

### TINGRI Tigri Snowland Hotel
*Gang Ga Zhen Xi Ca* **Tel** *(0892) 826 2711* **Rooms** *35*

Tibetan-owned Tingri Snowland Hotel is located on the west end of Tingri, and has friendly staff who cook superb Tibetan and Western food. Hot showers are available in the evening only, but the excellent views of the Himalayas from the hotel make this a more special place to stay.

### TSETANG Xuege Binguan
*Hubei Rd 1* **Tel** *(0893) 782 8888* **Fax** *(0893) 782 7777* **Rooms** *74*

While reception staff at other hotels in town call the police to see if you're "allowed to stay," the staff at Tsetang's three-star hotel try the revolutionary approach of welcoming their guests. The mid-sized rooms are spotless, beds are firm, and the bathrooms compact but clean. Try the four-lane bowling alley for entertainment.

# WHERE TO EAT

*Yin* and *yang* Rice Bowl

Can any other nation rival China's obsession with food? Instead of "How are you?" Chinese people greet each other with *"Ni chi fan le ma?"* – "Have you eaten yet?" Once your travels begin, you may ask yourself a similar question – have you really eaten Chinese food before? For the Middle Kingdom serves up cuisine of such variety and delight that mealtimes there will soon dissolve the taste memories of the pale imitations of Chinese food from back home. As you travel around the country you will enjoy a veritable culinary gazeteer. From the wheat noodles, lamb kabobs, and Peking duck of the north, venture east to taste the braised crabs and abalone of Shanghai, west to try the fiery feasts of Sichuan, and south to "dot the heart" with a thousand different Cantonese *dim sum*.

Eating together, an important part of any meal or snack

## A DIVINE PLEASURE

Food is a divine pleasure runs a traditional saying. China's fascination with food stems from the ancient worship of gods and spirits, when emperors were carried to temples or sacred peaks to guarantee good harvests with sacrifices of meat and rice wine. Today, any event can prompt a feast where families can bond, relationships grow, disputes be resolved, and business deals reached. For Chinese people everywhere, food is not just a social lubricant, but the cornerstone of their culture.

## A FAMINE CUISINE

One of China's perennial problems has been how can such a large population feed itself (currently a fifth of the world's people) when less than 10% of its land is arable? The answer lies in centuries of innovation and efficiency in the fields and in the kitchen. The Chinese have developed a "famine cuisine," cherishing wild plants like bamboo

shoots, lotus roots, seaweed, fungi, or moss, and utilizing every part of domesticated or wild animals. Bustling markets and even some mealtimes are not for the squeamish, but the daring will learn how fish heads, pig's trotters, chicken intestine, duck webs, sea slugs, and bull testicles can be prepared as delicacies. Imagine how many lives scorpions, deep-fried and full of protein, could save in a famine?

## THE FIRST FAST FOOD

Although boiling and steaming dominate Chinese cooking, it is best known for the stir-fry. Restaurants tend to follow the less economical traditions of the elite, not the simplicity of everyday fare, but the stir-fry still reflects the efficiency of Chinese food. Meat and vegetables are cut into small pieces and fried briefly in hot oil, thus saving on fuel and equipment without sacrificing taste. There was little saving in work time, but labor is one resource of which China has plenty.

## THE CULINARY ARTS

According to records China's earliest master of gastronomy, Yi Yin, cooked for the first Shang emperor way back in the 16th century BC. One cookbook from the sixth century AD still sets standards for today's chefs, like a mouthwatering recipe for roasting suckling pig that should "melt in the mouth like ice." Over the centuries, countless men of letters sang the glories of food. Song Dynasty poet Su Dongpo penned a famous ode to pork and today Dongpo Pork remains Hangzhou's most celebrated dish. On your travels you can learn the stories behind many other famous dishes. The ancient philosophy of *yin* and *yang* – the blending of contrasts and duality of nature – applies to culinary matters in China as much as to spiritual ones. Achieving the right harmony of *yin* (soft, cold, dark, and feminine) and *yang* (strong,

Scorpion kebabs – cooking renders the sting ineffective

**Steaming food on the street – simple, fast, and efficient**

hot, bright, and masculine) will ensure good health not just a good meal. Cooling *yin* foods – for example most vegetables, crab, beancurd – must complement warming *yang* – meat, chilies. Hence in menu planning, there should be meat dishes as well as vegetable, hot and cold, sweet and sour, plain and spicy. Even meat dishes rarely contain meat alone, while the basic ingredients of stir-frying – scallions and ginger – are *yin* and *yang* too. Additionally a balanced diet should include appropriate proportions of both *fan* (grains) and *cai* (vegetables) and not too much meat. Many aspects of the culinary arts are thus governed by concepts and philosophies that seem to permeate all of Chinese life.

**Rice and chopsticks**

## YOU ARE WHAT YOU EAT

Nutritionists were attached to the Zhou court back in the seventh century BC, for the Chinese have long recognized the medicinal value of food. In the Chinese chef's repertoire there is a dish or an ingredient for every poorly organ or ailment. Some foods that are meant to boost your *qi*, such as ginseng and bird's nest soup, require a small leap of faith as to their efficacy; others such as iron-rich duck blood are more obvious. In some cases, as in

other societies, animal parts are believed to strengthen the human equivalent – try duck brain for more intelligence, ox tongue for eloquence, and bull's testicles for greater sexual potency.

## THE FIVE FLAVORS

The Chinese are not really recipe-bound. Amid the drama of the flaming stir-fry, they seem to take a more flexibile approach, finely judging the right quantity of each ingredient. But nevertheless, Chinese chefs are very particular about flavor, aroma, color and texture. Each of these properties has been elevated to an art form with special vocabulary and sets of rules. If *xian* captures the soul of a food (an elusive, sweet but natural freshness), *cui* is the goal of most Chinese cooking

(a crisp crunchiness like the skin of perfect Peking duck). Trained Chinese palates distinguish five different flavors – sweet, sour, bitter, pungent, salty – and only the right combinations work. Foods rich in flavor combine well with texture foods of little taste, such as sea cucumbers and shark's fin, which absorb and heighten the foods cooked with them.

## SYMBOLISM IN FOOD

In a culture obsessed with symbolism, and eating, there are many foods that have earned special meaning and must be consumed on certain occasions. Round mooncakes, dotted with moon-like duck egg yolks, are a must for the family reunion at Mid-Autumn Festival. At the important Spring Festival dinner, the whole family cooks *tangyuan*, round sweet dumplings made of glutinous rice flour, because *yuan* can also mean "reunion." Fish is particularly auspicious, because the character for fish (*yu*) sounds like the one for "abundance" and offers the hope of good fortune in the year ahead. Meat dumplings (*jiaozi*) are another New Year favorite, especially in the north, as their shape is said to resemble a golden symbol of prosperity. Birthdays are often celebrated with noodles, a symbol of longevity, while red beans are a metaphor of longing and love. And to celebrate new arrivals, parents hand out bundles of eggs painted red for luck – an even number to celebrate a boy, an odd number for a girl.

**Cooking chinese-style – balancing colors, tastes, and textures**

# Types of Restaurants

Whether you are looking to eat in the splendor of an imperial pavilion in Beijing, a chic Shanghai café, or a busy Sichuan teahouse, you will find a restaurant boom taking place in China. Freed from state control, entrepreneurs are thinking up tempting new ways to indulge in the country's favorite pastime. You never have to walk far to find restaurants in China and when you do, do not let first appearances put you off – in contrast to the delicacy of the food, many gourmet restaurants boast simple decor and harsh lighting. Look instead for happy crowds of diners and a different concept of "atmosphere." In Chinese eyes, the more lively and noisy *(renao)* a restaurant is, the better.

Typical restaurant – busy and noisy with a utilitarian decor

## OPEN ALL HOURS

Early to bed, early to rise was the pattern of Chinese lives until the 1990s, leaving some foreign visitors caught out when planning mealtimes. While Chinese stomachs still demand food earlier than their Western counterparts, social and professional hours are diversifying. You can breakfast on the street by 6am, but all hotels should serve breakfast until 10am or later. Lunch is typically from 11:30am until 2:30pm, after which some restaurants shut until the evening shift starts around 5:00 pm. In the evening closing times can be very late, while some places never shut. Booking is rare except for the most popular and high-end establishments. Usually you can simply turn up; if the restaurant is full, you may have to wait until a table comes free or have a drink at the bar. Sometimes the owner will come to your rescue by setting up a makeshift table in the corner, or even out in the backyard.

## HOTEL FOOD

If you are tired and hungry, and staying at one of China's more expensive hotels, then room service can provide comfort with imitations of Western food. But try to make it downstairs, as most hotels offer a range of cuisines within the premises.

In the main cities, some of the best restaurants are located in hotels, and you can sample some excellent upscale Chinese cuisine. Contrary to opinion, hotel restaurants do not always serve overpriced, deliberately bland Chinese food to appease foreign palates. However, home to one of the world's top cuisines, China has a lot to offer. The more intrepid diner who makes a few forays outside the comfort of four-star hotel restaurants will be sure to reap handsome dividends.

## STREET FOOD

As China smartened up for the Olympics and the World Expo, street vendors must sometimes play hide-and-seek with the authorities. Yet their portable stalls form a vital part of the everyday life of China, selling cheap and popular foods such as breakfasts of dough sticks *(youtiao)* and beancurd *(doujiang)*, or snacks like scallion pancakes *(jianbing)*, sweet potatoes *(shanyu)* roasted in old oil drums, deep-fried beancurd cubes *(zhadoufu)*, and local fruits.

A reliable way to locate delicious street food is to stroll through a night market *(yeshi)*, a culinary and visual feast where clouds of steam escape from bamboo steamers and the sky glows red from the flames of oil drum stoves. The sizzle of cooking and clamor of vendors shouting for business should stir your appetite and if deep-fried scorpions or cicadas on skewers prove too exotic, be assured that plenty of other foods will take your fancy. If the food is hot and freshly cooked for you, hygiene problems are rare. The market off Wanfujing Dajie *(see p94)*, in Beijing, is the most famous, but track down night markets wherever you go, to enjoy the local delicacies and specialties.

Dunhuang night market – food stalls for shoppers buying spices, silks, and carpets

**Stall-holder making some *xiaochi* or "little eats" in Dalian**

## LITTLE EATS

Cheap and nourishing snacks such as those found at night markets are known collectively as *xiaochi*, or "little eats." Restaurants that specialize in them are called *xiaochidian*; they sell different types of noodles or dumplings, stuffed buns or pancakes. Open early for breakfast, they may serve simple stir-fried dishes too, and shut only when the last guest leaves. The setting is usually basic, but the food is hearty, tasty, and very reasonably priced. Every city has its own local varieties, but the ultimate "little eats" are the *dim sum* of Cantonese cooking *(see p282)*.

**Pretty colored dumplings**

## FAST FOOD

The popularity of fast food giants McDonald's, Pizza Hut, and Kentucky Fried Chicken, now found in all cities, has spurred Chinese firms to compete. Yonghe King is an impressive Taiwanese chain serving up all-day breakfasts of soya bean milk, *congee* (a savory rice porridge), and spring onion pancakes, while 85°C is a rapidly-expanding coffee, cake, and bread chain. If the street stalls are a little too basic, food courts in department stores or malls are worth exploring and are clean and usually air-conditioned.

## THEMED RESTAURANTS

As urban tastes grow ever more sophisticated, restaurateurs race to catch up, opening restaurants with a special theme, cuisine, or setting, like a train carriage or mock prison. The character of these places is often nostalgic, such as the old Beijing style (Lao Beijing), where each guest is loudly greeted, and staff in pre-Revolution uniforms clatter the teacups in welcome on your table. The walls of Cultural Revolution restaurants are covered with bitter-sweet memorabilia of that era, while many Sichuan eateries have concentrated on rustic decor to increase the appeal.

## THE OTHER CHINA

There is not only a wide spread of regional cuisines across Han China, but also a whole range of ethnic specialties offered by the many minority nationalities from the Korean border to the Tibetan plateau. The minorities' restaurants are an "exotic" attraction for Chinese as well as foreign tourists.

In Dai restaurants, offering the Thai-like cuisine of southern Yunnan, guests are greeted with scented water, given a lucky charm, and later invited to join in the singing and dancing. In Uighur restaurants, serving food from the Muslim northwest, belly dancing is sometimes on show.

## VEGETARIAN SURPRISE

The Chinese understanding of a good life is inextricably associated with meat. They find it hard to understand why someone who could afford to eat meat would choose not to. Nevertheless, you will find a few vegetarian restaurants in big cities, often attached to Buddhist temples, serving excellent vegetarian dishes to worshipers and non-worshipers alike. Many of these have meaty names, and are made in exact imitation of their meat-filled namesakes. Ordinary restaurants can lay on good vegetarian meals too, as long as you can repeat: *"Wo chi su"*, ("I eat vegetables") a few times and don't mind the odd bit of meat or chicken stock turning up in your bowl every now and then.

## FOREIGN FOOD

Western restaurants, now found in all major cities, typically offer Indian, Thai, Italian, and French, or a fusion of international food. Some have justifiably earned wide acclaim, such as Maison Boulud in Beijing, and M on the Bund in Shanghai.

In smaller cities, western restaurants are harder to find, although Italian cuisine is the most common – ravioli and spaghetti are easy concepts for the dumpling- and noodle-loving Chinese to appreciate. Other Asian cuisines, namely Korean, Japanese, and Thai, are also well-represented, and more readily accepted.

**Uighur bread stall in the market at Linxia, Gansu**

# Food Customs and Etiquette

Confucius was renowned for his silence at meals. The good news, however, is that 2,500 years later, the Chinese are actually quite informal at meal times. In fact, a busy Chinese restaurant can be a deafening place as waiters crash plates about and diners shout orders at the waiters. It may seem daunting but just join in and expect praise for your chopstick skills – even if you struggle, your willingness to try will be appreciated.

Business dinner in a private room, still an enjoyable event

## EARNING SOME FACE

The Chinese do not expect visitors to be fully versed in proper banquet etiquette, but awareness of a few essentials can earn "face" both for yourself and your host, whatever the occasion. The other guests will appreciate that you have some respect for Chinese culture and traditions.

When attending, or hosting, a formal meal, note that the guest of honor is usually placed on the seat in the middle, facing the door. The host, traditionally positioned opposite the guest, now more often sits to his or her left.

If you come as a guest, be punctual and do not sit down until you are given your seat – seating arrangements can be very formal and based on rank.

Once seated, do not start on the food or drink before your host gives the signal. Some of the delicacies on offer may test your courage; be gracious and try everything, it is an insult if the food is untouched; but leave some food on the plates. Empty bowls imply that the host is too poor or mean to lay on a good spread.

## THE ART OF ORDERING

If you are someone's guest, you may be asked to order something, or state some sort of preference – if you do not do so, a ten-course banquet could soon appear. Feel free to name your favorite dish, or point at the object of your desire, often swimming in a fish tank at the entrance to the restaurant. Freshness is all important in Chinese cuisine.

English language menus are becoming more common, and an increasing number of restaurants actively encourage visitors to get out of their chairs and choose ingredients from tanks, cages, and supermarket-type shelves. Your Chinese friends (and waiters and onlookers) will likely be delighted by any interest you show in the whole experience. In the end, when language or phrase book fail, point at whatever appeals on other tables, or even head into the kitchen to find what you need.

A meal might begin with cold starters such as pickled vegetables, ten-thousand-year old eggs, seasoned jellyfish, or cold roasted meats.

When selecting main courses, remember to aim for harmony and balance – an equilibrium of *yin* and *yang*. For example, with sweet and sour pork, you might order a spicy chicken dish. Different cooking methods are also important: a steamed fish or roast pork add variety to a series of stir-fried foods. You shouldn't need to ask for a side order of vegetables as they are usually part of the dishes – unless you want something specific.

The last dish, or *cai*, is usually soup. Then comes *fan*, a grain staple such as rice, noodles, or bread *(mantou)*, without which a Chinese diner may feel they have not eaten. At informal meals you can have rice at the start of the meal, but not at a banquet, or your host will assume his dishes are inadequate.

Desserts are not a Chinese tradition, but fresh fruit is almost always served in Chinese restaurants, especially at banquets, and succulent fruit is available nationwide.

Filling up on rice at an informal meal in a market, Dali

## INVITED TO DINNER

A formal meal often takes place in a private room and usually begins with a toast. The host serves his guest with the choicest morsels, and then everyone is permitted to help themselves. Serving chopsticks or spoons are sometimes provided; otherwise you can simply use your own pair.

Confucius said that it was uncivilized to have knives on the table, but if you are really struggling most restaurants will readily provide you with knives and forks.

The host almost always orders more dishes than necessary. While it is polite to try everything, don't feel it is necessary to finish it all.

## GOOD NEIGHBORS

It is courteous to keep your neighbors' tea cups filled. To thank an attentive neighbor, tap your first two fingers together on the table. This tradition dates back to the Qing Qianlong emperor, who liked to tour the country in disguise. Once, at a teahouse, he took his turn to pour the tea. His companions, who should have been pressing their foreheads to the floor, maintained his disguise by tapping their fingers in a mini-kowtow. If you don't want your cup refilled then don't empty it.

**Crabs – difficult to eat with chopsticks**

## DOS AND DON'TS

The Chinese are fairly relaxed about table manners. Slurping shows appreciation, enables better appreciation of flavor, and sucks in air to prevent burning the mouth. Holding your bowl up to your mouth, to shovel rice in, is another practical solution. You may happily reach across your neighbors, but do not spear food with your chopsticks, and do not stand them upright in a bowl of rice either, as it looks like an offering for the dead. If you have finished with the chopsticks lay them flat on the table or on a rest. You

## HOW TO HOLD CHOPSTICKS

1) Place the first chopstick in the crook of your thumb and forefinger. Support it with the little and ring fingers, and keep it there with the knuckle of the thumb.
2) Hold the second chopstick like a pencil, between middle and index fingers, anchored by the pad of your thumb.
3) When picking up food, keep the lower stick stationary and the tips even. As the index finger moves up and down, only the upper stick should move, using the thumb as an axis.

**Third finger acting as a rest for the lower stick**

**Thumb and first finger controlling the top stick**

shouldn't suck greasy fingers, or use them to pick bones out of your mouth – spit bones or shell onto the table, into the saucer that was under your bowl, or into a napkin. Toothpicks are ubiquitous, but do cover the action with your free hand. And don't be shy about shouting for attention.

Eating alone is very strange to the Chinese way of thinking. Eating in a group – sharing the dishes and the experience – greatly increases the enjoyment.

## THE END OF THE MEAL

A platter of fresh fruit and steaming hot towels signal the end of the meal is coming. Just as you should await the start of a meal, do not stand up before your host, who will rise

**An old lady demonstrates the perfect noodle technique**

and indicate that the dinner has ended and ask if you've had enough. The answer is "yes."

The person who invited you usually shoulders the full weight of the bill, so accept graciously. Offering to pay is fine, even polite; insisting too hard suggests that you doubt the host's ability to pay.

The capitalist habit of tipping was wiped out after Mao's Communist Party took over. Politically acceptable today, it is still rare, as is "going Dutch."

Prices are fixed and written down in most restaurants, and on bills, although there is the occasional story of restaurants overcharging foreigners.

There is no service charge except in the more upmarket and expensive restaurants, which are also the only places likely to accept international credit cards.

## THE BUSINESS OF BANQUETS

The business banquet is the apex of the Chinese dining experience, and almost all significant deals are clinched at the banquet table. In addition to the above, further rules apply: arrive 15 minutes early; if you are applauded as you come into the room, applaud back; reply to the welcome toast with your own short speech and toast; avoid sensitive subjects; show respect to your elders and superiors by ensuring that the rim of your glass is lower than theirs when clinking glasses and drain your drink in one swift movement.

# What to Drink

**Fresh tea leaves**

Tea, of course is the most popular drink in China. There are countless arguments for drinking the infusion of the bush *Camellia sinensis*, and just as many legends about its origin *(see p293)*. While tea is the most popular drink, there is a wide range of others for the visitor. Beer is popular with meals but wine is also drunk in many upmarket restaurants. Chinese spirits can range from the extremely pleasant to the almost dangerous. Likewise approach the "health tonics" like snake wine with caution – as if the reptilian "sediment" in the bottle isn't enough, they can be fiercely alcoholic.

**Tea plantation in the Fujian hills, South China**

## TYPES OF TEA

Green is the most common tea, baked immediately after picking. Flower tea is a mixture of green tea with flower petals. Black tea colors during the fermentation process and the reddish brew that results explains its Chinese name – red tea. The most highly prized is oolong, a lightly fermented tea. Brick tea is black or green, pressed into blocks. Eight Treasure tea *babaocha* has many ingredients including dates, dried longan, and wolfberry, and Tibetans enjoy yak butter tea.

*Gaiwan or three-piece tea cup*

**Lid keeps leaves in the cup, not the mouth**

**Saucer to prevent fingers burning**

**Black:** hongcha, *actually called "red tea" in Chinese.*

**Green:** lucha, *uses leaves dried without fermentation.*

**Pu'er:** *from Yunnan, is compressed into "bricks."*

**Flower:** huacha *a mix of petals – jasmine, rose, and chrysanthemum.*

**The famous "Hairy Peak" green tea**

**Coffee:** *as café culture enters China, coffee drinking is fashionable among the middle classes. Starbucks may have an outlet inside the Forbidden City, but freshly-ground coffee is rare outside major hotels.*

**Tea and Coffee drink:** *those who want a fashionable coffee drink, but cannot do without their daily shot of tea, can try this blend of tea and coffee.*

## SOFT DRINKS

Even as a cold drink tea is dominant. Iced tea is very popular, especially with the young. Besides the usual array of fruit juices, there is pomegranate juice in Xinjiang, hawthorn juice in Beijing, and lychee and sugar cane juice down south. As well as the global drink brands there are local challengers like Tianfu Cola, and the energy drink Jianlibao, made with honey. As China overcomes its dairy aversion, milk and yoghurt drinks multiply, as well as soyabean *(doujiang)* and Hainan's famous coconut milk.

**Bamboo cane juice**

**Iced green tea**

**Coconut milk drink**

## BEER

Europeans first introduced beer to China in the early 20th century; in the 21st, China has taken over as the world's biggest brewer, so you are never far from a very acceptable light lager, and even a darker brew. Each city usually has its own local brewery.

**Tsingtao beer**

**Yanjing beer**

## WINE

Although grape seeds traveled the Silk Roads, China has historically preferred grain alcohol. The quality is rapidly improving, and red wine is almost exclusively consumed – it is considered good for the heart, and a lucky color too.

**Great Wall**    **Dragon Seal**

## SPIRITS

For millennia the Chinese have been distilling grains into *baijiu* or "white spirits" ranging from strong to deadly. Classified into three types: the *qingxiang*, or light bouquet, group includes Fenjiu from Shanxi; Guizhou's famous Maotai is a classic *jiangxiang*, soy bouquet, while *nongxiang*, strong bouquet, is championed by Sichuan giant Wuliangye.

*Maotai "eight times fermented and seven times distilled" is favored for toasts at banquets. At the other end of the scale* erguotou *is cheap and effective – the people's drink.*

**Maotai**    **Erguotou**

## RICE WINE

Despite being called "wine," some care is required as this can vary in strength from a mild 15–16 % alcohol, to the double- or triple-fermented wines at up to 38 % ABV. Good rice wine is best drunk warm and goes well with cold starters.

**Shaoxing rice wine**

*Shaoxing: This is among the best of the* huangjiu *(yellow spirits), noted for its moderate alcohol content (about 16%) and mellow fragrance.*

**Strong rice wine**

## DRINKING CULTURE

Teahouses are enjoying a bit of a revival in China, as appreciation of tea culture recovers after years of proletarian austerity. While *cha* (tea) stimulates quiet contemplation, *jiu* (alcohol) lubricates noisy celebrations. Despite reveling in the drunkenness of their poets such as Li Bai *(see p28)*, the Chinese have not been as badly affected by alcoholism as many other societies. Public drunkenness is frowned upon – except maybe in the ever more popular karaoke bars. Traditionally only soup was drunk with meals, but this is changing, especially when eating with foreigners. "*Gan bei!*" or "dry the cup" is the clarion call to toasting bouts and drinking games. Beware the legendary capacity of the northeast Chinese, and don't drink alone or on an empty stomach.

**The Jazz Club, Hong Kong – typical of the thriving big city bar scene**

# Choosing a Restaurant

Chosen for their excellent food, good value, and convenient or interesting location, the restaurants in this guide cover a wide price range. They are listed by area in the same order as the chapters appear in this book. Where a restaurant has both an English and Chinese name, the English name is given first.

**PRICE CATEGORIES**
The following price ranges are the equivalent of a meal for two made up of a range of dishes, served with tea, and including any service charges.

¥ Under ¥100
¥¥ ¥100–¥250
¥¥¥ ¥250–¥500
¥¥¥¥ Over ¥500

## BEIJING

### Ding Tai Fung (Ding Tai Feng)                                       ¥
*Hujiayuan Yibei Building 22* **Tel** *(010) 6462 4502*

Internationally acclaimed Taiwanese chain restaurant serving wonderful Shanghainese cuisine and specializing in delicious *xiao long bao* (dumpling soup). Slick decor across two storeys, numerous private rooms and an open kitchen/steamer room to entertain diners. Service is attentive and some of the servers speak English.

### Han Cang                                       ¥
*Ping'an Dadao, opposite North Gate of Beihai Park and on east bank of lake* **Tel** *(010) 6404 2259*       **Map** 1 C3

This bustling, two-storey establishment with huge outdoor dining area enjoys a good location facing the Qian Hai (lake). Han Cang is always packed with locals and foreigners enjoying simple, tasty Hakka dishes. An army of waiters briskley delivers house specialities, including foil-wrapped fish and salt-baked shrimp.

### Qin Tang Fu                                       ¥
*Chaoyangmen Nan Xiaojie 59, Chaoyang* **Tel** *(010) 6559 8135*

This charming, rustic restaurant is busy and noisy, and serves regional cuisine from Shaanxi province. The food is filling, delicious, spicy, and inexpensive. Try the *rou jia mo* (pork burgers), *paomo* (lamb and bread soup), or spicy noodle soups. The menu is in English but staff may struggle to understand you.

### Yuxiang Renjia                                       ¥
*Chaoyang Men Wai Dajie 20, 5th floor of Lianhe Dasha (behind Bellagio Restaurant)* **Tel** *(010) 6588 3841*

One of a chain of restaurants scattered all over the city, at least as good and far cheaper than its more famous competitors, of which there are many. Despite the chain mentality, the restaurant retains a charming village theme. This is real Sichuanese food – oily, intensely spicy, and addictive. The smoked duck is a must.

### Beijing Roast Duck Restaurant (Beijing Dadong)                                       ¥¥
*Building 3, Tuanjiehu Beikou, Dong San Huan* **Tel** *(010) 6582 2892*

There's no finer Beijing duck than that served here – full-flavored and with just the right balance between tender meat and crispy skin. This restaurant surpasses similar Quanjude establishments dotting Beijing and is very popular. Typical Sichuan dishes can also be sampled here.

### Dali Courtyard                                       ¥¥
*Xiaojingchang Hutong 67, Dongcheng* **Tel** *(010) 8404 1430*

As it is hugely popular, this is one of the few restaurants in Beijing where booking is essential. The focus is on regional dishes from Yunnan province, and goat's cheese, cured ham, and spicy fish dishes feature heavily. There is no menu – the chefs decide what to serve depending on what's in season. In summer, there is pleasant courtyard seating.

### Huajiayiyuan                                       ¥¥
*Dongzhimen Nei Dajie 235, Dongcheng* **Tel** *(010) 6403 0677*

The words noisy, fun, and atmospheric sum up this Beijing institution, popular with locals and tourists alike. Aside from the tasty and inexpensive food, the restaurant puts on entertainment like noodle-making and tea-pouring ceremonies in the evening. Staff is friendly and speak good English.

### Huang Ting                                       ¥¥
*Jinyu Hutong 8 (in Peninsula Hotel)* **Tel** *(010) 8516 ext. 6707*       **Map** 2 E5

Old Beijing recreated with thousands of bricks from demolished hutong, along with wooden screens, carved stone friezes, and door guardian stones. Dishes such as deep-fried prawns with wasabi-mayonnaise show a Hong Kong influence, but also include a classic Beijing roast duck.

### Lotus in Moonlight (Hetang Yuese Sushi)                                       ¥¥
*Liufang Nanli 12* **Tel** *(010) 6465 3299*

Practically glowing with health, enhanced by the light-filled interior, this vegetarian restaurant is hugely popular for its range and creativity. Options vary from fake (soy product-based) meat dishes to innovative vegetable combinations, complemented by an extensive tea selection.

**Key to Symbols** *see back cover flap*

### My Humble House (Sai She)

*W307/1F Oriental Plaza West Tower, Dong Cheng Tel (010) 8518 8811*

Map 4 D1

This smart branch of the Singapore chain serves intriguing fusion cuisine in a chic, modern setting. Beautiful presentation throughout, from the decorative pond in the light-filled atrium to the lines of poetry weaved into the descriptions of the dishes.

### Pure Lotus (Jin Xin Lian)

*Holiday Inn Lido 3f, Jiangtai Lu Tel (010) 8703 6668*

The dining room of this branch of a vegetarian restaurant chain features striking Eastern-inspired artworks and fittings to match similarly presentable "meat inspired" food. Offerings include vegetarian mutton (made of tofu), pork dishes (made with beans), and vegetarian Peking duck.

### Three Guizhou Men (San Ge Guizhouren)

*Guanghua Xili 6 (behind Bellagio restaurant) Tel (010) 6507 4761*

The Three Guizhou Men offers genuine Guizhou cuisine which is uncompromisingly spicy and sour. This is generally too coarse for foreign tastes but the chef has blended the traditional dishes with more conventional Chinese flavors to create something really rather enjoyable. Stylish and atmospheric.

### The Tree (Yinbide Shu)

*Bei Sanlitun 43, behind 3.3 Mall Tel (010) 6415 1954*

This cozy pub, in the heart of the Sanlitun nightlife, serves good wood-fired pizzas and a selection of Belgian beers on tap. Enjoy soothing acoustic tunes from Filipino cover bands and gaze at abstract nude portraits on the walls. Regulars swear by the Flemish-style bitterballen pizza. Courtyard open during the summer months.

### Cepe

*Jinchengfang Jie 1 (in Ritz-Carlton Hotel) Tel (010) 6601 6666*

Clusters of silver mushrooms hang from the ceiling in this restaurant specializing in contemporary Italian cuisine. The menu here is noted for its excellent pasta, fish, and beer dishes, all with an emphasis on mushrooms, which are cultivated in the restaurant's own humidor.

### China Grill

*Park Hyatt Hotel, Jianguomenwai Daije 2, Chaoyang Tel (010) 8567 1234*

As it is located on the 66th floor, the awe-inspiring 330° view of Beijing is the star selling point here, although the food is good too. The Western menu offers lots of grilled items, but a recommended dish on the Chinese menu is sweet and sour black cod. Service is excellent.

### Hazara

*Face Bar, Dong Cao Yuan 26, Gongli Nan Lu, Chaoyang Tel (010) 6551 6788*

Beijing's best Indian restaurant offers delicious, if expensive, Northern Indian curries, including tasty cashew nut curry, in a stunning setting, with antiques sourced from across India. There is also an English menu. Service is excellent. Part of the Face complex, which has a number of bars and restaurants, set in a converted schoolhouse.

### Made in China (Chang'an Yi Hao)

*Dong Chang'an Jie 1 (in Grand Hyatt Hotel) Tel (010) 8518 1234 ext. 3608*

Map 4 D1

Brick walls hung with cooking implements give the impression of eating with the family. At open kitchens, ducks roast and nimble fingers speedily make disks of dough to be spooned with fragrant filling to make the little pasta parcels known as *jiaozi*, a Beijing specialty. Superb.

### Whampoa Club

*Jinrong Jie 23A, Haidang Tel (010) 880 88828*

This is the most fashionable restaurant in Financial Street, Beijing's answer to Wall Street. It offers reinvented local specialties, lightened for modern tastes and at designer prices. The atmosphere at night is wonderful, due to the twinkling lights in the seductive dining area, and there's a stylish bar for post-dinner cocktails.

### Court Yard (Siheyuan)

*Donghuamen Dajie 95 Tel (010) 6526 8883*

Map 2 F5

Once proclaimed one of the world's top dining places, Beijing's most famous fusion restaurant isn't quite the revelation it's made out to be, but it is nevertheless excellent. The menu changes regularly, with emphasis on execution over innovation, and the wine list is unrivaled. Browse the art gallery while you're there.

### Domus

*Nanchizi Dajie 115, Chaoyang Tel (010) 8511 8015*

This beautifully designed restaurant, near the Forbidden City, is stylish and sexy. The Chinese owners spent a lot of money converting a courtyard, hidden down a historic Hutong alley, into a modern restaurant and bar. The menu is inspired by traditional French cooking. The dining room is darkly lit, while the upstairs bar and café is light and airy.

### Jaan

*Dong Chang'an Jie 33 (in Raffles Beijing Hotel) Tel (010) 6526 3388*

Map 4 D1

With the best of a combination of locally and globally sourced ingredients, this restaurant offers a delightfully imaginative modern French menu led by fish and seafood dishes that are presented with bravura. Elegant decor with tall French windows and crystal chandeliers plus an original 1920s dance floor.

## Jing

🏨🍴 ⑤⑤⑤⑤

*Jinyu Hutong 8 (inside Peninsula Hotel)* **Tel** *(010) 8516 2888 ext. 6714*

**Map** *2 E5*

There's impressive variety and no shortage of innovation and quality in this food which travels from all over Asia and Europe. The focus here is on the visual – few restaurants in China can even dream of being so stylish. Admire the modern metal-and-glass interior with multiple open kitchens.

# HEBEI, TIANJIN, & SHANXI

## CHENGDE Xin Qianlong Dajiudian

📋 ⑤

*Da Jingyuan Dasha, Xinhua Lu* **Tel** *(0314) 207 6768*

Like many other restaurants in Chengde, this one stresses regional game and wild mountain ingredients in a pleasant environment and at low prices. Try the dumplings stuffed with local game – a nice variation on a standard dish, which make for a quick, cheap, and satisfying meal.

## CHENGDE Qianyang Dajiudian

⑤⑤

*Pule Lu 18* **Tel** *(0314) 590 7000*

Familiar Chinese cooking methods are applied to ingredients stressing Chengde's origins as a hunting resort for the Qing emperors In this hotel-based restaurant. Emphasis is on local game (venison, pheasant, and wild boar). Local produce like mountain mushrooms and herbs are artfully employed.

## DATONG Dongfang Mianshi Guan

📋 ⑤

*Yingze Jie* **Tel** *(0352) 203 9940*

Expect a 10-minute wait, though it's well worth it. The hordes start piling in at 11:30am to slurp up *dao xiao mian* – Datong's specialty noodles – from classic lime green bowls while sitting on bright orange stools. Free tanks of broth available for refills. A good place to visit if you are looking for culinary authenticity.

## DATONG Yonghe Hongqi Meishicheng

📋🏨 ⑤

*Yingbin Dong Lu 8* **Tel** *(0352) 510 0333*

Datong's best-known restaurant (known in English as Red Flag Food City) is outrageously large, with six hostesses greeting diners on their way in. It specializes in local Shanxi dishes such as oat noodles as well as spicy Sichuan and Hunan cuisine. A giant rock garden dominates the center of the dining space.

## JI'NAN Luneng Ju Ji Wang

📋 ⑤

*Heihuquan Xi Lu 65* **Tel** *(0531) 611 9212*

Everything from snake to steak. Point and choose from various roasted meats, Chinese-style sushi, traditional stir-fry, fresh seafood, and various Shandong cold dishes. Save room for the creatively different dumplings such as chrysanthemum flower and shrimp, or the specialty salted chicken. Impeccable service.

## PINGYAO Dejuyuan Folk-style Guesthouse (Dejuyuan Mingfeng Binguan)

🏨 ⑤

*Xi Da Jie 43* **Tel** *(0354) 568 5266*

English menus and pictures simplify ordering at this often packed restaurant-cum-hotel lobby. The kitchen usually modifies the normally salty and spicy Pingyao specialties to foreign tastes. Pingyao cold beef is recommended, as is the *you mian kao lao* – a steamer of large, hollow noodles with a dipping sauce.

## PINGYAO Yuanheng Jiujia

📋 ⑤

*Xi Da Jie 111* **Tel** *(0354) 568 7052*

The stale atmosphere of a typical Chinese restaurant, but a place to eat local dishes with local people on Pingyao's main street. No English menus, but typical Pingyao specialties can be found here, including *qiao mian wan tuan* – a thin pancake cut into strips and served in a soup. Shanxi-style dishes are also available.

## SHIJIAZHUANG Quanjude

📋 ⑤⑤

*Heping Xi Lu 108* **Tel** *(0311) 8783 4014*

A bright, modern restaurant located in a guesthouse, this famous duck specialist chain serves Beijing's signature dish in more pleasant surroundings than the Beijing premises, and for lower prices. Shandong dishes are also available for those wanting to stray from duck fare.

## SHIJIAZHUANG The Greenery Café (Lüyin Ge Kafeiting)

🏨🍴 ⑤

*Zhongshan Dong Lu 195, inside the Yanchun Garden Hotel* **Tel** *(0311) 8667 1188*

For those seeking a break from standard Chinese, here's a selection of pan-Asian and Western expat favorites, from Malaysian chicken to spaghetti Bolognaise, and excellent set breakfasts. The restaurant is themed with general transport decor and you can enjoy the strange option of eating inside an aircraft fuselage.

## TAIHUAI (WUTAI SHAN) Fo You Yuan Quan Su Zhai

📋🌱 ⑤

*Wuyue Miao Dong Ce* **Tel** *(0350) 654 6283*

Everything vegetarian (but not vegan), from simple potato and greens to tofu and beans disguised as chicken wings or BBQ pork. Diners often find themselves eating with monks, as the restaurant is very popular with the local monastic community. Only open in the tourism season: March–April.

**Key to Price Guide** *see p582* **Key to Symbols** *see back cover flap*

### TAIHUAI (WUTAI SHAN) Yinhai Shanzhuang Canting

*Taihuai Zhen* **Tel** *(0350) 654 3794*

A sparse, windowless restaurant located within the Yinhai hotel, with a peculiar simple/smart divide. Considered by locals to be the fanciest in town, but serves simple mountain fare like pheasant, rabbit, and local wild vegetables and mushrooms. Beijing duck and Cantonese food are also available, as are vegetarian dishes.

## SHANDONG & HENAN

### KAIFENG Diyilou Baoziguan

*Sihou Jie 8* **Tel** *(0378) 599 8655*

Seemingly every family restaurant in Kaifeng advertizes *guangtang* (soup-filled) dumplings, but this is the upmarket choice. So popular, it has spawned a dumpling empire stretching to 40 outlets across China. Typical flavors include Chinese leek and pork, and spicy chicken. Service attentive, serving up to 1,000 clientele.

### KAIFENG You Yi Xin

*Gulou Jie 22* **Tel** *(0378) 595 6677*

This is a typical Chinese restaurant in the sense that the atmosphere is not impressive, but the food is of very high quality. Diners are able to sample simple country dishes from Henan; it is hard to define Henan cuisine exactly, but the Chinese categorize it as being neither extremely sweet, spicy, sour, nor salty. Service is friendly.

### LUOYANG Mudan Ting

*Zhongzhou Xi Lu 15, 2nd floor* **Tel** *(0379) 6468 0028*

Not as famous as Zhenbutong, but more conveniently located and with English menus. Up to 20 courses of various soups are served in the "flowing" water banquet and Korean-style BBQ meats are available. Music and dancing performances often accompany dinner. Service is much friendlier than elsewhere.

### LUOYANG Zhenbutong Fandian

*Zhongzhou Dong Lu 369* **Tel** *(0379) 6395 2338*

Well-known water banquet takes center stage at this famous restaurant. Since it opened in 1902, Zhenbutong has been awarded gold medals by international food critic associations. Stairs lead past pictures of the celebrities and statesmen who have eaten here, including former Chinese premier Zhou Enlai.

### QINGDAO La Villa Bar & Restaurant (Weila Faguo Canguan)

*Xianggang Zhong Lu 5 Hao* **Tel** *(0532) 8388 6833*

Busy every day from early until late, La Villa's bar offers lounge-like comfort in a well-restored stone villa. Catering to more Western tastes, patrons may dine in private, in the strikingly-lit bar, or al fresco. Snack on tapas, or dine on an impressive range of salads, soups, pizzas, and spaghetti. Open all day.

### QUFU Queli Hotel Dining Room (Queli Binshe Canting)

*Queli Jie 1* **Tel** *(0537) 486 6660*

Features Kong Family dishes originally prepared for visiting officials and special occasions. English explanation for several dishes. Also serves Confucian *dim sum* – various fried, savory, and sweet bites. Traditional Chinese music accompanies most meals. Located in the Queli Hotel.

### QUFU Confucia Dining Room (Kongfu Xiyuan Canting)

*Ban Bi Jie 8* **Tel** *(0537) 442 3666*

This rather ordinary restaurant stands not far from the West Garden Hotel, and in stark contrast to the elegant hotel to which it's connected. It specializes in Kong Family cuisine, a branch of Shandong style, emphasizing the use of dark colors and strong flavors. The picture menu is necessary to facilitate ordering if you don't speak Chinese.

### TAI'AN Taishan Restaurant (Taishan Caiguan)

*Hongmen Lu 20, Daizongfang* **Tel** *(0538) 626 7888*

A fine restaurant to eat a meal at before or after a hike up Tai Shan, and therefore conveniently located close to its entrance with a rather spectacular backdrop. Features typical Shandong food, liberally utilizing soy sauce, vinegar, and salt. Stewed dishes get high ratings, as does the local Tai Shan beer.

## SHAANXI

### XI'AN Fanji Lazhi Roudian

*Zhubashi Jie 45* **Tel** *(029) 8727 3917*

A diner from another era – you'll be transported back to the days of ration coupons by the state-run ambience. Since this is the most renowned vendor of Xi'an's favorite snack – a lightly spiced pork hamburger (rou jia mo) that tastes much better than it sounds – it is the ideal venue in which to try it. Closed at weekends.

### XI'AN Highfly Pizza (Gaofei Bisa)

*Huanchen Nan Lu 73* **Tel** *(029) 8841 0626*

Excellent Western-style breakfasts (with real muesli!) and decent approximations of home comforts such as hearty soups, pasta, and pizzas smothered in cheese are the main reasons for dining here. Pizzas are delivered to your hotel for a small surcharge. Ideal if you are after some respite from Chinese cuisine. One of two branches in the city.

### XI'AN Lao Sun Jia

*Dong Guan Zhengjie 78* **Tel** *(029) 8240 3205*

The best place to try Shaanxi cuisine's most famous dish – *yangrou paomo* (lamb and bread soup) – is on the third floor of this bustling restaurant (one branch of many across the city). Shred your bun into tiny pieces; let the waitress add the broth; add chilli and coriander to taste. The point-and-order eatery on the second floor is superb value.

### XI'AN The Tang Dynasty (Tang Yue Gong)

*Chang'an Lu 75* **Tel** *(029) 8782 2200*

The light southern Chinese cuisine is elaborately prepared and named, from the "Princess' Pin" to the "Pearls of Cathay." The musical entertainment, showcasing instruments and costumes of the Tang Dynasty, is a stunning spectacle. Dinner of Shaanxi classics starts at 6:30pm sharp, and the show starts at 8:30pm – reservations are essential.

# SHANGHAI

### Nan Xiang Steamed Bun Restaurant (Nan Xiang Mantou Dian)

*Yu Yuan Rd 85* **Tel** *(021) 6355 4206*

Come by 10:30am or after 3pm or be prepared to wait; but the pork and crab dumplings are worth it. Walk past the line-up on the stairs to an upstairs, more pricey dining room with a much shorter wait: they will still want you out as soon as you've eaten. A rare, long-standing institution (founded 1900) that actually lives up to its reputation.

### 1221

*Yan'an West Rd 1221* **Tel** *(021) 6213 6585*

1221 serves up a Canton-influenced and less oily version of Shanghainese dishes including a refreshing pork and papaya soup, or a spicy boiled beef with warm sesame loaf. Western and Japanese influences make this popular, if not a favorite of expats. Away from the center of town but worth the effort.

### Bao Luo

*Fumin Rd 271* **Tel** *(021) 6279 2827*

Don't be put off by the musty entrance. This restaurant is a favorite of local gourmets (plus renowned chef Jean-Georges Vongerichten) and is justifiably acclaimed for its cheap and classic Shanghainese dishes such as the divinely sweet stir-fried eggplant in pancakes.

### Crystal Jade (Fei Cui Jiujia)

*South Block Xin Tiandi, Lane 123, Xingye Lu* **Tel** *(021) 6385 8752*

Exceptional Cantonese, Shanghainese, and other Chinese food in this upmarket Xintiandi complex. Highlights include the spicy, nutty *dan dan mian* (made from one long, fresh noodle), superb Shanghainese dumplings, and the many varieties of steamed buns. Bookings are essential on weekends.

### Dong Bei Ren

*Shanxi South Rd 1* **Tel** *(021) 5228 9898*

This colorfully decorated cheap-eats hall serves wholesome northeast dishes, including simply prepared *jiaozi* (meat dumplings) and surprisingly flavorful tofu. Bottles of *baijiu* (white spirits) are a popular accompaniment so tables do tend to get rowdy at times.

### Element Fresh (Xin Yuan Su)

*4/5f, KWah Centre, Huaihai Zhong Rd 1028* **Tel** *(021) 5403 8865*

If you are tired of street noodles, Element Fresh provides the perfect tonic with its large salads and sandwiches. Try a crunchy Niçoise washed down with freshly-squeezed carrot and apple juice. This KWah Centre location is the best of the chain and boasts an expansive terrace as well as the city's leafiest views.

### Fulton Place

*Yongjia Rd 570* **Tel** *(021) 3461 1775*

Talented American chef Marc Johnson creates stylish contemporary European cuisine in a distinctly British-styled restaurant. The setting evokes the drawing room of a country manor house with patterned wallpaper and wooden furniture. One of the various snack plates makes a good place to start. Mains include roast lamb. Closed Sunday.

### Gu Yi

*Fumin Rd 87* **Tel** *(021) 6249 5628*

The unassuming corner of Julu and Fumin roads now boasts exceptional eateries, among them Gu Yi. Bland palates beware since everything in this outstanding Hunanese restaurant comes full of chillies, from pork ribs to cold pressed chicken, to a side dish of cucumbers.

**Key to Price Guide** *see p582* **Key to Symbols** *see back cover flap*

## Lost Heaven Yunnan Folk Cuisine (Huama Tiantang Yunnan Canting)
*Gaoyou Rd 38* **Tel** *(021) 6433 5126*

Set in a charming, three-storey villa on a French Concession backstreet, Lost Heaven has quickly gained a devoted following thanks to its comfortable southeast Asian decor, attentive staff, and wide selection of rustic dishes. The dishes represent the cuisine of Yannan's minority groups with an emphasis on fish, chicken, and vegetables.

## Vegetarian Lifestyle (Zao Zi Shu)
*Fengxian Rd 258* **Tel** *(021) 6215 7566*

Zao Zi Shu boasts no eggs, meat, fish, fowl, or MSG. Fake meat dishes are prominent, most of them created with tofu, and many of the patrons are monks in flowing robes. After eating, you can browse the restaurant's New-Age bookstore that stocks a variety of titles from Buddhist literature to vegetarian cookbooks.

## Wagas
*Donghu Rd 7* **Tel** *(021) 5466 1488*

One of a chain of relaxed cafés serving breakfast, lunch, and dinner to an eclectic clientele. Think gourmet sandwiches, pasta dishes, Asian plates, fresh juices, cakes, and pastries, all served up MSG- and preservative-free. Drinks include illy coffee and a selection of wines and beers. Popular with laptop users due to its free Wi-Fi access.

## Whisk Choco Café
*Huaihai Rd 1250* **Tel** *(021) 5404 7770*

Despite the name, chocolate is not the only thing this petite and friendly cafe has to offer. Run by a New Zealander, the cafe serves good quality coffee and a prosciutto caprese panini to die for. Hot chocolates and wonderfully decadent desserts complete the satisfying picture.

## Mr & Mrs Bund
*The Bund 19* **Tel** *(021) 6323 9898*

Created by French celebrity chef Paul Pairet, this Bund-front restaurant focuses on modern European cuisine, including some of Pairet's famed molecular gastronomy. The menu is vast, as are the cocktail and wine lists. One of the city's best-value upscale eateries. Reservations recommended.

## Palladio (Paladuo)
*Nanjing West Rd 1376, (inside Portman Ritz-Carlton)* **Tel** *(021) 6279 8888*

Sumptuous menu of extravagant Italian dishes with hints of Napoli; meals should be taken at a gentle pace, although briskly served business set lunches are excellent value for money too. Vast wine list worth serious consideration — thrice winner of Wine Spectator award of excellence. Highly recommended.

## Shintori Null II (Xinduli Wu Er Dian)
*Julu Rd 803* **Tel** *(021) 5404 5252*

Rustic paths wind through bamboo to the sliding metal door of this former warehouse. Inside is an industrial chic space and possibly Shanghai's best Japanese food. Enjoy the beefsteak in pu-leaf – a winning variation on Beijing Duck – but leave room for the green tea tiramisu. Situated on the quiet Julu Lu.

## South Beauty 881 (Qiao Jiang Nan)
*Yan'an Middle Rd 881* **Tel** *(021) 6247 5878*

South Beauty 881's setting, an ornately decorated mansion with roof terrace and vast gardens, threatens to overwhelm the Sichuan/Cantonese menu. However, some of the hot and spicy items, particularly the seafood dishes, have remarkable flavors and are innovative in presentation.

## Vedas
*Jianguo West Rd 550* **Tel** *(021) 6445 8100*

Set in a quiet corner of the French Concession area, this clean and comfortable Indian restaurant has quickly established itself as Shanghai's leader in *biryanis*. The management is superb, the presentation stylish, and the samosas, curries, and breads flavorful. The Maharaja Lounge offers more intimate dining.

## Whampoa Club (Huangpu Hui)
*5th Floor, Three on The Bund, Zhongshan Dong Yi Rd 3* **Tel** *(021) 6321 3737*

Completely comprehensive menu of traditional Chinese favorites in top-notch surroundings, some given a surprising modern twist (such as fried almond-and-cocoa spare ribs) or simply reinvented to accentuate the flavors. A tea sommelier offers 50 different fine teas from around China.

## Yucca
*26F Sinan Mansions, Sinan Rd* **Tel** *(021) 3368 9525*

Located in Sinan Mansions, a collection of restored heritage villas in the French Concession area, Yucca is a hip, brash, and extremely popular cocktail and tapas lounge in a vibrant, colorful setting. The tapas menu features delicious new takes on traditional Mexican and Latin American dishes.

## Haiku by Hatsune
*Taojiang Rd 28B, near Hengshan Rd* **Tel** *(8612) 6445 0021*

This Beijing restaurant brand has brought its elegant, stylish interiors, and modern Japanese food to a small, funky space in the French Concession. Service is excellent. The long, low tables are great for groups of friends, the sake and beer are superb, and the large menu ranges from California-style sushi rolls to several vegetarian options.

### Jean Georges (Rangqiaozhi)    🔲🍽️    ¥¥¥¥¥
*4th Floor, Three on The Bund, Zhongshan Yi Rd 3* **Tel** *(021) 6321 7733*

The Shanghai branch of Jean-Georges Vongerichten's garlanded New York restaurant offers French with hints of Asia (lemongrass, coconut), each dish small but perfect in every way. Try the seasonal set menu which makes the best of available ingredients, and something from the 5,000-bottle wine cellar.

### M on The Bund (Mishi Xi Canting)    🔲🍽️    ¥¥¥¥
*7th Floor, Guangdong Rd 20* **Tel** *(021) 6350 9988*

Regarded as the pioneer of top-of-the-range foreign food outside the big hotels, Michelle Garnaut serves European and Middle-Eastern flavors which has made her Hong Kong restaurant legendary, including a soft-as-butter salted lamb. Atop a 1920s bank overlooking the river, the bar is also popular.

### The Yongfoo Elite (Yongfu Hui)    🔲    ¥¥¥¥
*Yongfu Rd 200* **Tel** *(021) 5466 2727*

The abalone-heavy Shanghai and Cantonese menu is a little pricey, but dining here is worth the expense. The Yongfoo Elite is housed in an ancient former British Consulate building and reputedly took two years to furnish. The results are extraordinary, from the verandah shaded by an ancient magnolia to the ornate candelabras.

# JIANGSU & ANHUI

### HEFEI The Golden Lotus (Jin Lian Ge)    🔲    ¥¥
*Wuhu Rd 199* **Tel** *(0551) 228 6200*

The decor may be unremarkable, yet this hotel restaurant is in the prettiest part of Hefei, looking across to the Baogong Temple and Children's Palace. Cantonese dishes dominate the menu, local Anhui delicacies such as *caocao chicken*, cooked with traditional Chinese herbal medicines, also available.

### NANJING Dingshan Yixian    ¥¥
*Zhongshan Dong Rd 458, 2/F* **Tel** *(025) 8445 6622*

Consistently recommended by locals as one of the best places in town to sample Jiangsu's Huaiyang cooking style. The decor is average but the food is tasty home-cooking and includes duck and meatball dishes. If you're feeling adventurous, try fried soft-shell turtles with white eggs and beancurd. English menu.

### NANJING Great Nanjing Eatery (Da Pai Dang)    🗐    ¥¥
*Shizi Qiao Jie 2* **Tel** *(025) 8330 5777*

Offers up the full selection of Huaiyang specialties all produced in a home-cooked style in an earthy selection of chinaware. Specialties include jelly-like tofu in a lobster sauce (*xihuang dofu*) and pig's lung soup (*zhufei luobo tang*). If this doesn't suit, there are plenty of other options just along the street. No English menu.

### NANJING Behind the Wall    🗐🍽️    ¥¥¥
*Shanghai Rd 150* **Tel** *(025) 8368 6481*

A friendly, relaxed restaurant perfect for al fresco eating during the summer thanks to its gorgeous, softly-lit patio dining area. Very popular with the expat crowd for its use of fresh ingredients; filling, well-cooked portions and live jazz at the weekends. European fare and some Mexican dishes also available.

### NANJING Ming Yuen    🔲    ¥¥¥
*B/F, Shangri-La Hotel, Cha Er Rd 90* **Tel** *(025) 5880 2888 ext 21*

A great place to get acquainted with the province's local Huaiyang cuisine in a high-class environment through a menu focusing on fresh seasonal river food such as perch and shrimp. Other Huaiyang specialties include duck and eel dishes. Also staple Cantonese dishes available such as shark's fin and abalone. English menu.

### NANJING Nihero Cantonese Cuisine (Yue Hong He)    🗐    ¥¥¥
*Suning Universal Shopping Centre 11/F, Hunan Rd 18* **Tel** *(025) 5792 3588*

One of the most popular upscale Cantonese restaurants in town, on the upper floors of a shopping arcade. Renowned for the freshness and quality of its ingredients. There is no English menu but the waitresses will happily point out the most delicious dishes. Strong on seafood dishes, sushi is also available.

### NANJING Sui Yuan    🔲    ¥¥¥
*1/F, Grand Metro Park Hotel, Zhongshan Dong Rd 319* **Tel** *(025) 8480 8888 ext 7760*

Consistently high standards are served up in this five-star restaurant focusing on regional fish dishes such as Huaiyang eel and other local dishes like Nanjing roasted duck and "Lion's Heads" – *shizi tou (see p180)*. A selection of *dim sum* is available. English menu. The walls are adorned with colorful Jiangsu artwork.

### SUZHOU The Bookworm    🗐🇻🍽️    ¥¥
*Gun Xin Fang 77* **Tel** *(0512) 6526 4720*

The Bookworm café offers much more than just food and is a great place to hang out or sample some local culture. There is a large selection of international and Chinese food options for breakfast, lunch, and dinner. A wide variety of books are available for loan and free Wi-Fi access. There is also an annual Literary festival held every March.

### SUZHOU Chuanfulou Dajiudian

*Guanqian Jie Bifeng Fang 1* **Tel** *(0512) 6522 8877*

Nestled in Suzhou's gastronomic heartland, Sichuan and Suzhou dishes are presented in a variety of stone pots and porcelain plates in a spotless yet charming setting. Highlights of the comprehensive menu include *Chuan Fu* roast beef (sizzling and invigorating) and simple yet stunning stir-fried local mushrooms.

### SUZHOU Deyue Lou

*Guanqian Jie Taijian Nong 8 and 43* **Tel** *(0512) 6523 8940*

This renowned 400-year-old restaurant has twice appeared on Chinese cinema screens. It's probably the best place to sample squirrel-shaped mandarin fish and other Suzhou specialties. Presentation is outstanding – particularly the dumplings, some of which come shaped like hedgehogs or geese.

### SUZHOU Wang Si Wineshop (Wang Si Jiujia)

*Guanqian Jie Taijian Nong 23* **Tel** *(0512) 6522 7277*

Despite its tired interior, the Wang Si Wineshop serves memorable local cuisine, with an emphasis on the ingredients' medicinal properties. Try one of the wild vegetable dishes or the succulent "beggar's chicken" wrapped in lotus leaves and baked in clay. Absolutely fresh ingredients and flavors.

## ZHEJIANG & JIANGXI

### HANGZHOU Zhangshengji

*Shuangling Rd 77* **Tel** *(0571) 8602 6666*

A partial picture menu makes ordering the light and delicate local cuisine very easy. The palatial multi-story restaurant is always busy with local people, and unlike the restaurants favored by tour guides, prices are low and the quality high. Expect a variety of Hangzhou and Huaiyang dishes with strong emphasis on fish.

### HANGZHOU Crystal Garden (Yuqilin)

*Dongpo Rd 12* **Tel** *(0571)8706 7777*

Smart, brightly-lit three-story interior atrium with traditional square tables and wooden stools. A picture menu with English makes ordering very easy; try steamed mince pork and roe balls, or chicken in rice wine. Conveniently located in central Hangzhou. Tables are scattered over two balconied floors above a central well.

### HANGZHOU Shang Palace (Shang Gong)

*Bei Shan Rd 78, inside Shangri-La Hotel* **Tel** *(0571) 8797 7951*

Local Hangzhou favorites such as Beggar's Chicken and Dongpo pork prepared alongside the lightest and most delicate of Cantonese specialities, all perfectly executed, and served in opulent surroundings. Luxurious traditional Chinese motifs decorate this pleasant restaurant located inside the Shangri-La Hotel.

### HANGZHOU Va Bene (Huabinni)

*Nan Shan Rd 147, Xi Hu Tiandi* **Tel** *(0571) 8702 6333*

An Italian heads the large open kitchen of this latest incarnation of the Hong-Kong-based Italian, set amongst lakeside groves of maple and bamboo in Hangzhou's answer to Shanghai's trendy restaurant scene. Try beef *carpaccio* or salmon with horseradish, pizzas from as little as ¥30, and a set menu from ¥220.

### NANCHANG The New Oriental Hotel (Xin Dongfang Dajiudian)

*Binjiang Nan Rd 18* **Tel** *(0791) 670 9999*

Not a hotel, but a palatial four-story restaurant opposite the Teng Wang Ge with different rooms and every kind of Chinese food conceivable, from *dim sum* to hot pot. Spicy fish head tofu is the local specialty. The owner is so rich that he also owns the province's only Rolls-Royce, parked in the lobby.

### NANCHANG Yuan Dong Dajiudian

*Fuzhou Rd 95* **Tel** *(0791) 621 8888*

Once Nanchang's most celebrated restaurant, now dowdy and left behind by more service-oriented newcomers, the Yuan Dong at least stays open late and serves well-executed spicy local dishes. Ingredients and pre-prepared dishes are on display at the entrance, making pointing to order easy.

### PUTUO SHAN Seafood Restaurants

*At the docks*

The small, simple restaurants dotted along the two roads that lead up from the dock offer a wide variety of seafood as fresh as it is possible to find. The fish are still alive in buckets or swimming in tanks until selected to be your main dish, and cooked to order.

### PUTUO SHAN Xilei Xiao Zhuang

*Xianghua Jie 1* **Tel** *(0580) 609 1512*

Many of Putuo Shan's restaurants cater for the pilgrim market with extensive vegetarian menus alongside the meat dishes for mere tourists. There's plenty of choice in the Chinese dishes on offer here for herbivores and carnivores alike. Comfortable surroundings, located inside the Xilei Xiao Zhuang Hotel.

### WENZHOU Haigang Meishi Fang

*Wang Jiang Dong Rd* **Tel** *(0577) 8819 7199*

On a two-story barge moored opposite Jiangxin Island, this has even better views than the Jingwangjiao, and the same raw ingredients, methods, and minimalist pricing. Point to order, then sit on white plastic chairs (open-air on the upper deck) to eat. Take advantage of the location and indulge in fish and seafood.

### WENZHOU Jinwangjiao Dajiudian

*Wang Jiang Dong Rd* **Tel** *(0577) 819 7008*

Point to your desired fish or seafood, mention or mime a cooking method, and select other dishes from those on display. Visitors to China sometimes seem scared to venture beyond the pseudo-Western restaurants in their hotels, but the fresh seafood on offer here, at less than half the price, is reason enough to be a little more adventurous.

## HUNAN & HUBEI

### CHANGSHA Boton (Bodun Xicanting)

*Wuyi Dadao 591* **Tel** *(0731) 8227 7518*

Relief for those who find Hunan food too crude and too hot, in comfortable modern surroundings with steaks and approximations of other Western favorites, as well as good if expensive coffee. Be entertained on the stylish couches by occasional live easy-listening music, with piano and saxophone. Nice.

### CHANGSHA Huo Gong Dian

*Wuyi Dadao 93* **Tel** *(0731) 411 6803*

Everything Hunanese from pickles to seafood is brought round with rapidity and efficiency in trolleys. This serving method and a picture menu make ordering easy. Expect everything to be spicy hot, except the sweet rice dish *ba bao zhou*. Also serves Cantonese dishes such as *dim sum* and duck soup.

### WUHAN Fang Fang Caiguan

*Jiqing Jie 1, Hankou* **Tel** *(027) 8281 0954*

Excellent food, and for a small fee you can be serenaded by local musicians singing current pop hits or Chinese classics. This is the oldest and largest restaurant, conspicuous by its giant yellow tent, and yellow theme. Try the *caiyu lianou* (fish and lotus root) or *ya bozi* (duck's neck), both local favorites.

### WUHAN Mr. Xie Restaurant & Pub (Xie Xiansheng Canting)

*Jianshe Dadao 548* **Tel** *(027) 8577 7288*

Mr. Xie worked for several years in the U.S. restaurant business and returned to open a restaurant in the heart of Wuhan. A partial menu is available in English, and the owner himself often greets guests. Always packed with locals and foreigners. Try the steamed Wuchang fish (*qingzheng Wuchang yu*), a local favorite.

### WUHAN Sunny Sky (Yanyangtian)

*Jiefang Dadao 588, Baofeng Lukou* **Tel** *(027) 8375 0706*

Sunny Sky's muted, tasteful decoration helps balance the din of the main room. The food is excellent and the Chinese menu has a few pictures. Dishes to try include the *suzha oujia* – deep-fried, battered slices of lotus root sandwiched around a pork filling, and *nongjia xiaochaorou*, a spicy pork dish.

### WUHAN Changchunguan Sucaiguan

*Wuluo Rd 269, Wuchang* **Tel** *(027) 8885 4229*

This pleasant restaurant, the name means Eternal Spring in English, copies the decor of the adjacent Daoist temple and produces all manner of vegetarian dishes. The *xiaopinpan* is a sampler platter with small portions of several of the most popular dishes. Also try the *lazi tianluo*, a vegetarian version of spicy river snails, a local favorite.

## FUJIAN

### FUZHOU Juchun Yuan Dajiudian

*Dong Jie 2* **Tel** *(0591) 8750 2328*

*Fo tiao qiao*, or "Buddha jumping over the wall," a stew of more than twenty mostly rather expensive ingredients, is Fuzhou's sole claim to culinary fame. The original restaurant has been reincarnated inside a modern hotel of the same name in the city center, but the Ming-era recipe survives. Focus on the specialty stew.

### XIAMEN Nan Putuo Si

*Inside the Nan Putuo Si (temple)* **Tel** *(0592) 208 5908*

Justly famous restaurant for not imitating meat dishes but bringing out the best in a wide variety of fresh vegetables, legumes, and tofu, in simple surroundings. Buy a set meal at the ticket office, hand the receipt to the waitress and all will be brought to you. Caters principally for the monks and Buddhist visitors to the temple.

**Key to Price Guide** *see p582* **Key to Symbols** *see back cover flap*

### XIAMEN Guan Hai Canting ⓨⓨ

*Lujiang Dao 54 (on top of the Lujiang Binguan)* **Tel** *(0592) 202 2922*

Quality may be higher at restaurants inside the city's four-star hotels but so are the prices, and none have the views of the Guan Hai ("view the sea") restaurant. There's an emphasis on fresh seafood but there's also standard dishes from around China and a nod to Xiamen's links to Hong Kong in all-day trolleyed *dim sum*.

## GUANGDONG & HAINAN

### GUANGZHOU Mao Jia Fandian 🚩 ⓨ

*Tian He Bei Lu 181* **Tel** *(020) 8525 0519*

Rambling interior with artificial trees, ponds, and bridges. Features the spicy Hunan foods that Chairman Mao – represented by a shrine-like interior, a bronze bust, and pictures of his home – favored. *Hong shao rou* (fatty pork), Marshall's duck, baked pigs' feet, and "stinky tofu" served by eager staff.

### GUANGZHOU Taste Of India (Yinsi Weishiguan Jiulang) Ⓥ ⓨ

*Tao Jin Lu 165* **Tel** *(020) 8350 7688*

Serves the best Indian food in Guangzhou, endorsed by expat Indians. Evening buffet starts at 6:30pm, and the menu features Arabic salad, Goan fish curry, and mutton vindaloo. Watch Indian cricket matches on TV or view the fish in the aquarium while dining in the comfort of Taste of India's plush furniture.

### GUANGZHOU East River Seafood Restaurant (Dong Jiang Hai Xian Jiu Jia) 🚩 ⓨⓨ

*Yan Jiang Zhong Lu 9* **Tel** *(020) 8429 7510*

Best of 18 franchises in Guangdong, this is where Cantonese go to eat seafood. There is a fresh fish market and a fresh juice stand on the first floor, and a surprisingly limited menu for such a large restaurant – try the East River beancurd in hot pot, or hand-shredded salt chicken. Bars on each floor of this seafood palace for those less interested in eating.

### GUANGZHOU Guangzhou Jiujia ⓨⓨ

*Wenchang Nan Lu 2* **Tel** *(020) 8138 0388*

This long-established warren of dining rooms has meals to suit all budgets, from pocket money-priced *dim sum* and set meals, to the most elaborate and expensive of Cantonese food order-to-impress dishes. Always busy, and with a limited English menu available. Enjoy navigating around this multi-story dining bedlam.

### GUANGZHOU Qiaomei Shijia Ⓥ ⓨⓨ

*Shamian Nan Jie 52* **Tel** *(020) 8121 7018*

Qiao Mei's staff say every dish is special, but seafood remains their strongest point, with shark fin soup with chicken and pork, fried sea cucumber, or double-boiled tortoise with Tian Shan snow lotus. Other delights include eels scrambled with pepper, double-boiled chicken with caterpillar fungus, and golden grilled baby pigeon.

### GUANGZHOU Taotao Ju 🗐 ⓨⓨ

*Dingshipu Lu 20* **Tel** *(020) 8139 6111*

Eating snake (and snake blood) is a Cantonese tradition and Taotao Ju offers snake in soup and other forms alongside a menu of more familiar Cantonese dishes. Slightly smaller and more dignified than other long-standing Guangzhou restaurants, it still has the authentic raucous bustle of the Cantonese way of life.

### HAINAN Haigang Dajiulou 🚩 ⓨⓨ

*Xinfeng Lu 128, opposite the Mingri Hotel, Sanya* **Tel** *(0898) 3828 3333*

With a Hong Kong manager, this Cantonese option in Sanya city boasts good food in a comfortable, immaculate setting. There are no sea views but this is more than compensated for by an open kitchen and strong emphasis on the freshness of the seafood. Try the fishhead soup or Zhongshan pigeon.

### HAINAN Heyou Seafood Restaurant (Haikou Heyou Haixiangguan) 🚩 ⓨⓨ

*Haixiu Dadao 28, Haikou* **Tel** *(0898) 6676 0006*

A highly regarded seafood restaurant, which once catered for military officials – hence the red star adorning the ceiling of the main dining room. Choose live fish or crustaceans from one of the many tanks. The steamed lobster in garlic is a highlight. Try the Hele crab, one of Hainan's four signature dishes.

### HAINAN The Spice Garden (Xiangliaoyuan Yazhou Canting) 🚩🍽 ⓨⓨ

*2/F, Sheraton Sanya Resort, Yalong Bay National Resort District, Sanya* **Tel** *(0898) 8855 8855 ext. 8411*

Southeast Asian seems an appropriate choice of cuisine in Hainan, which feels more like the southeast than the rest of China. Seafood laksa brims with fresh fish and prawns, and the *tom yum* soup tingles the lips. Coconut palms and umbrellas shade the expansive outside deck. The best-located restaurant in the Sheraton Sanya Resort with sea views.

### HAINAN Symposium (Sofitel Da Judian) 🚩🍽 ⓨⓨ

*Sofitel Boao, Dong Yu Island, Boao, Hainan* **Tel** *(0898) 6296 6888 ext. 63*

Inventive Chinese dishes served in a stylish setting. As the name implies, Symposium is popular among political and business leaders attending the Boao Forum for Asia, not least for its view of the Jade Belt Beach. Hainan specialties abound, from simple seafood dishes to quick-boiled Wenchang chicken.

# HONG KONG & MACAU

## HONG KONG Tim Ho Wan

*Shop 8, Tai Yuen Mansion Phase 2, Kwong Wa St 2–20, Kowloon* **Tel** *(852) 3196 9100*

Crowds wait in line round the block to eat at this seemingly insignificant dumpling house. They are hungry for lotus leaf-steamed rice, *cha sui* pastries, pork buns, and *fun qwor* dumplings, served with constantly flowing *pu'er* tea. Prepare for a long wait to eat at the cheapest Michelin-starred restaurant in the world.

## HONG KONG Gaylord

*1/F Ashley Centre, 23–25 Ashley Road, Tsim Sha Tsui, Kowloon* **Tel** *(852) 2376 1001*     **Map** *1 B4*

Chintzy curry houses abound in this area but the Gaylord is one of the classier ones. Flavors are full without being too fiery. The dishes taste freshly prepared and the spices are freshly toasted. The delights emerging from the Tandoor oven are well worth trying. Northern Indian dishes also available.

## HONG KONG Woodlands

*Wing on Plaza, 62 Mody Road, Tsim Sha Tsui, Kowloon* **Tel** *(852) 2369 3718*     **Map** *1 B4*

The food far excels the expectations of either the distinctly unlovely decor or the menu prices at Woodlands – an entirely vegetarian and alcohol-free place although there's a wide choice of juices and lassi yoghurt drinks. The buffet (*thali*) is a good way to go, but you're unlikely to be disappointed whatever you choose.

## HONG KONG DiVino

*73 Wyndham Street, Central* **Tel** *(852) 2167 8883*     **Map** *2 B3*

Rustic Italian menu in a stylish setting with a few tables al fresco, somewhat of a rarity in Hong Kong. DiVino's straightforward dishes are enhanced by the freshest of imported ingredients including a memorable creamy buffalo mozzarella and excellent swordfish. Popular with expats.

## HONG KONG Kung Tak Lam

*10th floor, World Trade Centre, 280 Gloucester Rd, Hong Kong Island* **Tel** *(852) 2890 3127*     **Map** *3 E3*

Kung Tak Lam sources its supplies from its own farms for this restaurant in the World Trade Centre and its other branch in Tsim Sha Tsui. Fresh, inventive yet quintessentially Chinese flavors are the essence of this excellent vegetarian restaurant. Don't be put off by the dowdy but unpretentious interior; do try the delicious pumpkin stew.

## HONG KONG Luk Yu Tea House

*Ground floor, Luk Tea Building, 24–26 Stanley Street, Central, Hong Kong Island* **Tel** *(852) 2523 5464*     **Map** *2 B3*

Smart surroundings and Cantonese cuisine about as authentic as it gets are the main attractions, and the old world charm of the building doesn't hurt either. Bird's nest and abalone are options for the affluent, the *dim sum* are excellent value, as are many of the consistently good staples (*prawn fu yung* and roast pigeon).

## HONG KONG Shang Palace

*Kowloon Shangri-La, 64 Mody Road, Tsim Sha Tsui, Kowloon* **Tel** *(852) 2733 8754*     **Map** *1 C4*

This is fine dining Chinese style. The flavors are subtle, and the dishes, culled from a range of regions and Chinese cuisines, are given great, effective twists, such as the tender, deep-fried shrimp rolls or the flavorful roast pig's neck with honey. Admire the elaborate, opulent red Chinese decor.

## HONG KONG Yung Kee

*32–40 Wellington Street, Central, Hong Kong Island* **Tel** *(852) 2522 1624*     **Map** *2 B3*

Up there with Luk Yu Tea House, this centrally located, authentic Cantonese restaurant, is a larger, more impersonal, and often more crowded place, yet the cuisine is invariably fresh and the standards unwaveringly high (no frozen produce is used). The chefs often win local culinary awards.

## HONG KONG Gaddi's

*The Peninsula, Salisbury Road, Tsim Sha Tsui, Kowloon* **Tel** *(852) 2315 3171*     **Map** *1 B4*

If you must have the best, don your jacket (compulsory for men) and head here for an intense and creative culinary adventure in a lavish chandelier-festooned dining room. Rich, classic French food prepared with the finest ingredients and a sensational wine list. Prices, needless to say, are stratospheric.

## HONG KONG Miso

*Shop 15, Basement, Jardine House, Central, Hong Kong Island* **Tel** *(852) 2845 8773*     **Map** *2 C3*

You can't get better Japanese food for less in Hong Kong than at Miso. The sushi and sashimi are superb, although there are plenty of other options such as grilled mixed skewers. Appropriately for its name, the miso soup is superb, and the desserts are luscious. Service is terrific too. A sure-fire winner.

## HONG KONG Petrus

*Island Shangri-La, Pacific Place, Central* **Tel** *(852) 2820 8590*     **Map** *3 D4*

Petrus offers a contemporary French menu that is imaginative but unfussy. There is a wonderful old-world elegance here, with large windows offering panoramic views and attentive but discreet service. The same excellence is applied, without compromise, to an extensive vegetarian menu.

**Key to Price Guide** *see p582* **Key to Symbols** *see back cover flap*

### HONG KONG Pierre 🚗🍴 ⓦⓦⓦⓦ
*5 Connaught Road, Central (in Mandarin Oriental Hotel)* **Tel** *(852) 2825 4001* **Map** *2 C3*

The impressive black marble and silver leaf interior on top of the Mandarin Oriental offers impressive, floor-to-ceiling views over the harbor. The menu is modern French and repeated visits are necessary to get the measure of Michelin three-star chef Pierre Gagnaire's limitless creativity.

### HONG KONG Spoon by Alain Ducasse 🅅🚗🍴 ⓦⓦⓦⓦ
*Intercontinental, 18 Salisbury Road, Tsim Sha Tsui* **Tel** *(852) 2313 2256* **Map** *1 C5*

550 Venetian glass spoons hang from the ceiling of this much-garlanded restaurant with its modern versions of French classical food. From *foie gras* to *feuillat aux framboises*, all is superb. A vast wine list is full of surprises – simply put yourself in the hands of the oracular sommelier.

### HONG KONG Top Deck 🚗🍴 ⓦⓦⓦⓦ
*Top Floor, Jumbo Kingdom, Sum Wan Pier Drive, Aberdeen* **Tel** *(852) 2552 3331*

The top floor of the touristy floating restaurant Jumbo, reached by a two-minute ferry ride, has been turned into a separate first class seafood establishment with everything from *bouillabaisse* to Boston lobster. Dining is occasionally accompanied by live jazz.

### MACAU Clube Militar 🚗🍴 ⓦⓦ
*Avenida da Praia Grande 795* **Tel** *(853) 2871 4009*

The Clube Militar dates back to 1870, with ceiling fans stirring the soupy air, creaking wooden floors, and walls lined with pictures of Macau past. Much of the remaining Portuguese community comes here for Portuguese staples such as chili and coconut-laced African chicken, washed down with a crisp Portuguese white wine.

### MACAU Espaco Lisboa 🚗🍴 ⓦⓦⓦ
*Rua das Gaivotas 8, Coloane* **Tel** *(853) 2888 2226*

Tucked away in a Coloane village, a ¥20 taxi ride away from the Macau peninsula, this rustic little restaurant is proudly presided over by its Portuguese chef-owner. The Espaco Lisboa is a reminder of pre-development sleepy Macau and offers a menu of solid Portuguese staples.

### MACAU Naam 🚗🍴 ⓦⓦⓦⓦ
*Avenida da Amizade (in Mandarin Oriental Hotel)* **Tel** *(853) 2856 7888*

Naam enjoys a wonderful setting amongst the lush tropical gardens of the Mandarin Oriental resort hotel. The restaurant's largely Thai staff conspire with Thai chef Nui to produce not only an utterly authentic menu, but a completely Thai experience.

### MACAU Robuchon a Galera 🚗🍴 ⓦⓦⓦⓦ
*2–4 Avenue de Lisboa* **Tel** *(853) 8803 7878*

Said to have the best wine cellar in Asia, this restaurant belonging to celebrated Michelin-starred French chef Joel Robuchon is easily the best and priciest (still cheaper than any Hong Kong equivalent) place in town for Western food. The cuisine is sublime Portuguese and modern European with, needless to say, a French bias.

## SICHUAN & CHONGQING

### CHENGDU Ginko Restaurant (Yinxing Chuancai Jiulou) 🚗 ⓦⓦ
*Lin Jiang Zhong Lu 12* **Tel** *(028) 8555 5588*

A three-story affair with a lounge on the first floor, main dining room on the second and private rooms on the third. Try the specialty Sichuan roast duck (*zhang cha ya*), spicy chicken (*ma la tu ji*), and steamed fish (*qing zhen gui yu*). The main dining room has large picture windows facing the river, lined with lights at night.

### CHENGDU Huang Cheng Lao Ma 🚗 ⓦⓦ
*Er Huan Lu Nan Duan 3, 20* **Tel** *(028) 8513 9999*

A five-story building with a tea lounge in an expansive atrium area, as well as a museum, babysitting facilities, and stage for entertainment. One room has a hot pot buffet on a rotating conveyor. Reservations are necessary on weekend nights. Probably the best place for Sichuan hot pot, which is not as fiery as Chongqing hot pot.

### CHENGDU Shunxing Ancient Tea House – Chengdu Snack City 🍴🚗 ⓦⓦ
*Shawan Lu 258, Chengdu International Exhibition and Convention Centre Mall area, 3rd floor* **Tel** *(028) 8769 3202*

Covering a huge area in total, this restaurant/teahouse offers a pleasant and authentic atmosphere to enjoy Sichuan's well-known snack specialties, easily substantial enough for a whole meal. Provides nightly performances of Sichuan opera including the whole show of amazing face changing, acrobatics, and tea.

### CHENGDU Sichuan Mantingfang Langting Guibin Huisuo 🚗 ⓦⓦ
*Erhuan Lu 15, Nan San Duan* **Tel** *(028) 8519 3111*

The well-appointed interior and artful division of space with dividers and columns cleverly avoid the big-room syndrome so often a part of most restaurants. This classic Chinese restaurant ensures excellent but subdued service, and tasty food. This will appeal to those looking for some traditional yet unusual fare.

### CHENGDU Hailingge Grand Restaurant (Hailingge Dajiudian)

*Shang Nan Da Jie 4, Tianfu Guangchuang, Floors 2 & 3* **Tel** *(028) 8612 3111*

Known to serve the best regional Chinese in Chengdu, this has an impressive and grand feel. Service is impeccable and food is artistically arranged for a pleasant experience. Try the "Happy Family" *(hai ling ge quan jia fu)* specialty dish, combining various meats and seafood. Interior is primarily white walls and brightly-lit rooms.

### CHENGDU Old Chengdu Mansion Restaurant

*Qinghua Lu 37–41* **Tel** *(028) 8732 0016*

Located just over 1 mile (2 km) west of the city center, next to Du Fu's cottage, is this theater-restaurant in an antique-style teahouse setting strung with lanterns. Tables are arranged in the central atrium and in booths around the walls. The menu features mild Chinese banquet dishes and fiery Sichuanese classics. Reservations recommended.

### CHONGQING Chongqing Dezhuang Huoguo, Qi Xing Gang Branch

*Zhong Shan Lu 148* **Tel** *(023) 6352 1934*

Take advantage of its reputation as one of the most famous Chongqing hot pot restaurants, and part of a nationwide chain. The lively atmosphere, "four-alarm" spicy hot ingredients, and attentive service make for a good place to enjoy this searing local specialty. An ideal place to stop if visiting the Liberation Mounument.

### CHONGQING Da Du Hui Wai Po Qiao

*Fengwei Lu Building, 7th Floor* **Tel** *(023) 6383 5988*

Located on the 7th floor of the Fengwei Lu building and serving a variety of Chongqing specialties and snacks. If the location's ambience is lacking, the artful presentation of the dishes makes up for it. Take advantage of delicious regional meat dishes using smoked pork *(lao shao zhi zheng la rou)* or duck.

### CHONGQING Tao Ran Ju Dajiulou

*Zhou Rong Plaza, Floors 6 & 7* **Tel** *(023) 6379 2466*

Spread over two floors, this restaurant makes a convenient stop-off point en route to the Liberation Monument. Part of a nationwide chain, the menu features classic Sichuan cuisine including a number of unusual dishes like fried snail or taro root and chicken stew. Traditionally furnished and attentive staff.

### CHONGQING Xiaotian'e Ba Yu Shi Fu

*Ming Zu Lu 22, Xin Chongqing Guangchang, 6th Floor* **Tel** *(023) 6545 8328*

Nationwide chain restaurant is one of Chongqing's most popular hot pot restaurants. Those unable to take their spices should order the half white/half red hot pots, ask the staff to remove most of the chili peppers, and put only meats in the red side. The interior is decorated in a typical Chinese restaurant-style.

### LE SHAN Dengqian Fandian

*Binjiang Lu 158* **Tel** *(0833) 242 0000*

Close to Dafo boat dock, this restaurant serves an accomplished range of rural Sichuanese food, from basic snacks such as spicy beef steamed in ground rice to hot pot, and they pride themselves on locally made tofu. There are good fish dishes too, but these are sold by weight so check the prices. Reservations are recommended.

## YUNNAN

### DALI Café de Jack's

*Bo'ai Lu 82* **Tel** *(0872) 267 1572*

Cleaner and more upscale than Dali's typical backpacker haunts, this friendly Dali institution has a menu ranging from Chinese and Bai minority dishes to simple Western favorites. Good for breakfast to full-scale Bai banquets with pleasant balcony seating from which to watch the world go by.

### DALI Jim's Peace Café (Jimu Heping Kezhan)

*Boai Lu 63* **Tel** *(0872) 267 1822*

This is one of the original café-guesthouses to cater specifically for foreign visitors. From the menu to the decorations, it's like dining in Lhasa itself, with better Tibetan dishes than Western ones. Reservations are necessary for the specialty – a 20-dish Tibetan banquet (groups of six or more only).

### KUNMING The Brother Jiang (Qiao Xiang Yuan)

*Qingnian Lu 87* **Tel** *(0871) 515 157*

This chain features the most famous dish of Kunming and four set menus make it simple to order the minimum (ten) or maximum (sixty) number of ingredients required. Serving bowls are big. "Crossing-the-bridge" noodles comprise fiery hot (temperature-wise) chicken or duck soup served with an array of raw accompaniments.

### KUNMING Yu Quan Zhai

*Yuantong Jie 22* **Tel** *(0871) 511 1809*

Located a few doors along from a Buddhist temple, don't be fooled by the meaty English words on the menu like "vegetarian duck"; all the dishes at this popular restaurant are completely vegetarian, artfully imitating flesh using vegetable protein. The serving sizes can be huge, be careful not to order too much.

**Key to Price Guide** *see p582* **Key to Symbols** *see back cover flap*

### KUNMING New Yun Yuan Restaurant (Xin Yun Yuan Jiulou)

*Qingnian Lu 452* **Tel** *(0871) 315 9668*

Considered by locals as one of the best in Kunming for its vast range of both Yunnan and other regional Chinese favorites. The 184-item menu (in English) runs from stewed dog to fried pigeon and beyond, and is noted for its barbequed fish specialty. The second floor houses private dining rooms.

### KUNMING Shiping Huiguan

*Cui Hu Nan Lu Zhong He Xiang 24* **Tel** *(0871) 362 7444*

Worth a visit, even if not eating there, just to see an original Chinese two-story courtyard home. Best to try this restaurant in a group with a Chinese-speaking guest as there's no English menu, no pictures, and no English spoken. The earthenware-stewed chicken is a favorite among staff and should not be missed.

### KUNMING 1910 Gare du Sud

*Houxin Jie 8* **Tel** *(0871) 316 9486*

Both traditional and modern Yunnanese cuisine is served at this restaurant in a former colonial-era train station building. Dishes include innovative takes on rural Yunnanese dishes; try steamed ham, vegetable soup served inside a pumpkin shell, or spicy stewed chicken. Open 5–10pm. Booking recommended.

### LIJIANG Lijiang Naxi Yinshi Wenhua Cheng

*Fuhui Zhong Lu* **Tel** *(0888) 518 2870*

A friendly atomosphere can be found here thanks to the mix of local and tourist diners. The restaurant serves a feast of traditional Naxi cuisines and snacks, with dishes such as whole chicken, deep-fried wheat cake, and yak. The ancient-style architecture, along with the traditional singing and dancing adds a festive air.

### LIJIANG Sakura Café (Yinghua Wu)

*Xinhua Jie, Cuiwen Duan 123* **Tel** *(0888) 518 7619*

This very friendly, low-key café has earned the reputation of being one of the best in the old city. Its 354-item bilingual menu offers plenty of choice and includes German, French, and local wines. The cuisine itself ranges from Asian and Western-style to Middle Eastern (Israeli) fare. Closer to home, try the delicious stuffed flatbread.

## GUIZHOU & GUANGXI

### GUIYANG Siheyuan

*Qianling Xi Lu 79* **Tel** *(0851) 682 5419*

This is basic Guizhou food at rock bottom prices, in a clumsily adapted courtyard house; loud and friendly, rough and ready. Industrially spicy dishes such as shredded beef with shredded peppers, and milder dishes like potato pancakes rolled and stuffed with bean paste, then dusted with coconut.

### GUIYANG Guizhou Long

*Jiandao Jie 23* **Tel** *(0851) 586 3333*

One of Guiyang's smartest restaurants, with four stories of elegant private dining rooms complete with towel warmer and TV (optional). Serves a wide range of well-executed Guangdong, Sichuan, and Shanghai favorites. Located amongst Guiyang's other smart restaurants with views across a soupy river to a small, battered temple.

### YANGSHUO Cloud 9

*Cnr Chengzhong Lu & Xi Jie* **Tel** *(0773) 881 3686*

This excellent restaurant might make you wish you could eat Chinese food more often. Dishes from the Guangxi countryside feature heavy taro-pork stews, edible flowers and plenty of chilis, and fresh fruit. Medicinal soups made with special herbs are popular and sell out early.

## LIAONING, JILIN, & HEILONGJIANG

### CHANGCHUN Xiangyang Tun

*Dong Chaoyang Lu 433* **Tel** *(0431) 889 82876*

The overwhelming local favorite, and for good reason – the place turns out well-executed fare at dirt cheap prices. Dishes are simple but flavorful, a few even frightening, but most simply delicious. Pork ribs (*dapaigu*) are popular. Service is warm and patient with foreigners.

### DALIAN Mingzhu Revolving Restaurant

*Shen Li Square 8, Bohai Pearl Hotel, Zhongshan* **Tel** *(0411) 8812 8888*

Situated at the top of the Bohai Pearl Hotel, this revolving restaurant is one of Dalian's most famous places to eat. The stunning views of the city are matched by the impressive cuisine, prepared by an award-winning chef. The food is local Dalian, specializing in seafood.

### DALIAN Tian Tian Yugang

*Renmin Lu 10* **Tel** *(0411) 8280 1118*

Simply the finest place to sample the city's famous seafood. Prices are high, but there's a visually delightful selection of ocean life on offer, presented live in a room full of aquariums. Servers are helpful with suggestions on how to have selections prepared to best delight your tastebuds. Quality seafood and knowledgeable staff.

### DANDONG Fuhong Erhao Gong Guan

*Two blocks west of Yalujiang Qiao* **Tel** *(0415) 345 8888*

Dishes here are shockingly creative considering the city's remoteness. Sichuan is the main influence, with hints of Macau and Cantonese. Located on the Yalu River, the dining room is pleasantly bright and clean, with good views of North Korea from the window tables, although views are not necessarily picturesque.

### HARBIN Dongfang Jiaozi Wang

*Shangzhi Da Jie 168* **Tel** *(0451) 8484 9111*

Quite simply the best dumpling restaurant in the region, if not the country. The *jiaozi* (dumplings) here are exceedingly simple, but perfectly delicious, and criminally cheap. This is the original branch of a rapidly expanding chain, often imitated but as yet unmatched. Glimpse the show through glass-fronted kitchens.

### HARBIN Portman (Boteman Xicanting)

*Xiqi Daojie 53* **Tel** *(0451) 8468 6888*

Not exactly authentic Russian food, but close enough. With a distinctly European feel, the place is consistently packed, as much for the beer (which is brewed on site) and live entertainment as the food. But the food is worth a visit – hearty and comforting, especially if you're battling the vicious winter.

### JILIN Liyade Shifu

*Jiyuan Shangchang on Jiefang Da Lu* **Tel** *(0432) 6201 7999*

Dining options in the city are notoriously slim, but the well prepared Hui Muslim food here is worth a venture out of the hotel. Unlike Uighur Muslim cuisine, the Hui version is closer to other Chinese styles, heavy on garlic and chili. Expect plenty of meat-based dishes and don't miss the *shousi yangrou* (hand-torn mutton).

### SHENYANG Laobian Jiaozi House (Laobian Jiaozi Guan)

*Zhongjie 206* **Tel** *(024) 2486 5369*

Supposedly founded 170 years ago in a different building long since redeveloped, this is the most famous dumpling restaurant south of Harbin. Provides some respite from the frenzy of the shopping district. The dumplings are done in the simple northeastern style, with dozens of filling options to choose from.

## INNER MONGOLIA & NINGXIA

### HOHHOT Jinhuolu Shaokao Cheng

*Dongying Niu Jie Beikou* **Tel** *(0471) 232 8216*

Opened only a few years ago, this is a simple, matter-of-fact kind of place. The main draw of the restaurant is the popular Mongolian barbeque; servers help grill assorted meats on a hotplate in the middle of the table, somehow producing little or no smoke – a method originally used by Mongolian horsemen, using shields for grilling.

### HOHHOT Xin'anju

*Xin Cheng Bei Jie* **Tel** *(0471) 660 8888*

The very helpful English menus here are well organized into Shandong, Shaanxi, Sichuan, as well as Mongolian sections. Specialties, including leg of lamb, can be washed down with agreeable house wines. Nicely decorated dining room with carved wooden walls and red Chinese knots.

### HOHHOT Little Fat Sheep Hotpot (Xiaofeiyang Huoguo)

*Wulanchabu Dong Lu Zhaojun Huayuan Shizi Lukou* **Tel** *(0471) 490 1998*

With hundreds of branches around the country, Xiaofeiyang is the acknowledged king of Mongolian hot pot. The restaurant places great emphasis on the quality of its cuisine, and diners are encouraged not to use dipping sauce, which dampens the natural flavor of the lamb. Individual hot pots are also available.

## GANSU & QINGHAI

### DUNHUANG Charley Johng's Cafe

*Mingshan Lu 21* **Tel** *(0937) 388 2411*

Located in downtown Dunhuang, next door to the Feitian Hotel, Charley Johng's offers a wide selection of Western and Chinese food. The staff speak English and there is a menu in English. The restaurant is simply decorated, but clean and comfortable. There's a small Internet section and bike rentals can be arranged from here too.

**Key to Price Guide** *see p582* **Key to Symbols** *see back cover flap*

### JIAYUGUAN Lin Yuan Jiudian ¥¥

*Xinhua Nan Lu 32 **Tel** (0937) 620 3555*

Even by Chinese standards, hotel restaurants in Jiayuguan are diabolical. Not to worry – the light, immaculately presented Cantonese and Huaiyang cuisine at this four-story restaurant means that it is usually full-to-bursting with locals – always a promising sign, so take heart. No English menu.

### LANZHOU Mingde Gong ¥¥

*Qing Yang Lu 171 **Tel** (0931) 843 3599*

This flagship restaurant for Gansu cuisine (*long cai*), a fusion between home-style Chinese fare and lamb-based dishes from the northwest, ironically draws most of its chefs from Guangzhou. It has a vast first floor dining hall, and opulent private rooms; service is attentive throughout, although there is no English menu.

### TIANSHUI Tianshui Maiji Dajiudian ¥¥

*Tianshui Huoche Zhan Guangchang Xi Ce **Tel** (0938) 492 0000*

There is little in the way of good restaurants in Tianshui, and the town is perfect for a stopover on the way to visiting the caves at Maiji Shan. This restaurant, located in the Maiji Hotel, is the best available option. There is decent Chinese food, and the staff are friendly, though they can't speak English and there's no English menu.

### XINING The Greenhouse ¥

*Xia Du Da Jie 222-22 **Tel** (0971) 820 2710*

Located in downtown Xining, this is the first real coffee house in town. There is a full menu of lattes, cappucinos, and other imported coffee drinks, as well as fresh home-made donuts, pastries, and sandwiches. The menu is in English and the staff also speak English.

## XINJIANG

### KUQA Wumai'er Hong Meishi Cheng ¥

*Tuanjie Lu 70 **Tel** (0997) 712 4634*

Uighur food is hot and hearty and includes whole chicken dishes, thick "pulled" noodles, dumplings, rich stews, rice pilaf, pigeon dishes, and kabobs. Finish off with a fresh fruit salad. This restaurant is hugely popular with locals who are always delighted to welcome foreign visitors.

### TURPAN Oasis Hotel (Lüzhou Binguan) ¥¥

*Qingnian Lu 815 **Tel** (0995) 855 3110*

Whole roast lamb and other hearty meaty Uighur specials with mountains of flat bread and noodles enough to fill the hungriest traveler. For those in need of variety there is a mainstream Chinese restaurant and a small coffee shop located in the same building.

### URUMQI The Texas Cafe (Dekesasi Xicanting) ¥

*Nan Men Mashixiaoqu **Tel** (0991) 281 0025*

The food here is mainly Tex-Mex, with dishes such as enchiladas and nachos, but there are also burgers, imported beers, and freshly made cakes. There's free Wi-Fi and a book exchange. The café is located in a grapevine-covered alley across from the computer market, and has a great Xinjiang feel to it. English menu.

## TIBET

### LHASA New Mandala Restaurant ¥

*West of Barkhor Square, 2nd floor **Tel** (0891) 634 2235*

New Mandala offers some of the best Nepali and Tibetan food in Lhasa, along with some Western food. The staff is friendly and speak English well, and the menu is in English too. There are fantastic views of Barkhor Square, and in summertime tables are available on the roof where the views are even better.

### LHASA Snowland Restaurant ¥

*Dan Jie Ling Rd 4 **Tel** (0891) 632 0821*

Snowland Restaurant is one of the most popular restaurants in Lhasa, and serves a wide, well-priced range of Tibetan, Western, Chinese, and Nepali dishes. Try the yak pepper steak and potato momos (dumplings). Staff all speak English and the menu is also in English.

### SHIGATSE Gongkar Tibetan Restaurant ¥

*Xuegiang Rd **Tel** (0892) 882 1139*

A popular hangout for travelers, the Gongkar offers cheap, tasty Tibetan food. The staff don't speak English but there is an English menu. The specialties are dumplings (momos) and noodle dishes, plus there is also yak tongue soup for the more adventurous diner.

# SHOPS & MARKETS

China's rich artistic heritage is reflected in its stunning range of characteristic works of art – from stylized landscape paintings and calligraphy to delicate ceramic bowls and exquisitely carved bamboo. With the burgeoning of tourism and the official encouragement of enterprise, Chinese cities are alive with shops and markets selling an often bewildering array of trinkets and souvenirs. Even though the market is flooded with cheap imitations, many objects are still made by age-old

**Statue of Buddhist deity**

techniques, and authentic items are not hard to find. Perhaps some of the most unique souvenirs are those produced by China's ethnic minorities, particularly their accomplished embroidery. The major cities have seen the emergence of malls and department stores, which provide certificates of authenticity for items such as jewelry and semi-precious stones (although still no guarantee). Many large hotels also have souvenir shops, although these tend to stock over-priced, upmarket items, such as silk and jade.

## OPENING HOURS

Shops in China are usually open from 8:30am until fairly late in the evening – around 8pm – while winter timings are generally 9am to 7pm. High street stores and malls tend to open from 10am to 10pm regardless of the season. They can be very busy in the evening once offices have closed. The opening and closing times of shops varies from place to place; in some areas they open as early as 8am, and stay open until well after 8pm. Local food shops and markets selling fresh produce remain open for business from early in the morning until late at night. Some shops remain closed on public holidays such as the three-day Chinese New Year (Spring Festival), National Day (October 1), and New Year's Day (January 1), although most malls remain open.

**An array of calligraphy brushes for sale in a Beijing market**

## HOW TO PAY

Chinese currency is the *yuan renminbi* or "people's money" (shortened to RMB). One *yuan* is divided into 10 *jiao* or *mao*, each of which is divided even farther into 10 *fen*. Credit and debit cards are widely accepted in malls,

shops, hotels, restaurants, and bars. Likewise, ATMs are widespread in every city including at most major banks, such as Bank of China, ICBC, HSBC, Citibank, and Bank of Communications. ATMs should display in both Chinese and English, or give you the option to display in English only. The commission and exchange rates charged for ATM withdrawals depend on your bank so it is worth checking before your visit.

Most major banks have exchange desks for foreign currency and traveler's checks (although checks are less used now). These are also found at airports, in larger hotels, and in certain stores. Keep your exchange receipts as you will need them to convert your spare *renminbi* into another currency before leaving the country (*see pp620–21*).

## BARGAINING

Bargaining is a common practice in China, especially in street markets, night bazaars, and souvenir stands. It is even worth trying in the smarter, more expensive hotels, modern shops, department stores, and government emporia. Stallholders are notorious for charging visitors thrice the "real" price, and sometimes their starting price may be up to ten times the cost. Make a comparison of prices and be conscious of what others are paying, particularly local Chinese.

**Bustling Nanjing Road with its brightly colored billboards, Shanghai**

An upmarket department store in Zhaoqing, Guangdong

## DEPARTMENT STORES & BOUTIQUES

The consumer revolution in China has led to the mushrooming of upmarket brand stores, shopping plazas, and fashion boutiques in every city, especially Beijing and Shanghai. Brands from D&G to Gap, Zara, Apple, and Hershey chocolates can now be found in the leading retail cities of Shanghai and Beijing, as well as the many malls in other Chinese cities.

As in most developed countries, there is heavy emphasis on high-end items such as electrical goods, designer fashion, perfumes, jewelry, and watches, while large stores, such as Carrefour, Marks & Spencer, IKEA, and Walmart, offer foods, souvenirs, and household goods at reasonable prices.

## SHOPPING MALLS

Like in all fast-emerging Asian nations, mall shopping is a favored urban leisure pursuit. In most Chinese cities, glassy retail plazas dominate the downtown areas. They are usually built to a similar design and house a mix of upmarket brands, coffee shops, fast food outlets, and local eateries, with a giant supermarket in the basement. In the central business districts of the largest cities, upscale shopping malls are attached to luxury hotels. While the malls multiply, China's department store heritage is fast diminishing.

## MARKETS

The best way to experience China's diversity and its many ethnic cultures is to visit the bustling local markets, especially in rural areas. Held on specific days of the week, these are locally known as *ganji*, which means "going to market," or *gangai*, meaning "going to the street."

Selling carpets at a market in Linxia, Gansu

Traditionally, people from the surrounding countryside came into town on market days to buy or sell their farm produce. Nowadays however, rural markets are expanding their scope, and it is not uncommon to see stalls selling a range of household items from toothbrushes to woks and cooking pots. While some markets still follow the lunar calendar, which is confusing for most visitors, many have shifted to a more regular schedule. Such markets are busiest between mid-morning and mid-afternoon. The variety of food, souvenirs, and domestic items on sale is astounding, but be prepared to bargain hard.

## ANTIQUES

Unless you're an expert, buying antiques in China is a rather risky proposition. Many Chinese cities have flourishing antiques markets, but most of the items on sale will undoubtedly be fake. However, as long as you don't mistake them for the real thing, it is fun to browse and bargain for cheap replicas. The state-run antique shops, like the Friendship Stores, are in decline – and never had any bargains anyway. Shops in the foyers of art galleries and museums also sell works of art such as scroll paintings, calligraphy, and attractive silk scarves. In China, objects dating to 1795 or earlier may not be legally exported, so make sure any antiques (of a later date) that you purchase carry a red wax seal permitting export. Always keep the receipts as they may be required at Customs.

A souvenir shop in Qingcheng Shan park near Chengdu

# What to Buy in China

**Opera mask**

Market stalls and small shops sell interesting souvenirs in tourist centers throughout China. Traditionally styled items can be found just about everywhere, while many other crafts are regional. You can find beautifully intricate embroidery in the southwest, prayer wheels and flags in Tibet, carpets in Xinjiang, and ginseng in the northeast. When shopping in markets it is essential to bargain. Friendship stores and gift shops at factories usually have fixed, but inflated, prices.

**A collection of Mao statuettes in many different poses**

## CALLIGRAPHY

A skill as revered as painting, calligraphy is an ancient Chinese art that is a fluid form of self-expression. Master calligraphers practice their art assiduously, and one of their works could be very expensive. Less costly examples of calligraphy are widely available.

**Marble chops** *are traditionally used to imprint a calligrapher's seal on to a work. At many craft markets vendors create personalized chops by carving a character version of a person's name on the base.*

**Scrolls** *painted with elegantly striking script make excellent souvenirs. Skilled calligraphers will paint chosen sayings in different styles or you can purchase pre-painted works.*

**Lid of ink stone**

**Ink stick**

**Writing brush**

**Base of ink stone**

**Writing** *brushes should have a defined tip and firm fur bristles. Ink sticks made of soot are ground down and mixed with water on an ink stone.*

**Painted** *on paper or silk with simple brushstrokes, painting is one of the most important traditional arts. Many paintings now have contemporary touches.*

## CERAMICS

Chinese ceramics are known the world over. They have been mass produced for hundreds of years, with fired pots being passed through a line of artisans, each adding a layer to the glaze. Porcelain, a fine, translucent ceramic, was invented during the Sui dynasty, and high quality pieces are still produced.

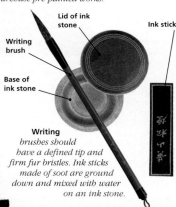

**Jingdezhen** *in Jiangxi has been one of the main producers of porcelain since the 10th century (see pp254–5). It still produces fine pieces, although some of the cheaper wares may be decorated by stencil.*

**Yixingware,** *or purple sand pottery from Ding Shan in Anhui (see p218), is usually a dark reddish brown, but can also be green, buff, or gray.*

## SILK

Woven from the strands that make up a silk worm's cocoon, silk is also a Chinese invention *(see pp208–9)*. Clothes made of silk, such as ladies' *cheongsams*, are widely available, but be aware that silk sold in markets is likely to be rayon. Beautiful embroidery on silk is also available.

**Silk embroidered coasters**

**Silk bags**

**Silk-covered cushions**

**Jade,** *a semi-precious stone, is associated with immortality. These pendants are green, but the lustrous gem can also be gray or brown.*

## OTHER TRADITIONAL HANDICRAFTS

Occasionally created by skilled craftsmen but often mass produced, Chinese handicrafts are almost always highly intricate and of vibrant color. The variety of goods on offer is staggering, from delicate miniature glass bottles to the bold graphics of communist memorabilia.

**Lacquerware jewelry box**

**Decorative tassel**

**Carved wooden fan**

*The best paper cuts are made in a few minutes by a master craftsman with a pair of scissors. Most paper cuts are mass produced, with many simultaneously cut to a pattern.*

**Glass snuff** *bottles were popularized during the Qing dynasty, when snuff usage was common. Using a hooked brush, artisans paint miniature scenes inside.*

**Cloisonné** *vases, boxes, and jars have been copper-enamelled: copper is faced with pieces of colored enamel and fired, creating a shiny finish.*

**Baoding balls** *are weighted and sometimes contain a chime. The two balls are maneuvered in one hand, strengthening grip and massaging the channels through which* qi *runs (see p232).*

**Mao memorabilia** *is based on designs that existed during Mao's rule. Some is authentic, but most communist souvenirs are produced for the tourist market.*

**Mao badges**

**Mao lighter**

**Tea,** *often sold in colorful tin caddies, is available everywhere. Tie guanyin and other oolong teas of Fujian are very fine. Pu'er is a specialty of the southwest.*

# ENTERTAINMENT

The Chinese work hard, but they also take their leisure seriously, and have a range of traditional and modern entertainment. The vast tradition of performing arts reflects China’s rich cultural heritage, and includes Chinese opera, theater, shadow puppetry, and the circus. Many types of dance and music derive from ethnic cultures, adding to the diversity of entertainment. China’s increasing westernization has meant that young people in particular enjoy the same leisure activities as their western counterparts, including contemporary films and music concerts. Karaoke is hugely popular, and most towns and cities have numerous bars, where visitors can sing along to popular Chinese and Western songs, accompanied by the latest videos. The Internet has opened up new avenues for on-line entertainment, with many people carrying smartphones, iPads, and PSPs. Casino gambling is only permitted in the specially administered region of Macau, and horse racing is popular in Hong Kong (see p332).

**Traditional dancer posing**

Passing the time with a game of *xiangqi* on the sidewalks of Xi’an

## GAMES

Playing games in public parks is a timeworn Chinese custom, and though visitors may feel too inhibited to challenge locals to a game, they are great fun to watch. Some Chinese games date back thousands of years. The most well-known game is *mahjong*, which uses plastic tiles, originally made of bamboo or ivory. The rules are similar to rummy, with players trying to create identical, or consecutively numbered, sets. More advanced versions of the game have special tiles representing the four winds, four dragons, seasons, and flowers. When a game is in full swing, the quick movements of the participants make the tiles click and clatter – a popular translation of *mahjong* is “chattering sparrows.”

Chinese checkers *(xiangqi)* is another popular game. Here, there are two opposing sets of round counters. The board is divided into squares by nine vertical and ten horizontal lines. The board game Go *(weiqi)* dates back more than 4,000 years. Also known as encirclement chess, it involves two opposing sides, each with a set of circular stones, struggling for territory.

## SPECTATOR SPORTS

The most popular sports at schools and colleges are basketball, badminton, and table tennis (ping pong), and the Chinese excel internationally in the latter two. Soccer is also played and followed with enthusiasm. The top European clubs have a strong fan-base in China, and Chinese soccer players are now being recruited by them. Fitness centers and gyms are becoming increasingly popular in cities. Traditional martial arts such as *tai ji quan* are popular amongst the older generation, and people practice early in the morning in parks, squares, and gardens.

## TRADITIONAL FORMS OF THEATER

Beijing opera *(jingju)* is a world famous traditional art form unique to China (see pp74–5). It is highly stylized, and characters wear elaborate costumes with special make-up and masks. Performances usually take place on a simple stage with few props.

The Chinese circus has a worldwide reputation for its highly-trained gymnasts who perform breathtaking routines that showcase their unnerving flexibility. Displays of balance

Actors in a Beijing opera, performing in opulent costumes

often involve household props, such as brooms, plates, and chairs, with one of the most popular tricks being performed by 20 or so acrobats piled precariously on a bicycle. These routines are often combined with acts involving caged and tame animals, but the current trend is toward a purer display of acrobatics.

Some forms of traditional dance still exist, especially among China's ethnic groups. Some relate to shamanistic or other religious rituals, and often involve the wearing of special masks.

## SHADOW PLAYS & PUPPET THEATER

Shadow plays *(piyingxi)* are popular, and usually involve the use of leather puppets with jointed limbs. These are manipulated close to a white sheet and lit from behind, throwing their shadows on to the sheet. The performance is accompanied by singing and music. Plays with wooden puppets *(mu'ouxi)* involve elaborate and colorfully dressed marionettes, glove puppets, or puppets on the end of rods.

## TRADITIONAL MUSIC

Chinese music can be traced back as far as the Shang era. Ancient sets of 65 bells from the 5th century BC have been unearthed. During the Tang dynasty, the traditional musical forms began to take root and music was also an important part of Confucian education.

Traditional instruments include strings, winds, and percussion. String instruments played with the fingers, plectrum, or bow are the Chinese violin, horizontal harp, and many-stringed zithers, such as the *zheng*. The lute-like *pipa* is one of the most important stringed instruments. The most common bamboo flutes are the vertical *(xiao)* and horizontal *(di)*. The *hulusu* made from a gourd and

**Crowds enjoying the many bars along Lan Kwai Fong, Hong Kong**

bamboo is popularly used in folk music. The *sheng*, one of the oldest Chinese instruments, has up to 17 bamboo pipes and a vibrating reed. Another ancient instrument is the earthenware *xun*. Dating back 8,000 years, and sometimes made of bone or ivory, it has a mouthpiece and a series of holes for varying the tones. Percussion Instruments include gongs, chimes, drums, woodblocks, and xylophones.

**A musician strums the lute-like *pipa***

## KITE FLYING

Kite flying is a major hobby in China, especially on public holidays when parks, gardens, and even city squares are crowded with displays of colorful and fantastically-shaped kites, soaring to considerable heights. Birds and dragons are the most common kite designs.

## BARS, DISCOS & KARAOKE

Bars, nightclubs, and karaoke lounges have sprung up all over urban China. Some bars specialize in live bands, and these are very popular with expats, foreign visitors, and

urban Chinese – be warned that drinks are expensive. Coffee bars are also increasingly popular with young people, although the older generation remain faithful to their green tea and traditional teahouses.

## ROCK & POP MUSIC

China's rock scene is young and rebellious, and only really gained a foothold during the 1980s, when it played a central role at the Tian'an Men Square protests. Still not accepted by state-run radio stations, bands rely on the Internet and word of mouth.

Canto-pop, Hong Kong's popular music tradition, has sugary lyrics of love and loss, sung in Cantonese. Many Canto-pop singers become hugely popular pin-ups, as have a new generation of Mando-pop stars, singing in Mandarin, from Taiwan and the mainland.

## CINEMA

China has traditionally produced many good films, based mainly on folk tales, romantic love stories, or strong patriotic themes. Chinese cinema has also opened up to embrace international tastes, including those of both Hollywood and Bollywood, and movies such as Zhang Yimou's extremely popular *Hero*, released in 2004, blended martial arts with impressive special effects. All cities show foreign movies, although they are often censored.

**Delicate kites for sale catching the breeze from the Yangzi, Wuhan**

# SPORTS & SPECIALIST HOLIDAYS

As the Olympic host for 2008, Beijing was the showpiece city for a nation that celebrates sporting heroes with the fervor once reserved for political icons – soccer and basketball have become big spectator sports. The spending power and leisure interests of China's booming middle classes translate into more sporting choices for visitors too –

**Flowers in bloom**

there's skiing, golf, rock climbing, and more. Courses in martial arts can be found in most tourist centers, or head to the hallowed halls of the Shaolin Temple to find a master. Organized tours ply the major sights of the country, but for a really memorable experience consider booking a trip that has a fascinating focus, whether photography, whitewater rafting, costume, or horse trekking.

## THE OLYMPIC GAMES

The 2008 Beijing Olympics made a dramatic impact on the capital, with infrastructure improvements and massive construction projects transforming the city in the run-up to the games. Beijing promised a "Green Olympics, Hi-tech Olympics, People's Olympics," so visitors enjoyed acres of parkland and futuristic stadiums. Half of the main Olympic Park area, at the apex of an extended imperial axis running north-south through the city, is being turned into woodland and lawns.

At the 2008 Olympics, 43 world records and 132 new Olympic records were set. China won 100 medals, 51 of them gold, and so the Games were declared a logistical success.

In 2010, the Asian Games took place in Guangzhou, and in 2015, Beijing's National Stadium will host the World Athletics Championships.

## SPECTATOR SPORTS

China has gone soccer-mad. Although ancient records describe a game of kick-ball with three players on each side, and paintings show a Song emperor juggling a ball with his feet, soccer is a recent phenomenon here. The Chinese Professional Soccer League was established in 1994, and the **China Super League**, an elite group of teams, kicked off in 2004. The Super League has a massive fan base, but has run

into problems with corruption and sponsorship. **Basketball** is also gaining in popularity and its profile has been boosted by Chinese NBA stars such as the towering Yao Ming.

The annual Rugby Sevens tournament in March is a massive – and very rowdy – event in Hong Kong, with international teams playing almost 70 games over three days. The **Hong Kong Rugby Football Union** plays regular fixtures during the rugby season, which runs from November through March.

Both Shanghai and Beijing now host the **Rolex Masters** tennis tournaments.

Shanghai hosted the **Formula One Grand Prix** for the first time in 2004. Tickets are expensive, but 80 percent of the circuit is visible from the stands.

For a Chinese flavor, track down the Minority Nationalities Traditional Sports Games. Ethnic groups play unusual sports from dragon boat racing to elephant tug-of-war.

## GOLF

Golf grows in popularity in China, despite initial Communist Party reluctance to embrace this elitist, land-hungry sport. Visiting golfers can enjoy over 200 courses nationwide. **Mission Hills** has 15 separate courses in two tournament locations at Shenzhen and Haikou; while the course on Jade Dragon Snow Mountain near Lijiang, Yunnan, is one of the world's highest. Perhaps the most alluring is the beautiful **Spring City** course near Kunming. Most courses are open to the public, and prices are similar to those in Western countries.

## SWIMMING

China has plenty of coast-line but lacks the beach culture of its southeast Asian neighbors. However, Hainan Island is touted as China's Hawaii, and the resorts there are improving fast, while Beihai in Guangxi boasts a

**Horse trek up the steep sides of Tiger Leaping Gorge, Yunnan**

Traversing the sand dunes of Mingsha Shan by camel, near Dunhuang, Gansu

very long stretch of sand. Closer to the capital, enjoy Beidaihe, long the Communist Party's summer retreat, or the seashores of the lovely city of Qingdao.

## DOWNHILL SKIING

The Chinese are discovering the thrill of downhill skiing. The best natural snow and ski resorts lie in Heilongjiang and Jilin provinces. **Yabuli**, about 100 miles (160 km) from Harbin, is one of the most established resorts, and **Club Med** has opened its first winter sports resort there. In the Beijing suburbs at least 10 slopes, mostly with man-made snow, attract skiers, and Shanghai has one of the world's largest indoor facilities. Large feet may cause problems with equipment rentals, and watch your back – complete novices abound.

## CHOOSING A TOUR

A multitude of tour companies ferry groups of photo-snapping tourists through the top sights of China. If you are thinking of booking a tour, do your research carefully; it is essential to find one that suits you well. Beyond the obvious essentials of types of accommodation, transport, the size of the group, and the itinerary, be sure to ask about the tipping policy,

which can sometimes add a sizeable unexpected cost to your trip. Also query the frequency of shopping stops, the bane of all organized trips in China. These detours (from which your guide may be earning a commission) can cut sightseeing time short and will become increasingly boring.

There's a wide choice of tour companies to travel with. **Abercrombie and Kent** is an established international group, which has provided well-organized trips for decades. **Steppes Travel**, which is particularly strong on the Silk Routes and Tibet, provides suggested itineraries that it is happy to adapt. The company also organizes special interest tours, such as those that seek out the intricate embroidery and beautiful textiles of Tibet and Guangxi. **Mongol Global Tours** organizes trips focusing on costumes and special itineraries for photographers. **Myths and Mountains** has some well thought-out

itineraries that cover Yunnan and Tibet, and also organizes horse trekking. **Wild China** organizes tours nationwide, including trips to remote Tibetan monasteries in western Sichuan and through the dense jungle and rural hamlets of Xishuangbanna.

## TRAIN SPOTTING

With such an extensive rail network, China has been a favorite destination of train lovers for years, particularly as it continued to run steam locomotives well after other nations discontinued their use. Sadly the last line to run steam, the Jitong railway, no longer does. Tours to highly industrialized areas still operate though, as many private lines at mining pits still use steam. China now has a national super high-speed rail network, which has revolutionized rail travel (see pp628–9). Train spotters have a strong internet presence – check the web for details.

Boarding a traditional raft kept afloat by inflated sheep stomachs, Yellow River

Hot air balloon floating amongst the karst peaks of Yangshuo, Guangxi

## CYCLING

Although the curse of the automobile threatens the bicycle kingdom, China remains a great place to saddle up. You will see more from a bike than a bus, and gain greater insight into the lives of the locals. A well-organized tour should provide alternative transport if you become exhausted or fall ill, and will have all the fix-it gear and able mechanics to deal with problem chains and derailers. Itineraries are set at different levels, from easy to challenging, and some companies provide bikes, while others ask that you bring your own wheels to keep costs down. For biking tours, consider specialist operators like **Bike China Adventures** who are based in Chengdu, **Bike Shanghai** and **Cycle China**.

In rural areas, renting a bike for a day or two is the best way to see sights just outside of town and get a feel for countryside life. There are plenty of bike-hire shops in most places, and many hotels can also arrange bike rental. In cities remember to park in designated areas (retain the token) and keep to cycle lanes where possible.

## MARTIAL ARTS

China attracts thousands of martial arts enthusiasts hoping to find the roots to their practice. Many head for famous Shaolin Temple in Henan *(see p158)*, where Bodhidarma is said to have

first taught the monks exercises that developed into *shaolin quan* during the 6th century. The temple is surrounded by kung fu schools, which have courses that range from a week to six months or longer. The less well-known monastery on Wudang Shan in Hubei *(see p272)*, said to be the home of *tai ji quan*, also has schools of martial arts.

Most forms of kung fu taught in China are watered-down versions of the original martial forms, which have become popular and effective ways to keep fit. If you are looking for pure fighting technique, you may have more luck overseas, or possibly, in Hong Kong. In Beijing, Shanghai, and other big cities, courses are advertized in listings magazines, but although there are plenty of sports institutes in China with classes, you may have difficulty finding an English-speaking instructor. Head to one of the traveler havens, such as Yangshuo, Dali, or

Lijiang, and you are certain to find capable instruction in English. Of course, you can always try joining the leagues of kung fu practitioners at daybreak in the nation's parks, particularly if your interest is *tai ji quan*.

If you want to fight with more than your bare hands, paintballing is growing in popularity – try the listings magazines in the large cities. For those who really need to let off steam, anti-aircraft guns and AK-47s are available for renting at the firing range en route from Beijing to the Great Wall at Badaling.

## CLIMBING

Most of China's sacred and scenic mountains, such as Tai Shan and Huang Shan, have steps, cable cars, and crowds all the way to the summit. Some of the mountains have less-used paths that make for pleasant hiking, but if you are a serious mountaineer, you will need to head to western China. The true roof of the world awaits in Tibet – topping Mount Everest will require patience and official approval, but treks to Everest base camp in the Rongbuk Valley are offered by several travel operators. Other spectacular climbs include Gongga Shan in Sichuan and also Muztagh-ata in Xinjiang (an easier climb and you can ski down), but, again, seek permission first.

More feasible is rock climbing at Yangshuo in Guangxi, where the limestone crags that inspired poets down the centuries now inspire climbers up the peaks. Asia's fastest developing sport climbing

A class of soon-to-be kung fu masters, Shaolin Temple, Henan

**Panda at the Breeding Center near Chengdu**

area combines a wide range of climbs with beautiful views, winding rivers and great accommodations.

A few intrepid spelunkers have been exploring the extensive karst cave network of Guangxi. A small industry of caving tours has developed, although, for the most part, the itineraries are geared to the experienced spelunker.

## TREKKING & CAMPING

The fascinating southwest offers some of the best trekking possibilities in the country, such as exploring the jungle of Xishuangbanna or visiting remote Tibetan monasteries. Horse-riding

trips are possible in the heavenly mountains of Xinjiang and the national parks of Sichuan. Check with specialist tour companies and the **Northwest Yunnan Ecotourism Association.** Whitewater rafting trips are popular in the southwest and in Tibet. If you are thinking of signing up, check the comapny's credentials and past history, and ensure that high-quality helmets, life-jackets, and, if necessary, wetsuits are provided.

Camping independently in China is tricky, and not recommended. However, the lack of legal camping facilities may be about to change, because caravan culture has just reached China. RVing is still in its birthing stages and as the industry develops, trailer parks and camp grounds are certain to appear. Restrictions on foreign drivers mean that motorhoming is not yet an option for non-residents.

## WILDLIFE & BIRD-WATCHING

Spot a panda at the Wolong Nature Reserve (see p369) or in the Breeding Center (see p360), where efforts are made to conserve the threatened species. Bird-watching tours head to Qinghai province for Bird Island on Qinghai Hu (see p499), and to parks such as Zhalong National Reserve (see p452), in the northeastern province of Heilongjiang, and Xixi Wetlands Park near Hangzhou, a natural sanctuary for birds and wildlife.

China's environment was savaged in the 20th century by political campaigns to move mountains with manpower; in the 21st, rampant economic growth threatens both biodiversity and cultural diversity, and conservation efforts are growing to save China's unique wildlife and ways of life. To support a responsible approach to tourism and the environment, consider tours and eco-lodges offered by organizations such as the Northwest Yunnan Ecotourism Association, based near Lijiang in Yunnan.

# DIRECTORY

## SPORTS

**Basketball**
www.nbachina.com

**Formula One**
www.icsh.sh.cn

**Rugby**
www.hkrugby.com

**Soccer**
www.sinosoc.com

**Tennis**
www.rolexmasters.com

## GOLF

**HSBC Champions Golf**
www.hsbcgolf.com

**Mission Hills**
1 Mission Hills Road, Shenzhen.
Tel (0755) 2802 0888.
1 Mission Hills Blvd, Haikou.
Tel (0898) 6868 3888.
www.missionhills china.com

**Spring City**
Tangchi, Yilang, Yunnan, PRC 652103.
Tel (0871) 767 1188.
www.springcity resort.com

## DOWNHILL SKIING

**Yabuli**
100 miles (160 km) east of Harbin, Heilongjiang.
Tel (0451) 5345 8888.
www.yabuliski.com

## TOUR COMPANIES

**Abercrombie & Kent**
www.abercrombie kent.com
In the US:
1520 Kensington Road, Suite 212, Oak Brook, IL 60523-2156.
Tel 1-800 554 7016.
In the UK:
Sloane Square House, Holbein Place, London, SW1W 8NS.
Tel (0845) 070 0615.

**Mongol Global Tours**
4141 Ball Road, no. 187.
Cypress, California, USA 90630. Tel 866 225 0577.
www.mongolglobal tours.com

**Myths & Mountains**
976 Tree Court, Incline Village, Nevada USA 89451.
Tel 1-800 670 MYTH.
www.www.journeysto china.com

**Steppes Travel**
51 Castle Street, Cirencester, Gloucestershire, UK GL7 1QD.
Tel (01285) 880 980.
www.steppestravel.co.uk

**Tibetan Connections**
www.tibetanconnections. com

**Wild China**
Room 801 Oriental Palace, 9 East Dongfang Road, North Dongganhuan Road, Chaoyang District, Beijing.
Tel (010) 6465 6602.
www.wildchina.com

## CYCLE TOURS

**Bike China Adventures**
6 Yi Guan Miao Fang Cao Jie, Wangfu Huayuan 64-1-17, Chengdu.
Tel 1-800 818 1778.
www.bikechina.com

**Bike Shanghai**
www.bikeshanghai.com

**Cycle China**
www.cyclechina.com

## ECOTOURISM

**Northwest Yunnan Ecotourism Assoc.**
Tel (0139) 8882 6672.
www.northwest yunnan.com

# SURVIVAL
# GUIDE

# PRACTICAL INFORMATION

China is going through an explosion in both international and domestic tourism. While there have been gradual improvements in the quality of tourist services, some of the remoter sights can still be difficult to reach independently, and most accessible sights get very crowded, especially during the summer season. Due to the absence of a nationwide non-profit network of tourist information centers, visitors often have to rely on hotels for guidance.

**Symbol of the China Tourist Board**

In the larger cities the tourist infrastructure, including transportation, hotels, and restaurants, is on a par with international standards. The remoter areas, however, provide fairly basic accommodations and may not be equipped to cater to the needs of the international tourist. Communication also poses difficulties, as English is not spoken widely and its usage is generally restricted to major cities, tour groups, four- and five-star hotels, and restaurants catering to tourists.

## WHEN TO GO

Although there are great climatic disparities within China, spring and fall are generally the best months to travel. The peak tourist season, however, is during summer (June to September), best avoided if you don't like the heat – it is baking hot in North China, steamy in the Yangzi region, and sweltering in South China. Winter is fiercely cold in North China, particularly in the northeast. Winters in South China are more pleasant, especially on the perennially warm Hainan Island and parts of Yunnan province. Climate and rainfall charts are found on pages 48–9. Planning a trip to coincide with the holiday and festival periods (see pp44–7) can lead to a fun and colorful trip experiencing China at its liveliest. However, tickets for air, train, and bus transport can be very difficult to acquire, as half of China will be traveling as well. Tourist sights are swamped with local sightseers, and most hotels and guesthouses raise their rates.

## WHAT TO TAKE

The clothes you need will depend on the time of year that you visit. In northern China, from November until March, you will require a down jacket, gloves, sweater, warm socks, thermal leggings, sturdy footwear, and lip balm. During the same season in the south, you still need a sweater and warm clothes, even as far south as Hong Kong. In summer, across most of China, you only need loose-fitting shirts or t-shirts, and thin trousers. Shorts will also do, though not many Chinese wear them. Bring a first-aid kit (see p618), raincoat, sun hat, deodorant, pocket knife, flashlight, and some good reading material.

## ADVANCE BOOKING

The boom in domestic tourism means it is wise to book ahead year-round, but especially during the peak holiday periods between May 1 and October 1, and the Chinese New Year. Booking in advance using the internet can secure you good deals on accommodations. Unless traveling on short intercity routes, train tickets should be bought a few days before travel, as seats can be in short supply. Train tickets can only be purchased up to five days in advance of the day of travel. Bus tickets need not be booked in advance, but airplane tickets should be, especially during major holiday periods.

## VISAS & PASSPORTS

A passport, valid for at least six months, and a visa are necessary to enter the People's Republic of China. Most foreign nationals don't require a visa for entering Hong Kong and Macau but will need one if traveling on to mainland China. Chinese embassies and consulates around the world issue a standard single-entry, 30-day visa, although multiple-entry visas, and 60-day visas can also be obtained, depending on the purpose of your visit. Visas cannot be issued at the border. When completing the visa application form, you must clearly specify what parts of

**Temperate weather at a tea garden in Chengdu**

◁ **Scores of cyclists pedaling through Beijing**

China you plan to visit. Avoid mentioning Tibet, or Xinjiang, even if you plan to visit these regions, as you may be questioned about your occupation and intent of visit – the list you provide is non-binding. Always carry your passport, as it is an essential document for checking into hotels, and the Public Security Bureau *(see p616)* may insist on seeing it. Photocopying the visa page and the personal information page will speed up replacement in case your passport is lost or stolen. Visa extensions are sometimes granted for 30 days by the foreign affairs branch of local PSBs throughout the country. Note that heavy fines are levied if you overstay your permitted period in China.

## PERMITS

Some areas of China are either totally or partially off-limits, and may require a permit from the PSB, include Lushun (Liaoning), Xanadu (Inner Mongolia) and parts of Shennongjia (Hubei). Check with the PSB before going to western Sichuan, where the rules of access are not fixed.

All travel to Tibet has to be arranged beforehand through a travel agency in China, who will arrange a permit for you. If you want to travel outside of Lhasa, the agency will have to arrange a tour guide, private vehicle and driver, and any additional permits. It is easiest to arrange this from Xining or Chengdu.

## EMBASSIES & CONSULATES

Most countries have embassies in Beijing and consulates in Hong Kong, Shanghai, and Guangzhou, and to a lesser extent, in Chengdu, Chongqing, Qingdao, and Dalian. Consular offices can re-issue passports and assist in case of emergencies, such as theft, imprisonment, and hospitalization. Your hotel can put you in touch with your embassy or consulate, or try (www.travelchinaguide.com).

## CUSTOMS INFORMATION

When entering China, visitors are entitled to a duty-free allowance of 70 fluid ounces (2 liters) of wine or spirits, 400 cigarettes, and a certain amount of gold and silver. Foreign currency exceeding US$5000, or its equivalent, must be declared.

Items that are prohibited include fresh fruit, rare animals and plants, and arms and ammunition. Chinese law specifies limits on the export of certain items, such as herbal medicines. Also, objects predating 1795 cannot be taken out of China, while antiques made after that date will need to have an official seal affixed. Although foreign visitors are largely left alone, it is not advisable to take in politically controversial literature, especially to sensitive areas such as Tibet where there have been instances of books being confiscated.

**Shang-dynasty bronze tripod**

## IMMUNIZATION

Ensure that all of your routine vaccinations are up to date, such as tetanus and polio. It is advisable to also get vaccinated against Hepatitis A and B, and typhoid. Only visitors traveling from countries where yellow fever is endemic must provide proof of vaccination against the disease. Malaria medication is a good idea for those visiting rural areas, especially Yunnan and Hainan, as is a Japanese encephalitis vaccination. Try www.mdtravelhealth. com for up-to-date travel-health information and more advice on immunization.

## INSURANCE

It is advisable to take out an insurance policy for medical emergencies as well as theft before leaving home, checking with your insurance company that it is entirely valid in China. The policy will

# DIRECTORY

### CHINA INTERNATIONAL TRAVEL SERVICE (CITS)

www.cits.net

**Beijing**
1 Dongdan Beidajie.
*Tel (010) 6522 2991.*

**Dalian**
Central Plaza Hotel,
145 Zhongshan Lu.
*Tel (0411) 8368 7843.*

**Guangzhou**
185 Huanshi Xi Lu.
*Tel (020) 8666 6889.*

**Shanghai**
1277 Beijing Xi Lu.
*Tel (021) 6289 8899.*

**Suzhou**
251 Ganjiang Xi Lu.
*Tel (0512) 6515 1369.*

**Xi'an**
50 Chang'an Bei Lu.
*Tel (029) 8524 1864.*

cover the loss of baggage, tickets, and, to a certain extent, cash and checks. However, before signing an insurance policy, look for one that excludes coverages you will not require during your stay in China. Insurance is also essential to cover any adventure activity or sport that you may undertake during your trip.

**Classic *tai hu* rock formations lining the shore in Yu Yuan (Jade Garden), Shanghai**

## TOURIST INFORMATION

With the exception of the major cities, China has yet to recognize the value of professional Tourist Information Centers, either at home or abroad. Those that exist in Beijing and Shanghai are often under-funded, poorly staffed, and unreliable, although they are useful for obtaining free maps. The state-approved **China International Travel Service** (CITS) (*see p611*), originally set up to cater to the needs of foreign visitors, today functions as any other local operator, offering nothing more than tours, tickets, and rented cars. A limited choice of government-run travel agencies abroad promote China tourism. However, they fail to offer professional and unbiased advice, instead steering customers toward group tours and standard hotels.

## ADMISSION CHARGES

Virtually every sight in China carries an admission fee. While many major museums are now free to enter, most temples and parks, smaller museums, palaces, historical monuments, sacred mountains, and wildlife reserves can only be entered after paying a fee. While temples charge anything from ¥5 to ¥80, prices of all other entry tickets vary. It is often hard to see where the money goes as many of China's temples and monuments appear severely neglected. Non-Chinese visitors often have to pay a higher

admission charge, and you may still encounter a foreign visitor surcharge. Most sights, such as parks and temples, simply have a main ticket for entry *(men piao)*, but further tickets may need to be purchased for access to individual sights within the complex. Alternatively, a "through ticket" *(tao piao)* can be bought for access to all the sights. Occasionally there are further fees for storing bags. The sale of tickets often ceases half an hour or so before the sight closes for the day. Guides swarm around entrances to major sights and will latch onto you, even if you're not interested. It is advisable to test their English first, as many just repeat fixed lines, parrot fashion, relating to the sight in question, and are unable to answer further queries.

**Road sign in both pinyin and Chinese characters**

## HOLIDAYS & OPENING HOURS

Even though New Year's day (January 1) is a public holiday in China, the main holiday periods are during the Lunar New Year (Spring Festival) and October 1 (National Day) holidays (the May holiday is just a single day). Each holiday period officially lasts three days, although most businesses and banks remain shut for seven days. Accommodation prices rise as domestic tourism peaks. Tourist sights, however, remain open during these times.

## LANGUAGE

The official language of China is *Putonghua* (literally "common tongue"), based on the dialect spoken in Beijing, and known outside China as Mandarin Chinese. *Putonghua* doesn't specifically belong to any one region, and is used across the country for communication between speakers of China's numerous dialects. Unlike other dialects, such as Cantonese, *Putonghua* can be used throughout China. Since the vast majority of Chinese people do not understand English, it is largely useless for communication outside of hotels. The tonal nature of *Putonghua* makes it difficult for English speakers to become accustomed to the language. Pinyin, a romanization system, helps in the recognition of sounds and has diacritical marks to indicate tone. A few basic phrases in *Putonghua* are listed on pages 668–72.

## FACILITIES FOR THE DISABLED

If you are a wheelchair user, China is not a recommended destination for you. With the exception of Hong Kong and, to some extent, Macau, China offers very basic facilities for the disabled, both in public transport and accommodation. Public buildings and places of interest are rarely fitted with ramps or rails, although this is slowly improving. Many of the pavements in urban areas are littered with obstacles and occasional potholes, and have high curbs, making wheelchair access troublesome.

The scarcity of safe crossing points on urban roads drives pedestrians onto overhead walkways; otherwise they have to join the crowds surging through the traffic. Rooms with services for disabled visitors are only available at the better hotels, although elevators are common in most hotels over three stories high.

**Façade of the impressive Shaanxi History Museum, Xi'an**

## FACILITIES FOR CHILDREN

The Chinese love children, and they are usually welcome everywhere in China. Even though baby-changing rooms are extremely rare, and very few restaurants have child seats, traveling with very young children can have its advantages as people will generally go out of their way to accommodate you in most places and situations. Supermarkets are well supplied with diapers, baby wipes, bottles, creams, medicine, clothing, infant milk formula, and baby food. However, the baby food is of a sweeter variety and nearly always processed. The Chinese very rarely give pacifiers to their children, but you can find them in department stores in larger cities. Also bring a set of plastic cutlery for your child, as some restaurants and eating places only have chopsticks.

## PHOTOGRAPHY

Everyone in urban China uses digital cameras now so film-developing stores are, as elsewhere, a novelty rather than the norm. While 35mm color print film is available almost everywhere, don't expect to find color slide or high-speed film outside of the large cities. Camera batteries are widely available in department stores in big cities, though it is best to bring your own supply. Many photo stores in Hong Kong, Macau, and mainland China provide transferring of images from a digital camera onto a disc.

Photographing people in China is generally not a problem, but it helps to first ask for their permission. Photography is rarely allowed within temple halls and museums, or at archeological sites, and signs indicate where photography is not permitted. In case you don't find a sign with such restrictions marked in English, it is advisable to ask around.

Children with their parents enjoying a meal

Photographing politically-sensitive images may result in the confiscation of your film and it goes without saying that photography of military sites is banned. As far as the regulations go, photography from aircrafts is banned, and so is taking photographs of airports, harbors, and railroads. However, barring the military installations, most of the other restrictions are seldom enforced.

If you are discreet and respectful, then you should encounter no problems.

## ELECTRICITY

The electrical current in China is 220 volts. You will see a variety of plugs in China, including two flat prongs (the same as American plugs), or three flat prongs (the same as Australian ones). The British three square-pin arrangement is rare outside of smart hotels, and it is therefore advisable to carry a travel conversion plug, readily available in most of the larger cities. A power-surge cable will protect laptops against voltage fluctuations, which are common in China. It is best to avoid cheap batteries, as they are very shortlived. Instead, buy a battery charger and rechargeable batteries, which can be easily found in most Chinese stores. Blackouts are not unheard of in China, so, given the erratic powercuts, it is wise to carry a flashlight.

**Plugs with two and three prongs**

## TIME & CALENDAR

Despite its size, China occupies only one time zone, and there is no daylight saving time. Midday in Beijing is also midday in far-flung parts of China, including Lhasa and Ürümqi, which are along the same latitude as countries that are two and three hours behind China. China time is seven or eight hours ahead of Greenwich Mean Time (GMT), two or three hours behind Australian Eastern Standard Time, 15 or 16 hours ahead of US Pacific Standard Time, and 12 or 13 hours ahead of US Eastern Standard Time. The Western Gregorian Calendar is used for all official work, although the lunar calendar is still used for calculating the dates of festivals.

## MEASUREMENTS & CONVERSION CHARTS

The metric system is most commonly used in all parts of China.

**Imperial to Metric**
1 inch = 2.5 centimeters
1 foot = 30 centimeters
1 mile = 1.6 kilometers
1 ounce = 28 grams
1 pound = 454 grams
1 pint (US) = 0.473 liters
1 gallon (US) = 3.785 liters

**Metric to Imperial**
1 centimeter = 0.4 inches
1 meter = 3 feet 3 inches
1 kilometer = 0.6 miles
100 gram = 3.53 ounces
1 kilogram = 2.2 pounds
1 liter = 2.11 pints (US)

# Etiquette

Despite rampant modernization, China remains a traditional society governed by strong family values. Although the cities and towns give the outward impression of Western modernity, their inhabitants retain a deep-seated and family-oriented conservatism. Confucian values promote respect for elders and those in positions of authority, and reinforce notions of conformity. Religious observance is also an important part of people's lives, but is largely separate from mainstream social behavior. The Chinese are, above all, welcoming and generous, and visitors are often amazed at their hospitality. If invited to someone's home, a gift of chocolates, French wine, or a carton of cigarettes will be greatly appreciated.

## GREETING PEOPLE

While shaking hands is not customary in China, Chinese men may shake your hand or expect their hand to be shaken by foreign visitors. Although the Chinese are not particularly tactile in their greetings, bodily contact is quite common between friends, even of the same sex. It is quite common to see young men and women walking arm in arm, or with their arm around another's shoulder. The usual Chinese greeting is *ni hao* (how are you?) or *nimen hao* in its plural form, to which you reply *ni hao* or *nimen hao* – the polite form is *nin/ninmen hao*. Chinese people can be very direct, and will not blanch at asking you how much you earn, how old you are, or whether you are married. Such questions are seen as nothing more than taking a friendly interest in a new acquaintance. When proffering business cards, the Chinese do so politely, using the fingertips of both hands, and receive cards in the same manner. It is a good idea to take some business cards, with your particulars in Chinese on one side and in English on the reverse, as there will be many occasions to give them away.

## BODY LANGUAGE

Once they reach the age of 30 or 40, the Chinese tend to dress conservatively, favoring dark and inconspicuous colors such as brown and black. In cities and towns, people wear jeans, t-shirts, and skirts, and many youngsters also dye their hair. Locals expect foreign visitors to dress and behave a little flamboyantly, so don't worry too much about what you wear, but try to avoid looking scruffy. It is also acceptable for both sexes to wear shorts in hot weather.

**Advice for burning incense**

On the beach, nudity and women sunbathing topless are rarely seen as Chinese beach culture is quite modest.

## FACE

Reserved in manner and expression, the Chinese also harbor strong feelings of personal pride and respect. The maintenance of pride and the avoidance of shame is known as saving face. Loss of face *(mianzi)* creates great discomfort and embarrassment for the Chinese, so although you may often be frustrated by bureaucratic red-tape and delays, remember that arguing may make matters worse. Instead, try tackling difficult situations by being firm but polite, and use confrontation only as a last resort.

## PLACES OF WORSHIP

Although there are no dress codes for Buddhist, Daoist, or Confucian temples, visitors to mosques should dress respectfully – avoid wearing shorts or short skirts – and cover their upper arms. Buddhist, Daoist, and Confucian temples are relaxed about visitors wandering about, but do be considerate toward worshipers. Also, check whether you can take photographs within temple halls, as this is often not permitted. Taking photographs in courtyards, however, is usually not a problem. Some Buddhist and Daoist temples are active, and you should show respect towards the resident monks.

## DOS & DON'TS

If invited out for dinner, expect to see the diners competing to pay the entire bill, rather than dividing it up between them. It is a good idea to join in the scramble for the bill, or at least make an attempt – your gesture will be appreciated, though almost certainly declined. The Chinese avoid talking about politics, and it is best to follow suit.

The courtyard of the Jade Buddha Temple in Shanghai

## ANNOYANCES

The Chinese habit of staring, especially in smaller towns and rural areas, can be a little annoying. However, the intent is rarely hostile. Staring was common even in Beijing until the 1990s, and although it is rare in cities today, it helps to remember that China was closed to foreign nationals until the early 1980s. Another annoyance that visitors face in smaller towns are the constant calls of "Hellooo!" or *laowai* (foreigner). It is best to either ignore them or smile, as saying hello often results in bursts of laughter. In large cities, people often strike up conversation to practice their English. Sometimes, art students try and coerce you into visiting over-priced art galleries, which you should firmly decline to do.

Although line-ups are beginning to replace the usual mêlée at ticket offices, be prepared for a lot of pushing and shoving.

Since the outbreak of SARS in 2002, public health organizations have made considerable efforts to curb the habit of spitting. It is still widespread, however, especially in rural areas. Spitting is common on buses and trains, and it is not considered rude to spit in mid-conversation, so do not take offense.

Bric-à-brac to be haggled over on display at a street market in Tianjin

## SMOKING & ALCOHOL

Smoking is now banned in public places in China, such as restaurants, hotels, railway stations and theaters. However, as the world's largest producer and consumer of cigarettes *(xiangyan)* these rules are difficult to enforce in China. Despite the appearance of no-smoking zones, many people choose to ignore them, and towns and cities remain shrouded in a haze of cigarette smoke. Many business owners resent banning their customers from smoking on their premises.

Smoking is also banned on domestic flights and in train carriages. The Chinese are very generous when it comes to offering cigarettes, so remember to be equally generous in return. They also enjoy drinking alcohol, and there is no taboo against moderate intoxication. The usual accompaniment during a meal is beer *(pijiu)*, or white spirit *(baijiu)*. People in cities are increasingly drinking wine, and it is available in most large supermarkets. If someone raises a toast to you *(ganbei!)*, it is good form for you to toast the person back at a later stage.

**A spirit consumed at business banquets**

## BARGAINING

As a foreign national in China, it is essential to bargain *(jiangjia)*. You may often be overcharged – sometimes by large amounts – in markets and anywhere else where prices are not indicated. In some restaurants, the English menu has more expensive rates than the Chinese one. You may be able to bargain to reduce your hotel room-rate, especially during the low season. When bargaining, there is no need to be aggressive. Instead, firmly state your price – which should never be unrealistic – and walk away if the vendor doesn't agree. Shopkeepers will often agree to the price once they realize they're losing a

potential sale. The prices in large shops and government emporia *(guoying shangdian)* are usually fixed.

## TIPPING

Tipping is very rare in China, Hong Kong, and Macau, so there is no obligation to leave a tip *(xiaofei)* and people don't usually expect one. Some smarter restaurants include a service charge on the bill.

## BEGGING

China's imbalanced economic progress and huge population of rural poor have resulted in large numbers of beggars all over the country, especially in cities. Foreign visitors naturally attract their attention, and groups of children are often sent by their parents to extract money. The best strategy is to ignore them and walk away.

**A beggar in Lhasa with colorful Buddhist regalia**

# Personal Security & Health

The Police Force in China is called the Public Security Bureau (gonganju), abbreviated to PSB. Foreign nationals are unlikely to encounter the PSB, unless extending their visa, applying for a permit to a restricted area, or reporting loss or theft. China is a police state, so the PSB is riddled with corruption and overwhelming bureaucracy. Not all police stations (paichusuo) have English-speaking staff, so try to take along an interpreter if reporting a crime, although it is best to contact your embassy or consulate first for guidance. Throughout mainland China, call 110 for the police. Protect your valuables and important documents at all times, stay and eat in clean places, and drink only mineral water. For medical attention, it is better to opt for a private clinic rather than one of the many government hospitals.

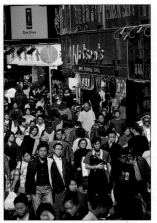

**Crowds in the busy shopping district of Causeway Bay, Hong Kong**

## GENERAL PRECAUTIONS

Traveling in China is generally safe. Even though crime has burgeoned since the 1980s economic liberalization, with millions of unemployed migrants flocking to the cities, foreign visitors are unlikely to be the victims of crime, apart from petty theft. Tourists on buses and trains, particularly those in the hard-seat class (see p629) and on overnight journeys, are tempting targets for thieves. Guard your camera and valuables, wear a money belt at all times, and secure your luggage to the rack on overnight train journeys.

Hotels are, more or less, a lot more secure than dormitories, even though it is not unusual for things to go missing from hotel rooms. You could use the safes or storage areas that most hotels offer, but do insist on a receipt. If staying in a dormitory, never leave your essentials and important documents lying around, and be cautious about giving too many details to fellow travelers.

When walking in crowded streets, avoid wearing anything expensive or eye-catching, and keep your wallet in the bottom of your bag, but never in a backpack. Be discreet when taking out your wallet; it is best to carry only as much cash as you need for the day. Keep an eye on your belongings while visiting public washrooms, as quite a few travelers have had very unpleasant experiences.

Keep cash, traveler's checks, passport, and visa documents in a money belt – ones that lie flat and are meant to be worn under clothing are best. Also, remember to make photocopies of the personal information and China visa pages of your passport and any other important documents and store them separately from the originals.

## SECURITY

Hosting the Olympics saw China upgrade security at airports, railway and metro stations, and at some sights, but it is rarely intrusive. At certain sights, you will be asked to deposit your bag before making a visit. Always carry your passport with you for identification.

## WOMEN TRAVELERS

China is usually regarded as a very safe destination for women. In general, Chinese men are respectful toward women, and it is unlikely for them to experience any serious form of sexual harassment. That said, never take your safety for granted, and though independent travel is safer in China than in many other countries, traveling in a group is always wiser, as lone travelers are more likely to be mugged or assaulted. However, if you do travel alone, stay on your guard when visiting rural and far-flung areas, and avoid wandering about alone in quiet and deserted places, especially after dark.

As far as clothing goes, it is best to observe the clothing and behavior of local women, and adapt as closely as possible. It helps to dress modestly, especially in Muslim regions and rural areas.

If possible, avoid hotel dormitories and opt for single rooms in hotels located near the center of town on well-lit streets. To avert an undesirable encounter, carry a whistle or learn a few basic self-defense moves.

## GAY AND LESBIAN TRAVELERS

The gay and lesbian scenes in China's main cities, in particular Shanghai, Beijing, and Hong Kong, are growing and diversifying, with clubs, bars, and venues increasing in number. However, China is still a highly conventional society,

**Beijing PSB officer**

and homosexuality is largely disapproved of and misunderstood. Homosexuality is legal, but there are no laws to protect gays, and police periodically crack down on meeting places. Even in cities, it is inadvisable for gays and lesbians to be open with their sexuality, despite the tactile relationship many Chinese have with friends of the same sex.

## HOSPITALS & MEDICAL FACILITIES

It is important to take out comprehensive medical insurance before arriving in China. China's state hospitals vary considerably in quality; the better-equipped hospitals *(yiyuan)* can be found in the cities and large towns, but even at the best, communication can be problematic. Cities with large expatriate communities have private hospitals, where there are exclusive clinics with English-speaking staff to

**Distinctive green cross of a pharmacy**

attend to non-Chinese visitors. Consider contacting your embassy for a list of approved hospitals. In general, medical services are reasonably cheap throughout China, but many hospitals may levy a certain amount of "foreigner surcharge" that could ensure

better care. Whatever the type of institution, you will be expected to pay cash at the time of being admitted.

Pharmacies *(yaodian)*, identified by green crosses, are found all over China. Many of them stock both Western medicine *(xi yao)* and Chinese medicine *(zhong yao)*, and can treat you for minor injuries or ailments. Take adequate supplies of any prescription drugs you require, and also remember to take the chemical – not brand – name of all prescriptions, in case you need to restock. In large cities such as Beijing and Shanghai, prescriptions may not be required for a range of medicines, including antibiotics and sleeping pills. Some large hotels have in-house clinics to help guests with diagnosis, medical assistance, and prescriptions. Large modern hotels may also be able to provide a Chinese speaker to accompany you to the hospital.

Those interested in traditional Chinese medicine *(see p232)* for treating chronic ailments can visit the traditional institutes attached to local hospitals and medical colleges. Some hotels, too, offer traditional Chinese treatments.

## PUBLIC BATHROOMS

Public bathrooms are typically of the squat variety and are squalid, filthy, and rarely cleaned, unless watched over by an attendant. There is little privacy – doorless cubicles, separated by low walls, are the norm. Toilet paper is a rarity – don't

**Sign pointing the way to the facilities**

forget to carry your own supply. Toilet paper should be put in the receptacle, if provided, rather than down the toilet, as septic systems are often unable to handle paper products. You will be expected to pay a few *jiao* for using the facilities. Use hotel and fast-food restaurant bathrooms whenever you get the opportunity.

## HYGIENE TIPS

The rigors of travel require a few extra hygiene considerations. Carry a small bar of handsoap or a tube of concentrated camping soap with you all the time. A packet of wet wipes always comes in handy.

Warts are easily picked up from poorly cleaned shower stalls. You will often find a pair of flipflops under your hotel bed. These are meant to be worn in the shower, but you might consider packing a pair of your own.

---

# DIRECTORY

### IN AN EMERGENCY

**Tel** Police 110.
**Tel** Fire 119.
**Tel** Ambulance 120.

### HOSPITAL & MEDICAL FACILITIES

**Beijing**
Hong Kong International
Medical Clinic,
9th floor, Office Tower,
Hong Kong Macau
Center, Swissotel,
2 Chaoyang Men Bei Dajie.
**Tel** *(010) 6553 2288.*
**www**.hkclinic.com

International SOS, Suite
105, Wing 1, Kunsha
Building, 16 Xin Yuan Li,
Chaoyang. Clinic appts:
**Tel** *(010) 6462 9112.*

**Guangzhou**
Can-Am International Medical Center, 5th floor, Garden Tower, Garden Hotel,
368 Huanshi Dong Lu.
**Tel** *(020) 8386 6988.*
**www**.canamhealthcare.
com

**Hong Kong**
Queen Elizabeth Hospital,
30 Gascoigne Rd,
Yau Ma Tei.
**Tel** *(0852) 2958 8888.*

**Shanghai**
Parkway Health, 203/4
West Retail Plaza,
Shanghai Center, 1376
Nanjing West Road.
**Tel** *(021) 6445 5999.*
**www**.parkwayhealth.cn

### EMBASSIES IN BEIJING

**Australia**
21 Dongzhi Men Wai
Dajie.
**Tel** *(010) 5140 4111.*

**Canada**
19 Dongzhi Men Wai
Dajie.
**Tel** *(010) 5139 4000.*

**Ireland**
3 Ritan Dong Lu.
**Tel** *(010) 6532 2691.*

**United Kingdom**
11 Guanghua Lu.
**Tel** *(010) 5192 4000.*

**USA**
55 Anjia Loulu.
**Tel** *(010) 8531 4000.*

### TRAVEL HEALTH

**Masta**
**Tel** *0870 606 2782.*
**www**.masta.org

**MD Travel Health**
**www**.mdtravel
health.com

Sitting in the shade at the Botanical Gardens, Hangzhou, Zhejiang

## HEAT, HUMIDITY & POLLUTION

During summer, it is hot all across China. If you're traveling during this time drink plenty of fluids to prevent dehydration, and increase your intake of salt to compensate its loss through sweating. Wear loose-fitting cotton clothing and sandals, remember to bring a sunhat and sunglasses, and use plenty of sunscreen. Most hotels, except the very cheapest, have rooms equipped with air- conditioning, and virtually all restaurants are air conditioned as well. Prolonged exposure to the sun can cause heat stroke, a serious condition with high body temperature, severe headaches, and disorientation. To avoid heat rashes and fungal infections caused by humidity, wear clean, loose clothes made of natural fibers, and open sandals.

Many of China's cities, including Beijing, experience chronic levels of atmospheric pollution. This aggravates chest infections, and asthmatic travelers should always carry their own medication.

## COLD & HYPOTHERMIA

Winter can be severe through most of north China. High-altitude travel in particular can expose you to extreme cold, and travelers to Tibet and other mountainous regions must be prepared for sudden changes in temperature. A waterproof and windproof layer is vital in cold conditions, as is adequate warm clothing, including thick socks, boots, jacket, gloves, and most importantly, a hat. The symptoms of hypothermia, which include shivering, dizziness, exhaustion, and irrational behavior, are brought on by prolonged exposure to the cold. Be aware of fingers and toes going white or numb, the first indications of frost bite, and rub them vigorously if they do.

**A motorcyclist wrapped up against pollution**

## FIRST-AID KIT

Organize a basic first-aid kit, which should include all personal medication, aspirin or painkillers for fevers and minor aches and pains, tablets for nausea and movement sickness, antiseptic cream for cuts and bites, an anti-fungal ointment, Band-Aids, gauze and tensor bandages, a pair of scissors, insect repellent, and tweezers. Also carry antihistamines for allergies, anti-diarrhea tablets, water purification tablets, disposable syringes, oral rehydration solution, and a thermometer. Taking a supply of antibiotics is a good idea. Most of these items are readily available at Chinese pharmacies.

## STOMACH UPSETS & DIARRHEA

Usually caused by a change of diet, water, and climate, diarrhea is common among visitors. Chinese food, which can be quite oily and spicy, does require some getting used to for many people. If the change of diet is affecting you, stick to Western food and simple boiled food, such as plain rice, until the diarrhea subsides. Most importantly, drink lots of fluids, as diarrhea quickly leads to dehydration – oral rehydration solution (ORS) is an effective remedy. If you do not have any ORS, stir half a teaspoon of salt and three teaspoons of honey or sugar into a mug of boiled water.

To decrease your chances of stomach upset, avoid raw salads, cut fruit, cold cuts, roadside kabobs, fresh juice, and yogurt. It is important to avoid drinking tap water even in big cities, apart from Hong Kong. Drink boiled water, or bottled mineral water after checking that the seal is intact. Most international brands of carbonated drinks are widely available. Although street food can look tempting, it is safer to abstain unless it is hot and freshly cooked in front of you.

A good pharmacist can recommend standard diarrhea medication, such as Imodium, though if the attack is severe, it is best to consult a doctor. A popular and effective Chinese medicine for upset stomachs is *Huangliansu*.

## SARS & FLU

In 2003, severe acute respiratory syndrome (SARS) spread throughout China and then to Toronto, Canada. China managed to contain the disease with a strict identification and quarantine program. Since then, there have only been minor, localized outbreaks of the disease. Another SARS outbreak is unlikely, but should one occur, do not travel to the affected area.

Bird flu, or avian influenza, is a serious problem in east Asia, but unlikely to affect travelers. Do not visit

**A food stall with a tempting but risky display**

any poultry farms, avoid birds at outdoor markets, and eat only poultry and eggs that have been thoroughly cooked.

In 2009, China underwent a mass vaccination program against swine flu (H1N1) for at-risk individuals (such as young children and pregnant women). The World Health Organisation (WHO) provides up-to-date information on serious diseases. If you develop symptoms of pneumonia or flu after your trip, see your physician immediately.

## SEXUALLY TRANSMITTED & OTHER INFECTIOUS DISEASES

After years of denial, Chinese authorities have begun to publicly admit to the alarming spread of HIV – the virus that causes Acquired Immune Deficiency Syndrome (AIDS) – via unprotected sex, drug use, and infected blood banks. Nonetheless, considerable ignorance about the disease and its prevention still exists in rural areas, and most prostitutes working in the cities are from rural China. Long-term visitors to China are screened for HIV infection.

Hepatitis B, also transmitted through contact with infected blood, is spread through sexual contact, unsterilized needles, tattoos, and shaves from roadside barbers. However, it can be prevented with a vaccine.

When visiting a clinic, ensure that the doctor opens a new syringe in front of you. You may even want to bring your own disposable syringe for the doctor to use. Any procedure using needles, such as tattooing or ear-piercing, is best avoided.

## WATER-BORNE DISEASES

Visitors must be on their guard against dysentery. Bacillary dysentery is accompanied by severe stomach pains, vomiting and fever, whereas amoebic dysentery has similar symptoms but takes longer to manifest. Vaccination against Hepatitis A is advisable before leaving home, especially if you plan to visit rural areas. Other water-borne diseases, such as cholera and typhoid, can also be prevented with vaccines. Schistosomiasis (bilharzia), a disease caused by a water-borne parasitic worm found in south and central China, can be avoided by not swimming in fresh water. Drink bottled mineral water at all times, and avoid ice cubes.

**Bottled mineral water**

## RABIES

The deadly rabies virus is spread via the bite of an infected animal. If you are bitten, clean the bite with an antiseptic solution, and seek medical help at once. Treatment involves a course of injections. A rabies vaccine is only necessary if you are visiting high-risk areas for a long period and likely to come into contact with animals. Do not have this vaccine, unless advised by your doctor.

## INSECT-BORNE DISEASES

Mosquitos are rife during the summer in China. In the southern part of the country, mosquitos can carry a number of diseases. If you are visiting an area with a high risk of malaria, take preventive anti-malarial drugs before, during, and after your trip. Contact MASTA (Medical Advisory Services for Travellers Abroad) and check the MD Travel Health website *(see p617)* for information on malaria medication. Dengue fever and Japanese B encephalitis are also carried by mosquitos. To guard against mosquito bites, apply mosquito repellent, and wear clothes that cover as much of your arms and legs as possible.

## ALTITUDE SICKNESS

A lack of sufficient oxygen at altitudes higher than 8,000 ft (2,500 m) can cause attacks of Acute Mountain Sickness (AMS) – severe headaches, dizziness, and loss of appetite. These symptoms subside within a day or two, but if they persist beyond 48 hours, you must descend to a lower altitude immediately and seek medical help. To avoid altitude sickness ascend slowly, drink plenty of fluids, and avoid alcohol and sedatives.

**Trekking at high altitudes on Chomolungma (Mount Everest)**

# Banking & Local Currency

**24-hr banking sign**

China provides a wide range of banking facilities and money exchange services, which are available in large cities, international airports, major banks, and top-end hotels. Always keep some cash to hand for transport, restaurants, and purchases, as traveler's checks and credit cards cannot be used everywhere, especially in rural areas. ATMs that accept international cards are easy to find in all major cities. Foreign banks like Citi, HSBC, and Standard Chartered are expanding their branch networks in major Chinese cities.

## BANKS & BANKING HOURS

The Bank of China has the most extensive network in the country. Several other major banks operate nationwide, including the Industrial and Commercial Bank of China, the China Construction Bank, and China Merchants Bank. Banks are normally open 9am–4:30pm or 5pm Monday to Friday, but there are variations between places, and some banks are open on Saturdays. All banks remain closed for the first three days of the Chinese New Year, with reduced hours during other Chinese holidays.

## AUTOMATED TELLERS

Automated Teller Machines (ATMs) that accept foreign cards are common in all major cities of mainland China, plus Hong Kong and Macau, so can be relied upon for easy access to cash. In more remote areas of China, ATMs may not all accept international cards; visit your card issuer's website for locations. In cities, ATMs are located in banks, shopping malls, five-star hotels and airports. Some ATMs also dispense cash against credit cards. Cash withdrawn from ATMs is subject to the same exchange rate as credit cards, and there may be a limit to how much you can withdraw per day.

**Hong Kong & Shanghai Banking Corporation (HSBC) ATMs**

## CHANGING MONEY

Chinese currency is non-convertible; it is not widely available internationally and cannot be used outside the country. You will have to exchange your money in China (most major currencies are accepted), and then convert any left-over *renminbi* back before you leave. You can exchange currency at banks and international airports and most decent hotels will change money for guests. All exchange operations are linked to the Bank of China so rates do not vary between them. Keep exchange receipts so that you can re-convert any surplus *renminbi* before leaving China. The Chinese "black market" for exchanging foreign currency offers only marginally better rates than banks. Dealing with the shady characters involved is not worth the hassle or risk, and you may end up with counterfeit *renminbi*.

Hong Kong dollars are convertible and available outside the country. They are accepted in Macau and most southern Special Economic Zones.

## CREDIT CARDS

Credit cards are widely accepted in upmarket restaurants, hotels, and high-street stores, but always check before attempting to make a purchase that your foreign card is accepted. The accepted cards are MasterCard, Visa, Japan Credit Bureau (JCB), Diners Club, and American Express. Air tickets

---

# DIRECTORY

**BANK OF CHINA**

**Beijing**
Asia Pacific Building,
8 Yabao Lu, Chaoyang District, 100020.
1 Fuxing Men Nei Dajie, 100818.

**24-hr ATMs**
*Arrivals Hall, Capital Airport.*
*Corner of Sundongan Plaza,*
*Wangfujing Dajie.*
*Corner of Oriental Plaza,*
*1 Dongchang'an Jie.*

**Shanghai**
39/F, Bank of China Tower,
200 Yincheng Rd, Central,
Pudong, 200120.

**Hong Kong**
2A Des Voeux Road,
Central.
24–28 Carnarvon Road,
Tsim Sha Tsui.

**HSBC**

**Beijing**
Block A, Beijing COFCO
Plaza 8,
Jianguo Men Nei Dajie,

Dong Cheng District,
100005.

**Shanghai**
HSBC Tower,
101 Ying Cheng East Rd,
Pudong, 200120.

**24-hr ATMs**
*Shanghai Center, 1376*
*Nanjing Xi Lu.*

**CITIBANK**

**Shanghai**
Marine Tower,
1 Pudong Avenue,
Pudong, 200120.

**24-hr ATMs**
*Adjacent to the Peace*
*Hotel, Zhongshan Dong Lu.*

**AMERICAN EXPRESS**

**Beijing**
Room 2101,
China World Tower One,
China World Trade Center,
1 Jianguo Men Wai Dajie,
100004.

**Shanghai**
Room 206, Retail Plaza,
Shanghai Center, 200040.

can be bought by credit card from the Civil Aviation Administration of China (CAAC) offices, but train tickets have to be paid for in cash. Cash advances can be made on credit cards at the Bank of China.

## TRAVELER'S CHECKS

Traveler's checks are safer to carry than cash and offer a better exchange rate, but you will have to pay a commission. All major brands are accepted in China, and American Express and Visa are the most widely used. They can be encashed at major branches of the Bank of China, and at larger hotels, but are not accepted at most hotels and restaurants. Keep the proof of purchase slips and a record of the serial numbers in case of loss or theft. Hold on to encashment slips, so you can convert spare *renminbi* to another currency before leaving the country.

## CURRENCY

China's currency is called *yuan renminbi*, literally People's Currency. One *yuan* divides into 10 *jiao*, which divides into 10 almost worthless *fen*. In colloquial Chinese, *jiao* is called *mao*, and *yuan* is *kuai*. The most common coins in-clude 1 *yuan*, 5 *jiao*, and 1 *jiao*, while the bills in circulation are 1, 2, and 5 *jiao*, and 1, 2, 5, 10, 20, 50, and 100 *yuan*. There are also some *fen* coins and notes, but this tiny denomination is rarely accepted. Try not to acquire too many damaged notes, as they may be difficult to get rid of. Counterfeiting is widespread, and shopkeepers regularly scrutinize large denominations. Hong Kong dollars divide into 100 cents, and Macanese *patacas* into 100 *avos*.

**Bank Notes**
*The more recently minted bills have Mao Zedong on one side and a well-known heritage sight on the other. The older bills depict the traditional dress of various ethnic minorities.*

1-yuan note

5-yuan note

10-yuan note

20-yuan note

50-yuan note

100-yuan note

**Coins**
*Chinese coins are not widely circulated. There is a 1 yuan coin, some jiao denominations, as well as tiny and lightweight fen.*

5 jiao      1 jiao      1 yuan

# Communications

China has an efficient postal network with a variety of services, including registered post and express mail. Telecommunication systems are reasonably advanced and international telephone calls can be made from all but the cheapest hotels. The Internet is hugely popular, and cafés with Wi-Fi access are widespread. The government, however, polices the net, and websites that it considers controversial may be blocked. Foreign newspapers and magazines are sold in five-star hotel bookstores, and in some supermarkets and bookshops.

**Wheelchair-accessible phone booth, Beijing**

## INTERNATIONAL & LOCAL TELEPHONE CALLS

Public telephones do exist in China but are rarely used in the cities – China has the largest number of mobile phone users in the world. If you do use a public telephone, card phones that accept a wide variety of phonecards are available in large cities, and are the cheapest way of making calls. IC (Integrated Circuit) cards come in denominations of ¥20, ¥50, and ¥100. They are largely used for domestic calls. They can also be used for international calls, though the rates are not very good. IP (Internet Phone) cards come in denominations of Y100 and offer the cheapest rates for international calls.

If you buy a local SIM card you can hook your GSM cellphone up to the Chinese system in minutes (North Americans need unlocked tri- or quad-band phones). Top-up cards are available on

almost every street corner. Phones can also be purchased for modest prices (all have English menus) and there is a thriving second-hand market. Most international mobile networks have "roaming" partnerships with Chinese phone companies, but it is a good idea to check the call rates before you travel.

## INTERNET

Personal computer ownership is widespread in China, and Internet cafés *(wangba)* have almost become a thing of the past. China has rapidly become a very wired nation; most urbanites carry a smartphone and laptop or iPad. Many smart, modern cafés and coffee shops offer free Wi-Fi and are frequented by China's laptop fraternity. Similarly, free broadband access for those with their own computers is commonplace in most hotels of a reasonable standard, as well as in the majority of youth

hostels. Overseas websites and blogs are carefully monitored in China and often blocked. Websites can only be accessed if the virtual private network is paid for.

## POSTAL SERVICES

The postal service in China is, for the most part, reliable, and the domestic service is reasonably fast. It takes less than a day for mail to reach local destinations, two or more days to inland destinations, while the international postal service takes up to 10 days to send airmail and postcards overseas. Visitors can send mail by standard or registered post *(guahaoxin)*, while EMS (Express Mail Service) is a reliable way to send packages and documents abroad and within the country.

Main post offices are open seven days a week, from 8am to 8pm, while smaller ones usually close earlier or for lunch, and remain shut on the weekends. Large hotels usually have post desks.

Take your mail to the post office, rather than dropping it in a mailbox. It will help postal staff sort your letter if you write the country's name in Chinese characters. Aerograms and packaging materials for parcels are available at post offices.

Reliable poste restante services are available all over China. You will need some form of identification – preferably your passport – to retrieve your mail. Envelopes should be addressed with the surname underlined and in

**Internet cafés are quickly being replaced by Wi-Fi access in regular cafés**

A choice of Chinese newspapers on display at a newsstand

capitals. Chinese addresses always start with the country, then the province, city, street, house number, and name of recipient. The postcode should be written at the end.

## COURIER SERVICES

Courier services are widely available, but less so in small towns and remote areas. While it is preferable to send large, bulky items by regular land, sea, or air cargo, important letters, documents, and smaller parcels are best sent through a courier agency. **United Parcel Service** (UPS), **Federal Express**, **DHL Worldwide Express**, and **China Post** are international courier agencies with a wide network.

**Mail box, Beijing**

## NEWSPAPERS & MAGAZINES

The *China Daily* is China's official English language newspaper. Its reputation for being dry remains, but its scope and coverage has greatly improved. The state-run *Shanghai Daily* offers good coverage of events in the city. Most international newspapers and magazines can be found at tourist hotel bookstores and a small selection of supermarkets and bookstores. Titles available include the *International Herald Tribune*, the *Financial Times*, *Time*, *Newsweek*, and the *Economist*. In Beijing, Shanghai, Tianjin, Guangzhou, and other large

cities, look out for expat entertainment and culture magazines, which offer the best news on local events. The *Shanghai Daily* also covers entertainment, dining options, and cultural events.

## TELEVISION & RADIO

The state-run television network, Chinese Central Television (CCTV), has two English-language channels. CCTV9 is tolerable despite its biased news and does have some interesting programs. Some English programs are also broadcast on CCTV4. Cable and satellite television is available in most international chain hotels, and you will find BBC News 24 or CNN everywhere. Chinese programs range from

historical costume dramas and tepid soaps to domestic travel, wildlife programs, war films, and heavily biased news programs.

There is also a wide Chinese-language radio network, but only a few local English-language programs. You will need a shortwave radio to pick up the BBC World Service, Voice of America, and other international programs. The BBC has closed its Chinese language World Service broadcasts. English broadcasts are often subject to disruption.

### DIRECTORY

**China Post**
*Tel* 11185.
www.ems.com.cn

**DHL Worldwide Express**
*Tel* 800 810 8000 (toll free nationwide). www.dhl.com

**Federal Express**
*Tel* 800 988 1888 (toll free nationwide). www.fedex.com.

**General Post Office**
134 Changjiang Lu, Dalian.
Near Bell Tower, Bei Dajie, Xi'an.

**International Post Office**
Jianguo Men Bei Dajie, Beijing.
Sichuan Bei Lu, Shanghai.

**United Parcel Service**
*Tel* 800 820 8388 (toll free nationwide). www.ups.com

## USEFUL DIALLING CODES & NUMBERS

- To call China from abroad, dial your international access code, China's country code (86), the area code omitting the first 0, followed by the local number.
- Neither Hong Kong nor Macau have area codes; they only have country codes – 852 and 853 respectively.
- To make an inter-city call, dial the area code of that city and the local number. For Beijing, dial 010; Shanghai, 021; Guangzhou, 020; Chongqing, 023; Kunming 0871.

- To make a local call, omit the area code.
- To make an international call from China, dial 00, the country code, the area code omitting any initial 0, and the local number.
- Country codes: UK 44; France 33; USA & Canada 1; Australia 61; Ireland 353; New Zealand 64; South Africa 27; Japan 81.
- Dial 115 for international directory assistance.
- Dial 114 for local directory enquiries in Chinese; dial the area code followed by 114 for numbers in another town.

# TRAVEL INFORMATION

**M**ost visitors to China arrive by air, though overland routes exist with train links to neighboring Russia, Mongolia, Kazakhstan, and Vietnam, and a bus link to Pakistan. It is also possible to arrive by sea; there are regular ferries from Japan and South Korea to China. Traveling within the country – even to remote areas – is possible by air, train, road, and, on a few routes, by boat. China has a huge, rapidly expanding rail network, although tickets – especially for sleeping berths – can be rare during the holiday periods. Bus travel is improving, with buses covering the entire country, including a number of "luxury" buses that offer reasonable comfort. Mired in bureaucracy, renting a car is not advised; foreigners are restricted from driving in many areas and the condition of many roads is very poor.

**Arriving in China with luggage**

## ARRIVING BY AIR

All major international airlines fly to China. **Air China**, the country's main international carrier, has quite basic service and facilities, but has a near-spotless safety record and its flights, to most of the world's major airports, are competitively priced. North American and European carriers such as **United Airlines**, **British Airways**, **Virgin**, **Lufthansa**, **KLM**, and **Air France**, have regular flights to some, or all, of China's three main – and most sophisticated – airports at Hong Kong, Shanghai, and Beijing. Flights to the other parts of the Far East, Australia, and New Zealand are offered by Singapore Airlines, Japan Airlines, **All Nippon Airways**, Korean Air, **Qantas**, **Cathay Pacific**, Air New Zealand, and others. Both Virgin and British Airways fly direct to Shanghai. Cheap flights to China are also available via Air China, China Eastern, Aeroflot (via Moscow), Malaysia Airlines (via Kuala Lumpur), and Air Asia, Jetstar, and Tiger Airways (from Southeast Asia).

## INTERNATIONAL FLIGHTS & AIRPORTS

China's four main international airports are at Hong Kong, Beijing, Shanghai, and Guangzhou. The Chinese government is investing a considerable amount of money to provide its international airports with state-of-the-art features. Beijing Capital Airport has three impressive terminals – terminal three was designed by architect Norman Foster and opened in time for the 2008 Olympics. In 1999, Pudong Airport was built in Shanghai, making it the first city in China to have two international airports. Macau, too, has an international airport on Taipa Island, although most visitors arrive via boat from Hong Kong. Other international airports offering flights to overseas destinations include Changchun (Nagoya, Seoul, and Tokyo), Changsha (Seoul), Chengdu (Amsterdam, Bangkok, Kathmandu, Singapore, and Tokyo), Chongqing (Nagoya, Seoul, and Singapore), Dalian (Hiroshima, Munich, Sendai, Seoul, and Tokyo), Guangzhou (Kuala Lumpur, Los Angeles, Sydney, Singapore, Paris, and other destinations), Guilin (Seoul and Bangkok), Haikou (Bangkok, Osaka, and Seoul), Hangzhou (Bangkok, Kuala Lumpur, Seoul, Tokyo, and Amsterdam), Harbin (Seoul, Khabarovsk, and Vladivostok), Kunming (Bangkok), Lhasa (Kathmandu), Nanjing (Bangkok, Seoul, Singapore, and Frankfurt), Qingdao (Osaka, Seoul, and Tokyo), Shenyang (Osaka and Seoul), Shenzhen (Bangkok, Manila, and Tokyo), Tianjin (Nagoya and Seoul), Xi'an (Nagoya, Pusan, Seoul, and Tokyo), Xiamen (Manila, Singapore, Osaka, and Tokyo), Ürümqi (Almaty, Bishkek, Islamabad, Moscow, and Novosibirsk), and Wuhan (Seoul).

## AIR FARES

Air fares vary according to the airline and the season. The peak season for international flights to China is between June and September, when prices are most expensive. Reasonably priced tickets are also hard to find during the holidays: Chinese New Year and the first week of October. While flying via another country is cheaper than flying

**State-of-the-art terminal at Beijing Airport**

direct, traveling by a Chinese airline such as Air China or China Eastern will be cheaper than international airlines. Plenty of discount tickets are available for long-term travel, which are valid for 12 months with multiple stopovers and open dates. The best deals can usually be found online (try www.ctrip.com and www. elong.com). Numerous travel agencies across the world have websites, making it easy to compare prices. Tickets can be booked through ticket offices, travel agents, and hotels, but travel agents – especially those away from hotels and areas used by expats – tend to offer the best prices.

## ON ARRIVAL

On the airplane, visitors are given a customs arrival form to complete, combining immigration, customs, and health information, which has to be submitted along with their passport at the airport immigration counter (between the plane and the arrivals hall).

International airports throughout China offer a limited range of facilities, but you will find foreign exchange counters, ATMs, public telephones, left-luggage services, restaurants (though rather overpriced), very limited shops, and toilets. Airport tourist information centers in China are of varying degrees of usefulness, and are often manned by staff who speak poor English.

## GETTING FROM THE AIRPORT

Airports are linked to the city by express train or by bus routes which make several stops in town. Avoid the overpriced taxi touts who try and force their services on foreign visitors. Instead, head for the taxi rank where trips into town are charged by the meter. Four- and five-star hotels usually run shuttle buses to their hotels and the Civil Aviation Administration of China (CAAC) runs buses to their office in town.

## CHECK-IN

The check-in time for international flights is officially two hours before departure. Most passengers are allowed 40 pounds (20 kg) of baggage, while first-class passengers may be allowed 66 pounds (30 kg). One additional item of hand luggage weighing up to 11 pounds (5 kg) is also usually permitted. Baggage allowance depends on the destination, and travelers to North America are generally allowed more luggage. If you are carrying heavy luggage, check with your airline to make sure that your luggage is within the weight limit, as excess baggage charges can be very high.

**AIR CHINA**

Logo of China's national airline, Air China

## DEPARTURE

Departure tax is included in the price of an airplane ticket and a fee is no longer payable at airports.

## DIRECTORY

### AIRLINE OFFICES

**Air China**
*Tel 4008 100 999, toll free nationwide.*
**www**.airchina.com.cn

**Air France**
*Tel 4008 808 808.*
**www**.airfrance.com.cn

**All Nippon Airways**
*Tel (010) 6505 3311, Beijing.*
**www**.ana.co.jp

**British Airways**
*Tel (800) 7440 031, Beijing.*
*Tel (800) 4400 031, Shanghai.*
**www**.britishairways.com

**Cathay Pacific**
*Tel 400 888 6628.*
**www**.cathaypacific.com

**Delta**
*Tel 400 814 0081.*
**www**.delta.com

**KLM**
*Tel 4008 808 222, Beijing & Shanghai.* **www**.klm.com

**Lufthansa**
*Tel (010) 6468 8838, Beijing.*
*Tel (021) 5352 4999, Shanghai.*
**www**.lufthansa.com

**Qantas**
*Tel 800 819 0089.*
**www**.qantas.com.au

**United Airlines**
*Tel (010) 8468 6666, Beijing.*
*Tel (021) 331 4567, Shanghai.*
**www**.united.com

**Virgin Atlantic**
*Tel (021) 5353 4600, Shanghai.*
**www**.virgin-atlantic.com

| AIRPORT | TEL INFORMATION | DISTANCE TO CITY CENTER | AVERAGE JOURNEY TIME |
|---|---|---|---|
| Beijing Capital Airport | (010) 6454 1100 | 16 miles (25 km) northeast | 40 mins (taxi) |
| Hongqiao Airport (Shanghai) | (021) 5114 6655 | 12 miles (19 km) west | 30 mins (taxi) |
| Pudong Airport (Shanghai) | (021) 6834 5328 | 28 miles (45 km) east | 45 mins (taxi) |
| Hong Kong International Airport | (0852) 2181 8888 | 20 miles (32 km) west | 25 mins (train) |
| Macau International Airport | (0853) 2886 1111 | 3 miles (5 km) northwest | 15 mins (taxi) |

# Domestic Air Travel

The arrival of cheap, high-speed train travel in China has led Chinese airlines to step up the competition in terms of both the cost and comfort of their services, especially on the popular Shanghai–Beijing route. The extensive domestic flight network involves numerous regional airlines flying to over 150 airports. The main cities of Beijing, Nanjing, Chengdu, Tianjin, Chongqing, Hong Kong, Shanghai, Dalian, Guangzhou, and Xi'an are particularly well connected to airports throughout the country. Domestic air tickets are straightforward to buy, so wait until you arrive in the country and then shop around for discounts. Flight cancellations and delays due to bad weather are common, especially in winter and on less traveled routes in the more remote provinces, so remember to reconfirm your ticket and the time of your flight.

## DOMESTIC AIRLINES

A few private airlines operate from Hong Kong and Macau, but most other airlines in China are administered by the Civil Aviation Administration of China (CAAC). There are currently about ten domestic carriers operating in China. (The initials in parentheses are the airline code or flight-number prefix.) Some of the domestic airlines, such as **China Southern** (CZ), and **China Eastern** (MU), also fly international routes. You can buy domestic flights from these airlines overseas, but rates are far better when booked in China. Other domestic airlines include **Sichuan Airlines** (3U), Shenzhen Airlines (4G), Hainan Airlines (HU), and Xiamen Airlines (MF).

The CAAC is driving service improvement throughout the industry, especially on board, and changes are noticeable from even just a few years ago. Unfortunately, frequent delays and cancellations still occur. Announcements are both in Chinese and English if there are foreign nationals on board. In-flight service can be brusque, and foreign visitors have

**Logo of Hainan Airlines**

felt neglected in the past but service has improved greatly.

Air China's international flying safety record is good, and now almost all domestic airlines have fleets of new aircraft, which means safety records have improved further. Older aircraft are sometimes used in China's peripheral regions. Before you choose to book with a particular airline, you may wish to ask what kind of plane you will be boarding.

The baggage allowance is 44 pounds (20 kg) for economy class and 66 pounds (30 kg) for first and business class. You are also allowed up to 11 pounds (5 kg) of hand luggage, although airlines almost never weigh it. The

charge for excess baggage is 1 percent of the full fare per 2.2 pounds (1 kg).

## DOMESTIC AIRPORTS

Air travel is becoming much more convenient in China as new airports are being built and old ones renovated and expanded. It has been made a national priority to upgrade all city airports, and state-of-the-art facilities are now available at Beijing Capital Airport, Shanghai's Pudong International Airport and Hongqiao Airport, Guangzhou Baiyun International Airport, and the Hong Kong International Airport at Chek Lap Kok. These modern airports easily compare with the best airports in the world. Airports in some major tourist cities, such as Xi'an, Hungzhou, Tianjin, Kunming, Chengdu and Nanjing also sport up-to-date facilities. Many new airports are being built in cities across China, including a second in Beijing. A few private airlines operate from Hong Kong and Macau, as well as from the mainland, including the fast-expanding low-cost carrier Spring Airlines and the Hainan Island-based Hainan Airlines, but most other airlines are administered by the CAAC.

## GETTING TO & FROM THE AIRPORT

The distance from airports to city centers varies considerably in China, so

**Flight attendants aboard Sichuan Airlines en route to Chengdu**

factor this into your journey time. Also, always allow time for unforeseen delays en route. In many large cities and towns, you can reach the airport or travel from the airport into town on a CAAC bus, which departs from and arrives at the CAAC office in town. In larger cities, such as Beijing, Shanghai, and Hong Kong, dedicated bus and train services run from town to the airport. Hong Kong, Shanghai and Beijing airports all have express train links to the city. Shanghai's Hongqiao and Pudong Airports are connected to the city's metro system (line 2). For faster travel to and from downtown, the high-speed Maglev train connects with Longyang Road metro station (also line 2), near the Pudong commercial/ residential centre.

Taxis wait for passengers outside the arrivals hall. Make sure you head for the taxi rank and avoid the numerous touts who will try to direct you towards their own car. Insist on the driver using the meter. Drivers rarely speak English so have your destination written in Chinese characters or keep the phone number of your accommodation on hand so the driver can call for directions. If you have booked accommodation, check whether your hotel offers transport to and from the airport.

### CHECK-IN

For most domestic flights, the check-in time is at least an hour and a half before departure, although very few passengers arrive that early. Make sure all your bags are tagged, and do not pack sharp objects, such as scissors, tweezers, nail files, or knitting needles,

**Road signs to the airport, Hong Kong**

in your hand luggage. The airport tax for domestic flights is usually ¥50, and is paid at the time of purchasing the ticket.

### TICKETS, RESERVATIONS & CANCELLATIONS

Each domestic airline has a booking office in most cities, as well as a reservation counter at each airport. Tickets can be booked through ticket offices, travel agents, online via www.ctrip.com, www.elong. com, and www. travelzen.com, or the travel desks of some of the better hotels – you should not be charged a booking fee. Travel agents tend to offer the best discounts. Credit cards are accepted by many travel agents and CAAC offices. Visitors are required to show their passports when purchasing tickets. There is generally no shortage of tickets unless you are flying between Hong Kong and a mainland destination, except in the run up to and during the Chinese New Year, and the week-long holiday periods after October 1, when it is advisable to book well ahead.

A combined international and domestic timetable is published by CAAC in both English and Chinese. These publications can be bought at most airline offices and CAAC outlets. Individual airlines also print their own timetables, available at booking offices throughout the country. Flight schedules are revised in April and October each year.

Ticket prices are calculated according to a one-way fare, and a return-ticket is simply double the single fare. Discounts on official fares are the norm, so it is best to check with travel agents for good deals. You are likely to get a better deal on a flight if you buy your ticket from an agent in the city you are

departing from. Business class tickets cost 25 percent more than economy, while first class tickets cost 60 percent more. Children over the age of 12 are charged adult fares, while there are special discounted fares for younger children and infants.

If you wish to return or change your air ticket, you can get a refund as long as you cancel at least 24 hours before departure, and return your ticket to the same agent who sold it to you. Even if you miss your flight, you are entitled to a refund of 50 percent of the full fare. You may be asked to buy travel insurance from your ticketing agent. However, it is generally not worthwhile, as the claim amount is very low.

# Traveling by Train

China is a vast country and, for many travelers, train journeys are an excellent way to see the countryside and get to know the people. Trains are punctual, fast, and relatively safe, and are a reliable transport option. Since 2009, China has been rolling out an extensive network of high-speed "bullet" trains running on key intercity routes. Journey times are much shorter, but ticket prices are higher. Trains are usually crowded so it is advisable to either buy your ticket well in advance, or ask your hotel or travel agent to arrange your bookings.

## THE RAILWAY NETWORK

Since the cost of air travel is beyond the reach of most Chinese, traveling by train is the preferred alternative, especially over long distances. China has an efficient and extensive rail network that covers every province including Hainan Island, connected to the mainland by a special train ferry, and mountainous Tibet, connected to Qinghai by a new railway line. Hong Kong is also connected to mainland China by rail. Depending on which type of ticket you purchase, Chinese trains can be quite comfortable, and there are fast services running between most large towns and cities.

## TRAINS & TIMETABLES

Although trains in China are commendably punctual, trying to decipher a Chinese timetable is an impossible task, unless you can read Chinese. Timetables are published in April and October each year, and are available at railway station ticket offices. A good online

Platform food stall, Yinchuan train station

timetable can be found at www.travelchinaguide.com. Stations can be frustrating places, and visitors will need patience to deal with them. Trying to locate English-speaking staff on platforms is difficult, even in large cities such as Beijing and Shanghai. Telephoning stations with enquiries is pointless unless you speak Chinese.

Each train is identified by a train number, written on the outside of each carriage, that indicates its route and destination. As a rule, incoming and outgoing trains running between two destinations are numbered sequentially. For example, train K79

travels from Shanghai to Kunming, while train K80 runs from Kunming to Shanghai.

Trains are of five types: those with numbers prefixed by the letter "T" or "K" are express (*te kuai*) or fast (*kuai*) trains, and those whose numbers have no prefix are ordinary (*pu kuai*) trains, with frequent stops. "G" indicates direct high-speed trains, while "D" is used for high-speed trains with stops. Express trains have carriages of all classes, and are the most modern and comfortable, with few stops and superior services. All long-distance trains are equipped with sleepers.

There is no smoking permitted within compartments, except in hard-seat carriages, although most trains allow passengers to smoke in the corridors. Most trains have dining cars, and staff will continuously push trolleys through the carriages selling noodles, snacks, mineral water, coffee, and newspapers. The noise level in carriages is often very high, as music and announcements are regularly broadcast over the speakers. China's modern fleet of trains are much cleaner than the old ones and have air conditioning. The older trains can be very dingy indeed; prepare yourself for sordid and filthy bathrooms.

## CLASSES

Chinese trains have four classes. The most luxurious class is **Soft Sleeper** (*ruan wo*), with four comfortable berths per compartment. Offering more privacy, security, and cleanliness than

Grand Soviet-style Taiyuan train station

Modern glass and steel train station, Changzhou

less-expensive classes, soft sleeper tickets are very pricey, and are not much cheaper than air tickets on certain routes.

For long journeys lasting over six hours, **Hard Sleeper** (*ying wo*) is the best way to travel. Consequently, these tickets are the hardest to procure, and you'd be lucky to get one on short notice. Hard sleeper can be an economical choice when traveling between cities overnight, as it saves the cost of a night in a hotel.

Carriages consist of doorless compartments, each with six bunks. Tickets are of three types – upper berth (*shang pu*), middle berth (*zhong pu*), and lower berth (*xia pu*), with a small price difference between each. The lowest berth is the most expensive, while the top one is the cheapest. The best berth, however, is the middle one. The upper bunk has little head-room and is closest to the speakers. During the day, the lower bunk acts as seating and fills with fellow passengers. Pillows, sheets, and blankets are provided by the railways, as are two thermos flasks of boiling water, which you can replenish yourself from the massive boiler at the end of each carriage. Once aboard the train, the inspector will exchange your ticket for a metal token, and return the ticket at the end of the journey.

The cheapest class is **Hard Seat** (*ying zuo*), which seats three people side-by-side on lightly cushioned seats. Although fine for short journeys, spending more

than four hours in a hard-seat carriage can be quite unpleasant. Carriages are usually crowded and dirty, the speakers blare endlessly, lights remain on at night, and compartments are filled with smoke. It is possible to upgrade (*bu piao*) once aboard the train, if there are seats available in the class of your choice. Note that hard-seat tickets bought on the same day are usually unreserved.

Available only on certain routes, **Soft Seat** (*ruan zuo*)

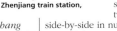
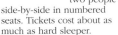
Booking office sign, Zhenjiang train station,

carriages are much more comfortable and spacious than hard seat, and seat two people side-by-side in numbered seats. Tickets cost about as much as hard sleeper.

## TRAIN TICKETS, FARES & RESERVATIONS

When buying tickets, it is essential to plan in advance. On most routes, it is vital to buy tickets at least two or three days before you travel, although tickets are available

about five days before departure. On short routes, you may be able to secure a ticket just before departure, but it is safest to buy ahead. Tickets on longer routes sell out, especially those for hard sleepers.

Train fares are calculated according to the class and the distance traveled. All tickets are one-way, so you will need to buy another ticket for the return journey, although return tickets are gradually being introduced for the high-speed intercity routes. Joining the crowds at station ticket counters can be very trying, so unless the station has a separate ticket office for foreign visitors, which is the case at Beijing train station, consider asking your hotel, tourist office, or travel agent to buy tickets for you. Black-market operators buy tickets in bulk, and then re-sell them at a mark-up outside railway stations. If you're buying tickets on the black-market, check the dates of travel, destination, and class printed on the ticket carefully.

Before boarding the train, visitors wait in a hall before filing past ticket-checkers to the platform. Retain your ticket as inspectors will ask to see it again, just before you reach your destination. Note that getting hold of tickets during the Chinese New Year (Spring Festival), and the May and October holiday periods can be very difficult, and it is inadvisable to travel during these times.

A uniformed guard minding a double-decker train, Dalian

# Traveling by Bus & Ferry

China's extensive network of road transport connects most cities, as well as distant, rural areas. Bus travel is essential for reaching places that are not served by train. Tickets are both easier to procure and are cheaper than train tickets, and there is a wider choice of departure times, stops, and itineraries. The absence of a national operator, however, means that numerous competing businesses exist, coupled with minimal regulation. Furthermore, driving is often rash, vehicles are poorly maintained, and road conditions can be bad, especially in the more remote areas. A small network of passenger ferries serves ports along China's coastline and some of the inland waterways.

## LONG-DISTANCE BUSES

There are still many parts of China that are not accessible by train, making it necessary to make the long haul by road. In Fujian, where rail services exist, but are infuriatingly indirect, bus travel makes a lot of sense. In Guizhou and Guangxi, the more interesting areas inhabited by ethnic minorities are only accessible by bus and the tropical area of Xishuangbanna in Yunnan is best explored by bus or taxi. You will also need to take a bus (unless you are flying) to reach Lijiang in northern Yunnan and all of western Sichuan. Getting around Tibet will require long bus journeys, as will exploring the northwestern frontier of China if you want to get beyond the towns on the main train line. Numerous sights throughout China are off rail lines.

Many smooth, wide highways now link some of the major cities, making some bus travel, particularly on the east coast, reasonably comfortable. In some cases, the bus is now a faster way to reach your destination than the train.

All cities and most large towns have at least one long-distance bus station (*changtu qiche zhan*) where state-run buses arrive and depart. Private bus firms may have set up a few of their own bus stations in town; often, one of these is located next to the train station. Other stations may be located on the edges of town – the North or East Bus Station will usually serve destinations to the north or east. Determining which of these stations serves the place you are trying to reach can be tricky, so you will need to ask around. Destinations are displayed in Chinese characters on the front of buses.

Long-distance buses vary enormously in quality, age, and comfort. You may find that several buses are running along the same route, so make sure you are sold a ticket for the fastest, most comfortable bus, or cheapest bus, if you prefer. Note that in general, long-haul bus journeys are taxing. Road conditions are often poor and road works are common, slowing the journey considerably. Drivers can be reckless and bus crashes are distressingly frequent. The noise level can be deafening, with music blaring and the driver leaning on the horn, so take earplugs. Most buses are choked with cigarette smoke.

**Ordinary buses** (*putong che*) are the cheapest and have basic wooden, or lightly padded, seats. These buses stop often, so progress can be slow. They provide little space for baggage – there's no room under the seats and the luggage racks are minuscule. Suitcases and backpacks are usually stacked next to the driver, and you may be charged.

**Sleeper buses** (*wopu che*) speed through the night making few stops, so reach their destination in good time. They usually have two tiers of bunks, or seats that recline almost flat. The older models can be quite dirty. Lower bunks (*xia pu*) cost more than the upper bunks (*shang pu*), but are worth the extra cost as you are less likely to be thrown from your bed when the driver takes a corner at speed.

Shorter routes are served by rattling **minibuses** (*xiao ba*), which depart only when every spare space has been filled by a paying passenger. Crammed to the roof, minibus trips can be quite uncomfortable.

**Express buses** (*kuai che*) are the best way to travel. Some are luxury (*hao hua*), have air conditioning, and enforce a no-smoking policy. Luggage is stowed in a hold, which is fairly safe, given the few stops that are made en route.

In certain parts of China – in Gansu and Sichuan, for instance – you may be required to purchase insurance from the People's Insurance Company of China (PICC) before being allowed on a bus. Usually, however, it is included in the price of the ticket. This insurance waives

**Bus stop, Hong Kong**

A basic long-distance bus (*putong che*) awaiting passengers, Qinghai

A ferry on the Huangpu River, sailing through Shanghai

any responsibility of the government bus company should you be injured in a bus crash; it does not cover you in the event of an accident.

## BUS TICKETS & FARES

Traveling by road is generally much cheaper than traveling by train. Tickets are sold at long-distance bus stations and, unless you are hoping for a seat at the front of a luxury bus, do not need to be bought in advance. Tickets for private buses and minibuses are either purchased on board the bus or from touts nearby. Main bus stations invariably have computerized ticket offices, and the queues are much shorter than those experienced at train stations.

Promotional river cruise sign
outside tourist office

## FERRIES, BOATS & CRUISE SHIPS

A small network of coastal routes survives in China, and vessels still ply the Yangzi River, but the increased convenience of traveling by air, road, and rail has reduced the variety and frequency of sea- and river-ferry sailings in China.

The most popular river route is the trip along the Yangzi between Chongqing and Yichang, through the Three Gorges *(see pp352–4)*. An overnight ferry service for tourists runs along the Grand Canal between Suzhou and Hangzhou, and Wuxi and Hangzhou *(see p217)*. There are no regular passenger ferry services up the Yangzi River available to foreign visitors until Wuhan.

Popular coastal ferry routes include boats to Hainan Island from ports in the province of Guangdong (including Guangzhou) and Beihai in Guangxi. A large number of vessels ply between Hong Kong and Macau, many of which are high-speed and operate round the clock. Macau is also connected to ports in Guangdong, while Hong Kong is linked to Zhuhai and several ports on the Pearl River delta. Within Hong Kong, a medley of craft run to the outlying islands. There are quite a few vessels connecting Hong Kong with the rest of China, but services are becoming less frequent. Because of the prohibitively long overland routes, ferries link the booming northeastern city of Dalian with Yantai and Tianjin. Yantai and Weihai on the eastern tip of Shandong peninsula are accessible from Shanghai, Dalian, and Tianjin. Note that ferry timetables may change frequently and services may have been added or terminated.

Several international sea routes link China to other countries. From Japan, Kobe is connected to both Tianjin and Shanghai on the east coast, while ferries also link Osaka with Shanghai. From South Korea, the port of Inchon is connected to the Chinese ports of Dalian, Weihai, Qingdao, Shanghai, and Tianjin.

Shanghai's expanding international ferry terminal welcomes increasing numbers of cruise ships, with the fast-developing cruise industry forming a key part of the city's plan to become an international shipping center. By 2016, Shanghai expects to welcome 500 cruise ships annually, bringing 1.2 million visitors to the city. Costa and Royal Caribbean already use the city as an Asian base port, and several other Asia-Pacific cruise routes – including to Russia, Taiwan, and Southeast Asia – are expected to open in the next few years. Cruise passengers arriving in Shanghai should now be able to shop in duty-free stores at the port.

Tourist boats docked on the vast Qinghai Lake

# Local Transport in Cities

**Hong Kong's MTR logo**

Transport options vary greatly between cities in China. Many of the largest metropolises have complex networks with subway systems, which, in many cases, are in the process of being extensively expanded. In Beijing and Shanghai, the subway *(ditie)* is the best way to get around, while in Hong Kong, the transport system is well-integrated, and subways, trains, and buses are all convenient options. In most cities, buses are slow and usually packed, but are very cheap. Taxis *(chuzu qiche)* are a necessity for most travelers, and, despite the language barrier and misunderstandings with drivers, are the most convenient way to get around. Bicycles once ruled the roads of China's cities and although not as popular today, they are still one of the best ways to explore.

## BEIJING'S SUBWAY

The subway system in Beijing underwent major development in preparation for the 2008 Olympic Games. The system has been expanded and includes an express rail line which goes direct to Beijing Capital Airport.

The subway is a swift way to get around this spread-out city. The system is easy to use, although walks between lines at interchange stations can be long. Currently there are two different fares: one ticket for ¥3 covers trips on lines 1 and 2; the ¥5 ticket covers lines 2 and 13. Buy your paper ticket at the ticket booth near the entrance. Tickets are undated and you should show your ticket to the attendants at the entrance to the platform. The current ticketing system is based on the distance traveled. Line 13 now has automated ticket gates, as will any other lines that open up in the future.

## SHANGHAI'S SUBWAY

The rapidly expanding Shanghai subway system is clean and efficient, with the first line built in 1995. The 11 lines currently in operation are expected to increase to a total of 22 by 2020. Lines 1 and 2 are most useful to the tourist, with line 2 connecting the

**Sign for Beijing subway**

city's two airports, Pudong and Honqqiao; the raised Line 3, or Pearl Line, travels the western outskirts of the city. Fares for Lines 1 and 2 range between ¥3 and ¥6, depending on the number of stops traveled. Check the map to determine your fare and then buy a ticket from the booth or machine. You can also buy ¥50 pre-paid tickets. Put your ticket into the slot at the barrier and the gates will open. Retrieve your ticket on the other side of the gate and hold on to it – you will need it at the destination exit. The much-touted Maglev (magnetic levitation) runs between Pudong Airport and the eastern end of Line 2 and reaches speeds of 270 miles per hour (430 km/h). Check the times of departure.

## HONG KONG'S MTR & KCR

Integrated and efficient, Hong Kong has the best public transportation system in the country. The city is easy to get around using all of its forms of transport – MTR (subway), KCR (overland train), buses, trams, and ferries – and most signage is in English. You can buy single tickets for your journeys, but each type of transit requires a separate ticket. Alternatively, you can buy an Octopus card, an electronic card that allows you to hop on and off most of the system. You can buy these for a minimum of HK$150 including a HK$50 deposit, which is refunded when you return the card. Touch the card to the electronic reader at each ticket collection point and the fare will be deducted from your card. You can easily add credit at MTR and KCR stations.

The underground Mass Transit Railway (MTR) currently has seven lines, with many more planned. The fare increases with distance traveled, except on the Airport Express Line where a higher fee is charged. If you buy a single ticket, insert it into the turnstile and retrieve it on the other side. Hold on to your ticket as you will need it to exit the system. If you have an Octopus card simply touch the card to the yellow reader on the turnstile.

The Kowloon–Canton Railway (KCR) now has three lines that comprehensively cover the New Territories. KCR East Rail was the original line and heads north into mainland China. Do not go past Sheung Shui (the second last stop), if you do not have documentation to enter the mainland.

## BUSES & TRAMS

City bus networks are extensive and cheap. The buses *(gonggong qiche)*, however, are almost always overcrowded – so much so that you are unlikely to be able to see out of the windows. These conditions are perfect for thieves, so stay

**Motor-rickshaw for hire, Harbin**

Bicycles in Beijing – the traditional way to get around the city

well-aware of your belongings. Consider using buses only for short straight-forward journeys. Avoid them if you are trying to get from one end of town to the other – you are likely to get stuck in traffic.

Bus routes can be tricky to navigate, particularly as most routes and destinations are listed in Chinese only. Hong Kong has the most comfortable and easy to use bus system, although traffic can be as bad here as anywhere else. Hong Kong also has an old tram line that runs from Sheung Wan to Causeway Bay on Hong Kong Island. Dalian has a few trams as well. Maps of bus and tram routes are widely available, especially in and around train stations.

## TAXIS

The best way to get about in cities that don't have sub-way systems is by taxi (*chuzu qiche*). Taxis are found in large numbers in all Chinese cities – often congregating near train stations – and can be hailed easily in the street. Guests staying at hotels can also ask the reception desk to summon a taxi. When arriving at airports, avoid the touts who immediately surround you, and head instead to the taxi rank outside where you are less likely to be over-charged. Also, make sure the driver uses the meter

(*biao*) or negotiate a flat rate in advance. Taxis rarely have rear seat belts (*anquan dai*), so sit in front if you are traveling alone. Few taxi drivers speak English, so it is wise to have your destination written down in Chinese, which the staff at your hotel will gladly do for you.

Fares vary slightly from city to city, but taxis generally offer both good value and convenience. In many cities, different models of cars will have different rates. Tipping the driver is not necessary.

Taxis can also be hired for the day – a convenient way to see sights just out of town. Agree on a price beforehand, and make sure your driver is clear on the extent of your itinerary. In Tibet, you may find that hiring a jeep and driver is the only way to get to some sights. It is customary to pay for the driver's lunch.

In smaller towns, motorcycle rickshaws (*sanlun motuoche*) and bicycle rickshaws

A city taxi in Beijing

(*sanlun che*) are a convenient and entertaining way to get around town. Do not take these in major cities – they cost about the same as a taxi and frequently target tourists for substantial rip-offs. In some small towns, they are the only form of transport. Agree on the fare before climbing aboard.

Motorcycle taxis are a very quick way to cover longer distances, although they are really only practical if you are traveling alone with little luggage. Insist on the driver providing you with a helmet.

## CYCLING

Hiring a bicycle is one of the best ways to explore towns and their environs. Bike lanes are common (although not always respected by drivers) and roadside repair

stalls are everywhere. Beijing, with its spread-out sights and flat terrain, is the most cycle-able of the big cities, but you may find the traffic intimidating. Hangzhou has the best bike hire system, with dozens of kiosks to hire official public bicycles from. Make sure that any bike you rent has a lock. Handy bike stands are found in big cities and have an attendant to watch the bikes for a nominal fee.

## ROAD NAMES

Main streets, avenues, and thoroughfares are often divided into different sections based on the four cardinal points. For example, Zhongshan Lu (Zhongshan Road) may be divided into Zhongshan *Xi* Lu (West Road) and Zhongshan *Dong* Lu (East Road). Similarly, you may also see Zhongshan *Bei* Lu (North Road) and Zhongshan *Nan* Lu (South Road). Apart from *lu* (road), other key words are *jie* (street), *hutong* and *xiang* (lane or historic alleyway). Road names in large cities such as Beijing may also display the pinyin translation, but in smaller towns and remote destinations, only Chinese is used. The use of pinyin is being phased out and in many large cities sign-age will be in Chinese script and English only.

Taxis and buses on a busy street in the center of Macau

# General Index

# Acknowledgments

DORLING KINDERSLEY would like to thank the following people whose contributions have made the preparation of this book possible.

**PUBLISHING MANAGERS**
Kate Poole, Scarlett O'Hara

**MANAGING EDITORS**
Vicki Ingle, Anna Streiffert

**PUBLISHER**
Douglas Amrine

**PRODUCTION CO-ORDINATOR**
Linda Dare

**ADDITIONAL CONTRIBUTORS**
Calum Macleod, Helen Glaister, Sarah Waldram, Martin Walters

**EDITORIAL ASSISTANTS**
Katherine Haw, Alka Thakur

**CARTOGRAPHIC DESIGNER**
Alok Pathak

**CARTOGRAPHIC PROOFREADER**
Tony Chambers

**ARTWORK REFERENCE**
Other Shore Arts Inc.

**PROOFREADER**
Stewart Wild

**PROOFREADER, CHINESE**
Jiewei Cheng

**INDEXER**
Hilary Bird

**DESIGN AND EDITORIAL ASSISTANCE**
Emma Anacootee, Claire Baranowski, Sonal Bhatt, Tessa Bindloss Gary Bowerman, Caroline Evans, Anna Freiberger, Lydia Halliday, Rose Hudson, Helena Iveson, Olivia King, Priya Kukadia, Maite Lantaron, David Leffmann, Neil Lockley, Carly Madden, Nicola Malone, Rosie Mayer, Peter Neville-Hadley, Sangita Patel, Marianne Petrou, Pollyanna Poulter, Supriya Sahai, Meredith Smith, Josh Summers, Janis Utton, Conrad Van Dyk, Ros Walford, Christine Watts, Jamin York, Gui Zhiping

**DTP**
Shailesh Sharma, Vinod Harish

**DIGITAL MEDIA TEAM**
Nishi Bhasin, Manjari Rathi Hooda, Pramod Pant, Mahesh Singh

**ADDITIONAL PHOTOGRAPHY**
Max Alexander, Geoff Brightling, Chen Chao © Rough Guides/Tim Draper, Andy Crawford, Gadi Farfour, Steve Gorton, Colin Keates, Dave King, Stephen Lam, Ian O'Leary, Jane Miller, Hugh Thompson, Walia BPS, Paul Williams

**PHOTOGRAPHY PERMISSIONS**
The Publishers thank all the temples, monasteries, museums, hotels, restaurants, shops, and other sights for their assistance and kind permission to photograph their establishments.

**PICTURE CREDITS**
Key: a-above; b-below/bottom; c-centre; f-far; l-left; r-right; t-top.

Works of art have been reproduced with the permission of the following copyright holders:

*Zhang San Feng* from *The Explanation of Taijiquan Shi Yi* by Dong Yingjie scanned by Chip Ellis with thanks to Gordon Jolly 273cl.

4CORNERS IMAGES: SKME/Grandadam Laurent 10bc, SIME/Hans-Peter Huber 11bl.

AKG-IMAGES: Archives CDA/St-Genes 254tr; Han Kan 208cla; Laurent Lacat 53tr; VISIOARS 462cl.

ALAMY IMAGES: 524tl; Pat Behnke 74br, 613tr; Tibor Bognar br left front endpaper, 306; Peter Bowater 33cr; Jon Bower 307bc; China Span / Keren Su 352cal; David Crausby 620c, 630cr; Nick Dawson 44bc; Eagle Visions/Craig Lovell 524tl; Eye Ubiquitous/Trevor Page 351cr; First Light/Ken Straiton 73tc; Robert Harding World Imagery 153cl; Dallas & John Heaton cal left front endpaper, 182; Iain Masterton 623t; Colin Monteath 510br; Jake Norton 619br; Panorama Stock cbr right front endpaper, 103bc, 128br, 132bc, 160, 288–9, 462br; /Li Jiangshu 110br; / Ru Suichu 102bc; /Zhang Zhenguang 206tr; Rochaphoto 507car; David Sanger 464tr; Sami Sarkis tr right front endpaper, 120; Alex Segre 186bl, 195bl; Snap 2000 Images/David Robinson 89c; Valery Rizzo 42bl; View Stock China 11cr, 122c, 153cbl; Matthew Wellings 45b; Ron Yue 44tc, 46cr.
ANCIENT ART & ARCHITECTURE COLLECTION: 477bc.
ARDEA.COM: Chris Martin Bahr 22tl; Mary Clay 23bra; David Dixon 20bra, 344cl; Kenneth W. Fink 22bl; Nick Gordon 23cl; Pascal Goetgheluck 411cal; Joanna Van Grulsen 20cbl, 20bla; C Clem Haagner 22cbl; Keith & Liz Laid 344car; Tom & Pat Leeson 21br; Adrian Warren 361car; M. Watson 22bla, 23br, 403br.
THE ART ARCHIVE: Bibliotheque Nationale de

Paris 53cra, 217cra, 464–5, /Marc Charmet 28tr;
British Library 26br, 28bl, 57tr; British
Museum/Eileen Tweedy 74tr; Freer Gallery of
Art 38–9, 57cr, 280cla; Genius of China
Exhibition 38tr, 51bc, 54bl, 464bl, 464cla;
Musée Thomas Dobrée Nantes/Dagli Orti 63tl;
National Palace Museum of Taiwan 30cl;
Palace Museum Beijing 432–3; Private
Collection Paris/Dagli Orti 135bc; School of
Oriental & African Studies/Ellen Tweedy
422bl; William Sewell 263tr.

STEVEN BAIGEL: 533br.
BENOY BEHL: 523bc.
BIBLIOTECA NAZIONALE CENTRALE, Rome: 232cbl.
BIBLIOTHÈQUE NATIONALE DE FRANCE, Paris: 26tr,
36ca.
WWW.BRIDGEMAN.CO.UK: 30cr, 31cra, 31c, 36tr,
36cbl, 37cal, 37cbl, 43tr, 262tr, 434bl, 62cbr,
433bl; Bibliotheque des Arts Décoratifs, Paris
293tc, 433br; Bibliothèque Municipal, Poitiers
209tr; Bibliothèque Nationale Paris 4tr, 8–9,
28cl, 31tr, 60bcl, 62bc, 143bc, 471cb; British
Museum 487br; Giraudon 54br; James Gray
(1757–1815) 433crb; Miss E. M. Gregson 345br;
Hermitage 495cb; Illustrated London News
434clb; National Palace Museum, Taipei,
Taiwan 471car; Private Collection 209tl, 262cl;
Société Asiatique, Collège de France, Paris
293cal; V & A Museum 432bl; Yu Zhiding
(1647 – p.1709) The Depiction of the Poet
Wang Yuang (1634–1711) watercolor 178tr
(d).
BRITISH LIBRARY, London: 57tl. © THE BRITISH
MUSEUM: 29tcr, 38br, 38bc, 38bca, 39tr, 39bc,
39bl, 39br, 39cra, 56–7, 522bc.

CHINA STOCK: bcr right front endpaper, 53bl,
59c, 59bl, 64bl, 65car, 256br, 294, 416br;
Dennis Cox tl right front endpaper, 436; Liu
Liqun 5tr, 36cb, 36br, 353tl, 353car, 403car,
414cl; Liu Xiaoyang 268ca.
CHINAPIX: 186tr; Zhang Chaoyin 534cl, 534bc.
CHINA SPAN: Keren Su 179cl, 217cl.
CORBIS: 63c, 66bl, 67tc, 86c, 101tl; Archivo
Iconografico, S.A. 433cra; Asian Art &
Archaeology Inc. 51ca, 52clb, 54ca, 56cbl,
58bc, 58tc, 464crb; Tiziana and Gianni
Baldizzone 29cra, 546t; Dave Bartruff 262bl,
575br, 578t; Bettman 37tr, 65tl, 65br, 66tl,
159bl, 197br, 250bc, 257tl, 297crb, 297cra,
377br, 446br, 491tc; Bohemian Nomad
Picturemakers cbl left front endpaper, 238,
575tl; Bohemian Nomad Picturemakers/Kevin
R Morris 217cbr; Bowers Museum of Cultural
Art 153tc; Burstein Collection 30br, 50, 53clb,
55tc, 60bl, 208bc, 495br; China features 544bl,
/Li Gang 19tr; Christie's Images 52tr;
ChromoSohm INC/Joseph Sohm 106bc; Pierre
Colombel 156–7, 487cbr, 496tr, 496cal, 496cra,
496cbl, 496bl, 496crb, 496br, 497tl, 497cal,

497cbl, 497bl; Dean Conger 135cra, 243br,
507cl, 579c; The Cover Story 463tl; Ric
Ergenbright 217bl; Macduff Everton 67bl,
67cr, 195tc; Eye Ubiquitous/Bennett Dean
395tr, 540bc; /Julia Waterlow 28br, 462cbl,
510tl; Free Agents Limited 34tr, 435car; Alain
Le Garsmeur 608–9; Lowell Georgia car right
front endpaper, 140; Christel Gerstenberg
208cbl; Philip Gould 280tr; Peter Guttman
513tl, 513tr; Historical Picture Archive 293cbl,
433tr; Angelo Hornak 495bl; Dave G. Houser
43bl; Hulton Collection 243bl, 434cal, 543tr;
Hanan Isachar 24b; Langevin Jacques 442–3;
Robbie Jack 41bl; Wolfgang Kaehler 133bl,
154tr, 434tr, 434br, 434–5c, 435cbr; Kelly–
Mooney Photography 97tc; Christine Kolisch
532tr; Earl & Nazima Kowall 25tr,
33tl, 45t, 454br, 455cr, 455cl, 455cbr, 455br,
455bl, 515cl, 462bl, 579bc; Daniel Lainé
393cbr; Charles & Josette Lenars 59tr, 145tl;
Paul W. Liebhardt 407bl; Liu Liqun 16tc, 25br,
109tc, 193clb, 305tc, 353cbl, 463bl; Chris Lisle
533c; Craig Lovell 525br, 535br, 540tr; Ludovic
Maisant 393cfl; Lawrence Manning 263bl; Tom
Nebbia 412br; Papilio/John R. Jones 504tl;
Louie Psihoyos 453bl; Carl & Ann Purcell 24tr,
31cbr, 505br; Red link/Mu Xiang Bin 189b;
Reuters 32bl, 42br, 47tc, 269br,
574br, 626br; Roger Ressmeyer 94c, 94cr;
David Samuel Robbins 535bl; Galen Rowell
514tc, 524c, 524–5, 524bc, 525c, 533tc; Royal
Ontario Museum 38bl, 39crb, 56ca, 60t, 254br,
255tl, 411cr; Royalty–Free 43bc; Sean Sexton
Collection 197bl; Stapleton Collection 75tr;
Keren Su 1, 24clb, 42cl, 235cl, 235br, 236cal,
237br, 268br, 354br, 406br, 406clb, 407br, 407tl,
407cr, 413tl, 462–3, 506cl, 510cl, 512cbl; Vince
Streano 423bl; Swim Ink 263tl; Robert van der
Hilst 181cl, 495cl; Ron Watts cal left front
endpaper, 202; Reza Webistan 515br; Nevada
Weir tcl left front endpaper, 463cr, 502, 509tl;
Nick Wheeler 232br; Janet Wishnetsky 465br;
Alison Wright 456–7, 491cbl, 514br; Michael S.
Yamashita 179br, 209crb, 411br; Liang
Zhuoming 504bc; Xinhua Photo 453br.
CPA MEDIA: 62t, 64tr, 197tc, 197cl, 297tc,
432cbl, 433tl; David Henley 225car, 229cbr;
Meng Qingbiao/Chinese Government (1961)
65cbr; Oliver Hagreave 297cbl; Oliver
Hagreave/Bibliothèque Nationale Paris 60clb.

DREAMSTIME.COM: Piero Cruciatti 598 bl,
Cupertino 187tl, Brad Rickerby 318-319r,
Tyhoonski 176b; DK IMAGES: British Museum
37tcl, 38cal, 219bl, /David Gower 208tr, /Alan
Hills 38tl, 219cbl, 219cr, 232car; Glasgow
Museum/Ellen Howdon 523car; The Jazz Club
581br; MTR (Mass Transit Railways) 632tl; Judith
Miller Archive 254bl, /Wallis & Wallis 10tc; /
Sloan's 254bl, 487bl; courtesy National Maritime
Museum/David Spence 149bc, /James Stevenson
37cbr; courtesy of Pitt Rivers Museum/ Geoff

Brightling 36tl; private collection 339ca, 457ca, 515tc; courtesy of Science Museum 37bl, /Dave King 37bc; Yorkshire Museum/Harry Taylor 453cbr.
TIM DRAPER: 404–5, 421br.
RAY DUNNING: 219c.

EYE UBIQUITOUS: Bennett Dean bl left front endpaper, 396.

FOTOE: 30tr, 297cb; A Chun 352bc; An Ge 21cr; Wang Yizhong 383cbl; Wu Dongjun 406–7; Yang Xingbin 376tl; Ying Ge 352car; Yu Zhi Xin 147br; Zhang Weiqing 30bl.

GETTY IMAGES: AFP 42–3; Walter Bibikow tcr right front endpaper, 78; China Photos 66lt; Robert Harding tr left front endpaper, 466; Image Bank bcl left front endpaper, cbl left front endpaper, 68–9, 244–5, 258, 270–1, 348; 426–7; Image Bank/Angelo Cavalli 624bl; Image Bank/Yann Layma 10cla; National Geographic 52cla, /Louis Mazzatenta 453car; Photographer's Choice/John Warden 107tc; Photographer's Choice/Nikolay Zurek 263cl; David Silverman 363cr; Stone 2–3, 274–5; Stone/Vince Streano 10cr; Travel Ink 231tl; Berthold Trenkel 389tl.

SALLY & RICHARD GREENHILL: S.A.C.U. 64tl, 65tr, 64br, 64cl.

HAINEN AIRLINES: 626cl; HEMISPHERES IMAGES: Frank Guizou 11tl
NIGEL HICKS: 168–9, 278bc; 338–9, 344clb, 344cbr, 344bl, 344br, 371tc, 452br, 504c, 505tl, 506tr, 506bl, 508tl.
HONG KONG TOURISM BOARD: 311tc, 320bc, 325t.

IMAGINE CHINA: 66cbr, 109bc, 122bc, 262–3; Adrian Bradshaw 195cla, 453cal; Chen Shuyi 95b; Chen Yun 491br; CNS 75cr; Dong Jinlin 264tr; Fan Chongzhi 281tl, 281tr, 281car; Fang Zhonglin 192clb; Gong Weizhi 87cr; Guangyao 178cr; Hu Qingming 153br; Huang Jinguo 179cr; Huang Shaoyi 280bc; Huang Yizhu 356cal; Jia Guorong 219cbr; Jiang Chao 33car; Jiang Guohong 40br; Jiang Ren 159car; Jin Baoyuan 179tr; Kan Kan 30cb; Lang Congliu 229tc; Li Jiangsong 29br; Li Wei 254cal, 254cbr, 281cbr; Liang Weijie 440tl, 440bc; Lin Weijian 178bl, 186cl, 186cr; Ling Long 46br; Liu Jianming 376br; Liu ling 253br; Liu Liqun 128tl, 264cl, 264bl, 354cla; Liu Quanju 46tl; Liu Zhaoming 474br, 474tc; Long Hai 74bc, 75bcr, 189tc, 219br; Luoxiaoyun 454tl; Lu Baohe 293bl; Ma Kang 511tl, 512tr; Olivia Savoure

512cal, 513br, 522tr; Shen Yu 178br, 198bc, 280tl, 622bl; Shui Xiaojie 272br, 412car; Tang Jianwei 272tl; Wang Jianxin 75bcl, 360tl; Wang Mengxiang 424cr, 425br; Wei Hui 41cr; Wu Changqing 104tr, 297cal; Wu Hong 41br, 85br; Xiong Yijun 23cr; Xu Ruikang 179tc; Yan Shi 145b; Yang Xi 228cl, 281cr; Yin Zi 26–7; Yuan Yanwu 32–3, 273tc; Yue Sheng 525tl; Zeng Yun 280cbl; Zhan Xiadong 525tr; Zhang Fenquan 441br; Zhang Guosheng 91bl; Zhang Jie 297bl; Zhang Xing 281br; Zhang Xinmin_Xinjiang 505c, 508bl, 509br; Zhang Yongzhe 209br; Zhou Kang 97c, 190tr; Zhu Xuesong 265tl, 265cr, 265br; Zhuge Ming 447bl, 524tr; Zou Xian 32br; Zuo Shan 383br.

INSTITUTE OF HISTORY & PHILOLOGY: Academia Sinica 26clb.

KOBAL COLLECTION: Columbia 41tr; Tomson films 41tl.
WWW.KUNGFUMAGAZINE.COM 2005: 159tc, 159crb, 159clb.

DAVID LEFFMAN: 424tl.
LEONARDO MEDIABANK: 551tl.
LIBRARY OF CONGRESS, Washington, D.C.: 393bl.

MAGNUM: Rene Burri 256tr; Steve McCurry tl left front endpaper, 526.
MARY EVANS PICTURE LIBRARY: 33cbr, 275t, 491cbr, 491cr; Kieou King 232c.

NASA: 153cr.
NATIONAL TRUST PHOTOGRAPHIC LIBRARY: John Hammond 293cr.
NATURE PICTURE LIBRARY: Bernard Castelein 20ccrb; G & H Denzau 21cl, 460bc; Elio Delia Ferrera 403bl; Martha Holmes 22cl; Pete Oxford 20br, 23bl, 411tc; David Pike 403cal; Jose B. Ruiz 22bra, 22br; Warwick Sloss 22crb; Lynn Stone 20cr, 20bl; Solvin Zankl 23cbl; Xi Zhinong 403cb.
NATURAL VISIONS: Heather Angel 345crb, 361crb.
NATIONAL GEOGRAPHIC IMAGE COLLECTION: Doug Stern 168bc; Joseph Rock 390bc.
NHPA: 20cl; James Warwick 361br.

OSF/PHOTOLIBRARY.COM: 21bl; Deni Bown 21bla; Irvine Cushing 21bra; Robert A. Lubeck 23cbr; Richard Packwood 403tc; George Reszeter 23bla; Konrad Wothe 21clb.
PANOS PICTURES: 27cra.
THE PEAK: 313cr, 313tl.
MARIANNE PETROU: 522cl.
PHOTO12.COM: OIPS 109c, 111cl; Panorama Stock 22cr, 98bc, 105tl, 106c, 425tc, 432br; Panorama Stock/Zhao Guangtian 464tl, 464clb.
PHOTOLIBRARY.COM: Jiangshu Li 25cr; James

Montgomery 14; Keren Su 43c, 44cl; Ming Li 424bl; Panorama 463br; Xin Li 463tr.
PHOTO SCALA, Florence: British Museum 522tl.
POPPERFOTO.COM: 64–5c, 197cra, 197cb.
POWERSTOCK: age fotostock 126–7, 72–3;
Digital Vision Royalty Free 280–1.

By permission of THE RANDOM HOUSE GROUP LTD: 263br.
RED GATE GALLERY: 95tc.
THE RED MANSION LTD: Cang Xin "The Unification of Heaven and Men (Ice)" 40cal;
Fang Lijun "Series 2 no 2" 40–1; Zhan Wang "Torso" 40cbl.
REUTERS: 353br; Jason Lee 111tr.
ROBERT HARDING PICTURE LIBRARY: 199tc, 513bl;
Nigel Blythe 512bc; Gina Corrigan tcr left front endpaper, 478; Panorama Stock 61tc, 488–9, 516–7; A.C. Waltham 524bl.

SCIENCE & SOCIETY PICTURE LIBRARY: 27b.
SHAANXI HISTORY MUSEUM: 56br, 56clb, 166b, 167cra, 167cbr.
SHANGHAI MUSEUM: 190tl, 190cal, 190c, 190cbl, 191cl, 191cr, 191tc.
SINOPIX PHOTO AGENCY: Lou Linwei 42tr, 168br;
Saigo-Jones 361tc.
THE SWATCH ART PEACE HOTEL: 187cla.

TERRACOTTA ARMY MUSEUM: 168tl, 168cbl, 169tl, 169car, 169br, 169cfr.
TERRA GALLERIA PHOTOGRAPHY: Quang Tuan Luong 362tr, 362car, 363br, 363t, 364tr, 366–7, 378–9.
THAMES & HUDSON LTD: Photo Eileen Tweedy 28–9.

TIBET IMAGES: Neville Hopwood 522cr.
TIBET HERITAGE FUND: Andre Alexander 531tc;
Yutaka Hirako 531ca.

TOPFOTO.CO.UK: 256cla, 256clb; British Museum 31bc, 63bl; Sven Hedin Foundation 495cr; The Museum of East Asian Art/HIP 61b, 465cl.
Courtesy of THE TRUSTEES OF THE V&A: 209bc, 464br; Ian Thomas 208–9, 209cl.

THE WELLCOME INSTITUTE LIBRARY, LONDON: 32cbl, 55cbr.
WERNER FORMAN ARCHIVE: 55c; Forest of Stelae Museum, Xi'an 465cr; P'yongyang Gallery, North Korea 31cla; Peking Palace Museum 58cb; Private Collection 53br, 61c, 63br;
Private Collection/Sotheby's 1986 57br;
Tanzania National Museum 465bl; Victoria & Albert Museum 55b; Yang-Tzu-Shaw 54cbr.

BRIAN K.H. YIM: 321cl.

Jacket – Front: PHOTOLIBRARY: Christian Kober;
Back: AWL IMAGES: David Bank clb; Danita Delimont Stock cla; DORLING KINDERSLEY: Nigel Hicks bl; Colin Sinclair tl; Spine: PHOTOLIBRARY:
Christian Kober t.

All other images © Dorling Kindersley. For further information see: www.dkimages.com

## SPECIAL EDITIONS OF DK TRAVEL GUIDES

DK Travel Guides can be purchased in bulk quantities at discounted prices for use in promotions or as premiums.
We are also able to offer special editions and personalized jackets, corporate imprints, and excerpts from all of our books, tailored specifically to meet your own needs.

To find out more, please contact:
(in the United States) **SpecialSales@dk.com**
(in the UK) **travelspecialsales@uk.dk.com**
(in Canada) DK Special Sales at **general@ tourmaline.ca**
(in Australia)
**business.development@pearson.com.au**

# Glossary

## ARCHITECTURE

**cheng** city; also means city wall
**chorten** or stupa, a Buddhist tower containing sacred objects
**dian** pavilion
**dougong** elaborate bracket attaching column to beam
**ge** storied pavilion
**gompa** Tibetan monastery
**gong** palace; usually denotes a Daoist temple
**gulou** drum tower
**hutong** alleyway
**ling** tomb
**lou** storied building
**men** city gate
**miao** temple, usually Confucian
**mu** tomb
**nanmu** cedar with much-valued straight trunk used for columns
**paifang** ornamental gateway
**pailou** ornamental gateway
**qiao** bridge
**si** temple, usually Buddhist
**siheyuan** courtyard house
**Spirit Tower** pavilion at entrance to an imperial tomb
**Spirit Way** straight road leading to an imperial tomb and lined with guardian statues
**stele** free-standing stone slab or pillar engraved with text
**stupa** a Buddhist tower containing sacred objects
**ta** pagoda
**tang** hall
**yuan** garden
**zhanglou** bell tower

## CULTURE

**celadon** pottery with greenish glaze
**cloisonné** enamelling, in which the enamel is raised and separated by fine pieces of wire
**erhu** two-stringed fiddle
**huaju** spoken theater
**jingju** Beijing Opera
**lacquer** wood glazed with sap from the lac tree which is carved before completely dry *(see p292)*
**lusheng** bamboo instrument with numerous pipes
**model opera** operas based on a proletarian heroic model, promoted by Mao's wife Jiang Qing during the Cultural Revolution
**pipa** lute-like instrument
**porcelain** translucent ceramic ware made from clay containing kaolin and feldspar, and fired at high temperatures *(see p254)*
**sancai** tri-glazed pottery, usually yellow, green, and white, prevalent during Tang dynasty

**sanxian** three-stringed lute
**sheng** modern instrument based on the *lusheng* with 17 to 37 pipes
**suona** double-reeded wind instrument, similar to an oboe
**taotie** pattern on Shang bronze; possibly representing a mythical man-eating beast
**xiao** bamboo flute
**xun** rounded clay wind instrument
**zheng** many-stringed zither

## HISTORY & POLITICS

**cadre** Communist party bureaucrat
**canton** a small territory where foreign traders were required to reside during 18th and 19th century
**Communist Party** ruling party in China since 1949
**concession** an area of land ceded to a foreign government
**Cultural Revolution** radical attempt to socialize China's culture, 1966–76 *(see pp64–5)*
**Gang of Four** high-profile group responsible for some of the Cultural Revolution's worst excesses *(see p65)*
**Great Leap Forward** Mao's disastrous policy to force the collectivism of agriculture (1958–60), resulting in widespread famine
**Kuomintang** (KMT) founded by Sun Yat Sen; fought the Communists for 25 years under Chiang Kai Shek; moved to Taiwan where it is still a major party
**Legalism** fascistic political philosophy dominant during the Qin dynasty based on the idea that man is undisciplined and must be controlled through fear
**Little Red Book** Mao's sayings compiled by Lin Biao, head of the PLA, in 1966 as a treatise for Red Guards and the PLA
**Long March** Epic tactical retreat of the Communist Party from Nationalist forces in 1935 *(see p256)*
**Nationalist Party** the Kuomintang
**People's Liberation Army (PLA)** Communist military forces
**Red Guard** unruly movement approved by Mao during the Cultural Revolution to weed out counter-revolutionaries and destroy evidence of the past
**soviet** regional Communist base, e.g. Jiangxi Soviet
**Special Administrative Region (SAR)** Regions, such as Hong Kong and Macau, provided with a high degree of autonomy and a capitalist economy

**Special Economic Zone (SEZ)** areas, such as Shenzhen, set aside in the 1980s for a capitalist test of a freer economy and to attract foreign investment
**triad** a secret society, especially one involved in organized crime

## NATURAL FEATURES

**chi** lake or pool
**dao** island
**dong** cave
**feng** peak
**gongyuan** park
**gou** gully
**hai** sea
**haitan** beach
**he** river
**hu** lake
**jiang** river
**karst** limestone landscape with irregular peaks, underground streams, caves, and sinkholes *(see pp412–13)*
**pubu** waterfall
**shan** mountain
**shui** water
**shuiku** reservoir
**tan** pool
**xi** stream
**xia** gorge

## RELIGION & PHILOSOPHY

**A-Ma** Macau's Goddess of the Sea; see Tianhou
**Amitabha Buddha** Buddha of boundless light
**Analects** (*Lunyu*) major work compiled by Confucius's followers of his sayings
**arhat** or luohan; one of the Buddha's 18 disciples
**Avalokitesvara** bodhisattva of compassion
**bagua** eight trigrams ranged around a *yin-yang* symbol; a codification of *qi* *(see pp30–31)*
**Bodhidarma** Indian monk who traveled to China in the 6th century and started the Chan (Zen) sect of Buddhism
**bodhisattva** Buddhist deities who have postponed nirvana to help others
**Bon** indigenous animistic faith of Tibet *(see p522)*
**Buddha** the awakened one, originally the Indian Gautama Buddha; in Chinese and Tibetan schools the Buddha has numerous forms *(see pp30, 487, 522–3)*
**Buddhism** religion based on the teachings of the 6th-century BC Indian teacher Gautama Buddha

**Chan** School of Buddhism spread by Bodhidarma; popular in Japan as Zen Buddhism

**Chenresig** Tibetan name for bodhisattva Avalokitesvara

**Confucius** or Kong Fuzi (551–479 BC); developed the philosophy of Confucianism, which was then spread by his followers

**Confucianism** dominant philosophy prescribing a structured society based on filial relationships *(see p30)*

**Dafo** Great Buddha

**Damo** Chinese name for Bodhidarma

**Dao** in Daoism the way that permeates reality; a single cosmic force

***Daode Jing*** Daoist *The Way and Power Classic* attributed to Laozi

**Daoism** philosophy expounding non-action and living in harmony with the Dao or Way; became a pantheistic religion *(see p31)*

**dharmapala** protector deities of Tibetan Buddhism

**Dipamkara** in Tibetan Buddhism, the past Buddha

**Eight Immortals** Daoist adepts each with a superhuman power

**feng shui** a form of geomancy that determines the flow of *qi* through a physical place *(see p31)*

**fo** a Buddha in Putonghua

**Gelugpa** Most powerful Tibetan Buddhist sect, headed by the Dalai Lama; also called the Yellow Hat sect

**Guanyin** bodhisattva of compassion in Chinese Buddhism

**Guardian Kings** four protective deities of the cardinal directions; often stationed at the entrance of a temple

**Guru Rinpoche** spreader of Buddhism through Tibet

**Jampa** the future or Maitreya Buddha in the Tibetan pantheon

**Jampalyang** bodhisattva of wisdom in Tibetan Buddhism

**Jowo Sakyamuni** in Tibetan Buddhism, the present Buddha

**karma** in Buddhism, the merit accrued by a person's actions, determining their destiny

**kora** circuits of holy sites made by Tibetan Buddhists to accrue merit

**Laozi** first Daoist who may have lived during the 6th century BC and produced the *Daode Jing*

**Laughing Buddha** Milefo, the future Buddha

**luohan** or arhat; one of the Buddha's 18 disciples

***Lunyu*** Confucian writings, the *Analects*

**Mahayana**, Greater Vehicle, dominant form of Buddhism in China and Japan with ritual and devotional practices, and worship of bodhisattvas

**Maitreya** the future Buddha; the Buddha that has yet to come

**mandala** an esoteric diagram of circles and squares around a central focal point used as a meditation aid and forming an important part of Tibetan Buddhist iconography

**Manjusri** bodhisattva of wisdom

**Marmedze** the past or Gautama Buddha

**Mazu** Goddess of the Sea; see Tianhou

**Milefo** the future or Maitreya Buddha represented as the plump Laughing Buddha

**nirvana** in Buddhism, having broken from the cycle of rebirth; attained via the extinction of desire and individual consciousness

**Nyingma** oldest Tibetan Buddhist sect founded by Guru Rinpoche

**Padmasambhava** Guru Rinpoche

**Puxian** bodhisattva of universal benevolence; rides an elephant

**qi** concept of vital force and cosmic energy *(see pp32–3)*

**Sakyamuni** the past Buddha; Gautama Buddha

**sutra** sacred Buddhist writing; a discourse of the Buddha

**thangka** Buddhist painting on silk, originally used as objects of meditation and portable teaching tools

**Theravada** (Hinayana, Lesser Vehicle) school of Buddhism practiced in Southeast Asia and India emphasizing the importance of an ascetic way of life

**Tianhou** Daoist Empress of Heaven and Goddess of the Sea, equal to Buddhist Guanyin *(see p149)*

**Tinhau** Tianhou in Hong Kong; see Tianhou

**trigram** one of the eight sets of three broken *(yin)* and unbroken *(yang)* lines combined in pairs to make hexagrams for divination using the *Yijing*

**Wenshu** bodhisattva of wisdom

**yang** masculine, sun, positive; interacts with the complementary opposing force of yin

***Yijing*** classic ancient text, *The Book of Changes*, made up of oracles consulted for divination; source of Daoist and Confucian philosophies *(see p33)*

**yin** feminine, moon, negative; interacts with the complementary opposing force of *yang*

## MISCELLANEOUS

**bei** north

**binguan** tourist hotel

**bowuguan** museum

**CAAC** Civil Aviation Administration Authority

**canting** restaurant

**Cantonese** dialect of Chinese spoken in the south

**cheongsam** a tight-fitting dress with a high collar and slit skirt

**CITS** China International Travel Service; organization for international tourists, whose main interest is selling tours and tickets

**CTS** China Travel Service; organization similar to CITS

**cun** village

**da** big

**dadao** wide street or boulevard

**dajie** avenue (literally "big road")

**dong** east

**fandian** hotel or restaurant

**fen** smallest denomination; there are 100 *fen* to a *yuan*

**ger** round tent used by nomads of the steppe; a yurt

**jiao** there are 10 *fen* to one *jiao*; and 10 *jiao* to one *yuan*; also called *mao*

**jie** street

**jinguan** hotel

**kuai** colloquial word for *yuan*

**laowai** foreigner

**lokbar** traditional heavy wool Tibetan robe

**lu** road

**mahjong** popular rummy-like game played with small tiles

**mao** colloquial term for *jiao*

**nan** south

**Pinyin** a standardized system for transliterating Chinese characters into the roman alphabet

**PSB** Public Security Bureau; branch of the police force that deals with foreigners

**PRC** People's Republic of China

**Putonghua** Mandarin; the form of Chinese that is the official language of China

**qigong** martial art concentrating on the control of breath and *qi*

**renminbi** currency; literally "the people's money"

**sheng** province

**shi** city or municipality

**tai ji quan** (supreme ultimate fist) martial art made up of slow, flowing movements *(see p273)*

**xi** west

**yuan** China's currency; divided into 10 *jiao* and 100 *fen*; also called *kuai*

**zhong** middle

# Phrase Book

The Chinese language belongs to the Sino-Tibetan family of languages and uses characters which are ideographic – a symbol is used to represent an idea or an object. Mandarin Chinese, known as Putonghua in mainland China, is fairly straightforward as each character is monosyllabic. Traditionally, Chinese is written in vertical columns from top right to bottom left, however the Western style is widely used. There are several romanization systems; the Pinyin system used here is the official system in mainland China. This phrase book gives the English word or phrase, followed by the Chinese script, then the Pinyin for pronunciation.

## GUIDELINES FOR PRONUNCIATION

Pronounce vowels as in these English words:

| | |
|---|---|
| a | as in "father" |
| e | as in "lurch" |
| i | as in "see" |
| o | as in "solid" |
| u | as in "pooh" |
| ü | as the French u or German ü (place your lips to say oo and try to say ee) |

Most of the consonants are pronounced as in English. As a rough guide, pronounce the following consonants as in these English words:

| | |
|---|---|
| c | as ts in "hats" |
| q | as ch in "cheat" |
| x | as sh in "sheet" |
| z | as ds in "heads" |
| zh | as j in "Joe" |

Mandarin Chinese is a tonal language with four tones, represented in Pinyin by one of the following marks ¯ ´ ˇ ` above each vowel – the symbol shows whether the tone is flat, rising, falling and rising, or falling. The Chinese characters do not convey this information: tones are learnt when the character is learnt. Teaching tones is beyond the scope of this small phrasebook, but a language course book with a cassette or CD will help those who wish to take the language further.

## DIALECTS

There are many Chinese dialects in use. It is hard to guess exactly how many, but they can be roughly classified into one of seven large groups (Mandarin, Cantonese, Hakka, Hui etc.), each group containing a large number of more minor dialects. Although all these dialects are quite different – Cantonese uses six tones instead of four – Mandarin or Putonghua, which is mainly based on the Beijing dialect, is the official language. Despite these differences all Chinese people are more or less able to use the same formal written language so they can understand each other's writing, if not each other's speech.

## In an Emergency

| | | |
|---|---|---|
| Help! | 请帮忙！ | Qing bangmang |
| Stop! | 停住！ | Ting zhu |
| Call a doctor! | 叫医生！ | Jiao yisheng |
| Call an ambulance! | 叫救护车！ | Jiao jiuhuche |
| Call the police! | 叫警察！ | Jiao jiingcha |
| Fire! | 火！ | Huo |
| Where is the hospital/police station? | 医院/警察分局在哪里？ | Yiyuan/jingcha fenju zai nali？ |

## Communication Essentials

| | | |
|---|---|---|
| Hello | 你好 | Nihao |
| Goodbye | 再见 | Zaijian |
| Yes/no | 是／不是 | shi/bushi |
| … not … | 不是 | bushi |
| I'm from… | 我是…人 | Wo shi … ren |
| I understand | 我明白 | Wo mingbai |
| I don't know | 我不知道 | Wo bu zhidao |
| Thank you | 谢谢你 | Xiexie ni |
| Thank you very much | 多谢 | Duo xie |
| Thanks (casual) | 谢谢 | Xiexie |
| You're welcome | 不用谢 | Bu yong xie |
| No, thank you | 不，谢谢你 | Bu, xiexie ni |
| Please (offering) | 请 | Qing |
| Please (asking) | 请问 | Qing wen |
| I don't understand | 我不明白 | Wo Bu mingbai |
| Do you speak English? | 你会讲英语吗？ | Ni hui jiang yingyu ma？ |
| I can't speak Chinese | 我不会讲汉语 | Wo buhui jiang hanyu |
| Please speak more slowly | 请讲慢一点 | Qing jiang man yidian |
| Sorry/Excuse me! | 抱歉／对不起 | Baoqian/duibuqi |
| Could you help me please? (not emergency) | 你能帮助我吗？ | Ni neng bang zhu wo ma？ |

## Useful Phrases

| | | |
|---|---|---|
| My name is …. | 我叫… | Wo jiao … |
| How do you do, pleased to meet you | 你好，很高兴见到你。 | Ni hao, hen gaoxing jiandao ni |
| How are you? | 你好吗？ | Ni hao ma？ |
| Good morning | 早上好 | Zaoshang hao |
| Good afternoon/ good day | 下午好/你好 | Xiawu hao/ Ni hao |
| Good evening | 晚上好 | Wanshang hao |
| Good night | 晚安 | Wan an |
| Goodbye | 再见 | Zaijian |
| Take care | 保重 | Bao zhong |
| Keep well (casual) | 注意身体 | Zhuyi shenti |
| The same to you | 你也是 | Ni yeshi |
| What is (this)? | （这）是什么？ | (zhe) shi shenme？ |
| How do you use this? | 你怎样用这个东西？ | Ni zenyang yong zhege dongxi？ |
| Could I possibly have …? (very polite) | 能不能请你给我 …？ | Neng buneng qing ni gei wo … |
| Is there … here? | 这儿有 … 吗？ | Zhe'r you … ma？ |

| Where can I get ...? | 我在哪里可以得到 ...? | Wo zai na li keyi de dao ...? |
| How much is it? | 它要多少钱? | Ta yao duoshao qian? |
| What time is ...? | ... 什么时间? | ... shenme shijian |
| Cheers! (toast) | 干杯 | Ganbei |
| Where is the restroom/toilet? | 卫生间 / 洗手间在哪里? | Weishengjian/ Xishoujian zai nali? |
| Here's my business card. | 这是我的名片。 | Zhe shi wo de mingpian. |

## Useful Words

| I | 我 | wo |
| woman | 女人 | nüren |
| man | 男人 | nanren |
| wife | 妻子 | qizi |
| husband | 丈夫 | zhangfu |
| daughter | 女儿 | nü'er |
| son | 儿子 | er'zi |
| child | 小孩 | xiaohai |
| children | 儿童 | er'tong |
| businessman/ woman | 商人 / 女商人 | shangren/ nüshangren |
| student | 学生 | xuesheng |
| Mr./Mrs./Ms. ... | 先生 / 太太 / 女士 | xiansheng/taitai/ nüshi |
| big/small | 大/小 | da/xiao |
| hot/cold | 热/凉 | re/liang |
| cold (to touch) | 冷 | leng |
| warm | 暖 | nuan |
| good/not good/ bad | 好 / 不好 / 坏 | hao/buhao/ huai |
| enough | 够了 | goule |
| free (no charge) | 免费 | mianfei |
| here | 这里 | zheli |
| there | 那里 | nali |
| this | 这个 | zhege |
| that (nearby) | 那 | na |
| that (far away) | 那个 | nage |
| what? | 什么? | Shenme? |
| when? | 什么时候? | Shenme shihou? |
| why? | 为什么? | Wei shenme? |
| where? | 在哪里? | Zai nali? |
| who? | 谁? | Shui? |
| which way? | 哪个方向? | Nage fangxiang? |

## Signs

| open | 开 | kai |
| closed | 关 | guan |
| entrance | 入口 | rukou |
| exit | 出口 | chukou |
| danger | 危险 | weixian |
| emergency exit | 安全门 | anquanmen |
| information | 信息 | xinxi |
| restroom/toilet (men) (women) | 卫生间 / 洗手间 （男士）（女士） | Weishengjian/ Xishoujian (nanshi) (nüshi) |
| occupied | 占用 | zhanyong |
| free (vacant) | 空闲 | kongxian |
| men | 男士 | nanshi |
| women | 女士 | nüshi |

## Money

| Could you change this into? please. | 请你把它换成 ...，好吗? | Qing ni ba ta huancheng ... hao ma? |
| I'd like to cash these travelers' checks. | 我想把旅行支票换成现金。 | Wo xiang ba lüxing zhipiao huancheng xianjin. |
| Do you take credit cards/travelers' checks? | 你收信用卡 / 旅行支票吗? | Ni shou xinyongka/ lüxing zhipiao ma? |
| bank | 银行 | yinhang |

| cash | 现金 | xianjin |
| credit card | 信用卡 | xinyongka |
| currency | 外汇兑换处 | waihui duihuanchu |
| exchange office | | |
| dollars | 美元 | meiyuan |
| pounds | 英镑 | yingbang |
| yuan | 元 | yuan |

## Keeping in Touch

| Where is a telephone? | 电话在哪里? | Dianhua zai nali? |
| May I use your phone? | 我可以用你的电话吗? | Wo keyi yong nide dianhua ma? |
| Mobile phone | 手机 | shouji |
| sim card | 卡 | sim ka |
| Hello, this is ... | 你好，我是 ... | Nihao, wo shi |
| I'd like to make an international call | 我想打个国际长途电话。 | Wo xiang da ge guoji changtu dianhua. |
| Where can I get online? | 我可以在哪里上网? | Wo keyi zai nali shangwang? |
| airmail | 航空 | hangkong |
| e-mail | 电子邮件 | dianzi youjian |
| fax | 传真 | chuanzhen |
| internet | 互联网 | hulianwang |
| postcard | 明信片 | mingxinpian |
| post office | 邮局 | youju |
| stamp | 邮票 | youpiao |
| telephone booth | 电话亭 | dianhua ting |
| telephone card | 电话卡 | dianhua ka |

## Shopping

| Where can I buy ...? | 我可以在哪里买到 ...? | Wo keyi zai nali maidao ...? |
| How much does this cost? | 这要多少钱? | Zhe yao duoshao qian? |
| Too much! | 太贵了! | Tai gui le! |
| I'm just looking | 我只是看看。 | Wo zhishi kankan. |
| Do you have ...? | 你有 ...? | Ni you ... ma? |
| May I try this on? | 我可以试穿吗? | Wo keyi shi chuan ma? |
| My size? | 我的尺寸? | Wo de chicun? |
| Please show me that. | 请给我看看那个。 | Qing gei wo kankan na ge. |
| Does it come in other colors? | 有没有其它颜色? | You meiyou qita yanse? |
| black | 黑色 | heise |
| blue | 蓝色 | lanse |
| brown | 棕色 | zongse |
| green | 绿色 | lüse |
| purple | 紫色 | zise |
| red | 红色 | hongse |
| white | 白色 | baise |
| yellow | 黄色 | huangse |
| cheap/expensive | 便宜 / 贵 | pianyi/gui |
| audio equipment | 音响设备 | yinxiang shebei |
| bookstore | 书店 | shudian |
| boutique | 时装商店 | shizhuangshang– dian |
| clothes | 衣服 | yifu |
| department store | 百货商店 | baihuo shangdian |
| electrical store | 电器商店 | dianqi shangdian |
| fish market | 鱼市 | yu shi |
| folk crafts | 民间工艺品 | minjian gongyipin |
| ladies' wear | 女式服装 | nüshi fuzhuang |
| local specialty | 地方特产 | difang techan |
| market | 市场 | shichang |
| men's wear | 男式服装 | nanshi fuzhuang |
| newsstand | 报摊 | baotan |
| pharmacist | 药剂师 | yaojishi |
| picture postcard | 图片明信片 | tupian mingxinpian |
| sale | 廉价出售 | lianjiachushou |
| souvenir shop | 纪念品店 | jinianpin dian |
| supermarket | 超市 | chaoshi |
| travel agent | 旅行社 | lüxing she |

## Sightseeing

| | | |
|---|---|---|
| Where is …? | … 在哪里？ | … zai nali? |
| How do I get to …? | 我怎么到 …？ | Wo zenme dao … ? |
| Is it far? | 远不远？ | Yuan bu yuan? |
| art gallery | 美术馆 | meishu guan |
| reservations desk | 订票台 | dingpiao tai |
| bridge | 桥 | qiao |
| city | 城市 | chengshi |
| city center | 市中心 | shi zhongxin |
| free entry | 免费入场 | mianfei ruchang |
| gardens | 花园 | huayuan |
| hot spring | 温泉 | wen quan |
| tourist information office | 旅游信息处 | lüyou xinxi chu |
| island | 岛 | dao |
| monastery | 寺院 | siyuan |
| mountain | 山 | shan |
| museum | 博物馆 | bowuguan |
| palace | 宫殿 | gongdian |
| park | 公园 | gongyuan |
| port | 港口 | gangkou |
| river | 江，河 | jiang, he |
| ruins | 废墟 | feixu |
| shopping area | 购物区 | gouwu qu |
| shrine | 神殿 | shendian |
| street | 街 | jie |
| temple | 寺庙 | si/miao |
| tour, travel | 旅行 | lüxing |
| town | 镇 | zhen |
| village | 村 | cun |
| province/county | 省／县 | sheng/xian |
| zoo | 动物园 | dongwuyuan |
| north | 北 | bei |
| south | 南 | nan |
| east | 东 | dong |
| west | 西 | xi |
| left/right | 左／右 | zuo/you |
| straight ahead | 一直向前 | yizhi xiangqian |
| between | 在 … 之间 | zai … zhijian |
| near/far | 近／远 | jin/yuan |
| up/down | 上／下 | shang/xia |
| new | 新 | xin |
| old/former | 旧 | jiu |
| upper/lower | 更高／更低 | genggao/gengdi |
| middle/inner | 中间 | zhongjian |
| in | 在 … 里 | zai … li |
| in front of | 在 … 前面 | zai … qianmian |

## Getting around

| | | |
|---|---|---|
| airport | 机场 | jichang |
| bicycle | 自行车 | zixingche |
| rickshaw | 人力车 | renliche |
| I want to rent a bicycle | 我想租一辆自行车 | Wo xiang zu yiliang zixingche. |
| Ordinary bus | 公共汽车 | gonggong qiche |
| Express bus | 特快公共汽车 | tekuai gonggong qiche |
| Minibus | 面包车 | mianbaoche |
| Main bus station | 公共汽车总站 | gonggong qiche zong zhan |
| Which bus goes to …? | 哪一路公共汽车到 … 去？ | Nayilu gonggong qiche dao … qu? |
| When is the next bus? | 下一辆公共汽车是什么时候？ | Xiayiliang gonggong qiche shi shenme shihou? |
| Please tell me where to get off? | 请告诉我在哪里下车？ | Qing gaosu wo zai nali xia che. |
| car | 小汽车 | xiaoqiche |
| ferry | 渡船 | duchuan |
| ferry dock | 渡口 | du kou |
| baggage room | 行李室 | xingli shi |
| motorcycle | 摩托车 | motuoche |
| one-way ticket | 单程票 | dancheng piao |
| return ticket | 往返票 | wangfan piao |

| | | |
|---|---|---|
| taxi | 出租车 | chuzuche |
| ticket | 票 | piao |
| ticket office | 售票处 | shoupiao chu |
| timetable | 时刻表 | shikebiao |

## Trains

| | | |
|---|---|---|
| What is the fare to …? | 去 … 的票价是多少？ | Qu … de piaojia shi duoshao? |
| When does the train for … leave? | 去 … 的火车什么时候开车？ | Qu … de huoche shenme shihou kai? |
| How long does it take to get to …? | 去 … 要多少时间？ | Qu … yao duoshao shijian? |
| A ticket to …, please | 买一张去 … 的票。 | Mai yizhang qu … de piao |
| Do I have to change? | 我要不要换车？ | Wo yao buyao huanche? |
| I'd like to reserve a seat, please | 我想预定一个座位。 | Wo xiang yuding yige zuowei |
| Which platform for the train to …? | 去 … 的火车在哪个站台？ | Qu … de huoche zai nage zhantai? |
| Which station is this? | 这是什么车站？ | Zhe shi shenme chezhan? |
| Is this the right train for …? | 这火车是不是去 …? | Zhe huoche shi bushi qu … ? |
| train station | 火车站 | huoche zhan |
| express train | 直达快车 | zhida kuaiche |
| fast train | 快车 | kuai che |
| ordinary train | 普通列车 | putong lieche |
| line | 线路 | xianlu |
| local train | 地方列车 | difang lieche |
| platform | 站台 | zhantai |
| reserved seat | 预定座位 | yuding zuowei |
| subway | 地铁 | ditie |
| train | 火车 | huoche |
| unreserved seat | 未预定的座位 | wei yuding de zuowei |
| hard seat | 硬座 | yingzuo |
| soft seat | 软座 | ruanzuo |
| hard sleeper | 硬卧 | yingwo |
| soft sleeper | 软卧 | ruanwo |
| upgrade ticket | 升级车票 | shengji chepiao |

## Accommodations

| | | |
|---|---|---|
| Do you have any vacancies? | 你们有没有空房间？ | Nimen you meiyou kong fang jian? |
| I have a reservation | 我有预定的房间。 | Wo you yuding de fangjian |
| I'd like a room with a bathroom | 我想要一个有卫生间的套间。 | Wo xiang yao yige you weishengjian de taojian |
| What is the charge per night? | 每晚的收费是多少？ | Mei wan de shoufei shi duoshao? |
| Are the taxes included in the price? | 价格有没有包括税？ | Jiage you meiyou baokuo shui? |
| Can I leave my luggage here for a little while? | 我可以把行李放在这里一会儿吗？ | Wo keyi ba xingli fang zai zheli yihui 'er ma? |
| Can I have a look at the room? | 我可以看一看房间吗？ | Wo keyi kan yi kan fangjian ma? |
| air-conditioning | 空调 | Kongtiao |
| bath | 洗澡 | xizao |
| check-out | 退房 | tui fang |
| deposit | 定金 | dingjin |
| double bed | 双人床 | shuangren chuang |
| hair drier | 吹风机 | chuifeng ji |
| hot (boiled) water | 热（开）水 | re (kai) shui |
| hotel (upscale) | 饭店 | fangdian |
| hotel (downscale) | 旅馆 | lüguan |
| hostel | 招待所 | zhaodaisuo |
| room | 房间 | fangjian |
| economy room | 经济房 | jingji fang |
| key | 钥匙 | yaoshi |
| front desk | 前台 | qiantai |

| | | |
|---|---|---|
| single/twin room | 单人 / 双人房 | danren/shuangren fang |
| single beds | 单人床 | danren chuang |
| shower | 淋浴 | linyu |
| standard room | 标准房间 | biaozhun fangjian |
| deluxe suite | 豪华套房 | haohua taofang |

## Eating Out

| | | |
|---|---|---|
| A table for one/two/three, please | 请给我一 / 两 / 三个人的桌子。 | Qing gei wo yi/liang/san ge ren de zhuozi |
| May I see the menu? | 请给我看看菜单。 | Qing gei wo kankan caidan |
| Is there a set menu? | 有没有套餐? | You meiyou taocan? |
| I'd like …. | 我想要 … | Wo xiang yao … |
| May I have one of those? | 请给我这个。 | Qing gei wo zhege |
| I am a vegetarian | 我是素食者。 | Wo shi sushizhe. |
| Waiter/waitress! | 服务员! | Fuwuyuan! |
| What would you recommend? | 你建议那几个? | Ni tuijian na jige? |
| How do you eat this? | 这个怎么吃? | Zhege zenme chi? |
| May I have a fork/knife/spoon | 请给我一把叉 / 刀 / 汤匙。 | Qing gei wo yiba cha/dao/tangshi |
| May we have the check please. | 请把帐单开给我们。 | Qing ba zhangdan kaigei women |
| May we have some more … | 请再给我们一些 … | Qing zai gei women yixie … |
| The meal was very good, thank you | 饭菜很好吃,谢谢。 | Fancai hen hao chi, xiexie |
| assortment | 混合餐 | hunhe can |
| packed lunch | 盒装午餐 | hezhuang wucan |
| breakfast | 早餐 | zaocan |
| buffet | 自助餐 | zizhucan |
| chopsticks | 筷子 | kuaizi |
| delicious | 好吃 | haochi |
| dinner | 晚餐 | wancan |
| to drink | 喝 | he |
| a drink | 一杯饮料 | yibei yinliao |
| to eat | 吃 | chi |
| food | 食品 | shipin |
| full (stomach) | 饱 | bao |
| hot/cold | 热 / 冷 | re/leng |
| hungry | 饿 | e |
| lunch | 午餐 | wucan |
| set menu | 套餐 | taocan |
| spicy | 酸辣 | suan la |
| hot (spicy) | 辣 | la |
| sweet | 甜 | tian |
| mild | 淡 | dan |
| Western food | 西餐 | xi can |

## Places to eat

| | | |
|---|---|---|
| cafeteria/canteen | 自助餐馆 / 餐厅 | zizhucanguan/canting |
| coffee shop | 咖啡店 | kafei dian |
| Internet café | 网吧 | wang ba |
| local bar | 当地酒吧 | dangdi jiuba |
| noodle stall | 面铺 | mianpu |
| restaurant | 餐馆 | canguan |
| restaurant (upscale) | 饭店 | fangdian |
| tea garden | 茶室 | chashi |
| vegetarian restaurant | 素菜馆 | sucai guan |

## Food

| | | |
|---|---|---|
| apple | 苹果 | pingguo |
| bacon | 咸肉 | xianrou |
| bamboo shoots | 笋 | sun |
| beancurd | 豆腐 | doufu |
| bean sprouts | 豆芽 | dou ya |
| beans | 豆 | dou |

| | | |
|---|---|---|
| beef | 牛肉 | niurou |
| beer | 啤酒 | pijiu |
| bread | 面包 | mianbao |
| butter | 黄油 | huangyou |
| cabbage | 卷心菜 | juanxincai |
| cake | 蛋糕 | dangao |
| chicken | 鸡 | ji |
| candies | 糖果 | tangguo |
| crab | 蟹 | xie |
| duck | 鸭 | ya |
| eel | 鳗 | man |
| egg | 蛋 | dan |
| eggplant | 茄子 | qiezi |
| fermented soybean paste | 酱 | jiang |
| fish | 鱼 | yu |
| fried egg | 炒蛋 | chao dan |
| fried tofu | 油豆腐 | you doufu |
| fruit | 水果 | shuiguo |
| fruit juice | 果汁 | guo zhi |
| ginger | 姜 | jiang |
| ham | 火腿 | huotui |
| hamburger | 汉堡包 | hanbaobao |
| haute cuisine | 美味佳肴 | meiwei jiayao |
| hors d'oeuvres | 冷盆 | leng pen |
| ice cream | 冰淇淋 | bingqilin |
| jam | 果酱 | guojiang |
| lobster | 龙虾 | longxia |
| mackerel | 鲭鱼 | qingyu |
| mandarin orange | 柑橘 | gan ju |
| meat | 肉 | rou |
| melon | 瓜 | gua |
| mountain vegetables | 山地蔬菜 | shandi shucai |
| noodles | 面 | mian |
| egg noodles | 鸡蛋面 | jidan mian |
| wheat flour noodles | 面粉面 | mianfen mian |
| rice flour noodles | 米粉面 | mifen mian |
| octopus | 章鱼 | zhangyu |
| omelet | 煎蛋饼 | jiandanbing |
| onion | 洋葱 | yangcong |
| oyster | 牡蛎 | muli |
| peach | 桃子 | taozi |
| pepper | 胡椒粉, 辣椒 | hujiaofen, lajiao |
| pickles | 泡菜 | paocai |
| pork | 猪肉 | zhurou |
| potato | 土豆 | tudou |
| rice | 米饭 | mifan |
| rice crackers | 爆米花饼干 | baomihua bing'gan |
| rice wine | 米酒 | mi jiu |
| roast beef | 烤牛肉 | kao niurou |
| salad | 色拉 | sela |
| green salad | 绿菜色拉 | lücai sela |
| mixed salad | 混拌色拉 | hunban sela |
| salmon | 鲑鱼, 大马哈鱼 | guiyu, damahayu |
| salt | 盐 | yan |
| sandwich | 三明治 | sanmingzhi |
| sausage | 香肠 | xiangchang |
| scallion | 韭葱 | jiucong |
| seaweed | 海带 | haidai |
| shrimp | 虾 | xia |
| snapper (fish) | 笛鲷 | didiao |
| soup | 汤 | tang |
| soy sauce | 酱油 | jiangyou |
| squid | 鱿鱼 | youyu |
| steak | 牛排 | niupai |
| sugar | 糖 | tang |
| toast | 烤面包 | kao mianbao |
| trout | 鳟鱼 | zunyu |
| vegetables | 蔬菜 | shucai |
| watermelon | 西瓜 | xigua |
| yoghurt | 酸奶 | suannai |

## Drinks

| | | |
|---|---|---|
| beer | 啤酒 | pijiu |
| black tea | 红茶 | hong cha |
| coffee (hot) | （热）咖啡 | (re) kafei |
| black | 不加牛奶 | bu jia niunai |
| coffee with milk | 加牛奶 | jia niunai |
| filter | 过滤 | guolü |
| cappuccino | 卡普契诺咖啡 | kapuqinuo kafei |
| cola | 可乐 | kele |
| green tea | 绿茶 | lü cha |
| iced coffee | 冰咖啡 | bing kafei |
| lemon tea | 柠檬茶 | ningmeng cha |
| milk | 牛奶 | niunai |
| mineral water | 矿泉水 | kuang quanshui |
| orange juice | 橙汁 | cheng zhi |
| soya drink (milk) | 豆浆 | dou jiang |
| tea (Western-style) | 茶（西式） | cha (xi shi) |
| tea with milk | 加牛奶的茶 | jia niunai de cha |
| water | 水 | shui |
| whiskey | 威士忌 | weishiji |
| wine | 葡萄酒 | putaojiu |
| yoghurt drink | 酸奶饮料 | suannai yinliao |

| | | |
|---|---|---|
| 21 | 二十一 | ershi yi |
| 22 | 二十二 | ershi er |
| 30 | 三十 | sanshi |
| 40 | 四十 | sishi |
| 100 | 一百 | yi bai |
| 101 | 一百零一 | yi bai ling yi |
| 200 | 二百 | er bai |
| 300 | 三百 | san bai |
| 400 | 四百 | si bai |
| 500 | 五百 | wu bai |
| 600 | 六百 | liu bai |
| 700 | 七百 | qi bai |
| 800 | 八百 | ba bai |
| 900 | 九百 | jiu bai |
| 1,000 | 一千 | yi qian |
| 1,001 | 一千零一 | yi qian ling yi |
| 2,000 | 两千 | liang qian |
| 10,000 | 一万 | yi wan |
| 20,000 | 两万 | liang wan |
| 100,000 | 十万 | shi wan |
| 1,000,000 | 一百万 | yi bai wan |
| 123,456 | 十二万三千四百五十六 | shier wan san qian si bai wushi liu |

## Health

| | | |
|---|---|---|
| I don't feel well | 我感觉不舒服。 | Wo ganjue bu shufu |
| I have a pain in ... | 我 ... 疼。 | Wo ... teng. |
| I'm allergic to ... | 我对 ... 过敏。 | Wo dui ... guomin |
| acetaminophen (paracetamol) | 扑热息痛 | purexitong |
| aspirin | 阿司匹林 | asipilin |
| asthma | 哮喘 | xiaochuan |
| cold | 感冒 | ganmao |
| condom | 避孕套 | biyuntao |
| cough | 咳嗽 | kesou |
| dentist | 牙医 | yayi |
| diabetes | 糖尿病 | tangniaobing |
| diarrhea | 腹泻 | fuxie |
| doctor | 医生 | yisheng |
| fever | 发烧 | fashao |
| flu | 流感 | liugan |
| headache | 头疼 | touteng |
| hospital | 医院 | yiyuan |
| medicine | 药品 | yaopin |
| mosquito coil | 蚊香 | wenxiang |
| mosquito netting | 蚊帐 | wenzhang |
| traditional Chinese medicine | 传统中医 | chuantong zhongyi |
| pharmacy | 药店 | yaodian |
| prescription | 处方 | chufang |
| sanitary pads | 卫生巾 | weishengjin |
| stomach ache | 胃痛 | weitong |
| tissues | 纸巾 | zhijin |
| toothache | 牙疼 | yateng |

## Numbers

| | | |
|---|---|---|
| 0 | 零 | ling |
| 1 | 一 | yi |
| 2 | 二 | er |
| 3 | 三 | san |
| 4 | 四 | si |
| 5 | 五 | wu |
| 6 | 六 | liu |
| 7 | 七 | qi |
| 8 | 八 | ba |
| 9 | 九 | jiu |
| 10 | 十 | shi |
| 11 | 十一 | shiyi |
| 12 | 十二 | shier |
| 20 | 二十 | ershi |

## Time

| | | |
|---|---|---|
| Monday | 星期一 | xingqiyi |
| Tuesday | 星期二 | xingqi'er |
| Wednesday | 星期三 | xingqisan |
| Thursday | 星期四 | xingqisi |
| Friday | 星期五 | xingqiwu |
| Saturday | 星期六 | xingqiliu |
| Sunday | 星期天 | xingqitian |
| January | 一月 | yiyue |
| February | 二月 | eryue |
| March | 三月 | sanyue |
| April | 四月 | siyue |
| May | 五月 | wuyue |
| June | 六月 | liuyue |
| July | 七月 | qiyue |
| August | 八月 | bayue |
| September | 九月 | jiuyue |
| October | 十月 | shiyue |
| November | 十一月 | shiyiyue |
| December | 十二月 | shi'eryue |
| Spring | 春 | chun |
| Summer | 夏 | xia |
| fall/autumn | 秋 | qiu |
| winter | 冬 | dong |
| noon | 中午 | zhongwu |
| midnight | 午夜 | wuye |
| today | 今天 | jintian |
| yesterday | 昨天 | zuotian |
| tomorrow | 明天 | mingtian |
| this morning | 今天上午 | jintian shangwu |
| this afternoon | 今天下午 | jintian xiawu |
| this evening | 今天晚上 | jintian wanshang |
| for the whole day (continuous) | 一整天 | yi zheng tian |
| every day | 每天 | mei tian |
| month | 月 | yue |
| hour | 小时 | xiaoshi |
| time/hour (duration) | 时间 | shijian |
| minute | 分钟 | fenzhong |
| this year | 今年 | jin nian |
| last year | 去年 | qu nian |
| next year | 明年 | ming nian |
| one year | 一年 | yi nian |
| late | 晚 | wan |
| early | 早 | zao |
| soon | 很快 | henkuai |
| now | 现在 | xianzai |

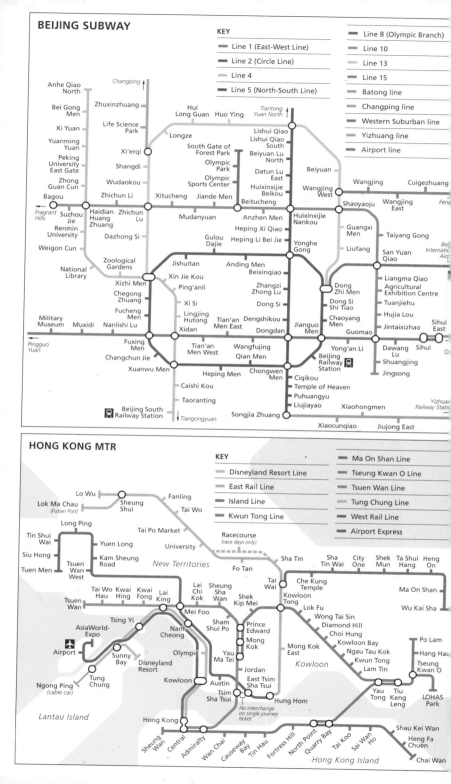

# BEIJING SUBWAY

**KEY**

- Line 1 (East-West Line)
- Line 2 (Circle Line)
- Line 4
- Line 5 (North-South Line)
- Line 8 (Olympic Branch)
- Line 10
- Line 13
- Line 15
- Batong line
- Changping line
- Western Suburban line
- Yizhuang line
- Airport line

# HONG KONG MTR

**KEY**

- Disneyland Resort Line
- East Rail Line
- Island Line
- Kwun Tong Line
- Ma On Shan Line
- Tseung Kwan O Line
- Tsuen Wan Line
- Tung Chung Line
- West Rail Line
- Airport Express